Did the cultural transformation of the later Roman Empire really involve migrating barbarian tribes bearing a distinguishable Germanic culture? Previous studies of this question have begun from the assumption that barbarian groups were ethnic groups or the seeds of ethnic groups. In contrast, this case-study of the Goths of Italy in the late fifth and early sixth century begins from the assumption that the ethnographic language used to describe the barbarians makes them look like ethnic groups to twentieth-century observers.

Since this ethnography was classicizing, biblical and, above all, ideological, the ancient texts that use it must be constantly questioned and compared with other evidence for ancient communal behavior. Ostrogothic Italy provides a large and comparatively neglected body of data on individual behavior and group allegiances. The prosopographical appendix to this book groups together evidence for 379 individuals who could be considered "Goths" under various institutional ideologies at play in sixth-century Italy. The chapters successively examine these ideologies and their impact upon "Goths" and "Romans," that is, the Italians who inhabited the regions of Italy in a time of political, social and religious upheaval.

The inquiry suggests new ways of understanding the appearance of barbarian groups and the end of the Western Roman Empire, as well as proposing new models of regional and professional loyalty and group cohesion in the period.

Cambridge Studies in Medieval Life and Thought

PEOPLE AND IDENTITY IN
OSTROGOTHIC ITALY, 489–554

Cambridge Studies in Medieval Life and Thought
Fourth Series

General Editor:

D. E. LUSCOMBE

Leverhulme Personal Research Professor of Medieval History, University of Sheffield

Advisory Editors:

R. B. DOBSON

Professor of Medieval History, University of Cambridge, and Fellow of Christ's College

ROSAMOND McKITTERICK

Reader in Early Medieval European History, University of Cambridge, and Fellow of Newnham College

The series Cambridge Studies in Medieval Life and Thought was inaugurated by G. C. Coulton in 1921; Professor D. E. Luscombe now acts as General Editor of the Fourth Series, with Professor R. B. Dobson and Dr Rosamond McKitterick as Advisory Editors. The series brings together outstanding work by medieval scholars over a wide range of human endeavour extending from political economy to the history of ideas.

For a list of titles in the series, see end of book.

PEOPLE AND IDENTITY
IN OSTROGOTHIC ITALY,
489–554

PATRICK AMORY

CAMBRIDGE
UNIVERSITY PRESS

PUBLISHED BY THE PRESS SYNDICATE OF THE UNIVERSITY OF CAMBRIDGE
The Pitt Building, Trumpington Street, Cambridge CB2 1RP

CAMBRIDGE UNIVERSITY PRESS
The Edinburgh Building, Cambridge CB2 2RU, United Kingdom
40 West 20th Street, New York, NY 10011-4211, USA
10 Stamford Road, Oakleigh, Melbourne 3166, Australia

First published 1997

Printed in the United Kingdom at the University Press, Cambridge

Typeset in Monotype Bembo 11/12 pt

A catalogue record for this book is available from the British Library

Library of Congress cataloguing in publication data

Amory, Patrick, 1965–
People and identity in Ostrogothic Italy, 489–554
Patrick Amory.
p.   cm.
Includes bibliographical references.
ISBN 0 521 57151-0 (hc)
1. Goths–Italy–History.   2. Italy–History–476–774.   I. Title.
DG504.A56 1997
945'.01–dc20   96–2952 CIP

ISBN 0 521 57151 0 hardback

WV

For my parents

What are we waiting for, assembled in the forum?

    The barbarians are due here today.

Why isn't anything going on in the senate?
Why are the senators sitting there without legislating?

    Because the barbarians are coming today.
    What's the point of senators making laws now?
    Once the barbarians are here, they'll do the legislating.

Why did our emperor get up early,
and why is he sitting enthroned at the city's main gate,
in state, wearing the crown?

    Because the barbarians are coming today
    and the emperor's waiting to receive their leader.
    He's even got a scroll to give him,
    loaded with titles, with imposing names.

Why have our two consuls and praetors come out today
wearing their embroidered, their scarlet togas?
Why have they put on bracelets with so many amethysts,
rings sparkling with magnificent emeralds?
Why are they carrying elegant canes
beautifully worked in silver and gold?

    Because the barbarians are coming today
    and things like that dazzle the barbarians.

Why don't our distinguished orators turn up as usual
to make their speeches, say what they have to say?

    Because the barbarians are coming today
    and they're bored by rhetoric and public speaking.

Why this sudden bewilderment, this confusion?
(How serious people's faces have become.)
Why are the streets and squares emptying so rapidly,
everyone going home lost in thought?

    Because night has fallen and the barbarians haven't come.
    And some of our men just in from the border say
    there are no barbarians any longer.

Now what's going to happen to us without barbarians?
Those people were a kind of solution.

C. P. Cavafy, "Waiting For The Barbarians"
(trans. Edmund Keeley and Philip Sherrard)

CONTENTS

PREFACE

The transformation of the Roman Empire in the fifth and sixth centuries poses some of the knottiest questions in history. The role of divided communities, peoples and ethnicity in this transformation looks like the toughest of these knots in our ethnicity-obsessed world today. This case-study of one of the most famous barbarian groups, Theoderic's Goths in Italy between 489 and 554, does not pretend to solve the ethnicity question, merely to make what I hope will be a thought-provoking, if occasionally polemical, contribution to the current lively debates. In questioning certain entrenched assumptions and vocabulary relating to the barbarians of late antiquity, I do not propose a new single model, only a new method of inquiry. The evanescent and ever-changing Goths of sixth-century Italy provide only one glimpse of the varieties of community and the impact of ethnographic texts on late antique Mediterranean and European societies. The Italian developments need not mirror the experience of the other barbarian groups in other parts of the Empire.

I hope that this book synthesizes several areas of research that have remained somewhat out of touch with one another: notably the theories of the German and Austrian ethnogenesis historians, the recent British and American work on late Roman frontier regions and military culture, and the deep enquiries into texts, manuscripts and literary strategies of early Byzantinists and early medievalists from the late 1960s onward. In particular, I hope that I have responsibly used all this research to set the barbarians of the fifth and sixth centuries into the rich cultural Mediterranean milieu of late antiquity described with such power and passion by Peter Brown.

It is therefore particularly important to me to extend my heartfelt thanks to the following people for reading and criticizing chapters of this book: George Boulukos, Peter Brown, Marios Costambeys, Nick Everett, Peter Heather, Yitzhak Hen, Alen Mattich, Walter Pohl and Ian Wood. None of them is responsible for any of the opinions contained within, and in some cases they disagree with me strongly. I can only hope that our differences will continue to provoke the fruitful and challenging discussions that we have had thus far.

Hugh Elton was kind enough to provide me with a copy of his book, *Warfare in Roman Europe*, in advance of publication. Peter Heather, Michael Maas, Ralph Mathisen, Walter Pohl and Johan Weißensteiner also all generously gave me copies of articles before they reached print. All proved enormously helpful, even where we have differed, and I have learned much from their insights.

I am also most grateful to Fred Amory, Tom Brown, Patrick Geary, Catherine Hills, Caroline Humfress, Doug Lee, Peter Linehan, Michael Maas, Ralph Mathisen, John Moorhead, Steven Muhlberger, Tom Noble and Lawrence Okamura for their advice and help on various points contained within.

Particularly valuable were the incisive comments of Chris Wickham and Christopher Kelly, who brought their detailed knowledge of two different Italies to the Cambridge Ph.D. dissertation that was the basis of this book. No degree candidate could wish for more discerning and painstaking examiners.

Above all, I am entirely indebted to the wisdom, firm support and endless forbearance of my supervisor, Rosamond McKitterick, who put up with reading and criticizing these chapters at their original length. Without her help I could never have completed them.

RULERS A.D. 475–602

	Eastern emperors	Kings of the Balkan or Italian Goths	Popes★
475	Zeno	Theoderic the Great	Simplicius
483			Felix III
491	Anastasius I		
492			Gelasius
496			Anastasius II
498			Symmachus/(Laurentius)
507			Symmachus
514			Hormisdas
518	Justin I/Justinian I		
523			John I
526		Athalaric/Amalasuintha	Felix IV
527	Justinian I		
530			Boniface II/(Dioscorus)
533			John II
534		Amalasuintha	
534		Amalasuintha/ Theodahad	
535		Theodahad	Agapetus I
536		Witigis	Silverius
537			Vigilius
540		Hildebad	
541		Eraric	
541		Totila	
552		Teia	
556		. . .	Pelagius I
561			John III
565	Justin II		
575			Benedict I
578	Tiberius II		
579			Pelagius II
582	Maurice		
590			Gregory the Great
602	Phocas		

★Antipopes are in parentheses.

xiii

TERMINOLOGY AND VOCABULARY

I use certain words in a technical sense:

Identity: an individual's allegiance to a community, as manifested in behavioral and cultural traits. Deeper than this we can rarely penetrate. It need not mean anything similar to the overriding concern with personal affiliation of our own day.

Ethnicity: the anthropological term for group cohesion based on belief in shared ancestry and a shared past, with consequent common cultural traits and political goals.[1]

Ethnography: the literary, artistic or propagandistic depiction and representation of races in the classical sense (*ethnē, gentes, nationes*).[2]

Ideology: articulated systems of thought about the ideal community, propagated by powerful individuals and institutions.[3]

Barbarian groups: the *gentes* who laid claim to ancient ethnographic group-names and established kingdoms within Roman provinces in the fifth and sixth centuries. Neither the groups, their names nor their members need to have arrived from outside the Roman frontiers, at least in the immediate past of the group as currently constituted.[4]

---

[1] I thus use "ethnicity" in both the "weak primordialist" and "instrumentalist" sense: see pp. 14–18, below.

[2] I hope to demonstrate that ethnographic representation had ideological ends and ideological effect on individuals in fifth- and sixth-century Italy.

[3] I do not necessarily oppose it to truth or to reality. One must take the passage of time into account. Sixth-century ideologies had roots in specific political and social circumstances: they were ways of interpreting and therefore of attempting to change these circumstances, and very often they succeeded in doing so. In this sense, many forms of representation were ideological. On ideology see Paul Rabinow, "Representations are social facts: modernity and post-modernity in anthropology," in *Writing Culture: The Poetics and Politics of Ethnography*, ed. James Clifford and George E. Marcus (Berkeley, 1986), p. 240.

[4] "Barbarian" here is intended to be a neutral term: one could use Herwig Wolfram's phrase "federate armies," but they were not always federates and after a time, they were not all soldiers. I avoid the words "tribe" and "people" with their connotations of biological kin-groups and race, as well as the word "migration," which implies mass-movements on a monumental scale, and "invasion," which implies an organized challenge to one political entity by another

Germanic: properly used, this refers to a language family, not a culture, ethnic group or race. No evidence from the period indicates that speakers of different Germanic dialects or languages were aware that language ties gave them anything else in common: there was no "pan-Germanic" identity. I do not use the word "German" to refer to individuals or peoples; it is anachronistic for the period.[5]

Gothic language: refers to two phenomena. The first is the written language of Ulfilas's translation of the Gothic Bible and related liturgical sources. The second is the rarely attested spoken language of soldiers in the Balkans and Italy. The two were related, but had probably diverged widely by the sixth century; no contemporary source associates or identifies them.[6]

Ostrogothic: a political term used only to refer to the "Ostrogothic government" (the successive royal courts in Italy from Theoderic to Teia). It does not imply that this government was "Gothic" in any way: it continued the late Roman administration and employed many Italians. Neither the government nor any individuals ever called themselves "Ostrogothic."[7]

Goth and **Roman:** ideologically loaded terms and thus not used in this book without at least imagined inverted commas around them. When they are used of individuals, they refer only to individuals who fit into the ideology or criteria of identity under discussion at that point. In order to avoid circular argumentation, the groups commonly referred to in scholarly literature as Goths and Romans in Italy are called "the settlers" or "the followers of Theoderic," and the "Italians," "natives" or "indigenous population," respectively.

Similarly, in order to avoid confusion between Eastern "Romans" and Italian "Romans" (occasionally, but not invariably, portrayed as

(external) political entity. The words "group" and "movement" are mundane but carry few associations that could affect judgment of ethnicity. "Raid" and "battle" describe most hostile contacts between groups at the time; where appropriate, "war" is used. The one potential barbarian invasion was that of the Huns, on which see ch. 1, n. 66, below.

[5] The *Germani* of Tacitus were the inhabitants of the regions that we call Germany today; in late antiquity, the word referred to inhabitants of the provinces Germania I and II on the Rhine; for Procopius it meant "Franks"; "The collectivity of Germans is an anachronism if transposed to the sixth century or earlier" (Walter Goffart, "Rome, Constantinople and the barbarians," 1981, reprinted in Goffart, *Rome's Fall and After* (London, 1988), pp. 4–5.) On the Germanic culture-construct, see appendices 2 and 4.

[6] See chs. 3 and 7.

[7] See, however, ch. 3 on the political names Ostrogotha, Ostrogotho and Ustrigotthus. When necessary, "Ostrogoths," in the plural, is used to distinguish the Goths who followed Theoderic from the "Visigoths" in southern Gaul and in Spain and from other Gothic groups.

the same group in the sources), I refer to the Easterners by the anachronistic term "Byzantines," for which I apologize; it is preferable, at
any rate, to "Greeks," the favorite word for them in sixth-century Italy.

Catholic church: the church hierarchy admitting Nicaean definitions
of the Trinity. It thus includes both the Chalcedonian papacy and the
Eastern churches whether Chalcedonian or not, but not the Arian
churches.

Italian elites: these divide into two general groups.

> *Senator***:** refers not only to a member of the senate and the holder of
> the rank-grade *inluster*, but to the chief branches of ancient and
> powerful clans like the Anicii and the Decii, who intermarried. They
> were closely associated with the city of Rome. These families pre-
> served pride in their genealogies, maintained residences in Rome,
> cultivated literary style and classical education, and, by this period,
> wielded great influence over the papacy, with which they were fre-
> quently locked in conflict. They often owned vast wealth and estates
> on which they could retire to cultivate the virtue of *otium*. These
> families could expect to advance their sons rapidly to prestigious high
> office for brief periods without first enduring long careers in the
> palatine or military service. They might hold the urban praetorship,
> a year-long provincial governorship, the urban prefecture and a con-
> sulship, occasionally also serving in one of the palatine offices. If they
> did not succeed in achieving high office, they might be granted an
> honorary illustrate for admission to the senate. Unlike their counter-
> parts in Gaul, the Italian senators did not monopolize the episcopacy.
> They never became soldiers.
>
> *Parvenu***:** members of the provincial aristocracy, sometimes even *cur-*
> *iales*, sometimes cadet branches or distant relatives of senatorial famil-
> ies, but in any case families of which the male members had to devote
> entire careers to imperial or royal service in order to advance to high
> office and membership in the senate. They might advance via the
> army or the palatine ministries or the law-courts, or a combination
> of these routes. They could also receive provincial governorships,
> but are more frequently to be found in palatine *officia* or local regi-
> ments, from which they might move up to the position of *comes*
> *civitatis*, *magister officiorum*, the chief of one of the financial depart-
> ments, the quaestorship and the praetorian prefecture, even the con-
> sulate. For these last-named positions, the parvenus competed with
> the senators, who demanded them by right of high birth. Upon
> achieving the illustrate, of course, parvenus entered the senate, but

there is little evidence for intermarriage with senatorial clans. Alternatively, such families could produce bishops for local cities, although this phenomenon is much harder to trace than in Gaul. In sum, parvenus were careerists who rose slowly through the palatine and military ranks, possibly also through the church, and men who maintained local connections and loyalties to their cities and regions of origin.

The distinction between senator and parvenu may have become blurred in individual instances, but in general it is possible to identify members of either group. Needless to say, membership in either group did not automatically identify an individual's party-politics, beliefs or behavior. Neither group acted as a social class.[8]

There are no Germanic tribes, barbarian invasions or migrations of peoples in this book. This is not to say that such things cannot have existed, merely that their existence must be demonstrated once more. Despite their stubborn malingering in scholarly publications, the research of the past century has made them obsolete as terms. My more neutral vocabulary will, I hope, help to avoid prejudging the case until after full reassessments of the sources.[9]

---

[8] On senators and parvenus, see, for example, A. H. M. Jones, *The Later Roman Empire 284–602*, 2 vols. (Oxford, [1964] 1973), 1: 545–52; John Moorhead, *Theoderic in Italy* (Oxford, 1993), pp. 144–72, 200–4, 210–11, 222–45; Alexander Demandt, "The osmosis of late Roman and Germanic aristocracies," in *Das Reich und die Barbaren*, ed. Evangelos K. Chrysos and Andreas Schwarcz, Veröffentlichungen des Insituts für Österreichische Geschichtsforschung 29 (Vienna, 1989), pp. 75–86, with table after p. 86 (on senators' refusal to marry non-senatorial families); Patrick Amory, "Names, ethnic identity and community in fifth- and sixth-century Burgundy," *Viator* 25 (1994), 7–8; on their careers, John Matthews, "Anicius Manlius Severinus Boethius," in *Boethius: His Life, Thought and Influence*, ed. Margaret Gibson (Oxford, 1981), pp. 26–8.

[9] Further justification for this terminology will be found in chs. 1, 3 and 7. On "Germanic culture," see appendix 2.

ABBREVIATIONS

ACO	*Acta conciliorum oecumenicorum*
Agathias	Agathias, *Historiae*
Arelat	*Collectio Arelatensis* (under "Papal letters" in bibliography)
Auct. Prosp. Havn.	*Auctarium Prosperi Havniensis*
Auct. Havn. Extr.	*Auctarii Havniensis Extrema*
AV	*Anonymus Valesianus pars posterior*
Avellana	*Collectio Avellana* (under "Papal letters" in bibliography)
B.	T. S. Brown, "Prosopographical Index," in *Gentlemen and Officers*, pp. 250–82
BP, BV, BG	Procopius, *Bellum Persicum, Bellum Vandalicum, Bellum Gothicum* (see "Notes on citation" in bibliography, below)
Bury, HLRE	J. B. Bury, *History of the Later Roman Empire*, 2nd edition
CCSL	*Corpus Christianorum scriptorum, series latina*, Turnhout, 1953–
CIL	*Corpus inscriptionum latinarum*, ed. Theodor Mommsen et. al., Berlin, 1863–
CJ	*Codex Iustinianus*
Coll. Brit.	Ewald, "Die Papstbriefe der brittischen Sammlung" (under Papal letters in bibliography)
Cont. Marc.	*Continuatio Marcellini*
CSEL	*Corpus scriptorum ecclesiasticorum latinorum*, Vienna, 1886-
CT	*Codex Theodosianus*
Dig.	*Digesta*
Ennodius, *Pan.*	Ennodius, *Panegyricus dictus Theoderico regi* = *Op.* 263 (*Opusc.* 1), ed. Friedrich Vogel in Ennodius, *Opera* (see "Notes on citation" in bibliography, below)

ET	*Edictum Theoderici regis*
ETV	*Epistulae Theoderici Variae*
F-S	Otto Fiebiger and Ludwig Schmidt, *Inschriftensammlung zur Geschichte der Ostgermanen* (under "Inscriptions" in bibliography)
F-S, 2F	Otto Fiebiger, *Inschriftensammlung,* Zweite Folge (under "Inscriptions" in bibliography)
F-S, NF	Otto Fiebiger, *Inschriftensammlung,* Neue Folge (under "Inscriptions" in bibliography)
Förstemann	Ernst Förstemann, *Altdeutsches Namenbuch*
Gassò and Batlle	Pius M. Gassò and Columba M. Batlle. *Pelagii I pape epistulae quae supersunt* (under "Papal Letters" in bibliography)
GR	Gregory the Great, *Registrum epistolarum*
HE	*Historica Ecclesiastica*
ICUR	*Inscriptiones Christianae urbis Romae,* ed. Giovanni Battista de Rossi (under "Inscriptions" in bibliography)
ICUR, n.s.	*Inscriptiones Christianae urbis Romae,* nova series, ed. Angelo Silvagni, et al. (under "Inscriptions" in bibliography)
ILCV	*Inscriptiones latinae christianae veteres* (under "Inscriptions" in bibliography)
Jones, LRE	A. H. M. Jones, *The Later Roman Empire*
JK	Jaffé-Kaltenbrunner = Phillippe Jaffé, Samuel Loewenfeld, F. Kaltenbrunner and Paul Ewald, *Regesta Pontificum Romanorum* (see "Notes on citation" in bibliography, below)
Kauffmann	Henning Kauffmann, *Ergänzungsband zu Ernst Förstemann, Personennamen*
Le Blant	Edmond Le Blant, *Inscriptions chrétiennes de la Gaulle antérieures au VIIIe siècle* (under "Inscriptions" in bibliography)
LF	*Fragmentum Laurentianum (Laurentian Fragment)*
LP	*Liber Pontificalis,* 2nd edn, ed. Duchesne, 1: 117ff.
LP¹	*Liber Pontificalis,* 1st edn, ed. Duchesne, 1: 18–108
Mazzoleni	Danilo Mazzoleni, "Nomi di barbari nelle

	iscrizione paleocristiane" (under Inscriptions in bibliography)
MGH: AA	*Monumenta Germaniae Historica: Auctores antiquissimi*, ed. Theodor Mommsen et al., 1877–1919
MGH: SRG	*Monumenta Germaniae Historica: Scriptores rerum germanicarum in usum scholarum separatim editi*, 1841–
MGH: SRM	*Monumenta Germaniae Historica: Scriptores rerum merovingicarum*, ed. Bruno Krusch and Wilhelm Levison, 1885–1920
Mommsen, "OGS"	Theodor Mommsen, "Ostgothische
NA14 or 15	Studien," *Neues Archiv* 14: 225–49, 453–544; *Neues Archiv* 15: 181–6
Nov. Iust.	*Novellae Iustiniani*
Nov. Maj.	*Novellae Maioriani*, in *Novellae ad Theodosianum pertinentes*
Nov. Marc.	*Novellae Marciani*, in *Novellae ad Theodosianum pertinentes*
Nov. Theod.	*Novellae Theodosii*, in *Novellae ad Theodosianum pertinentes*
Nov. Val.	*Novellae Valentiniani*, in *Novellae ad Theodosianum pertinentes*
PA	Prosopographical Appendix, at end of book
Paul Diac., HL	Paul the Deacon, *Historia Langobardorum*
PDip	*I papiri diplomatici*, ed. Gaetano Marini (under "Papyri" in bibliography)
PG	*Patrologiae cursus completus, series Graec*, ed. J.-P. Migne et al., 161 vols., 1857–66
PItal	*Die nichtliterarischen lateinischen Papyri Italiens*, ed. Jan-Olof Tjäder (under "Papyri" in bibliography)
PL	*Patrologiae cursus completus, series Latina*, ed. J.-P. Migne et al., 221 vols., 1844–64
PLS	*Patrologiae cursus completus, series Latina, Supplementum*, ed. Adalbert Hamman et al., 5 vols., 1958–74
PRainer Cent	*P. Rainer. Cent. Festschrift zum 100-jährigen Bestehen der Papyrus-Sammlung der österreichischen Nationalbibliothek Papryus Erzherzog Rainer* (under "Papyri" in bibliography)

PLRE2	J. R. Martindale, *The Prosopography of the Later Roman Empire*, 2
PLRE3	J. R. Martindale, *The Prosopography of the Later Roman Empire*, 3
RE	*Real-Encyclopaedie der klassischen Altertumswissenschaft*, ed. A. Pauly, G. Wissowa, W. Kroll et al.
RICG	*Recueil des inscriptions chrétiennes de la Gaule antérieure à la Renaissance carolingenne* (under "Inscriptions" in bibliography)
Rugo	Pietro Rugo, *Le iscrizione dei secoli VI–VII–VIII esistenti in Italia* (under "Inscriptions" in bibliography)
Settimane di Studio	Settimane di Studio del Centro Italiano di studi sull'alto medioevo (Spoleto)
Schanz-Hosius	Martin Schanz, Carl Hosius and Gustav Krüger, *Geschichte der römischen Litteratur bis zum Gesetzgebungswerk des Kaisers Justinians*
Schönfeld	M. Schönfeld, *Wörterbuch der altgermanischen Personen- und Völkernamen*
SH	Procopius, *Secret History* or *Anecdota*
Thiel	Andreas Thiel, *Epistolae Romanorum pontificum genuinae* (under "Papal letters" in bibliography)
Tjäder	Jan-Olof Tjäder, editorial comments on *Die nichtliterarischen lateinischen Papyri*
Var.	Cassiodorus, *Variae*
VSeverini	Eugippius, *Vita Sancti Severini*
Wrede	Ferdinand Wrede, *Über die Sprahe der Ostgoten in Italien*

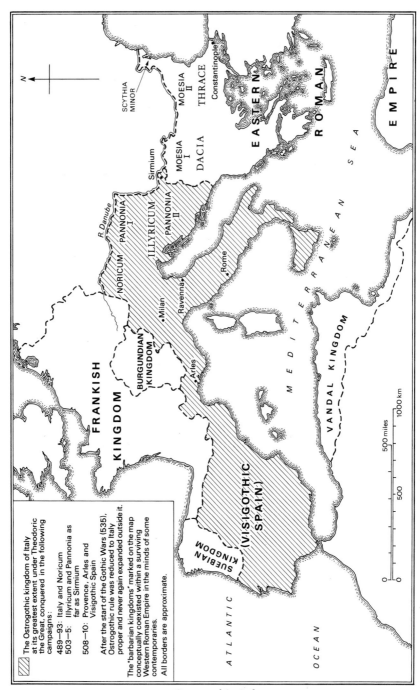

The Ostrogothic kingdom of Italy
at its greatest extent under Theodoric
the Great, conquered in the following
campaigns:

489–93: Italy and Noricum
503–5:   Illyricum and Pannonia as
         far as Sirmium

508–10: Provence, Arles and
         Visigothic Spain

After the start of the Gothic Wars (535),
Ostrogothic rule was reduced to Italy
proper and never again expanded outside it.
The 'barbarian kingdoms' marked on the map
conceptually coexisted within a surviving
Western Roman Empire in the minds of some
contemporaries.

All borders are approximate.

Ostrogothic Italy

INTRODUCTION: STUDYING THE BARBARIANS IN LATE ANTIQUITY

We are the prisoners of preconception and periodization. We imbue preconception in images of the barbarians that surround us in school and in popular culture from our earliest childhood. Whether a *New Yorker* cartoon depicting barbarians in horned helmets and furs confusedly invading a modern office, or Marinetti's fantasies of mustachioed Ostrogoths eating pasta out of holes in the ground with their hands,[1] imagery of barbarian primitivism, violence and, above all, imagery of difference from equally stereotyped Roman behavior, is impossible to avoid.[2] The Nazis celebrated their version of the violent heroism of "Germanic" barbarians,[3] and biker gangs today preserve vestiges of imagery associated with barbarians since the nineteenth century and before.

Despite decades of scholarship on the barbarians, we cannot easily escape these preconceptions, themselves inherited from the literary and artistic depictions of Graeco-Latin ethnography. Theoderic the Great was, alongside his classical education and the enormous subtlety and enlightenment of his propaganda and policy, an unpredictably violent man who murdered his predecessor and one of his courtiers with his own hands. Scholarly commentators have associated Theoderic's violence with his barbarianness,[4] although the Roman Emperor Valentinian III had similarly murdered his general Aetius fifty years earlier.

While preconception determines certain images of barbarians and Romans, periodization locks in an even more insidious conceptual break at the time of the fall of the Western Roman Empire, around A.D. 500, a break created by Renaissance humanists, transmitted in the twentieth century through the enduring works of Spengler and Durant, and preserved in the curriculum of European history in every school

---

[1] Filippo Tomaso Marinetti, *The Futurist Cookbook* [1932], trans. Suzanne Brill (San Francisco, 1989), p. 51.

[2] See S. J. B. Barnish on the high-flown rhetoric of Theoderic's minister Cassiodorus: "Most barbarians, and even Romans of the day, would have found even the simpler letters hard to understand." (*Cassiodorus: Variae*, trans. with commentary [Liverpool, 1992], p. xxxii).

[3] Herwig Wolfram, *History of the Goths*, trans. Thomas J. Dunlap (2nd rev. edn, Berkeley, 1988), p. 3.

[4] J. M. Wallace-Hadrill, *The Barbarian West 400–1000* (3rd rev. edn, Oxford, 1967), p. 33.

and university in the world. The notion of a break, in culture, politics or institutions, prevents us from seeing late antiquity as an integrated culture or set of cultures in its own right, and encourages us mentally to assign fifth- and sixth-century groups either to the toga or to furs and pantaloons. The notion of a break imperceptibly urges us to continue the seventeenth- and eighteenth-century dispute between Montesquieu and Le Nain de Tillemont, or the nineteenth-century dispute between Fustel and Dahn: were the Roman successor states "Roman" or "Germanic"? Were they more like the second century or more like the ninth century? Preconception encourages us to think of the sixth-century Romans as second-century men and women, and the sixth-century barbarians as ninth-century men and women.

This is the problem of artificially dividing world history into distinct "civilizations." One philologist is still able to imagine the contrast in sixth-century Italy between "the vivacity and rigour of Ulfilan Gothic culture" and "the decline of Graeco-Roman tradition."[5] Contemporaries did not always imagine the world to be divided up in this way. From our standpoint, we can see the richness and coherence of late antique culture in itself, as something *sui generis*, containing both "Ulfilan Gothic culture" and "Graeco-Roman tradition." They were cultural elements that influenced and determined each other, and each of which coexisted (in their late antique manifestations) with cultural traits not easily identifiable as either "Roman" or "Germanic."

In other words, it is time to set the barbarians fully into late antiquity. Historians of the fifth and sixth centuries now have a field of their own, a way to avoid both the preconceptions of cultural dichotomy and the traditional periodization. An enormous number of works on late Roman history and on late antique culture have appeared over the last two or three decades. These studies examine the period between 300 and 700 as a historical epoch in its own right, not as a period of transition. Peter Brown's vivid depiction of the fourth- and fifth-century penetration of spirituality into everyday life, and Dick Whittaker's nuanced study of frontier cultures as coherent interactive cultural zones throwing up new leaders and identities, can join the vast collection of artistic objects and settlement excavations that show us a world that was neither like the second century nor like the ninth century, but one where people had inherited imagery, literature and institutions of the past and, without necessarily seeing any change, had imperceptibly made these things their own. It was a period of innovation and creativity, the world that threw up Western notions of individual guilt and

---

[5] Piergiuseppe Scardigli, *Lingua e storia dei Goti* (Florence, 1964), p. 4.

conscience, the codex book, the lower-case alphabet that we still use today, the codification of law that determined subsequent legal science in Continental Europe, the triumph of monotheistic religion, and, not least, the ethnographic names that still mark and divide the political map of Europe.

How does the continuing late antique use of a dualistic classical ethnography, which distinguished between Romans and barbarians, fit into this world? The late Roman Empire was an antiquarianizing society at its wealthiest, most educated levels. But this antiquarianism re-used and recreated elements of past culture to fit new circumstances. It was a varied antiquarianism, itself in constant evolution. The use of classical ethnographic discourse in literature, law and ideology is one manifestation of this recycling of the past. Although some historians have argued that we must try to analyze the world in which late antique men and women lived as much as their ideas of "barbarian" and "Roman,"[6] there has as yet been little attempt to set classical ethnography into its correct niche within the rest of Mediterranean culture. The common assumption that it continued to remain stable in its attitudes and vocabulary shows that ethnography in late antiquity has been insufficiently studied.

A discourse in anxious flux, classical ethnography could not operate in the same way in a non-classical world any more than classical literary genres could satisfactorily describe Justinian's Constantinople without displaying strain.[7] In the wake of recent re-evaluations of classicizing literature in late antiquity, we must place classical ethnographic texts among other, non-ethnographic sources that described ancient community, all of which influenced each other. Only then can we understand both the relative importance of ethnography and the composition and formation of groups ethnographically described in the sources.

Classical ethnography describes only a small part of the story. The late Roman Empire was composed of both a Mediterranean-centered political world with a cosmopolitan and well-traveled elite that shared certain cultural characteristics and behavior based on (but not preserving unchanged) ancient traditions, and a huge variety of cultures, languages and allegiances in the vast geography through which they moved. It was a world in which rigid hierarchy, ceremony and manners competed

---

[6] e.g., James J. O'Donnell, "Liberius the patrician," *Traditio* 37 (1981), 32. Rather than ask what Romans thought of barbarians and vice versa, we must ask "what did the average citizen of the western empire, by this time a Christian from a Christian family, think of the *world* in which he found himself – without necessarily using categories like barbarian, Roman, or pagan?" (Jean Durliat, "Qu'est-ce que le Bas-Empire? II," *Francia* 18.1 [1991], 131).

[7] Averil Cameron, *Procopius and the Sixth Century* (Berkeley, 1985), pp. 19–32.

with institutional structures that allowed startling social mobility and opportunity for the ambitious.

Part of what we call the fall of the Roman Empire was the collapse of these political structures and the geographical shrinking of the range of social institutions, with the consequent narrowing horizons for everyone in the West. With this diminution of opportunity, long-silent local cultures suddenly find a voice in our sources, alongside the protests of some of the privileged people who had lost access to a broader source of power and prestige.[8] These cultures were not only "barbarian" or "Germanic." They included the Thracians and the Isaurians, the Moors and the Basques, identities – geographical, linguistic or political – that, like the barbarian groups, attached to ancient names in new manifestations of a smaller independence from imperial power. These were not, of course, the same identities that had existed in the regions before the Roman Empire conquered them, but ones that developed beneath the small, if permeable, elite class of classically educated administrators and careerists. When access to that supraregional class vanished, people looked to local routes to power and local identities. These people could speak Greek or Latin without always considering themselves Romans.

One of the most pervasive historical myths is that the Romans "Romanized" the Roman Empire. The impact of the Roman armies, literate elites and bureaucratic government was enormous – and enormously varied. Roman administrative and learned culture was received differently according to the local culture, language, geography and economics of the regions conquered by the Empire. It is like the European and Mediterranean reception of Christianity. We need to imagine a sort of live, evolving "Romanization," gradually laid down over a Mediterranean-sized field of different reactive cultures, and producing innumerable different reactions in different places over time.[9]

Did a single Roman people and culture confront diverse barbarian groups, as certain forms of classical ethnography – that elite viewpoint –

---

[8] This interpretation was advanced by Herwig Wolfram as early as 1970, building on the ideas of Rostovtzeff but emphasizing regional particularity over Rostovtzeff's class alienation. To my knowledge, no one has yet taken up Wolfram's suggestion and developed it, despite the subsequent barrage of studies on political and cultural regionalism in the late Empire. At the time, of course, Wolfram also saw the barbarian settlements as invasions, and believed that the barbarians carried new culture into the Roman Empire, whereas I would see most of this culture as aspects of regional diversity newly brought to light – without downplaying the conflicts and massive social disruption that obviously occurred. (See Herwig Wolfram,"The shaping of the early medieval kingdom," *Viator* 1 [1970], 16–18 with n. 80.)

[9] The most powerful statement of this view remains that of Peter Brown in *The World of Late Antiquity A.D. 150–750* (London, 1971), pp. 11–21, though the study of interaction between center and periphery goes back to Theodor Mommsen on the Roman provinces ("Ostgothische Studien," NA14: 225–49, 453–544 [1889]; NA15: 181–6 [1890]).

suggest? To accept the ethnographic viewpoint is to ignore not only the hundreds of regions, cities, cultures and languages within the vast Roman state, but also the overriding power of status and institutional affiliation among the salaried servants of that state.

What did the word "Roman" mean to the millions of inhabitants of the Mediterranean littoral and its hinterland? Many things: tax-exactions, law (not all of it) and overbearing ceremonial splendor; certainly the army. But when urban citizens were not in the law-courts or presenting a petition to a magistrate, such external concerns faded into the background. Among the civil servants and the military, fierce loyalties developed, not only to the emperors who changed so rapidly in the West, but also to the regiments and offices within which they and their fathers had served all their lives. At the same time, the rise of the Christian church introduced new and powerful institutional loyalties, in the West developing a cosmology in which the Roman Empire was no longer a providential manifestation of eternity.

Many of our preconceptions about barbarians must necessarily vanish when we set them into our newly focused, newly periodized picture of the late antique Mediterranean, a world in which a mosaic of different smaller identities resurfaces amidst the disruption of the deceptively smooth surface of Roman political culture. Appendix 4 shows how even the most sober scholars have succumbed to their prejudices – or to their wishful thinking – in examining reports and imagery of "barbarian dress." How is it possible that serious historians can classify imagery of eagles on soldiers' brooches as evidence of Germanic paganism, when the eagle was one of the oldest symbols of Roman imperial power, one associated with the military, and one in active revival in fifth- and sixth-century imperial art? The answer is, sadly, the mustachioed Ostrogoths devouring pasta.

I advocate this new approach. Let us set barbarian history into late antique culture and view an integrated world – one composed of many different and occasionally mutually opposed parts, but not one in the midst of a "break" or a "transition," and emphatically *not* one sinking into barbarism, or at least not sinking into a new barbarism brought by the barbarians. It was a world that contained what we sometimes call "Germanic" cultural traits as constituent parts of its own wider culture, parts so constituent that neither "Germanic" nor "non-Germanic" cultural traits as they existed in the fifth century would be imaginable had the other not existed.

In turn, a re-examination of cultural diversity within the Empire calls into question the role of assumed ethnic or cultural community as a binding or divisive force among the barbarian groups and the Roman provinces in which they lived. This book examines the meaning of community in the barbarian group most frequently used as a template for understanding all the barbarians: the Goths of Italy between 489 and 554.

OSTROGOTHIC ITALY: A NOTE ON THE POLITICAL HISTORY, 476–568

It is entirely characteristic of scholarship on the barbarians that there is still no single study of the political history of the Ostrogothic kingdom of Italy. Despite the richness of the source material and the importance of its cultural production, the Ostrogothic kingdom is an anomaly in the traditional periodization and regional division of historical scholarship in Europe. With the exception of a few books and a large body of specialist journal articles, one must study it through works on the later Roman Empire, on sixth-century Byzantium (itself a neglected field, astonishingly), on the barbarian kingdoms, or on (all) the Goths as a "tribe." These perspectives carry the obvious limitations of vantage-point and allottable space. Herewith an up-to-date summary.[10]

---

[10] Herwig Wolfram's *History of the Goths* studies the formation and composition of all the groups who laid claim to the name *Gothi* in late antiquity. Peter Heather's *Goths and Romans 332–489* (Oxford, 1991) covers the vicissitudes of Theoderic and his followers in the Balkans between 450 and 489. The political history of fifth-century Italy must be approached through J. B. Bury (*History of the Later Roman Empire from the Death of Theodosius I to the Death of Justinian*, 2nd edn, London, 1923), Ernst Stein (*Histoire du Bas-Empire de la disparition de l'Empire d'Occident – la mort de Justinien 476–565*, Paris, 1949–59), A. H. M. Jones (*The Later Roman Empire 284–602*, Oxford, 1973) and a number of scattered articles. John Moorhead's *Theoderic in Italy* (Oxford, 1973) addresses in great detail and clarity the political history of Ostrogothic Italy under Theoderic, between 489 and 526, but stops at Theoderic's death. The history of the senate under the Ostrogothic government through 554 receives a detailed but misconceived and misleading treatment in Sundwall's *Abhandlungen zur Geschichte des augehenden Römertums* (Helsinki, 1919). The period from 526 to 554, including the Gothic Wars, remains almost entirely neglected. Aside from Stein and Bury, one must use outdated works such as Hodgkin's nineteenth-century *Italy and Her Invaders* (Oxford, 1892), and Hartmann's *Geschichte Italiens im Mittelalter* I (Stuttgart, 1923). The Byzantine administration in Italy after the reconquest, from 554, on the other hand, is now well-covered by T. S. Brown's *Gentlemen and Officers: Imperial Administration and Aristocratic Power in Byzantine Italy, A.D. 554–800* (Rome, 1984).

Outside the works of Stein, Moorhead and T. S. Brown, study of the church and papacy have been left to ecclesiastical historians such as Erich Caspar and Eduard Schwartz. But a major problem with both the political and ecclesiastical literature is that historians, influenced by the idea of the primacy of race or ethnicity, have tended to explain ecclesiastical divisions and factions by ethnic and political divisions. On the basis of church disputes, entire pro-Gothic, pro-Italian and pro-Byzantine parties have been created in sixth-century Italy, often without a scrap of evidence.

In particular, historians have used the following events to align participants for or against the Gothic monarchy: the Acacian schism (484–519), the Laurentian schism (499–505), the elections of Pope Felix IV and of Boniface II (526 and 530), the schism between Boniface II and Dioscorus (530), the condemnation of that schism by Agapetus (535), and the deposition of Pope

The Western Roman Empire (between 455 and 476 effectively reduced to Italy) was ruled by a series of puppet emperors under the military regency of the generals Ricimer, Gundobad and Orestes. In 476, the Western Roman barbarian general Odoacer deposed and pensioned off the child-emperor Romulus Augustulus, and sent the Western imperial regalia to the Eastern emperor Zeno at Constantinople. Odoacer suggested that he himself might rule Italy under the sovereignty of the emperor at Constantinople.

Zeno eventually, if reluctantly, accepted this arrangement. He faced a number of political and military difficulties at home, not least the management of a number of warlike bands in the Balkan provinces of Pannonia, Moesia and Thrace. Several of these groups are called "Goths" in the sources. They were the remnants of soldiers or people attached to the short-lived confederation of the Huns under Attila, which had disintegrated in the 450s. Zeno played diplomacy with these warbands, alternately hiring them as allies of the Roman army and setting them against one another. Constantinople was frequently under siege from them during the 470s and 480s.

The leader or "king" of one of these groups of Goths in the Balkans, Theoderic the son of Thiudimir, had grown up at the imperial court at Constantinople as a hostage from 461 to 471. He came from a royal family called the Amals, which may have laid claim to a prestigious history of rule over groups called Goths. The Amals, based in Pannonia, already led a group of soldiers and their families that later sources called "Ostrogoths" as a means of distinguishing them from the Visigoths of Toulouse and Spain. Theoderic returned to the Balkans in 471. He and his soldiers spent the next fourteen years in and out of alliance with Constantinople.

In 488, Zeno appears to have suggested to Theoderic – perhaps as a way of getting rid of him – that he invade Odoacer's Italy and restore it to the Roman Empire (more specifically, to Zeno's rule). In 489, Theoderic and his army crossed the Isonzo in Istria and defeated Odoacer at Verona. The peninsula was effectively his except for the impregnable fortress of Ravenna. Italy continued to suffer the ravages of war and famine for the next four years. The Ostrogothic army

Silverius by Pope Vigilius and Belisarius (537). But if anything, these disputes occasionally illuminate the evolution of ecclesiastical conceptions of the ideal Christian community in Italy. This evolution was gradual, and the ideas contained within it were often mutually contradictory. In particular, as I shall argue, the association of Arianism with the Goths, despite the Arian affiliation of all the Ostrogothic royal families, did not become a feature of papal policy until the period of the Gothic Wars. Arianism was an issue separate from Gothic rule for most people at most times, and ecclesiastical faction rarely followed political faction. I make the arguments supporting this interpretation in ch. 6; see also ch. 4, n. 152.

recruited soldiers from the Pannonian and Italian provinces, and
absorbed the remnants of Odoacer's army. Theoderic besieged Odoacer
in Ravenna until 493, when he gained the city by treachery, and, after
agreeing to rule with Odoacer, murdered him at a dinner party.

Theoderic was now in control of Italy, but the emperor Zeno had
died in 491, and his successor Anastasius was not immediately amenable
to Theoderic's rule in the ancient home of the Roman Empire. It was
not until 497 that Anastasius recognized Theoderic as king, apparently,
like Odoacer, as a viceroy of the emperor in Italy. Anastasius sent the
Western imperial regalia back to the new king at Ravenna.

The new government at Ravenna was not all new. It continued to
use the same imperial administrative bureaucracy and many of the same
people who had served under the last Western emperors and under
Odoacer. Theoderic continued to honor the ceremonial prerogatives
of the senate at Rome, as Odoacer had done, and gained from Anastasius the right to nominate one of its members as a Western consul each
year. With the help of seasoned Italian politicians, such as the praetorian
prefect Liberius and Cassiodorus *père*, Theoderic arranged for members
of his army to be settled in Italy under some kind of reciprocal arrangement that may have involved the redistribution of tax revenues.

Theoderic's reign in Italy, from 493 to 526, is generally seen as a
period of prosperity and peace until just before its end. Although
Theoderic, members of his family and some of his followers subscribed
to the heretical Arian sect of Christianity, Theoderic tolerated and honored the majority Catholic church and the papacy at Rome. In the
year 500, he entered the city of Rome and celebrated his *tricennalia*, his
thirty-year anniversary of rule. He worshipped the relics of St. Peter at
the basilica on the Vatican Hill. He restored the walls and statues of
many cities, and embarked on a major building program in Ravenna,
including the Arian church now called Sant'Apollinare Nuovo. He fostered and probably actively encouraged an intellectual climate that led
to the production and reproduction of major works on philosophy,
theology and science. The king maintained steady neutrality in the
(Catholic) Laurentian schism, which divided the pope Symmachus from
the antipope Laurentius in 499 and 502, but finally intervened in Symmachus's favor in 507, after continuous riots and massacres in the city
of Rome. In the same year, the pro-Symmachan deacon Ennodius, later
bishop of Pavia, delivered a panegyric to the king suggesting that he
had singlehandedly revived the glory of the Western Empire.

Theoderic conducted a number of military campaigns in the name
of restoring lost territory to the Empire. He reconquered Sicily from
the Vandals in the early 490s. In 504, he launched a campaign in his

old home, Pannonia, and took over the Balkan provinces of Dalmatia and Savia. In 507, after Clovis and the Franks invaded the Visigothic kingdom of Toulouse, Theoderic entered the war and conquered Provence, the Narbonnaise and most of Spain, where he allowed his young Visigothic grandson Amalaric to rule as nominal king, and installed a regent from Italy named Theudis.

During this time, Theoderic, although doctrinally estranged from both sides, helped negotiations between the papacy and the Eastern churches on healing the Acacian schism. This split between the Western and Eastern churches had begun in 484, over methods of compromise with the monophysite heresy then popular in Alexandria and Syria. After the death of the pro-monophysite emperor Anastasius in 518, the churches were reunited under the new emperor Justin I and his nephew Justinian in 519.

Shortly after the reconciliation of the churches, things began to go wrong for Theoderic. He turned against his *magister officiorum*, the philosopher Boethius, in 523, on suspicion of treason, and had him imprisoned and executed. Shortly thereafter he forced Boethius's friend, the new pope John I, to travel to Constantinople to stop Justin and Justinian from enforcing long dormant imperial laws against the Arians in the Eastern Empire. At this same time, the Vandal king Thrasamund of Africa died, and the new king, Hilderic, began to mistreat Thrasamund's widow, Theoderic's sister Amalafrida. Theoderic, enraged, threatened Africa with war. Amalafrida died under suspicious circumstances in 525. In 526, Theoderic assembled a fleet and made preparations to invade Africa. These were cut short by his death from dysentery in August of 526.

Theoderic was succeeded by his grandson Athalaric, who was only ten years old. He ruled under the regency of his mother Amalasuintha, Theoderic's daughter. Because the Gothic army would not accept the militarily incapable leadership of a woman or of a minor, Amalasuintha appointed generals as co-regents. Our sources for Athalaric's short reign are not good, but apparently various military officers objected to his upbringing. Amalasuintha, classically educated herself, was not "bringing him up as a Goth," which probably meant that the young king was not receiving a military education. Amalasuintha handed him over to soldiers, where Athalaric led a life of debauchery and dissipation. He died in 534. Amalasuintha was then forced to accept the co-rule of her cousin Theodahad, not a military man either, but at least a man. The queen feared for her rule and for her life, and made overtures to Justinian, who had succeeded his uncle Justin as emperor in 527.

During the late 520s and 530s, the Eastern emperor Justinian embarked on a massive program of propaganda and repressive policy designed to create a single Catholic Mediterranean polity in the name of restoring the Roman Empire of the past. This program involved the first complete codification of Roman law, the building of new architectural projects such as Hagia Sophia in Constantinople, and the repression of all the many religions and Christian heterodoxies that did not conform to the emperor's own formulation of correct Christian doctrine.

Justinian's new policy of renewal inevitably suggested, for the first time, that the barbarian kingdoms of the West were no longer, in fact, part of the Roman Empire. The reconciliation of the Eastern and Western churches in 519 suggested a more momentous reconciliation: the reunion of the Eastern and Western Empires, administratively split since 395.

In 533, Justinian's armies invaded the Vandal kingdom in northern Africa on the pretext of restoring it to the Empire. In 535, Theodahad suspected Amalasuintha of turning Italy over to Justinian and had her imprisoned on a small island, where she was apparently murdered. Justinian, using this as a pretext, instructed his armies in Africa, under the general Belisarius, to reconquer Italy – even though it was nominally under his sovereignty anyway.

With Belisarius's invasion of Italy in 535, the Gothic Wars began, dividing the loyalties of the civilian inhabitants of the peninsula. The Byzantine armies told the Italian citizens of Syracuse and Naples that they had come to restore them to the Roman Empire; the Gothic armies reminded them how much they had benefited under the rule of Theoderic, legally recognized as the servant of the Roman emperors. This pattern, resembling the predicament of modern civilian populations caught between native guerilla forces and the occupying army of a colonial power, was to continue throughout the Wars.

The first stage of the Gothic Wars, from 535 to 540, did not go well for the Gothic army. Theodahad, clearly incapable of leading an army in battle, was deposed and murdered by his general Witigis in early 536. Witigis, who married Amalasuintha's daughter for the purposes of Amal legitimacy, was then chosen as king by the Gothic army. Meanwhile, Belisarius had advanced toward Rome and taken it. Witigis unsuccessfully besieged Belisarius in Rome from 536 to 537, and Belisarius besieged Witigis in Ravenna from 539 to 540. After the capitulation of Ravenna in 540, Belisarius sent Witigis in chains to Constantinople, where the ex-king subsequently retired with honor.

In 540, the Gothic Wars might have ended, but some sections of the Gothic army held out in northern Italy, in Verona and Pavia. This army was leaderless – its last three rulers had all tried to leave troubled Italy for a comfortable life in Constantinople; Witigis succeeded. But the Gothic army clearly wanted to retain its special corporate identity, necessarily in an Italy autonomous in some sense from the East. The army offered the kingship to Belisarius, who refused it. At the same time, a financial officer named Alexander arrived from the East as part of the new Byzantine administration in Ravenna. He enraged Italians of any sympathy with the typically outrageous Justinianic tax demands necessary for the maintenance of the emperor's constant wars and building projects.

No member of the Amal dynasty was left who had not defected to Byzantium.[11] After electing and deposing two ineffectual and unreliable kings, Hildebad and Eraric, the Gothic army offered its leadership to a young relative of the Spanish king Theudis, who was named Totila. His election probably owed something to the hope of bringing Theudis in on the Gothic side. But Spain stayed resolutely neutral in the conflict, successfully maintaining a renewed independence for the Visigothic kingdom. That kingdom would outlast Ostrogothic Italy by a century and a half.

In a series of swift and efficient campaigns, Totila reconquered almost all of Italy. Under Totila, the Gothic Wars continued from 541 to 552. Both the Gothic and Byzantine sides committed many atrocities, alienating large sections of the Italian civilian population, which could not afford to withhold its nominal support from whichever army happened to be occupying the region. Regions switched hands continually. Surrendered troops on either side joined the army against whom they had been fighting. There were frequent mass desertions in both directions. Totila besieged and occupied Rome twice, in 546–7 and in 550. In the winter of 550, the city of Rome was entirely depopulated for the first time in its history.

In 552, Totila was defeated and killed at the battle of Busta Gallorum by the Byzantine eunuch general Narses. Some Gothic troops, under the new king Teia in Cumae, continued resistance through the end of 552. Teia's younger brother Aligernus, continued to hold out until 554, when he joined the Byzantines against the Frankish troops of Theudebert I, who had occupied large sections of northern Italy in the last phases of the Gothic Wars.

Narses continued to pacify regions of Italy until the Franks were

---

[11] In the Prosopographical Appendix (PA), see **E**bremud, **A**malafridas, ***M**atasuentha (who married Justinian's cousin Germanus), possibly ***T**heudegisclus and ***T**heudenantha. Every Ostrogothic ruler from Amalasuintha onward, except for Teia, defected or considered defecting to Byzantium.

completely driven out in 561. At this point, some parts of northern Italy were in schism with both the papacy and Constantinople over the Three Chapters Controversy, which may have led them to ally with new groups of ex-Byzantine soldiers and barbarian freebooters coming in from Pannonia, the Lombards. In 568, Lombard groups overran northern and central Italy, which had long been devastated from over two decades of warfare, and continued to raid and seize different cities in different areas. The foundations of these raids eventually led to the formation of a Lombard kingdom based on Milan in the north, and two Lombard duchies in the middle of Italy, based at Spoleto and Benevento.

The Byzantine government treated its sections of Italy no longer as the ancient home of the Roman Empire, but as a military frontier province governed by a military official at Ravenna called the exarch. The regions are thus usually called the Exarchate of Ravenna. They included Rome, Ravenna, and a narrow strip of land between the two, the Via Flaminia, as well as Genoa, the area that would become Venice, southern Italy and Sicily. Italy did not form a single state again until the year 1870.

After the 550s, no individual called a Goth ever appears again in Italy.[12]

---

[12] The only possible exceptions: PA Widin (dating uncertain, 552/561), Wililiwa (613/641, but uncertain label: the reading "Goth" in the papyrus is a hazardous emendation). On Widin, see ch. 5, below.

Chapter 1

ETHNICITY, ETHNOGRAPHY AND COMMUNITY IN THE FIFTH AND SIXTH CENTURIES

Fifth- and sixth-century use of classical ethnographic ideologies – in propaganda, literature, theology and art – created the Goths of Italy. This re-use of elements from the heritage of Mediterranean ethnographic culture "created" the Goths not only for us, for whom they so frequently seem a concrete and stable community or tribe, but also for men and women of the period, for whom distinct advantages or disadvantages accrued from accepting the label Goth at different times and in different places.

Ancient ethnographic description of barbarian groups such as the Goths need not always have described ethnicity. Ethnicity is not the only form of community in a society, or the necessary primary identity for an individual. He or she may belong to several different groups, the relative importance of which can shift according to the circumstance of the moment. These different communities within society attracted ethnographic description in late antiquity. A soldier in Italy in 510 could belong to the Catholic church, own tax-bearing property and speak the Latin language. As a soldier he could be called a "Goth" by the king, as a Latin-speaking taxpayer a "Roman," as a member of the Catholic church and an inhabitant of Italy, a citizen of the *imperium Christianum* – or of the province of Lucani et Brutii and the episcopal see of Reggio. At different moments in his life, different labels would be of use to him or to the powers who chose to classify him in such ways. Some of these identities were more permanent than others, and over the lifetime of the Ostrogothic regime, he might be forced to choose his loyalties.

Prosopography – the study of individual behavior – illuminates the impact of ideology upon these varieties of communal allegiance. German and Austrian theories of early medieval ethnogenesis have partly demonstrated the importance of political ideology in the formation of some communities, which these theories see as "ethnic." By using prosopographical data and by questioning the assumption that ancient ethnography describes our term "ethnicity," I hope to complicate the ethnogenesis model considerably.

Regional, professional and institutional loyalties in Italy were as important in binding communities together as the loyalties described by the ethnographic terms "Goth" and "Roman," and were far less subject to ideological redefinition. Ethnographic ideology, which itself only occasionally emphasized descent, attempted to construct new communities by redefining profession and region in ethnographic terms: soldiers as Goths under Theoderic, obedient inhabitants of Italy as Romans under Justinian. Individual reactions to these ideologies show how evanescent and changeable were these new allegiances, and how persevering were the old submerged communities of *civitas* and profession in sixth-century Italy.

ETHNICITY: THE IDENTITY OF PEOPLES IN ANTHROPOLOGICAL TERMS

In current anthropological consensus, ethnicity means the definition of a group through cultural difference, usually on the basis of its belief in common descent and a shared past. It is thus, effectively, an irrational *belief* in biological "race," existing concurrently with other identities in society. It is at heart a subjective phenomenon, but it is justified by the group through its objectively visible cultural traits and concrete practices. Political leaders and groups can manipulate myths of the past to create or transform ethnicity. Thus groups of people in any given region can define themselves as the descendants of common ancestors, and explain cultural similarities such as language, dress, religion or law as due to this common descent. Common descent is articulated in a myth about the group's ancestry, regional origin and shared suffering through the generations.[1]

---

[1] Here I draw together the most commonly found elements in anthropological definitions of ethnicity; although there are of course dissenters, few anthropologists or historians would define as ethnicity any sort of primordial tie based on real biological descent or on any single cultural feature, even so important a cultural feature as language. The spectrum runs from scholars who emphasize "primordial ethnicity," a group-identity based on culture that is always there, to those who emphasize "instrumental ethnicity," a group-identity based on the political circumstances of the moment. In either view, status-differences and overlapping allegiances complicate the primary position of ethnicity within a society. The consensus view is that of Anthony D. Smith, *The Ethnic Origins of Nations* (Oxford, 1986), now updated in "The politics of culture: ethnicity and nationalism," in the *Companion Encyclopedia of Anthropology: Humanity, Culture and Social Life*, ed. Tim Ingold (London, 1994), pp. 706–33, esp. 707–8; see further Richard Jenkins, "Social anthropological models of inter-ethnic relations," in *Theories of Race and Ethnic Relations*, ed. John Rex and David Mason (Cambridge, 1986), pp. 170–86. Both build on the classic work of Frederik Barth, *Ethnic Groups and Boundaries: The Social Organization of Cultural Difference* (Boston, 1969). On the influence of familial and kin structures (arguing for ethnicity as an evolutionary and biological phenomenon), see Pierre L. van den Berghe, "Ethnicity and the sociobiology debate," in ibid., pp. 246–63, whose arguments, I believe, may demonstrate

It is clear that these differences exist within people's minds, because we do not believe any longer in biological determinism. "Race" is a word inexactly used to indicate groups in European history.[2] In the prescient words of Norman Baynes, writing in 1943: "I confess that as soon as the word 'race' is introduced into any discussion, I realize that my only safe course lies in a resolute silence, for I have never been able to understand the precise significance of that ambiguous term."[3] Race ought to refer only to categorization on the basis of perceived physiological difference.[4] This book is concerned with cultural constructions of community, not with breeding-stocks. Race is the insidious subtext of ethnicity, and we must constantly remind ourselves that whatever ethnic groups believe about their own ancestry, that ancestry does not determine cultural characteristics.[5]

the influence of biological ties not in a physical sense, but in a cultural sense. More recently, John and Jean Comaroff advocate an extreme instrumentalist position in *Ethnography and the Historical Imagination* (Boulder, Colorado, 1992), pp. 49–67. Further references are to be found in the notes below.

[2] The term "race" is still too frequently used to refer to barbarian groups, as if differences between barbarians and Romans were immediately physically obvious: see Peter Heather, *Goths and Romans 332–489* (Oxford, 1991), pp. 324, 325 ("the extent to which Visigoths and Ostrogoths were multiracial has been considerably overstated") and 326; John Moorhead, *Theoderic in Italy* (Oxford, 1993), p. 72 ("the imposition of race on a dichotomy which had already existed") and p. 85 ("marriages across racial lines"). Among other authors see Henry Chadwick, *Boethius: The Consolations of Music, Logic, Theology and Philosophy* (Oxford, 1981), p. 58. On other periods, places and groups in late antiquity, see Kenneth G. Holum, *Theodosian Empresses: Women and Imperial Dominion in Late Antiquity* (Berkeley, 1982), p. 9 (equating "non-Roman extraction" with "race"); T. S. Brown, *Gentlemen and Officers: Imperial Administration and Aristocratic Power in Byzantine Italy, A.D. 554–800* (Rome, 1984), pp. 67–8 (in the midst of a far more nuanced discussion than this terminological slip might suggest); Judith W. George, *Venantius Fortunatus: A Poet in Merovingian Gaul* (Oxford, 1992), p. 16; Alan Cameron, Jacqueline Long and Lee Sherry, *Barbarians and Politics at the Court of Arcadius* (Berkeley, 1993), p. 323, for whom the barbarians were "ethnic," "ethnicity" being equivalent to "race." ("Racial prejudice is always at least latent in any society with a sizable minority of a different ethnic origin.")

[3] Norman H. Baynes, "The decline of Roman power in Western Europe: some modern explanations," in Baynes, *Byzantine Studies and Other Essays*, (London, 1955), pp. 91–2.

[4] On race as a subjective construct see, for example, J. Milton Yinger, "Intersecting strands in the theorisation of race and ethnic relations," in Rex and Mason, *Theories of Race and Ethnic Relations*, pp. 20–41, arguing for a distinction between "socially and biologically defined races," the latter of interest to the biologist and physical anthropologist (p. 21), the former "a special case of ethnicity" (p. 20).

[5] Recently, genetics – a perfectly respectable field – has allowed non-specialists to make the connection between ethnicity and race once more. This connection appears, for example, in a review of a prize-winning book on odd genetic groups or genetic islands within European countries: see Steve Connor's review of *The Language of Genes* by Steve Jones (London, 1993) entitled "We know where they're coming from" (*The Independent*, 26 May 1994, p. 23). The article is decorated with pictures of individuals from various countries wearing what might be called national dress: a Scotsman with a flat cap, a Finnish woman with braids and an embroidered shirt, a Karenni woman with a set of neck-rings and a Surui man with facial paint. The article explains that through genetics we can detect "the biological remains of [an] early civilisation," for example, the Etruscans, in the blood cells of modern Umbrians. Similarly, genes in

Ethnicity is thus a historically determined phenomenon. Its stability is always in question. It is constantly in flux. In the process of ethnogenesis, ethnic identity can submerge, and reappear – with new definitions – under various circumstances. These circumstances include the outbreak of war, famine or other disasters, and the related formation of political consciousness among a group. When two groups, whether affiliated hitherto or not, are forced into sharing limited material resources, ethnicity *may* assume a preponderant role in dividing and defining each of them.[6]

So we must also take care that we do not assume that ethnicity is the paramount concern of any given group identified by the sources, even if it *is* described in ethnographic terms. A group described in ethnographic terms, if it existed, may really have been a regional community, a religious sect or a social class.[7]

It is not easy to determine subjective ethnic identity from objectively visible culture. Ethnicity can manifest itself in a wide variety of cultural traits, and a wide variety of cultural traits were at different times associ-

---

the north of England identical to ones found in inhabitants of Norway provide evidence for the Viking settlements. These people are the "living descendants of long-extinct civilisations." But "man's wonderful genetic diversity has come under threat" from interbreeding, so "scientists want to preserve blood samples from some of the world's remotest ethnic groups." The assumption that genetic relatedness determines culture and ethnicity is clear, and completely false. If any remnants of Etruscan or Viking *culture* survived in these areas, this culture can owe nothing to genes, or nothing that we can connect with genes in the state of our present knowledge of genetics. Nevertheless, the idea that genetics determined a special "Germanic" Christianity has already appeared in James C. Russell, *The Germanization of Early Medieval Christianity: A Sociohistorical Approach to Religious Transformation* (Oxford, 1994), p. 14. The notion of race continues to loom large in historical scholarship. We must guard against it.

[6] M. E. Burgess, "The resurgence of ethnicity: myth or reality?" *Ethnic and Racial Studies* 1 (1978), 265–85; W. E. Mühlmann, "Ethnogonie und Ethnogenese: theoretisch-ethnologische und ideologiekritische Studie," in *Studien zur Ethnogenese*, Abhandlungen der rheinisch-westfälischen Akademie der Wissenschaften 72 (Opladen, 1985); Anthony D. Smith, "War and ethnicity: the role of warfare in the formation, self-images and cohesion of ethnic communities," *Ethnic and Racial Studies* 4 (1981), 375–97; Smith, "The politics of culture," pp. 711–13. The "instrumentalist" definition sees ethnicity as an entirely political creation, at least in its origins, e.g. John and Jean Comaroff, *Ethnography and the Historical Imagination*, pp. 50–67, esp. 54–9. Due in part to such political redefinitions, the edges of an ethnic group are always bleeding and healing, as people leave it or join it through accepted devices such as intermarriage, emigration or rational choice determined by social or political exigency. On the other hand, see Yinger, "Intersecting strands," against rational choice theory: such choices must struggle against categorization by others. Recently, Patrick Geary has argued that what we call "ethnicity" was actually a situational construct in Merovingian Gaul, in which case the question arises whether such ties can usefully be called "ethnic" at all: "Ethnicity as a situational construct in the early Middle Ages," *Mitteilungen der anthropologischen Gesellschaft in Wien* 113 (1983), 15–26. Here is where an examination of ancient ethnography can help avoid prejudging the case.

[7] On the existence of ethnicity simultaneously with other social ties, next to which it may have a greater or lesser importance, see A. H. Halsey, "Ethnicity: a primordial social bond?" *Ethnic and Racial Studies* 1 (1978), 124–8.

ated with the name "Goth" by different observers. While the consistent possession of any of these cultural traits would not prove that their possessors constituted an ethnic group, neither does their absence or inconsistency in itself prove that their possessors were *not* an ethnic group. The Gothic language survived in the Crimea in the early modern period. But it survived among people who did not call themselves Goths.[8] More recently, on Cape Cod, a group of Americans culturally indistinguishable from other Massachusetts residents persuaded courts that they had claims on land because they preserved the ethnic memory of tribal identity as the Mashpee, and were therefore a tribe – or, in the view of one anthropologist, recreated themselves as a tribe on the basis of believed common descent in order to take advantage of material circumstance.[9] If historians in the distant future attempted to determine the Mashpee identity from cultural artefacts of the 1970s, they would find little on which to base their inquiry, aside from the court records. The Mashpee re-arose or re-formed during a crisis – or were created anew by that very crisis. Such redefinitions and use of past names can occur at any time, as the recent events in Bosnia demonstrate.[10] There

---

[8] Despite the use of the name *Gothia* for the region during the Byzantine Empire, this never seems to have translated into calling people there Goths (see A. A. Vasiliev, *The Goths in the Crimea*, Medieval Academy of America Publications 29 [Cambridge, Mass., 1936], pp. 70–252); by the time that our source, the ambassador of the Holy Roman Empire Ogier-Ghislain de Busbecq, arrived, the name Goth had vanished, but the language survived. Mühlmann, "Ethnogonie und Ethnogenese," pp. 15–16, warns against the identification of linguistic groups with ethnic groups.

[9] James Clifford, "Identity in Mashpee," in James Clifford, *The Predicament of Culture: Twentieth-Century Ethnography, Literature and Art* (Cambridge, Mass., 1988), pp. 277–346.

[10] In Bosnia, identities forcibly submerged since the Nazi occupation have apparently burst to the fore once more. This would be a naive interpretation. What has actually happened is that political leaders have used elements of history of the Nazi occupation and before to recreate an ethnic community. Despite the intermarriage between Serbs, Croats and Muslims, children of mixed families are expected to "choose" their "real" identity and stick to the political side thus delineated. People who in no way considered themselves to be Serbs ten years ago suddenly find themselves engaged in a bloody war defending their Serb interests. Their own children will grow up in this firmly defined group, holding quite a different notion of their group allegiance from their parents. On this process of redefining identity in former Yugoslavia, see Tony Barber, "Young men in no rush to join old battle," *The Independent on Sunday* 76 (7 July 1991), 17. Similar processes are going on in the conflict between Armenia and Azerbaijan: Robert Cullen, "Roots," *The New Yorker* (15 April 1991), 55–76. For conflicting interpretations of the primordiality of the identities of the warring groups in Rwanda, see Alex de Waal, "The genocidal state: Hutu extremism and the origins of the 'final solution' in Rwanda," *Times Literary Supplement* 4761 (1 July 1994), 3–4 (creation of Hutu and Tutsi ethnicities by the imposition of Western ideas during the colonial period), and Jean-Luc Vellut, "Ethnicity and genocide in Rwanda" [reply to de Waal], *Times Literary Supplement* 4763 (15 July 1994), 17 (ethnic and cultural divisions between Hutu and Tutsi extend back for centuries – wrongly, however, declaring that "ethnicity is a loan-concept from classical antiquity"; ethnicity in this sense is a loan-concept from the nineteenth-century *imagination* of classical antiquity, overlaid with twentieth-century anthropological ideas); see further de Waal, "Ethnicity and genocide in Rwanda"

is no question that there are Serbs in former Yugoslavia who have always called themselves Serbs, who lived through the Second World War and have always hated Croats. But their community is in a process of warlike and expansive self-redefinition. The "primordial" ethnic identity is proving itself surprisingly flexible.[11]

ETHNOGRAPHY: CLASSICAL LITERARY AND SCIENTIFIC FORMS OF IMAGINED COMMUNITY

Classical ethnographies defined communities not only by descent but also by profession, religion and, above all, by geography.[12] "Ethnography" is in fact our name, not that of the ancients, for the study of

[reply to Vellut], *Times Literary Supplement* 4764 (22 July 1994), 15; the fact that the rebel leader in Rwanda has both Hutu and Tutsi ancestry suggests that postcolonial anthropologists may be closer to the truth. None of these predicaments need offer parallels for Ostrogothic Italy, of course: the point is to underline the models that we have in our minds today, consciously or not, for the cohesion of groups described by ethnography.

[11] The final alternative notion, that we should simply use the late antique vocabulary for describing peoples, and thus avoid projecting modern analytical structures onto the past, seems to me naive. Some historians have recently complained about "methodologies imported into the study of ancient history from the social sciences by way of modern history": John Vanderspoel, review of *From Empire to Commonwealth: Consequences of Monotheism in Late Antiquity* by Garth Fowden, *Bryn Mawr Classical Review* 5.2 (1994), 13. But historical study, since the days of Pirenne and Bloch, has consistently used categories borrowed from the social sciences, whether "language," "society" or "bureaucracy," along with their accompanying expectations. We know that the Romans did not explain the genesis and classification of languages in the way we do, but we nonetheless study Latin syntactical development according to our modern expectations of how such development occurs. Particularly when we study late antiquity, we are forced to fill in the gaps between source material in order to answer questions about the period. We naturally fall back on our own models in order to fill these gaps, and so long as we realize the limitations of those models and the possibility that they do not apply to the period, it is surely better to define them explicitly than to rely on unspoken assumptions. We could simply use the word *gentes* to describe the barbarian groups, but in fact the use of this word was neither universal nor consistent, and we cannot be exactly certain what it meant: Herwig Wolfram, *History of the Goths*, 1979, 2nd rev. edn, trans. Thomas J. Dunlap (Berkeley, 1988), pp. 11–12. We are forced to use the language of the present-day social sciences as admittedly inadequate tools to discuss past social behavior. Perhaps when this behavior does not match expectations, historians can have something to teach social scientists.

[12] That ethnographic description was often ideological and often sterotyped does not mean that it never contained accurate observations about the groups or regions that it purported to examine; it was an essential tool of imperial diplomacy and tactics: A. D. Lee, *Information and Frontiers: Roman Foreign Relations in Late Antiquity* (Cambridge, 1993). But just because details could be correct does not mean that we must accept the whole *framework* for describing foreign groups and places as a transparent or objective template. The Byzantine historian Agathias was capable of recounting authentic characteristics of people who lived in sixth-century Gaul, but his classification of them as *Phrangoi*, "Franks," is an ethnographic and literary categorization that must be examined within the context of the history of such categorizations, with the cultural baggage that they carried for the observer. On Agathias, see Averil Cameron, "Agathias on the early Merovingians," *Annali della Scuola Normale di Pisa* 2nd ser. 37 (1968), 134–5.

peoples or communities. It did not form a separate literary or mental category of its own. In classical literature, the study of peoples was subsumed either under *geographia* or *chorographia*, that is, the two types of geography,[13] or else under history, and frequently both. It could thus be a topic of philosophy/science, or of literature, or of both. The literary historical genre *origo gentis*, from Tacitus to Jordanes, ties in geography as an inextricable characteristic of the group described. "De origine *et situ* Germanorum" is the title of Tacitus's work.[14] Pliny considered it essential to supply the *situs* of every people whose *mores* he described.[15]

In one influential form of ancient ethnography, climate determined the behavior of individuals and their classification into peoples. *Gentes* were indeed seen as being made up of *stirpes* and *genera*, clans or families, or even lineages, but these families did not transmit their *gens*-affiliation by descent: their place of habitation was far more important.[16]

In ethnogeography, as typified by the works of Pliny, Pomponius Mela and Ptolemy,[17] the excesses of barbaric *gentes* were a result of their

[13] On the ideologies inherent in Roman geographical works, see C. R. Whittaker, *Frontiers of the Roman Empire: A Social and Economic Study* (Baltimore, 1994), pp. 12–18.

[14] And it begins, famously, by locating *Germania* as *place* divided from *peoples*: "Germania omnis a Gallis Raetisque et Pannoniis Rheno et Danuvio fluminibus, a Sarmatis Dacisque mutuo metu aut montibus separatur . . . " Tacitus, *Germ.* 1.1, ed. J. G. C. Anderson (Oxford, 1938).

[15] Pliny, *Nat. Hist.*, Books 2–6, ed. and trans. H. Rackham, W. H. S. Jones and D. E. Eichholz, 10 vols. (Cambridge, Mass., 1938–62).

[16] On the political and ideological uses of ethnographic vocabulary, that is, *Romanus, gens, natio, populus, patria* and various ethnographic group-names, see the detailed but overschematizing and philological account of Suzanne Teillet, *Des Goths – la nation gothique: les origines de l'idée de nation en Occident du Ve au VIIe siècle* (Paris, 1984), pp. 17–38; cf. Herwig Wolfram, review of Teillet, *Francia* 13 (1985), 724–6. I am unpersuaded by Teillet's argument, detailed though it is; she does not pay sufficient attention to the varying rhetorical and ideological uses of the terminology that she describes. Elsewhere I have attempted to examine such terminology, and even within a single source its meanings can be complex indeed: Patrick Amory, "The meaning and purpose of ethnic terminology in the Burgundian laws," *Early Medieval Europe* 2 (1993), 1–28. On the etymological connotations of descent in *natio, gens* and *genos* (but not *ethnos*), known to some late antique writers but coexisting with other definitions, see p. 24 with n. 42, below.

[17] For an exceptionally clear summary of ethnogeography in general, see Gilbert Dagron, " 'Ceux d'en face': les peuples étrangers dans les traités militaires byzantins," *Travaux et Mémoires* 10 (1987), 207–15: "Geography commands ethnology" (p. 215); James S. Romm, *The Edges of the Earth in Ancient Thought* (Princeton, 1992), pp. 44–9; also J. P. V. D. Balsdon, *Romans and Aliens* (London, 1979), pp. 59–60. On climatic theory, see K. Trüdinger, *Studien zur Geschichte der griechisch-römischen Ethnographie* (Basel, 1918), pp. 37–8, 51–2. On the Greek origins of ethnogeographic climatic theory and its influential propagation in a text by a writer in the Hippocratic school (the anonymous *perì aéron hudáton tópon*), see J. G. C. Anderson in Tacitus, pp. xiii–xv. On ethnogeography in specific works, see Klaus Erich Müller, *Geschichte der antiken Ethnographie und ethnologischen Theoriebildung* 2 (Wiesbaden, 1982), pp. 123–37 (Pomponius Mela), 141–2 (Pliny). On the relationship between ethnography, medicine and claims of Roman superiority, see Y. A. Dauge, *Le barbare: recherches sur la conception romaine de la barbarie et de la civilisation*, Collection Latomus 176 (Brussels, 1981), *passim* and pp. 806–10.

placement on the cold or hot edges of the world. In the temperate Mediterranean, the civilized man could master his own temper and thus achieve a state of wisdom, *prudentia*, with which to master the barbarians outside.[18] The Mediterranean, "center of the world," providentially became the enclosed heart of the Roman Empire, *mare nostrum*, a unity naturally different from the turbulent plurality of the varied extreme temperatures to the north and the south.[19] Climate "permet de placer la Romanité au centre du tableau et d'annuler en elle toute marque d'ethnicité."[20] When they used this particular framework, geographers distinguished between provinces within the Empire, and peoples without.[21] Ethnogeography explained the providential domination of Mediterranean men – always men – through the beneficial effects of a moderate climate. Cities and lawful governance were the exterior reflection of the peaceable and firm control that the Mediterranean man had within himself.[22]

To the north and south of the Mediterranean, by no accident in the regions just beyond the Roman imperial frontiers, unfortunate men lived without cities in the harsh extremes of the Sahara Desert, the Carpathians, the Alps and the Black Forest. Horribly hot or cold, the men from these regions could never learn to control themselves, and hence never learned to live in cities, govern themselves by laws or to control their emotions. They had no education.[23]

Since geography determined the characteristics of *gentes*, the same regions kept pouring forth barbarians with the same characteristics.

---

[18] On the "interior barbarian," see Dauge, *Le barbare*, pp. 307–78, 806–10. "There is in each of us a barbarian tribe, extremely overbearing and intractable" (Themistius, *Or*. 10, ed. H. Schenkls, rev. Glanville Downey and A. F. Norman, *Themistii opera* 1 [Leipzig, 1965], p. 199; in *The Goths in the Fourth Century*, ed. Peter Heather and John Matthews, trans. David Moncur [Liverpool, 1991], pp. 38–9).

[19] Pliny, *Nat. Hist.* 2.80.189–90; Pomponius Mela, *De chorographia*, ed. K. Frick (Leipzig, 1880), 1.1–24 and *passim* – though both these authors characteristically go on to describe a plurality of people and customs even in the Mediterranean. Roman imperial writers inherited pre-imperial ethnographic description of regions that would become Roman provinces from the Greek writers like Posidonius and from writers of the Republic, and they did not jettison such description to fit a newer theory that resulted from imperial ideology of Roman superiority, on which see below.

[20] Dagron, " 'Ceux d'en face,' " pp. 215–16.

[21] However, as we shall see, the Roman unity/barbarian plurality model coexisted with older models allowing plurality of *gentes* within the Empire.

[22] On control of the body, see Michel Foucault, *The History of Sexuality* 2: *The Use of Pleasure*, 1984, trans. Robert Hurley (New York, 1985), pp. 97–139; Peter Brown, *The Body and Society: Men, Women and Sexual Renunciation in Early Christianity* (New York, 1988), pp. 9–12.

[23] Pliny, *Nat. Hist.* 2.80.189–90. Different characteristics, chiefly physiological traits, might be added to these for each barbarian group described in ethnographic texts as living beyond the frontiers, but there was also a broad difference between south and north; southerners were weaker than the Romans, northerners more stupid (Balsdon, *Romans and Aliens*, pp. 59–60).

Even though these barbarians bore a different name, they were essentially the same and might even be given the same name, the so-called "doctrine of transference." Thus the Scythians in these texts, the people northwest of the Danube delta and the Black Sea, may have changed their name to "Goths" in the third century, but from the Roman viewpoint they were still Scythians at heart, because they continued to emerge from the same unforgiving geography.[24] When they came into the Roman Empire, however, either by entering Roman service or as captured slaves, the barbarians could – within a generation – shed their ancient characteristics and become Romans.[25]

But different *gentes* also existed within the Empire itself, as these same texts show. Roman imperialist ethnogeography, opposing the middle of the world to the extremes, coexisted with older forms of ethnography. The schematism of imperialist ethnogeography suited it for imperial ideology and *paideia*, but not for actual description of the Mediterranean world. Ethnographies of the Greeks and of the Roman Republic had considered other inhabitants of the Mediterranean and other areas that later became part of the Empire barbarians. These contradictorily survive in Roman ethnographies that oppose a civilized center to barbaric north and south.[26]

Some *gentes* in the interior of the Empire never stopped being considered barbarians, such as the groups called Isaurians and the Basques.[27] Conversely, barbarian regions outside the Empire were considered to

---

[24] Wolfram, *Goths*, p. 7; Dagron, "'Ceux d'en face'," p. 215; Anderson in Tacitus, pp. xxix–xxxii.

[25] Aurelius Victor attributed the success of Rome to activity of immigrants and imported skills: *De caesaribus* 11.13, ed. Franz Pichlmayr (Leipzig, 1911), as Walter Goffart points out in "The date and purpose of Vegetius' *De re militari*," 1977, reprinted in Goffart, *Rome's Fall and After*, p. 71. Although this need not have been a particularly easy or pleasant experience before 212, due to the legal difficulties and barriers imposed in the process of becoming a citizen (Balsdon, *Romans and Aliens*, pp. 83–96), it was one through which people from large parts of the Empire as well as people from outside the Empire had to go; in cases before 212, where the entrant was not seeking citizenship, or in all cases of immigration after 212, the very variety of the Empire ensured that becoming a "Roman" in the broad geographical and subject-political sense was not traumatic or difficult in itself. In late antiquity, "Roman citizenship" becomes an archaic phrase, loaded with ideological overtones, but not legal privilege; see Amory, "The meaning and purpose of ethnic terminology," pp. 15–17, to which add *Nov. Theod.* 16, contra e.g. R. C. Blockley, *East Roman Foreign Policy: Formation and Conduct from Diocletian to Anastasius*, ARCA 30 (Leeds, 1992), p. 82 (on Theoderic), and Heather, *Goths and Romans*, pp. 164–5 (on Theodosius and fourth-century Goths), both supporting themselves on classicizing works, which use phrases involving *civitas* and *polis* as indications of Roman cultural superiority.

[26] Balsdon, *Romans and Aliens*, pp. 29–54, 60–70.

[27] Walter Goffart, "The theme of '*the* barbarian invasions' in later antique and modern historiography," in Goffart, *Rome's Fall and After*, p. 113 with n. 7.

lie under the power of the emperor.[28] The early fourth-century Verona List refers to the "barbarian *gentes* who multiplied under the emperors," including *externae gentes* with the inhabitants of the Mediterranean,[29] and other texts similarly do not differentiate between *gentes* outside the Empire, and *gentes* such as the Africans, Italians and Thracians, traditionally considered "Roman."[30]

If climatic ethnogeography was the language of providential imperial victory and expansionism,[31] other forms simply stressed the diversity of the *oikoumene*. In the tradition of theogony, peoples and dynasties were descended from gods, a literary notion transmitted by Homer and Vergil.[32] Other literary works deployed satirical virtue-based ethnographies, such as those of Tacitus and Salvian.[33] The *gentes* could provide merely a mass of rhetorical allusions and topoi, as in Avitus or Gregory of Tours.[34] Amidst such variety the meaning of "Roman" did

---

[28] Whittaker, *Frontiers*, pp. 14–18.

[29] Goffart, "Rome, Constantinople and the barbarians," p. 4.

[30] Vibius Sequester, *De fluminibus*, 317–61, ed. Remo Gelsomino (Leipzig, 1967), also listing Apuli, Getae, Sauromatae, Teutones, and so on.

[31] Most recently, Romm, *The Edges of the Earth*, pp. 120–71. On depictions of barbarians in imperial victory ideology, see Sabine MacCormack, *Art and Ceremony in Late Antiquity* (Berkeley, 1981), pp. 71–2, 216–17; Whittaker, *Frontiers*, pp. 28–30, 37, 241–2. On the functions of victory ideology over barbarians, see Michael McCormick, *Eternal Victory: Triumphal Rulership in Late Antiquity, Byzantium and the Early Medieval West* (Cambridge, 1986), p. 4: "The ruler's military success confirmed his right to rule."

[32] *Origo gentis Romanae*, ed. Franz Pichlmayr in his edition of Aurelius Victor (Leipzig, 1911), pp. 4–22; this text can perhaps also be seen as an antiquarianizing return to an idea of *Italy* as a providential place for the origins of Rome: "Primus in Italiam creditur venisse Saturnus" is the first line of the text (§1.1); in the two main codices it is a prolegomena to the *De viris illustribus urbis Romae* (Pichlmayr, p. 23) – but since the MSS are very late (fourteenth and fifteenth century), the attachment of the two texts need not be a late antique phenomenon.

[33] The literary genre of "inverse ethnocentrism" in which the author incidentally upheld traditional values by pointing up the ridiculousness of inverting them, is most recently discussed by Romm, *The Edges of the Earth*, pp. 46–9, 70–7; see also Karl Christ, "Germanendarstellung und Zeitverständnis bei Tacitus," 1965, reprinted in Karl Christ, *Römische Geschichte und Wissenschaftsgeschichte 2: Geschichte und Geschichtsschreibung der römischen Kaiserzeit* (Darmstadt, 1983), pp. 140–51; Michael Maas, "Ethnicity, orthodoxy and community in Salvian of Marseilles," in *Fifth-Century Gaul: A Crisis of Identity?*, ed. John Drinkwater and Hugh Elton (Cambridge, 1992), pp. 275–84. Cf. also Themistius (Goffart, "Rome, Constantinople and the barbarians," p. 16): Themistius implies that the raid of the barbarian is no worse than the exactions of the tax-collector.

[34] Patrick Amory, "Ethnographic rhetoric, aristocratic attitudes and political allegiance in post-Roman Gaul," *Klio* 76 (1994), 440–6, although Augustine's theology allowed him to see everything ugly or evil as beautiful and holy if one saw it, properly, as part of a divine whole within which everything had a purpose. In *De civitate dei* (ed. Bernard Dombart and Alfonsus Kalb, 1928 [5th edn, Stuttgart, 1981]), Augustine states: "clean and unclean are contained within the church's unity" (15.27); heresies are necessary to show which people are of sound condition; all elements of the world are essential, only some directly effective (16.2 , similarly 18.51); monstrous races seem ugly to us because we cannot see the beauty of the whole (16.8). On the conceptual expansion of the church to include the entire world, see below, n. 39.

not narrow and grow fixed,[35] but rather gained a plethora of uses, whether ideological or rhetorical.[36] Varieties of ethnographic meaning multiplied in late antiquity when Christianity began to provide the divergent Eastern and Western ethno-geographies with new classifications.[37] Eusebian ideals in the East promoted a Roman Empire determined by the Christian religion, and of barbarians defined as heretics.[38] In contrast, Augustine and the papacy in the West prophesied a universal *civitas dei* in which all *gentes*, even barbarians, would belong to the Church.[39]

---

[35] As Herwig Wolfram argues, "The shaping of the early medieval kingdom," *Viator* 1 (1970), 2, n. 6.

[36] Thus *Romanus* could refer to the city of Rome, to the Roman Empire, to Roman citizens, to *Romani* as a *gens, natio* or *populus*. It could have political or religious overtones or both, enmeshed in its ethnogeographic meanings. By the fifth and sixth centuries, the papacy and some Western Catholics had begun to adopt it for the church and its members. See Manfred Fuhrmann, "Die Romidee der Spätantike," 1968, and Michael Seidlmayer, "Rom und Romgedanke im Mittelalter," 1965 (both reprinted in *Rom als Idee*, ed. Bernhard Kytzler, Wege der Forschung 656 [Darmstadt, 1993], pp. 88–123, 158–87). *Romanus* = "Catholic" (see chs. 6 and 7). From the late 520s, Justinian claimed the entire politico-religious heritage of the word *Romanus* in the providential tones of victory ideology; such ideology insisted that all inhabitants of former provinces were Romans, but in the end associated "Roman" particularly with the government at Constantinople (see ch. 4). Of course, over several centuries, Greek-speaking Christian subjects of the Byzantine emperors learned to call themselves *Rhomaioi*, "Romans," an ethnogenesis that produced an identity lasting until the early nineteenth century; see further Johannes Koder, "Byzanz, die Griechen und die Romaiosyne – eine 'Ethnogenese' der 'Römer'?" in *Typen der Ethnogenese unter besonderer Berücksichtigung der Bayern* 1, ed. Herwig Wolfram and Walter Pohl, Denkschriften der philosophisch-historischen Klasse 201, Veröffentlichungen der Kommission für Frühmittelalterforschung 12 (Vienna, 1990), pp. 103–13.

[37] This is visible in Christian texts, influenced by biblical genealogies of peoples, from earliest times. The third-century chronicle of Hippolytus suggested an ethnography based on the inheritance of the world by the offspring of Noah. Such models could still be influenced by ethnogeography: Hippolytus followed his genealogy of Noah's descendants with a geography of the Mediterranean world. On Hippolytus, see Steven Muhlberger, *The Fifth-Century Chroniclers: Prosper, Hydatius, and the Gallic Chronicle of 452*, ARCA 27 (Leeds, 1990), pp. 13–14.

[38] The cosmology of Eusebius is a syncretism of Christian and ethnogeographic mental conceptions in which the Roman Empire itself took on the identity of the providential Christian community via the person of the emperor, continuing both the emperor-cult and victory ideology in a new framework that incorporated Hellenistic ideas of sacral monarchy. See Norman H. Baynes, "Eusebius and the Christian Empire," [1933] in Baynes, *Byzantine Studies and Other Essays* (London, 1955), pp. 168–72; Norman H. Baynes, "The Hellenistic civilization and East Rome," [1945], ibid., pp. 9–10, 17–18; Francis Dvornik, *Early Christian and Byzantine Political Philosophy: Origins and Background*, 2 vols., Dumbarton Oaks Studies 9 (Washington, D.C., 1966), 2, pp. 611–58. Victory ideology itself, with all its pagan overtones, took on a noticeably Christian tint; see MacCormack, *Art and Ceremony in Late Antiquity*, esp. 145–58; and McCormick, *Eternal Victory*, pp. 100–11. Note the use of ethnographic Christian-state providentiality even in a Western law issued in Italy by Glycerius in 473, which prohibits simony to avoid offending divinity, so that the *Romana gens* may not meet misfortune (Edict of Glycerius to Himelco, ed. Gustav Haenel, *Corpus legum* §1226 [Leipzig, 1857], p. 260).

[39] The *City of God* directly challenged the use of an ethnography of Roman superiority in a Christian world, and announced that Christianity would spread to all peoples: *De civitate dei* 20.11, see also 18.32, 18.47–9; Augustine, *ep.* 93.31 ("The church shall be preserved to the

The word *gens* itself was transformed. Biblical models supplied the notion of a "people under arms,"[40] and *gens* translated biblical peoples in Jerome's Vulgate in the late fourth century. A *gens* could be a blessed or a wicked people – the Israelites or the Philistines. This usage dovetailed nicely with the classical ethnographic notion that the barbarian *gentes* were warlike, producing a new confluence of meanings in legal and literary texts.[41] In the midst of the Gothic Wars, Theoderic's former minister Cassiodorus twice explained that *gens* came from *genus*, and was a group descended from one family, a group sharing common ancestry. But he made these equations in his exegesis on the psalms, to explain the Vulgate word *gentiles* ("nations" in the Authorised Version).[42] Cassiodorus's etymology of *gens* is tied to the biblical and pseudotheogonistic concept of the patriarch and his offspring. The

end, until it includes all peoples, even barbarian ones"), ed. A. Goldbacher, 5 vols., CSEL 34, 44, 57–8 (Prague, Vienna and Leipzig, 1885–1923); Norman H. Baynes, "The political ideas of St. Augustine's *De Civitate Dei*," [1936] in Baynes, *Byzantine Studies and Other Essays*, pp. 288–306; R. A. Markus, *Saeculum: History and Society in the Theology of Saint Augustine* (Cambridge, 1970), pp. 35–40, 60–1. Augustine synthesized the concepts of an expanding Christianity and a doomed earthly Empire, against conservatives who wished to maintain an unpolluted Christianity as an elect, minority sect (Peter Brown, "Pelagius and his supporters: aims and environment," [1968] in Brown, *Religion and Society in the Age of Saint Augustine* (London, 1972), pp. 203–7. Augustine, of course, was a product of the late fourth century, and he continues the Eusebian equation of church and state in his demands for secular religious coercion (Markus, *Saeculum*, pp. 133–53, esp. 147–8).

Eusebianism survived in the West, but competed with Augustinian ideals (see ch. 6). Augustine's cosmology was spread by his disciple and secretary to Leo the Great, Prosper of Aquitaine, whose *Call of All Nations* celebrated and demanded, for the first time, the evangelism of the barbarians via the new Rome, seat of the pope: "But the grace of Christianity is not content with the boundaries that are Rome's. Grace has now submitted to the sceptre of the Cross of Christ many peoples whom Rome could not subject with her arms" (*De vocatione omnium gentium* 2.16, PL 51 [Paris, 1861]). Prosper's enormously influential and popular *Chronicle* played down the devastations of civil war and barbarian disruption in favor of the triumph of the church (Muhlberger, *The Fifth Century Chroniclers*, pp. 126–35). See also Muhlberger, pp. 102–10: an Augustinian view of secular history suffuses the work. On the mixture of the ideas of Augustine and Leo in Prosper, see R. A. Markus, "Chronicle and theology: Prosper of Aquitaine," in *The Inheritance of Historiography*, ed. Christopher Holdsworth and T. P. Wiseman (Exeter, 1986), pp. 31–41. Augustine's ideas were transmitted to subsequent papal supremacists such as Gelasius (see ch. 6).

Augustine's ideas had a massive impact on Western views of the ideal community and virtually none on Eastern views (Berthold Altaner, "Augustinus in der griechischen Kirche bis auf Photius," 1952, reprinted in Altaner, *Kleine patristischen Schriften*, ed. Günter Glockmann, Texte und Untersuchungen 83 [Berlin, 1967], pp. 57–98.

40 The phrase is Herwig Wolfram's from his article "Gothic history and historical ethnography," *Journal of Medieval History* 7 (1981), pp. 312–13, 316, adducing the use of *origines gentis* to show the influence of royal genealogies from pagan gods on the creation of such peoples, on which see pp. 34–9, below (ethnogenesis theory).

41 *Gentiles* as troops: CT 7.15.1, on which see Jones, LRE I: 651–2. *Gentiles* as pagans: CT 16.5.43. *Gentiles* as foreigners: CT 12.12.5. On *gentes* and *gentiles* as heretics, see Amory, "Ethnographic rhetoric, aristocratic attitudes and political allegiance," pp. 440–4.

42 Cassiodorus, *Expositio Psalmorum* 2.9; 78.1.

"seed of Israel" denotes "the full complement of all *gentes*."[43] Elsewhere in his commentary, which is influenced by that of Augustine,[44] and by contemporary papal politics,[45] he declares that *omnes gentes* have been called to join the Catholic church, "assembled from different parts of the world."[46]

Consequently, armies and soldiers began to attract the vocabulary of ethnography. *Gens* comes to mean "army," *barbarus* to mean "soldier," even in the imperial rhetoric of fifth-century legal texts.[47] These equations were doubtless related to the settlement of mercenary bands from outside the frontier within the Empire for the first time, who supposedly replaced regular "Roman" troops, the "barbarization of the Roman army."[48] But it is also part of a new way of thinking about the profession of soldier – what we could call the "militarization of ethnography."[49] The full synthesis of Western "professional" and "biblical" ethnography appears in Isidore of Seville,[50] whose notions would prove dominant in the Middle Ages, but which were already blossoming in the fifth and sixth centuries.

[43] Ibid., 21.25.
[44] Ibid., *praef.*
[45] See ch. 6.
[46] Cassiodorus, *Expositio Psalmorum*, 116.1.
[47] *Gentiles* as troops, see above, n. 41. *Barbarus* as soldier: CJ 12.20.5 (the *scrinium barbarorum*, which recruited soldiers among the barbarians, with William Sinnigen, "*Barbaricarii, barbari* and the *Notitia dignitatum*," *Latomus* 22 [1963], 806–15); CT 11.30.62: appeals by *barbari* are to be heard by their prefects; CT 3.14.1: the *barbari gentiles* whom the *provinciales* of Thrace were forbidden to marry were clearly soldiers. Alaric's troops are *foederati* when fighting on behalf of the emperor, *barbari* when rebelling against him: CT 5.7.2; 7.16.2; 10.10.25; 15.14.14. The equation is clearer in the post-Roman law-codes; see Amory, "The meaning and purpose of ethnic terminology," pp. 9–10, 24–6 (with similar prohibition on marriage). The equation of *barbarus* with "soldier" appears in non-military texts earlier because the late antique laws ideologically use the word *barbarus* as a synonym for "enemy"; see Sven Rugullis, *Die Barbaren in den spätrömischen Gesetzen: eine Untersuchung des Terminus "barbarus,"* Europäische Hochschulschriften, ser. 3: Geschichte und ihre Hilfswissenschaften 513 (Frankfurt, 1992). Note also the tendency of Roman regiments to gather ethnographic names (see p. 28, below).
[48] See pp. 28–9, below.
[49] Sixth-century Syriac sources use the word "Goth" to mean soldier, but even more commonly, "Roman" (Peter Brown, personal communication).
[50] Isidore defines an army as a people under arms: "Exercitus multitudo ex uno genere, ab exercitatione belli vocata" (*Etym.* 9.3.58), and defines a *gens* as a group from one place: "Gens est multitudo ab uno principio orta, sive ab alia natione secundum propriam distincta, ut Graeciae, Asiae" (*Etym.* 9.2.1); these *gentes* are also, but secondarily, defined etymologically from *gigno* and *nascor* (9.2.1), and they are descended from the peoples of the bible (9.2.2); peoples, we have learned, are *gentiles* ripe for Christianity (8.10.3–4), and language comes after the geographical wanderings of the sons of Noah (9.2.3–9.3.56).
    This interpretation differs fundamentally from that of Dietrich Claude, "Gentile und territoriale Staatsideen im Westgotenreich," *Frühmittelalterliche Studien* 6 (1972), 17. Claude emphasizes *Abstammungsgemeinschaft*, descent, over geographical origin; Isidore does the reverse. Claude does allow that Isidore mentions geographical origin, but only in a footnote (n. 114).

OTHER COMMUNITIES WITHIN THE ROMAN EMPIRE:
PROFESSION, REGION, AND STATUS

The ethnographic texts of late antiquity themselves occasionally suggest non-ethnic ways of understanding the barbarian groups: the categories of profession and region. Recent work on the military origins of the barbarian groups, and on localizing tendencies at work within the late Roman Empire, suggest that profession and region were just as important foci of communal identity as belief in common descent. The *gentes barbarae* multiplied *within* the Empire at the same time as regiments of the Roman army in disrupted frontier regions were growing increasingly alienated or isolated from the imperial centers. As centralizing and homogenising imperial ideology declined in the West, the distinction between "army" and *gens* was becoming increasingly blurred not merely in rhetoric, but also in reality.

The barbarian groups who first appear as corporate entities within the Roman Empire in the late fourth century emerged from the military milieu of the Roman frontier regions. We now know that these frontiers were not lines or barriers, but broad economic and cultural zones, containing provinces and communities quite different from the Mediterranean centers of Rome or Antioch.[51] On, or rather in, these frontiers, which were important recruiting-grounds, "Roman soldiers" were scarcely distinguishable from "barbarian soldiers."[52] The inadequate vocabulary differentiating between regular and irregular (or "allied") troops in the fifth-century Roman army[53] conceals the unre-

---

[51] On frontiers, see Benjamin Isaac, "The meaning of the terms *limes* and *limitanei*," *Journal of Roman Studies* 78 (1988), 125–47, and Whittaker, *Frontiers*, *passim*, esp. 226–8. The polemical criticism of these historians by Everett L. Wheeler, "Methodological limits and the mirage of Roman strategy," *Journal of Military History* 57 (1993), 7–41, 215–40, does not convince me. Wheeler uses a transhistorical notion of "strategy" to condemn both authors as reductionist "new historians" who take "the high road" toward sources in order to "demilitarize" history, and who refuse to believe in objectivity (13–21), none of which is valid in the slightest. Wheeler himself uses sources with little attention to bias and meaning, for example his citation of *Dig.* 49.15.24 to support the idea that "Germans were officially recognized as public enemies (*hostes*) as opposed to brigands (*latrones*) in Roman law" (25–6); in fact this third-century law – an ideological and archaicizing framework, of course – cites *Germani* not as declared enemies of Rome but as an example of a possible enemy, perhaps with an earlier time in mind; the distinction between *latrones* and *hostes* here does not put *Germani* in the latter category permanently: it distinguishes between forms of conflict (exterior, interior; formal, informal) and especially the fate of individuals captured by either type of army.
On archeological frontier cultures, see Guy Halsall, "The origins of the *Reihengräberzivilisation*: forty years on," in Drinkwater and Elton (eds.), *Fifth-Century Gaul*, pp. 196–207.
[52] "Roman soldiers" and "barbarian soldiers": Whittaker, *Frontiers*, pp. 192–278; Thomas S. Burns, *Barbarians Within The Gates of Rome* (Bloomington, Indiana, 1994), p. 146.
[53] *Foederati* an uncertain term with no essential meaning of "barbarian": Olympiodorus, *frag.* 7.4, in *The Fragmentary Classicising Historians of the Later Roman Empire*, ed. R. C. Blockley, 2 vols.

liability of the late Roman army in general from the emperor's point of view.[54] Private armies and the rise of warlords who were also land-lords made it easy for ambitious rebels and usurpers to build bases of power in regions distant from the imperial court.[55]

Professional identity, mandated by emperors intent on separating the civilian and military branches of government, strengthened new military elites. Laws on the army required the heritability of the profession of soldier and the army's complete withdrawal from civilian life.[56] These laws may have aided the appearance of a strong military aristocracy from the late third and early fourth century. This aristocracy intermarried with the imperial dynasties and with barbarian leaders, to the extent that the behavior and culture of all these people is not categorizable by ethnographic classification.[57] The leaders of these groups were related to each other, to the emperor and to Latin-named military aristocrats of obscure origin. As they assembled private property and private armies, their imperial titles, such as *magister militum*, became *de facto* hereditary alongside their profession. Eventually, the power of the military dynasty might outgrow the original imperial commission, forcing the emperor to negotiate constantly with the military leaders and play one off against the other, as occurred in the late fifth- and early sixth-century Balkans.[58]

ARCA 6 and 10 (Liverpool, 1981–3), with Whittaker, *Frontiers*, p. 272; above, n. 47, on the varying vocabulary for Alaric and his troops. For different definitions of *foederati* in the fourth and fifth centuries, see Heather, *Goths and Romans*, pp. 108–13, 253–4. On the historiographical myth of an imperial "federate policy," see Burns, *Barbarians*, pp. xvii–xix.

[54] In general on the late Roman army, see J. H. W. G. Liebeschuetz, *Barbarians and Bishops: Army, Church and State in the Age of Arcadius and Chrysostom* (Oxford, 1990), pp. 7–85, although it will be clear that I do not agree that "the Roman government came to rely to such a large extent on barbarians" (11): this statement assumes that it was easy to identify a barbarian. But if borders, frontier regions and identities were as diverse as recent work suggests, the "recruitment of barbarians" can also be seen as the assumption of quasi-autonomy, and of ethnographic identities different in name from that claimed by the emperor, by regiments of the army. On Liebes-chuetz's rather uncritical use of ethnogenesis theory, see Amory, "The meaning and purpose of ethnic terminology," pp. 1–2, nn. 4 and 6. Burns argues that frontier societies in areas such as Raetia had become entirely militarized from the late fourth century (Burns, *Barbarians*, pp. 112–47).

[55] Whittaker, *Frontiers*, pp. 243–78.

[56] Heritability: CT 22.1–12. Separation of soldiers and civilians: CT 1.5.10; 1.6.11; 1.7.4; 1.15.7; 2.1.2; 2.1.9; 8.4.28; 9.2.2; *Nov. Theod.* 4; *Nov. Marc.* 1.7. Despite the laws on the subject, civilians and soldiers were in close contact; see Ramsay MacMullen, *Soldier and Civilian in the Later Roman Empire* (Cambridge, Mass., 1963), pp. 119–51. A similar situation prevailed in Ostrogothic Italy, as we shall see, despite government rhetoric to the contrary.

[57] Alexander Demandt, "Magister militum," *RE* Suppl. 12 (Stuttgart, 1970), 553–788; Alexander Demandt, "The osmosis of late Roman and Germanic aristocracies," *RE* Suppl. 12 (Stuttgart, 1970), pp. 75–86 with table after 86.

[58] Demandt, "Magister militum," cols. 785–6. Parallel to the unmanageability of the Balkan armies in the late fifth century is the contemporary loss of legitimacy of the late Western puppet-

A cosmopolitan institution – a regiment in Anatolia might contain men from Narbonne, Bergamo, north Africa and Britain – the fourth- and fifth-century army nonetheless had collected ethnographic and regional names among its regiments. There was the "regiment of the Persoarmenians," "the regiment of the Heruls," "the regiment of the Batavians" and so on.[59] We might attribute this process to recruitment from among barbarians.[60] But such recruitment had been going on since the third century. And the parallel practice of naming regiments after gods (*Herculani, Joviani*)[61] shows that theogonistic ethnographic conceptions influenced the army as well, a vision of Roman providentiality deployed by the soldier-emperors Diocletian and Constantine.

Like the late Roman regiments among which some of them were counted, the barbarian groups were small and composed of professional soldiers.[62] The extent to which they also included families, slaves and camp-followers is unknown, at least at the time of their initial appearance in the Empire.[63] At any rate, our groups were not entire nomadic

emperor vis-à-vis other barbarian (or military) leaders who did not support his kingmaker, leading to the anomalies of the former *magister militum* Aegidius in northern Gaul refusing to support his opponent Ricimer's candidate Libius Severus, or the similar behavior of the Visigothic king Euric; see Herwig Wolfram, "Gotisches Königtum und römisches Kaisertum von Theodosius dem Großen bis Justinian I," *Frühmittelalterliche Studien* 13 (1979), 12–13; Ian Wood, "The end of Roman Britain: continental evidence and parallels," in *Gildas: New Approaches*, ed. Michael Lapidge and David N. Dumville (Woodbridge, Suffolk, 1984), pp. 24–5. On the implications of these developments for understanding the origin and original composition of Theoderic's Balkan Goths, see ch. 8, below.

[59] *Heruli seniores*: ILCV 464, 548; *numerus Batavorum seniorum*: ILCV 460, 480–1, 499; *Numerus felicum Persoarmeniarum*: PA Tzitta 2.

[60] Thus the units bearing barbarian names in the *Notitia Dignitatum*, ed. Otto Seeck (Berlin, 1876), such as the Vandali, Sarmati, Iuthungi at *Or.* 28, or the Germani, Franci, Quadi, Chamavi, Alamanni at *Or.* 31, are taken to be "barbarian units." But we have no proof that that these units included only people who called themselves by these names, or that the units themselves did not eventually lend such labels to their recruits, given that service in them was meant to be hereditary. See Jones, LRE I: 620: "initially no doubt these units were raised from the tribes or areas from which they took their names, but there is no reason to believe that any attempt was made to maintain their tribal or local character, and in general Germans seem to have been mixed with Romans in most units."

[61] Jones, LRE I: 53.

[62] A point first demonstrated by Hans Delbrück, *History of the Art of War* 2, *The Barbarian Invasions*, [1921], 3rd edn, trans. Walter J. Renfroe, Jr. (Lincoln, Nebraska, 1980), pp. 285–99; see further Walter Goffart, *Barbarians and Romans A.D. 418–584: The Techniques of Accommodation* (Princeton, 1980), p. 5 with n. 3, pp. 231–4; Whittaker, *Frontiers*, pp. 210–11.

[63] Influenced by the late-nineteenth century successes of Germanic philological history, Delbrück was able to write, "Historical scholarship sometimes appears to move in circles. There was a time when scholars refused to believe in the migrations of whole peoples but regarded the bands that took possession of the Roman provinces as the large retinues of individual warlords. The sources proved that concept to be erroneous. It was really the entire peoples who moved out, abandoned their ancient homeland, and sought a new one" (Delbrück, *History of the Art of War* 2, p. 394). Historical scholarship really does move in circles, for the consensus has again moved around to viewing the barbarian groups as professional warbands, at least in origin and

peoples, and their relationship to the settled (non-nomadic) societies well beyond the northern frontiers remains uncertain.[64] These warbands were subsequently employed by the Roman emperors and the Roman army, and each of the groups who established a settlement and then a kingdom on Roman soil were invited to that settlement by an agent of the imperial government or its internal adversaries.[65] The significant exception, the Hunnic confederation of Attila, was a polyethnic and political organization actively opposed to the emperors; it did not survive the death of Attila, and its remnant groups followed the pattern of warbands in search of imperial employment.[66]

These small military groups were not stable in name, membership or purpose over the period between the late fourth century and the sixth century. In particular, the continuity of the many groups called "Goths" – such as the Tervingi who entered Thrace in 376 and the

---

at the core (see below, pp. 34–5), although the pendulum appears to be swinging back again (below, nn. 77–80).

Frontier studies and regionalism offer a way out of Delbrück's circle: if the Empire is not seen as a hermetically sealed, homogenous entity punctured by visibly different aliens, then the appearance of powerful self-defined groups on frontiers, different from urban inhabitants on the Mediterranean, can be seen as a natural result of waning control from the centre. This does not deny, of course, the occurrence of huge disruption, suffering and social upheaval in the Empire; it simply attributes it to internal warfare and changing ideologies as much as to migration and invasion.

[64] As constituted when they first appear in the sources, the barbarian groups came from frontier regions on either side of the Roman "border," not huge distances from the north. Not one of the southern European groups retained any documented political or cultural ties with any community to the north (on the question of the "tribal memories" supposedly contained in Jordanes, see ch. 8, below).

The regions that are now Germany were not boiling over with nomadic tribes, but housed a settled, agrarian economy: see Malcolm Todd, *The Northern Barbarians* (London, 1975), pp. 116–17, 131; Malcolm Todd, *The Early Germans* (Oxford, 1992), pp. 19, 62–79; Günter P. Fehring, *The Archaeology of Medieval Germany: An Introduction*, trans. Ross Samson (London, 1991), pp. 148–79; Barry Cunliffe, *Greeks, Romans and Barbarians: Spheres of Interaction* (London, 1988), pp. 189–90 (although he goes on to accept the historicity of migrations); Whittaker, *Frontiers*, p. 214; and Goffart, *Barbarians and Romans*, pp. 3–34. To the east of Budapest, north of the Danube, communities practiced pastoral and transhumant agriculture, not nomadism; see Hugh Elton, *Warfare in Roman Europe A.D. 350–425* (Oxford, 1996), ch. 1. I am deeply grateful to Professor Elton for supplying me with a copy of this book in advance of publication.

[65] Whittaker, *Frontiers*, pp. 202–14, 243–78 (in a book emphasizing "pressure" on the frontiers rather more than it needs to); Goffart, "Rome, Constantinople and the barbarians," pp. 1–32; and Goffart, "The theme of 'the barbarian invasions'," pp. 111–32 (although I see these invitations as short-term responses to immediate problems rather than the long-term dismantling of the Empire envisaged by Goffart).

[66] Otto J. Maenchen-Helfen, *The World of the Huns: Studies in Their History and Culture*, ed. Max Knight (Berkeley, 1973); Goffart, "Rome, Constantinople and the barbarians," p. 10: "The Huns are an exception and should be treated as such," a statement with which few would disagree. Even the Huns were probably less nomadic than has been believed (Elton, *Warfare*, ch. 1). On *Attilani*, see PA *Mundo*; for the history of some post-Attilanic groups in the Balkans, see ch. 8, below.

Greuthungi who entered Pannonia near the same time – with subsequent groups bearing the name "Goth," is unlikely. Warbands laid
claim to names, and with those names, prestige and history, in their
search for food and employment.[67]

The "barbarian" groups of the late Empire were mobile mercenary
warbands frequently in the service of the emperors, and just as frequently in the service of usurpers and army officers renegade or otherwise. They were forced to shift for themselves as support in one quarter
dried up. This process involved a huge amount of violent social disruption in the provinces through which they moved, and in which they
settled for periods of tribute-collecting or active service in the Roman
army.

The culture of the barbarian groups does not allow itself to be inserted
in a bipartite Roman-Germanic framework. Some of the barbarian
groups carried some cultural traits different from those found in the
Mediterranean centers of Rome or Antioch, such as Germanic languages
or Arian belief, but varying cultural traits had always existed among the
diverse regions of the Roman Empire. There was no single late antique
"Germanic culture" based on language, religion, law, material goods or
naming traditions: this philological myth still influences too many studies.
Cultural similarities among the barbarian groups different from those of
the literate centers were at least partly products of dynamic frontier
societies and of long-unattested provincial cultures newly brought to
light by the crumbling of the imperial superstructure.[68]

Increasing regionalism in the Empire aided the process of the alienation of the "Roman" troops. At the same time as elites in Gaul, the
Balkans and Africa were beginning to collaborate with soldiers who
looked like enemies from the Mediterranean viewpoint,[69] we can begin
to see cultural particularity in the regions of the Empire more clearly.

---

[67] Wolfram, *Goths*, pp. 1–116 and *passim*; Heather, *Goths and Romans*. See further below, pp. 34–
9, on ethnogenesis theory.

[68] On the fallacies of the Germanic culture-construct, see appendix 2, below.

[69] CR 5.7.1; 9.14.3; CJ 4.41.2; Orosius, *Historia adversus paganos* 7.41.4, 7, ed. C. Zangemeister,
CSEL 5 (Vienna, 1882–9); Priscus, *frag.* 11, lines 407–51, ed. Blockley, *Fragmentary Classicising
Historians* 2: 266–72; Jill Harries, "Sidonius Apollinaris, Rome and the barbarians," in *Fifth-
Century Gaul*, pp. 305–6; note also H. S. Sivan, "Sidonius Apollinaris, Theodoric II and Gothic-
Roman politics from Avitus to Anthemius," *Hermes* 117 (1989), pp. 85–94; Whittaker, *Frontiers*,
pp. 192–3. On desertion or collaboration with the barbarians, François Paschoud, "Le mythe
de Rome à la fin de l'empire et dans les royaumes romano-barbares," in *Passaggio dal mondo
antico al medio evo da Teodosio a San Gregorio Magno*, Atti dei Convegni Lincei 45 (Rome, 1980),
pp. 132–8; W. H. C. Frend, "The monophysites and the transition between the ancient world
and the Middle Ages," in ibid., p. 342: defection might be seen as treachery in the East, but
was excusable in the West due to intolerable conditions. This can be made more specific, in
light of the Arvandus affair: behavior that seemed reasonable in Gaul was treason from the
viewpoint of the senate at Rome (see Harries).

Coptic and Celtic languages revive, and non-Latin names begin to appear in the Mediterranean aristocracy.[70] The Romanization of the Roman Empire is revealed as a superficial veneer on top of a mosaic of cultures and identities, themselves changed indeed by centuries of Roman rule, but not by any means homogeneous.[71]

Social divisions also split the Empire horizontally, although it is needless to say that the interests of the non-mobile lower classes were always local. The same was true of the dwindling middle classes by the time of the late Empire. Whereas the aloof senatorial aristocracy and the careerist palatine and military elites partook of a Mediterranean-wide *paideia* and access to broad opportunities for the ambitious, the rural *coloni* and municipal *curiales* were increasingly tied to their place of birth and to the professions of their fathers. If these laws were meant to increase imperial influence in the localities,[72] they also had the reverse effect of increasing the local allegiance of the people forced to stay in those localities. The *curiales* could and did escape their burdens in the fourth and early fifth centuries, but suffered from the increase of magnate power and the decline of town populations.[73]

Restricted to their localities, occasionally speaking languages different from those of their masters, the poor made themselves known through city riots and rural uprisings. But even these manifestations of discontent were used by local elites for their own purposes, whether Syrian and Egyptian bishops attempting to increase their power,[74] or increasingly powerful rural warlords in Africa or northern Gaul.[75] The best ways

[70] Ramsay MacMullen, "Provincial languages in the Roman Empire," 1966, reprinted in MacMullen, *Changes in the Roman Empire: Essays in the Ordinary* (Princeton, 1990), pp. 32–40; MacMullen, "The Celtic renaissance," 1965, in ibid., pp. 41–8; on Egypt, see also Roger Bagnall, *Egypt in Late Antiquity* (Princeton, 1993), pp. 230–60 (though I am uneasy about his frequent use of the term "ethnicity").

[71] Ramsay MacMullen, "Notes on Romanization," 1984, reprinted in *Changes in the Roman Empire*, pp. 56–66. On Isaurians and Basques, see n. 27, above, and on the official depiction of Isaurians as bandits, see Jones, LRE I: 25, 116 and 192 (cf. n. 51, above, on *latrones* and *barbari*). On the various groups in the Balkans, see ch. 4, pp. 127–31, below. On the survival of Thracian and Illyrian languages there, see Dimiter Detschew, *Die thrakischen Sprachreste*, Österreichische Akademie der Wissenschaften, philosophisch-historische Klasse: Schriften der Balkankommission, Linguistische Abteilung 14 (Vienna, 1957); and Anton Mayer, *Die Sprache der alten Illyrier* 1, *Einleitung, Wörterbuch der illyrischen Sprachreste*, same series 15 (Vienna, 1957). On Illyrian's probable survival in modern Albanian, with Latin and Slavic borrowings, see John Wilkes, *The Illyrians* (Oxford, 1992), pp. 278–80.

[72] Peter Heather, "Literacy and power in the migration period," in *Literacy and Power in the Ancient World*, ed. Alan K. Bowman and Greg Woolf (Cambridge, 1994), pp. 185–6 with n. 39.

[73] Jones, LRE I: 737–57, on *curiales*.

[74] Peter Brown, *Power and Persuasion in Late Antiquity: Towards a Christian Empire* (Madison, 1992), pp. 71–117.

[75] The literature on revolt, Bacaudae and Circumcellions is too huge to be addressed here. See Whittaker, *Frontiers*, p. 264; Raymond Van Dam, *Leadership and Community in Late Antique*

out of the locality had been via the army or the palatine service. But the palace was now in Toulouse or Carthage or Lyons, and the army now belonged to the landlord himself, or, at best, to his local military patron.

If professional and social divisions were endemic in the later Empire, the regional particularity that they eventually embraced began at the frontier provinces, in northwestern Gaul, Noricum and the Balkans, where the barbarian groups first appear. In these distant and unfamiliar regions, even soldiers of the Roman army could be seen as "strangers in an alien life" from the viewpoint of Constantinople.[76] These were words (*peregrini* and *alieni*) traditionally used to describe barbarians, now barely distinguishable from "Romans" who lived on or near the *limes*. The interests of the periphery did not always match those of the center. Was it "collaboration" when provincials worked with men who offered more immediate threats and opportunities than the distant and demanding administrations on the Mediterranean?

A nuanced view of the composition and formation of these barbarian groups within the Empire must explain how a professional group – an army – comes to bear an ethnographic name at a time when the Empire itself, in its newly visible diversity, begins to look like a subject for the classical ethnography of *barbaricum*. Such an explanation might or might not decide to use ethnicity as an explicative tool. But it would have to move to individual analysis of the groups, the regions where they

Gaul (Berkeley, 1985), pp. 40–2; and John Drinkwater, "The Bacaudae of fifth-century Gaul," in Drinkwater and Elton (eds.), *Fifth-Century Gaul*, pp. 208–17 (disagreeing with Whittaker and van Dam). On revolt and dissidence in general, see Ramsay MacMullen, "The historical role of the masses in late antiquity," in MacMullen, *Changes in the Roman Empire*, pp. 250–76; and Brown, *Power and Persuasion*, pp. 71–117. Internal pressure and political subjection of the *curiales* and lower classes have been seen as an explanation for the fall of the Roman Empire: see G. E. M. de Ste. Croix, *The Class Struggle in the Ancient Greek World from the Archaic Age to the Arab Conquests*, 1981 (corrected impression, London, 1983), pp. 453–503. See, further, Chris Wickham, "The other transition: from the ancient world to feudalism," 1984, reprinted with additions in *Land and Power: Studies in Italian and European Social History, 800–1200* (London, 1994), pp. 20–2; the comments on de Ste. Croix by P. A. Brunt, "A Marxist view of Roman history," *Journal of Roman Studies* 72 (1982), 162 (pointing out that unrest cannot be shown to have increased significantly in late antiquity), and Perry Anderson, "Geoffrey de Ste. Croix and the ancient world," 1983, reprinted in *A Zone of Engagement* (London, 1992), pp. 19–24, (in which Anderson advocates more attention to the "external" disruption by the barbarians, on which Wickham offers a less simplistic model); and Liebeschuetz, *Barbarians and Bishops*, pp. 242–52 (persuasively advocating more attention to the autonomy of the army and the attractions of the church). As historians begin to address dissent, collaboration and autonomy on the basis of region and institution rather than on the assumption that the Empire was an effective and monolithic superstate, the role of revolt in the partial dismantling or rejection of imperial administration might become clearer.

[76] *Nov. Theod.* 4.

are first attested, and the regions where they eventually settled. The dichotomy "Roman vs. barbarian" does an injustice both to the diversity of Roman regions and to the diversity of the barbarian groups.

HISTORIOGRAPHY OF THE COMPOSITION AND FORMATION OF THE BARBARIAN GROUPS IN LATE ANTIQUITY

Despite this recent work on region and profession in relation to the barbarian groups and the transformation of the Roman armies, the historiography of the barbarian groups and kingdoms often continues to take ideological imperial ethnography at its word. "Barbarian" and "Roman" are too frequently accepted as simple descriptive terms, ones identifying people and groups easily visible to men and women in late antiquity.[77] The notion of barbarian culture, translated into the nineteenth-century philological construct "Germanic culture," continues to provide an easy way to translate classical ethnography into modern terms.[78] Simple ethnicity – the term usually left undefined – is in resurgence as an explanation for barbarian group coherence.[79] On the Continent, where recent archeological theory has made little headway, excavation continues to provide quantities of material culture, inexorably catalogued and classified according to the ideological and stereo-

---

[77] For example, Blockley, *East Roman Foreign Policy*, pp. 99–100, 121: "the distinction between Roman and barbarian was . . . held to be a fact by the majority of Romans" (p. 100), generalizing from quite varied elite texts written in the imperial ideological and ethnographic rhetorical tradition between the fourth and sixth centuries. One wonders just who this "majority of Romans" was.

[78] See appendix 2, "The Germanic culture-construct," below.

[79] These works make no clear distinction between ethnicity and culture, subjective and objective distinguishing traits. Most serious are the arguments of Heather, *Goths and Romans*, pp. 309–30, who explicitly opposes much of ethnogenesis theory (on which see below): the late fifth-century Balkan Goths of Theoderic became an ethnic group through shared suffering, and can be distinguished through their Arianism, Germanic language and distinctive material culture. But there is no proof that all or even a majority of Theoderic's followers in the Balkans were Arian or spoke a Germanic language (or only a Germanic language); material remains do not provide a reliable guide to distinctive cultural groups in society, let alone ethnicity (see note 80). As for shared suffering, this may or may not create ethnic cohesion, but I do not think that the scanty Balkan sources allow us a sufficient window into subjective group self-consciousness. We can first analyze this in Theoderic's group in Italy. The processes of recruitment, absorption of other armed bands and intermarriage in a group that was certainly *at least* a regional army suggest that ethnic cohesion is questionable without further proof. For other examples of the resurgence of ethnicity as an explicative tool (ignoring ethnogenesis theory), see Barry Hague, "Cultures in collision: the barbarization of the western Roman Empire in ideology and reality (*c.* 370–530 A.D.)," Ph.D. thesis, Cambridge, 1987; David Frye, "Gundobad, the *Leges Burgundionum*, and the struggle for sovereignty in Burgundy," *Classica et Medievalia* 41 (1990), 199–212; and Moorhead, *Theoderic*, pp. 66–113 (in an otherwise excellent survey of political history). Note too the careless use of "ethnic" and "racial" in the works cited in n. 2, above.

typed group-names of classical ethnography: Frankish brooches and Gothic combs.[80] These artificial, mutually opposed cultures and ethnicities are sometimes invoked to support a picture of natural political conflict between "Romans" and "Germans," and hence the old myths of migration and invasion in the late Empire.[81] If migration and invasion are vanishing in recent scholarship, this is only infrequently accompanied by revisions in views about barbarian or Germanic culture and ethnicity.[82]

Many studies still pay too little attention to the Austrian and German theories of ethnogenesis developed over the last several decades.[83] In particular, Reinhard Wenskus and Herwig Wolfram have deployed anthropological ideas on subjective community and political purposes of oral tradition to suggest that barbarian groups could metamorphose from political and professional groups into ethnic groups.[84] For them, the late antique barbarian groups were not originally tribes, but armies, "peoples under arms," in the service of the Empire. This professional identity gave them their mobility and their attraction for potential recruits.

In order to attract followers, Wenskus and Wolfram argue, barbarian kings combined the prestige of their Roman military offices with an extra-Roman *Traditionskern* to found a myth about the glory of their royal lineage and mythical descent from pagan gods. With continued

---

[80] See appendix 3, below, especially the section "Archeology and the ethnic ascription tradition."

[81] Much of Blockley's *East Roman Foreign Policy* is based on the assumption that "Romans" and "Germans" were naturally opposed political groupings (see n. 77, above); invasions of conquest, for example in Elton, *Warfare in Roman Europe*, ch. 2, though not linked to barbarian culture, but see *passim* and conclusion for the assumption that the Empire was destroyed by conflict with external enemies; vast migrations and invasions: see the works of Volker Bierbrauer (appendix 3, below, nn. 1–2); no migration, but inevitably opposed political groupings based on cultural differences: Heather, *Goths and Romans*, pp. 317–30.

[82] Important revisions about barbarian migration and invasion are to be found in Whittaker, *Frontiers*, pp. 192–278, esp. 192–4, 243–4, and in Burns, *Barbarians*, pp. 112–47. But note Burns on "artifacts stylistically characteristic of east Germans, that is to say Gothic speakers" (p. 139), artifacts belonging to recruits who were "kinsmen" of inhabitants outside the Empire – and this in a study elsewhere critical of using material goods as a key to identity (see p. 134 on the so-called "Elbgermanen"). Whittaker is far more nuanced on identity in frontier regions, but mysteriously fails to take account of ethnogenesis theory, which would enrich his picture greatly.

[83] The seminal work is Reinhard Wenskus, *Stammesbildung und Verfassung: Das Werden der frühmittelalterlichen Gentes* (Cologne, 1961). *Verfassung* is difficult to translate into English, and probably ought to be rendered "political composition." The word comes from the German academic tradition of *Verfassungsgeschichte*, "constitutional history" – essentially, sociopolitical history (the study of the influence of political leaders on social structures). See Samson, "Translator's Introduction," in Fehring, *Archaeology of Medieval Germany*, p. xvii.

[84] Wenskus's book is still not sufficiently well-known in Anglophone scholarship, partly because of its length and its impenetrable German: see Herwig Wolfram, Review of *Goths and Romans* by Peter Heather, *Francia* 20.1 (1993), 257–8.

military success, material reward and the charisma of the king would combine to transform the royal clan and its polyethnic armed following into a nascent *gens*, a people cleaving to an ancient ethnographic group-name. After settlement in one region, recruitment from among the natives and the displacement or absorption of local tradition by the settlers, full ethnogenesis could occur: the army under its military king (*reiks, rex*) would now consider itself an ethnic group, a people, a race. Among subsequent generations born in that region, it would seem as if their people had always existed. The original arrival of the king and his followers would eventually become a full-blown migration myth. They also drew on elements of classical ethnography in building their myths of royal descent, so much so that the different sources of these myths, Germanic or Graeco-Roman, are no longer distinguishable.[85]

For Wolfram, the ultimate myth of royal prestige and tribal origins survives in the *Getica* of Jordanes, a sixth-century Byzantine Goth, writing in Latin, who is claimed to have summarized the lost *Gothic History* of Cassiodorus. Wolfram believes that Cassiodorus, writing under Theoderic in Italy in the 520s, recorded his master's views of the Gothic past. Both Wolfram and Wenskus rely heavily on the *Getica* as a container not of pristine Gothic tradition but of what a sixth-century Gothic king wished the world to believe was Gothic tradition. In the *Getica*, according to Wenskus and Wolfram, we possess the active manipulation of a *Traditionskern* by a barbarian war-leader in the process of constituting his people.[86]

---

[85] In addition to Wenskus, see Wolfram, *Goths*; Wolfram, "Gothic history and historical ethnography," pp. 309–19; Wolfram, "The shaping of the early medieval kingdom," *Viator* 1 (1970), 1–20; Wolfram, "Gotisches Königtum und römisches Kaisertum," pp. 1–28. See also the essays in *Typen der Ethnogenese* 1; Pohl, *Die Awaren*; and the summary of ethnogenesis scholarship by Walter Pohl, "Tradition, Ethnogenese und literarische Gestaltung: eine Zwischenbilanz," in *Ethnogenese und Überlieferung: Angewandte Methoden der Frühmittelalterforschung*, ed. Karl Brunner and Brigitte Merta (Vienna, 1994), pp. 9–26. Crucial to the imperial context of Wolfram's theory are his studies on the use of legitimating titles by barbarian groups, particularly *rex* (Gothic *reiks*), the quasi-imperial military rulership with overtones of popular leadership, legitimized by real imperial military offices such as *magister militum* and *patricius*: see Herwig Wolfram, *Intitulatio* 1, *Lateinische Königs- und Fürstentitel bis zum Ende des 8. Jahrhunderts*, Mitteilungen des Instituts für Österreichische Geschichtsforschung Ergänzungsband 21 (Graz, 1967), 40–89, closely linked to his studies on the vocabulary of rule implied among fourth-century Balkan groups called Goths in Ulfilas's Gothic translation of the Bible, on which see ch. 7, n. 11 with accompanying text. (I do not believe that the insights on this particular fourth-century Balkan culture necessarily apply to sixth-century groups called Goths.) See also Wolfram, "Gotisches Königtum und römisches Kaisertum," pp. 1–4, 18–28 on the interplay of titulature and legitimacy among the barbarian rulers, a typically brilliant and wide-ranging survey. On the rhetoric of rule of Theoderic the Great and its relationship to the emperorship, see below, ch. 2.

[86] Herwig Wolfram, "Einleitung oder Überlegungen zur Origo Gentis," in *Typen der Ethnogenese* 1: 19–33; Herwig Wolfram, "*Origo et religio*: ethnic traditions and literature in early medieval texts," *Early Medieval Europe* 3 (1994), 19–38. The four potential levels of importance of Jordanes

Over-reliance on the *Getica* is the main weakness of the ethnogenesis school. It is impossible to point to any other origin saga dating from the sixth or seventh century that is not influenced by the *Getica* itself, aside perhaps from the *Origo gentis Langobardorum*. Outside the *Getica*, one must use much later texts, such as Widukind of Corvey, the *Nibelungenlied* or the stories about Dietrich von Bern, all dating from the tenth century and later. Other fifth- and sixth-century sources show barbarian kings in the process of recruitment and attempting to enhance their prestige. But they do not show them propagating myths of origin. One must rely on the evidence of personal names in genealogies or the problematic descriptions of Graeco-Latin sources influenced by classical ethnography.

Both the authenticity and the motives of the narrative contained within Jordanes's *Getica* have come under attack. Walter Goffart challenges the idea that Jordanes faithfully transmitted the words or the meaning of Cassiodorus's *Gothic History*. Peter Heather, who does not accept Goffart's views, suggests that only parts of the *Getica* reflect the desires and propaganda of Theoderic. James O'Donnell argues for its Christian providential overtones, and Brian Croke for its similarity to contemporary military histories produced in sixth-century Constantinople.[87]

Furthermore, there are anthropological objections. František Graus long ago pointed out that Wenskus privileges kings over peoples as

are thus as follows: if he summarized Cassiodorus faithfully, then we might possess in him a chain going back to the oral traditions of the Goths themselves. If Jordanes actually preserves no oral traditions (on the questionable use of "orality" in this debate, see below, ch. 8, pp. 295–8), then he might still preserve what Theoderic wanted the Italians to believe were oral traditions. If Jordanes actually preserves none of Cassiodorus's ideology, then he might still preserve Cassiodorus's work, writing as a contemporary of Theoderic and Athalaric. If he actually preserves none of Cassiodorus's work, then he might still preserve precious material on what it meant to be a Goth – albeit a Goth from the Balkans in Constantinople – since Jordanes describes himself as a Goth.

[87] Walter Goffart, *The Narrators of Barbarian History (A.D. 550–800): Jordanes, Gregory of Tours, Bede and Paul the Deacon* (Princeton, 1988), pp. 28–111; Peter Heather, "Cassiodorus and the rise of the Amals: genealogy and the Goths under Hun domination," *Journal of Roman Studies* 79 (1989), 103–28; Heather, *Goths and Romans*, pp. 34–67; James J. O'Donnell, "The aims of Jordanes," *Historia* 31 (1982), 223–40; Brian Croke, "Cassiodorus and the *Getica* of Jordanes," *Classical Philology* 82 (1987), 117–34. Shortly to come will be a stylistic analysis of the *Getica* that purports to prove that every phrase can be traced back to Cassiodorus, announced by Johann Weißensteiner, "Cassiodor/Jordanes als Geschichtsschreiber," in *Historiographie im frühen Mittelalter* 1, ed. Anton Scharer and Georg Scheibelreiter, Veröffentlichungen des Instituts für Österreichische Geschichtsforschung 32 (Vienna, 1994); I am grateful to Dr Weißensteiner and Walter Pohl for providing me with a copy of this paper in advance of publication. Of all these, I find Croke the most convincing, but Jordanes will not be addressed in this book until the last chapter due to the continuing controversy over every aspect of his work, his distance in space and time from most of the events examined, and his lack of interest in Ostrogothic *Italy*.

bearers of traditions. The notion that charismatic leaders can urge people to give up their knowledge of their own pasts and adopt a new one is intriguing, but is not consistent with our knowledge of folklore, which persists orally and simultaneously with elite traditions. Wenskus seems to ignore the effects of permanence and locality in his overemphasis on mobile groups.[88]

Graus marked the way toward a further problem with the ethnogenesis theory: a certain blurriness on both the exact size of the *Traditionskern* and on the moment when ethnogenesis takes place. What, exactly, was in the "kernel of tradition?" What *had* been passed down from generation to generation? Perhaps it was as little as a list of kings and gods, later synthesized into a theogonistic genealogy. But it also seems to have contained vague memories of earlier places in Bosporan caps or long hair.[89] The place of cultural elements such as language and religion remains unclear in the ethnogenesis framework. Wolfram believes that the Gothic language and Arian belief could help bind Goths and proto-Goths together. But there is little evidence that the Gothic kings actively promoted such ideas.

The very group-names adopted by barbarian kings, Wolfram argues, are Germanic in linguistic origin, even if they have centuries of attestation in Graeco-Latin texts.[90] But what if the group-names came to the attention of the late antique kings *through* Graeco-Latin texts?[91] Ethnographic group-names are scattered through historical, panegyrical, epigraphical and geographical texts. They were not always attached to connotations of odium and stupidity: virtue-based ethnography could allow the barbarians a primitive purity compared to the Romans, and most texts allow the barbarians bellicosity, which could have appeared a virtue to a military commander.

Moreover, the extent to which the group-names were already contaminated by non-Germanic elements, or were not Germanic from the beginning, remains understudied. *Ostrogothi* first appears in a written text as *Austrogothi*, so its usual (Germanic) translation, "Goths from the East," could be replaced by a Latin amplification of the Germanic word *Gothi*, producing "Goths from the South." No group is known to have called itself "Ostrogoths" (rather than "Goths"), but outsiders might

---

[88] František Graus, review of *Stammesbildung und Verfassung* by Reinhard Wenskus, *Historica* 7 (1963), 185–91, esp. 187–8.

[89] Wolfram, *Goths*, pp. 102–3, 290–5, 301, 337. On "Phrygian caps" see below, appendix 4, p. 342 with nn. 28–30. On *capillati* and "long hair," see below, ch. 3, p. 94 with n. 43, and appendix 4, pp. 344–6.

[90] Wolfram, "*Origo et religio*," pp. 19–38.

[91] See below, ch. 8, pp. 296–7 with n. 99.

use that name for Theoderic's group, while Theoderic himself deployed
the name in his family and his mythical ancestry. Even if parts of such
names are Germanic, they can show a mixture of other languages current within the Roman Empire. A dependent group of Sarmatians
called the Limigantes probably derived its Latino-Celtic name from its
settlement on the Danube *limes*.[92] Just as the vocabulary and syntax of
Ulfilas's Gothic Bible is influenced by Greek vocabulary and syntax,[93]
the names of groups on the frontier of the powerful and literate Empire
could absorb non-Germanic linguistic elements from a world that itself
contained a variety of languages and dialects.[94] The group-names *Thraci*,
Veneti and *Itali* are not of Latin linguistic origin either, but nobody
would argue from this that people called by these terms in late antiquity
preserved ancient traditions or memories. The significance of group-
names from the northern frontier being "Germanic," in a larger culture
where these group-names were bandied about and used by groups
unconnected with one another, may be small in evaluating the heritage
of "non-Roman" tradition or culture.

Finally, there is the question of how to define "full" ethnogenesis.
If ethnic groups are always in flux, if their membership and definitions
of membership are always changing, then they are constantly under-
going ethnogenesis. To insist on constant change is, of course, an
extreme position. The issue for historians is whether a group remains
a discrete community from which members believe they accrue
distinct advantages for a reasonably long period of time, during which
period the definitions of membership do not change noticeably and
during which period the body of the group does not show a particularly
large turnover.[95] These limits – "reasonably long," "noticeably," "particularly large" – are liable to different interpretations by different
people.

When, in other words, does ethnogenesis take place? At what points
in the history of the groups using the ethnonym *Gothi* did those groups
become ethnic groups? If the change in membership and definitions of

---

[92] Whittaker, *Frontiers*, p. 178; Whittaker sees this as a "Roman nickname," but why need it be?
[93] See below, ch. 7.
[94] Thus if any oral tradition did exist among groups within the Roman Empire, that tradition
had to exist in constant dialogue with literate tradition, as anthropological models suggest; see
below, ch. 8, pp. 296–8, with references.
[95] This is the view of Heather, *Goths and Romans*, pp. 323–30, opposing that of Wolfram, on
Theoderic's Goths in the Balkans. But few groups in late antiquity are known to have been
as varied and flexible as this group (see ch. 8, below, and Wolfram, *Goths*, pp. 258–302); Heather
connects Theoderic's Balkan Goths with earlier groups called Goths, but all these groups are
only observable through texts produced outside the groups, or through texts produced in the
sixth century such as Jordanes or the Gothic Bible.

membership is too rapid, it might be worthwhile to look for other explanations of the group and its name besides ethnicity.

METHODOLOGY: THE IMPACT OF IDEOLOGY ON COMMUNITY

In order to distinguish between past ethnographic representation and past community, this study examines the impact of ideology on individual behavior in a single region. I successively examine the related and interreacting ideologies of community held by the Ostrogothic rulers, by various Italian writers, by the Eastern emperors and by the Catholic and Arian churches in light of the inheritance of classical ethnographies and the notion of a civilized Mediterranean Empire facing a pluralistic world of barbarians outside. The age of Theoderic and Justinian witnessed a massive revival of ethnographic conceptions and ethnographic texts.[96]

These ideologies could be effective. They could change the way that people saw themselves. Contemporary rulers were aware of the power of words. Leaving aside the studies that argue for a higher literacy rate in late antiquity than was previously suspected,[97] both imperial government and church had a variety of ways of communicating written documents to popular audiences, through inscription, proclamation of laws, liturgy and imagery.[98] In this manner the written word could travel. In an era when the establishment of a single, correct doctrine had become a paramount concern, Justinian extended a paralyzing eye over the writing produced in his Empire. Procopius knew that he could never openly publish his *Secret History*. Pope Vigilius was forced to smuggle out his

---

[96] This topic has received much attention in the East, but little in the West. On Byzantine ethnography and its use in victory ideology under Justinian, see Dagron, "'Ceux d'en face',", pp. 207–32; Maria Cesa, "Etnografia e geografia nella visione storica di Procopius di Cesarea," *Studi classici e orientali* 32 (1982), 189–215; Cameron, "Agathias on the early Merovingians," pp. 95–140; Cameron, "Agathias on the Sassanians," *Dumbarton Oaks Papers* 23–4 (1969–70), 1–150; Cameron, *Procopius*, pp. 218–22 and *passim*; Michael Maas, "Terms of inclusion: Christianity and classical ethnography from Justinian to Heraclius" (forthcoming); I am grateful to Professor Maas for making a copy of this paper available to me in advance of publication. The Byzantine uses of ethnogeography are examined further in ch. 4, alongside the Western evidence for the revival of ethnography, geography and the copying of classical ethnogeographic texts in Italy.

[97] Bowman and Woolf (eds.), *Literacy and Power in the Ancient World*; Rosamond McKitterick (ed.), *The Uses of Literacy in Early Medieval Europe* (Cambridge, 1990); Rosamond McKitterick, *The Carolingians and the Written Word* (Cambridge, 1988), p. 24 with n. 5 and references.

[98] On government see Brian Croke, "City chronicles of late antiquity," in *Reading the Past in Late Antiquity*, ed. G. Clarke et al. (Sydney, 1990), pp. 116–31 with references. On the church see Michel Banniard, *Viva Voce: Communication écrite et communication orale du IVe au IXe siècle en Occident latin*, Collection des Etudes Augustiniennes, Série Moyen-Age et Temps Modernes 25 (Paris, 1992).

arguments against the condemnation of the Three Chapters to the bishops of the West, and John of Ephesus sent out the chapters of his monophysite *Ecclesiastical History* piece by piece from his prison in Constantinople.[99] A similar freeze may have quelled the discussion of Arianism as heresy under Theoderic in Italy.[100]

The other chapters test the effectiveness of these ideologies. I use the Prosopographical Appendix (hereafter PA) as a body of data from which to examine the behavior of everyone who could be labeled a "Goth" according to the ideologies and mentalities outlined in the first part.[101] The PA therefore includes a varied assemblage of individuals, since these ideologies all defined Goths in different ways, according to name,[102] profession, religious adherence, language or dress. Finally, there is the crucial evidence that an individual was identified as a Goth by someone else, or (almost non-existent outside the royal families) that someone identified himself as a Goth.

There is one major control on this comparison of individual behavior against ideologies, which is that the Goths as a group are identifiable in the sources as, at the very least, an army that arrived in Italy in 489 under the leadership of Theoderic the Great. Whatever their feelings about themselves as a group, they were initially a band of soldiers and their families, the followers of a king, and settlers in a new land. There is, in other words, an initial objective difference, between settler and native, on which to build our vision of what it meant to be a Goth in Italy between 489 and 554.

"Goth" at the outset denoted soldiers who arrived in Italy in 489. The first Italian Goths constituted an army. They were probably not

---

[99] On Procopius and John of Ephesus, see Cameron, *Procopius*, pp. 16–17; on Vigilius, see ch. 6, pp. 230–3, below.

[100] In general, see Moorhead, *Theoderic*, pp. 91–3; Moorhead allows that relations between Arians and Catholics may simply have been good in Theoderic's early reign; I agree, with reservations: see ch. 6, pp. 195–205, below.

[101] For more detail on the methodology of the Prosopographical Appendix, see PA, Methodology and Purpose.

[102] A Germanic name has been considered a waterproof identification of a Goth, even when people had both a Germanic and Latin names themselves or in their families, invalidating most previous prosopographical work on people who might be identified as "Goths." This is a constant problem in PLRE, and also invalidates some of the conclusions of Moorhead, *Theoderic*, pp. 83–97 on intermarriage and religious affiliation, as well as most of the conclusions of Gerd Kampers, "Anmerkungen zum Lateinisch-gotischen Ravennater Papyrus von 551," *Historisches Jahrbuch* 101 (1981), 141–51, esp. 143–7. On this subject, see further below, ch. 3, pp. 87–9, and ch. 7, pp. 251–6, 270–4. Assuming that personal names determine identity has led to some ridiculous circular arguments, particularly in Horst Ebling, Jörg Jarnut and Gerd Kampers, "Nomen et gens: Untersuchungen zu den Führungsschichten des Franken-, Langobarden- und Westgotenreiches im 6. und 7. Jahrhundert," *Francia* 8 (1980), 687–745, against which see Amory, "Names, ethnic identity and community," pp. 2–3 with nn. 8–12.

very numerous, perhaps 20,000 people at most (although all figures are guesses), and certainly a mere fraction of the population of Italy.[103] This army had picked up recruits in both the Pannonian and Italian provinces. It absorbed the remnants of Odoacer's army. It contained groups with "non-Gothic" labels, such as the Rugians and the Gepids. Wolfram's assertion that the army was "polyethnic" (that is, diverse) upon its arrival must stand. It was a motley crew, and any study of Gothic ethnicity or ethnogenesis in Italy must assume that the Goths did not arrive as an army already cohering to a single, overwhelming ethnic identity.[104] It seems to me impossible for a mobile army to be a stable endogomous breeding group: the rate of attrition is too high, and the question of where the women come from is paramount. Whether it managed to be a stable cultural or ethnic formation in the face of attrition and recruitment is the question that this book addresses.

Despite Theoderic's rhetoric about the army, to which he always referred as *exercitus Gothorum*, the army continued recruiting after settlement, whether from without or within Italy or both. This process of recruitment affected its "polyethnicity" and therefore any formation of a single identity among people labeled Goths. Relations between the settlers and the natives were influenced by the circumstances of settling an army in Roman provinces. Whether this army received land, as was traditionally thought, or shares of tax-assessments, as Walter Goffart argues,[105] or both, as seems possible, day-to-day relations between the new (and old) soldiers and the old civilians were clearly mediated by this relationship.

We do not know how many civilians there were with Theoderic: some wives and families, as well as secretaries,[106] priests (Arian or Catholic), and slaves, just as in late Roman regiments.[107] That the soldiers of Theoderic's armies had families with them is not, of course, certain, only probable, and the presence of families does not mean that this group was an ethnic group.[108] What modalities were used to keep

---

[103] This is by no means a new assumption; I suspect that it is further confirmed by the fairly low proportion of Germanic names in Italy throughout the period, as shown, for example, in inscriptions. See ch. 3, below.

[104] Here I part with the arguments of Peter Heather: see n. 79, above. The identity of the people who arrived in Italy from the Balkans with Theoderic in 489 is the subject of ch. 8, below.

[105] Goffart, *Barbarians and Romans*, pp. 58–102.

[106] Such as Theoderic's Greek-named secretary in the Balkans in the 470s, Phocas (PLRE 2 Phocas 2). It may be significant that no wives or families are attested by name in any source.

[107] MacMullen, *Soldier and Civilian*, pp. 119–51.

[108] Delbrück believed that families must indicate cohesion as a people (see *History of the Art of War* 2: 394 [quoted above at n. 63]), still accepted by many writers on the basis of Procopius's claim (fifty years later, of course) that the Goths arrived in Italy with their women and children

families together within a mobile band of soldiers, and how might the presence of families foster or disrupt group cohesion?

The Ostrogothic kingdom of Italy lasted for sixty-five years by the longest possible calculation. Political Methusalehs like Liberius, Cassiodorus and Narses straddled it with ease. Although sixty-five years is not a very long time to allow an identity to change, and not a very long time to allow an identity to form, it nonetheless encompasses three generations, perhaps more. The first part of the Ostrogothic kingdom, from 493 to 535, may, moreover, have been a period of stability and prosperity in Italy.

Given the time-frame, there exists the putative *possibility* that a single ethnic identity formed among the people called Goths in Italy between 489 and 554. There also exists the *probability* that one did not form, and that allegiances of all sorts could switch very rapidly, particularly in light of the many political changes of the period, and the consequent number of ideological shifts that we see in the propaganda focused on sixth-century Italy. Allegiance-switching seems to have become the rule, not the exception, during the twenty-year Gothic Wars, as each side preyed on the loyalties of the hapless Italian civilian population.

Nonetheless, belief in descent is a powerful constructor of identity. It can be learned in one's earliest childhood from one's own parents. The evidence of intermarriage, of the use of different names or different religious affiliations within families, is one of our most valuable tools for penetrating the relative importance of labels like "Goth" attached at different times to naming traditions and religious affiliations.

Against this background of ideology, chronology and family, I place individual behavior and cultural traits, especially the instances when criteria of "Gothic" identity match up or fail to match up consistently in a single social group or in a given individual. Are all soldiers under Theoderic, who saw his army as composed of "Goths," Arians? Do they all have Germanic names? Do individuals change their religion or their names? Do people have matching criteria themselves, but different criteria in their family? What is the relationship between these ideological criteria and political events?

(BG I(5).I.12); see for example Francesco Giunta, "Gli Ostrogoti in Italia," in *Magistra barbaritas*, ed. Giovanni Pugliese Caratelli (Milan, 1984), p. 71.

Chapter 2

THE RAVENNA GOVERNMENT AND ETHNOGRAPHIC IDEOLOGY: FROM *CIVILITAS* TO *BELLICOSITAS*

The government of Theoderic propagated a stylized ideology of professional identity that used the vocabulary and assumptions of classical ethnography. It was a means of conceptualizing and therefore ordering Italian society along ethnographic lines for the purpose of achieving a consensus of governance among the settlers and the indigenous population. This ideology was to affect both the social roles and the behavior of Theoderic's subjects. It functionally distinguished soldiers (Goths) from civilians (Romans), and philosophically attempted to influence the behavior of individuals thus labeled "Goth" or "Roman." The philosophy of *civilitas*, two nations living together in peace but performing different functions,[1] originated in the minds of Theoderic and of his advisers; it was innovative as a synthesis, but drew on earlier Roman ideas of law and ethnography.[2] *Civilitas* ideology already existed in the 490s, soon after the conquest of Italy, and was thus not a product of the rhetoric of Cassiodorus or Ennodius, but of the king and the people around him throughout his reign.

Beginning in the 520s or earlier, this ideology appears less frequently in governmental sources. At the same period, Ravenna began to stress the history and characteristics of the Gothic people independent of Roman influence. This second approach would increase the distance between those whom the government defined as Goths and those

---

[1] There are many definitions of *civilitas* in the scholarship, all unsatisfactory. Wolfram, *Goths*, p. 296, defines *civilitas* as "the social, legal and economic coexistence of Romans and foreigners based on the law." Wolfram's formula of ethnic interdependence based on the rule of law is closer to the mark than Traube's "status rei publicae iustus," Momigliano's definition of it as preservation of Roman civilization, or Moorhead's "rule of law." See Ludwig Traube, index to Cassiodorus, ed. Theodor Mommsen, MGH: AA 12 (Berlin, 1894), s.v., p. 521; Arnaldo Momigliano, "Cassiodorus and Italian culture of his time," [1955] reprinted in Momigliano, *Studies in Historiography* (New York, 1966), p. 191 with n. 60; and Moorhead, *Theoderic*, pp. 78–80. Odo John Zimmermann defines *civilitas* as "the state" or "the universality of citizens" from only two uses of it, not taking into account the general context in Cassiodorus: *The Late Latin Vocabulary of Cassiodorus* (1944; reprint, Hildesheim, 1967), pp. 88, 179.

[2] Such a combination of old material with new ideas was characteristic of Theoderic's policies. See especially Moorhead, *Theoderic*, pp. 252–3.

whom it defined as Romans; it would also contribute to souring relations with Byzantium.

In setting forth this ethnographic ideology, Theoderic's advisers borrowed from Roman law the terminology of obligation to the state, investing the words with new ethnographic meaning: *civilitas, utilitas, libertas* and *devotio*. The choice of legal culture is significant. Theoderic based both the successful cohabitation of his army with the population of Italy and his own ambiguous constitutional (and ecclesiastical) position on the supremacy of Roman law over all other forms of human organization. It was this state that had propelled his family into eminence; it was this body of law that was transforming the meaning of the word *barbarus* from "hostile foreigner" to "servant of the Roman state."

Theoderic's ideology of ethnographic coexistence naturally drew on the late antique synthesis of legal conceptions of public service and of fiscal obligation. The consensual, republican terms of Roman law had gathered a sense of debt. It was no accident that laws on taxation could provide terminology to describe a state of ethnographic peace, since once barbarians were defined as soldiers and provincials as civilians, those same laws described their relationship, both fiscal and social. Theoderic's ideology thus extended a conceptual ethnographic divide down to the level of the taxpayers and the soldiers that they supported. This divide was then used to draw these two groups together in a reciprocal financial contract, which was described in the exalted language of the jurisconsults. Such propaganda was meant not only to establish goodwill in the potentially dissonant relationship between settler and native, but to consolidate Theoderic's power as the emperor-like ruler of Italy and "fount of *civilitas*." He was literally the source both of lawful behavior and of the ideological system ostensibly meant to maintain such behavior.

It may nevertheless seem superfluous to analyze the ethnographic ideology of Theoderic's government in Italy when its outlines are so well known.[3] The prevailing historical analyses, however, do not attempt to distinguish between governmental ethnographic ideology and its effects in execution. Historians have taken ideology for reality.[4] Worse, they fail to distinguish between this ideology and the communal reality that underlay it.[5] Political ideology can influence communities in com-

---

[3] See the references at n. 12, below.

[4] James J. O'Donnell, "Liberius the patrician," *Traditio* 37 (1981), 60: "The earlier pattern had been for military affairs to be controlled entirely by Goths, and civil affairs entirely by Romans" (on the appointment of Liberius as *patricius praesentalis* in 533).

[5] With the single exception of Wolfram, *Goths*, pp. 288–90. Moorhead, *Theoderic*, pp. 71–5, unfortunately presupposes that differences between Goths and Romans were inherently obvi-

plex ways, since politics can play a major role in the birth of ethnic consciousness.[6] Furthermore, ideologies of ethnography are shaped by the societies within which their progenitors are reared. They are not timeless: they change and react according to political circumstance.

Even Wolfram combines two aspects of Cassiodorus's rhetoric that occur in different contexts, and at different periods, in Theoderic's reign. "Theodoric's state, the dominion over 'Goths and Italians,' combined the *principatus populi Romani* with a *regnum gentis*. The king wanted his Goths to recognize *civilitas*, the rule of law. In this regard the Goths were to imitate Romans, not the reverse."[7] Although Theoderic did imagine his rule as legitimized from two sources, I do not agree that at all times during his reign he conceived of his *kingdom* as a new and radically different ethno-social construction.

Only in the royal letters addressed within his kingdom, and especially during the period documented by Cassiodorus's quaestorship (507–11), did Theoderic propagate the image of the Goths living under Roman law. In their very relationship with the Italian population, the Goths displayed their superiority over the other *gentes*. The Italians and the Goths together, in fact, were seen as living in a thriving Roman Empire, the *res publica*. The valor of the Goths was to contribute military security to a mutually beneficial relationship.[8]

In contrast, in letters addressed to other barbarian kings, and during the later part of Theoderic's reign (523–6), the rhetoric of governance shifts to emphasize the superiority of the Gothic *gens* over other *gentes* through their warlike virtues and through the splendor of the royal Amal blood. In this formulation, the king appears more and more often as a war-leader by virtue of descent. This tendency culminates with the bellicose assertions of Witigis. But it has already begun under Theoderic.[9]

These two governmental viewpoints share common emphases, of course, such as the military excellence of the Gothic army, and the social role of the Goths as soldiers. But the first envisages the continu-

---

ous, envisaging Theoderic's program as "the imposition of race on a dichotomy which had already existed [viz. soldier–civilian]" (p. 72); it is unclear what he means by "race." But earlier studies, as Moorhead notes, simply took the evidence of the *Variae* as descriptive rather than prescriptive, and simply described Theoderic's Italy as being divided between soldier-Goths and civilian Romans (p. 71, n. 23). To these add, for example, J. B. Bury, *History of the Later Roman Empire*, 2 vols. (2nd edn, London, 1923), I: 455–6; Ludwig Schmidt, "Die comites Gothorum: ein Kapitel zur ostgotischen Verfassungsgeschichte," *Mitteilungen des Instituts für Österreichische Geschichtsforschung* 40 (1925), 129–33 (an attempt to fit the complex administrative framework of Ostrogothic Italy into Theoderic's ethnic ideology).

[6] See, generally, Rex and Mason (eds.), *Theories of Race and Ethnic Relations*, esp. pp. 170–86.
[7] Wolfram, *Goths*, p. 290.
[8] See below, pp. 50–9.
[9] See below, pp. 61–78.

ation of the Roman Empire under Theoderic in Italy, while the second does seem to imagine a *regnum gentis*, the ethnographically defined army-nation in perpetual readiness for battle. The rhetoric defining each viewpoint is quite different, and does not occur in the same letters of the *Variae*.

ETHNOGRAPHIC IDEOLOGY AND THE RAVENNA GOVERNMENT

This subtitle begs a number of questions. Why have an ethnographic ideology? What did Theoderic's government set out to accomplish with it? Who was the audience for its ethnographic propaganda? The answers are complicated and lie within the program that Theoderic set out upon his establishment of the kingdom of Italy.

Certainly, there is no doubt anymore that Theoderic, as well as his advisers, were the fount and origin of the extraordinary Ostrogothic governmental experiment in *civilitas*. The seeds may have been sown during his upbringing and education as a hostage at Leo's court at Constantinople in the 460s, to which he adverted later.[10] The evidence for the Ostrogothic governmental program appears as early as the 490s, long before Cassiodorus was old enough to become quaestor, and only shortly after Liberius joined the administration. Theoderic may have been illiterate, in Latin at least, if we are to believe a story told identically of Justin I, that he could only write the word "legi" using a gold stencil.[11] But as with Charlemagne centuries later, this detail – unlikely

---

[10] Ennodius, *Pan.* 11 (3); Cassiodorus, *Var.* 8.9.3, where Cassiodorus has Athalaric refer to his grandfather's education. See Wolfram, *Goths*, pp. 262–3. Pierre Riché, *Education and Culture in the Barbarian West*, trans. John J. Contreni (Columbia, SC, 1976), discusses Theoderic's education in detail. I do not agree with Riché that the king was necessarily only interested in the sciences. Nor do Riché's citations from the mid-sixth century Jordanes prove that Theoderic was deliberately imitating his philosopher-ancestors (p. 58 with nn. 38–9). If these particular statements of Jordanes do depend on Cassiodorus, then they only prove that the king was concerned to promulgate a certain image of the Goths among the Italians; the emphasis on Amal ancestry, moreover, may have appeared only late in Theoderic's reign (see below, pp. 64–72, esp. pp. 68–9). Riché also stresses that the renaissance of Hellenism in Theoderic's Italy was superficial and limited (Riché, ibid., p. 44), which is true, but from the viewpoint of ideological analysis, it is more interesting that a Greek education could still be seen as the foundations of classical culture and, more specifically, as a component of Roman wisdom: see *Var.* 1.45.3 (praising Boethius for "making Greek learning Roman"), and the reference in Ennodius's panegyric just cited, with pp. 116–17, below. A more positive position than Riché is taken by O. Pecere, "La cultura greco romana in età gota tra adattamento e trasformazione," *Teodorico il Grande e i Goti d'Italia*, Atti del XIII Congresso Internazionale di Studi sull'Alto Medioevo, Milan, 2–6 November 1992 (Spoleto, 1993).

[11] AV 14.79. The story is told in a hostile tone (connecting the king's illiteracy with his "obrutus sensus"), and occurs precisely at the point where the Anonymus turns against Theoderic. On the much debated question of Theoderic's literacy, see Riché, *Education and Culture*, p. 57 with nn. 32–3, and Moorhead, *Theoderic*, pp. 104–5 with references (both favoring literacy).

as it seems anyway – may have been irrelevant to his ability to influence cultural developments. In all the speeches attributed to the king, in all his actions and in his entire policy through 519, his own initiative shines through.

Theoderic's domestic policy is well known, and ethnographic ideology was a major aspect of it.[12] Like the emperor whom he strove to resemble in his imagery and propaganda, he strove for peace and prosperity, and, above all, consensus to his military–civilian rule over the ancient Roman center. It was therefore essential to reconcile the Italian population to the settlement of the Goths.

After his conquest of Italy, the Gothic king installed a large, formerly mobile army in his new realm. Whether or not this army represented a unified ethnic group, a large part of it was composed of non-Italians used to continuous warfare and eking out survival in harsh conditions. Achieving peaceful coexistence was not going to be easy, and the disturbances of the early 490s, not to mention the frequent subsequent references to troops pillaging the Italian countryside en route elsewhere,

---

[12] There is no room to summarize Theoderic's policy here. In general, see Moorhead, *Theoderic*, pp. 32–113; Johannes Sundwall, *Abhandlungen zur Geschichte des ausgehenden Römertums* (Helsinki, 1919), pp. 190–229; Wolfram, *Goths*, pp. 286–306; Wilhelm Ensslin, *Theoderich der Grosse* (Munich, 1947); and the *Atti* of the XIII Congresso (1993). Specifically, on the Gothic settlement, see Goffart, *Barbarians and Romans*, pp. 58–102, amplified by Jean Durliat, "Le salaire de la paix sociale dans les royaumes barbares (Ve–VIe siècles)," in Herwig Wolfram and Andreas Schwarcz (eds.), *Anerkennung und Integration: zu den wirtschaftlichen Grundlagen der Völkerwanderungszeit, 400–600*, Denkschriften der philosophisch-historischen Klasse 193 (Vienna, 1988), pp. 29–71, with the partial rebuttals of S. J. B. Barnish, "Taxation, land and barbarian settlement in the Western empire," *Papers of the British School at Rome* 54 (1986), 170–95; Dietrich Claude, "Zur Ansiedlung barbarischer Föderaten in der ersten Hälfte des 5. Jahrhunderts," in *Anerkennung und Integration*, pp. 13–16; and Ian Wood, "Ethnicity and ethnogenesis of the Burgundians, appendix: the settlement of the Burgundians," in Herwig Wolfram and Walter Pohl (eds.), *Typen der Ethnogenese unter besonderer Berücksichtigung der Bayern* 1, Denkschriften der philosophisch-historischen Klasse 201, Veröffentlichungen des Instituts für österreichische Geschichtsforschung 12 (Vienna, 1990), pp. 65–9. On Theoderic's civilian and military administration, see A. H. M. Jones, "The constitutional position of Odoacer and Theoderic," *Journal of Roman Studies* 52 (1962), 128–30; William G. Sinnigen, "Administrative shifts of competence under Theoderic," *Traditio* 21 (1965), 456–67. Jones, LRE 1: 254, and Theodor Mommsen, "OGS," NA 14 (1889), 516, hold that Theoderic's "maiores domus regiae" were a royal household in the "Germanic" sense. This is pure conjecture. Mommsen himself admitted possible Roman precedents for the institution (p. 516, n. 1). On Theoderic's delicate use of imperial ceremonial, see Ensslin, *Theoderich*, pp. 157–65; Wolfram, *Goths*, pp. 286–8; McCormick, *Eternal Victory*, pp. 273–84; and Moorhead, *Theoderic*, pp. 39–51. On his policy of religious toleration, see Wolfram, *Goths*, pp. 327–8; Moorhead, *Theoderic*, pp. 97–100; T. S. Brown, "Everyday life in Ravenna under Theoderic: an example of his 'tolerance' and 'prosperity?,' " XIII Congresso, Milan, 3 November 1992. On the Jews, see below, pp. 60, 80–1. On Theoderic's behavior in the Acacian and Laurentian schisms, see Thomas F. X. Noble, "Theoderic and the papacy," XIII Congresso, Milan, 4 November 1992, and below, ch. 6. On his quasi-imperial building and restoration policy, see Cristina La Rocca, "La politica edilizia di Teoderico," XIII Congresso, Milan, 5 November 1992; further, Moorhead, *Theoderic*, pp. 140–4 with references.

show that the king faced a gargantuan task in reconciling his "two peoples."[13]

Theoderic's ideology of mutual coexistence appears in the *Variae* as *civilitas*, a word with complex overtones, which etymologically invoked the consensual organization of a Mediterranean *civitas* or *polis*.[14] Theoderic's *civilitas* conceives of two distinct but co-dependent groups living together in Italy – the Goths and Romans. In explaining this ideal to both the Italians and the Goths, the government drew on the familiar language of Roman law and classical ethnography.

The audience, as always, comprised the ruling classes of Italy, the addressees of the *Variae* and the recipients of his edicts, his *comites*, bishops, senators, generals and *saiones*, whether Romans or Goths. These were the people who received the royal commands, who were present at the recitations of the panegyrics of Ennodius and Cassiodorus, who corresponded with the king about the Laurentian schism. The government's rhetoric of ethnography in the Ostrogothic kingdom was aimed at the whole of civil society.

The basis of the royal ethnographic ideology was that any worthwhile Gothic culture was learned from the Romans and was, essentially, Roman culture. In defending it by arms, therefore, Goths protected the interests of one integrated society under one law.[15] What the Goths brought to this equation was not any culture of their own, but military success. This is not to say that there was no distinct "Gothic" culture in Italy – or non-Roman military culture, or at least a culture originally attached to Theoderic's followers from the Balkans, for all these terms beg questions – but that almost no surviving document produced by the Ostrogothic government mentions Gothic culture as such. Any indigenous *prudentia* among Theoderic's Goths formed no part of the royal ideology of ethnographic roles in Italian society.[16]

In its practical expression, this ideology implies that Goths defend the Roman state, all inhabitants of which live under Roman law.

---

[13] Moorhead, *Theoderic*, pp. 27–8, 77–8. The instances of seizures of land cited by Moorhead demonstrate tension between soldier and civilian, and not necessarily between two ethnic groups – Moorhead is himself seduced by the royal ideology that all soldiers were Goths and all civilians Romans. See below, p. 80 with n. 193; see also the comment in n. 24.

[14] See below, pp. 116–17.

[15] "Delectamur iure Romano vivere quos armis cupimus vindicare," *Var.* 3.43.1. "Laus Gothorum est civilitas custodita," *Var.* 9.14.8. When he installed the *comes* of the conquered Pannonia Sirmiensis, the king warned him that "set among the perverse customs of the nations you are able to demonstrate the justice of the Goths, who have always been surrounded by praise, because they accepted the wisdom of the Romans, and possessed the valor of the *gentes*": *Var.* 3.23.3. Interestingly, this representative of the Goths had a Latin name: PA Colosseus; on names, see chs. 3 and 7.

[16] Contra Wolfram, *Goths*, pp. 286–7, 324–7.

Therefore, the army is composed of Goths, and the civilian population is composed of Romans. The extent to which this ideology *determined* membership of one group through profession, rather than birth, is a major question of this study, to be addressed in the subsequent chapters on the behavior of individuals.

One caveat: Cassiodorus selected and polished the letters of the *Variae* in the Ravenna of the late 530s, long after the events they describe. Do they remain a reliable source on Theoderic's policy? It seems that any polish extended only to the probable elimination of many personal names, and of protocol and eschatocol, as well as to the possible addition of excurses on natural phenomena.[17] It could not have served Cassiodorus's literary or political purposes to insert a whole ideology regarding ethnographic identity into (especially) the early letters. In addition, he was compiling them in the besieged Ravenna of 538, when such a policy was obviously in ruins. His own sentiments at the time, as implied by the preface to his *De anima*, suggest that he still regretted the failure of Theoderic's reconciliatory ethnographic policy.[18] The *Variae* may then have partly been meant to commemorate it.[19]

---

[17] On the authenticity of the *Variae* as actual chancery documents, see Stefan Krautschick, *Cassiodor und die Politik seiner Zeit* (Bonn, 1983), pp. 41–5; Moorhead, *Theoderic*, pp. 2–3, 145 with n. 29; J.J. O'Donnell, *Cassiodorus* (Berkeley, 1979), p. 59. Franz Staab, "Ostrogothic geographers at the court of Theoderic the Great: a study of some sources of the Anonymous Cosmographer of Ravenna," *Viator* 7 (1976), 55, is even willing to ascribe the predominance of scientific excursuses in the first part of the *Variae* to Theoderic's own interest in scientific and historical topics. G. Vidén, *The Roman Chancery Tradition: Studies in the Language of "Codex Theodosianus" and Cassiodorus' "Variae,"* Studia Graeca et Latina Gothoburgensia 46 (Göteborg, 1984), notes that Cassiodorus's letters continue to reproduce the conservative bureaucratic style of the fifth century.

[18] Moorhead, *Theoderic*, p. 113 with n. 212, citing *De anima* 18: "Invidit, pro dolor, tam magnis populis, cum duo essent, et adhuc temporales persequitur quos impio ambitu fecit esse mortales," J. W. Halporn (ed.), CCSL 96 (Turnhout, 1973), p. 574, lines 10–12. The *De anima* is mentioned in the preface between Books 11 and 12 of the *Variae* as coming immediately after it, and is attached to the *Variae* in one of the MS traditions: James J. O'Donnell, *Cassiodorus* (Berkeley, 1979), p. 114. O'Donnell, pp. 127–8, sensibly notes that the conflicting interpretations of the two *populi* as either "the Ostrogoth–Roman kingdom of Italy and the Byzantines" or "Catholic Romans and Arian Goths in Italy" "blur an important reality, namely the connection between the Catholic Romans in Italy and the Catholic Romans coming from the East." True enough, but we must realize that some people called "Goths" could be Catholics, as we shall see in the following chapters, a situation known to the Catholic Cassiodorus, still or just recently in the service of the Gothic kings. It is impossible to imagine the newly committed Christian Cassiodorus as opposing Catholics and Arians on equal terms, but quite possible to imagine him opposing the Byzantine and Gothic armies then struggling over Italy as peoples equally to be pitied before God. Letters written in Books 10 and 12 of the *Variae* support the kingship of Theodahad and Witigis in the first phase of the wars during the late 530s. The appearance of *populi* in a religious text does not mean that it need refer to religious groups.

[19] I am unconvinced by P. S. Barnwell's argument that the *Variae* are fabricated documents designed to glorify a fictitious political career; see Barnwell, *Emperors, Prefects and Kings: The Roman West, 395–565* (London, 1992), pp. 166–9. Aside from their authentic bureaucratic style

CASSIODORUS'S *VARIAE* AND GOVERNMENTAL ETHNOGRAPHIC IDEOLOGY

I shall first analyze Cassiodorus's use of rhetoric in support of the *civilitas* system, particularly for the period when he was quaestor (507–11). Theoderic's letters to other barbarian kings modify the style used in letters to Italians. Next I shall note inconsistencies in other places where one would expect *civilitas* rhetoric to appear. Finally, I shall examine the chronological development in the later *Variae*, from 523–37. For in the *Variae* we see a definite evolution from the early Theoderican viewpoint of ethnographic accommodation to a greater emphasis on the warlike attributes of the Goths in the letters of Athalaric's successors. This evolution was doubtless linked to the evolving political conditions of the day as much as to changing attitudes toward ethnicity.

Cassiodorus's rhetoric was ideally suited to expressing Ostrogothic ethnographic ideology, since its roots in classically influenced late antique style contributed a rich fund of images of warlike barbarians. The *barbarus ferox* was an essential ingredient of classical Roman ethnographic literature, an object of satire as much as a worthy foe for the imperial armies. Some of this sort of language found its way into the fifth- and sixth-century writing of Sidonius, Avitus and Ennodius, despite its occasional jarring context.[20]

In contrast to these writers, Cassiodorus uses ethnographic rhetoric to fuse the former *extera gens* of the Goths to the social structure of the *res publica*. Since the Goths have an inborn vocation for fighting, they are suited to defend the Empire; since they obey Roman law, they lose any of the pejorative connotations of barbarians, such as immoderation and lawlessness. *Gothi* are superior to the *gentes*. In return, as effectively the army of Rome, they gain the old Roman connotations of an efficient *invictus exercitus*.

The rhetoric of the *Variae* also integrates barbarian soldiers into the framework of the Roman state by using the legal language of public obligation, both fiscal and abstract. Together Goths and Romans thrive in the *res publica* in a state of *civilitas* (peace and the restraining rule of Roman law) through *utilitas* (each performing his reciprocal *munera* or burdens). If Cassiodorus possessed a large stock of imagery of the supposed valor of barbarians, he had even greater legal-rhetorical resources

and vocabulary, the *Variae* present too much circumstantial detail and document too many subtle changes in royal policy. Barnwell suggests no convincing motive for their alleged forgery. See further the review by R. W. Burgess, *Bryn Mawr Classical Review* 4.3 (1993), 1–5. On the *Variae* as a reliable guide to Theoderic's policy, see Krautschick, *Cassiodor*, pp. 118–22.

[20] Amory, "Ethnographic rhetoric, aristocratic attitudes and political allegiance," pp. 444–6.

on the eternity of the Roman Empire and its superiority to the rest of the world. Both Goths and Romans benefit from it in his writing.

Cassiodorus's depiction of Theoderic's *civilitas* ideology can thus be divided into two parts, functional (legal) and philosophical (ethnographic). A unified vision appears, appropriately enough, in a formula. It is the formula of the office of *comes Gothorum per singulos civitates*, an official whose role has been debated.[21] It postulates a jurisdictional division between Goths and Romans. Since Goths are *permixti* with provincials, Theoderic is sending a count to prevent *indisciplinatio* among *consortes*. He is to decide cases between two Goths "secundum edicta nostra," and between a Goth and a Roman after talking to a "prudens Romanus" or jurisconsult, whereas Roman–Roman cases are to go before the local *cognitor* or provincial governor.[22] Since the next part of the letter makes it clear that the Goths in question were soldiers,[23] this legal division is between soldiers and civilians, who fell, as always in Roman law, into two separate jurisdictions (but did not thus fall under different laws).[24]

---

[21] *Var.* 7.3. Theodor Mommsen, "Ostgothische Studien," NA 14: 502–3; Schmidt, "Die comites Gothorum," pp. 129–31 (assuming that other *comites* were the *comites Gothorum* referred to elsewhere); Wolfram, *Goths*, pp. 290–1. This *comes* seems to have been a military watchdog. Since the Goths referred to were soldiers stationed among provincials, probably receiving allotments of taxation, the *comes Gothorum* was clearly a linchpin in maintaining *civilitas*, and it is appropriate that this rhetoric occurs in the formula of his office. Schmidt's notion that he judged only unmobilized Goths (p. 129) is unsupported by the text. On *comites Gothorum*, note that this whole formula is such a statement of ideology that the office as such may not have existed; the formula merely provided a template of behavior for *comites* "of the Goths," in other words, in *civilitas* ideology, for *comites* "of the army."

[22] *Var.* 7.3.1.

[23] *Var.* 7.3.7. See also nn. 26–7, below.

[24] So much misunderstanding prevails on this subject that it deserves a full note. Mommsen long ago recognized the professional division at work in this letter; see "Ostgothische Studien," NA 14: 528–9, citing *Nov. Theod.* 4, *Nov. Marc.* 1.7, CJ 12.35.18 preface. The novel of Theodosius mirrors Cassiodorus's formula exactly: soldiers are to be tried by the *magister militum*, civilians by the provincial governors, while cases involving both a soldier and a civilian are to be heard by a military court.

This formula is not a proof of "personal law" in Italy: law under the Ostrogoths was territorial, as the edicts of both Theoderic and Athalaric make clear; ET prologue: "ut salva iuris publici reverentia et legibus omnibus cunctorum devotione servandis, quae barbari Romanique sequi debeant, super expressis articulis, edictis praesentibus evidenter cognoscant;" similarly in Athalaric's *Var.* 8.3.4: "Gothis et Romanisque apud nos ius esse commune" (Piergiuseppe Scardigli, *Lingua e storia dei Goti* [Florence, 1964], p. 286, thinks this statement of territorial law represents a brand-new state of affairs, offering no supporting evidence and wrongly attributing this letter to Theoderic); 9.18.12: "But lest, by touching on a few laws, I should be supposed not to desire the maintenance of the rest, I decree that all edicts, both my own, and the lord my grandfather's [Theoderic's], that were drafted with honored deliberation, as also the ordinary public laws, are to be kept with full force and rigor ... The ordinary rule of the laws and the integrity of my commands are everywhere to be upheld," trans. S. J. B. Barnish (Liverpool, 1992), p. 120. The imperial constitutions continued to be the basis of justice: *Var.* 9.18.1 enforces the novel of Valentinian III on the violent occupation of someone else's estates, an abuse

Since Romans and Goths were *consortes*, they were partners in the Ostrogothic settlement agreement. Romans paid taxes, and Goths collected them; Romans produced food, Goths fought. This is the functional division envisaged. The potential stresses are obvious, and therefore the need for a *comes Gothorum*, a military official to mediate (with Roman legal assistance).

But Cassiodorus goes beyond the mere functional distinction common in the barbarian kingdoms. The above conditions prevail "ut unicuique sua iura serventur et sub diversitate iudicum una iustitia complectatur universos. Sic pace communi utraeque nationes divinitate propitia dulci otio perfruantur."[25] Two nations are to live as one, with different judges, that is, different functions, in mutual peace and sweet leisure.

The emphasis on law is the Roman side of the equation, what the Goths receive in return for their defence of the Empire, and the close of the formula brings in these key words to sum up the philosophy. "Non amamus aliquid incivile:" laws, not arms, must solve disputes. The king addresses the two groups together as a single *populus*. To the Goths, he announces that the Romans are their neighbors, and that their lands are "joined in charity." He urges the Romans to love the Goths, who defend the *universam rem publicam* in time of war.[26]

Theoderic's kingdom thus appears as the Empire: Roman in its law, containing two *nationes*, but one *populus*, interdependent and joined

common to both Romans and Goths, as Pope Gelasius I commented in the 490s, referring to farms "quae vel a barbaris vel a Romanis inconvenienter invasa sunt;" Gelasius, JK 685 = *ep.* "Ad cumulum vero" (Thiel, fr. 35, pp. 501–2); on the probability that having a *sors barbara* made such abuses easier, see below, n. 193. Personal law is still accepted by Adriano Cavanna, "Diritto e società nei regno ostrogoto e longobardo," in *Magistra barbaritas*, pp. 356–8, and in sundry works on non-legal subjects. "In Theoderic's Italy territorial law, from which no one was exempt, was in force" (Wolfram, *Goths*, p. 289).

A similar inherited division between military and civilian law in the other barbarian law-codes may have created the impression that personal law existed elsewhere in sixth-century Europe. In fact, the expression is an anachronism when discussing the post-Roman world: see Amory, "The meaning and purpose of ethnic terminology," pp. 10–15, 19–23.

The question of Jordanes's *belagines*, supposed ancient Gothic customs (Jordanes, *Getica* 69, ed. Theodor Mommsen, MGH: AA 5.1 [Berlin, 1883]), which is still accepted, for example, by Riché, *Education and Culture*, p. 71, n. 130 and by Cavanna, "Diritto e società nei regno ostrogoto e longobardo," p. 359, is irrelevant here, since no evidence whatsoever shows that they existed in Theoderic's Italy. *All* the Italian evidence does show that Goths were subject to the same law as Romans.

The *ecclesia legis Gothorum Ravennatis* of PItal 33 and 34 refers to the Arian church of Ravenna: *lex* here has a purely religious sense, against Piergiuseppe Scardigli, *Die Goten: Sprache und Kultur* (Munich, 1973), p. 300; see, for example, Wolfram, *Goths*, pp. 210, 462 with nn. 307, 309. The Arian church and its role in Gothic identity is the subject of ch. 7.

[25] *Var.* 7.3.1–2.
[26] *Var.* 7.3.3.

together. The neatness of the construction of the letter, and the express-
iveness of its language and antitheses, are the work of Cassiodorus. But
the sentiments thus expressed were the consistent ethnographic philosophy of the king and his government.

Cassiodorus's other letters attest both the functional and philosophical
propagation of this ideology. The functional ethnographic division of
Italian society, in this view, is that Goths are soldiers, and Romans are
civilians. The Italian *exercitus* is the *exercitus Gothorum*: the two terms
are synonymous.[27] The duty of this army, of these Goths, is to preserve
civilitas within the *res publica* by securing its borders against the *extera
gentes*.[28]

Theoderic's kingdom is still the *res publica Romana*,[29] or, when talking
to the East, one of two Empires.[30] The Roman role within this system –
and here the *possessores* are meant – is to pay taxes and thus supply the
army with food and salary.[31] This role can even apply to the senate,
who are urged to pay taxes "quod nos salva civilitate dissimulare non
possumus, ut sine acerbitate belli rebus suis exuantur oppressi et illi
magis pereant, qui rei publicae parere festinant."[32] The assumptions of
useful reciprocity between king and senators, between Goths and
Romans, within one *res publica* and one state of *civilitas*, are clear.

---

[27] *Var.* 1.4.17; 3.38.2: "Vivat noster exercitus civiliter cum Romanis"; "Gothi" in 4.36.3 clearly
refers back to the "exercitus" of 4.36.2; the *millenarii* of 5.27 are the *Gothi* of the address of
5.26: they "accept the donative" in 5.27.1 and are called *exercituales* in 5.26.2 and *exercitus* in
5.27.2 (on the identity of *millenarii* and *universi Gothi* in these letters, see Goffart, *Barbarians and
Romans*, pp. 82–7). (Note that 5.26 and 5.27 date from the 520s [Krautschick, *Cassiodor*, p. 77]:
they document, however, not the propagation of ethnic ideology so much as the terminological
repercussions of the use of this kind of rhetoric over the previous thirty-odd years, i.e. Goths =
soldiers.)

[28] *Var.* 2.5: The army serves the *utilitas rei publicae* by securing the borders and keeping the *gentiles*
and *barbari* outside.

[29] *Var.* 1.20.1, 3.18.2: Magnus v.s., in being repatriated to the Ostrogothic kingdom, is returning
"ad Romanum . . . imperium."

[30] *Var.* 1.1.4, 2.1.4. This fiction was convenient to retain even under Theodahad in 535 (10.21.2)
and Witigis in 536 (10.32.4).

[31] *Var.* 4.36 to the praetorian prefect Faustus: taxes on the *provinciales* of Alpes Cottiae are to be
remitted; Theoderic himself will pay the [thus reduced] *stipendium* of the Goths. 5.14.6–8: in
the interest of the *utilitas publica*, "former barbarians" in Savia, governed by a *iudex Romanus*
(provincial governor) and *comes Gothorum* (military official), must now pay taxes because they
have acquired land. "Barbarus" here clearly means soldier; on the rare inconsistency in Cassiodorus of using the term instead of *Gothi* (note that Cassiodorus was not always consistent), see
the examples given below, n. 188. It is, however, fully consistent with the usage of the *Edictum
Theoderici* (see below, pp. 79–81). 5.27.2: the *millenarii* of Picenum and Samnium are urged to
preserve the meadows of the *possessores* since this is the source of their pay, "ut ab armatis
custodiatur intacta civilitas;" on *millenarii*, see above, n. 27. Later, under Athalaric, it helps the
Reatians and Nursians (Goths) if the Romans are kept in peace, because the king's treasury
will increase, and thus the Gothic donatives multiply (*Var.* 8.26.4).

[32] *Var.* 2.24.5.

Not only are the Romans supposed to produce quietly, but *possessores* in particular are not *allowed* to become soldiers. The very definition of a Roman is a civilian. "Restrain, therefore, the reckless tumult of the *possessores*. Let them love tranquillity, since no one is driving them into danger. While the Gothic army wages war, let the Roman be at peace. What is enjoined on you is the aim of the fortunate: it is to prevent the savage *genus* of the *rustici* from being carried away by lawless ventures when they escape the routine of their work . . . Let them draw the steel, but steel to till the fields . . . It will be the greatest glory of the defenders if, while they guard the regions mentioned, the civilians continue to cultivate the lands of their own country."[33]

The role of the Goths as warriors defending the state takes us to the philosophical side of *civilitas* ideology. Theoderic combined opposing classical ethnographic motifs to suggest that in keeping barbarians out of the Empire, the Goths themselves were no longer barbarians. They are a *gens* or *natio*, certainly, but they possess the *Romanorum prudentia* alongside their *virtus gentium*,[34] with the result that they alone of all the non-Roman peoples can lay claim to *iustitia*.[35] Innate military valor allowed the Goths to achieve their unique position as defenders of the Roman state.[36] But it is Roman law that is reiterated as the very foundation of *civilitas*, on both sides of the agreement between Goths and Romans.

The superiority of the Gothic army of Italy to the *gentes* that they strive to keep out appears again and again throughout the *Variae*.[37] Theoderic urges "all the barbarians and Romans" in reconquered Pannonia not to fight, *pro regni nostri utilitate*,[38] for the sake of *civilitas* and hence *pax*. They should imitate the Goths, who show pugnaciousness abroad and modesty at home ("intus"), by observing law, since they

---

[33] *Var.* 12.5.4–5, trans. Barnish, p. 164 (I have retained certain Latin words). The letter is from 535–6, and the regions are Lucania and Bruttii, so the orders contained partly originate from fear of the Byzantine army, then in Sicily and threatening southern Italy. But even this late, the rhetoric still perfectly sums up *civilitas* ideology and in fact uses the word (12.5.6: "sic enim prosperrime geri non sentietis bellum, si vobis sit communiter de civilitate consilium"). The letter evokes an ideal situation – clearly some peasants *were* joining the army, perhaps on the wrong side! – and in all its details coincides perfectly with the evidence from 507–11. I cite it here because it is the most complete summary of the role of the Roman *possessor* in wartime. Further on this letter, see n. 170, below.

[34] On *prudentia* as Rome's successful answer to barbarian *virtus*, see Dauge, *Le barbare*, pp. 806–10.

[35] *Var.* 3.23.3, 7.25.1.

[36] *Var.* 1.24.1, 1.38: "To Goths, valor makes full age;" 5.24 (using the Roman-sounding "Schola Martia" as a metaphor for military valor).

[37] Further on victory ideology in Theoderic's government, see McCormick, *Eternal Victory*, pp. 273–84, and below, pp. 115–17.

[38] *Var.* 3.24.2.

now have a new *iudex*.[39] The formula for the office of general of the Raetian border, the *dux Raetiarum*, emphasizes that, beyond the border, he is to secure *libertas* "contra feras et agrestissimas gentes." Within, his *milites* are to live with the *provinciales iure civili*, "because that shield, our army, ought to preserve peace for the Romans."[40]

The Goths achieve their superiority through living under Roman laws; therefore, Ostrogothic Italy, the *regnum* of Theoderic, is the very home of *civilitas*, and through its reconquests reintegrates lost provinces into the Roman Empire. The senate should observe *ius Romanum*, which moderates the behavior of the *exterae gentes*, Italy itself being *ipsa sedes civilitatis*.[41] The reconquered provinces of Gaul[42] should obey Roman law, to which they have now at last been restored. The people there should vest themselves in togas. "Exuite barbariem, abicite mentium crudelitatem, qui sub aequitate nostri temporis non vos decet vivere moribus alienis." For "iura publica certissima sunt humanae vitae solacia." Destined for "civilem regulam," the Gauls can now repudiate *gentilitas*, the opposite of Roman *civilitas*.[43] In another letter regarding these provinces, Theoderic announces that he delights that those whom he defends live under *ius Romanum*, "for what is the profit from the removal of barbarian confusion, if people do not live under *leges*?"[44] The senator Arigernus, having, in the cause of *utilitas*, restored *civilitas* to these very Gallic provinces, now comes back to supervise *iustitia* and *leges* at the city of Rome, apparently in the military position of the *comes urbis Romae*.[45]

In participating so fully in the Roman *res publica*, a whole body whose members were necessarily interdependent and indivisible,[46] the Goths secure that most precious of Roman traits, *libertas*, the right to Roman law, and the consequent civilizing moderation of barbarian ferocity.[47]

---

[39] *Var.* 3.24.4.
[40] *Var.* 7.4. On *libertas*, see references at n. 47, below.
[41] *Var.* 1.27.1.
[42] Provence and Narbonensis, formerly part of the Visigothic kingdom.
[43] *Var.* 3.17. Cf. the parallel implications of Ennodius's use of *civilitas*, p. 116, below.
[44] *Var.* 3.43.1, on enforcing Roman laws on runaway slaves in Gaul.
[45] *Var.* 4.16; PA **Arigernus**.
[46] *Var.* 9.2.1, admittedly a post-Theoderican document, but one expressing an old idea.
[47] Chaim Wirszubski, *Libertas as a Political Idea at Rome* ([1950], reprint Cambridge, 1960), p. 7: *libertas* "is not an innate faculty or right of man, but the sum of civic rights granted by the laws of Rome," hence it contains ideas of restraint and moderation; in the Principate, it was considered a peculiarly Roman property, coterminous with citizenship (pp. 3–6). John Moorhead, "*Libertas* and *nomen Romanum* in Ostrogothic Italy," *Latomus* 46 (1987), 161–5, esp. 165: "confronted by the *gentes barbarae*, the function of the Gothic troops was clear: they fought *pro libertate*, while it was the responsibility of the duke of Raetia to act so that life could be enjoyed within the Gothic state *secura libertate*."

The senate is the *aula* or *curia libertatis* in Cassiodorus.[48] The Gothic army was also a special preserve of *libertas*, although this quality receives more emphasis in the letters of the 520s than in the 500s. Various soldiers enjoyed the "liberty of our army" or the "liberty of our Goths."[49] In a somewhat obscure injunction to his administrators in Spain in the later part of his reign, Theoderic complains that some of the Goths stationed in cities have been forced into *servitia*: "it is not fit to seek services from freemen whom we send to fight for *libertas*."[50]

The Gothic army fights for the *utilitas publica*, another term borrowed from Roman law. It has a doubly rich connotation. First, it evokes Roman imperial universalism. The emperor's responsibility had been defined by Ulpian as "pro utilitate humani generis."[51] When Theoderic applied *utilitas* to his army, he arrogated the emperor's natural right to universal sway, spreading the uplifting values of *civilitas*. But in the course of the fifth century, the growing focus of imperial government on the imposition and regulation of tax burdens and fiscal obligations meant that they had come to attract the term *utilitates publicae*. Furthermore, in Roman private law, the services rendered by a landowner to his tenants came to be called *utilitates*.[52] This double etymological shift documents the blurring of public and private characteristics of late and post-Roman society in the spheres of tax and rent.[53] Hence the responsibilities formerly identified with the imperial government were now also associated with great landlords, who had become state institutions. *Utilitas* occurs as both a philosophical and a fiscal term in the

---

[48] *Var.* 6.4.3, 6.16.3, 8.22.4, 9.25.3 and, outside the *Variae*, Theoderic's *praeceptum* of 507, ETV 9: "reparator libertatis, senatus urbis Romae." Four of these are addressed to the senate or to a senator, which implies flattery – but the term must have possessed some potency in Italian society; one of Witigis's letters to the East complained that Roman *libertas* was suffering from force of arms, i.e. the Byzantine invasion: 10.33.3; cf. Moorhead, *"Libertas* and *nomen Romanum,"* pp. 161–2. See also *Var.* 9.22.3, where the Decii are praised as a great family, the *auxilium libertatis* (cited by Moorhead, ibid., p. 163).

[49] Anduit enjoys the *libertas* of the army at 5.29.1: since he has become blind, it is now being threatened by his enslavement; Costula and Daila have enjoyed the liberty "Gothorum nostrorum" (5.30). These letters date from the 520s.

[50] *Var.* 5.39.15. This letter could be late; Book 5 contains documents from both the 500s and the 520s. Krautschick, *Cassiodor,* p. 77, does not attempt to date it.

[51] Michael H. Hoeflich, "The concept of utilitas populi in early ecclesiastical law and government," *Zeitschrift der Savigny-Stiftung für Rechtsgeschichte* 98, Kanonistische Abteilung 67 (1981), 37–8.

[52] Ibid., pp. 67–8.

[53] Walter Goffart, "From Roman taxation to medieval seigneurie: three notes," [1972], reprinted in Goffart, *Rome's Fall and After* (London, 1989), pp. 167–211, esp. 174–7, 188–9, 199–201; Goffart, "Old and new in Merovingian taxation," [1982], reprinted in Goffart, *Rome's Fall and After,* pp. 213–31.

Variae,[54] referring as much to the authority and duties of the king as
to those of his greatest subjects. The term, used in one sense, must have
evoked the other, if indeed the two meanings had not already been
conflated altogether.[55]

Given that the constant association of *utilitas* with ethnographic ideology must be related to the Gothic settlement, perhaps based on taxation,[56]*utilitas* in ethnographic matters must then have been meant to
evoke the reciprocal duties of Roman civilians and Gothic soldiers in
Theoderic's state. If Goffart is correct, the state effectively sloughed off
to private landowners one of its major responsibilities: the upkeep of
the army. Aside from the importance of maintaining an army for public
utilitas in the imperialist sense, by reiterating the word constantly in
reference to the relations between Goths and Romans, Theoderic was
recalling to each group their duties to the commonwealth, fiscal and
philosophical. Cassiodorus's *utilitas* meant, both abstractly and con-
cretely, "responsibility to the state." For Goths this meant fighting in
the army; for Romans, performing their *munera*: paying taxes. The
church had adapted this language from Roman law rather similarly in
the mid-fifth century.[57]

Libertas, utilitas, civilitas: it sounds like an Ostrogothic version of the
motto of the Jacobins. The simile is apt in that Theoderic conceived
of a whole philosophy of social organization. But in a precise reversal
of revolutionary France, these virtues flowed from the king. Like the

---

[54] Philosophical: *Var.* 1.17.1 (Goths and Romans to build themselves houses in the fort at
Dertona); 2.6.1 (sending an ambassador to the East); 3.27.3 (urging the *consularis* of Campania
to fulfill his duties honorably); 3.34 (the Massilians should obey their new count in anything
he proposes "pro publica utilitate"). Fiscal: 2.23 (it does not behove those who serve the *publicae
utilitates* to be burdened with extra *onera*); 3.25.2 (Simeonius to reorganize the collection of the
siliquaticum in Dalamatia; note philosophical use of *utilitas* in §1 of this letter); 12.6.2 (Cassiodorus
as prefect to those administrating the prefectural *tituli*: "Publicis utilitatibus servite fisci" [surely
the right reading: see Mommsen, apparatus, p. 365]).
[55] Note *Var.* 2.20, on bringing "frumentis fiscalibus oneratas" from Ravenna, beginning "Omnes
decet gratanter impendere quod publicas videt utilitates posse respicere . . ." Also *Var.* 2.32.1,
associating *utilitates publicae* twice with the senate in the first two lines, and then ordering them
to help the *patricius* Decius in draining the Pontine Marshes, an activity which "virtus publica
refugit, manus privata suscepit" (2.32.3). That these two concepts were already confused is
implied by the following letter, which remits taxes to Decius on any lands he might recover
from his work (2.33.1: "sine fisco possideas"). (For Decius's subsequent grateful inscription to
Theoderic, explicitly calling him "Augustus," see n. 65, below.)
[56] Whether one accepts the Goffart thesis or not. According to older theories, those parts of Italy
where the Goths did not receive tax-free lands paid the government a tax called the *tertium*;
according to Goffart's thesis, the Gothic soldiers received this tax directly, rather than lands.
[57] Hoeflich, "The concept of utilitas populi," pp. 59–71, esp. 68–70. An example in Ennodius:
Op. 235 (*ep.* 5.13, from early 506), p. 183, line 12: "utilitates sanctae Romanae ecclesiae,"
referring to church monies (ed. Friedrich Vogel, MGH: AA 7 [Berlin, 1885]).

emperors, he was the *auctor civilitatis*,[58] and his quaestor, the speaker of his voice, was the *templum civilitatis*.[59] These phrases imply not only that Theoderic was the literal "author" of this system, which no doubt he was, but that all the virtues of the dual ethnographic system flowed from his kingship. In a phrase perhaps borrowed from Cassiodorus, Jordanes attributes to Theoderic's chosen heir, Eutharic, "prudentia et virtus," wisdom and valor, the twin supports of Ostrogothic ethnographic ideology.[60]

As Wolfram has pointed out, Theoderic provides the epitome of the type of post-Roman military kingship.[61] As both commander of the army and viceroy of the Roman state, he was the natural leader of each of the groups into which he conceived his society to be divided, and thus he was the natural force to unite them. All the careful policy outlined above, of accommodation and strict government, of ethnographic rhetoric and ideology, was aimed at this goal, as was his delicate use of ceremonial, to assert his own authority in a society mesmerized by ritual and tradition, without offending the Eastern emperor.[62]

In practice, Theoderic's rhetoric, and the hazy arrangements under which the emperor legitimated his rule, made the king into a virtual emperor himself. The word *civilitas* had a long history as a specifically imperial virtue, the guarantee that the autocrat would not overstep the bounds of lawful rule. Its association with the soldier-king demonstrated that he was more than a soldier, that he had the right to rule the civilian population of Rome itself.[63] In an age when the Eastern emperor could

---

[58] *Var.* 8.2.2; *civilitas* was traditionally an ideal trait of emperors (whatever its specific meaning at different periods), Andrew Wallace-Hadrill, "The emperor and his virtues," *Historia* 30 (1981), 313–14; Eutropius, *Breviarium* 18.2 (of Jovian), on which see H. W. Bird, *Eutropius: Breviarium* (London, 1993), p. xliii (but "graciousness" or "courtesy" are probably not adequate renderings of *civilitas* in Eutropius). Other imperial virtues associated with Theoderic in the *Variae* and Ennodius are *clementia, iustitia, libertas, pietas, providentia, securitas, tranquilitas, victoria,* and *virtus* (a Roman as well as barbarian attribute: Dauge, *Le barbare,* index s.v. *virtus* and *vera virtus*), these imperial virtues listed in Wallace-Hadrill, "The emperor and his virtues," p. 323: see Traube, index to Cassiodorus, ss.vv; Vogel, index to Ennodius, ss.vv.

[59] *Var.* 6.5.5. The king and quaestor were, of course, the fount and the voice of law, the standard Latin meaning of *civilitas*, but it is impossible for the word not to have overtones of ethnographic coexistence in the *Variae*.

[60] Jordanes, *Getica* 298; cf. *Var.* 3.23.3: "Romanorum prudentia . . . et virtus gentium;" also *Var.* 11.13.4, where the senate describes Theodahad as "Romanis prudentia carum, gentibus virtute reverendum." The first parallel is noted by Moorhead, *Theoderic,* p. 201 with nn. 129, 132, who sees only concealment of Eutharic's vices here. A model for Ostrogothic kingship is the more likely basis.

[61] Wolfram, *Goths,* pp. 288–90.

[62] Best summed up by Ensslin, *Theoderich,* pp. 157–65; McCormick, *Eternal Victory,* pp. 269–84; Moorhead, *Theoderic,* pp. 39–51.

[63] On *civilitas* as an imperial virtue, see Andrew Wallace-Hadrill, "*Civilis princeps*: between citizen and king," *Journal of Roman Studies* 72 (1982), 32–48; I am grateful to Christopher Kelly for

be called *rex Romanorum*, and when both the Vandal king Gelimer and the emperor Justinian could be called *basileus*,[64] it was natural that one Roman senator could erect an inscription to Theoderic calling him by the otherwise unattested title *augustus*.[65] Even the Byzantine author Procopius, writing later under the revived imperial ideology of Justinian, could say, "Theoderic was in name a usurper (*tyrannos*), in reality nevertheless a genuine emperor (*basileus*) just like those who have distinguished themselves in this office from the beginning."[66] Theoderic's own rhetoric encouraged such imagery of rule.

These, then, are the outlines of the *civilitas* ideology, with regard to both function and philosophy, in Ostrogothic Italy. The evidence of Cassiodorus also suggests that Theoderic's government was not always consistent in propagating *civilitas* ideology, particularly according to the destination of the letters. In the later part of his reign, and under his successors, such ideology fell away completely.

The main factor governing the appearance of ideological inconsistency in the early *Variae* of 507–11 is the destination of the letter. Whereas *civilitas* ideology is most common in letters addressed to military and civilian officers sent to govern regions of the kingdom, particularly those newly conquered, to *possessores* and soldiers stationed in Italy, and to the Roman senate, inconsistencies appear most frequently in the letters addressed by Theoderic to other barbarian kings, and in those addressed to other groups in Italian society, such as the Jews. Although the *Variae*, both in 507–11 and 523–37, use the formulaic

pointing this out to me. See further ch. 4, below, on *civilitas* in Ennodius's panegyric to Theoderic.

[64] Wolfram, "Gotisches Königtum und römisches Kaisertum," pp. 7, 21–2.

[65] The notion of Pierre Courcelle ("Le tyran et le philosophe d'après la 'Consolation' de Boèce," in *Passaggio dal mondo antico al medio evo da Teodosio al San Gregorio Magno*, Atti dei Convegni Lincei 45 [Rome, 1980], p. 208 with n. 81), that Theoderic called *himself* Augustus on the basis of the inscription erected by Decius Basilius (CIL 10.6850) at times of tension with the East seems to me to have implications that are too broad: "Despite the degrees to which some of his subjects were prepared to assimilate Theoderic into the category of emperor, for official purposes he remained cautious" (Moorhead, *Theoderic*, p. 48, explicitly rejecting at n. 64 the idea that this inscription is evidence that Theoderic called himself Augustus). Theoderic did not call himself emperor, but he did encourage the propagation of victory ideology about himself.

[66] Procopius, BG 1(5).1.29, on which see Wolfram, "Gotisches Königtum und römisches Kaisertum," p. 1; earlier, Procopius says that Theoderic "did not claim the right to assume either the garb or name of emperor of the Romans, but was called 'rex' to the end of his life, for thus the barbarians are accustomed to call their leaders, still, in governing his own subjects, he invested himself with all the qualities which appropriately belong to one who is by birth an emperor" (1[5].1.26) ("his own subjects" clearly refers to all the inhabitants of Italy here): although the statement about Theoderic's restraint in regard to ceremonial and titulature is clearly correct, the entire statement is influenced by Justinianic ideology and appears in a preface justifying Justinian's right to invade Italy; on this, see chapter 4, below.

phrase "Goths and Romans" to mean "anyone,"[67] many other groups
had always existed in Italy. Certain letters acknowledge this diversity. A
letter to the Jews of Genoa dictates that Roman laws must be respected
regarding the Jews. The word *civilitas* appears twice.[68] Similarly, the
Jews of Milan are to be protected by the laws, since *civilitas* must be
preserved.[69] These letters allow the Jews to live according to their own
laws, as they had under the Empire.[70] These laws were, of course,
religious in origin, not parallel to the twin jurisdictions of the Goths
and Romans, both under Roman civil law.[71]

Theoderic links his religious tolerance to Roman tradition. The delicate procedure for finding the arsonists who burned a Jewish synagogue
in Trastevere must be conducted with extreme care, so as not to injure
Romana gravitas.[72] The word *civilitas* can merely mean universal lawful
concord under Theoderic's tolerant rule, and here acknowledges other
communities in Italy besides Roman civilians and Gothic soldiers.

In other circumstances, Cassiodorus varied the application of *civilitas*
rhetoric to suit the addressee. One example is the style of the first
twenty-one formulae of Book 6. Beginning with the consul and continuing down to the *rector* of a province, the vision of these thoroughly
Roman offices never mentions Goths or even the words "arms" or

---

[67] A necessary corollary of *civilitas* ideology. See *Var.* 4.47.2; 5.5.2; 7.39.2; 8.2.7; 8.3.4; 8.4.2; 8.6.2; 8.27.2.

[68] *Var.* 4.33.1–2.

[69] *Var.* 5.37.1.

[70] See ET 143, and below, n. 196.

[71] CT 2.1.10 (Arcadius, 398); similarly, 16.8.13 (Arcadius and Honorius, 397). Note 16.8.21 (Theodosius II, 412, 418, 420): Jews are to be protected, but not to be admired or encouraged on that account, a very similar tone to the *Variae* letters on the burned synagogue. The extent to which the Diaspora Jews had already become an ethnic community, as well as a religious affiliation, remains unclear. Judaism was still a proselytizing religion in seventh-century Spain (Roger Collins, *Early Medieval Spain* [London, 1983], pp. 129–42) as it had been in the third- and fourth-century Mediterranean (Martin Goodman, "Proselytising in Rabbinic Judaism," *Journal of Jewish Studies* 40 [1989], 175–85). Although there is no evidence for conversion to Judaism in sixth-century Italy, the existence of Jewish senators and a Jewish legal adviser at Theoderic's court suggests more integration than was the case in later medieval Jewish com- munities; the Greek and Latin names of some of these men at least imply that they were descended from converts, although caution is necessary here. Jewish senator from the late fourth or early fifth century (Cham v.c., "vir mire bonitatis," *Année Epigraphique* [1976], 67, no. 247); from 494/5, the vir clarissimus Telesinus and his relative Antonius, converted to Christianity, Gelasius, JK 654 = *ep. fr.* "Vir clarissimus Telesinus" (Thiel 45, p. 508); legal adviser: Symmachus *scholasticus*, AV 94. Moorhead, however, points out that the Anonymus elsewhere opposes "Iudaeus" not to "Christianus" but to "Romanus" (81f.) (*Theoderic*, pp. 98–9). This usage suggests a consciousness of ethnic difference as well as religious, although note that in Spain, for example, "Romanus" had come to mean "Catholic" (Gregory of Tours, *Gloria martyrum* 78–9, ed. Bruno Krusch, MGH: SRM 1.2 [Hanover, 1885]).

[72] *Var.* 4.43.3.

"soldier."[73] By implication these offices are thus purely civilian, as indeed they had been since Diocletian. But otherwise, the concept of a dual society is avoided, and the word *civilitas* appears only once.[74] Although the day-to-day letters addressed to particular holders of these offices stressed the royal ethnographic ideology repeatedly, as we have seen, the formulae carefully maintain the fiction of an unchanged Roman political culture.

Cassiodorus's diplomatic letters vary in other ways. In contrast to Theoderic's letters to the Emperor, which depict his own *gens* as superior through its natural alliance with Rome,[75] his letters to other barbarian kings assert Gothic superiority through military valor and the leadership of the Amal *stirps*, the royal family. Although some historians see Theoderic's "barbarian policy" as innovative, a diplomacy based outside the Roman Empire, freed from the norms of Roman diplomatic discourse and founded on marriage alliances and the extra-Roman custom of royal adoption *in armis*,[76] the rhetoric of royal diplomacy never addressed other kings as equals. Perhaps "to the *gentes* Theodoric appeared just like an emperor;"[77] but to Avitus and Sigismund he was merely the *rector Italiae*, an obstacle to messages sent Eastward.[78] Theoderic could comport himself like an emperor to the *gentes*, on the basis of his alliance with Italy and Roman law, but he might also emphasize his military achievements and the glory of his dynasty.

One constant in Cassiodorus's diplomatic letters to other kings is a condescending, at times sneering, tone.[79] From 507 to 511, it is based on the Gothic monopoly on *Romanitas*; in the later period, on the pre-eminence of the Amal *stirps*. Thus, in the first part of his reign, Theoderic borrowed from *civilitas* ideology in his dealings with barbarian kings, and later on, emphasized the might of Gothic blood.

In these earlier years, the king stressed the Romanness of his rule to foreigners in the same way that he did at home. In commanding Boethius to make a water-clock for Gundobad, king of the Bur-

---

[73] *Var.* 6.1–6.21.

[74] *Var.* 6.5, the formula for the quaestorship, called the *templum civilitatis*. This is surely due to the conception of the quaestor's peculiarly close position to the king: see p. 58, above.

[75] *Var.* 1.1; 2.1; the Burgundian kings pursued a similar diplomacy (see Avitus of Vienne, *epp.* 93–4, ed. Rudolf Peiper, MGH: AA 6.2 [Berlin, 1883]).

[76] Wolfram, *Goths*, pp. 306–27; Wolfram, "Il regno di Teoderico in Italia e nelle area adiacenti," XIII Congresso, Milan, 2 November 1992; Dietrich Claude, "Teoderico il Grande nel quadro europeo e mediterraneo: le sue relazioni diplomatiche," XIII Congresso, Milan, 2 November 1992.

[77] Wolfram, *Goths*, p. 307.

[78] Avitus, *ep.* 94; p. 101, line 26.

[79] Peter Heather (personal communication).

gundians, Theoderic announced, "Let the *exterae gentes* recognize, through you, that we [*nos*] have such noblemen as the sort who are read as authors."[80] *Nos* makes Boethius and Theoderic part of the same society, and by implication includes Theoderic in the praise of Graeco-Roman culture earlier in the letter.[81]

So far, so good: this inclusiveness in Roman cultural superiority is part and parcel of the *civilitas* ideology. In the next letter, to accompany the clock to the Burgundian king, Cassiodorus continues to make Theoderic emphasize the point. Theoderic arrogantly assumes the role of the representative of Rome: "Habetote in vestra patria, quod aliquando vidistis in civitate Romana." Through Gundobad's participation in such wonderful products of Italian culture as the water-clock, Burgundy may even be able to lay aside her *propositum gentile*.[82] In praising this *prudentia* on the part of the Burgundian king, Cassiodorus implies that his kingdom and subjects are not quite up to scratch. Certainly, the letter, accompanying an expensive diplomatic gift, one requested by Gundobad in the first place, must have been meant to accomplish concord between the two realms. But this concord, from the Ostrogothic viewpoint, assumed Italian superiority on the basis of its Roman heritage.

These particular letters still mirrored *civilitas* in pushing barbarity outside Italy and away from the Goths. The Burgundians remain an *extera gens*. The harpist which Theoderic requested from Boethius for Clovis will tame "gentilium fera corda."[83] The assumptions are obvious: there is no special relationship between Theoderic and the other barbarian kings.

But the royal letters dating from early 507,[84] which attempt to avert the war which finally broke out between the Franks and the Visigoths, invoke very different ideals for the same ends. Here we find no mention of Roman culture or Italian superiority. In the letter accompanying the harpist, Theoderic congratulates Clovis on his warlike valor and the recent triumphs over the Alamanni by his *gens Francorum*.[85] As one who has seen many wars "feliciter," Theoderic also proffers fatherly advice on moderation. Instead of appealing to Roman superiority the Gothic

[80] *Var.* 1.45.12.
[81] *Var.* 1.45.3-4.
[82] *Var.* 1.46.2. See Amory, "The meaning and purpose of ethnic terminology," pp. 27-8.
[83] *Var.* 2.40.17.
[84] Schmidt, "Comites Gothorum," 133-4, argues that these letters must be earlier. He suggests either redating Cassiodorus's quaestorship on this basis, or attributing them to an earlier quaestor. His points are interesting, but I think that the letters can remain in early 507. See further Krautschick, *Cassiodor*, pp. 53-8; Moorhead, *Theoderic*, p. 177, n. 12 with references.
[85] *Var.* 2.41.1-2.

king tells Clovis, "cede itaque suaviter genio nostro, quod sibi gentilitas communi remittere consuevit exemplo."[86] The condescension is clear. One wonders whom Cassiodorus and Theoderic thought were advising the Frankish king. To anyone who could understand the implications of the Latin, the letter would be tremendously insulting.[87] Perhaps it is of a piece with the Ostrogothic policy of alternately bullying and cajoling that we begin to find in the subsequent diplomatic letters.

Theoderic is less patronizing in those letters where he alludes to a similar framework of barbarian royal kinship which had no clear relationship to the *civilitas* ideology. In a subsequent, rather more polite, missive to Clovis, Theoderic stresses that he and the Visigothic king Alaric are relatives, and that indeed an affinity exists between all the (barbarian) kings which they should respect by leaving each other in peace.[88] Similar sentiments occur in his letters to Alaric[89] and to the Burgundian king Gundobad,[90] and in a form-letter delivered to the kings of the Heruls, the Warni and the Thuringians.[91] This affinity was real, in that almost all the barbarian kings were related to one another. The notion that kinship would halt violence between kings sounds ridiculous to anyone who has read Gregory of Tours, but there was no reason to think it might not be effective in 507.

But the careful diplomacy of marriage alliances to which Theoderic alludes in these letters has no clear connection to the ideological role of the Goths within Italy: that of keeping out the *exterae gentes*. The Burgundians might be an *extera gens* when the king talked to Boethius, and the Franks a *fera gens*, but when talking to Clovis, Theoderic praises the warlike virtues of the Franks in the highest terms, and implicitly compares them to those of the Goths. While the rhetoric does not allow the Franks equal place with the Goths, it is not downgrading them solely because of their lack of Roman culture and law – which is what we would expect from *civilitas* ideology.

A similar rhetoric, free from *civilitas*, prevails in Theoderic's other letters to the kings of the Thuringians and the Heruls, preserved as *Variae* 4.1 and 4.2. True, the letter to Hermanafrid, the Thuringian king, in bestowing Theoderic's niece Amalaberga in marriage, emphasizes that she is "litteris doctam, moribus eruditam," Roman qualities. But the word "Roman" does not appear. Rather, "Habebit felix Thor-

---

[86] *Var.* 2.41.2.
[87] Particularly to those Gauls who saw themselves as representatives of Roman culture.
[88] *Var.* 3.4.
[89] *Var.* 3.1.
[90] *Var.* 3.2.
[91] *Var.* 3.3.

ingia quod nutrivit Italia,"[92] and with this acquisition, the Thuringian king "should now shine even longer through the fame of the Amal blood."[93] The good qualities of (Roman) education are now intrinsic to Theoderic's family – a conceit visible in the letter to Boethius about the clock – and it is thus through Amal alliance, not alliance with the *res publica*, that the Thuringians will prosper.

In this letter, the familiar tone of condescension appears: Hermanafrid may be "de regia stirpe," but will shine more brightly "claritate Hamali sanguinis," and, indeed, so will his people: Amalaberga "nationem vestram meliore institutione componat."[94] The letter concludes with thanks for a gift of superb Thuringian horses, a gift "decus regiae potestatis."[95]

Theoderic offers no marriage alliance to the less important Heruls. Instead, he establishes a "barbarian" alliance which stresses his own authority: adoption of the Herul king "per arma," which "is always held to be a great honor *inter gentes.*"[96] This adoption is "more gentium" – the sort of *mos* from which Theoderic takes great care to distance himself in the *civilitas* letters – and accompanies appropriate gifts of arms, shields "et reliqua instrumenta bellorum."[97] The letter stresses the warlike power of both *gentes*, and hearkens back to ancient times, when the Goths had helped Heruls as allies.[98]

Then as now, the Goths were to be the supreme partners in the

---

[92] *Var.* 4.1.2.

[93] *Var.* 4.1.1: "claritate Hamali sanguinis fulgeatis." Most MSS actually have "imperialis" for "Hamali," a suggestive reading which would strengthen the argument here. See Moorhead, *Theoderic,* p. 45 with n. 51 (in the context of Theoderic's near-portrayal of himself as an emperor).

[94] *Var.* 4.1.1.

[95] *Var.* 4.1.4.

[96] *Var.* 4.2.1.

[97] *Var.* 4.2.1. *Adoptio per arma* was not necessarily actually a *mos gentium,* of course: here we encounter the ethnographic association of *gentes* and warfare. Since this sort of adoption was used by Roman emperors for barbarian kings (Zeno and Theoderic, or Justin I and Eutharic, for example), Dietrich Claude describes it as "eine Verbindung der bei den Germanen seit alters gebräuchlichen ehrenden Waffengabe mit Elementen des römischen Adoptionsgedankens" (Claude, "Zur Begrundung familiärer Beziehungen zwischen dem Kaiser und barbarischen Herrschern," in *Das Reich und die Barbaren,* p. 39), but since these emperors came from the same military background and even the same families as the kings whom they adopted, it might make more sense to replace "Germanic custom" with "frontier military custom." I am grateful to Walter Pohl for pointing out this study to me.

[98] *Var.* 4.2.3. The Goths had recently encountered Heruls as enemies in the following of Odoacer, so, if the same people are meant, the letter may refer to the mid-fourth century subjection of the Heruls by Ermanaric, recorded in *Get.* 116–18; it may thus constitute a rare confirmation of the existence of parts of Jordanes's version of Gothic history in Theoderic's kingdom. Heather (in "Cassiodorus and the rise of the Amals," pp. 110–13, and *Goths and Romans,* pp. 24–5, 88) has shown that the Ermanaric section is one of the least reliable parts of Jordanes's text.

agreement. "Summus enim inter gentes esse crederis, qui Theoderici sententia comprobaris."[99] Nevertheless, the Goths and Heruls share a heritage: "Nota sunt enim Erulis Gothorum deo iuvante solacia: gentes autem sibi olim virtutum pignora praestiterunt."[100] Moreover, and most surprisingly, the ambassadors will explain the rest of the message "patrio sermone,"[101] presumably in Gothic.[102]

This letter takes us far from the values of Roman law, the special role of the Goths in keeping out the *gentes exterae*, and the Roman heritage of the Goths among *gentes*. In fact, it constructs precisely the opposite viewpoint. The Goths are united to the Heruls by their extra-Roman history, by the non-Latin language of their *patria*, by the fiction of royal blood-ties, and by their success in arms. We could not be farther from *civilitas* ideology. The only remaining element is the pre-eminence of the Gothic *gens*, and that on a very different basis.

Two letters to Thrasemund, king of the Vandals, dating from 510 or 511, mention neither Italy, nor the Romans, nor, indeed, the Goths. The emphasis is on royal family connections. In the first letter, Theoderic upbraids the Vandal king for sheltering Gesalecus, bastard son of Alaric II and pretender to the throne of conquered Visigothic Spain. Since Thrasemund is Theoderic's brother-in-law through his marriage to Amalafrida, the letter treats the incident, fully politicized, as a personal affront. Thus Cassiodorus slips Theoderic into the first person singular, a very rare move: "Stupeo vos his beneficiis obligatos Gesalecum . . ."[103] These "beneficia" are the gift of Theoderic's sister, "generis Hamali singulare praeconium."[104] In the second letter, Theoderic thanks Thrasemund for acceding to his requests.[105] In both letters the stress is on the governance of the two kingdoms involved, and on the relationship between the two kings.[106] Theoderic returns Thrasemund's gifts as if they were from a friend to a friend rather than diplomatic

---

[99] *Var.* 4.2.2.

[100] *Var.* 4.2.3.

[101] *Var.* 4.2.4.

[102] A language presumed by linguists to be comprehensible by both Goths and Heruls: see Rudolf Much, "Heruler," in *Reallexikon der germanischen Altertumskunde* 2 (Strasbourg, 1913–15), pp. 518–19. Scardigli, *Lingua e storia*, pp. 309–11, points out that we have no remains of the language spoken by the Heruls, but Herul names share East Germanic roots with those of the Goths. See, however, chs. 3 and 7 on the differences between military spoken "Gothic" and the written classical Gothic discussed by Scardigli.

[103] *Var.* 5.43.2. On the dating, see Krautschick, *Cassiodor*, pp. 59, 77.

[104] *Var.* 5.43.1.

[105] *Var.* 5.44.

[106] *Var.* 5.43.3: "regnum vestrum"; 5.44.3: "fecimus utrique regalia"; 5.43.4: "animus parentum nostrorum"; 5.44.4: "parentes."

offerings.[107] This kind of rhetoric serves an intimate diplomacy and a personal conception of rulership.

It is difficult to document government policy during Cassiodorus's absence from office from 511 to 523. But in 519, the government was still promoting elements of *civilitas* ideology within Italy. Cassiodorus published his short *Chronicle* to congratulate Theoderic's nephew and heir Eutharic Cilliga on his reception of the consulate and his adoption by the emperor Justin I. These events coincided with the reconciliation of the Eastern and Western churches and the end of the Acacian schism. In the *Chronicle*, Cassiodorus describes Theoderic's advent into Rome in the year 500 as that of an emperor, and emphasizes the happiness of both Goths and Romans at Eutharic's honors of 519.[108] Cassiodorus's intervening notices document both Theoderic's military measures and his emperor-like work of civic restoration.[109]

The *Chronicle* nonetheless does not quite propagate the same ideology visible in so many of the early *Variae*. The terms *civilitas*, *libertas* and *utilitas* do not appear. Cassiodorus makes no explicit reference to the reciprocal functions of Gothic soldiers and Roman taxpayers, to Gothic valor or to the overarching structure of Roman law and prudence. The chronicle celebrates not the military victories of the Goth Eutharic, but his accession to a civilian honor, the consulship – albeit one appropriate for the heir of the exconsul Theoderic. One can just perceive a similar approach in the few surviving fragments of Cassiodorus's panegyric to Eutharic, delivered in 518 or 519 to celebrate the same occasion.[110]

More unusually, the *Chronicle* makes reference to Gothic history. For the first time, the Gothic past is an object worthy of study, instead of a barbarous darkness from which Roman *prudentia* and *ius* brought them into light. This is not the "splendor of the Amal blood" that appears in Theoderic's diplomatic correspondence. It is a record of the successes of the Goths, of any sort, against the Roman people. It thus sets the Goths into Roman history. While it does tone down any possible bitter-

---

[107] *Var.* 5.44.4.

[108] Cassiodorus, *Chron.* 1339, 1364, ed. Theodor Mommsen, MGH: AA 11 (= Chronica Minora 2) (Berlin, 1894).

[109] Victories against the Bulgars and Franks: 1344, 1349 (implying with the conquest of Sirmium and of Gaul that the empire received back its rightful borders); and rebuilding in Rome and of Ravenna: 1339, 1342. Cassiodorus thus sparsely but equally records each of these traits of Theoderic.

[110] *Orationes* ed. Ludwig Traube, in Mommsen's edition of Cassiodorus's *Variae*, pp. 457–84. One section praises the restoration of the *res publica*, particularly the recovery of Gaul (Cassiodorus, *Oratio* 1, p. 466, lines 14–20); quasi-imperial language appears ("triumphator," p. 466, line 14, *principes*, p. 466, line 2). There is no reference to *civilitas* – but the text is not complete. Another section clearly compares Eutharic to great consuls of the past (p. 467, lines 1–21), just as the *Chronicle* places him in his rightful place in the series.

ness caused by, for example, Alaric's sack of Rome, and deftly removes references to Arianism, the entire notion would have been alien to the internal rhetoric of Theoderic's propaganda ten years previously.

The dual approach of the *Chronicle* may document Theoderic's movement toward a different way of conceiving Amal rule in formerly Roman Italy. True, 519, with its royal consul and ecclesiastical peace, "must have seemed [a year] of bright promise for the Ostrogothic kingdom."[111] But in another source Eutharic appears as an evil villain, connecting him with ominous anti-Jewish disturbances at Ravenna and pro-Arian reprisals against the Catholics there.[112] Of course, this later source generalizes a local disturbance to all of Italy in order to lead up to a tragic account of Theoderic's last days.[113] As late as 522, when both of Boethius's sons were consuls, Theoderic's relations with the senate were still good. Nonetheless, the Anonymus Valesianus story suggests that not all Italy was as happy with the Ostrogothic kingship as Cassiodorus suggests. Such suggestion of opposition is absent from the earlier part of Theoderic's reign. In such a dimly perceptible climate of change the king may have begun to promote, within Italy, an ideology more similar to that of his earlier diplomatic letters. This new approach emphasized the royal family and the historical legacy of the Gothic people.

At some point within this period, Theoderic commissioned Cassiodorus to write a history of the Goths. The date of this lost work is controversial. It may not have been written until after Theoderic's death, but the suggestion to write it came in the last part of his reign.[114] With his history Cassiodorus "made Gothic history Roman,"[115] suggesting that it resembled the *Chronicle*. But Cassiodorus's later recitation of the Amal relatives of Theoderic's daughter Amalasuintha[116] suggests that he had done more research into, or invention of, an independent, non-Roman Gothic past. He himself declares that he has described the

---

[111] Moorhead, *Theoderic*, p. 202.

[112] AV 80–2.

[113] It is a tendentious and chronologically condensed account dating from mid-century; see Moorhead, *Theoderic*, pp. 217–19, and S. J. B. Barnish, "The *Anonymus Valesianus* II as a source for the last years of Theoderic," *Latomus* 42 (1983), 585, 596.

[114] Most recently, Krautschick dates it to 519, with subsequent revision in 551, while Goffart dates it to 533: see Krautschick, *Cassiodor*, pp. 21–40, and "Zwei Aspekte des Jahres 476," *Historia* 35 (1986), 364–7; Goffart, review of Krautschick, *Cassiodor*, *Speculum* 60 (1985), 989–90, and *The Narrators of Barbarian History* (A.D. 550–800) (Princeton, 1988), pp. 32–5. Moorhead's assertion that the history must date from after Theoderic's death assumes that Cassiodorus composed the last paragraph of the *Anecdoton Holderi*; as Krautschick points out (*Cassiodor*, p. 79), this could have been the work of the excerptor.

[115] In Cassiodorus's own words: *Var.* 9.25.5.

[116] *Var.* 11.1.19.

origin, places and customs of the Goths, which implies more than the *Chronicle* provides.[117] Such a *Gothic History* must have gone further than the *Chronicle*, which gave the Goths a past framed by Roman consulships and emperors.

Cassiodorus's lost *Gothic History* was contemporary with Theoderic's new emphasis on royal descent and on the uniqueness of a Gothic *gens* glorified by its own past, rather than the *gens* that had assimilated Roman wisdom. For the first time, Theoderic and his successors propagated this message in Italy, particularly in letters to the senate.[118] The king still depicted his authority as quasi-imperial, but now based it on a fictitious history that gave him splendor and prestige independent of Roman traditions. The shift is momentous. It can be corroborated again by the *Variae* after 523.

When Cassiodorus reappears as a chancery source again, in Theoderic's diplomatic letters of 523–6, *civilitas* ideology has been shunted aside completely in favor of imagery of valorous *gentes* allied by military success to the glorious name and family of the Amals. Theoderic thanks the king of the Warni for his gift of swords, and wants to join "facientes gentium nostrorum" together.[119] The emphasis is on valor and warlike success; neither the Romans nor the *res publica* appear.[120] A letter to the Hesti cites *fama nostra* – and Tacitus, a Cassiodoran touch – but does not mention Theoderic's Roman realm.[121]

This approach reaches its climax in Athalaric's letter to the Vandal king Hilderic in 526 – an instructive contrast to the endless reiterations of *civilitas* rhetoric in Athalaric's internal letters of the same year.[122] Here, the Amal family and *Gothi nostri* are welded together. "Our Goths feel the insult"[123] of the imprisonment of Amalafrida, "generis nostri decus egregium."[124] The threat is unconcealed. The Hasdings had had the honor of alliance with the "purple dignity of Amal blood,"[125] and they have abused it grievously. The letter implicitly threatens war unless

---

[117] Goffart, *Narrators*, pp. 37–8, suggests serial biographies like those of the Roman emperors, which does not seem sufficient.

[118] Moorhead, *Theoderic*, p. 109. See further below, pp. 72–4.

[119] *Var.* 5.1.3. Krautschick, *Cassiodor*, pp. 59, 77, wants to redate these letters to 507–11, not impossible, but unlikely, given the rhetoric.

[120] Despite a Cassiodoran reference to Vulcan: *Var.* 5.1.2.

[121] *Var.* 5.2 (*fama nostra*: 5.2.1; Tacitus: 5.2.2). The citation of Tacitus occurs in the scientific discussion of the origins of amber; since it comes from *Germania* 45, it might just constitute an acknowledgement of a world view based on a Roman–barbarian dichotomy – but none of this crops up in the letter.

[122] See pp. 71–2, below.

[123] *Var.* 9.1.2.

[124] *Var.* 9.1.1.

[125] *Var.* 9.1.2.

Hilderic can offer an excuse – although Theoderic had already been planning a retaliatory invasion[126] – and concludes with dire threats and a biblical reference to the slaughter of Abel.[127] Once more, the diplomatic emphasis is on Gothic power through the splendor of the Amal family and its military prowess; any connections with other parts of the world flow through the personal relationship of the Amal king with foreign rulers. Aside from the assumptions of Gothic valor, of course, there is nothing overtly "ethnographic" about this letter compared with the *civilitas* letters, but it proposes an entirely different cosmology and order of society compared to the ethnographic basis of the *civilitas* letters. The contrast is therefore important.

Cassiodorus and his masters applied different ethnographic rhetoric to situations inside and outside Italy respectively. But the Amal–Gothic–*gentes* rhetoric also begins to appear in letters within Italy when Cassiodorus reappears as a source in 523.[128] After a brief disappearance at the beginning of the reign of Athalaric, it becomes the norm through 538, the end of the chronological period covered by the *Variae*.

This shift in the propagation of an internal ethnographic philosophy must have some connection with the political circumstances of the end of Theoderic's reign. I do not wish to exaggerate a supposed change in the disposition of the king or of his attitude toward certain of his Roman subjects. From his murder of Odoacer – "The man has no bones in his body"[129] – onward, Theoderic had always found it easy to be ruthless. He executed his count Odoin in the Sessorian palace in Rome in 500,[130] and killed his count Pitzia with his own hands in 514 (and later regretted it).[131] He was careful to impose equal proscriptions on erring magnates, whether the influential praetorian prefect Faustus Niger or his nephew Theodohad, and in both cases used his personal agents, the *saiones*, to impose his will.[132]

---

[126] John Moorhead, "The last years of Theoderic," *Historia* 32 (1983), 119–20.

[127] If we can accept Hodgkin's reading of *Var.* 9.1.4: "vindicet nunc superna maiestas scelus quali-bet arte commissum, quae ad se clamare profitetur fraterni sanguinis impiam caedem" as referring to the Cain and Abel story (Thomas Hodgkin, trans., *The Letters of Cassiodorus* [London, 1886], p. 385).

[128] This change has nothing to do with Cassiodorus's new position as *magister officiorum*: he wrote the 523–6 letters for the current quaestor, apparently because his rhetorical style was so valued: *Var. praef.* 7; *Var.* 9.25.8.

[129] John of Antioch, fr. 214a, ed. C. Müller, FHG 4–5 (Paris, 1868–70).

[130] AV 12.68; *Auctarium Prosperi Havniensis* s.a. 504, ed. Mommsen, MGH: AA 9, Chronica Minora (Berlin, 1982); Marius of Avenches, *Chronicon* s.a. 500.3, ed. Mommsen, MGH: AA 11 (as above); on the date, see Wolfram, *Goths*, p. 502, n. 223.

[131] *Auctarium Prosperi Havniensis*, s.a. 514.

[132] *Var.* 3.20; 4.39: despite apparent differences in language, the *saiones* probably only communicated orders in both instances.

But Theoderic's actions in the early 520s fall under a different heading. There is a sense that the king is out of control.[133] In acting against
Albinus, Boethius and Pope John he alienated the leaders of the very
Italian institutions that he had worked so hard to conciliate in the early
part of his reign. Albinus was a member of the Decii, one of the two
most prominent senatorial families. Boethius, a member of the Anicii
and the king's *magister officiorum*, was in his own words the spokesman
for the senate, or at least for a part of it,[134] and John had journeyed to
Constantinople to spread a little of Theoderic's religious tolerance in a
land where it would shortly be sorely needed.[135]

Neither case represents the culmination of alienating interests building up through Theoderic's reign.[136] Boethius's circle need not have
been politically "philobyzantine" for favoring Greek theology. The
Laurentian schism – if its divisions actually outlasted their origins by
seventeen years – had not revolved primarily around the question of
compromising with the party of Acacius at Constantinople.[137] Finally,
with his diplomatic reticence, Theoderic himself had supported the
papacy's attempts to reunify the Eastern and Western churches right up
through its success in 519.[138]

Whatever the origins of Theoderic's change in internal policy, it
seems to me indisputable that the absence of *civilitas* rhetoric in the
royal letters of 523–6 must be related to it.[139] Just as telling is the abrupt

[133] Previously favorable sources like the *Anonymus Valesianus* and the *Liber Pontificalis* now turn
against him. Both were produced later, in 540s Italy, and mirror each other in depicting a
golden age for Italian Catholics in Theoderic's early reign. But even the contemporary first
edition of the *Liber Pontificalis* stops wavering on the king and turns against him decisively with
the life of John I (522–5). Ch. 6 deals with ecclesiastical attitudes.

[134] Boethius, *De consolatione* I, prose 4, ed. H. F. Stewart and E. K. Rand (Cambridge, Mass.,
1918); AV 14.85; Matthews, "Anicius Manlius Severinus Boethius," pp. 29, 37–8.

[135] These events are best summed up by Moorhead, "The last years of Theoderic," pp. 114–16,
and "The Decii under Theoderic," *Historia* 33 (1984), 112–15.

[136] Contra Moorhead, "The Decii under Theoderic," "The last years of Theoderic," "The Laurentian schism: East and West in the Roman church," *Church History* 47 (1978), 126–9. Moorhead has since modified his views, *Theoderic*, pp. 115–39, 158–72, 219–26.

[137] The Laurentian schism receives full discussion in ch. 6, below; it suffices here to stress that
the main issues discussed at the time were the alienation of secular property to the church and
the role of lay leaders in church governance; senatorial factions and circus parties may have
played a role as well. Ernst Stein, in *Histoire du Bas Empire*, 2 vols. (Paris, 1949–59), 2: 136–
7, is sensibly cautious about drawing connections, even if his placement of the patrician Symmachus among Pope Symmachus's supporters probably no longer stands.

[138] Noble, "Theoderic and the papacy."

[139] Chs. 4, 5 and 6 will argue that *civilitas* ideology was dropped for two reasons: first, that it failed
to describe adequately the reality of mingled civilian and military society in Italy, and second,
that the reunification of Eastern and Western churches reopened the possibility that civilian
Catholic Italians could be "Romans" in the sense of direct subjects of the emperor. This last
development came gradually and was only fully realized with Justinian's invasion of Italy in

reappearance of such expressions, in a self-consciously stiff and formulaic way, in Athalaric's rather desperate first series of letters to the powers of his realm, an attempt to mould a new consensus after the splits and cracks of Theoderic's last years. The artificiality of the expression of this rhetoric is as telling as its subsequent abrupt disappearance, followed by new forms of ideology in the letters written for Theodahad and Witigis, who faced more opposition to their royal authority, both from within and without, than had their predecessors.

On the accession of Athalaric, who failed to gain the imperial recognition that Theoderic and Eutharic had received, Cassiodorus wrote a series of conciliatory letters to all the major constituents of Italian society. These show the reappearance of *civilitas* rhetoric in the governmental documents. This rhetorical revival was not accompanied by a revival of policy.

Athalaric's initial publications carefully use the language of Theoderic's early reign. In the letters to the senate and to the people of Rome, the king is the *auctor civilitatis*, as Theoderic had been.[140] Athalaric has been elected by the *generalis consensus*, the *suavissimus consensus*, of the Goths and Romans (presumably at Ravenna).[141] Athalaric promises to do justice and to treat the *populi* with equal clemency, and specifically, to apply *ius commune* to both Goths and Romans, and not to let anything divide them.[142] There follows a re-statement of Theoderic's functional ethnographic ideology: "nisi quod illi labores bellicos pro communi utilitate subeunt, vos autem habitatio quieta civitatis Romane multiplicat."[143]

All the elements of *civilitas* ideology are here: the Goths and Romans living together under one law, performing different functions under an equitable king, distinguished implicitly as *populi* from the *gentes* outside.

535: see ch. 4 on the late gestation of the idea of Reconquest, chs. 3 and 5 on soldiers firmly bound into Italian society, and ch. 6 on the slow and stuttering Catholic acceptance of imperial claims in Italy. Also important was Theoderic's use of parvenus in high office from 511 to 521 (Moorhead, *Theoderic*, pp. 151–8): men like Cyprian came from families who had provided both soldiers and bureaucrats for generations, and the functional rhetoric of *civilitas* did not describe them well. Cyprian was willing to take on attributes of "Gothic" identity (see below and ch. 5; PA Cyprianus). *Civilitas*, with its appreciation of the Roman past, the senate and Republican office, appealed to the non-military senatorial aristocracy and men like Cassiodorus who admired that world, but the senators were excluded from office for this entire decade, as Moorhead has shown. By the time they returned, with the consulship of Boethius's sons in 522, the chancery was no longer promoting *civilitas* rhetoric.

[140] *Var.* 8.2.2.
[141] Since these phrases occur in the letters to Rome: *Var.* 8.2.7; 8.3.3.
[142] *Var.* 8.3.4.
[143] *Var.* 8.3.4.

These sentiments are repeated painstakingly, in similar language, in the letters to the Romans of the Italian provinces,[144] to Liberius the prefect of Gaul,[145] and to the Gallic provincials.[146]

The significant exception in this series is the letter to the "diversis Gothis per Italiam constitutis," which seems rather influenced by the rhetoric of Theoderic's diplomatic letters and of his later years. It makes no mention of Romans or of Goths, but dwells instead on the "Hamalorum regalem prosapiam, blatteum germen, infantiam purpuratam" of Athalaric.[147] The emphasis is on the superiority of the blood of the Amals and their divine right to rule.

The letter to the Goths stands out strikingly in the series of Athalarican *civilitas* letters beginning Book 8 of the *Variae*. It demonstrates that Athalaric's government thought that *civilitas* rhetoric was no longer appropriate in dealing with the army of Italy. *Civilitas* rhetoric would appear only twice more in letters to the Goths.[148] One of these letters shows not only that Theoderic's ethnographic ideology was having little effect, but that governmental policy now allowed the count of the Goths to judge cases between two Romans if they consented. Such "consent" would amount to a successful claim by civilians to the benefit of military forum, a right as non-existent under Roman law as it had been under Theoderic.[149] It represents a major departure from the practice of Athalaric's grandfather.

The remaining letters of the *Variae*, from 526 to 537, are more notable for omitting any form of ethnographic rhetoric than for propagating it. But where ethnographic rhetoric does occur, it strays far from the ideals of *civilitas* ideology. In a letter to the senate of Rome from the end of 526, Athalaric praises the *patricius* Tuluin for being "Gothorum nobilissima stirpe," which is foremost among the nations.[150] True, the

---

[144] *Var.* 8.4.2.

[145] *Var.* 8.6.2.

[146] *Var.* 8.7.3.

[147] *Var.* 8.5.2.

[148] *Var.* 8.26.4, on the benefits of protecting the Romans because donatives multiply, and, reiterating the formula of the *comes Gothorum* (7.3), 9.14.8, to the count of Syracuse: "Gothorum laus est civilitas custodita," and "Vos armis iura defendite, Romanos sinite legum pace litigare."

[149] *Var.* 9.14.7 upbraids Gildila, *comes civitatis Syracusanae*, for judging cases between two Romans, a situation clearly forbidden by *Var.* 7.3 (assuming, with Schmidt, that the *comes Syracusanae civitatis* refers to the same officer as the *comes Gothorum* of *Var.* 7.3, "Comites Gothorum," p. 129). "Etiam his invitis" implies that if the two Romans had been willing, they could have received trial in the (military) court of the *comes Gothorum* (as Schmidt notes, ibid.). Restriction of military forum: CT 2.1.9 (Arcadius, 397), military courts not to hear civil cases; similarly, the formula for the *comes, Var.* 7.3.1. Krautschick, *Cassiodor*, pp. 48–9, dates the formulae tentatively to the period of Cassiodorus's quaestorship under Theoderic (507–11), and the letter to Gildila to "soon after 30 Aug. 526," directly after Athalaric's accession, pp. 89, 103.

[150] *Var.* 8.10.2.

senate is still the *atria libertatis*, but it is being opened to a Goth – not just a man with a Germanic name, but a Goth famed for his ability in war and his ability in defeating other *gentes*. Indeed, "convenit gentem Romuleam Martios viros habere collegas."[151] This sort of prose may seem superficially similar to *civilitas* rhetoric in its marriage of the civilian Roman to the warlike Goth, but in fact it is different. It evokes the bellicosity of the ancient Romans, in a classicizing image to be sure, but in a manner alien to the concept of reciprocal ethnographic functions. Moreover, the Romans are called a *gens*, just like the Goths, and by implication, like the other warlike *gentes* against whom Tuluin has been fighting. None of the elevating connotations of Roman law or of a Gothic–Roman *populus* appears. Rather, by admitting Tuluin to the senate, the fathers confer their *libertas* upon him, and this *libertas* is military, like the *libertas* of Gothic soldiers. Compare Arigernus, commended to the senate in 507–11. He also distinguished himself in war, but he did so through the lessons that he had already learned in the senate. Cassiodorus made no mention then of Goths or of *gentes*.[152]

Athalaric's letter to the *patricius* Cyprian breaks *civilitas* rules by praising him for educating his children in the *gentilis* style, teaching them arms and, indeed, the Gothic language.[153] Cyprian himself receives praise for having filled military and civil office with equal success.[154] "Sic victoriam Gothorum non tam numero quam labore iuvisti."[155] Praise for a man called a Roman, who crossed the functional borders of *civilitas* in this way, does not exist in sources from the earlier period of the kingdom, although Cyprian had fulfilled his military service in the Sirmium campaigns of 504–5.[156]

Cyprian was not the only "Roman" to have served in a military capacity,[157] but this is almost the first letter in the *Variae* to praise a man called a Roman – not merely a man with a Latin name – for such service. Significantly, the previous exception, from 524, in the last years of Theoderic's reign, was a pair of letters commending Cyprian to the senate. There, Theoderic spoke highly of Cyprian for his military service, the service of his father Opilio, and for his fluency in three languages, presumably, again, Latin, Greek and Gothic.[158] Just a little earlier, in 523, Cyprian's brother (also called Opilio) appears to have

---

[151] *Var.* 8.10.11.
[152] *Var.* 4.16: see above, p. 55.
[153] *Var.* 8.21.6–7: "Pueri stirpis Romanae nostra lingua loquuntur."
[154] *Var.* 8.21.1–5.
[155] *Var.* 8.21.3.
[156] On which, see PLRE2 Cyprianus 2, p. 332, PA Cyprianus.
[157] Wolfram, *Goths*, pp. 291–2 with n. 218; p. 300 with n. 263.
[158] *Var.* 5.40.5; 5.41.

occasioned the king's wrath. In order to deflect the royal anger, the two informed on Boethius.[159] The scheme worked. First Cyprian, and then Opilio, rose to *comes sacrarum largitionum* in 524–5 and 526–7; in 527, Cyprian was appointed *patricius*, one of the highest honors of the state.[160]

Given the people involved, and their enmity to the victims of Theoderic's purges, it is difficult not to conclude that the eclipse of *civilitas* rhetoric bears some relationship to the political events of the early to middle 520s. During and after these events, with the exception of the palliating letters to major constituencies at the very beginning of Athalaric's reign, the government seems to have decided to emphasize the values of Gothic military success and native Gothic characteristics over a reciprocal division of Italian society into warlike Goths and civilian Romans. With whomever the government chose to associate it, valor had become an absolute good.

Throughout Books 8 and 9 of the *Variae*, references to Gothic deeds of valor, Amal blood and recollections of the past occur even more frequently than in the earlier letters. In the letter to the senate which Cassiodorus wrote in Athalaric's name to announce his own promotion to the praetorian prefecture, the words *civilitas* and *utilitas* do not occur. Cassiodorus does receive credit for funding the Gothic soldiers out of his own pocket when the *provinciales* could not meet the burden; the Goths should be the defenders, not the ravagers, of the provinces.[161] This reference shows that some conception of a functional division of society survived. But otherwise the letter concentrates on Cassiodorus's personal service to the king. Cassiodorus had restored fame to the Amals. In the most famous phrase of the *Variae*, "he made Gothic history Roman."[162] Scholars have disputed what this sentence implies about the content of the lost *Historia Gothorum*.[163] But in its context, the phrase can only mean that the Amal dynasty was now recognized as equal to, if not superior to, the Roman senators in historical significance. "Commendat enim suam gentem, qui oratione placabili permulcet regiam summitatem."[164] It is thus part of the general tendency in the later *Variae* to exalt the family of Theoderic and not just the person of the king, and to see the components of the Ostrogothic kingdom

[159] Boethius, *de consolatione* 1, prose 4; PLRE2 Cyprianus 2, p. 333, Opilio 4, p. 808. The exact course of events is hardly clear; for a recent account, see Moorhead, *Theoderic*, pp. 219–35.
[160] PLRE2 Cyprianus 2, p. 333; Opilio 4, p. 808; PA Cyprianus, Opilio.
[161] *Var.* 9.25.9.
[162] *Var.* 9.25.5–6.
[163] See Goffart, *Narrators*, pp. 35–8 with references; Heather, *Goths and Romans*, pp. 52–61; Moorhead, *Theoderic*, p. 160.
[164] *Var.* 9.25.2.

merely as two *gentes* with no special virtue in their relationship. Only in the former conception can the Amals be compared favorably with the Roman past so celebrated by Theoderic in the early part of his reign. We have reached a new philosophy of rule in the Gothic government of the Italian peninsula.

However successful Theoderic had been in inculcating his ideology, any system of mutual obligation and respect was breaking down in Theodahad's reign, not least because the invasion of Italy by a Byzantine army – a "Roman" army promoting its own propaganda[165] – confused the loyalties of the Italian provincials.[166] In 535, Theodahad wrote to the *populus Romanus*, who were complaining that he had sent soldiers to Rome. He advises them not to reject those whose task is to defend and to protect *civilitas* every day:[167] it was not some "strange new nation" who greeted the plebs, but the one (the Goths) whom they had always known.[168] The letter does not mention the Goths, and appears to have been an attempt to revive the *civilitas* mentality when it was clearly in its death throes.[169]

Cassiodorus's prefectural letters of 533–7, contained in Books 11 and 12, rarely mention ethnographic issues, although there are a few evo-cations of *civilitas* rhetoric.[170] In one of his last letters, to the Ligurians

---

[165] Reconquest ideology will be addressed in ch. 4; on its reception, see ch. 5.

[166] Most famously illustrated by the divisions within Naples during Belisarius's siege in 536: see Procopius, BGI(5).8.7–40, ed. J. Haury, trans. H. B. Dewing (London, 1914); see below, ch. 5.

[167] *Var.* 10.14.1.

[168] *Var.* 10.14.3; Hodgkin's translation.

[169] Theodahad's letters in the *Variae* otherwise do not mention *civilitas*, but given the king's well-known affection for Roman letters, it makes sense that he might have sympathized with it. There does survive a metrical poem of Maximian that addresses the king in panegyrical terms, praising both his *sapientia* and his *virtus*, his victories over the *gentes* in war and, better, his cultivation of *quies* among his *populi*, Maximian, "Quisquis ad excelsi," ed. H. W. Garrod, "Poesos saeculi sexti fragmenta quattuor," *Classical Quarterly* 4 (1910), 265, poem 3, esp. lines 17–23. But despite the use of the word *utilis*, this is imperial victory rhetoric, not *civilitas*. There is nothing on Goths or Romans, merely *milites* (*populi* is the standard word for the subjects of the emperor, e.g. Const. *Tanta*, address); *gentes* are the enemy (there is nothing about internal *gentes*, or two *gentes* in one *populus*); no fiscal-legal language appears. Further on Theodahad's classical learning, see below, PA ★Theodahadus and ch. 5. On the identification of the author of these four poems with Maximian, see S. J. B. Barnish, "Maximian, Cassiodorus, Boethius, Theodahad: literature, philosophy and politics in Ostrogothic Italy," *Nottingham Medieval Studies* 34 (1990), p. 16, n. 3 with references.

[170] *Var.* 11.13.4, the senate to Justinian: Theodahad is "Romanis prudentia carum, gentibus virtute reverendum." If this phrase implies the Goths to be one of the *gentes*, then it does not sit well with *civilitas* ideology. On the other hand, 12.5 does use the rhetoric of Theoderic's early years. The army's *maxima laus* is not to despoil the *possessores*, to revere law, and to maintain *civilitas* (12.5.5–6). "Dum belligerat Gothorum exercitus, sit in pace Romanus" (12.5.4). Significantly, the letter was written while Belisarius's army was in Sicily, threatening Lucania and Bruttii; the addressee, a *spectabilis* Valerianus, had complained to Cassiodorus about having to supply the Gothic army. Such situations were ripe for the resurrection of *civilitas* rhetoric. But they did not always attract it; see the discussion of *Var.* 12.28, below.

wiped out by famine in 535–6, Cassiodorus rouses them with memories of the king's generosity toward them during the Burgundian raids. Despite the Burgundians' *feritas gentilis*, the *imperium* had risen again,[171] through the Goths' *belli studium*, which had also succeeded against the Alamans.[172] We once more see an implicit contrast between the Goths and the other *gentes*.

This contrast, however, does not evoke *civilitas* rhetoric. It is more similar to Theoderic's letters to barbarian kings. It stresses the valor of the Goths, but says nothing of their *prudentia Romana* (despite the reference to the *imperium*). Nor is any reciprocal relationship envisaged between Ligurians and *Gothi*: the provincials are to give thanks to the king, their ruler. The words *Romanus* and *civilitas* do not occur.

We know that in the middle of 537 the bishop of Milan along with a party of Ligurian noblemen approached Belisarius, then under siege in Rome, and offered to detach not only Milan but also all of Liguria from Gothic rule and restore it to the Empire.[173] Cassiodorus's letter, although dating from the previous year, clearly attempts to forestall such treachery.[174] His aim is thus not to define Goths and Romans and bind them together in a single society, but merely to retain the personal loyalty of the provincials to the king in time of war, while at the same time to distribute practical famine relief. This letter is a measure of the times of trouble in Italy. The opportunity for social engineering, plausible in Theoderic's well-defended, prosperous kingdom, was gone. *Civilitas* rhetoric was now only useful to soothe those senators to whom it might appeal naturally.[175] In dealing with the *possessores* of the area around Milan, not to mention the provincial aristocracy, who may or may not have thought of themselves as Romans with all the accompanying baggage, a rhetoric both more immediately relevant and practical had become appropriate. A comparison with Theoderic's early letters to the *possessores* shows how things had changed.[176]

---

[171] *Var.* 12.28.2.

[172] *Var.* 12.28.3.

[173] Procopius, BG 2(6).7.35–8. Procopius was still in Italy at this time (Cameron, *Procopius*, p. 188), so he could have been an eyewitness, but he had recently been sent on expeditions to Naples (BG 2.[6].4.1–3) and to Campania (BG 2[6].4.19); he does not record the date of his return to Rome. Presumably he came back with Antonina and the provisions which they had collected in Campania; these arrive a bit before the bishop of Milan in the narrative: BG 2(6).7.1–12. In any case, there is no reason to doubt this particular report.

[174] Note that BG2(6).12.28 suggests that not all Ligurians may have favored going over to the Byzantines. Ch. 5 discusses this issue further.

[175] See p. 71, above.

[176] Or even with the rather nostalgic *civilitas* rhetoric used to the *vir spectabilis* Valerianus about the *possessores* in Lucania and Bruttii around the same time, discussed above, p. 54 with n. 33, and p. 75 with n. 170.

Lastly, we must consider the ultimate index of change, the letter of Witigis to the Goths upon his accession in 536.[177] Wolfram has noted that Witigis's election represented a change from those of his predecessors: military prowess, rather than Amal blood, was the basis of his claim to kingship. "With great clarity Vitigis established his rule as that of a king of the army."[178] While we may doubt that any Tacitean division between the *nobilitas* and the *virtus* of the Germanic king played any role here, or that Witigis's elevation represented a revival of ancient customs of Gothic royal election, the rhetoric used about his accession to the throne is new. In fact, it represents the culmination of tendencies begun in Athalaric's letter to the Goths,[179] and which also appeared in a letter to the senate justifying the rule of Amalasuntha after Athalaric's death.[180] It is continued in the fragments of the panegyric delivered by Cassiodorus in 536 to Witigis and Matasuntha. Unlike his previous oration to Eutharic, this piece dwells on warfare and deeds of glory, stressing Witigis's rise from his position as swordbearer to Theodahad, amidst *Gothi*, swords and blood.[181]

Witigis, unlike his effeminate predecessors, has been chosen king amidst a circle of spears, on a shield, in the open field rather than the audience chamber, "more maiorum."[182] The letter is all about the Goths. There is no Athalarican nonsense about having been chosen by "Goths and Romans alike." The *army* has chosen the king. Witigis hearkens back to Theoderic, not as restorer of *civilitas* to the *res publica*, but as a great king whom Witigis will imitate.[183] The letter is concerned solely with military glory, as befitted a time when the kingdom was under severe threat from the Byzantine army. The election of Witigis,

---

[177] *Var.* 10.31.
[178] Wolfram, *Goths*, pp. 342–3; quotation, p. 343.
[179] *Var.* 8.5; see above, p. 72.
[180] *Var.* 11.1, dating from 533. The letter is a justification for female rule; it dwells on her moral and personal virtues, but particularly her success in defending the kingdom. She has made the Danube Roman again (11.1.10) and has "quod habet eximium uterque sexus" (11.1.14). The reference to Goths and Romans equally (11.1.14) makes this letter sound different from those of Athalaric and of Witigis, but this difference is surely due to its destination, the senate instead of "all the Goths." The stress, in the end, is on her warlike character and virtue; a list of the moral qualities of her Amal ancestors (11.1.19) distinguishes her letter from that of Witigis and brings it closer to the earlier one of Athalaric, as we might expect. No ideology of ethnography appears.
[181] Cassiodorus, *Oratio* 2, pp. 473–84; on the Eutharic oration (*Oratio* 1), see above, p. 66 with n. 110. *Oratio* 2 is less fragmentary than its predecessor, and the total absence of pseudo-imperial description, any mention of Roman law and *civilitas* is striking in such long sequences. The emphases on blood, honor and the Goths match the contemporary letters, and I think that we can safely see *Oratio* 2 as mirroring the official sentiments contained in them.
[182] *Var.* 10.31.1–2.
[183] *Var.* 10.31.5.

finally, serves the *arma Gothorum* and the *utilitas gentis*.[184] *Utilitas*, a virtue of Theoderic's ethnographic ideology of accommodation, has been made into a purely Gothic necessity. Under the force of political circumstance, the royal attitude toward ethnographic groups has changed completely.[185]

The picture drawn here, of a royal ideology and policy of ethnographic accommodation, of its inconsistency, and of its gradual disintegration with the political fortunes of the Ostrogothic government, comes from the writings of Cassiodorus. It might thus be thought that this picture could represent the views of Cassiodorus's own class, the provincial parvenu aristocracy, or that it is only applicable to those brief periods when he held office, from 507–11 and from 523–37. I have chosen to start with Cassiodorus, however, only because his *Variae* shed the most complete light on governmental policy. The other sources from the Ostrogothic kingdom complement his evidence on ethnographic ideology and show not only that these governmental attitudes date from the time before Cassiodorus achieved his first office, but that in their application and vicissitudes they mirror the depiction of the *Variae*.[186] Only for the latter period are we forced to rely entirely on Cassiodorus.

THE *EDICTUM THEODERICI* AND GOVERNMENTAL ETHNOGRAPHIC IDEOLOGY

After the *Variae*, the second main source relating to Theoderic's government is the brief compilation and emendation of Roman vulgar law known as the *Edictum Theoderici*.[187] Like the *Variae*, the *Edictum* defines

---

[184] *Var.* 10.31.4.

[185] It may also be significant that here, and only here, does Cassiodorus use the classicizing word *Getae* for *Gothi*, with its connotations of a warlike past; *civilitas* texts like the writings of Ennodius always call Theoderic's group *Gothi*, and reserve *Geta* for Ricimer or the Visigoths: Walter Pohl, "I Goti d'Italia e le tradizioni delle steppe," *Teoderico il Grande e i Goti d'Italia*, Atti del XIII Congresso internazionale di studi sull'alto medioevo, Milan, 2–6 November 1992 (Spoleto, 1993), p. 245. I am grateful to Dr Pohl for sending me a copy of an offprint while the *Atti* remained unavailable to me.

[186] Further evidence that the *Variae* attest Theoderic's policy, and not merely the rhetoric (let alone the policy) of Cassiodorus as his minister, appears in the reception of Ravenna ideology in Italy, particularly the works of Ennodius, which are examined in ch. 4.

[187] For years the authorship and authenticity of this undatable law-code was accepted without question as the work of Theoderic the Great, see, for example, Rudolf Buchner, *Die Rechtsquellen*, supplement to *Deutschlands Geschichtsquellen im Mittelalter: Vorzeit und Karolinger*, ed. Wilhelm Wattenbach and Wilhelm Levison (Weimar, 1953), p. 14. But in 1953 Piero Rasi pointed out that only the title – itself only attested in the explicit – attributes the code to Theoderic (Piero Rasi, "Sulla paternité del c.d. Edictum Theodorici regis," *Archivio Giuridico* 145 [1953], 105–13), and since then the *Edictum* has occasioned more controversy than any

the mutual obligation of Roman and Goth in terms of profession and through technical words uniting fiscal and social obligation.

In the Edictum, *barbarus* means a "soldier in Theoderic's army," which is the meaning of *Gothus* when it occurs in Cassiodorus's *civilitas* rhetoric.[188] The *Edictum* follows the functional vision of the *Variae* in seeing *barbarus* as a tax-collecting soldier serving the Italo-Roman state. In the dry language of the *Edictum*, "Barbaris, quos certum est reipublicae militare, quomodo voluerint et potuerint, faciendi damus licentiam testamenti, sive domi sive in castris fuerint constituti."[189] Barbarians are

other early medieval source; see the summary of scholarship in Clausdieter Schott, "Der Stand der Leges-Forschung," *Frühmittelalterliche Studien* 13 (1979), 34–5: the code has been attributed to Odoacer, Gundobad, Aegidius, Syagrius, the praetorian prefect Magnus of Narbonne, Amalasuntha, Majorian, Eparchius Avitus, and Theoderic II of the Visigoths. Rasi finally called it a forgery of Pithou, the sixteenth-century humanist whose edition, based on two lost manuscripts, is the only witness to the text. On Pithou and the MSS, see Friedrich Bluhme, MGH: Leges in folio 5 (Hanover, 1889), pp. 146–7. Many of the theories proposed in the 1950s and 1960s have fallen by the wayside. Most influential has been Giulio Vismara's attribution of the code to another Theoderic, Theoderic II of the Visigoths, who reigned from 453 to 466 (Giulio Vismara, "Romani e Goti di fronte al diritto nel regno ostrogoto," *Settimane di studio del Centro Italiano di studi sull'alto medioevo* 3 [= *I Goti in Occidente: Problemi*] [1956], 407–63); Vismara, *Edictum Theoderici*, Ius Romanum Medii Aevi I,2 b aa α [Milan, 1967]). Vismara's viewpoint has found its way into standard works such as the *Handwörterbuch zur deutschen Rechtsgeschichte*: Hans-Jürgen Becker, "Edictum Theoderici," in vol. 1 (Berlin, 1971), cols. 801–2. In 1969, however, Hermann Nehlsen wrote a brilliant rebuttal of Vismara, followed up by further argument in 1972 (Hermann Nehlsen, review of Giulio Vismara, *Edictum Theoderici*, *Zeitschrift der Savigny-Stiftung für Rechtsgeschichte, Germanistische Abteilung* 86 [1969], 246–60; Nehlsen, *Sklavenrecht zwischen Antike und Mittelalter: germanisches und römisches Recht in den germanischen Rechtsaufzeichnungen* 1, *Ostgoten, Westgoten, Franken, Langobarden*, Göttinger Studien zur Rechtsgeschichte 7 (Göttingen, 1972), pp. 120–3. No answer to Nehlsen has yet appeared. At a conference in Milan in 1992, Vismara refused to address the point: Giulio Vismara, "Il diritto nel regno ostrogoto d'Italia," XIII Congresso, Milan, 4 November 1992; similarly, "Il diritto nel regni dei Goti," in *I Goti*, Catalogue of the Exhibition at Milan, Palazzo Reale, 28 January–8 May 1994 (Milan, 1994), pp. 368–72. Despite the tendency for Italian literature on the subject to ignore Nehlsen, there can be no question that his arguments outweigh those of Vismara. The discussion presented here also further supports Nehlsen's attribution of the *Edictum* to Theoderic the Great, since it clearly mirrors aspects of the *Variae*.

[188] Twice Cassiodorus slips into using *barbarus* to mean "soldier" or "Goth": *Var.* 3.24 (cited by Nehlsen, review of Vismara, pp. 225–6); 1.18.2. Cassiodorus avoids *barbarus* in general: for the inferior peoples outside Italy, he uses *gentes* or *gentes exterae* (*Var.* 1.27; 7.4). He was aware of the ancient negative connotations of *barbarus* (3.17.1), but the word need not always have been pejorative in sixth-century Italy. Gelasius could write a friendly letter to Theoderic referring to the Goths as *barbari* (below, p. 000). Two high-born ladies, Barbara, the correspondent of Ennodius and perhaps tutor of Amalasuintha, and Barbaria, the *inlustris femina* and patron of the cult of Severinus, bore names derived from *barbarus* (Ennodius, *Opp.* 393, 404/*epp.* 8.16; 8.27; Eugippius, *Vita Sancti Severini* 46, ed. Rudolf Noll and Emil Vetter [Berlin, 1963]). Of course, great families have been known to give ambiguous names to their children. One recalls the Texan patroness of the arts, Ima Hogg. Also note two notable sixth-century Italians called Bacauda (PLRE2: 207–8), surely not a complimentary name if any memory of the Gallic Bacaudae survived in Italy. See further chs. 3 and 7, below, on the many meanings of personal names.

[189] ET 32; see *Dig.* 29.1.

conceived as soldiers who "serve the republic;" like Roman soldiers, they have the right to make wills. Presumably the reference is to the old soldier's will,[190] which the *Edictum*, among other sources, now offers as an option to civilians as well.[191] Such legal inconsistency is typical of vulgar law, however, as is the incoherent preservation of certain classical forms. Here the law recognizes the right of a soldier to make a will, wherever he happened to be stationed – the origin of the separate form for military testaments.[192]

Having defined a *barbarus* as a soldier, the *Edictum* goes on to oppose and compare *barbari* with *Romani*, the other part of the functional division of *civilitas* rhetoric. Neither a Roman nor a barbarian should seize real estate belonging to someone else.[193] No one should transfer a lawsuit to either a Roman or barbarian *potens*, nor should they mingle a Roman or barbarian *potens defensor aut suffragator* in such a suit.[194] Since *barbarus* has already been defined as soldier, the first law may refer to transferring cases to military courts or vice versa, but it could just as well be legislating against the involvement of undue pressure from magnate patrons in provincial courts, a common late Roman abuse.[195] The second law seems to refer to such a situation. More significant for this analysis is the apparent assumption that "barbarus et Romanus" sums up the possible ingredients of Italian society, a basic tenet of the royal ethnographic ideology, and one, as we saw, not rooted in fact. The *Edictum* also confirms the protection accorded to the Jews in Theoderic's Italy, inherited from late Roman law, and reaffirmed in the

---

[190] W. W. Buckland, *A Manual of Roman Private Law* (Cambridge, 1925), pp. 223–4; Burns, *History*, p. 127.

[191] ET 28, allowing either 5 or 7 witnesses; see also CT4.4.1 (Constantine, ?326). On wills, see Ulrich Nonn, "Merowingische Testamente: Studien zum Fortleben einer römischen Urkundenform im Frankreich," *Archiv für Diplomatik* 18 (1972), 14–15. The separate soldier's will apparently lived on in Byzantium until the time of Justinian; Buckland, *Manual*, p. 224.

[192] Since there had to be provision for them to be witnessed on the field, even orally, as the soldier lay dying (Nonn, "Merowingische Testamente," pp. 7–8).

[193] ET 34. Such seizures were common in late antique society, but the *Variae* associates the problem most often with the relationship between Gothic soldiers and Roman *possessores* (1.18.2; 7.4.3; 8.26.4; 8.28; 12.5.6; and see above, nn. 13, 24), a situation which the allotment of tax revenues in lieu of land encouraged: see Wolfram, *Goths*, p. 224 (on the Visigothic settlement) and Goffart, *Barbarians and Romans*, pp. 89–100 (on the Ostrogothic settlement), also citing (at p. 94) Boethius, *de consolatione* 1, prose 4, on his efforts to protect people harassed by the "covetousness of the barbarians." Goffart is surely right to connect this statement with cases like that of Tanca (*Var.* 8.28). A tax-collecting armed soldier quickly established a relationship of power over a tax-paying civilian. Moreover, the right to collect some of the revenues of a property could easily be confused with ownership of it as the classical legal distinction between possession and usufruct broke down; on this development, see Ernst Levy, *West Roman Vulgar Law: The Law of Property* (Philadelphia, 1951), pp.19–72.

[194] ET 43–4.

[195] Jones, LRE I: 502–4.

Variae.[196] Even elsewhere in the laws, the phrase "servus cuiuslibet nationis" leaves more possibilities open, and, indeed, in allowing national labels to the unfree, departs from the concept of functional ethnicities enshrined in the Burgundian laws.[197]

But Jews and slaves, while members of society and thus necessary participants in the general recipe for peace, did not play a functional role in the central relationship between the military and civilian portions of the population. Essentially, these groups were not part of civil society. The philosophical parts of the concise *Edictum* argue that universal prosperity is best achieved under law through the peaceful cohabitation of barbarian and Roman.

Thus the prologue announces that many complaints come to the king that laws are not being observed in the provinces. Although nothing can be done injustly *sub legum auctoritate*, in the interest of general *quies*, the king "appends" the following edicts in the interest of "salva iuris publici reverentia et legibus omnibus cunctorum devotione servandis, quae barbari Romanique sequi debeant."[198]

All the basic ingredients of *civilitas* philosophy are here, once we add the functional division envisaged by the content of the *Edictum* itself. The prologue is typically delicate in its attitude toward Roman law and the royal role in propagating it. Roman law, that reverend subject, is already complete in itself. The king is most interested in making certain that people, both barbarians and Romans, obey it and show it *devotio*. If he adds a few *edicta* (nothing so grand as *constitutiones*), it is for the purpose of maintaining general peace. These edicts, of course, as we have seen, supplement the Theoderican view, as expressed in the *Variae*, of the ethnographic division of Italian society.

The epilogue is more forthright, perhaps suggesting that the attribution of the *Edictum* to Theoderic only in the explicit was part of the original intention. It also assumes a loftier, more rhetorical style.[199] Now the first emphasis is on the two ethnographic groups: "Haec quantum occupationes nostrae admittere, vel quae nobis ad praesens occurrere

---

[196] ET 143: "Circa Iudaeos privilegia legibus delata serventur. . .eos iudices habere necesse est . . ." On the Jews in Theoderic's Italy, see above, pp. 59–60. All the evidence shows that the Jews both occupied a special position in Roman law, and were allowed to use their own laws among themselves.

[197] Since *Romanus* and *Burgundio* in the Burgundian laws seem to apply chiefly to *consortes* in the settlement process (Amory, "The meaning and purpose of ethnic terminology," pp. 8, 24–5), slaves are never given such meaningful labels: Amory, "Names, ethnic identity and community," p. 4.

[198] ET prologue, continuing: ". . . super expressis articulis, edictis praesentibus evidenter cognoscant."

[199] As Nehlsen notes, review of Vismara, p. 251.

potuerunt, cunctis tam barbaris, quam Romanis, sumus profutura complexi: quae omnium barbarorum, sive Romanorum debet servare devotio." *Devotio* is again the necessary attribute: obedience to laws. It applies to everyone in society, as the edict next makes clear: "of whatever dignity, or wealth, or power, or office or honor." After repeating this injunction in a variety of different ways, the epilogue concludes, "quia quod pro omnium provincialium securitate provisum est, universitatis debet servare devotio."[200]

In combination with the functional division of society enshrined within the *brevitas edicti*,[201] this epilogue continues to propagate the ethnographic ideology contained with many of the letters of the *Variae*. All society, divided into *barbari* and *Romani*, is to observe Roman *iura* and *leges*. The realm envisaged consists of the *provinciae*, the Roman provinces ruled by Theoderic, in fact, the *res publica*[202] – not a *regnum*. The king is the prime supporter of the law that he has inherited; he adds to it for the same purposes for which it was formulated. By observing this Roman-royal law with *devotio*, the population will ensure the *securitas* of the realm.

Devotio and *securitas*: the words may be different, but the ideals are the same as Cassiodorus's *utilitas* and *civilitas*. Like *utilitas*, and from the same cultural evolution, *devotio* had come to mean not only obedience but also tribute or tax.[203] Like *utilitas*, *devotio* also still meant the obligation owed by every citizen to the emperor.[204] Although the *Edictum* merely demands *devotio* to the law, the *Variae* depict Theoderic as the fount of law, and law as the foundation upon which an ethnographically dual society should rest. The equation is natural in a rhetoric that links stability to the upkeep of a strong leader with an army. *Devotio* still described the obedience of soldiers to their leader in Theoderic's Italy.[205] The *Edictum* emerged from the same governmental ethos as did many of the early administrative letters contained in the *Variae*.

EARLY USE OF ROYAL IDEOLOGY BY THE CATHOLIC CHURCH

As early as the 490s, we find echoes of royal ethnographic ideology reflected in the papal letters. When two clerics of Nola took their case

[200] ET epilogue.
[201] ET epilogue. This is more modesty, although a fair enough description.
[202] ET 32.
[203] Zimmermann, *Late Latin Vocabulary of Cassiodorus*, p. 180; Pier Maria Conti, *"Devotio" e "viri devoti" in Italia da Diocleziano ai Carolingi* (Padua, 1971), pp. 40–9.
[204] Conti, *"Devotio,"* pp. 28–32.
[205] Ibid., pp. 26–8, 33–6 (military *devotio*); 94–122 (*devotio* under Theoderic). Conti's discussion of the latter topic is partly weakened by his assumptions about "Roman" and "Germanic" culture.

to the king's (lay) court in 496, Pope Gelasius complained to the king's mother, Ereleuva that they were supported by "barbarians" who took the case for them "contra civilitatem."[206] *Civilitas* here refers not only to the laws on the separation of lay and clerical jurisdiction,[207] but also to the division between military and civilian courts.[208] Felix and Petrus broke "divinas humanasque leges" by hiding their clerical status in appealing to the king, *not only* in crossing jurisdictions, but also by "bringing in barbarians."[209] Wolfram comments that Gelasius was protesting against the judgment of clerics by barbarians,[210] but given the repeated injunctions in the *Variae*, especially the formula of the *comes Gothorum*, against Goths judging Romans, along with the evidence for a military-civilian split in the *Edictum*, Gelasius was protesting against the judgment of *civilians* by barbarians, i.e., by soldiers.[211] There was a *lex humana* on this issue to which he could appeal. It was not that Gelasius cared so much about the principle of distinct military and civilian jurisdictions, but that he could use this principle as a further lever to pry the erring clerics out of Theoderic's court and back to the papal court at Rome, where he felt they belonged. The phraseology of the letter to Ereleuva makes his aims quite clear.

In the end, unsurprisingly, Theoderic, the pope's "son," and "that most outstanding man," returned the stubborn clerics to Gelasius for his examination. Theoderic had thus supported *civilitas*, and here the term has the same technical meaning as it does in the *Variae*. Among his flurry of letters on the subject, Gelasius had written to the king, reminding him that he has supported imperial laws in the past.[212] Unfortunately, only a small piece of this letter survives. The pope may have

---

[206] Gelasius, JK 743 = *ep.* "Felix et Petrus" (Thiel *frag.* 13, p. 490).

[207] The issue of lay and ecclesiastical jurisdiction exercised Gelasius exceedingly, and crops up again and again in his letters. See especially JK 664 = *ep.* "Valde mirati sumus" (Thiel 26, pp. 392–422), §1, p. 393, §6, p. 409 on non-interference of laity in ecclesiastical cases, along with the other letters on the Nola case, cited below; further, JK 714 = *ep. in.* 19 (Loewenfeld 19, p. 10), and JK 631 = *ep. in.* 3 "Religionis probatur iniuria" (Loewenfeld 3, p. 2), all stressing the importance of the inheritance of canon law for apostolic succession and church independence. On Gelasius's ideals and his attitude toward Theoderic, see further ch. 6.

[208] This is clearly the burden of Gelasius's letter; cf. a letter of Athalaric's government that responds to renewed complaints from the clergy of Rome that they were being dragged into lay courts: it never mentions *civilitas* or uses *civilitas* ideology: *Var.* 8.24.

[209] Gelasius, JK 721 = *ep.* "Felicem et Petrum" (Ewald 46, pp. 521–2).

[210] Wolfram, *Goths*, pp. 292–3.

[211] As early as 1880, Ewald (n. 6 on p. 521, referring to the letter to Ereleuva) had already explained the situation quite correctly: "Barbari in dieser Zeit der technische Ausdruck für Truppen der Leibwache."

[212] Gelasius, JK 722 = *ep.* "Certum est, magnificentium" (Thiel *frag.* 12, pp. 489–90). Another letter bearing on the situation is JK 723 = *ep.* "Frater et coepiscopus" (Thiel *frag.* 11, p. 489), urging two fellow-bishops to support the bishop of Nola in this affair.

been reminding the king of his duties in maintaining the ethnographic division of society expressed by *civilitas* ideology.

Similar outcrops of governmental ethnographic ideology occur in letters relating to the Laurentian schism in 501. The complicated events of that autumn led up to a series of synods attempting to decide who was the legitimate pope, Symmachus or Laurentius. An earlier synod at St. Peter's was broken up with violence, and there was rioting in the streets of Rome. In August 501, Theoderic sent three of his *maiores domus* to Rome in order to ensure that the impending new synod would take place in safety.

The letter accompanying these royal ambassadors from Ravenna to Rome dwells much on Roma, the *Romana ecclesia*, the *senatus et Romanus populus* (twice), and declares that it is not tolerable that, of all the cities of Italy, Rome alone should not possess tranquillity.[213] In a nice reversal of Cassiodoran-style ethnographic rhetoric, the king compares the chaos of the city with the peace of the state and quiet of the *gentes*:

Est quidem pudenda cum stupore diversitas Romanum statum in confinio gentium sub tranquillitate regi et in media urbe confundi, ut desideratur civilitas in arce Latii, quae est sub hostium vicinitate secura.[214]

The king is ironically amazed that Rome, secure from enemy attack, and the citadel of *civilitas*, should lack this virtue in comparison with the rest of his realm and with the *gentes* outside.

In Theoderic's dealings with the church, as elsewhere in Italian society, we never fail to encounter the repetition of a governmental ideology of accommodation between groups of people traditionally believed to be incompatible. It is crucial to reiterate that these sentiments did consist of a philosophy of social construction, grounded to some extent in real mutual appreciation, but by the same token not always conforming to reality. If social reality faithfully reflected governmental ideology, then the ideology would serve no purpose. It remains to be seen how this ideology did affect the coexistence of Theoderic and his followers with the indigenous population of Italy, in the period while it was propagated, and in the subsequent period when it appears less frequently in the governmental sources.

---

[213] Theoderic, *Praeceptio regis IIII missa ad synhodum* = *Acta synhodi a. DI 2*, ed. Theodor Mommsen, MGH: AA 12, pp. 421–2.
[214] Ibid., p. 422.

CONCLUSION

Theoderic's ethnographic ideology was new and adapted to current circumstances, even if it was a synthesis of older elements: barbarians as soldiers, the consensual observation of law as the foundation of peace and of good government, the blurring of public and private in taxation and social responsibility. It emerged, so far as we can tell, after Theoderic's conquest of Italy between 489 and 493. No source associates such an ideology either with Odoacer's kingdom or with Theoderic's warband in the Balkans. Nor can we find such conceptions in the other post-Roman barbarian states.[215] The Ostrogothic government formulated something unique.

To what extent were even Theoderic and his ministers *aware* that they were modifying Roman legal and classical ethnographic conceptions of the barbarian in describing ideal relations between Goths and Romans?[216] Themselves formed by the combination of classicizing education with the socio-cultural milieu of late antiquity, they may have found notions of fiscal *utilitas*, and of barbarians possessing *prudentia*, entirely natural. In fact, to anyone brought up on classical ethnography, the *prudentia* of the Goths could have appeared a *sine qua non*, since they had in fact become the rulers of the heartland of the Roman Empire. Without *prudentia* they could not have succeeded. Of course, Theoderic may have realized that certain aspects of his ideology did not correspond to reality, for example, the ideal of a society composed of only two groups, or the idea that all Romans were civilians. Nevertheless, the imperceptibility of change in certain cultural notions, including ideals of the limits of the Christian world, eased transitions to new ways of thinking about community.

---

[215] True, the soldier–civilian rhetoric used to accommodate the barbarians finds echoes in the laws of the Burgundian kingdom. But there this terminology is purely functional. The laws deal with professions and with their financing by the government and the population. There is no overlaid rhetoric. Even the functional division of society in Burgundy finds no echoes in the literary sources. See Amory, "The meaning and purpose of ethnic terminology," pp. 1–28; Amory, "Ethnographic rhetoric, aristocratic attitudes and political allegiance," pp. 452–3.

[216] Whittaker, *Frontiers*, p. 206, argues that Roman emperors believed in their own propaganda.

Chapter 3

INDIVIDUAL REACTIONS TO IDEOLOGY I:
NAMES, LANGUAGE AND PROFESSION

It is not easy to analyze individual responses to the label "Goth" since no one outside the royal families and the Arian church hierarchy ever declares himself or herself a Goth in the surviving sources. An alternative method is to assemble all the attested individuals who fall into one of the criteria of identity outlined by the various ideological descriptions of the Goths. I have done this in the Prosopographical Appendix (PA).[1]

Quantitative analysis of the 379 individuals in the PA is not possible in most categories. Half of the individuals listed are attested only by either Cassiodorus or Procopius. Aside from the problems of the bias of these sources (they propagate governmental ideologies), each tends to turn up specific types of people. Cassiodorus reveals Latin-speaking soldiers with Germanic names; we do not know their religion. Procopius reveals soldiers whom he calls Goths, with Germanic names, fighting on the Gothic side; we do not know their religion or their language. Neither source tells us much about spouses or family. We learn about spouses and family from people in inscriptions and papyri, but little about profession.[2]

Nevertheless, one generalization emerges. The survey shows an enormous number of certain Latin-speakers, a group including every attested Gothic-speaker. Granted, they are attested in Latin sources, but the complete absence of reference to interpreters and the very small number of references to a Gothic language shows that communication was not a problem. We can assume that all inhabitants of Italy spoke Latin or a dialect of it, including the south, where Greek continued to be spoken. Bilingualism perhaps existed in the Gothic army and in the Byzantine army, drawn from regions all over the East.[3]

---

[1] On the methodology of the PA, see PA, "Method and purpose"; PA III, "Totals."

[2] On the problems of the sources, see PA III, "Totals."

[3] PA III, "Totals": 72 per cent of the individuals surveyed are known to have spoken Latin, including almost none of the 20 per cent of the total attested only in Procopius, whose evidence is of course for the later period when Latin would have become *more* common, not less – if there *were* any people who did not speak it. No individual is known *not* to have spoken Latin. Gothic speakers, all of whom also spoke Latin: PA **B**essas, Cyprianus, **A**nonymus 17, ***A**malasu-intha, *Theodericus (**A**nonymus 17 possibly spoke Greek rather than Latin, but he in any case

There were two other stable forms of behavior among the individuals under discussion. First, most soldiers in Italy bore Germanic names.[4] Second, no Catholic clergyman in Italy bore a Germanic name.[5] These two quantitative conclusions are based on two best-documented groups in Italian society.

Personal names can have many functions. In late antiquity, they could demonstrate family, prestige, humility, fashion, religion or profession, and several of these at once.[6] A name chosen for a specific meaning, such as Inportunus, could be retained in the family and lose that original meaning. People could, and did, change their names, at marriage, baptism, taking monastic vows, and conversion.

It might seem simple to see the Goths in Italy: they were the people bearing Germanic names. This has been the assumption of most works on the Goths in the past two centuries, even when there is no other corroboration.[7] After all, the language called "Gothic" was a Germanic language, the Gothic Arian church used a bible and a liturgy in this language, the royal families bore Germanic names, and many of the people who arrived in Italy in the 490s bore Germanic names.

But this approach is simplistic. It does not take into account the passage of time once the settlers arrived in Italy, or the many other

---

may be an instructive type rather than an individual: see below, p. 000). Similarly all the individuals who knew written Gothic, which I argue was a different language, also knew Latin: see below, ch. 7, pp. 251–6.

[4] PA III, tables 1–2, 4.

[5] Ch. 7, below, pp. 264–6.

[6] On family, see Martin Heinzelmann, "Les changements de la dénomination latine á la fin de l'antiquité," in *Famille et Parenté dans l'Occident médiéval*, Actes du colloque de Paris (6–8 juin 1974), Collection de l'Ecole Française de Rome 30 (Rome, 1977), pp. 22–4. On prestige, see Iiro Kajanto, "The emergence of the the the late single-name system," in *L'onomastique latine*, Colloques internationaux du CNRS 564 (Paris, 1977), pp. 421–30; senatorial names made up many *cognomina* rather than just one, and included archaicizing *gentilicia* hearkening back to Republican days; similarly, the claimed genealogy of Theoderic himself: Norbert Wagner, "Namengebung zur Amalergenealogie," *Beiträge zur Namenforschung* n.s. 14 (1979), 26–43, and Wagner, "König Theodahad und die amalische Namengebung," *Beiträge zur Namenforschung* n.s. 21 (1986), 433–50. On names relating to humility, see Iiro Kajanto, "The problem of names of humility in early Christian epigraphy," *Arctos* 3 (1962), 45–53; for example, the "vituperative" names of Christians, such as Inportunus, Speciosus, etc. On religion, see ch. 7, below; in addition to the "vituperative" names, there were characteristic names like Clemens and Benedictus, and "theophorous" names like Adeodatus and Theophilus. On names of fashion and profession in late antiquity, see Iiro Kajanto, *The Latin Cognomina*, Societas Scientiarum Fenica: Commentationes Humanarum Litterarum 36.2 (Helsinki, 1965), and Kajanto, *Supernomina: A Study in Latin Epigraphy*, same series 40.2 (Helsinki, 1966). On names of profession in the early Middle Ages, see Karl Ferdinand Werner, "Liens de parenté et noms de personne: un problème historique et méthodologique," in *Famille et Parenté*, pp. 14–18, 25–32.

[7] e.g., Brown, *Gentlemen and Officers*, s.n. Gundeberga, p. 262; also p. 76 on Guderit (= PA Guderit 3); very frequently in PLRE, e.g. PLRE2 Hildevara, Liwirit (both = PA); F-S 2F 12, p. 12 with n. 1 (on PA Ariver); Tjäder 1: 344, 464, n. 27 (on PA Sisivera); Kampers, "Anmerkungen," pp. 143–7; Moorhead, *Theoderic*, pp. 89–97 *passim*.

meanings of names including naming strategies, or the fact that both Germanic and Graeco-Latin names could exist within one family, including the royal family. It does not take into account the workings of ideology, which propose specific definitions of Goth into which not everyone with a Germanic name fitted. Was a civilian born in 503 with a Germanic name a Goth? Was a Byzantine general in 546 with a Germanic name a Goth? Was Pope Boniface II (father's name: Sigibuldus) a Goth?

The dangers of using names as the key to identity are great. They are compounded when historians assume, as they do, that the Latin names of Arian clergymen indicate Goths who have taken Latin names, or Roman Arians, or that a man with a Latin name who could write Gothic was a Goth who had taken a Latin name.[8] One historian calls all marriages between individuals with Germanic names and individuals with Latin names "marriages across racial lines."[9]

We cannot always tell whether a name was Germanic or not. A Germanic name might be Gothic, or might belong to one of the other Germanic languages. Even this point is tricky, since one's personal name need not come from the language that one speaks, and it can survive in families that no longer speak the language that engendered the name.[10] Although individuals could have both Germanic and Graeco-Latin names, one source will give only one name even for people like senators, who had many names. Sometimes two names could be the result of a name-change, and sometimes both names were borne simultaneously.[11]

Personal names could be irrelevant to identity, and could also be strategic responses to ideology. They are most important insofar as they are clues to family. But families containing both Germanic and Graeco-Latin names upset even this theory. We need a nuanced, qualitative approach, examining a number of examples and comparing the evi-

---

[8] Tjäder 2: 95 and references at PA **L**atinus and **A**nonymus 1; Kampers, "Anmerkungen," pp. 143–7; on these men, see ch. 7, pp. 251–6.
[9] Latin-named Arian clergymen were Goths according to Moorhead (*Theoderic*, p. 86) but Romans according to Tjäder (2: 95) and Wolfram (*Goths*, p. 325) (on PA **P**aulus 2 and **P**etrus). A Gothic-writing Latin-named man was a Goth according to Tjäder 2: 260, n. 31; Brown, *Gentlemen and Officers*, p. 76; and Moorhead, *Theoderic*, p. 86 with n. 88. Marriages "across racial lines," Moorhead, *Theoderic,*, p. 85.
[10] Brown, *Gentlemen and Officers*, pp. 67–8, 76: "Caution is necessary in tracing Goths, since not all Goths held Gothic names." Brown actually says "Teutonic peoples," not "Germanic languages," but neither ethnographic group-names nor political communities seem to have matched up with the divisions of Germanic languages, even in regions where these definitely existed as forms of oral communication. On the perennial confusion between Germanic "peoples" and "languages," see below, p. 105; appendix 2, pp. 327–8; and above, ch. 1, n. 8.
[11] Below, ch. 7, pp. 263–7.

dence of names vis-à-vis individual behavior and the chronological progression of ideology in Italy.

Germanic names are associated with the Goths in Italy for the following five reasons.[12] First, there is a dramatic upsurge in the quantity of Germanic names attested in Italy from the 490s. This increase suggests that many of Theoderic's followers bore Germanic names. Second, Theoderic and his own family, the self-described leaders of the Goths in Italy, themselves all bore Germanic names (if sometimes alongside Latin names). Third, Germanic names are preponderant among attested individuals who could be described as Goths according to other criteria: soldiers, Arian clergymen and individuals called "Goth" in the sources. Fourth, not one member of the Catholic clergy in the whole period bore a Germanic name, suggesting that they avoided these names because they were associated with the self-described Gothic Arian church. Fifth, forgeries of Augustinian letters from Ostrogothic Italy attribute names to "Goths" that are all Germanic.[13]

Because Germanic names were associated with the settlers and their families in 489, they offer us a control on other evidence for Gothic identity and allegiance. Because people knew when names were Germanic – as the evidence of the Catholic clergy and the Augustinian forgeries shows – their adoption and use by families can sometimes suggest the assumption of Gothic identity by those families.

Nonetheless, possession of a Germanic name does not prove that its owner considered himself a Goth any more than does the profession of soldier or adherence to Arianism. The interesting phenomenon is the coincidence or non-coincidence of Germanic names with other

---

[12] Note, however, that contemporaries could not always identify Germanic names (which, of course, they would not have called "Germanic" but in Italy, "Gothic," in Africa, "Vandal" and so on). See below, n. 98.

[13] Upsurge of Germanic names in the 490s: most clear through inscriptions; cf. F-S, "Ostgoten" section; ILCV. Theoderic's family: PA II. Germanic names among "Goths" otherwise attested: see PA III, tables 1–2, 4 (soldiers), 7 (Arian clergymen), PA I–II, individuals with criterion [D] (mostly also with criterion N – though this is partly due to Procopius, the main source to declare that an individual is a Goth, and nearly all of his Goths were soldiers). Catholic clergy: see ch. 7. Augustinian forgeries: see Frank M. Clover, "The pseudo-Boniface and the *Historia Augusta*," in *Bonner Historia-Augusta Colloquium 1977/1978*, Antiquitas, 4th ser. 14 (Bonn, 1980), pp. 86–8; the names are Herpa, Gudila and Sonia, the last two attested in individuals from Ostrogothic Italy (PA **G**udila 1–4, **S**una; note also **S**uniefridus/Sunjaifrithas, and for Herpa, note the Erpamara at Jordanes, *Get.* 43 with the emendation of Ferdinand Wrede, *Über die Sprache der Ostgoten in Italien*, Quellen und Forschungen zur Sprach- und Culturgeschichte der germanischen Völker 68 [Strasbourg, 1891], p. 119 ["et Erpamara . . ."]).

criteria such as the profession of soldier at different periods during the lifetime of the Ostrogothic kingdom. Here we can perceive patterns.

Although many people called Goths bore Germanic names, not all of them did. Virtually all families with Germanic names also had members with Graeco-Latin names, including the Amal family.[14] Furthermore, Germanic names in Italy between 489 and 554 are a low percentage of the attested total of names: most families had only Graeco-Latin names.[15]

Consonant with the sixth-century Italian ("Gothic") military possession of Germanic names is the evidence of the Eastern armies and of the Italian army from before Theoderic's arrival. In Thrace and Illyricum, a majority of soldiers bore Germanic names. Of the officers in the Byzantine army in Italy during the Gothic Wars, a third bore Germanic names.[16] Historians attribute this phenomenon to the "barbarization of the Roman army" during the fifth century. This may be in some sense true, since the late Roman army was active on and recruited from frontier areas such as Thrace, thus favoring an increase in non-Graeco-Latin names. But such a process was a self-fulfilling prophecy. As it became usual for soldiers to bear Germanic names in the Mediterranean, so more military families may have given their children Germanic names.[17]

---

[14] PA III, table 11. Two exceptions are definitively all Germanic, both royal: the family of PA ⋆ Totila (⋆Theudis and ⋆Hildebadus), and of ⋆Teia (⋆Aligernus and Fredigernus). Possible exceptions: the sons of PA Tzalico were Gudila 4 and •••ri, but the latter name might not be Germanic; the sons of Gundihild bore Germanic names but were appointed a guardian named Flavianus; if Mustela was really the daughter of Mustila and <Fravi>ta, it is noteworthy that the spelling of her name (as opposed to that of her mother) is also the same as a Latin name (q.v.).

[15] This is impressionistic, but true, as any trawl through Silvagni's *Iscrizioni* or Diehl's ILCV will show. The traditionally quoted proportions of Greek and barbarian names versus Latin names in Italy hide an extremely small percentage of barbarian names (such proportions cited in, for example, Iiro Kajanto, *Onomastic Studies in the Early Christian Inscriptions of Rome and Carthage*, Acta Instituti Romani Finlandiae 2.1 [Helsinki, 1963], pp. 55–61; Peter Llewellyn, "The Roman clergy during the Laurentian schism [498–506]: a preliminary analysis," *Ancient Society* 8 [1977], 255). Moreover, these proportions (37 per cent in the fifth century, 43 per cent in the sixth century) are useless, since Greek names became very common in all Italian families from the late fourth century onward, through intermarriage, cultural interchange and above all the cult of saints and martyr-names; see Heikki Solin, *Die Griechische Personennamen in Rom: Ein Namenbuch*, 3 vols., CIL Auctarium (Berlin, 1980), and Brown, *Gentlemen and Officers*, pp. 67–8.

[16] PA III, table 2, commentary.

[17] Some Germanic names that occur in Ostrogothic Italy also occur in the Byzantine army in the Balkans, e.g. PLRE2 Tancus (PA Tanca, Tancila), PLRE3 Godilas 1 and 2 (PA Gudila 1–4, Gundila), PLRE3 Guduin (PA Guduin), PLRE3 Rhecitangus (cf. PA Rhecimundus). Balkan soldiers also might have a mixture of names in their families, e.g. PLRE3 Gibastes (hybrid Greek–Germanic) with daughter Anthusa; PLRE3 Alziola with daughter Bizantia. On possible

The connection of family with the linguistic origin of names may be linked to the connection between name and profession. In late antiquity, professions were supposed to be hereditary, and all members of the family took their status from the leading male. Thus the wife of a *comes* was a *comitissa*, even though she did not hold any office herself. She also took the rank-grade from her husband.[18] Wives of senators were called *senatrix*.[19] Even the wife of a bishop was an *episcopissa*.[20] The same could apply to the children. Ursulenthus, who died as an *infans* at Heraclea in Thrace in the fifth or sixth century, had already been enrolled in the *schola secunda scutariorum*. He was already a "guardsman" as a six-year-old, since his father was a guardsman in the same regiment.[21]

THE ARMY IN OSTROGOTHIC ITALY[22]

At the top level, the king was the commander-in-chief of the armed forces. There was a tight relationship between the monarch and the conceptual *Gothi* whom he had led, as soldiers, from the Balkans to Italy. Theoderic had borne the title *magister militum* under Zeno in the East, and never relinquished it in the West, since no other *magister militum* is attested in Italy after the reign of Odoacer. The *officium nostrum* mentioned in the *Variae* was the former *officium* of the *magister militum*, and all military officers now answered to the king.[23]

The king may have had a personal following with strong ties of loyalty to him, like the guardsmen of Aetius in the West, or the *dory-*

military naming strategies in sixth-century Gaul, see Amory, "Names, ethnic identity and community," pp. 26–8.
[18] *Dig.* 1.9.8. See further Susan Treggiari, *Roman Marriage* (Oxford, 1991).
[19] *Cont. Marc.* s.a. 548.
[20] *Acta Concilii Turonensis a. 567* §14(13), ed. C. de Clercq, in *Conciliae Galliae a. 511-a. 695*, CCSL 148A (Turnhout, 1963), p. 142.
[21] ILCV 564; PLRE2 Ursulenthus. Note MacMullen, *Soldier and Civilian*, p. 104 (stele of legionary with four-year-old son already clad with military belt). Cf. also PLRE3 Pastor 1, who died a *numerarius* (a civilian position) at the age of 15 – but he might well have already been working by that age.
[22] We know little about the internal organization of the army in Ostrogothic Italy, despite the rich administrative evidence contained in the *Variae*. Although the army had officers with the Roman titles *comes* and *dux*, there is no evidence for most of the lower imperial regimental grades, *tribunus, senator, primicerius* and so on. In fact, there is no attested regimental organization whatsoever. Named units (*numerus Batavorum*, etc.) vanish from Italy in the late fifth century and reappear at the time of the Gothic Wars. They were reintroduced by Justinian's armies. For a general overview of the Gothic army, see Wolfram, *Goths*, pp. 290–5, 300–6.
[23] Jones, "The constitutional position of Odoacer and Theoderic," pp. 128–30; Sinnigen, "Administrative shifts of competence under Theoderic," pp. 457–8, 461–4.

phoroi and *bucellarii* in the East, but no source attests such an institution.[24] Like the Eastern emperors, he had *spatharii* (sword-bearers) and *armigeri* (chief guardsmen),[25] but these need not translate into *bucellarii*. The imperial palace soldiers, the *scholarii*, *domestici* and *silentiarii*, continued to exist. Procopius claims that Theoderic reduced these regiments to ceremonial functions, but he claims the same, falsely, about the East at this period.[26] The post *comes domesticorum* was used as a *vacans* title to raise the holder to the illustrate,[27] but *vacantes* titles in the East coexisted with actual office-holders of the same title.[28]

To emphasize his quasi-imperial or vice-imperial claims, Theoderic also seems to have taken the military title *patricius praesentalis*, a shogun-like office peculiar to fifth-century Italy at the time of the puppet emperors. This patriciate combined actual military rule with effective civil rule, combining in its language the highest honorific, *patricius*, with the supreme military office *magister militum praesentalis*. It had been held by all the generalissimos of the Western Empire: Aetius, Ricimer, Gundobad, Orestes and Odoacer. After Theoderic's death, this title and the command of the armed forces, which could be held neither by the minor Athalaric nor the female Amalasuintha, went first to Tuluin and then to Liberius. After Liberius's defection to Justinian in 535, Theodahad must have held the office, but soon lost it and the kingship to Witigis. During the Gothic Wars, from Witigis onward, the king was always the commander-in-chief.[29]

---

[24] The *maiores palatii* cannot be defined as a *Gefolge* without further evidence; they seem to have been part of Theoderic's general ad hoc personal administration. Four were soldiers, one a civilian: PA Arigernus, Bedeulfus, Gudila 1, Tuluin, Wacca.

[25] On *armiger*, see Wolfram, *Goths*, p. 351; Moorhead, *Theoderic*, p. 101; PLRE3: 1383.

[26] Procopius, SH 24.15–23; 26.8, and Agathias 5.15.1–6, say that they had declined into mere ceremonial units, but see Michael and Mary Whitby, trans., *Chronicon Paschale, 284–628 A.D.* (Liverpool, 1989), p. 117, n. 351. The West: *Var.* 2.16.2, and Procopius *Anecd.* 26.27–8 (at the imperial palaces of Rome; he does not talk about Ravenna), but as Barnish, *Cassiodorus: Variae*, p. 98, n. 4, points out, *Var.* 1.10.1 and perhaps 6.6.1 imply that they still performed their function of defending the king (assuming that the *domestici* of the former shared the fate of the *scholares* of the latter). Moorhead, *Theoderic*, p. 254, however, accepts that they were now merely an ornamental guard, their function usurped by the "Gothic army." The distinction is crucial: if the *scholares* continued to be soldiers, then they were Goths by Theoderic's definition. Note that PLRE2 Romanus 8 and Rusticus 7, Eastern *comes domesticus* and *comes scholariorum* respectively, raided Italy with a fleet in 500; Odoacer's *comes domesticorum* Pierius commanded armies in 490 (*Anonymus Valesianus Pars Posterior* 53); PLRE2 Magnus 1 was an armed *silentiarius*.

[27] *Var.* 6.11.

[28] On *vacantes*, see Jones, LRE I: 535.

[29] Wilhelm Ensslin, "Der Patricius Praesentalis im Ostgotenreich," *Klio* 29 (1936), 246–9; Ernst Stein, "Untersuchungen zur spätrömischen Verwaltungsgeschichte," *Rheinische Museum* 74 (1925), pp. 390–1 (on Theoderic); Wolfram, *Intitulatio* I: 43–56, esp. 47 (on *patricius* and *magister militum praesentalis* in the West). Already, as so often, this solution to the title had been suggested in a few sentences by Mommsen, "OGS," NA 14: 506–7.

Ideology, organization and history combine to suggest that the army of Italy was composed of Goths. The role of the king, the disappearance of *numeri* in Italy and the name of the *exercitus Gothorum* show that the army in Italy retained the identity and putative function that it had had in the Balkans, a "people under arms," a troop of *foederati*, a band of soldiers and their families in the occasional service of the Roman Empire. Theoderic called children of his officers *iuvenes nostri*, destined to receive a military training and, doubtless, the inculcation in a military culture that the educated Athalaric was accused of missing.[30]

But the army had become larger than it had been in the Balkans, and had a wider range of tasks and regions to confront. This change in size led to the development of frontier forces and of military governors, both with Roman antecedents. Special frontier forces and military governors (called both *dux* and *comes*) appear in the reconquered provinces of the Narbonnaise, Rhaetia (the late Roman Rhaetia Secunda in the Central Alps), Noricum (the late Roman Noricum Mediterranensis, including modern Carinthia and Tyrol), Dalmatia and Savia (including much of modern Croatia and Serbia). Military *comites civitatis* took on civilian judicial functions in the cities of Italy, and the king's military couriers, the *saiones*, could penetrate all aspects of civilian life.[31]

Garrisoned in cities and *castra*, bound to civilians by the reciprocal arrangements of *consortium*, the soldiers of the Gothic army had daily contact with non-soldiers.[32] Theoderic ordered the soldiers and civilians of Nursia to build houses together in the *castrum*.[33] The *antiqui barbari* of Pannonia had married native wives, taking on the non-military obligation of paying taxes.[34] *Saiones* gave royal protection to civilians in

---

[30] *Var.* 1.38; Procopius, BG 1(5).2.8.

[31] On *comites* and *saiones* I am preparing a separate article.

[32] In general, see Wolfram, *Goths*, pp. 300–1, and the situation of closeness and tension assumed by the royal rhetoric examined in ch. 2, above. On the permanent garrisoning of many Italian cities, fortified during the turbulent fifth century, note the garrison of Syracuse at *Var.* 6.22 and Jordanes, *Rom.* 369, *Get.* 308, or those of the Cottian Alps at *Var.* 1.17 and Procopius, BG 2(6).28.28–35. Major cities at the outbreak of the Gothic Wars were garrisoned and, against Moorhead (*Theoderic*, p. 69, n. 12), I see no reason to suppose a general strategic mobilization otherwise unattested. I will be arguing for the existence of military officers with broad judicial portfolios, *comites civitatis*, in most cities, in the article (see n. 32) currently in preparation: these officers competed with the courts of provincial governors for legal cases whether military or civilian, despite Theoderic's apparent prohibitions of such activity. They clearly had armed retinues, and were probably the garrison-commanders of each city.

[33] *Var.* 8.26.

[34] *Var.* 5.14.6. The question of whether it was such marriages that made them *antiqui* remains open; suggested by Mommsen, "OGS," NA 14: 534, n. 4 (i.e. translate as "former barbarians"); Wolfram, in contrast, sees the *antiqui barbari* as barbarians settled in Pannonia before the arrival of the Goths: *Goths*, pp. 300, 320, an element of Theoderic's Goths' polyethnicity (i.e. translate as "old barbarians"); similarly, Jaroslav Šašel, "Antiqui Barbari: Zur Besiedlungsgeschichte Ostnoricums und Pannoniens im fünften und sechsten Jahrhundert nach den Schriftquellen,"

vulnerable positions, and sometimes exploited or abused them. The relationship between armed tax-collecting soldier or tenant, and tax-paying civilian or landlord, was fraught with tension. Occasionally the soldier seized the property of his civilian *consors*.[35]

The word Goth did not describe everyone in the army. Some smaller *gentes* conquered and absorbed by the Ostrogothic army retained their identity within it.[36] Procopius says the Rugian soldiers never intermarried with the Goths; they threw up their own king, Eraric, in 540, creating a certain amount of tension.[37] Some evidence shows that individual soldiers called "Gepids" resented the Goths;[38] Theoderic had fought the Gepids in Savia on his way to Italy in 488, and again in the Sirmian war of 504.[39] At the latter date, however, he gained the support of the Gepid prince Mundo, who had been ousted from his rightful throne.[40] At the time of the invasion of Gaul in 508, Theoderic arranged for the movement of a *multitudo Gepidarum* (soldiers) across northern Italy; perhaps this group had the status of a named regiment or of *foederati* within the army.[41] The Breones of the Alps were a geographical group known to classical ethnography, but in these times seem to have been a local militia or levy, perhaps also *foederati*, allied to the Gothic army in the border province of Raetia.[42] A former Italian *populus*, the Capillati, became a term for the soldiers of Italy.[43]

Some officers in the Gothic army came from native Italian families that had not arrived with the Goths from the Balkans. Liberius, who

---

in *Von der Spätantike zum frühen Mittelalter: Aktuelle Probleme in historischer und archäologischer Sicht*, ed. Joachim Werner and Eugen Ewig, Vorträge und Forschungen 25 (Sigmaringen, 1979), pp. 134–6.

[35] Goffart, *Barbarians and Romans*, pp. 93–9; see ch. 2, nn. 24, 193, above.

[36] Others, such as Alamanni, Suevi and Heruls, not to mention Romans or *provinciales*, lost their identity within the Gothic army: Wolfram, *Goths*, pp. 300–1.

[37] Procopius, BG 3(7).2.1–18. Heather, "Theoderic," p. 157, declares that "there is no reason to think them unique in" not intermarrying: but the reverse is surely true, since Procopius singles out this trait of the Rugians for special mention. On intermarriage of people identifiable as Goths, see further below. On Procopius and the Rugians, see further ch. 5, p. 178.

[38] Procopius, BG 3(7).1.43–8 (PA Velas, the murderer of Hildebad); 4.26.13; 4.32.22–8 (PA Asbadus, the murderer of Totila).

[39] Wolfram, *Goths*, pp. 280, 320–3.

[40] Brian Croke, "Mundo the Gepid: from freebooter to Roman general," *Chiron* 12 (1982), 125–35; this Sirmian "Gepid" leader went from being a Gepid prince to bandit to ally of Theoderic to ally of Justinian: PA Mundo.

[41] Wolfram, *Goths*, p. 301.

[42] Ibid.; also, Wolfram, "Ethnogenese im Donau- und Ostalpenraum (6.–10. Jahrhundert)," in *Frühmittelalterliche Ethnogenese im Alpenraum*, ed. Helmut Beumann and W. Schräder, Nationes 5 (Sigmaringen, 1985), pp. 118–22; see further PA Servatus, and *Var.* 1.11.

[43] Pliny, *Nat. Hist.* 3.5.47. Here I do not agree with arguments about the supposed Thracian origin of the *capillati* and of long hair among Goths: despite Wolfram, *Goths*, pp. 103, 301–2, the word only occurs in Italian sources. See further appendix 4, below.

served the Gothic kings for decades, and became *patricius praesentalis* in 533, was known to be a "Roman" and had begun his career under Odoacer. The same was true of the *silentiarius* and *comes domesticorum* Valentinianus. Cyprian, the enemy of Boethius, rose to prominence through his military career under Theoderic, and his family already had a history of imperial and royal service within Italy. Ursus, probably *dux Norici*, had ties of local pride and patronage to Teurnia, the metropolis of Noricum, where he dedicated a lavish series of church mosaics. He may well have come from the region.[44]

All these developments, and others less clear to us, changed the nature of a soldier's life and the cohesion of the army as an institution after its settlement in Italy. Soldiers initially received *sortes*, allotments, upon settlement.[45] They rapidly bought or otherwise acquired land as well, with accompanying local and fiscal burdens and duties. Upon retirement, they might acquire civil office or a pension. Their assimilation into civilian society left them open to civilian burdens, whether fair or unfair.[46] One blind ex-soldier was enslaved by two officers.[47]

An army is not a self-replacing breeding community, due to the hazardous nature of the profession and its all-male membership. The expansion of the army, which continued to recruit both inside and outside the frontiers, brought in people who had not experienced the epoch-making journey from the Balkans to Italy. Indeed, the army recruited on this very journey, and on its victory absorbed the remnants of the army of Odoacer.[48] In the 520s, Theoderic ordered recruitment of sailors to increase the Italian fleet.[49] Naval warfare had not been part of his military expeditions in the Balkans, but appears after his arrival in Italy in his war with Odoacer: he annexed Odoacer's navy as he absorbed Odoacer's defeated land troops.

There is no question that soldiers, although bound into civil society, shared a distinctive professional culture. The difficulty lies in saying what this culture was. We have seen that soldiers tended to have Germanic names. Were there other elements of "Gothic" identity bound into the "Gothic" army? At the very least, the soldiers shared the

---

[44] PA Liberius 3; **Valentinianus** (born early enough for *silentiarius* and *comes domesticorum* to have been real military offices, contra PLRE2: 1138, assuming that these were actually *only* titular and non-military offices at this time); Cyprianus; Ursus.

[45] Whether these *sortes* consisted of tax-assessments or lands does not affect this argument: see ch. 2 for the literature on this issue.

[46] Fair: *Var.* 5.14.6; unfair: PA **Guduin** 2, instructed to remove *onera servilia* from Costula and Daila (*Var.* 5.30).

[47] PA **Anduit**, *Var* 5.29.

[48] Wolfram, *Goths*, pp. 300–2.

[49] *Var.* 5.16: freemen recruited would receive a donative.

common bonds of a distinctive profession. These included dress and badge, the right to arms, and an upbringing or training in a military camp. Late Roman sumptuary laws dictated special dress for soldiers, and the *Notitia Dignitatum* shows a vast number of special badges and brooches indicating rank and regiment. Special dress doubtless persisted, and illustrations of the Gothic rulers in military dress suggest that this dress was similar to that worn by the Roman army in the fifth century.[50]

Children of officers received military training from their youth. The atmosphere of the training camp might have done much to inculcate professional pride and identity against the civilian world outside. But we have little detail about it. This is the "Gothic education" that the officers under Amalasuintha wanted Athalaric to have, rather than the classical education with which she provided him. Classical education, the special attribute of the resolutely non-military senate, was conceptually opposed to military ability, as in the career of Theodahad.[51] Some bowmen preparing for Theoderic's abortive invasion of Africa in 526 had just come out of training.

Dress marked soldiers as different, arms gave them undue power over civilians, and the world of the camp and the battlefield lent them esprit de corps and a common sense of identity – tied, during Theoderic's later reign, to the royal ideology of a military king and his splendid past. The "world" of *iuvenes nostri*, so different from the civilian world, must have included customs and traditions very different from those soldiers encountered in the cities, or among their *consortes* and civilian wives.

The right to bear arms was another differentiating characteristic inherited from the late Empire. Civilians were allowed to bear arms only under special circumstances. In 440, Valentinian III allowed the citizens of Rome to carry arms to defend themselves from the projected invasion of Geiseric. Majorian lifted the prohibition again in 456/457.[52] The circumstance persisted in Ostrogothic Italy, where Theoderic forbade Romans even to carry small knives.[53] The armed *saiones* were able to terrorize their civilian charges.

Military camp traditions are very difficult to identify. But there seems little reason to distinguish most of them from traditions among the late Roman army. Dress was similar; modes of battle do not seem to have included anything new; customs related to the election of the king-

---

[50] See appendix 4, below.
[51] See ch. 5, below.
[52] CT 15.15.1; *Nov. Val.* 9; *Nov. Maj.* 8, rubric (text of this law lost).
[53] AV 83, its most garbled section (on the events of 519).

commander were no different from the military aspects of the election of an emperor.[54]

SOLDIERS, CIVILIANS AND PERSONAL NAMES

The army was various in its membership, recruited actively, and went through much change over the years. It is then surprising that Germanic names remain so prevalent among its members. Can this be related to its prestige and history as a "Gothic" institution? Or does it merely show that the bulk of its members continued to be the descendants of the soldier-settlers from the Balkans in the 490s? Inherited names, both Germanic and Latin, may have existed in military families, along with a *Namenstrategie* to choose an appropriate name for a child destined for a certain profession.

We do not have a large number of attested common soldiers from Ostrogothic Italy, partly because the disappearance of *numeri* and of the lower rank designations in the Italian army makes them difficult to identify. Many of them may have been the Latin-named *viri devoti* in inscriptions and papyri, but *vir devotus* could also denote an individual in the civil bureaucracy.[55] Nonetheless, of the 18 named ordinary soldiers attested between 523/526 and 552 (none is attested earlier), only two have Graeco-Latin names, and both of those were sailors.[56] Most of the rest of the names are Germanic.[57] See PA III, Table 1.

Two of the ordinary soldiers in the 520s had wives with Latin names.[58] These are the only soldiers' wives we know, so intermarriage might have been common, as other evidence suggests. If the children of these marriages were to become soldiers, would they receive Germanic names? The evidence does not permit us to say. In low-ranking families whose professions we do not know, mixtures of both names appear from an earlier date than that of these soldiers.[59]

Given known intermarriage of soldiers and civilians,[60] and known

---

[54] See appendix 4, below. Even Wolfram, *Goths*, p. 343, appears to see Witigis's raising as a Gothic custom ("ancestral custom" for *mos maiorum*); but it was not, nor was it seen as such at the time.

[55] *Vir devotus* came to denote only soldiers in Byzantine Italy: Brown, *Gentlemen and Officers*, p. 134. It was standard for *saiones* (Conti, *"Devotio" e "viri devoti,"* pp. 118–22, claiming that here it was a "Germanic" trait), who combined bureaucratic and military functions.

[56] PA **A**ndreas and **S**ecundus.

[57] Exception: PA **C**occas (a Byzantine deserter; probably a Thracian name).

[58] PA **B**randila and **P**rocula; **P**atza and **R**egina.

[59] PA **D**umilda (son: **T**heodosus); **V**onosus (son: **A**river), **G**untelda (son: **B**asilius, his son: **G**untio); **T**hulgilo (children: **D**eutherius and **D**omnica), all *honesti* or of unstated rank. See PA III, table 11.

[60] *Var.* 5.14.6.

name-mixtures in both military and non-military families,[61] it is suggestive that none of the ordinary soldiers attested from the Gothic Wars,
in the next generation, has a Graeco-Latin name. This is, however, a
very small sample (11 names, 2 belonging to the sailors mentioned
above, both of whom were dead by 539).

The evidence for the names of officers in the Gothic army is much
richer, and, given the bias of the sources, shows a more reliable spread.
Out of 63 names, 12 are Graeco-Latin or biblical. These are evenly
spread between the period 489 to 554 (see PA III, table 2). But we
have little evidence for the *families* of officers. The probable *dux Norici*
in the first decade of the 500s, Ursus, had a wife with the strangely
similar name of Ursina. Perhaps she changed it upon marrying him.[62]
A *comes* with a Germanic name attested in an inscription in Milan in
512 had a daughter named Agatha, but he need not have been a military
comes.[63]

A useful comparison here is the naming behavior of certain Byzantine
officers from the Balkans whom some sources call "Goths." The Gepid
prince, bandit leader, Ostrogothic officer and Byzantine officer Mundo
had a son with the Greek name Mauricius who fought for Justinian in
the Gothic Wars. Mauricius's son was called Theudimundus, a Germanic name using his grandfather's name as an element. Here, as in
one family from Ostrogothic Italy, the Germanic name has skipped a
generation.[64]

Names skipping generations, the so-called *Nachbenennung* (or
variation) also occurred among the Latin names of the senatorial aristocracy of Rome,[65] but the family of another Balkan Byzantine officer
called a Goth was different. The father of the *magister militum* Vitalian
had a Latin name, Patriciolus, while Vitalian's own children received
Thracian names (Cutzes and Buzes) and a Germanic name (Venilus or
Benilus).[66] A third Illyrian Byzantine officer, Bessas, was described by

---

[61] PA III, table 11.
[62] PA Ursus, Ursina.
[63] PA Gattila, Agata.
[64] PA Mundo, Mauricius, Theudimundus; cf. Guntelda, Basilius, Guntio, a family also reusing
a Germanic name element that skipped a generation.
[65] The process is easiest to identify among the senatorial aristocracy, in which the multiple names
of individuals have been best preserved; it is a natural method of preserving genealogical claims
to family, particularly maternal ancestry. The patrician Symmachus's daughter's son (the son
of Boethius) was named Symmachus after his grandfather, a name taken by none of the
patrician's three daughters; the consul Gennadius Avienus's daughter's son was called Rufius
Magnus Faustus Avienus (the consul of 502), combining his father's name with that of his
maternal grandfather; the granddaughter of Proba and Probus (she the daughter of the Eastern
consul of 491) was called Proba; see PLRE2, stemmata 22, 23 and 3 respectively.
[66] PA Vitalianus 1.

Procopius as "one of the Goths who did not accompany Theoderic to Italy." His name was Thraco-Greek, but the names of two other officers from his village were Germanic. On the other hand, other contemporaries did not see Bessas as a Goth.[67]

In the early stages of the Gothic settlement, most of the attested officers with Latin names came from native Italian families. We have already discussed the Italian origins and careers of Liberius, Valentinianus, Cyprian and Ursus. We do not know the personal histories of the two other early examples.[68] Under the Gothic Wars, however, most of these officers had been born after 489, in the Italian kingdom.[69]

Civilians also bore Germanic names from the very beginning of Ostrogothic rule in Italy. We find Germanic names among royal tax-collectors, a treasurer and a *praerogativarius* of the praetorian prefect's office, eunuchs and attendants of the royal bedchamber, geographers, freedmen and freedwomen, and slaves.[70] Other civilians are only identifiable through the non-military rank-designation *vir honestus*, *honesta femina*. Leaving aside Arian clergymen, civilians with Germanic names form about 10 per cent of the total Germanic names attested in Italy at this time.[71]

Why did people take Germanic names or give them to their children? We can see some evidence of prestige naming among soldiers. Theoderic's own family laid claim to an illustrious ancestry of great warriors, first attested in Cassiodorus's letter to the senate for Amalasuintha in 533, publicizing her military heritage. This genealogy must go back to Cassiodorus's lost *Historia Gothorum*, written at Theoderic's request, and is thus part of Theoderic's late ideology of providential Amal military ascendancy.[72]

But the prestige of Amal names is not limited to soldiers fighting for the Goths, even if Theoderic did mean his followers to believe that they shared in Amal prestige. For example, Theoderic claimed an ancestor with the *gens*-name Ostrogotha, and he named one of his daughters Ostrogotho. His grandfather was named Vandalarius, hearkening back

---

[67] PA **Bessas**; cf. PLRE2 Froila and Blivila.
[68] PA **Colosseus** and **Servatus**.
[69] Assuming that most officers were under 46 when the war began, and under 65 by the time it ended: PA **Asinarius**, **Marcias**, **Moras 1**, **Moras 2**, **Romulus**, **Uraïas**, all first attested as active after 535 (**Herodianus** was a deserter from the Byzantines.)
[70] PA **Bauto** *conductor domus regiae* and **Witigisclus** *censitor Siciliae*; **Nonni** *arcarius* and **Bonila** *praerogativarius*; **Wiliarit 2** *eunuchus* and **Seda** *ignucus et cubicularius*; **Athanarid**, **Heldbebaldus** and **Marcormirus** *phyolosophi*; **Sifilo** and **Guderit 2** *liberti*; **Ranihilda**, slave.
[71] See PA III, table 10.
[72] Above, ch. 2, pp. 67–8, 74–5, 77 n. 180.

to Gothic supremacy over the Vandals, a topical issue in the 520s. Thus
we find a Gepid prince named Ustrigotthus, not active in the Gothic
Wars; the same prefix may appear in an inhabitant of Ravenna called
Otratarit who rented warehouse space under the Byzantine administration, and in an undated inscription belonging to a soldier called
[O]traustaguta; one of Aspar's relatives in Thrace in the 460s was called
Ostrys. A soldier in the Gothic Wars took the second name Vandalarius,
and one of Theoderic's officers in reconquered Gaul in 510 was called
Wandil. Actual Amal names seem to have been restricted to the royal
family, but Theoderic's great-nephew Amalafridas, son of the Thuringian king and Theoderic's sister Amalafrida, retained his name even while
fighting on the Byzantine side in the Gothic Wars.[73]

Also possibly prestigious and related to a sense of Gothic identity is
the common name prefix Gud-/Gund-, which seems to have the same
root as *Guta/Gotha/Gothus*.[74] It is not peculiar to military men but
appears among their names, including three of the *saiones*.[75] It also
appears among Byzantine officers from the Balkans, including the
fellow-countryman of Bessas, Godidisclus, another "Goth who did not
follow Theoderic to Italy."[76] But we also find Gud- in Burgundy and
Vandal Africa, one African example called a Goth by Procopius.[77] God-
is also part of the name of a man called a Thracian by Procopius.[78]

Soldiers could use a *Namenstrategie* when naming their children. An
Arian cleric writing in the Balkans in the 440s commented,

Sicut solent et barbarae gentes nomina filiis imponere ad devastationem respici-
entia bestiarum, ferarum vel rapacium volucrum, gloriosum putantes filios tales
habere, ad bellum idoneos et insanientes in sanguinem.
As they are accustomed, barbarous *gentes* give names to their sons appropriate
for the devastations of wild beasts, or of rapacious vultures, thinking it
glorious that their sons should have such names, suitable for war and raving
in blood.[79]

---

[73] PA ⋆Ostrogotho, Ustrigotthus, Otratarit, Visandus 1 Vandalarius, Wandil, Amalafridas.
[O]traustaguta: CIL 5.8740; see further PA Otratarit. PLRE2 Ostrys. Another possible prestige
name, from the second half of the sixth century, is Gainus of Parenzo; see under PA Acio
and cf. PLRE2 Gainas 1 and 2.

[74] Wrede, *Über die Sprache*, pp. 71–2.

[75] Officers: PA Guduin 2, Gundulf (a deserter from the Byzantines), Gundila, probably Gudila
3 and Gudila 4. *Saiones*: Gudinandus, Gudisal, Guduin 1. The two Guduins here might have
been identical: see PA Guduin 2.

[76] PLRE2 Godilas (= PLRE3 Godilas 1), Godidisclus, PLRE3 Godilas 2, Guduin 1.

[77] Burgundians: PLRE2 Gundobadus, Godigisel 2, Godomarus 1 and 2. Vandals: PLRE2 Godagis,
Godigisel 1, PLRE3 Godas (called a Goth by Procopius, BV 1.10.25)

[78] PLRE3 Godilas 2; see further below, p. 184.

[79] *Opus imperfectum in Matthaeum*, PG 56: 626 (Paris, 1862). On this anonymous Arian Latin text,
once attributed to Chrysostom, see ch. 7.

One historian saw in this a *usage Gothique*,[80] but it is no different from the use of prestigious Roman names in senatorial families, or the use of Graeco-Latin Christian names for sons destined for the church.[81] The custom described here is only *barbarous*, from the Christian point of view, because the desired qualities are warlike. We are looking at the usage of soldiers, not foreigners. Many successful soldiers in the fourth and fifth centuries had had Germanic names; in the late fifth and early sixth century, a large proportion of the Byzantine army had Germanic names. That pool of names was available to military families.

There were no hard and fast rules, but the predominance of Germanic names among both soldiers and officers suggests that the military of whatever origin leaned toward the use of Germanic names. The evidence of recruitment and side-changing suggests that as in the Eastern armies, this predominance of Germanic names was a matter of choice as much as descent. Germanic names were common in the Amal family that had led the army to victory from the Balkans, and in the Balkans themselves, Germanic names remained the rule for both Byzantine and non-Byzantine soldiers.[82]

Soldiers shared Germanic names with a smaller number of civilians. Soldiers' families, when they are attested, included Latin names as well.[83]

---

[80] Jacques Zeiller, *Les origines chrétiennes dans les provinces danubiennes de l'empire romain*, Bibliothèque des Ecoles Française d'Athènes et de Rome 112 (Paris, 1918), p. 478.

[81] On which see ch. 7. We must discount Norbert Wagner, "Germanische Namengebung und kirchliches Recht in der Amalerstammtafel," *Zeitschrift für deutsches Altertum und deutsches Literatur* 99 (1970), 1–16, who argues that Cassiodorus concealed Germanic name-giving practices in the Amal genealogy, in order to conceal uncanonical marriages between royal cousins! Wagner believes that Cassiodorus thus intended to win Catholic sympathies for the Amals under Athalaric. The list of assumptions here is enormous: the Amals must have used Germanic naming practices, these practices were not used by Romans, only "Germans" made uncanonical marriages (Wagner cites eighth-century sources on "Franks" and "Lombards," that is, Gaul and Italy, to suggest that cousin-marriage was a Germanic institution), and senators of the 530s might change their political sympathies to an Arian family because it followed Catholic canon law. Each of these assumptions is at least questionable. In particular, on "Germanic" naming practices (*Nachbenennung* is not easy to see in the Amal genealogy, so Wagner needs to excuse this); see next note.

[82] The whole theory of Germanic name-giving requires a new study free from the *kulturgeschichtlich* assumptions of Germanist philology. The principles of dithematism (bipartite names) and variation (*Nachbenennung*) were not in fact restricted to Germanic name-giving, let alone Germanic speakers. For the traditional view, see H. B. Woolf, *The Old Germanic Principles of Name-Giving* (Baltimore, 1939), still used by Wagner, "Germanische Namengebung," p. 9. *Nachbenennung* existed among the Roman senatorial aristocracy (above, n. 65). The phenomenon of giving one brother the full bipartite name and the other a hypocoristic form of it (Karl-mann, Karl) also existed among the Greeks (Rheskouporis, Rheskos), while both dithematic names and variation have existed in most Indo-European languages: Werner, "Liens de parenté et noms de personne," pp. 16–18 (calling for an empirical study free from preconceptions of era, region or ethnic unity).

[83] PA III, table 11.

Although ecclesiastical sources associate possession of a Germanic name with the label Goth,[84] the distribution of these same names throughout the Mediterranean soldiery, attached to individuals given many other ethnographic labels, suggests that the Germanic names of soldiers were a result of family and profession as much as an ethnographic label.

SOLDIERS, CIVILIANS AND LANGUAGE

One different cultural trait distinguishing the army might have been that the soldiers spoke the Gothic language, a Germanic tongue, and this would therefore explain the predominance of Germanic names in the army. But here we must tread very carefully. A spoken Gothic language is mentioned only four times in the Italian sources, only in military contexts, and only about individuals who also spoke another language. It need not have been identical to the written Gothic of the Arian churches.[85] Latin was the common language of Italy, and our spoken "Gothic" must have been a specialized, minority tongue.

First, if any soldiers spoke Gothic, then they were bilingual. As we have seen above, everyone in Italy spoke Latin. There can be no doubt about this. It is true that all the definite non-Arian clergy who are described as speaking Gothic were soldiers or members of the royal family. But all of them also spoke Latin, and some of them spoke Greek as well.[86]

Second, we must define what we mean by the phrase "Gothic language." The written language used by some members of the Arian clergy was an archaic, artificial and liturgical language. It was this archaism and artificiality that recommended it to the Arian churches, seeking to differentiate themselves from the Catholic church in Italy.[87]

---

[84] See ch. 7.

[85] It is striking that although Ulfilas's Gothic alphabet, related to runes, was preserved in Italy, not a single runic inscription is attested from Ostrogothic Italy – although runes are found on the fourth-century Danube and (very rarely) in Lombard Italy. On runes, see R. I. Page, *Runes* (London, 1987) and Heather, "Literacy and power in the migration period," p. 178.

[86] PA Bessas, Cyprianus, Anonymus 17, Anonymi 20+, ★Amalasuintha, ★Theodericus and possibly ★Totila. See PA III, table 12. Totila is doubtful, since the source is shaky in the extreme. In the sixteenth century, the humanist Petrus Alcyonius wrote that a cardinal (the future Leo X) said that *he* had seen a work by an unknown Greek historian who recorded that Attila (*sic*) planned to start forcing people to speak Gothic in Italy. "Attila" has been taken as a misunderstanding of "Totila." Aside from the problem of the emendation, the source is unnamed, unidentifiable with any attested Byzantine historian, and at least three removes from us. Nor does the story sit well with the portrayal of Totila as imitator of Theoderic in Procopius. See Schmidt, "Das germanische Volkstum," pp. 433–4; Wattenbach and Levison, *Deutschlands Geschichtsquellen* 1: 78, n. 151.

[87] See ch. 7. No Arian clergyman is described as *speaking* this language. The language of the Gothic Bible was based on a fourth-century Germanic dialect, was frozen in an artificial word-

The spoken language called "Gothic" and attributed to some sixth-century soldiers need not have had much in common with the written biblical and liturgical "Gothic." The spoken language presumably came from the Balkans, where groups speaking various Germanic dialects had settled since the late 300s. These dialects were mutually intelligible,[88] and no doubt absorbed Latin and Greek words from the Balkan Roman provinces even more than written "Gothic" did. This spoken Gothic influenced the Latin language in Italy very little. Few place-names in Italy can be traced to Gothic even in the current uncritical state of Italian toponymic scholarship.[89] Ennodius and Procopius both seem to have absorbed the word *balan*, a piebald horse from north of the Danube, which could have been a military borrowing. The fourth- or fifth-century military writer Vegetius referred to warhorses as *Toringi*, *Burgundiones* and *Hunnisci*, indicating that they had been imported for some time.[90] The Italian language today contains some Germanic words, like *albergo* ("inn"), but they seem to have been borrowed before the Ostrogothic settlement, and various others are undatable.[91] The word *saio* was imported into the Ravenna administration, but the office acquired duties not identified by the Germanic meaning of the word.

for-word translation of the Hebrew and Greek Scriptures, had absorbed Greek vocabulary and syntax, and was subsequently further adulterated by re-translation and emendation to reflect Latin word-order.

[88] William G. Moulton, "Mutual intelligibility among speakers of early Germanic dialects," in *Germania: Comparative Studies in the Old Germanic Languages and Literatures*, ed. Daniel G. Calder and T. Craig Christie (Woodbridge, Suffolk, 1993), pp. 9–28; more cautiously, Thomas L. Markey, "Germanic in the Mediterranean: Lombards, Vandals and Visigoths," in *Tradition and Innovation in Late Antiquity*, ed. Clover and Humphreys, p. 62: "the Germanic that confronted Romance . . . was probably never identifiable as one 'fixed' language, but was instead – in every instance of contact – a conglomerate of dialects with varying degrees of mutual intelligibility."

[89] And it is significant that none of the possible Gothic place-names is based on Germanic *vocabulary*: they are all formed either on the basis of a Germanic personal name plus a Latin word such as *mons*, *campus*, or simply on the basis of the word "Goth": see the lists in Ernst Gammilscheg, *Romania Germania* 2 (Berlin, 1935), 11–15, and Carlo Alberto Mastrelli, "I Goti e il gotico," in *I Goti*, pp. 278–9. On the problems of Italian toponymic studies (the criticisms of Mastrelli), see below, appendix 3; on the small number of possibly Gothic place-names, see Carlo Battisti, "L'elemento gotico nella toponomastica e nel lessico italiano," in *I Goti in Occidente*, pp. 621–49. Maria Giovanna Arcamone, "I Germani d'Italia: lingue e 'documenti' linguistici," in *Magistra barbaritas*, pp. 404–5, points out that Gammilscheg estimated seventy Ostrogothic place-names and 280 Lombard place-names, but Arcamone herself will only hazard Lombard place-names.

[90] Vegetius, *De re militari* 3.6; Goffart, "Date and purpose of Vegetius' *De re militari*," pp. 69–70.

[91] Moorhead, *Theoderic*, pp. 86–7 with n. 94 (misprinted in text as n. 95); Arcamone, "I Germani d'Italia: lingue e 'documente' linguistici," pp. 386–99 (such words could originate in Germanically influenced late Latin, Ostrogothic, Lombard or Frankish, and are only often first attested Romance or modern Italian; I might then adduce the possibility of Ottonian and medieval German influence); the list of Germanic words in modern Italian at pp. 399, 404. Mastrelli, "I Goti e il gotico," p. 278, provides a list of allegedly Gothic words, but allows that the attributions are shaky.

The word appears exclusively in the *Variae*; Ennodius did not see fit to use it in his correspondence with one *saio*.[92]

The connection between personal names and a *distinctively* Gothic or Ostrogothic language is slight.[93] In fact, out of four references to the spoken language, two attribute knowledge of it to men with non-Germanic names.[94] Ferdinand Wrede's attempt to prove that Germanic names in Italy derived from a distinctive Ostrogothic Gothic is vitiated by the automatic assumption that Gothic was a living language descended from that attested by Ulfila's Bible.[95] Philologists no longer accept that there was a particularly Ostrogothic Gothic.[96] The continuing use of dithematic names does not prove that such names continued to have linguistic meaning.[97] The nonsensical combination of Germanic elements in dithematic names including most of those in the royal family suggests that the dithematic naming tradition could survive without language.[98] The supposedly Germanic custom of *Nachbenennung*, as we have seen, existed in Latin names as well as Germanic ones.

Wrede's other assumption, that the Goths were already a people when they settled in Italy, still permeates most research on the Gothic language.[99] Wrede assumes that all names (recorded in Latin and Greek sources) attributed to people identified as "Goths" must be "seen through" to an original Ostrogothic form.[100] This assumption leads him and other philologists to ridiculous contortions. Procopius identifies a

---

[92] The word *saio* seems to mean "follower" in Germanic (Traube, index to Cassiodorus, s.v.). The *saiones* were royal couriers like the *agentes in rebus* or *comitiaci*, but they were armed (*Var.* 4.28) and were soon policing the realm and executing the king's orders (4.14; 4.47; 5.5), eventually taking part in court cases (8.24, 9.14, 9.18). By the 530s *saiones* seem to have permanently attached to courts as *executores* or *apparitores*; see 12.3. Ennodius corresponded with PA **T**riwila.

[93] More convincing is the philological distinction between East, West and North Germanic language-families on the basis of names, if we identify these languages with regions of Europe (the banks of the Danube and their hinterland, the Rhineland and northern Europe respectively) rather than with *gentes*. On these distinctions, see the summary of Arcamone, "I Germani d'Italia: lingue e 'documente' linguistici," pp. 381–2.

[94] PA **B**essas and **C**yprianus.

[95] Wrede, *Über die Sprache*, pp. 1–13.

[96] Scardigli, *Lingua e storia*, pp. 7–8.

[97] Peter Nichols Richardson, *German-Romance Contact: Name-giving in Walser Settlements*, Amsterdamer Publikationenen zur Sprache und Literatur 15 (Amsterdam, 1974), p. 64 with n. 7 and references. On dithematism in general, see above, n. 82.

[98] Moreover, there were hybrid Greek–Germanic names such as PLRE2 Gibastes, or probably hybrid Latin–Germanic names such as PA **S**arabonus. Contemporaries may not have found it any easier than we do to identify a name as Latin, Greek, Gothic or of other linguistic origin: possible examples are PA **C**occas, **M**arcias, **P**issas, **P**itzias (all also difficult to evaluate due to the textual transmission of the name). Many writers were under the impression that Theodahad's name was the Latin Theodatus: see PA *Theodahadus, PLRE2 Theodahadus.

[99] Scardigli, *Lingua e storia*, passim.

[100] Wrede, *Über die Sprache*, pp. 4–10, esp. 8–9.

Gothic soldier as Asinarios, a normal Greek spelling of the attested Latin name Asinarius. Wrede and Schönfeld assume that Procopius is Hellenizing an otherwise unattested Germanic *Asinareis, itself derived from the Latin Asinarius.[101] Why not accept that Asinarius simply had a Latin name?

Wrede assumes that the Ostrogoths in Italy spoke their own language, not a generalized Mediterranean or military Germanic dialect, because "die Scharen, welche unter Theoderic nach Italien zogen, waren kein buntes Völkergemisch wie die Massen des Odowacar, sondern sie bildeten eine einheitliche, fest zusammenhängende Nation."[102] Such statements condemn themselves in modern eyes anyway, but even Wrede ought to have been aware that Theoderic's army had absorbed "die Massen des Odowacar," not to mention Italian and Pannonian provincials, and that it had Latin names among its ranks as well as Germanic ones. Wrede displays his fundamental confusion between languages and peoples when he admits that there are problems in distinguishing between names developed from "Gothic" roots and those borrowed from other languages – "from other tribes," he says, revealingly. It was a conceptual problem for nineteenth-century German philologists that the German word for "tribe" (*Stamm*) is identical to that for linguistic stem (*Stamm*). But Wrede intends the identification here.[103]

In fact, one of four references to spoken Gothic in Italy mentions the fluency of the Byzantine officer Bessas, the Balkan Goth who did not follow Theoderic to Italy. Bessas also spoke Latin and Greek, and he was probably typical of the Balkan soldiers of whatever allegiance, who in the Byzantine army bore Latin, Greek, Germanic and Thracian names, even within the same family.[104]

Another reference to the language also attributes it to a soldier, but in an artificial story of Procopius. During Witigis's siege of Rome in 537 and 538, a Byzantine ("Roman") soldier fell into a pit outside the walls. A Gothic soldier also fell in. They conversed and became friends. They agreed that whichever side their discoverers belonged to, each would ensure the safety of the other. Gothic soldiers found them, so the Gothic soldier shouted up in Gothic that two Goths were in the pit. He allowed the Roman to be pulled up first, and after he himself

[101] Ibid., p. 92; M. Schönfeld, *Wörterbuch der altgermanischen Personen- und Völkernamen*, Germanische Bibliothek 3. Reihe (Heidelberg, 1911), p. 33.

[102] Wrede, *Über die Sprache*, p. 11.

[103] Ibid., pp. 12–13.

[104] PA Bessas. On Balkan military culture and personal names, see ch. 8.

had been pulled up, he explained the situation and arranged for the Roman soldier to have safe-conduct back to the city.[105]

The story reveals its own improbability simultaneously with the fact that bilingualism could be assumed by the author. First, the Gothic soldier could speak Latin or Greek (he conversed with the Roman soldier who could not speak Gothic). Second, the story is suspicious. It reads like a moral lesson on how both sides could get along. Neither does it make sense that the Gothic soldier could convince Goths that he was one of them by speaking their language. As we have seen, the Byzantine officer Bessas could speak Gothic, and indeed he is said to have shouted to the Gothic troops in this language at one point. Many other Byzantine officers also came from the Balkans, bore Germanic names, are identified as Goths, and presumably had similar facility in the language. Moreover, there had already been desertion in both directions, including "all the Goths settled in Dalmatia and Liburnia,"[106] who joined the ranks of the Byzantine general Constantianus. There were Gothic speakers in the Byzantine ranks if there were Gothic speakers anywhere, and knowledge of Gothic need have proved nothing about the allegiance of the men in the pit.

Given that all references to spoken Gothic occur in a military context, a Mediterranean-wide military context, perhaps this "Gothic" refers to the pidgin of the Mediterranean armies. As we have seen, Procopius attributes the name of the language to Byzantine soldiers, but also to the Vandals, Gepids, Visigoths and Goths (Ostrogoths), all of whom served as soldiers in the Mediterranean. Armies can develop a pidgin or cant of their own when moving around and taking in wide recruits speaking different languages. The Roman army of preceding centuries had had a specialized Latin with a large vocabulary incomprehensible to the layman.[107] Some of this Latin military slang had penetrated the fourth-century Balkan Germanic tongue that formed the basis of Ulfilas's translation of the Bible in the fourth-century Balkans.[108] Given the phenomenon of the *foederati*, recruitment outside the imperial frontiers, and the high percentage of Germanic names among soldiers from the fourth century onward, it would be very surprising if this

---

[105] Procopius, BG 1.29.11–20.
[106] PA Anonymi 34+; similarly Ebremud and Pitzas with their men. All deserted to the Byzantines by 537.
[107] R. Gordon and Mary Beard et al., "Roman inscriptions 1986–90," *Journal of Roman Studies* 83 (1993), 147.
[108] Wolfram, *Goths*, p. 113, but see ch. 7 below, on the influx of Latin into the Ulfilan text long after Ulfilas's death.

pidgin did not contain a large number of Germanic words and syntactical structures by the late fifth century, particularly in the Balkans.

Theoderic associated *nostra lingua* (never called "Gothic" by him) with the world of military training and the camp. Like the army itself, this language was associated with Theoderic's family, which itself came from the military world of the Balkans. Most members of this family are also attested as Latin-speaking, and some are attested as Greek-speaking. Theoderic, Amalasuintha, Amalaberga and Theodahad all received a classical education.

The king expresses astonishment and delight that the soldier and minister Cyprian learned *nostra lingua* and taught it to his children: learning the language was unusual. Another Italian commander much praised by the king, Liberius, is recorded as having done no such thing, but he seems to have had no difficulty leading troops. All the king's letters to soldiers and the army are written in Latin. To be sure, perhaps they were read aloud or translated, but we have references to no readers, translators or problems in communication. Nor need we hypothesize any.

With the army's absorption of Italian troops, intermarriage, recruitment and civilian connections, many soldiers need not have known a non-Latin tongue at all, let alone had the barely attested spoken Gothic as a first language. Its context in Procopius, despite that writer's rhetoric, suggests that Balkan soldiers in the Byzantine army brought "Gothic" back to Italy to some extent; the rapid desertions in both directions and intermingling of both armies would ensure that over the nineteen years of the Wars, it would become a feature in both camps.

This spoken Balkan military dialect is never called "Gothic" in the sources that attribute it to any given individual.[109] It was shared by some Byzantine soldiers, and by people who called themselves Vandals[110] –

---

[109] *Lingua nostra* for Theoderic and Athalaric (in the letter written for the latter when he was about eleven); *de tei patrioi glōssei* for Procopius (about PA **A**nonymus 17, BG 2[6].1.16), though *tei Gotthōn phōnei* about Bessas (BG 1[5].10.10).

[110] Spoken Gothic may have been stronger in Africa than in Italy, since we possess a fragment of a drinking song from there in the midst of a Latin poem: AL 279, which does call the language "Gothic"; one Arian Vandal bishop claimed that he could not speak Latin, a lie which his opponents soon saw through: Victor Vitensis 2.55, on which see Moorhead, *Theoderic*, p. 88; and in a disputation between an Arian and a Catholic, the Arian disputator exclaims "sihora armen!" ("domine miserere!") in Gothic: *Collatio cum Pascentio Ariano*, PL 33: 1162 (Paris, 1845); on which, see Scardigli, *Lingua e storia*, p. 8, n. 1; Frank M. Clover, "Carthage and the Vandals," in *Excavations at Carthage 1978, Conducted by the University of Michigan*, ed. J. H. Humphrey (Ann Arbor, 1982), p. 18. These last two examples, though, surely show the learned, priestly aspects of the written Gothic language as transmitted through Ulfilas's Bible: the Arian clergymen are speaking Gothic to make debating points and to emphasize

and who were only called Goths by ethnographic sources in the East who wanted to lump all Justinian's enemies together.[111] For Theoderic, the spoken language was a distinguishing feature of his army. But neither for him nor for them was it a barrier between them and the rest of the population. The evidence does not suggest that it was widespread, and it would be dangerous to give it undue weight as a distinctively Gothic cultural trait.

CONCLUSION

In the ideology of Ravenna, the army as an institution was supposed to be a separate ethnographic and professional community, but in fact was neither. Despite its glorious past associated with the name "Goth" and the family of Theoderic, the army was an extremely variegated body in constant flux, knit into the tight fabric of Italian civil society. To ambitious men it offered a career-route that allowed rapid advancement to the ear of its commander, the king of Italy. Latin-speaking, with civilian marriages and local property,[112] these soldiers of Italy offer considerable problems to anyone wanting to identify them as a homogeneous group with a single purpose.

the particularity of their church (see ch. 7, below). The African poem that calls a Germanic tongue Gothic may be evidence that names of languages did not match names of peoples, since there is no question that the Vandal royal family wished to disassociate themselves and their *gens* from the Goths.

[111] Procopius, BV 1(3).2.2–6, on which see ch. 4, below, pp. 141–2.

[112] Further instances of local marriages and property are examined in ch. 6.

Chapter 4

COMPLEMENTARY AND COMPETING IDEALS OF COMMUNITY: ITALY AND THE ROMAN EMPIRE

Other ideologies permeated the Italian air alongside the propaganda of the Gothic kings. In the secular world, the ethnographic labels "Roman" and "Goth" derived much of their power and importance from a political structure: the Roman Empire. But the Empire was changing faster than ideological rhetoric. For Italians, the presence of another Roman Empire in the East vied with ancient ethnographic and political ideas that Italy and Rome *were* the Roman Empire, ideas, in addition, cultivated by Theoderic under *civilitas*. Among elites, this paradox produced a delayed and ambivalent reaction to the *renovatio* ideology of Justinian, an ideology itself bound up not only with the idea of Rome but also with the notion of a Christian Empire.

The different Eastern and Western perceptions of Empire and ethnography reacted in various ways with the ideologies of Ravenna amidst the realities of Italian society, producing a multitude of ideas about the continuation or disruption of the Roman world. Historians once thought that the equation of the fall of the Western Empire with the advent of Odoacer, the first barbarian ruler in Italy, in 476, originated in the minds of the proudest senatorial families in Rome under Theoderic in the 510s and 520s, particularly that of Boethius's father-in-law, the historian Symmachus.[1] Recent work has demolished this thesis entirely. The emphasis on 476 first appears in the Chronicle of Marcellinus *comes*, the Illyrian secretary to Justinian, who composed it in the East in the 520s.[2] The year 476 was an Eastern fixation.

More recently, Bruno Luiselli has argued that no matter how minor the impact of the events of 476, the Eastern and Western elites between 450 and 526 came to think of a "fall" or an "end" to the Roman

---

[1] M. A. Wes, *Das Ende des Kaisertums im Westen des römischen Reiches* (The Hague, 1967), building on Wilhelm Ensslin, *Des Symmachus Historia Romana als Quelle für Jordanes*, Sitzungsberichte der Bayerischen Akademie der Wissenschaften, philosophisch–historische Abteilung 1948.3 (Munich, 1948).

[2] Stefan Krautschick, "Zwei Aspekte," pp. 344–71; Brian Croke, "A.D. 476: the manufacture of a turning point," *Chiron* 13 (1983), 81–119; and G. Zecchini, "Il 476 nella storiografia tardoantica," *Aevum* 59 (1985), 3–23, are all now accepted by current historiography, e.g. Moorhead, *Theoderic*, p. 159 with n. 94.

Empire.[3] In fact, the notion of a "fall" had existed for decades in various circles both Christian and secular, the natural result of the late Roman reverence for the past, the rhetoric of *renovatio* and Christian millenarianism.[4] Region and period determined different uses of the notion of a "fall": the reactions of Sidonius Apollinaris in southern Gaul in the 460s and 470s are qualitatively different from those of Ennodius in Italy in the 500s or those of Justinian in Constantinople in the late 520s.

No single political or ethnographic conception of the Roman Empire was ever accepted by all the elites of the Mediterranean. Different local literary, ideological, material and (as we shall see in chapter 6) religious conditions affected the meaning of the word "Roman," and hence the entire mental construction of ideal community and governance in the various provinces of the Empire and its successor-states. These ideals both affected and were affected by the political ideologies of the time. In turn, the appearance of such ideals in literary work shed instructive light on the personal mentalities of the people who wrote literature in the period, and serve as a valuable series of case-studies on the importance of ethnography and Romanity in the sixth-century Mediterranean.

CLASSICAL ETHNOGRAPHIC LITERATURE IN SIXTH-CENTURY ITALY

References and manuscript subscriptions show that classical ethnographic texts continued to find an audience in early sixth-century Italy. The last proof that Tacitus's *Germania* was being read in the West for three centuries comes from a reference in Cassiodorus's *Variae*.[5] Either Cassiodorus or Theoderic filled the royal letters with digressions on geography.[6] A royal official, Flavius Rusticius Helpidius Domnulus,

---

[3] Luiselli, *Storia culturale dei rapporti tra mondo romano e mondo germanico*, pp. 489–511.

[4] There were earlier notions of decline, for example pagan and Augustinian reactions to the sack of Rome in 410, on which see Peter Brown, *Augustine of Hippo* (London, 1967), pp. 291–3. The first articulated written statement that the Roman Empire had "fallen," however, comes from Zosimus, an Eastern writer, *c.* 500: Walter Goffart, "Zosimus, the first historian of Rome's fall," [1971] reprinted in *Rome's Fall and After*, pp. 96–8. On Zosimus, see below, p. 138 with nn. 166–7.

[5] *Var.* 5.2.2; F. Haverfeld, "Tacitus during the late Roman period and the Middle Ages," *Journal of Roman Studies* 6 (1916), 199; Walter Goffart, "The supposedly 'Frankish' table of nations: an edition and study," [1983] reprinted in Goffart, *Rome's Fall and After*, p. 153.

[6] Staab, "Ostrogothic geographers," pp. 55–7. Decades later at Vivarium, Cassiodorus recommended only two works of geography to his monks: the *Cosmographia* of Ptolemy, and Iulius Orator (on "maria, insulas, montes famosos, provincias, civitates, flumina, gentes"): *Institutiones* 1.25.1–2, ed. R. A. B. Mynors (Oxford, 1937). Cassiodorus may have encountered these works only in Constantinople, however, where he was doing research for the *Institutiones*; Averil Cameron, "Cassiodorus deflated," *Journal of Roman Studies* 71 (1981), 185.

produced a copy of the influential climatic ethnography of Pomponius Mela.[7] He also copied the *De fluminibus* of Vibius Sequester, a fourth- or fifth-century pedagogic list of "rivers, springs, lakes, forests, swamps, mountains and *gentes*."[8] It is a typical combination and ordering of topics in ethnogeography, but the section on *gentes* does not distinguish between those within and without the Roman Empire.[9]

Both the work of Mela and the *Natural History* of Pliny come down to us through fifth- and sixth-century Italian manuscripts.[10] A translation of a pseudo-Hippocratic medical text on foods produced in Italy at this time begins with a description of the regions of the world and how extreme climates affect growth and characteristics.[11] Three geographers, at the court of Theoderic in Ravenna,[12] produced what seems to have been a vast geographic survey of the known world, drawing on traditional ethnographic theory[13] and adding new information on distant regions apparently drawn from eyewitnesses.[14]

In some of the court activity we can perhaps perceive some of the fundamental changes in ethnographic conception bequeathed by the fifth century. The geographers at Theoderic's court did not distinguish clearly between Roman provinces and barbarian nations, between *patriae* and *gentes*.[15] Similar notions prevail in the "table of nations" that

[7] L. D. Reynolds (ed.), *Texts and Transmission: A Survey of the Latin Classics* ([1983], corrected reprint, Oxford, 1986), p. 290; PLRE s.n. Domnulus 2, pp. 374–5. Domnulus was *comes consistorianus*. On Pomponius Mela, see Müller, *Geschichte der antiken Ethnographie* 2: 123–37.

[8] Vibius Sequester, *De fluminibus, fontibus, lacubus, nemoribus, paludibus, montibus, gentibus per litteras libellus*; purpose: *praef.*, p. 1; date: François Laserre, "Vibius Sequester," in *Der kleine Pauly* 5 (Munich, 1975), 1251–2; transmission: Reynolds, *Texts and Transmission*, p. 290.

[9] *De fluminibus* §§317–61.

[10] Reynolds, *Texts and Transmission*, pp. 290, 308 with n. 3.

[11] *De observantia ciborum* 1.1–4, ed. Innocenzo Mazzini, *Romanobarbarica* 2 (1977), 315–16; on the date and place, see Mazzini's introduction, pp. 293–8. On the influence of the Hippocratic corpus on climatic theory and ethnogeography, see Anderson in Tacitus, pp. xiii–xv.

[12] The "Ostrogothic geographers" Athanarid, Heldebald and Marcomir, known through the references of the Ravenna Cosmographer. On their time and place, see Staab, "Ostrogothic geographers," pp. 29–30, 46–54.

[13] For example, the description of Britain as swampy (Ravenna Cosmographer, ed. Joseph Schnetz, *Itineraria Romana* 2 [Leipzig, 1940], 4.39); or of the Danes as the fastest men of all nations (4.13).

[14] Staab, "Ostrogothic geographers," p. 46: some information on the Finns appeared for the first time here. The linguistic evidence provided by Staab (pp. 57–64) is restricted to Germanic spellings used for some names, indicating that the geographers used Germanic speakers for sources on northern Europe, easily available in a court frequented by Thuringian ambassadors, and not that they wrote in Gothic, as Staab would have it: the Ravenna Cosmographer 4.13 attributes a Latin poem about the Danes to the Gothic geographers.

[15] For example, Saxonia at Ravenna Cosmographer 4.17, Italia at 4.29, patria Frigonum at 4.23, and an odd combination of a Roman province and a group of internal barbarians, Spanoguasconia, at 4.41. The transmission of this evidence through the Cosmographer admittedly makes it difficult to evaluate properly.

may well have been produced somewhere in the Ostrogothic king-dom.[16] It derives thirteen *gentes*, including both *Gothi* and *Romani*, from Tacitus's three kings.[17] Perhaps some less educated subject of Theoderic produced it, his confusion of traditional ethnography resulting from the king's battering repetition of the governmental eth-nographic ideology.

The court geographers and the author of the "table of nations" also shared points in common with authors in the East, causing at least one scholar to see the table as originating in Byzantium and passing through Ostrogothic Italy. General exchange of ethnographic literature did take place. The compiler of the *Collectio Avellana* may have attached a trans-lation of a Greek compilation of Jewish ethnography to his collection of papal letters.[18] Jordanes, writing in Latin in Constantinople in the 550s, used recent Western sources like the histories of Cassiodorus and the patrician Symmachus.[19] Some aspects of the "table of nations," like the grouping of certain *gentes* with the Goths, are paralleled by Eastern sources like Cyril of Scythopolis (writing *c.* 556).[20] Further Eastern eth-nography and geography will be discussed below.

It is therefore difficult to disentangle sixth-century Italian ethno-graphic literature from general Mediterranean literary culture. Any div-ision must become even more illusory once the Gothic Wars begin. No text was produced in an intellectual vacuum. On the other hand, Italian use of this literature was different, since the two areas had already seen different political and ecclesiastical developments.

ENNODIUS: ITALY AND EMPIRE

One Italian conception absent in the East was the Western Empire as "real" Empire, containing Rome, the seat of *civilitas* and her republican

---

[16] It first survives in an Italian manuscript of the early ninth century, and was composed *c.* 520; see Goffart, "Table of nations," pp. 141, 152. I do not find Goffart's arguments for a Byzantine origin convincing (ibid., pp. 157–63); he allows for possible production in Ostrogothic Italy (p. 158).

[17] Goffart, "Table of nations," pp. 145–6, 150.

[18] Anonymous Latin translation of Epiphanius of Constantia, *Liber de XII gemmis rationalis summi sacerdotis Hebraeorum* = *Collectio Avellana* 244, ed. O. Guenther, CSEL 35.1–2 (Vienna, 1895–8), pp. 743–73. Guenther suggests that it was a later addition (p. 743, n.), but offers no reasons. But Epiphanius was bishop of Constantia, that is Tomi, on the Black Sea, in the province of Scythia, whence came the Scythian monks with whom so many of the letters in the *Avellana* are concerned. On the ethnographic information on Scythia contained within, see below, n. 131.

[19] Jordanes, *Getica* 1 (Cassiodorus), 83–8 (Symmachus).

[20] Goffart, "Table of nations," p. 156.

traditions. For the parvenu provincial Ennodius,[21] Theoderic's kingdom signified the rebirth of the Western Empire under better auspices, at a time when the Greeks had fallen into heresy.[22] Italy had suffered devastation and civil war during Ennodius's youth (part of which he spent in Gaul); it had become "the spoil of victors." Nonetheless, it remained the heart of the Roman world to Ennodius, no matter who was ruling it. When that ruler was also restoring Illyricum, southeastern Gaul, Raetia and Spain to Italy's hegemony, he was actually a restorer of Roman power.[23] This rhetoric remains so powerful that scholars can refer to Theoderic's "*reconquering* southern Gaul," as if the Ostrogothic kingdom had been the legitimate manifestation of the Roman Empire in 508.[24]

So if from Constantinople it looked as if the Western provinces had dropped away, from Ennodius's viewpoint it could look as if the Western Empire itself, having shrunk to the size of Italy, could regain its natural borders without any reference to the East. Whereas the Anonymus Valesianus and the *Liber Pontificalis*, looking back from the 540s, reconstructed Theoderic's early reign as a golden age, Ennodius thought that he was living in a *saeculum aureum*.[25] His world, moreover, was more than just a Catholic Rome.[26] As churchman, lawyer and courtier, he enthusiastically supported Theoderic's rule as the renaissance of a Western Roman polity, the seat of ancient law, piety and tradition.

Ennodius supported Theoderic. At least one of his works was written for the government. The *Panegyricus Theoderico regi dictus* speaks the same language as Cassiodorus's works of ethnographic ideology.[27] It propagated *civilitas* on behalf of Ravenna.[28]

---

[21] John Moorhead, "Boethius and Romans in Ostrogothic service," *Historia* 27 (1978), 607–8. He also notes that no evidence associates Ennodius with Cassiodorus: not all parvenus moved in the same circles or shared the same views. Similarly, Momigliano, "Cassiodorus and Italian culture of his time," p. 188.

[22] Ennodius's *Panegyricus* represented his own views as well as the royal ideology; panegyric is a dialogue between ruler and ruled. See ref. in n. 26.

[23] Näf, "Das Zeitbewuβtsein des Ennodius und der Untergang Roms," pp. 106–12, citing Ennodius, *Op.* 370 (*ep.* 8.1, to Boethius), p. 268, lines 13–14, and comparing it with *Pan.* and *Op.* 458 (*ep.* 9.30).

[24] PLRE2: 705, emphasis mine.

[25] Näf, "Das Zeitbewuβtsein des Ennodius," citing *Pan.* 93 (21), p. 214, line 20, and *Op.* 458 (*ep.* 9.30), p. 319, line 25.

[26] Contra Näf, ibid., p. 122, who seems to contradict his earlier findings here.

[27] Ennodius, *Pan.*

[28] Sabine MacCormack, "Latin prose panegyrics," in T. A. Dorey (ed.), *Empire and Aftermath: Silver Latin II* (London, 1975), pp. 154–91. MacCormack (190–1) has a low opinion of Ennodius's panegyric, but the following discussion suggests that it was rather more formally impressive than she allows.

Ennodius recited his panegyric before Theoderic in 507,[29] a year of preparation for war and a period during which the government was promoting ethnographic ideology with vigor. Ennodius's panegyric unites two aspects of ideal rulership around the recurring word *civilitas*. On the one hand, it portrays Theoderic as a classically educated man who defends Roman law, restores the cities of Italy and reigns as an emperor in a restored *res publica*. On the other hand, it depicts the king as a successful war-leader and leader of his people who, through his conquest of Odoacer and his victories against Byzantium and the Gepids in Pannonia, protects the continuing Empire of the Romans and restores to it its rightful possessions.

The narrative interleaves episodes proving Theoderic's embodiment of these twin virtues, classical rulership and military prowess. True, it opens with no reference to the Goths, addressing Theoderic as "princeps venerabilis,"[30] begging him to "salve status reipublicae,"[31] and praising Theoderic's Greek education: "Educavit te in gremio civilitatis Graecia praesaga venturi";[32] with a classical upbringing in Constantinople, Theoderic was imbued with *civilitas* at an early age. But then Ennodius alternates between descriptions of Theoderic's military victories and of his achievements in rebuilding Italy and celebrating Roman law.[33]

Several themes from Cassiodoran rhetoric crop up. Theoderic's signal military achievement is his ability to protect Italy by cowing the nations, something Odoacer could not do.[34] In contrast, the Goths do not share the unpredictable and fierce characteristics of these peoples: they are a bulwark of strength, "Getici instrumenta roboris."[35] The Goths are identical to Theoderic's army.

---

[29] The traditional date; Sundwall prefers, more vaguely, 504–8 (*Abhandlungen*, pp. 42–3); McCormick suggests "perhaps in the spring of 507," *Eternal Victory*, p. 276.

[30] Ennodius, *Pan.* 1 (1).

[31] Ibid., 5 (2).

[32] Ibid., 11 (3).

[33] Ibid., 19–21 (5): victories over the Bulgars; 23–7 (6): the sad condition of Italy prior to Theoderic's arrival; 28–35 (7): victories over the Bulgars; 36–47 (8): war against Odoacer; 48 (9): apostrophe to Roma; 49–55 (10): Italy had suffered under Odoacer who unlike Theoderic could not control the barbarian peoples; 56–9 (11): Theoderic's policy of rebuilding; 60–73 (12–15): his military campaigns regaining lands from the Gepids, Alamanni and Vandals for Rome; 74–81 (16): his adherence to law and religion, like an emperor; 83–6 (19): the Goths protect Italy's leisure; 87–8 (20): most gloriously of all, Theoderic defends the law when he has finished the need for weapons.

[34] Ibid., 19 (5): the Bulgar ruler prostrate; 28–9 (7) the *audax gens* of the Gepids flees; 53 (10): hordes of Heruls tamed; 54 (10): Burgundians forced into treaty; 70 (13): Vandal depredations stopped; 72 (15): Alamanni peacefully absorbed. Hence 59 (11): "otia nostra magni regis sollicitudo custodit"; similarly, 87–8 (20).

[35] Ibid., 83 (19).

Like the senate or the emperor, Theoderic is the "vindex libertatis."[36] He is more than a successful general. Cato the Censor does not compare to him in military valour or even in *sapientia*.[37] He has raised cities from the ruins and roofed them "sub civilitate" with palatial generosity. He has rejuvenated Rome, that very mother of cities.[38] "Exhibes robore vigilantia prosperitate principem, mansuetudine sacerdotem."[39] It is a strange thing that Theoderic does not possess the proper names which victors were called of old. "My king should be by law called Alamannicus, but another is called by that name" – that is, the Byzantine emperor.[40] Most importantly, Theoderic preserves *civilitas* by ensuring the rule of law after he has finished defending it by arms.[41]

Ennodius emphasizes war and victory. Although he praises Constantinople as the cradle of *civilitas*, his bitterness against the emperor is clear in the section on the victory title "Alamannicus." The persistent attribution of quasi-imperial titles, let alone imperial character traits, suggest that the panegyric was recited at a time of tension with Byzantium.[42]

But Byzantium is not the only enemy: Theoderic is *victor* over the other *gentes*. The years 506–7 were the years of Theoderic's diplomatic letters to Clovis, Hermanafrid, Alaric and Gundobad, all attempting to avert war. The repeated emphasis on the ability of the Goths both to secure Italy and to restore her former imperial borders demonstrates an awareness of the impending conflict: the government knew that the fragile peace reigning around the kingdom of the Franks could not last long. The many descriptions of the recent Gothic successes in Raetia and in Pannonia Sirmiensis serve a similar purpose. The panegyric means to stir up its audience to patriotic support of further campaigns, and to raise the morale of the army, and of generals like Pitzia, in preparation for more war.

Impending war: this is the context of Ennodius's *Panegyricus*. How do the ethnographic attributes of the recital fit into this framework, and how do they compare with the *civilitas* ideology as expressed by

---

[36] Ibid., 42 (8).
[37] Ibid., 30 (7): Cato dealt merely with civil war, while Theoderic has restored the standing of Rome.
[38] Ibid., 56 (11).
[39] Ibid., 80 (17).
[40] Ibid., 81 (17): "Rex meus sit iure Alamannicus, dicatur alienus." Alienus = Anastasius: Ludo Moritz Hartmann, *Geschichte Italiens im Mittelalter* I (2nd edn, Stuttgart, 1923), p. 167, n. 11; Moorhead, *Theoderic*, p. 47 with n. 61. Anastasius did bear this title: Anastasius I, *ep.* "Si vos liberique" (Thiel, pp. 765–6). Chapter 6 discusses this letter further: below, p. 209 with n. 62.
[41] Ibid., 87–8 (20).
[42] McCormick, *Eternal Victory*, pp. 276–8. This tension probably went back at least to 504 (Moorhead, *Theoderic*, pp. 174–5, 182–8).

Cassiodorus around the same time? The panegyric does not refer to a functional division between Goths and Romans. Nevertheless, the recurring emphasis on the dual role of the king, appropriate for a panegyric, implies a functional division of his subjects. To be sure, the king's chief achievements are his victories over other nations, but these all serve the goal of keeping the people of Italy in peace. Since the king's army is identified as the Goths, the rest of the population, never called Romans, but associated with the ancient traditions of the city of Rome, consists of the grateful civilians.

The emphasis on royal victory serves the political needs of the moment. But the king is more than a mere war-leader. Imbued with *civilitas* through his upbringing, he repairs the ancient cities of Italy, respects religion, and ensures the rule of *ius* and *leges* after his conquests. In fact, he fulfills the role of a Roman emperor, governing through separate but reciprocal military and civilian administrations, uniting arms with law. As we have seen, Ennodius's language and import describe Theoderic as an emperor, without ever using the forbidden title Augustus.

Civilitas: the word derives from *cives* and *civilis*. It evokes the urban civilization of the Romans and its superiority through its propagation of *ius civile*, the civil law. Quintilian used it to mean "the art of government" and statesmanship, a translation of the Greek *politikē*.[43] Quintilian's *Institutes* formed the end of a gentleman's rhetorical training,[44] and since Ennodius adverted to Quintilian in a *dictio* on law,[45] he was familiar with his works. The opposite of *civilitas* in Quintilian's time, of course, was not Cassiodorus's *gentilitas*, which only received its meaning of "heathenism" and thus of "barbarity" in the ecclesiastical writers of the fifth century.[46] But by traditional implication, *civilitas*'s urban culture, knowledge of governance and basis in the law were alien to the barbarian.[47]

Ennodius was thus aware of the rhetorical paradox of making *civilitas* the prime characteristic of Theoderic's rulership. It stems from the king's upbringing in Constantinople and his promulgation and support of law. *Civilitas* is born in his education, blossoms with his consulship

---

[43] Quintilian, *Institutiones Oratoriae* 2.15.25; 2.15.33; 2.17.14, ed. Ludwig Radermacher, 2 vols. (Leipzig, 1965).
[44] Riché, *Education and Culture*, pp. 6, 40.
[45] Ennodius, *op.* 363 (*Dictio* 21), §§1–2.
[46] *Thesaurus linguae Latinae* (Leipzig, 1900–), 6.2, s.v., col. 1873, lines 46–53 (= *barbari* first in Ammianus); col. 1873, lines 59–63 (= "multitude of pagans" in Lactantius); col. 1874, lines 25–33 (= "barbarian pagans or heretics" in Ambrose, Rufinus et al.).
[47] Dauge, *Le barbare*, pp. 436–9, 534–6, 622–3.

of 484 in Byzantium, appears in his restoration of Rome and of the Italian cities, and finally in his zealous application of law.[48] In between each of these references occur the catalogues of Theoderic's successful battles, the praise of his generals and the valor of the Gothic army. Ennodius highlights each reference to *civilitas* with an attention-grabbing phrase,[49] and each reference serves to introduce a laudatory section on Theoderic's civilian policy, ending with his judicious mixture of *arma* and *lex*.

The whole structure of the panegyric, then, despite its topical emphasis on Gothic military achievement, links the king's wars with his Roman statesmanship in governing conquered Italy. Theoderic defends *civilitas* as a general, and embodies and restores it like an emperor. Despite the paradox from a classical point of view, the two forms of rulership are intertwined inextricably. The king as *auctor civilitatis*, ruling over two different but interdependent peoples, a rule based as much on valor in war as on Roman law and virtues of governance. Ennodius's letters to other representatives of the royal government function in the same way: they tell them what they want to hear. In a famous letter to Liberius, then praetorian prefect of Gaul, and a firm supporter of Ostrogothic government from its inception until the run-up to the Gothic wars,[50] Ennodius praises him for his earlier engineering of the Gothic settlement. "You have enriched the countless hordes of Goths with generous grants of lands, and yet the Romans have hardly felt it. The victors desire nothing more, and the conquered have felt no loss."[51]

The references to the "victors" and the "conquered" might imply a hierarchical relationship between Goths and Romans, yet this is not the point of Ennodius's letter. He goes on to praise Liberius for his conquest of Provence and the Narbonnais for Italy (508–10). "After many circles of years, you have brought *civilitas* to those who, before you, did not taste the savour of Roman liberty . . ."[52] This is an extraordinary statement to make about southern Gaul, which had been under

---

[48] Ennodius, *Pan.* 11 (3); 15 (4); 56 (11); 87 (20).

[49] References as for previous note: "Educavit te . . ." (after a long section on the edges of the civilized world known to Theoderic); "quis hanc civilitatem credat inter familiares tibi vivere plena executione virtutes?" Then "Trahit me ad aliam partem verabilium pars magna meritorum;" and finally, "Sed inter proeliares forte successus . . ., civilitatis dulcedini nil reservas?"

[50] PLRE2 Liberius 3, pp. 677–9; O'Donnell, "Liberius the patrician," pp. 31–72; see further ch. 5.

[51] Ennodius, *op.* 447 (*ep.* 9.23), §5, trans. Goffart, *Barbarians and Romans*, p. 70. Note the arguments of Goffart relating to this letter: pp. 70–6, 100: if he is right that it really describes tax-allocations rather than lands, then the letter further attests the functional division between *Gothi* and tax-paying Romans.

[52] Ennodius, ibid. §6, my translation; ". . . quibus civilitatem post multos annorum circulos intulisti, quos ante te non contigit saporem de Romana libertate gustare . . ."

Roman governance within living memory.[53] Moreover, Ennodius himself was of Gallic descent and had been born there. He is stating a
hyperbolic argument.

The rhetorical conception of the letter is that Italy has brought *civilitas*
and *libertas* to Gaul. Ennodius does not identify Italy as the Roman
Empire, or, except by implication, as the kingdom of Theoderic.[54] It
is, however, the seat of the Roman virtues of *civilitas* and *libertas*, not
an original conception, as we saw from the letters of Cassiodorus.
Moreover, Italy, about to welcome back Liberius,[55] is the grateful land
where Romans and Goths live in peace by the arrangements of reciprocal taxation devised, or at least implemented, by Liberius himself. The
conjunction of the reference to the Gothic settlement with the conquest
of Gaul by Italy cannot be accidental. The consensual values evoked
are those emphasized as primary goals of the royal government by Cassiodorus. Although the conception of two ethnographic groups living
together in peace is not the chief focus of this letter, it is tellingly
assumed to be a component of Italy's good government. Ravenna ideology again seeps through contemporary writings.

Even as a churchman and private individual, Ennodius believed in
civilitas and the continuing Western Empire. His *Vita Epifani* describes
a more restricted world than classical geography had done. One of the
only nearly contemporary[56] narratives of Italian events *c.* 460–500, it
shows no awareness of an end to the Western Empire.[57] Composed in
a rhetorical and encomiastic style, studded with rhetorical tropes, it was
intended for an educated audience.[58]

The *Vita* is also a witness to a related phenomenon: the emergence
of regional loyalties within the former Empire. Allegiance to the idea
of the West was partly a function of his identification with northern
Italy. In his depiction of Epiphanius's youth in the 460s, cities are the
major foci of loyalty and identity. Epiphanius "Ticinensis oppidi indi-

---

[53] Emilienne Demougeot, *La formation de l'Europe et les invasions barbares*, 2nd edn, 2 vols. (Paris,
1979), 2: 639–41: the cessions to Euric of the Auvergne, followed by the Arelate, fell in the
years 475–7. A 55-year-old man in 510 would have been an adult at the time of the cessions.
[54] The reference to the "potentissimus dominus" at Ennodius, ibid. §5.
[55] Ibid., §§6–7.
[56] Written in 503/4; Sundwall, *Abhandlungen*, p. 21.
[57] Näf, "Das Zeitbewuβtsein des Ennodius und der Untergang Roms," pp. 117–21.
[58] Augustin Dubois, *La latinité d'Ennodius* (Paris, 1903), pp. 18–19; Genevieve Marie Cook, trans.,
The Life of Saint Epiphanius by Ennodius, Studies in Medieval and Renaissance Language and
Literature 14 (Washington, 1942), p. 31. In occupying Italy, Theoderic "granted *Romanae libertatis ius;*" *Vita Epifani* (op. 80, opusc. 3) 122. The narrative is filled with praise of Theoderic,
"eminentissimus rex," "rex praestantissimus," etc., so it may have been written with the king
in mind as audience.

gena fuit."[59] The inhabitants of neighbouring cities like Milan are envi-
ous of Pavia for having received so virtuous a bishop.[60] We emerge
into the larger realm of politics and the *respublica* with the war between
Ricimer and Anthemius, but Ennodius revealingly describes these
events with the sentence "nutabat status periclitantis Italiae."[61] Whereas
Anthemius invokes the "amor reipublicae," Epiphanius calls the area
ruled by the Roman Emperor "vester regnum."[62] Similar attitudes prevail in the meeting with Euric in Toulouse, where the Italian prisoners
are called Romans, because, as Ennodius explains, they are from "Italia,
quo sit dominiorum antiquitas limitata confinio."[63] On the return of
Epiphanius, "light was restored to the waiting Italians."[64]

Italy is a geophysical entity, and *Romanus*, that conceptual, virtue-
laden realm, originates in the peninsula: Italy is a *sine qua non* for
Romans. In the *Vita Epifani*, the words "Ligurians" and "Italians" are
used far more frequently than "Roman;" the latter describes the superiority of the former.[65] "Romanus" can also describe superiority through
religion, although even this is related to geography. Thus the phrase
"catholicus et Romanus" is opposed to the "Graeculus" emperor
Anthemius,[66] and to the violent Rugi, who are associated with traditional topoi about the barbarians.[67] Catholic Italians are a fortunate
breed in Ennodius.

Ennodius's view of Eastern Romans as *Graeci* finds echoes in the
papal letters of Gelasius and those of the Western bishops in the Three
Chapters controversy, as well as Silverius's epitaph of his father Hormisdas.[68] In Burgundy, Avitus of Vienne referred to Anastasius as *Caesar
Graecorum* when he was not writing to the emperor himself.[69] Cassiodorus in the *Variae* remarked that the Greeks were known mainly for
their cunning.[70] The Goths' references to the Byzantines as "Greeks"

[59] Ennodius, *Vita Epifani* §7.
[60] Ibid., §§41–2.
[61] Ibid., §52.
[62] Ibid., §§65–7.
[63] Ibid., §88.
[64] Ibid., §94.
[65] e.g. ibid., §122: Italy is suffering because Theoderic will only allow "Romanae libertatis ius"
to those who support his side; signficantly, in pleading for a removal of these restrictions,
Epiphanius speaks only for "Liguria vestra" (§130). In the section on the Burgundians: "Audi
Italorum, supplicum voces;" "Audi Italiam, numquam a te divisam" (§157).
[66] See below, chapter 6, pp. 202–3, on the significance of this passage.
[67] Ibid., §117–18, "homines omni feritate immanes," not only in contrast to the "Romanus et
catholicus" Epiphanius, but also to the Goths.
[68] Below, chapter 6, pp. 213–4, 230–4.
[69] Avitus, *Contra Eutychianam haeresim* 1, ed. Rudolf Peiper, MGH: AA 6.2 (Berlin, 1883).
[70] *Var.* 5.40.5

in the concocted speeches in Procopius are surely based on knowledge of this Western usage.[71]

What we see in Ennodius is the breakdown in the ruling classes of a sense of climatically defined Mediterranean community and resurgence of the regional loyalties that lay beneath the surface of the cosmopolitan Roman gentleman. The ecclesiastical literature of 489 to 519 and beyond, examined in chapter 6, shows much the same phenomenon, for religious reasons, but with the same changes in ethnographic language. In Ennodius, Gelasius and the first edition of the *Liber Pontificalis* the new opposition of the geographical *Italia* with the linguistic *Graeci* appears repeatedly.[72] The term stresses the difference of the Easterners. If the East continued to see a divide between *Romani* and *Gothi* or *barbari* in the Western kingdoms, the inhabitants of those kingdoms were just as likely to distinguish themselves as *Itali* from the alien Greek-speakers of the East.

EUGIPPIUS: CHRISTIANITY, FRONTIERS AND EMPIRE

Eugippius, abbot of Lucullanum and an exact contemporary of Ennodius, also came from outside Italy but held different views about the state of the Roman Empire. He is the only writer in the West at this time to state that the Empire had come to an end at a previous date, unspecified, but in the 470s. Eugippius was part of the intellectual circle of Boethius and Dionysius Exiguus, with interests in Greek translation and contacts with the African Fulgentius. It is possible that he kept company with the deposed emperor Romulus Augustulus and his mother, now living in Lucullanum and dedicated to pious interests.[73]

Eugippius's views have thus been explained by the interests of his Italian friends.[74] However, Eugippius himself came from the border province of Noricum, and he implies that the Roman Empire had fallen because the garrison troops there were no longer being paid: "Per idem tempus, quo Romanum constabat imperium, multorum milites oppidorum pro custodia limitis publicis stipendiis alebantur."[75] Since no similar

[71] e.g. Procopius, BG 3(7).8.21, 9.10, 9.12.
[72] Below, chapter 6, pp. 199, 201–3, 208, 220.
[73] On Eugippius's connections with this circle, see Moorhead, *Theoderic*, pp. 207–10.
[74] Friedrich Lotter connects Eugippius's statement with Wes's thesis about Roman senatorial interest in 476: *Severinus von Noricum, Legende und historische Wirklichkeit*, Monographien zur Geschichte des Mittelalters 12 (Stuttgart, 1976), p. 207; Krautschick, "Zwei Aspekte," pp. 356–8, connects it with the possible nostalgic opinions of those around the former emperor Romulus. Lotter's acceptance of Wes unfortunately invalidates most of his conclusions on Eugippius (as opposed to Severinus).
[75] Eugippius, *VSeverini* 20.1.

concern ever appears in the writings of Dionysius or Boethius, it is more profitable to look at this statement as a reflection of Eugippius's personal experiences.[76]

Eugippius's personal history makes the *Vita Severini* a persuasive description of the end of Roman administration in a border province. Eugippius was a younger contemporary of Severinus, and an adult by the time of the evacuation of Noricum in 488.[77] He therefore experienced the suffering and destruction of Noricum himself, and his parents and friends had lived through the sackings and raids described in the *Vita*. The resulting tone of immediacy makes the narrative vivid and convincing. It may well be that Eugippius was scrupulous about maintaining the difference in his own and Severinus's attitudes toward barbarians: "It is a tribute to Eugippius that although he betrays his own prejudices, he does not allow them to distort his picture of his hero."[78]

In maintaining the observable difference between the views of Severinus in Noricum in the fifth century, and the related views of Eugippius in Italy in the early sixth, we must not lose track of the hagiographical purposes of the work. The "Romani" in the *Vita* are the Catholic inhabitants of the province,[79] the ones under Severinus's protection because their old support from Italy has vanished.[80] Victimized by the barbarians,[81] they are rescued by Odoacer and Pierius in 488 and evacuated en masse to Italy.[82]

Eugippius creates a rhetorical construction of Romanity in a frontier province, setting classical ethnographic terminology into the framework of the biblical persecution and exodus of a Christian people. Hence he makes frequent reference to Exodus, Genesis, the patriarchs and the Israelite escape from Egypt as a metaphor for the Roman escape from Noricum.[83]

Eugippius's text betrays the reality of which he may not have been conscious. His "Romans" are identical to the inhabitants of cities, which are not only the focus of threats from the Rugians, but also the centres of Christian belief.[84] Although he does not omit the hagiograph-

---

[76] R. A. Markus, "The end of the Roman Empire: a note on Eugippius, *Vita Sancti Severini*, 20," *Nottingham Medieval Studies* 26 (1982), 1–7.

[77] Lotter, *Severinus von Noricum*, pp. 22–31.

[78] Markus, "The end of the Roman Empire," p. 3.

[79] Eugippius, *VSeverini* 1.4; 27.1.

[80] Ibid., 20.1–2; 31.3–6.

[81] Ibid., 10.1–2.

[82] Ibid., 44.4–7.

[83] Ibid., 4.3 (Exodus); 40.5 (Genesis and the patriarchs), 43.1–2 (the patriarchs), 40.4 and 44.5 (the Israelite escape from Egypt).

[84] Ibid., 1.4, 31.6.

ical commonplace of the poor person aided by the saint, it is clear that Eugippius himself was well-educated and probably well-off, like his companions around the saint, and like his later friends in Italy.[85] Severinus wielded political influence in high places, despite the overlay of hagiographical topoi on this point.[86] Archaeology supports no large migration of people: the *Romani* who went to Italy with Odoacer were surely local elites and churchmen.[87]

Eugippius sees the end of the Roman Empire from the urban Christian point of view in Noricum. Like bishops in contemporary Gaul, Severinus was taking over the functions of provincial administration, including the conclusion of a new *foedus* with the Rugians. Since Eugippius situates this act against a gradual depiction of the collapse of the upkeep of imperial army garrisons,[88] for him the identification of Romans with urban Christians can only have been natural. Cities were decaying, contact with the collapsing imperial centre in Italy had vanished, and only saints were left to restore order.

These considerations call into question not only the identity of Eugippius's Norican Romans, but also his belief that the Roman Empire no longer still stood. On the first question, we can glimpse some "techniques of accommodation" between the Rugians and the Noricans. Severinus and King Feva discuss the fate of the Romans of Lauriacum, but not all of them, just the "Romani quos in sua sanctus Severinus fide susceperat."[89] They agree to distribute them through towns "benivola societate," a phrase that rings of Theoderic's *civilitas* in its functional sense.[90] We have already learned that one town, Comagenis, has its

---

[85] Note the *noblis presbyter* Primenius, a friend of Orestes, of *Ep. ad Paschasium* 8, and the *nobiles* around Severinus at *VSeverini* 32.2; Lotter would identify Severinus himself with the consul of 461: "Illustrissimus vir Severinus," *Deutsches Archiv* 26 (1970), 200–7; Lotter, *Severinus von Noricum*, pp. 223–60, though it remains difficult to explain why Eugippius would have professed ignorance of the saint's origin (*Ep. ad Paschasium* 7–11); E. A. Thompson, "The end of Noricum," in *Romans and Barbarians: The Decline of the Western Empire* (Madison, 1982), pp. 114, 117–18, rejects Lotter's thesis on this basis and on the problem of dates (convincing), but does not rule out a wealthy background for Severinus.

[86] Friedrich Prinz, *Frühes Mönchtum im Frankenreich: Kultur und Gesellschaft in Gallien am Beispiel der monastischen Entwicklung (4.–8. Jahrhundert)*, 1965, (augmented edition, Munich and Paris, 1988), p. 475; Markus, "The end of the Roman Empire," p. 2.

[87] Whittaker, *Frontiers*, p. 255. Walter Pohl warns me that archeology cannot prove or disprove migrations, with which I am fully in agreement. But the burden of proof here must surely be to demonstrate a large migration, which a close reading of Eugippius does not suggest. Aspects of archeological continuity and discontinuity in fifth-century Noricum have been well studied (see n. 110, below), but none of these need have anything to do with the withdrawal of thousands of people to Italy in the year 488.

[88] Markus, "The end of the Roman Empire," p. 4.

[89] Eugippius, *VSeverini* 31.6.

[90] E. K. Winter, *Studien zum Severinsproblem* (Klosterneuberg, 1959), pp. 434, 450.

own *foedus* with the barbarians, which restricts people's movements.[91] Since Feva's original goal was to add the Romans of Lauriacum to his *tributarii* towns, it seems clear that Romans were people who paid to support barbarians.[92] A subsequent remark makes clear that Feva's own people were an *exercitus*.[93]

It thus seems clear that some sort of conceptual functional division between *barbari* and *Romani* existed in Noricum in the 470s. Other remarks indicate that in the general conditions of lawlessness and confusion that prevailed, such arrangements were not always to the benefit of the unarmed.[94] The situation inadvertently revealed by Eugippius is more similar to that of Burgundy than of Ostrogothic Italy, where Ravenna overlaid such functional arrangements with a discourse of inherited cultural difference and peaceful consensus.[95]

Commentators have not noticed that Eugippius later seems to forget that he implied that the Roman Empire no longer existed. Severinus prophesies that the besieged "Romani" will migrate safely to a Roman province, without any loss of their *libertas*.[96] This "province," of course, turns out to be Italy, where Eugippius was living when he wrote this sentence, suggesting that in some ways he felt that he had escaped back into the Roman Empire.

But just because Italy was still a Roman province does not show that Eugippius shared the views of Ennodius and Cassiodorus. His only comment on Theoderic, then in Moesia, is neutral. Eugippius does not appreciate "barbarians," or, at any rate, the Rugians. Even when Rugians seek the advice of the saint, they get no accolades.[97] Although Odoacer orders the removal of the Roman population of Noricum to Italy, praise goes to the saint for prophesying the Romans' escape from "cotidiana barbarie frequentissima depraedatio."[98]

Eugippius's avoidance of praise for barbarian rulers is partly due to the hagiographical insistence on the inferiority of earthly honours.[99] But

---

[91] Eugippius, *VSeverini* 1.4.
[92] Ibid., 31.1.
[93] Ibid., 31.5.
[94] Ibid.
[95] Unlike in Ostrogothic Italy, the linguistic origin of names did not match profession or identity: we hear of a Catholic cleric named Bonosus, "genere barbarus" (Eugippius, *VSeverini* 35.1) and a soldier of the Rugian king Ferderuchus called Avitianus (44.2). Of course, exceptions occurred in Italy as well, although never openly among Catholic clergy. On names and soldiers in Italy, see chs. 3 and 5. On names and clergy in Italy, see ch. 7.
[96] Eugippius, *VSeverini* 31.6.
[97] Ibid., 5.1–4, 6.1–5, 8.1–6, 19.1–5, 40.1–6.
[98] Ibid., 44.5.
[99] Hence the prophecy of Odoacer's reign-length at 32.2, from Eugippius's vantage-point in 510 an ironic commentary on the transitoriness of earthly rule; cf. 5.2–4.

since humbler barbarian followers of the saint also receive short shrift,[100] one must conclude that Eugippius only sympathized with Noricans of his own background, who had suffered so much. An aura of supernatural menace and fate pervades the *Vita*. In the haunting scene where some desperate garrison soldiers finally decide to make the journey to Italy, after nothing is heard for a while, Severinus begins to weep. He declares that the river is sprinkled with blood, and indeed the bodies of the soldiers are found there, slain by the barbarians.[101]

Such imagery, without doubt chillingly real to Eugippius, creates an atmosphere of suffocating oppression. Eugippius's *Romani* are trapped creatures whose only support is their saint. The recital of doomed urban populations and abandoned cities concentrates the persecuted Romans more and more until, finally, escape appears in the form of exodus to Italy.

It is in the episode of the slaughtered garrison-soldiers that Eugippius refers to the fall of Roman power. Severinus's prophecy here, that the Roman soldiers have been killed, prepares us for his later prophecy that the Romans of Noricum will migrate to a Roman province after his death, the same chapter to imply that a Roman Empire still existed. The Roman Empire is part of the imagery of a Promised Land, lost to people for a generation, miraculously reappearing through divine intercession.

Eugippius was doubtless conscious of his literary structure. He may not have been so aware of his implications about the continuity of the Roman Empire. He was a religious man brought up in a distressed frontier society on the verge of collapse. Like his Norican *Romani*, he traveled to Italy to make a new life for himself, alongside the body of his venerated teacher. The *Vita Severini* shows the power of notions of classical ethnogeography: Italy is the center of civilization, which can only keep up Roman institutions on the northern frontier with the help of a centralized administration and army. When these go, the only remaining Romanity in Noricum is the Christian bishops and saints. Such notions lend themselves to providential interpretations: even the Roman cities perish; only Severinus and his followers finally remain. Eugippius's vantage point remains local, tied to his own provincial origin.

We might have expected Eugippius to support Theoderic, as the provincial Ennodius did, for restoring former provinces of the Western Empire to Italy. Theoderic did in fact reoccupy the southern Noricum

---

[100] Ibid., 6.5, where the "universa Rugorum gens" begins to consult Severinus regularly.
[101] Ibid., 20.

Mediterraneum, if not Noricum Ripense. But Eugippius's interests were wider than can be seen in the *Vita Severini*. Established at Lucullanum, he received a translation of Gregory of Nyssa from Dionysius Exiguus, prepared a selection of excerpts of St. Augustine, and corresponded with Fulgentius, Ferrandus and Proba.[102] When writing on his place of birth and the life of his teacher there, he imagined a disintegrating Empire and an embattled community led to salvation in Italy. The settled conditions in his new home allowed him to throw himself into the ecclesiastical and theological issues of the Catholic community of the Mediterranean, to the extent of debating theology with an Arian *"comes Gothorum."*[103] In the Italy of the 510s and 520s, the Norican problems were irrelevant to the new Christian opportunities available to churchmen with high-placed and overseas connections.

Involved as Eugippius was in circles of Greek intellectual interests, there appears in his text no political support for the Eastern emperor. The Rugian war of 487–8 that led to the Norican exodus may have been fomented by Zeno and the Byzantine court.[104] Despite his ethnogeographic picture of a crumbling Roman Empire in his homeland, Eugippius cannot have wanted the reinstallation of an emperor who had destroyed that homeland and who was in 510, moreover, heretical. Once more, we must avoid identifying religious or ethnographic views with political views.

The Italy within which Eugippius lived revered not only classical ethnogeography but also the writings of St. Augustine.[105] Eugippius himself produced a large compendium of selections of Augustine's work for the aristocratic virgin Proba, the sister of Boethius. Unlike Ennodius, who openly referred to Augustine as "the Libyan plague" and "the sandy snake" for his predestinarian doctrines, Eugippius considered Augustine's teaching on grace his most important work.[106] It was this

---

[102] Moorhead, *Theoderic*, 208–10; for Ferrandus, see n. 103.

[103] Ferrandus, *Epistula dogmatica adversus Arrianos alioque haereticos ad Eugippium* 1, ed. Angelo Mai, 1828, reprinted in PLS 4 (Paris, 1967), col. 24: Ferrandus was responding to a letter from Eugippius asking his opinion about how best to reply to the propositions put forth *ab arriano Gothorum comite*. See PA Anonymus 38.

[104] Michael McCormick, "Odoacer, the emperor Zeno and the Rugian victory legation," *Byzantion* 47 (1977), 212–22.

[105] On Augustine's writings in fifth-century Italy, see ch. 1; on the influence of Augustine on Gelasius and Hormisdas, and then again on the Western opponents of Justinian's legislation in the Three Chapters controversy, see ch. 6.

[106] Eugippius, *Excerpta ex operibus sancti Augustini*, ed. P. Knoell, CSEL 9.1 (Vienna, 1886), *praef.* (letter to Proba explaining the purpose of the compendium). Ennodius on Augustine: *Op.* 56 (*ep.* 2.19), §16, on which see Ralph W. Mathisen, "For specialists only: the reception of Augustine and his teachings in fifth-century Gaul," in *Augustine: Presbyter Factus Sum*, Collectanea Augustiniana, ed. Joseph T. Lienhard, Earl C. Muller and Roland J. Teske (New York, 1993), p. 33 with n. 24, attributing Ennodius's attitude to his Gallic ecclesiastical upbringing. I

very theology that led Augustine to suggest that grace could fall on all peoples, not just the citizens of the Roman Empire.[107] Eugippius included in his compendium that crucial chapter of the *City of God* that argued that the Church would spread to all peoples, *omnes gentes*.[108] He also included Augustine's interpretation of Thessalonians 1: 6–7 as a prophecy of the righteous downfall of the Roman Empire.[109] It is difficult to reconcile such beliefs with Eugippius's dismissive attitude toward the Rugians and barbarians in general, or with his equation of the Roman Empire with the Promised Land.

The *Vita Severini* only makes sense when read as the juxtaposition of two different kinds of rhetoric – ethnogeographic and Augustinian. The juxtaposition is effective. It may have been particularly so among Eugippius's well-educated, centrally located Italian audience. But we must not accept it as a realistic depiction of frontier life at the time of the disintegration of imperial administration on the Danube. It is obvious that Eugippius speaks as an inhabitant of cities, as a member of the educated elite, and as a Christian clergyman. It is just as obvious that his barbarians were defined as much by their profession of soldier as by the ethnographic names "Rugian" or "barbarian" – the former better seen as a political allegiance – and that his Romans included only a fraction of the non-military population of Noricum.

The little that we know about fifth-century Noricum outside Eugippius further suggests that not all the inhabitants shared Eugippius's views. The archeology of frontier zones shows a culture different from that of Mediterranean cities.[110] Like some of the "Romans" in the *Vita Severini*, frontier inhabitants could cooperate with barbarians, or with their equivalents, rebel generals and usurpers. The frontier soldiers had the duty of suppressing local unrest as much as keeping out barbarians. But sometimes they too took part in this unrest. In 430 and 431, Aetius

am grateful to Professor Mathisen for a copy of this article. Ennodius elsewhere cited Augustine approvingly, *Op.* 7 (*ep.* 1.4), §6 (the *Confessions*): apparently he only objected to the teachings on grace, a common standpoint in fifth-century Gaul.

[107] See ch. 1, n. 48.

[108] Eugippius, *Excerpta ex operibus sancti Augustini* 129 (use of *De civitate dei* 20.11, rebutting attempts to use classical ethnography to predict the coming of the Antichrist).

[109] Eugippius, *Excerpta ex operibus sancti Augustini* 131, esp. p. 475, lines 4–26.

[110] Romanization and Christianization changed Noricum without making it into a copy of other Western provinces, and the removal of imperial administration, as in Britain, removed much Romanizing culture; there were, moreover, regional differences within Noricum: Geza Alföldy, *Noricum*, trans. Anthony Birley (London, 1974), pp. 133–42, 213–27; Johann Haberl and Christopher Hawkes, "The last of Roman Noricum: St Severin on the Danube," in Christopher Hawkes and Sonia Hawkes (eds.), *Greeks, Celts and Romans*, Archaeology into History: Series 1 (London, 1973), pp. 97–149; Erich Zöllner, "Zusammenfassung: Noricum und Raetia I," in *Von der Spätantike zum frühen Mittelalter*, pp. 255–61, esp. 259 on specifically Pannonian and Norican forms of castles.

had to suppress an uprising of *Nori* – not *Romani* – in Noricum with military force.[111] Margin and centre could hold different views on the size and classification of political community.[112] Eugippius writes from the unusual standpoint of an educated man who has moved from margin to center.

VITALIAN, THE SCYTHIAN MONKS AND DIONYSIUS EXIGUUS: MEDITERRANEAN VIEWS OF THE BALKAN FRONTIERS

If the inhabitants of old Roman frontier provinces could look to post-imperial Italy as a safe and civilized hub despite its barbarian rulers, Mediterranean people no longer knew how to classify areas on the margin. This is particularly evident in their confused understanding of the peoples of the Balkans and Thrace, the areas from which Theoderic and his followers had come.

"Scythian" had designated any barbarian people from the area northeast of Greece since the days of Herodotus, and could still be used of Huns, Goths or Bulgars in the fifth and sixth centuries A.D. We cannot always tell to which group it referred, particularly when it is used to describe an individual. The suspicion arises that some of these sources did not know how to classify the individual in question. Worse, the Roman province north of Thrace (today Dobrudja on the Black Sea) had gained the name "Scythia minor." Inhabitants of this province could also be called Scythians.

Some of the provincial Scythians came to Italy, Dionysius Exiguus, and later his friends, the Theopaschite monks.[113] Their origins required excuses.[114] Dionysius, who shared the theological orientation of the Scythian monks, wrote to them that "Scythia, which is proved to be terrible both for its cold and its barbarians, has led forth men always burning with heat and marvellous in the placidity of their manners."[115] In complimenting the monks, he brings together an ethnographical topos about barbarians, who come from cold climes and cannot govern

---

[111] Hydatius, *Chron.* 93, 95; Sidonius, *Carm.* 7.233; Alföldy, *Noricum*, p. 214.

[112] Whittaker, *Frontiers*, p. 242.

[113] On the following, see further PA Dionysius, Iohannes 3 and Leontius.

[114] Cassiodorus, *Institutiones* 1.23.2, recommends the works of Dionysius, "Scytha natione, sed moribus omnino Romanus." Is it significant that Dionysius directly follows Eugippius (1.23.1) in this work?

[115] Dionysius Exiguus, *Ep. ad Iohannem et Leontium*, dedicatory letter to his translation of Cyril of Alexandria's letter to Successus, ed. Eduard Schwartz, ACO 4.2, Concilium Universale Constantinopolitanum sub Iustiniano habitum 2 (Strasbourg, 1914), p. xi.

themselves as civilized men can. He also admits Scythia as a home of barbarians.

Such comments might be dismissable as rhetoric, assimilating Herodotus's Scythia with the Roman province for the sake of a *bon mot*. But elsewhere we discover that the Scythian monks were associated with the eastern general and rebel Vitalian,[116] perhaps of his family,[117] and a third source describes Vitalian as a "Goth."[118] Past commentators have used this information, without further evidence, to class the Scythian monks as Goths,[119] or to explain the rapprochement between Vitalian and Theoderic in 515 as the result of their shared ethnic heritage.[120]

The situation is, however, even more complex. Vitalian is only called a "Goth" by a Syriac source, and appears in Greek and Latin ones as "Scytha."[121] Whereas Evagrius states that Vitalian commanded Huns, in Malalas these successively appear as "Huns and Bulgars," "Huns and Goths," and "Gothic, Hunnic and Scythian soldiers."[122] Malalas elsewhere connects "Scythians" with "Goths and Bessoi," the latter a classical ethnographical division of Thrace, so it is no surprise to find that he calls Vitalian a "Thracian."[123] Malalas was also aware of the history of the classical Scythians, explaining that 15,000 of them traveled to

---

[116] On whom see further PA **Vitalianus** 1.

[117] Dioscorus, *ep.* "Verum est," to Hormisdas (*Avellana* 216 = Thiel, pp. 868–71), §§2–3, p. 869.

[118] Zacharias, *Historia Ecclesiastica* 7.13; 8.2, ed. and trans. E.W. Brooks, *Corpus scriptorum Christianorum orientalium*, 3.6 (London, 1919–24).

[119] Viktor Schurr, *Die Trinitätslehre des Boethius im Lichte der "skythischen Kontroversen,"* Forschungen zur christlichen Literatur- und Dogmengeschichte 18.1 (Paderborn, 1935), pp. 142–3; Berthold Altaner, "Zum Schrifttum der 'skythischen' (gotischen) Mönche: quellenkritische und literarhistorische Untersuchungen," 1953, reprinted in Altaner, *Kleine patristische Schriften*, ed. Günter Glockmann, Texte und Untersuchungen 83 (Berlin, 1967); Chadwick, *Boethius*, p. 186.

[120] Notably Eduward Schwartz, *Publizistische Sammlungen zum Acacianischen Schisma* (Munich, 1934), pp. 249–51, 261–2; he translates "in Scythiae partibus" as "in der Gothenprovinz," p. 250, and defines Vitalian as "ein reichsuntertäniger Gothe," p. 249 with n. 2. Even more fancifully, Ludwig Schmidt defines Vitalian and the Scythian monks as Goths who stayed behind when Theoderic went to Italy: "Das germanische Volkstum in den Reichen der Völkerwanderung," *Historische Vierteljahrschrift* 29 (1934), 434–5.

[121] Evagrius, *Historia Ecclesiastica* 3.43, ed. J. Bidez and L. Parmentier (London, 1898); Marcellinus comes s.a. 514. Priscian, *De laude Anastasii imperatoris* 298–9, simply calls Vitalian and his troops *Scythicas gentes*; ed. Emil Baehrens, *Poetae latini minores* 5 (Leipzig, 1883).

[122] John Malalas, *Chronographia* 402, 404–5, ed. Ludwig Dindorf (Bonn, 1831), trans. Elizabeth Jeffreys, Michael Jeffreys and Roger Scott (Melbourne, 1986). Malalas 402 may be the source for Georgius Cedrenus, *Compendium Historiarum*, ed. Immanuel Bekker, 2 vols. (Bonn, 1838–9), 1: 632, lines 9–12, who also says that Vitalian commanded Huns and Bulgars, and occupied Thrace, Scythia and Moesia. On Cedrenus, see Roger Scott, "The Byzantine chronicle after Malalas," in *Studies in John Malalas*, ed. Elizabeth Jeffreys, Brian Croke and Roger Scott, Byzantina australiensia 6 (Sydney, 1990), p. 47.

[123] Ibid., 402. Similarly, note Ioannes Scytha, *magister militum per Orientem* from 483 to 498, cos. 498, whom Theophanes says commanded Thracians: PLRE2, s.n. Ioannes 34.

Egypt in the time of Sostris: "these Scythians have remained in Persia from that time to the present day; they were called by the Persians Parthians, which in the Persian language means Scythians. They preserve the dress, language and laws of the Scythians to the present day."[124]

A state of confusion reigned not only about the meaning of "Scythian" but also about the identities of the people who lived in Thrace. Born in nearby Lower Moesia, Flavius Vitalianus himself became *magister militum per Thracias* and launched several attacks from that region on Anastasius's Constantinople. He commanded the loyalty of the troops in that area and also that of the bishops, who were happy to rejoin the communion of Rome under his guidance three years before the resolution of the Acacian schism with the rest of the East. Although his father's name was Patriciolus, two of his sons had Thracian names and one had a Germanic name. His nephew, who was called John, was to play a major role under Belisarius in the Gothic Wars in Italy, alongside many generals called "Thracian," "Bessoi" or "Goths" by Procopius.[125]

An African annalist had a solution to this difficulty: Vitalian's distant troops were *barbari*.[126] Classical ethnography implied this equation: the general's followers were of diverse origins, one source calling them *foederati*.[127] They came from the uttermost corner of the Roman Empire, the provinces of Scythia and Thrace, or from beyond it, the Scythia of the ethnographers. Things looked similar to a Syriac author.[128]

The papal legates in Constantinople were willing to trust Vitalian, a clear papal ally, but not his monkish followers, about whom they professed constant suspicion. Even before Theopaschitism had become a problem, Dioscorus says that the Scythian monk Leontius merely "*calls himself a relative of the general.*" The bishops Germanus and Johannes write that they have met a Stephanus *comes*, who, "*as it is said*, is related to your son the general Vitalian."[129] Later on, after Dioscorus has recognized the danger of the monks' formula and their opposition to their

---

[124] Ibid., 26.
[125] PA **Vitalianus** 1, **I**ohannes 2; on the identity of Balkan soldiers in the Gothic Wars, see PA III, table 13 and table 2 commentary, PA **B**essas, Herodianus, with discussion in ch. 3 above and ch. 5 below.
[126] Victor Tonnennensis, *Chronica* s.a. 514. Victor traveled to Constantinople, and composed his chronicle there.
[127] John of Antioch, fr. 214e 1.
[128] Zacharias, *Historia Ecclesiastica* 8.2.
[129] Dioscorus, *ep.* "Verum est," §2, p. 869; Germanus and Johannes, *ep.* "In civitate Aulonitana," to Hormisdas (*Avellana* 213 = Thiel, pp. 849–51), §3, p. 851 (early March and 30 May 519 respectively). Emphasis added.

bishop, he expresses grave doubts about the position of their leader Maxentius: although he calls himself "abbot," he cannot say where his congregation is or in what monastery or under which abbot he himself became a monk.[130]

Little wonder that Dionysius could joke to the Scythian monks about their cold, barbarous homeland. From the Mediterranean perspective, it was an unknown region full of people of different identities.[131] But neither Dionysius nor the monks could be described as barbarians. Nor did either of them express any kinship with the Arian Goths who ruled Italy. Dionysius translated Greek texts for the West and produced collections of canon law; the monks prosecuted their case successfully with Vitalian and then with his enemy Justinian, if not with the pope. In his description of his experiences in Rome, Johannes the Scythian monk divides the world by regions: he is a Scythian, like Dionysius, because he comes from Scythia; Faustus of Riez is *Gallus*; Rome's fame is due to the papal see.[132] The monks distanced themselves from Arianism, but for doctrinal reasons, not because of any fear of being identified with the Goths of Italy.[133]

In fact, despite the chaos prevailing in the Balkans, the region, long since Latinized, was a centre for the production of Latin theological

---

[130] Dioscorus, *ep.* "Per Eulogium," to Hormisdas (*Avellana* 224 = Thiel, pp. 894–6), §4, p. 896 (15 October 519).

[131] As we have seen, when the *Collectio Avellana* was produced in mid-sixth-century Italy, someone attached a translation of the *Liber de XII gemmis* of the fourth-century bishop Epiphanius of Constantia (above, n. 18), the home of the Scythian monks. The text (§36, p. 753) explains that "the ancients were accustomed to call the seven northern beaches 'Scythia', where there are *Gothi et Dauni, Venni quoque et Arii usque ad Germanorum Amazonarum regionem*." "Arii" is very odd, and otherwise only attested in Tacitus, *Germania* 43 as living in the same region (otherwise in Persia: Lewis and Short s.v. Aria, p. 160, from Arrian, Strabo and Ptolemy); the association with *Germani*, for centuries now only associated with the Rhineland, is more evidence for the circulation of the *Germania*. The Amazons and Goths had long been associated with Scythia, of course, and were connected by the exactly contemporary Jordanes at this time. Ethnogeography had found its way into biblical and Hebraic ethnography and mysticism, which then traveled from Scythia to Italy. The appending of this translation to the *Avellana*, with its material on the Scythian monks (including the suspicious letters of Dioscorus), is more evidence for sixth-century Mediterranean ethnographic curiosity and confusion about Scythia and Scythians.

[132] Iohannes monachus Scytha, *Responsio adversus Hormisdae epistulam* 36–7, ed. Eduard Schwartz, ACO 4.2 = Concilium Universale Constantinopolitanum sub Iustiniano habitum 2 (Strasbourg, 1914), pp. 54–5. Schwartz identified this Johannes (the Scythian monk) with his abbot Maxentius, but F. Glorie has demonstrated that the two were different people, that this Johannes composed the *responsio* to Hormisdas, while Maxentius wrote the *Dialogi contra Nestorianos* (cited in next note), in his *Maxentii aliorumque Scytharum monachorum necnon Ioannis Tomitanae urbis episcopi Opuscula*, CCSL 85A, Scriptores "Illyrici" minores (Turnhout, 1978), pp. xl–xli.

[133] The Theopaschite formula was compared to Arianism by Trifolius: see below, ch. 6, n. 95. On distancing from Arianism, see Maxentius, *Dialogi contra Nestorianos* 2, ed. Schwartz, ACO 4.2: 39.

works. The Scythian monks, despite their Eastern geographical placement, were interested in the Western church and gaining the support
of the papacy.[134] Vitalian had shown the same interests.[135] The Theopaschite formula could be seen as a middle ground between Eastern
and Western definitions of orthodoxy, and the Balkans were the physical and cultural bridge between the East and the West.[136]

It is thus no surprise that the Graecophile Boethius, already a friend
of Dionysius, supported the monks' theology.[137] But the effort to construct a unified Catholic community did not make the monks' place of
origin or their descent fit into a classical ethnographic and geographical
framework, as we shall see. Hormisdas himself seemed confused about
the locations of the bishops who followed Vitalian to communion with
Rome in 515, on one occasion calling them "episcopi tam Dardani
quam Illyrici pene omnes nec non Scythae," at another "Thracibus,
Dardanis, Illyricis," and "de Thraciae et Scythiae Illyrique partibus" at
a third.[138]

The well-documented oddity of the Balkans reflects Mediterranean
views of the imperial frontiers as much as the smoothly rhetorical
descriptions of Noricum by Eugippius. The importance of the Balkans
for understanding the development of the two regions which it connected (namely, Constantinople and Italy) and the origin of Theoderic's
Goths will be further examined in chapter 8.

BOETHIUS: THE SURVIVAL OF THE EMPIRE ENTIRE

Boethius, unlike Dionysius's other friend, Eugippius, had close relations
with Theoderic and the Ravenna government. Unlike Ennodius,
Eugippius and Dionysius, Boethius had been raised in Rome, and came
from an ancient senatorial family. It is in these families that we would

---

[134] Altaner, "Der griechische Theologe Leontius und Leontius der skythische Mönch," pp. 383–5.
[135] Hormisdas, JK 774 = *ep.* "Cum Dei adiutorio" (*Avellana* 116–116a = Thiel 7, pp. 748–55), §3,
p. 749, referring to Hormisdas's lost letter, JK 776*, to Vitalian seeking the general's help in
presenting the papal proposals to Anastasius, from 11 August 515. On Vitalian's mixed religious
and political aims, see Bury, HLRE I: 349.
[136] Schurr, *Trinitätslehre*, pp. 229–30: "Durch diese Theologie einer dogmatischen Mitte wie auch
durch ihre Zweisprachigkeit stehen die Skythen vermittelnd zwischen Morgen- und Abend-
land." The Latin-speaking Scythian monks who came to Rome were not bilingual, however,
having to rely on their compatriot Dionysius for translations of Greek texts: Althaner, "Der
griechische Theologe Leontius," pp. 377–86; their leader Maxentius in Constantinople probably did know Greek, p. 386, n. 2.
[137] Schurr, *Trinitätslehre*, pp. 230–1.
[138] Hormisdas, JK 777 = *ep.* "Justum est" (Arelatensis 30 = Gundlach, pp. 43–4), p. 44, line 25;
Hormisdas, JK 784 = *ep.* "Qui de his" (Thiel 22, pp. 783–6), §3, p. 784; Hormisdas, JK 788 =
ep. "Inter ea quae" (Thiel 26, pp. 793–6), §3, p. 794. Dates: September 515, February 517
and April 517 respectively, all to Western bishops.

expect ancient ethnographic prejudice to be strongest, and many scholars have attributed such views to Boethius and other members of the senate.[139] But the identification of Boethius's views with those of Laurentians, philobyzantines or any other unattested anti-Gothic party is much too simplistic.[140] Arguments for the enmity of courtiers such as Ennodius and Maximian are fragile,[141] and Boethius's political views remain difficult to illuminate.

No evidence shows that Boethius himself wanted a political reunification of Italy with the East, nor even that he saw Italy as being divorced from the Empire.[142] He did have strong interests in Greek learning, friends in Constantinople and a desire to heal the Acacian schism. It is also probable that the excluded parvenus at court exploited Boethius's interests to suggest that his Eastern contacts were treasonable.[143] Theoderic, hard pressed on all sides by foreign powers, was in an unenviable position. He must have been aware that the correspondence of Justin and Hormisdas invoked an ideal world in which he had no place. Boethius was the victim of unjust suspicion.

Boethius's startling reply to his accusers, that he was defending the senate, does not show that he was contemplating political reunification

---

[139] Full references in Moorhead, *Theoderic*, pp. 166–72, 204–11, 219–45, 261–3.

[140] Nearly every historian of Ostrogothic Italy has used ecclesiastical dispute to establish the existence of pro- or anti-Gothic political factions, but unless we posit total concealment in the sources, no such factions existed. Examples are Sundwall, *Abhandlungen*, pp. 186–265; Momigliano, "Cassiodorus and Italian culture of his time," pp. 181–210; and Moorhead, *Theoderic*, pp. 114–72, 226–45. The actual intersection between ecclesiastical and secular politics was far more complex. As we shall see in ch. 6, the biggest change of the period was the reconciliation of the churches. Even though Theoderic had assisted in that reconciliation, the convergence of Catholic primate and Catholic emperor had potentially dangerous consequences for a barbarian ruler of the Arian faith. Nascent Reconquest ideology permeated even the letters of Hormisdas, a careful pope with the interests of the papacy foremost. The Eusebian Christian ideal remained powerful in people's minds. Theoderic's change in promoting a new ethnographic ideology starting in the early 520s may partially have been a reaction to the same political events that occasioned the fall of Boethius. See above, ch. 2, p. 70 with n. 139; below, ch. 6, pp. 216–21; cf. ch. 5, pp. 151–2.

[141] Ch. 6 below, n. 109.

[142] Contra Chadwick, *Boethius*, p. 68. Ecclesiastical interests are not the same as secular interests (though religious interests may be the same as political interests, as we have seen); nor was the senatorial Rome equivalent to Justinian's Rome. The burden of proof for Boethius's alleged conspiracy with the East lies with those who want to show it existed – and no source aside from the statements of his accusers themselves, including the pro-Boethius and pro-Justinian Procopius (BGI[5].1.32–9), suggests the Boethius contemplated treason. It is hardly surprising that Boethius's widow Rusticiana chose to support the emperor in the Gothic Wars (BG 3[7].20.29–31), but political circumstances had changed drastically since the early 520s. Her behaviour in the 540s tells us nothing about Boethius's views before his downfall in the 520s. See further ch. 6.

[143] Moorhead, *Theoderic*, pp. 226–35.

with the East.[144] Rather, it suggests that he still imagined himself as living within an *unbroken* Roman Empire, one whose ultimate sovereign reigned at Constantinople. He had been a consul of the Empire in 510, by Theoderic's nomination, and his sons were consuls in 522. In serving as *magister officiorum*, he was again serving the State, the *administratio publica*, as he says.[145]

Such an antiquarian vision of the political world matches Boethius's comments on the barbarians in the *Consolatio*. We need not assume that these were necessarily his beliefs earlier in his career. Rather, they are well-rooted prejudices and literary tropes that persecution had brought to the fore.[146]

It is revealing that Boethius applies characteristics to the barbarians that classical ethnography had allotted them. *Avaritia*, *violentia* and discordant music were three ethnogeographic reasons that barbarians were inferior to Romans, characteristics thought to be the result of a harsh climate and a wild place of habitation.[147] But of what does Boethius accuse the court officials? Of accepting bribes and favoring their friends, that is, taking *sportulae* and using *clientela* and *amicitia*. Moorhead suggests that the barbarians and the parvenus were unusually corrupt,

---

[144] Emilienne Demougeot, "La carrière politique de Boèce," in L. Obertello (ed.), *Atti del Congresso di Studi Boeziani* (Rome, 1981), pp. 83–108, and especially Moorhead, *Theoderic*, pp. 219–22, convincingly show that Boethius's *libertas Romana* was manipulated by his enemies to imply that he was scheming for reconquest, but nothing in Boethius's own narrative or his works indicates that he had such a desire. Moorhead's arguments for very early senatorial support for reconquest, here and in "*Libertas* and *nomen Romanorum*," pp. 161–8, must be re-evaluated in light of the arguments in ch. 2 for Theoderic's own use of the word *libertas*. Moorhead collapses Boethius's disgrace with Justinian's reconquest rhetoric, which had not yet appeared in 523, and Arator's *Acta Apostolorum*, commissioned in the 540s by the strongly pro-Justinianic Vigilius. On people who benefited from Boethius's death, see below, ch. 6, pp. 216–21. On Vigilius and Justinian, see below, ch. 6, pp. 227–34, and below, pp. 145–6.

[145] Boethius, *De consolatione* 1, prose 4; on the identification of this service with the office of *magister officiorum*, see Moorhead, *Theoderic*, pp. 229–30.

[146] Earlier in his life, in his treatise on music, he mentioned that Goths preferred harsher modes of harmony. More moderate Goths would prefer more moderate modes, "but at the present time there are virtually none of these." Quoted by Chadwick, *Boethius*, p. 92; *De musica, praef.* On Roman attitudes toward the Orpheus myth and its connection with the elements, with *cultura* and *natura*, see Dauge, *Le barbare*, p. 594. Also earlier in his life, Boethius had procured the harpist for Clovis to tame "the hearts of wild peoples" (*Var.* 2.40.17): it might seem from the statement of *De musica* that Theoderic's rhetoric that the Franks were barbarian and the Goths civilized had fallen on deaf ears. More likely, both texts use classicizing topoi.

[147] Dauge, *Le barbare*, pp. 432 (on *discordia*), 468–71, 620–2. On *avaritia*, note Tacitus's claim that his *Germani* were indifferent to money (*Germania* 5.3–5) until they learned from the Romans to like it (15.3), part of his satirical critique of Roman society by reversing traditional "Roman" and "barbarian" attributes. On the antecedents to Boethius's views on music, see Chadwick, *Boethius*, pp. 92, 101: "The theory of music is a penetration of the very heart of providence's ordering of things." Boethius's treatise was antiquarian and theoretical, unrelated to contemporary practice (pp. 78–101).

and it is true that they probably had more need of money and influence than members of senatorial clans.[148] But many studies have shown that this sort of corruption was institutionalized in the late antique bureaucracy.[149] One only has to read John Lydus's sad laments for the decrease in the amounts of the traditional bribes to understand that what we, and Boethius, call "corruption," was a way of life for late Roman courtiers, of barbarian origin or not.[150]

Boethius applied Cato-like standards to a world that had changed thoroughly, just as he assumed that correspondence with Constantinople, the capital, could not arouse any suspicion in Ravenna. His comments on the barbarians at court suggest that at heart, at any rate, he inhabited an archaic world of Roman superiority to the outsider. He understood the intrusion of new political realities differently from Theoderic or Ennodius.[151]

This extraordinary man may have resembled his father-in-law, the patrician Symmachus, about whom we could wish that we knew more, or some of his less worldly relatives, like Proba or Rustica. But in fact we do not know, and cannot know, to what extent Boethius's views were as unusual as he himself was in his bilingual scholarship and his broad intellectual interests.[152]

---

[148] Moorhead, *Theoderic*, pp. 234–5.

[149] Jones, LREI: 496–9, 502–4, 775–8; Paul Veyne, "Clientèle et corruption au service de l'Etat: la venalité des offices dans le Bas-Empire romain," *Annales: Economies, Société Civilisations* 36 (1981), 339–60; Karl Leo Noethlichs, *Beamtum und Dienstvergehen: Zur Staatsverwaltung in der Spätantike* (Wiesbaden, 1981), esp. pp. 214–22; Ramsey MacMullen, *Corruption and the Decline of Rome* (New Haven, 1988). Rather similarly, Courcelle, "Le tyran et le philosophe," p. 197, takes Boethius's complaints about rapacity toward provincials as a complaint about *hospitalitas*, but it is surely a complaint about *abuses* of *hospitalitas*, which was not a new phenomenon (see ch. 2 above); similarly, he believes that Boethius's complaints attest real tyranny on the part of Theoderic. We need additional evidence for such an interpretation besides the writings of a man imprisoned by the ruler, whether justly or unjustly.

[150] Maas, *John Lydus and the Roman Past*, pp. 31–2.

[151] This is not to say that Boethius lived in the past so much as that his world and viewpoints seem to have been very restricted, a specific *use* of antiquarianism. See John Matthews ("Anicius Manlius Severinus Boethius," pp. 37–8) and Momigliano ("Cassiodorus and Italian culture of his time," pp. 184–91), on the gulf separating Boethius from Cassiodorus, still a useful summary even now that Ensslin's thesis on Symmachus's authorship of Jordanes's *Romana* has been disproved. It is hardly surprising that Boethius comforted himself by opposing *tyranni* in the Roman republican and imperial (usurpers) tradition, to philosophers in the Greek tradition, now Christianized via Neoplatonism (Courcelle, "Le tyran et le philosophe," pp. 195–224).

[152] The extent to which even Boethius's antiquarianism affected his beliefs before the *Consolatio* remains unclear. It is more questionable still to extend Boethius's statements on barbarians (only attested, of course, in the *Consolatio*) to other senators, or to assume that disliking barbarians automatically indicated support for the emperor at Constantinople, e.g. Sundwall, *Abhandlungen* (p. 186) who wants to see Italian senators as sympathetic to Zeno because he was the leader of the Roman Empire, or (p. 202) senators as supporters of the antipope Laurentius because he was supposedly "pro-Byzantine"; Moorhead, "*Libertas* and *nomen Romanum*," pp. 167–8 argues that Arator was anti-Ostrogothic because he was of senatorial birth, and grandson of the

Ethnography affected people in subtler ways than just influencing their political views. The geographical unity of the Roman Empire was so obviously fragmented that older ethnographic terms like "Scythian" began to settle on Roman provinces, with consequent confusion of regional with ancestral origins. The descriptions of the Scythian monks, the feelings of Dionysius Exiguus and the position of Vitalian all show the increase of regionalism that Ennodius exemplifies in Italy, and Sidonius in Gaul. Hence the ideological attempts of Procopius, Agathias and Justinian to superimpose a classicizing ethnography on top of the new diversity recognized within the boundaries of the former Empire.

JUSTINIANIC *RENOVATIO* IDEOLOGY IN ITALY

While various ideals of Empire competed in Italy for attention, Constantinople, the surviving imperial center, gradually completed "the transfer of Roman ideology" to the East.[153] This transfer, which itself caused various changes in imperial ideology, strongly affected Eastern uses of the classical ethnographic tradition in literature and law. Eastern ethnogeography reaches its apex in the *renovatio* ideology of the emperor Justinian, which made its way to Italy during the Gothic Wars.

After the dormant fifth century, Eastern texts both official and unofficial again explain Roman and barbarian by a climatic dichotomy that supports the providentiality of the Mediterranean as Roman state.[154]

---

emperor Avitus; see also Matthews, "Anicius Manlius Severinus Boethius," pp. 32–8 (Boethius opposed Ostrogothic *civilitas* because he was "still very much a Roman senator, and a representative of the ancient world"); and Walter Ullmann, *Gelasius I. (492–496): Das Papsttum an der Wende der Spätantike zum Mittelalter*, Papst und Papsttum 18 (Stuttgart, 1981), pp. 217–18: Pope Gelasius ignored the Goths because he had nothing in common with them ethnically, linguistically, culturally or socially. Despite the demolition of the arguments of Ensslin and Wes (above, nn. 1–2) too many historians continue to assume that the fourth-century pagan world of the fourth-century Symmachus survived intact in his descendant, the sixth-century Symmachus, despite the vast difference of time, history and religion that divided the two: as Averil Cameron has shown for Byzantium in the classicizing works of Procopius, we must beware the overlay of topoi and genre, which in (some) sources encourage us to see the preservation of an unchanged, static "senatorial ethos" that determined every aspect of the beliefs of anyone who could be categorized a senator.

[153] Teillet, *Des Goths – à nation gothique*, p. 260.
[154] There is, however, more evidence for the persistence of classical ethnography in the fifth-century East than in the West, notably in the fragmentary classicizing Greek historians such as Priscus and Malchus. But in these writers, classical ethnography is not as consistent nor as tied to victory ideology as in Procopius and the mid-sixth-century historians. Notable are the reactions to the Western events of the year 476 in the Malchus and Candidus fragments; they are not seen as momentous in the way that they would be by Marcellinus comes, Procopius and Jordanes: Malchus, fr. 14, ed. Blockley 2: 419–20; Candidus, fr. 1, ed. Blockley 2: 469, lines 84–8. Ethnogeography e.g. at Priscus, fr. 66 (transmitted, however, through Procopius). Notable also is the vision of fifth-century Eastern church historians such as Theodoret, who saw the "Scythians" as harbingers of the apocalypse, already a threat to the *oriens Christianus*

This dichotomy attributes inferior culture to the barbarians on account of their geographic origins. But now this ethnogeography is Christianized. Via the Eusebian heritage and the notion of the emperor as vicar of Christ, Eastern sources can imagine the ethnographically superior Roman Empire as identical to the elect Christian Empire. One way to do this was to classify barbarians as heretics or pagans, an equation going back to Ambrose.[155] Various inconsistencies in this picture show that the revival of ethnogeography was artificial: its enduring heart would be the notion of an orthodox Empire.

Political allegiance and profession complicated this picture. In Procopius, the notion of Goths as uncontrollable warriors coexists uneasily with the fifth-century idea of barbarians as soldiers, the equation adopted by Theoderic. Simultaneously, for both Procopius and Justinian, political allegiance becomes the definition of barbarians or Romans. Goths or Vandals who were willing to join the emperor's army – itself made up of "barbarians" in the fifth-century professional sense – also became Romans in the political sense of obeying the emperor. In Procopius's narrative of the Gothic Wars, allegiance, profession and kinship are all competing, and confused, definitions of Goths, Romans and Italians.[156]

Eastern writers at the time of Justinian had the same access to classical ethnogeographic texts – and produced the same kinds of incoherent new ethnographic and geographic texts – as Western writers under Theoderic. Procopius and Agathias knew Herodotus, and Jordanes used a wide variety of earlier sources including Strabo and Mela.[157] The *Cosmographia* of Julius Honorius was written in about 500, perhaps by a Latin-speaker in an Eastern province.[158] At the same time appeared the *Isaurica* of Capito, an ethnography of a people within the Roman Empire,[159] and, later, the Christian geography of the Nestorian mer-

---

(a view combated in the West by Jerome and Augustine): Friedhelm Winkelmann, "Die Bewertung der Barbaren in den Werken der oströmischen Kirchenhistoriker," in *Das Reich und die Barbaren*, pp. 221–35; cf. the similar view of Goths in the mid-sixth-century work of Cyril of Scythopolis, now explicitly tied to Justinianic imperial ideology: see below, n. 181.

[155] See below, ch. 7, pp. 237–8 with nn. 6–7.

[156] See ch. 5, below.

[157] Herodotus in Procopius and Agathias: Cameron, *Procopius*, pp. 37–8; Cameron, *Agathias*, pp. 60–2. On Jordanes's sources, see Mommsen, in Jordanes, xxiii–xliv.

[158] Schanz-Hosius 4.2: 143, at any rate not near Italy, since the text is full of basic mistakes on Italian geography.

[159] It is now lost: *Suidas* κ.342; PLRE2 Capito; Eduard Schwartz, "Capito aus Lykien," RE3: 1527 (Stuttgart, 1899); significantly, he also produced a free Greek translation of Eutropius's *Breviarium* of Roman history: P. Gensel, "Eutropius, Historiker," RE 6: 1524–5 (Stuttgart, 1909), fragments of which survive, ed. Hans Droysen, MGH: AA 2 (Berlin, 1879), pp. 9–182, bottom half of pages. The parallels with Jordanes are striking: see below, ch. 8.

chant Cosmas Indicopleustes, who rewrote Ptolemy's ethnogeography in Christian terms.[160] It was the time of Justinian's recreation of a Chalcedonian Christian Empire and of Theodora's monophysite mission to Ethiopia: Eastern Christians were re-imagining the world. But less ambitious geographic interests also persevered. The *Ethnika* of Stephanus of Byzantium is an interminable etymological catalogue of towns, regions, peoples and cities within the Roman Empire. Stephanus repeats the story of Scythians and in Persia and Thrace; the Goths are a Scythian tribe to the north of the Black Sea, and so on. *Ethnē* exist within the Roman Empire, defined by cities, in the old Hellenistic polis-definition. The work is dotted with antiquarian knowledge, but concentrates on city and region.[161]

Justinian's ethnographic ideology of reconquest was a subsection in his exploitation of an old and powerful Roman political tool: the ideal of *renovatio*. Used by Constantine and Theodosius the Great, as well as by Theoderic himself, *renovatio* appealed to Roman political conservatism by cloaking novelty under the pretense of reviving a golden past. In all his political innovations, in streamlining Roman law or creating new civic officials, Justinian appealed to the past with historical digressions in his constitutions, in his use of obsolete but evocative titles like *praetor* and *aedile*.[162]

Reconquest would follow *renovatio* – although not until the 530s.[163] The political conditions of the age were beginning to make people in the East aware that imperial authority no longer encircled the Mediter-

---

[160] PLRE3 Cosmas 1; Wolfgang Buchwald, Armin Hohweg and Otto Prinz, *Dictionnaire des auteurs grecs et latins de l'antiquité et du moyen âge*, 1982, trans. and rev. Jean Denis Berger and Jacques Billen (Turnhout, 1991), s.n., p. 217; Cameron, *Procopius*, p. 27 (Cosmas, a "flat-earther," shows sixth-century traits more clearly than Procopius, whose classicizing genre produces antiquarian description).

[161] Stephanus of Byzantium, *Ethnika*, ed. August Meinecke, 1849 (reprint; Graz, 1958), s.v. Skythai (p. 578), Gotthoi (p. 212); on the author, see PLRE2 Stephanus 24. The work survives only in a lengthy epitome, but seems to give a good idea of the enormous whole, from the evidence of its use by Constantine VII and the *Suidas*; see further Buchwald, Hohweg and Prinz, *Dictionnaire*, s.n. Etienne de Byzance, p. 282. The epitome, by a certain Hermolaus, was dedicated to the emperor Justinian, though we do not know whether this was Justinian I or Justinian II; in either case, Stephanus himself certainly lived in the first half of the sixth century: PLRE2 Stephanus 24; PLRE3 Hermolaus.

[162] On *renovatio* in general, see Gerhart B. Ladner, *The Idea of Reform, Its Impact on Christian Thought and Action in the Age of the Fathers* (Cambridge, Mass., 1959). On Justinian's ideology of *renovatio*, see Cameron, *Procopius*, 19–23, 245–7; Michael Maas, "Roman history and Christian ideology in Justinianic reform legislation," *Dumbarton Oaks Papers* 40 (1986), 17–31; Maas, *John Lydus and the Roman Past*, pp. 83–96. On Theoderic's use of *renovatio*, see the brilliant analysis of Moorhead, *Theoderic*, pp. 252–8. The best characterization of Justinian and his politics is Tony Honoré, *Tribonian* (London, 1978), pp. 1–39, esp. p. 19.

[163] On the late gestation of reconquest ideology, see below, ch. 6, pp. 209–12, 224–5; Honoré, *Tribonian*, pp. 17–19 (the "age of hope" beginning after the Nika riots).

ranean, even in theory. In reconquering Africa, Italy and part of Spain, Justinian reorganized those provinces as militarized regions. He claimed that he was restoring the provinces to the Empire, and Roman *libertas* to the provinces, but in fact he was doing something quite different: using them as tributary states for the purpose of spreading a monolithic imperially directed Christian doctrine, and to increase his personal prestige and authority as Roman Emperor in a world where the Emperor was no longer the figure he had once been.[164]

This gap between rhetoric and practice enabled Justinian to gain some support from some indigenous elites of reconquered provinces, but it alienated others in the process. Since many Italians were far less aware of having left the Empire than Justinian wanted them to be, they were quite happy under the Goths, or at least happy with the idea of Italy a separate polity.

Contemporary Byzantine texts such as Procopius are suffused with this ideology because it was part of the cultural climate of Justinian's Constantinople. Since they were written by authors who also had viewpoints of their own, they themselves provide vantage-points on the reception of the official line. But Procopius's writings, part of the Byzantine sixth-century tradition of classicizing history in the mould of Thucydides, are also suffused with classical ethnographic assumptions and topoi.[165]

Despite the sporadic attempts of Constantinople to come to the aid of the beleaguered Western emperors in the mid-fifth-century, the Eastern emperors did not learn to think of the West as "lost" until the time of Justinian.[166] The road to this realization was complex. The first writer to see the Western provinces as lost was a pagan, Zosimus, writing in about 500 against the weakened military policy of the Christian Theodosian emperors.[167] The late fourth-century notion that the Mediterranean provinces should give up expensive defense on the frontiers perhaps began to weaken at about this time.[168] The Eastern armies were engaged

---

[164] Honoré, *Tribonian*, pp. 14–20; Averil Cameron, *The Mediterranean World in Late Antiquity A.D 395–600* (London, 1993), pp. 104–127; Cameron, *Procopius*, pp. 19–32; McCormick, *Eternal Victory*, pp. 67–8 ("a powerful reassertion of the image of the victor emperor").
[165] Averil Cameron, "History as text: coping with Procopius," in Holdsworth and Wiseman (eds.), *The Inheritance of Historiography*, pp. 53–66; Cameron, *Procopius*, pp. 33–46, 225–41 and *passim*.
[166] Walter Emil Kaegi, Jr., *Byzantium and the Decline of Rome*, (Princeton, 1968), pp. 3–58.
[167] Ibid., pp. 99–145; Goffart, "Zosimus: the first historian of Rome's fall," pp. 81–110.
[168] In Justinian's period, John Lydus, *De magistratibus* 3.40, complains that Constantine did not adequately defend Scythia and Moesia; hence they were overrun with barbarians, losing tax-revenues for the Empire, and thus increasing tax-burdens for all the other provinces. Compare, from the late fourth century, Themistius, *Or.* 8 and 10, arguing that the loss of provinces to the Scythians (Goths) reduced the tax-burdens for everyone else (cited by Goffart, "Rome, Constantinople, and the barbarians," p. 16, with comments at pp. 16–17). Note that for Lydus,

again in wars with Persia and in endless skirmishes in the Balkans, where the armies themselves were in constant conflict with one another. Throughout the reign of Anastasius, although Priscian (a Latin-speaking African) could refer to the wish that the Empire be reunited, the revolt of Vitalian, the Acacian schism and the Persian wars occupied the minds of those in power in Constantinople. The Western provinces were not yet legitimate objects of attention.[169]

After the advent of Justin I and Justinian in 518, the Mediterranean world appeared to have stabilized and regained its unity. The Acacian schism was ended in 519. Relations between Constantinople and Theoderic, and between Constantinople and the Vandals, were put on an excellent footing. The Balkans were temporarily quiescent. The new emperors moved to eliminate enemies within Constantinople such as Vitalian. In the next several years, the Persian wars would occupy the Eastern armies.[170]

The new ideas that had been gestating since 500, however, did not vanish. Justin and Justinian were devout Chalcedonian Christians, and their longing for orthodox homogeneity in a Eusebian imperial frame-work informed their entire policy. In the Chronicle of Marcellinus Comes, produced by Justinian's secretary in the year of his accession, appears the first reference to the notion that the Western Empire had fallen in the year 476, that is, the last year that saw a man in Ravenna bearing the title Roman emperor, and the first year that a self-identified non-Roman king ruled the provinces of Italy.[171]

Scythia is a *place* lost to the Empire, while for Themistius, the Scythians were barbarian hordes (Goths).

[169] Honoré, *Tribonian*, pp. 1–5; Bury, HLREI: 429–52. On Priscian's comments in *De laude Anastasii imperatoris* (265–9), Bury I: 467 inaccurately remarks that Priscian "sympathized with the national feeling of the Italians against Gothic rule," but what the panegyricist says explicitly is that both Romes should come to obey the emperor alone. Since the panegyric was delivered in 512, at the height of the Acacian schism and in the middle of the lead-up to the Chalcedon-ian Vitalian's revolt (to which Priscian refers: lines 298–9), this statement cannot be entirely and easily interpreted as nascent reconquest ideology, otherwise totally absent in Anastasius's reign. It must refer to the Acacian schism that infuriated the emperor so much; and indeed, despite the prevalence of victory ideology in the panegyric, this section refers specifically to religion (in the tone of Roman imperial religion and *renovatio*). On the date of the panegyric, see Moorhead, *Theoderic*, p. 171, n. 153. The interpretation of Priscian's statement by Chadwick (*Boethius*, p. 43) that it refers to "the well-known ambitions of Anastasius to reunite the bar-barian West under his authority and jurisdiction together with the Greek East" is entirely without foundation. I find even the more cautious comments of Moorhead, *Theoderic*, p. 171, and Croke, "A.D. 476: the manufacture of a turning point," p. 116, unconvincing.

[170] Stein, *Bas-Empire* 2: 264 suggests that Justinian recognized Athalaric in order to concentrate on the wars in the East; on the general distracting events of 518–32, see ibid., 2: 223–73, 287–310.

[171] Croke, "A.D. 476: the manufacture of a turning point," pp. 116–17; Krautschick, "Zwei Aspekte," pp. 367–8.

Classical ethnography and victory ideology could not explain such changes otherwise than as a loss to the Empire. Such ideas should have lost their strength with the disappearance of paganism and the political changes of the Mediterranean. But now they were being harnessed to the Eastern belief in a Christian Empire congruent with Christendom,[172] a notion that had been mooted for decades within the ancient framework of Roman law. The new providentiality of Justinian's ideas of empire brought the pervasive universalism of Eastern Christianity to notions of classical ethnography. The results were momentous.

In 533, Justinian's armies invaded Africa. His lawyers completed the Digest, the final block of Justinian's massive legal corpus, itself a recreation of the Roman past under the pretension of preserving it, a metaphor for his restoration of the Roman Empire.[173] The emperor announced his completion of Roman law in the resounding rhetoric of Roman providentiality, victory ideology and classical ethnography:

> In the name of the our Lord Jesus Christ
> Imperator Caesar Flavius Iustinianus Alamannicus Gotthicus Francicus
> Germanicus Anticus Alanicus Vandalicus Africanus
> Pius Felix Inclutus Victor ac Triumphator semper Augustus
> ad Senatum et Omnes Populos

So great is the providence of Divine Humanity toward us, that it always deigns to sustain us by acts of eternal generosity. For after the Parthican wars, eternal peace was laid to rest, and in the period since we invaded the Vandalic *gens* and Carthage, and indeed almost all Libya has again been brought back to the Empire, and a tempered compendium of the ancient laws, which until now were weighed down by old age, has at last stood forth in new beauty: which nobody before our rule had ever hoped for, nor did anyone think it even possible by human intelligence. For it is marvelous that consistency could be imposed upon Roman law – which, from the founding of the City until the time of our rule, that is, almost 1400 years, vacillated in internal contradictions extending even into the laws of the emperors – so that nothing contrary or repetitive should be discovered in it, and so that no twin laws ruling on the same subject should anywhere appear.[174]

The entire edifice of Justinianic ideology stands clear before us. The invocation to Christ and the antiquarianizing victory titles and address

---

[172] Kaegi, *Byzantium and the Decline of Rome*, pp. 176–223: paradoxically, for Christian writers, the Empire had not fallen, it was alive and flourishing in the East. Justinian could attach the notion of a flourishing Empire to the idea that the Western provinces were lost by assuming that the East would providentially and gloriously gain back the provinces of the West *because* the East was the Christian Roman Empire.

[173] Honoré, *Tribonian*, pp. 18–21; Maas, *John Lydus and the Roman Past*, pp. 39–48.

[174] Constitutio *Tanta*, in *Dig.* p. 131.

to the senate and Roman people sum up *renovatio*.[175] Already the titles Vandalicus and Africanus belong to Justinian, even though the Vandal Wars were still going on. Roman imperial *providentia* ensures that the emperor is still a semi-divine figure: his "divina humanitas" is itself the attribute of Christ in Nicaean and Chalcedonian terms. The emperor's benevolent interest (*liberalitates*) in his peoples, his *populi* (not *gentes*) is displayed through the parallel aims of rebuilding Roman law and rebuilding the Empire.[176] The appeal to 1,400 years of history recalls the past under the aegis of a return to a pristine time of unified perfection. Consistency was to be imposed throughout the Mediterranean – in law, religion and governance. The reference to the city of Rome can leave us in no doubt that the reconquest of Italy was next, as Amalasuintha and her courtiers feared. Victory ideology and its use of ethnography promised that recent blots like repetitions within the Roman law or the occupation of Libya by the *Vandalica gens* would be erased by the might of the triumphant emperor.

Procopius launches his history of Justinian's Western wars by justifying all of them – in Africa, Spain, the Balkans and in Italy – by grouping the four barbarian groups in those regions together and attributing to them common characteristics: Arianism, ferocity, non-Roman laws, physical characteristics, and identity with groups from a single geographic region of the past:

There were many Gothic *ethnē* in earlier times, just as also at the present, but the greatest and most important of all are the Goths, Vandals, Visigoths and Gepids. In ancient times, however, they were named Sauromatae and Melanchlaeni, and there were some too who called these *ethnē* Getic. All these, while they are distinguished from one another by their names . . . do not differ in anything else at all. For they all have white bodies and fair hair, and are tall and handsome to look upon, and they use the same laws and practice a common religion. For they are all of the Arian faith, and have one language called Gothic; and, as it seems to me, they all came originally from one *ethnos*, and were distinguished later by the names of those who led each group. This people used to dwell above the Ister River from of old. Later on the Gepids got possession of the country about Singidunum and Sirmium on both sides of the Ister River, where they have remained settled even down to my time . . . These barbarians became the most cruel of all men.[177]

---

[175] McCormick, *Eternal Victory*, p. 68, on the victory titles. Cf. below, ch. 6, p. 209 with n. 62, on Anastasius's diplomatic use of victory titles, and note Ennodius's discontent with the emperor's use of *Alamannicus* when it rightly belonged to Theoderic, discussed above.

[176] On *populus* and *gens* in rhetoric addressed to the Eastern emperor, see Amory, "Ethnographic rhetoric, aristocratic attitudes and political allegiance," p. 447; Amory, "Names, ethnic identity and community," pp. 12–13.

[177] Procopius, BV 1(3).2.2–6.

This text contains much of interest in it besides its propagation of revived ethnogeography. We learn that the Germanic tongue spoken by all these groups was called "Gothic." We learn that Arianism in the sixth-century Mediterranean was now associated with groups who came from the Danube. We learn that groups could be seen to be called after an eponymous leader – a notion not unfamiliar to the Romans of Romulus.

But most important is the ethnogeographic ideology contained in the passage, and its context.[178] Procopius describes these four "Gothic" groups as the tools of the downfall of the Roman Empire in the fifth century under Honorius and subsequently. Like ethnographic writers before him, he begins with a geographical description of the world. He then enumerates the regions which had once belonged to the Roman Empire. These regions are described as places, whereas the barbarians are *ethnē*: this is consistent ethnogeography, even more so than Pliny, who also saw *gentes* within the Empire. The barbarian *ethnē* all have similar northern features, fierceness in war and Arian belief – characteristics derived from their original habitation of one place, the Danube. Moreover, although the Empire made treaties with the barbarians, they broke them, "for faith with the Romans cannot dwell in barbarians,"[179] treachery being another traditional characteristic of barbarian behavior.[180] Procopius's views on Justinian's four enemy *ethnē* were by no means restricted to himself. They were current in various circles in the Eastern Mediterranean, and we find them in other ethnogeographic texts that used victory ideology.[181]

Justinian propagated several laws upon the conquest of Africa that

---

[178] Wolfram, in *Goths*, pp. 17–18 with n. 5, sees this passage and related Byzantine ethnography (below, n. 181) as descriptive reactions to groups formed by the ideologies of kings; I see them as part of *Justinian*'s prescriptive ideology.

[179] Procopius, BV 1(3).2.7.

[180] Dauge, *Le barbare*, pp. 432, 564–7, 737–40, 767–71 (an aspect of barbarian *discordia*, diversity).

[181] Related is Marcellinus comes's description of Odoacer as *rex Gothorum* in the usurpation of 476, now seen as crucial, "with the Goths henceforth holding Italy" (s.a. 476): a revision of history that allowed the illegitimacy of Gothic rule in Italy to be taken back into the fuzzy arrangements of the period in which Eastern writers now saw the West to have been lost to the Empire.

Procopius and other Eastern writers, like Marcellinus, saw 476 as a turning point: Cameron, *Procopius*, p. 199 with n. 82. The grouping of Goths, Visigoths, Gepids and Vandals also appears in two exactly contemporary writers: Jordanes (26, 42, 82, 94–8, with Wolfram, *Goths*, p. 18 with n. 8 – perhaps not as clear as Wolfram implies) and Cyril of Scythopolis, *Vita Sabae*, an Eastern anti-monophysite writer who used ethnographic assumptions and victory ideology. For Cyril, the Goths, Visigoths, Vandals and Gepids were all Arians, to be extirpated by Justinian, who was thus restoring the empire "of Honorius" (a similar view to that of the pagan Zosimus!): *Vita Sabae* 72 (175.20–176.7); see also 14 (97.5–21) on Justinian and the Saracens. Jordanes and victory ideology: *Get.* 313–16. Further on this grouping (which also appears in the "Table of nations"), see Goffart, "The supposedly 'Frankish' table of nations," pp. 155–6.

contain similar ethnographic ideology, several of them composed by himself.[182] In 534, he created the post of praetorian prefect of Africa for the conquered territory, announcing that Christ had decided that Africa should once again feel his *liberalitas* after 105 years of captivity by the Vandals, who were "at once enemies of the soul and of the body."[183] Through their Arianism and their barbarity, the Vandals had terrorized the Africans and the Catholic clergy. By freeing them *a iugo barbarico*, Justinian restored their *libertas*, a *libertas* as much Christian as Roman.[184] In a law from 535, the emperor announced that his law limited *incivile* behavior. Since God had delivered Africa to *Romanae dicioni* by Justinian's vigilance, all those who had suffered *a detentatoribus iniustis* under the Vandals, from the wars and calumnies that had almost destroyed *antiqua genera*, should know that peace had been restored.[185] Simultaneously Justinian announced severe penalties for Arian believers in Africa.[186]

The similarity between the language of Justinian and Theoderic is no accident. Both drew on the legal and cultural resources of the Roman past in propagating notions of the ideal state. Both used the imagery of *renovatio* and improvement through restoration of the good old ways. Both conquered adjacent regions in the name of restoring them to the Empire. The differences are two, but they are important: Theoderic did not use universal orthodoxy as a justification of his rule, and he was never able to claim the prerogative of the emperors in the sphere of divine providentiality. Justinian used universal religion and imperial divinity with great effect.

Only two of Justinian's laws for Italy survive, both from the end of the Gothic Wars. In order to understand Justinian's ideology there, we are forced to use the historians. Briefly, the justification for Justinian's conquest of Italy, as expressed in Procopius, has three strands. First, although Theoderic was a just ruler, Zeno and Anastasius had only meant him to rule Italy in the name of the emperors. But he had ruled it independently. Moreover, Theodahad's murder of Amalasuintha had robbed the Ostrogothic monarchy of any legitimacy that it had once had; Witigis's murder of Theodahad compounded this illegality. Second, the Goths were barbarians, and barbarian *ethnē* ought not to be governing parts of the Empire, least of all Italy and Rome, because

[182] CJ 1.27.1; 1.27.2; *Novellae App.* 3; 6; 9; Honoré, *Tribonian*, p. 25 with n. 268.
[183] CJ 27.1.1.
[184] CJ 27.1.1–10; quotation at §8. On the solecism here, Honoré, *Tribonian*, p. 24 with n. 266: "the self-satisfaction is considerable."
[185] *Nov. Iust.* 36.1.
[186] *Nov. Iust.* 37.

they are violent and ungovernable, the least suitable people to rule Italy. Third, the Goths were Arians, and heretics and heretical kings ought not to be ruling any part of the Empire, in the imperial name or not.[187]

Law (in the shape of legitimacy and treaty), classical ethnography and religion formed the basis for Justinian's reconquest of Italy. All three elements were framed in *renovatio*: Justinian was restoring lawful rule, expelling a barbarous people, and returning Italy to Catholic belief. Since Italy had known the ideology of law under Theoderic, had contained familiar and educated Goths who were not always classified barbarians, and was the home of the popes, the apostolic see and the Eternal City, Justinian's restoration of the past was an illusion.

The tendentiousness of this ideological stance led to endless problems in the East, let alone in the reconquest of Italy.[188] In Africa, of course, the Arian persecutions of the Vandal rulers, and their insistence that soldiers be Arians, delineated people called Vandals from people called Romans, and gave the imperial troops the advantage of a divided population.[189] In Italy things were not so clear. The Italians and the popes had long regarded themselves as more Catholic than the emperors. However attractive the notion of a Christian secular ruler, Augustinian universality and papal supremacy helped convince Italian Catholics that the emperor had no monopoly on correct belief. Aside from Theoderic's persecution of John I and Boethius, which aided several prominent people,[190] the kings behaved with exemplary discretion toward the church, and, unlike the emperors, did not interfere in the formulation of correct Catholic doctrine. Moreover, as we shall see, many soldiers were Catholics, so that the definition of "Goth" remained less clear than Justinian's ideology suggested.[191] These soldiers were welded to

---

[187] Procopius, BG 1(3).1–7. Much of this emerges from Procopius's tendentious picture of the conflict over the education of Athalaric and its consequences, on which, see ch. 5 below, pp. 155–61.

[188] e.g., Frend, "The monophysites and the transition between the ancient world and the Middle Ages," p. 365: the monophysite subjects whom Justinian was constantly trying to conciliate were "logically the most loyal upholders of the emperor and the authority of the emperor" until Justin's repressive enactments. The Tome of Leo presented endless problems to the emperors: it had become impossible to unite the Eastern and Western churches without alienating either the papacy or the monophysites. On Justinian and the Three Chapters, see ch. 6.

[189] Although even with this divided past, the African population was by no means firmly behind Byzantine rule; too many cultures and languages competed with the Greek-speaking Easterners: Averil Cameron, "Gelimer's laughter: the case of Byzantine Africa," in *Tradition and Innovation in Late Antiquity*, pp. 171–90. Further, see Walter Emil Kaegi, Jr., "Arianism and the Byzantine army in Africa 533–546," *Traditio* 21 (1965), 23–53, on the course of revolts immediately after the conquest (Arianism was not a major factor).

[190] Below, ch. 6, pp. 218–19.

[191] Below, ch. 7, p. 259 with n. 99, p. 272.

the cities and families of Italian civilians, and Justinian's armies would not find it easy to pry them apart.[192]

Some of the senators of Rome, and the papacy in the doubtful form of Vigilius, accepted Justinian's ideology. The role of the senators is less clear than many historians have wanted to believe.[193] Like everyone else in Italy, they were forced to make a choice of loyalties from which they could not retreat. Justinian offered not only the rhetoric of Empire to which they were accustomed (but which they were also accustomed to embody in themselves, without the support of Constantinople) but also material gain and safety in the East. By the time that they had made the choice to emigrate to Constantinople, no senator could return to Italy until it had been conquered by the imperial forces, as the various executions and massacres of senators by Gothic kings showed. Since they wanted to return to their homes and their lands, it is unsurprising that men like Cethegus urged Justinian to make a final effort to expel the Goths in 550. Their options in 550 were full reconquest, or exile with no hope of return.[194]

As we shall see, Vigilius gained his election in the reconquest, and owed his position to the direct interference of Theodora and Belisarius. He was also anti-Arian in the first part of his reign, precisely the period when Justinian agreed with him on the Chalcedonian-monophysite issue. While monophysitism seemed to be resolved, the papacy could concentrate on the Arian issue. In the first part of the wars, leading to the capture of Witigis, resolution of the Arian problem could not have seemed far off. In the second part of the wars, when Totila began to make good the Gothic losses, Vigilius could not afford to change his views on Arianism: he was at risk from both sides. Whether or not he actually believed that all Goths were barbarians and Arians, circumstances forced Vigilius into propagating such ideas. They helped his own position.[195]

Vigilius is the source for the only Italian pro-Justinianic propaganda that we know of outside the pleas of senators like Cethegus for the emperor to finish what he had started. This propaganda appears in inscriptions in the catacombs of Rome, and certain prayers added to

[192] Below, ch. 5, pp. 165–194.
[193] Ch. 5, pp. 165, 166–7, 174, 185.
[194] On Procopius's depiction of senatorial views in Constantinople, see Cameron, *Procopius*, pp. 197–8; here I clearly part with John Moorhead, "Italian loyalties during Justinian's Gothic war," *Byzantion* 53 (1983), 575–96, particularly 582–92, where, it seems to me, Moorhead takes the activities of a few aristocrats and generalizes them not only to all aristocrats but to the entire population of Italy, and assumes that the interests of the Catholic clergy were identical to those of senators, which, by the rise of the Three Chapters controversy, they clearly were not.
[195] See ch. 6, below, pp. 227–9.

the Roman mass. The inscriptions revive the doctrine of transference to identify Goths with Getae, and discuss Totila's siege of Rome in classicizing terms as a siege of the City by barbarians, who were moreover heretics in plundering the tombs of the saints.[196]

We do not know how Vigilius's propaganda was received, but it is safe to say that no other inscription or text produced by Italians about Goths resembles it in the slightest until the *Dialogi* of Gregory the Great, a figure by no means typical of his time.

Political allegiance was the effective aim of Justinian's ideology, whatever his ethnogeographic claims. Vandals and Goths who joined his army or retired from fighting became Romans.[197] At the end of the wars, Justinian's armies, which now included many men who had been in the Gothic army, put up official inscriptions of *renovatio* suggesting that Italy had been restored to the Empire.[198] Justinian's laws for Italy are less strident than the laws on Africa. Nineteen years of continuous war must have taught the emperor that ethnographic ideology did not always work – not in Italy. In 554, the laws and gifts of Amalasuintha, Athalaric and Theodahad were confirmed (Theoderic's reign being conceded as legitimate anyway), while those of the *tyrannus* Totila were all annulled. One chapter of the Pragmatic Sanction reads "from the time of king Theoderic up to those of the most wicked Totila"[199] – restrained indeed. *Ferocitas* and other barbarian traits are indeed associated with Totila and the Goths,[200] but there is none of the grand tone

---

[196] F-S 207–12, 216: the Goths are *barbari*, *Gethae* or *Getes*, a *gens infelix* (not an *exercitus*), who are also *impia*: "Hinc iter ad sanctos, quos impia turba Getarum, horrendum dictu, sedibus expulerat" (212); all the inscriptions are in metrical verse, a genre that favored the introduction of classicizing ethnography in itself – though some of the verses are also beginning to show rhyme. On the propagandistic effects of classifying Goths as *Getae*, note Procopius, BG 1(5).24.30, the Sibylline oracle on the defeat of the Goths by Justinian's army, reported in fragments of Latin. On the masses added by Vigilius to the Roman liturgy, see D. M. Hope, *The Leonine Sacramentary: A Reassessment of Its Date and Purpose* (Oxford, 1971), pp. 78–90.

[197] Below, ch. 5, pp. 168–71.

[198] Narses set up inscriptions on the Pons Salarius in 565 (two miles north of Rome) commemorating the restoration of Empire through the restoration of the bridge, referring to the *victoria Gothica* (i.e., the victory over the Goths) and to the restoration of *libertas* to the city of Rome and all Italy, threatened by the danger embodied in the broken bridge destroyed "a nefandissimo tyranno Totila;" a second inscription in metrical verse uses classical ethnography: "Qui [sc. Narses] potuit rigidas Gothorum subdere mentes, hic docuit durum flumina ferre iugum;" F-S 217a–b. Directly after about 550, an inscription was placed on the architrave of the main door to the basilica at the great cemetery of Manastirine in Split, reading "Deus noster propitius esto republicae Romanae," CIL 3.9626, on which, see Jacques Zeiller, *Les origines chrétiennes dans le province romaine de Dalmatie*, Bibliothèque de l'Ecole des Hautes Etudes: Sciences historiques et philologiques 155 (Paris, 1906), p. 157. See further PA **A**sbadus and the discussion in ch. 5, pp. 190–1 below.

[199] *Sanctio pragmatica pro petitione Vigilii* (= Nov. Iust. Appendix 7), 8.

[200] *Sanctio pragmatica* 15, 17.

of condescension found in the African laws. The very basis of Theoderic's *civilitas* is to remain:

Ut civiliter inter se causas audiant. Lites etiam inter duos procedentes Romanos vel ubi Romana persona pulsatur, per civiles iudices exerceri iubemus, cum talibus negotiis vel causis iudices militares immiscere se ordo non patitur.[201]

Not only are civilian and military legal cases to be kept separate, but civilians are still called Romans! And this process is described as managing disputes *civiliter*. Theoderic's view of the world continued to exercise influence in Italy. Justinian's *milites* are the same as Theoderic's Goths: the professional notion of the soldier as barbarian continued to exist. But ultimately, all Justinian's subjects were also Romans in the political sense.

CONCLUSION

Older ethnographic and geographic texts continued to exist in the Mediterranean even as its political unity dissolved. With the appearance of the new ideologies of community of Theoderic, of the Catholic church and of Justinian, there was an upsurge in the copying of old ethnographic texts and the production of new ones. Whichever way the influence ran, ethnography informed the ideologies of king, church and emperor.

Ethnography and ideologies of community were received in various ways by literary observers of the time. In Ennodius and Eugippius, they produced various explanations of the changes that had taken place in the world. On a wider level, traditional ethnography was shown to be inadequate for describing contemporary conditions in regions such as the Balkans, sporadically outside the control of either Theoderic or the Eastern emperors. A man like Boethius was capable of ignoring contemporary conditions entirely, accepting traditional ethnography to the extent of believing not only that he lived in the Roman Empire, but in an unchanged Roman Empire. His personal circumstances suggest that there were few other people like him. He paid for his antiquarian views.

The ideologies of both Theoderic and Justinian used elements of classical ethnography and of Roman law to impose a new consistency on their realms in the name of restoring a golden past. These ideologies ultimately failed, or rather produced different results from

---

[201] *Sanctio pragmatica* 23.

those expected, because they did not adequately mirror institutional, professional, religious and regional identities of the time. Justinian's Christian ethnography was taken over by his successors, at the eventual cost of losing the many provinces of the East that had a different conception of Christianity from the emperors. In Italy, the conflict between Justinianic, Theoderican and Catholic ideologies during the Gothic Wars would split the peninsula apart entirely.

Chapter 5

INDIVIDUAL REACTIONS TO IDEOLOGY II: SOLDIERS, CIVILIANS AND POLITICAL ALLEGIANCE

Around the year 539, a soldier named Gundila lost his property to the armies of the emperor Justinian. He regained it by petitioning Belisarius and converting to Catholicism under Pope Vigilius, in the year of Byzantine triumph, about 540. The Arian bishop of Rome certified that Gundila no longer belonged to his faith. Gundila immediately donated some of his land to the Catholic church of St. Maria in Nepi.

In the early 540s, Totila's armies swept back through central Italy, taking Nepi along with the rest of Umbria. Totila seized the land of Gundila and gave it to one of his officers, a *comes* named Tzalico. In 544 or 545, Belisarius reoccupied Nepi, and Gundila enlisted his support to regain his property. Belisarius, who may have forgotten about Gundila, gave the remaining property to the Catholic monastery of St. Aelia in Nepi. Gundila, now desperate, went back to plead with Pope Vigilius, who furiously informed the monks of St. Aelia that the property ought to return to the hapless soldier, who had already shown himself a good Catholic by donating part of it to the church. Once Gundila received his property back for the second time, he gave part of it to the monastery of St. Aelia anyway, and another part to the monastery of St. Stephanus. In the late 540s, Nepi fell into the hands of the Goths again, and Tzalico may have occupied Gundila's property for a second time.

In 557, after the end of the wars, the heirs of all sides launched an inquiry before a magistrate in Rome, to discover who had rightful claims on the property of Gundila. Pieces of it now belonged to Gundila or his heirs, and possibly to the heirs of Tzalico, as well as to two monasteries and a church. The heirs of Tzalico claimed that the property was theirs by the gift of Totila; the churches no doubt pressed their claim strongly. Since the fragmentary record of the inquiry has survived in the archiepiscopal archive of the Church of Ravenna, we can assume that the monasteries did not surrender the parts of the property that had been given them.

This fragmentary shred of papyrus[1] depicts Gundila as a man frantically attempting to belong to the right community at the right time. A "Goth" by virtue of his military position, his service under Witigis and his membership in the *ecclesia Gothorum*, he was forced to become a "Roman" under Belisarius. Not only that, but the imperial church advocated by Vigilius in his early years demanded that "Romans" be Catholics. Gundila received his property back from its second confiscation by Totila only by placating the Catholic church with yet more donations.[2]

Without property or salary one cannot survive. Both Gundila and Tzalico were forced to choose sides, to choose identities, not once, but many times. Gundila's allegiance was to his property and his locality. He was an important landowner in Nepi, important enough that the Pope took an interest in his conversion, rather than his bishop.[3] He proved himself a Catholic church patron in the city. But both Gundila and Tzalico suffered from the competing ideologies of a larger community in Ostrogothic Italy: the Catholic Empire of Justinian and Vigilius, the allegiance-based military communities of Belisarius and Totila, the ethnographic ideology of Justinian.

These ideologies were hard to live up to, since the participants in the dispute over the property did not possess all the traits of Gothic or Roman identity according to a given ideology. Gundila, indeed, began with a Germanic name, the profession of soldier, allegiance to Witigis and membership in the Arian church. Soon, he was a Catholic in the service of Belisarius and Vigilius, and a local church patron in Nepi. He still kept his Germanic name, so some modern scholars, if this document had not survived, would assume that he was a "Goth," with accompanying assumptions. The witness Sitza, in contrast to Gundila, had a Germanic name but was a Latin-speaking civilian, and had always been a Catholic. Tzalico seems to have lost his military position at the end of the wars, and by this time, of course, there was no possibility of allegiance to a Gothic king. Tzalico and his sons may have been Catholics as well.[4] There is no hint that any of the individuals involved spoke the Gothic language or had any difficulty with Latin. Most, if not all of them, must have been born in Italy; Gundila's acquaintance Sitza had been born in the 490s.

---

[1] Ital 49; on its interpretation, see Tjäder 2: 194–9, 298–302; PA Gundila, Sitza and Tzalico, and appendix 1 below.

[2] The inquiry took place three years after Justinian's Pragmatic Sanction denied the validity of all gifts and actions of the *tyrannus* Totila (*Sanctio pragmatica* 2), and two years after the emperor "reconciled" Arian ecclesiastical properties to his Catholic church: *PItal* 2 with Tjäder 1: 180–1; Agnellus, *Liber Pontificalis Ravennatis* 86, p. 334.18–20.

[3] A bishop of Nepi, for example, at *Acta Synhodi a. CCCCXCVIIII*, p. 401, no. 57 (Felix).

[4] If he and his sons, rather than Gundila, made the donation to the monasteries (see n. 7, below).

The participants in the dispute may have only imperfectly realized the demands made on their identities, as opposed to their behavior or allegiance. A striking feature about the document is that it does not mention group-allegiances aside from the *ecclesia Gothorum* (the standard name for the Arian church),[5] and that only in a matter-of-fact way that sounds strange after the polemic of the official sources. For the witness Sitza, bewildered and repetitive as he is, the powers of Italy appear as individuals and institutions, not members of larger communities called Goths and Romans. Gundila converted, as Sitza states repeatedly. He was *reconciliatus*, so why did his problems not cease? There is an element of fatality in Sitza's narrative. The sons of Tzalico "came," presumably in an assault on the city; likewise, Belisarius "came," Vigilius *furuit* upon hearing that the property was in the hands of the monasteries. From Sitza's viewpoint, Gundila was a mere tool in the hands of powerful men whose motives remained blank to him.

This "merkwürdige Geschichte aus einer verworrenen Zeit"[6] may not have occurred exactly as described above, but something very much like it did happen.[7] The episode is an example of ways in which individual behavior did not always attach to ethnographic groups, any more than ethnographic ideology consistently described such groups. Rather, individual behavior could reflect what was demanded of ethnographic groups to which an individual was thought to belong according to his possession of certain traits. In this intersection between ideology and reality, we can see something of what it meant to be called a Goth or a Roman in early sixth-century Italy, and in turn, the effectiveness and reception of ideologies.

GOTHS, ROMANS AND ITALIANS

The story of Gundila is merely one of the more explicit narratives of the consequences of ethnographic ideologies. The following examination of individual behavior among people labeled Goths in Italy further illuminates the fluidity of that label. Goths were not polyethnic, as Wolfram argues, but poly-everything. They were the ideological stick of the moment. Under Theoderic, the army was supposed to be the Goths, the Goths the army. But the army recruited on its entrance to Italy and

---

[5] But possibly also *Gothi*, meaning the army of Totila, at line 15, with Tjäder 2: 300, n. 12.

[6] Tjäder 2: 196.

[7] See PA **G**undila: the events must have occurred in the years indicated and with more or less these changes in allegiance; a slightly altered absolute chronology allows it to be possible that Tzalico or his sons donated some of Gundila's property to the Catholic monasteries. See further appendix 1, p. 321, n. 2 and discussion at pp. 322–5.

continued to do so once it was in Italy. Soldiers, to be sure, were identifiable as such, but were also tightly bound to the civilian population of Italy.

In Theoderic's later years, and under his immediate successors, the military and civilian populations were no longer distinguishable in Italy. People from Italian families were active at the highest levels of the military; people combined military and civilian positions. Further down on the social scale, intermarriage and the purchase of land gave soldiers local ties that competed with that of the *exercitus Gothorum*. One result was the imperilment of the army as a different and differently funded institution in society, which gave rise to the bellicose rhetoric of the Goths as *gens*, led by the glorious Amal family.

In the period leading up to the installation of Witigis, the Amal family proved disposable, and a different tendency took over: the glorification of the military in Italy. We have already seen that the military branches of government were taking over more and more functions. Individuals who formerly moved between the civilian and military spheres, between the "Roman" and "Gothic" identities defined by Theoderic, now had to choose allegiances. The choice proved too difficult for some of them, as the conflict over the education of Athalaric demonstrates. After the outbreak of the Gothic Wars, and the introduction into Italy of the *renovatio* ideology of Justinian, allegiance to one side or the other became the primary focus of survival for both civilians and soldiers; the two groups were, of course, often interconnected by marriage, friendship, ties of dependency and a common upbringing in the same region of Italy. The label "Goth" offered advantages and disadvantages to an individual in different times and places. Goths collected taxes and defended taxes under Theoderic, took part in a glorious past in the Italy of the 520s and 530s, and were the savage enemies of the "Roman" state in the 540s and 550s – or the saviors of Italy, if one needed to pacify the armies of Totila rather than those of Justinian.

In the twistings and turnings of the people of Italy, caught under political machinations described in language derived from classical ethnography, we can see no single discrete group of people called the Goths. Membership of the Goths changed alongside definition of the group, and against the background of competing definitions of the group.

PROFESSION AND ALLEGIANCE BEFORE THE GOTHIC WARS,
489–535

The relationship of profession to allegiance comes to the fore in one rather obscure event at the turning-point of Ostrogothic power: the controversy over Athalaric's education, when the army demanded that the young king be raised as a soldier. As we shall see, this event gathers in many of the most important military figures of the period.

This event shows some responses to Theoderic's ideologies, stemming from the careers of military parvenus at court and their families. Parvenus, insecure in society, had more reason to change their identities than well-established individuals born into senatorial families or ecclesiastical careers. These are people who seized opportunities for advancement and enrichment, people who were open to novelty.[8]

Two contrasting Italian examples are the careers of Liberius and of Cyprian. They were both Catholics, both of Italian families, both adults by the time of Theoderic's arrival in Italy. Both men came from the same careerist social background, the provincial aristocracy of Italy. This background did not guarantee success and high office, as did membership in the urban senatorial clans like the Anicii or the Decii. These men had to climb the career ladder via the bureaucracy or the army, even when their parents and ancestors had served in these institutions and thus reached membership of the senate.[9]

Liberius was a man who guided his life by ideologies, but his very career contradicted the *civilitas* policy that he helped build as praetorian prefect of Italy in the 490s.[10] A "Roman," he was probably in a military office under Odoacer. He subsequently took the quasimilitary post of praetorian prefect Galliarum in *c.* 510, and received the supreme command, *patricius praesentalis*, in 533. He thus took over the command of the entire Gothic army, previously held by Theoderic and Tuluin.[11]

For Liberius, service to the Ostrogothic state seems to have meant service to the *res publica*, as for Ennodius, and indeed as for Theoderic under *civilitas* ideology. He earned Theoderic's respect by staying loyal

[8] On parvenus and senators under Theoderic, see Moorhead, *Theoderic*, pp. 147–72, 226–35, a subtle and penetrating analysis. Further on parvenus, see ch. 1, n. 2.

[9] Social background: PA Cyprianus, Liberius; see Opilio, Anonymi 20+; see further PLRE2 Cyprianus 2, Liberius 3, Opilio 4; on Liberius, see O'Donnell, "Liberius the patrician," pp. 32–5, and on Cyprian and Opilio, Moorhead, *Theoderic*, pp. 232–5. On parvenus in general, see Momigliano, "Cassiodorus and Italian culture of his time," pp. 188–90, observations that remain sharp even though Momigliano's arguments about Cassiodorus and Jordanes, and the barbarian–Roman dichotomy are no longer accepted.

[10] On Liberius, *civilitas* and the Gothic settlement, see ch. 4.

[11] PA Liberius and Tuluin; on *patricius praesentalis*, see ch. 3, p. 124 with n. 29. O'Donnell, in "Liberius the patrician," pp. 60–1, for some reason sees Liberius as a civilian before his appointment (*Var.* 11.1.16 clearly indicates otherwise), and restricts the appointment to Gaul, without any evidence, making the date contemporaneous with Tuluin's appointment (although the letter referring to it is from 533), and doubting that "the supreme military commander of the Ostrogoths ... would be sent on a diplomatic mission to Constantinople very shortly after his appointment to command" (p. 61, n. 114) (but in the meantime Theodahad had become king, and though no soldier himself, would shortly lead troops).

to Odoacer until the end.[12] His defection to the East under Theodahad, while on embassy from Theodahad to Justinian in 534,[13] suggests deep dissatisfaction with the Ostrogothic government.

Liberius defected when *civilitas* rhetoric was in decline, in disgust at the murder of Amalasuintha, as he explained to Justinian.[14] He henceforth served Justinian enthusiastically, even when the emperor failed to realize his virtues.[15] His epitaph shows that he never regretted leaving the Ostrogothic kingdom to its fate – but also that he did not regret his earlier service to that kingdom.[16]

The family of Cyprian displays a different set of attitudes, but Cyprian, like Liberius, embodied a contradiction of *civilitas* ideology. Theoderic and Athalaric recognized him as a "Roman," yet congratulated him on his military service. He also served in both military and civil positions.[17]

Cyprian and his family, despite their Catholicism, took on some of the most notable characteristics of "Goths" by Theoderic's own definition: the profession of soldier, the military education of their children, and the knowledge of the Gothic language. In the later part of his reign, Theoderic commended Cyprian for his knowledge of the Gothic language. Under Athalaric, Cyprian was praised for raising his children as soldiers and for teaching them Gothic. "Pueri stirpis Romana nostra lingua loquuntur," says Theoderic through the medium of Cassiodorus.[18]

Cyprian's brother Opilio, who also went on the embassy from Theodahad to Justinian,[19] was the only member to defend Theodahad, and the only one to return to Italy.[20] One suspects that there was not as much opportunity for Opilio in Constantinople as there was for the prestigious Liberius and the other, senatorial, ambassadors. But Opilio and his family had also established their loyalties in the 520s. Did his

---

[12] *Var.* 2.16.

[13] Procopius, BG 1(5).4.24; since a later source records that he was received with the ceremonial due to a praetorian prefect (O'Donnell, "Liberius the patrician," p. 63, n. 120), the Eastern government perhaps did not recognize his Western military command, which would have required theoretical recognition from the emperor if it was still seen as equivalent to the post held by Aetius, Ricimer, Odoacer and Theoderic.

[14] Procopius, BG 1(5).4.22–5.

[15] O'Donnell, "Liberius the patrician," pp. 63–71; PLRE2 Liberius 3.

[16] Below, p. 159.

[17] PA Cyprianus; see also ch. 2, above, pp. 73–4.

[18] *Var.* 5.40.5; 8.21.6–7; 8.22.5; PA Cyprianus.

[19] It is unclear why S. J. B. Barnish, in "Maximian, Cassiodorus, Boethius, Theodahad," pp. 31–2, does not think this Opilio identical with Cyprian's brother: his career and allegiances make the identification entirely probable.

[20] Procopius, BG1(5).4.25; on his return to Italy, note his possible tomb at Rome, PLRE2 Opilio 4.

family's choice of "Gothic" traits determine his choice in 535? The court of Justinian was just then suffused with exultation surrounding the success of the emperor's recent great projects: the conquest of Africa, the codification of the law, the building of Hagia Sophia. The emperor and his advisers were laying great stress on the power of the renewed Roman Empire against the barbarian nations.[21]

The opportunities of men like Cyprian and Opilio narrowed with the advent of the Gothic Wars. Although Cyprian and his family were called "Romans," they had laid claim to characteristics that did not fit Justinian's definition of a Roman: speaking a barbarous tongue, unswerving loyalty to a Gothic king, and involvement in the death of a senator and a Catholic pope.[22]

Their Catholicism and connections did not make these choices any easier. Opilio subscribed the Acts of the Council of Orange with Liberius in 529, and was one of the recipients of the letter from John II justifying his *professio fidei* to the emperor, a group that also included Cassiodorus and Liberius. Opilio may moreover have married into the Decii, a senatorial clan with close ties to the papacy.[23] But the family had tied itself to the Amal kings and the Gothic army in a way that Liberius had not.

The beginning of this narrowing process is exemplified by the obscure conflict surrounding the education of Athalaric. This conflict, although difficult to date precisely, occurred at some point after the letters of praise for Cyprian and his sons, the emergence of Cyprian and Opilio in high office, and came just before the appointment of Liberius as *patricius praesentalis*, in the late 520s and early 530s.

Our source for the conflict over Athalaric's education is Procopius, who describes it according to the oppositions of classical ethnography. Procopius states that Amalasuintha, herself classically educated, confided the education of Athalaric to three old Goths, in order to "make her son resemble the Roman princes in his manner of life, and was already compelling him to attend the school of a teacher of letters (*grammatistēs*)."[24] Several of the Goths, however, were displeased by this,

---

[21] Ch. 4, pp. 140–1, above.

[22] We would like to know whether Procopius, himself an exponent of aspects of Justinianic ideology, would have identified Cyprian's sons as Romans or as Goths. Cassiodorus does not mention their names. These sons of Cyprian might lurk in the pages of the *Gothic Wars*, hidden under names like Uligasalus and Rhecimundus. Choosing Germanic names for his children would have been entirely consistent with Cyprian's choice of profession and language for them. For families with both Germanic and Latin names, see PA III, table 11; for a probable Germanic name in Ennodius's family, see PA Senarius.

[23] PA Opilio.

[24] Procopius, BGI(5).2.6–7, trans. Dewing 5: 17.

"for because of their eagerness to wrong their subjects they wished to be ruled by him more after the barbarian fashion."[25] They insisted that Athalaric receive a barbarian upbringing and be trained in the use of weaponry, so that he might be a fit leader for them, as Theoderic had been. Amalasuintha acceded to their requests, but when Athalaric leagued with them against her, she exiled three of them to the limits of the kingdom, where they continued their plotting against her. Shortly thereafter she made her plans to escape to Justinian. But then she managed to have the three conspirators murdered, and she decided to stay at Ravenna.[26]

Procopius telescopes the events of the ten-year period from 525 to 535 into a short story that almost seems to have taken place in the space of a few months. He sets the Athalaric incident, which must have occurred in the few years leading up to 534,[27] in the larger context of the fall of Boethius and the rise of Theodahad, both men trained in classical letters.[28]

Procopius's opposition of classical learning and barbarian ways is a prologomena to the outbreak of the Gothic Wars, and he uses it as a mechanism to show why barbarians ought not to be ruling sections of the Roman Empire. Not that a classical education makes a man good: Theodahad, who appears for the first time directly after the story just related, is described as both educated and rapacious, and secretly in agreement with Justinian to hand over Tuscany to the emperor in return for a wealthy retirement in Constantinople. Procopius explains that Theodahad's knowledge of philosophy made him unsuitable for warfare, and that Peter the Patrician used this argument to encourage him to defect to Justinian.[29] Procopius ties Amalasuintha's plans for Athalaric into her generous treatment of the children of the executed Symmachus and Boethius.[30] Procopius thus uses this story to explain both the falling-out of Theodahad and Amalasuintha (Theodahad's greed and fear versus Amalasuintha's rectitude) and the falling-out of Theodahad and the Gothic army (Theodahad's treachery and his lack of military experience, the latter a consequence of his interest in letters).

This rhetorical construction suggests that we cannot take Procopius's story literally, as the artificial repetition of groups of "three Goths"

---

[25] Ibid. 1(5).2.8, trans. Dewing 5: 17.
[26] Ibid. 1(5).2.11–29. See PA **A**nonymi 8, 9, 10 (the three old men), **A**nonymi 11, 12, 13 (the conspirators), ★**A**malasuintha.
[27] Wolfram, *Goths*, p. 336: "late 532/early 533."
[28] On Theodahad's education, see PA ★**T**heodahadus, and Barnish, "Maximian, Cassiodorus, Boethius, Theodahad," pp. 28–32.
[29] Procopius, BG 1(5).6.6–13.
[30] Ibid. 1(5).2.5.

already suggests. It is impossible to believe, for example, as the conspirators are said to have alleged, that Theoderic forbade the Goths to send their children to school, because it would wean them away from a warrior's courage.[31] The whole thrust of Theoderic's own rhetoric was to praise education and to celebrate the Goths' knowledge of Roman ways.[32] He himself ensured that Amalasuintha and Amalaberga received training in letters.[33] Procopius has inserted the allegation to strengthen his explanatory opposition – based on traditional ethnographic motifs – between classical education and barbarian soldierly virtue.

Is there a grain of truth in Procopius's story? The army's objection was that Athalaric was not being raised as a soldier. The three Goths were military men.[34] High officers were probably not motivated chiefly by "eagerness to wrong their subjects," and both Theoderic and the army valued a military education that may have included traditions unrelated to a classical education.[35]

Times had changed since the original propagation of *civilitas* rhetoric, and the army worried that the new king would not be able to lead them in battle when he came of age. It is entirely natural that Procopius described this situation in ethnographic terms: here he borrows from Theoderic's later ideological stance (which ignored classical education – but did not denigrate it) and combines it with that of Justinian (for whom the Goths were naturally savage and the enemies of Romans). Once young Athalaric joined the military men, he seems to have taken their views too, against those of his mother.

Athalaric, brought up like a Roman emperor, crossed the line in the reverse direction from the sons of Cyprian, Roman boys who were brought up like Goths. The notion that one could combine a classical education with military training, as Theoderic himself had done, does not seem to have occurred to any of the participants in the story; Procopius closes it out via the Justinianic ideology of Gothic savagery and lawlessness. But it may also be a sign of the anxious times. Amalasuintha surely realized that war was impending. Justinian conquered Africa in 533, the Frankish kings invaded Burgundy in 534. As in the careers of Liberius and Opilio, available political options were dwindling.

---

[31] Ibid. 1(5).2.14, accepted without a qualm by Chadwick, *Boethius*, p. 3, and by Riché, *Education and Culture*, pp. 63–4 (with phrasing implying other evidence, of which there is none, that Theoderic forbade Goths to get an education).

[32] See ch. 2.

[33] PA *Amalaberga, *Amalasuintha.

[34] Perhaps including PA Tuluin, *patricius praesentalis*: Wolfram, *Goths*, p. 336; Mommsen, "OGS," NA 14: 506–7; Ensslin, "Patricius," pp. 245–6, 248, is less certain. Other candidates might be PA Triwila and PA Liberius.

[35] Above, ch. 3.

The incident of Athalaric's education took place precisely before the period when Liberius was appointed commander-in-chief of the Gothic army. Procopius, although familiar with the patrician's activities, does not mention him in connection with the events – he did not fit into Procopius's vision of the Gothic military.[36] We would like to know whether Liberius was one of Amalasuintha's supporters, as we would expect from his loyalty to her after her death. If so, Procopius seems to have included him among "certain Goths who were energetic men and especially devoted to her."[37]

Where did Cyprian and Opilio fit into the conflict over Athalaric? The latter shortly emerges as the only supporter of Theodahad on the embassy to Justinian, so perhaps Cyprian and Opilio were among the "Goths" ranged against Amalasuintha. But we must beware of making easy judgments on factions.[38] It is perfectly plausible that Liberius, as a high-ranking officer, supported a military training for Athalaric, even though he was loyal to Amalasuintha politically. We might also expect Opilio, as a supporter of the classically educated Theodahad, to support a classical education for Athalaric. The evidence does not permit us to range people on either side, particularly in so polarized a picture as that of Procopius.[39]

It is probably due to this difficulty of choosing sides that the family of Cyprian and Opilio vanishes from history at the outbreak of the Gothic Wars. Opilio, the devout Catholic, must have found it very difficult to maintain his loyalty to the Gothic kings in the face of new papal support for Justinian. Unlike John II and Silverius, Pope Vigilius actively supported the emperor's policies during the opening stages of the Gothic Wars. Cassiodorus, another highly placed Italian Catholic, found himself supporting Vigilius in Constantinople, although Cassiodorus had remained loyal to Vigilius's enemy Witigis to at least 537–8, possibly to the end in 540. Cassiodorus at this point chose a religious

---

[36] Procopius, BG I(5).4.15 refers to him only as "a man of the Roman senate" (similarly Opilio, who had also held office under Athalaric), perhaps to exonerate him from personal service to the Gothic kings. Later Procopius again refuses to admit that Liberius had military experience, despite his own evidence to the contrary: see PA Liberius. On the collectivity of Liberius and Opilio with other men who had served the kings in John II's letter about his *professio fidei*, see ch. 6, below, pp. 218, 222–3.

[37] Procopius, BG I(5).2.25.

[38] See ch. 6, below.

[39] Of course, people probably had different views on different subjects, just like the partisans of the schisms, circus factions and disputed papal elections (see ch. 6, below). The difficulties of Barnish ("Maximian, Cassiodorus, Boethius, Theodahad," pp. 31–2) vanish if one accepts that faction membership or political partisanship need not restrict every other activity.

life, and gave up secular affairs.[40] We do not know which option Opilio chose.

Liberius, on the other hand, chose the "Roman" world of Justinian. He did not regret his service under the Gothic kings, and saw this service as "Roman" too, as his metrical epitaph shows.[41] This touching inscription, left at Rimini after 554, records that Liberius "rexit Romuleos fasces"[42] for many years, governed Gaul according to the rule of law, served in the army, and successfully arranged the Gothic settlement ("Ausoniae populis gentiles rite cohortes disposuit, sanxit foedera, iura dedit").[43] The word *iura* appears twice, and the poem begins with a reference to a *lex* of nature.

Liberius and his family thus saw fit to preserve, in the war-ravaged Italy after 554, the memory that he had arranged the Gothic settlement, supported the rule of law, and served faithfully under the Gothic kings – disposing all this information under the heading "running Roman offices." Such a view of his service was both Theoderican and Justinianic: the emphasis on *ius* and *lex*, the running together of the entire Mediterranean world under the heading "Roman," and the association of the Gothic army with *gentiles*. Astonishingly, the epitaph contains no reference to Liberius's well-recorded piety and Christian activities.[44] Perhaps he was disgusted with the church after his involvement with Justinian's difficulties with monophysites and with Vigilius's acceptance of the condemnation of the Three Chapters.[45]

A man also associated with the Athalaric incident was Tuluin, who may well have been a parvenu despite his or Cassiodorus's subsequent

---

[40] Cassiodorus, *Expositio Psalmarum, praef.* 1; O'Donnell, in *Cassiodorus*, pp. 103–30, points out that the notion that Cassiodorus abandoned Witigis after the massacre of Roman senators is unattested in any source and does not explain the composition of the *Variae*, which supports Witigis's rule (p. 104, n. 3). Cassiodorus eventually retired to his place of origin, his beloved Squillace, where he founded the monastery of Vivarium. But as praetorian prefect, he had kept up his interest in its welfare: O'Donnell, *Cassiodorus*, pp. 17–18 (interest as praetorian prefect), 177–22; Momigliano, "Cassiodorus and Italian culture of his time," p. 199; Pierre Courcelle, "Nouvelles recherches sur le monastère de Cassiodore," [1957] reprinted in Courcelle, *Opuscula Selecta* (Paris, 1984), pp. 137–54.

[41] CIL 11.382.

[42] "Rumuleos."

[43] It does not seem possible to equate this with the reorganization of Italy under Justinian in 554, as PLRE2: 680–1 does. Why would Justinian's armies be called *gentiles cohortes* and how could they be in a *foedus* when they were Roman troops in a Roman province? But it fits the Gothic settlement of the 490s perfectly.

[44] The reverse, in fact: it regrets that his great deeds might die with his physical remains.

[45] O'Donnell, "Liberius the patrician," perhaps overemphasizes Liberius's interest in the church; he certainly cannot explain the epitaph and (pp. 70–1) is forced to dismiss it as "filial piety and nothing more," concluding that "the only usable piece of information that it contains is that his wife was buried in the same tomb" (!).

claims to the contrary. Tuluin rose through the army, serving, like Cyprian, in the Sirmium war of 504–5. Like Cyprian, he became one of the king's most trusted counselors, and subsequently served as *dux* in Gaul in 508 and again in military operations there in 523–4.[46]

In 526, Athalaric's government appointed Tuluin *patricius praesentalis*, the chief of the armed forces in Italy. Tuluin had just recently married a daughter of Theoderic. The letter announcing Tuluin's appointment to the senate was originally sent in his name, not that of Athalaric, and it is clear that Tuluin must have been one of the most important members of the government in the late 520s, with Amalasuintha, Cyprian and Cassiodorus.[47]

Tuluin, the commander of the army, may have been a member of the military party in the conflict over Athalaric's education. Although Tuluin is only mentioned in the *Variae*, not in Procopius, Liberius was appointed to Tuluin's office, the *patriciatus praesentalis*, directly after the conflict. Procopius says that the "three Goths" who opposed Amalasuintha were exiled and killed. Tuluin does not appear in history after this event. He clearly posed a danger to Amalasuintha. Married into the royal family, holding the command of the armed forces previously held by Theoderic, and announcing this appointment to the senate in his own name, he had potential claims to the kingship. Tuluin's replacement, Liberius, had proved himself unfailingly loyal, and, was perhaps more sympathetic to the idea of a classical education for Athalaric. When Liberius finally defected to Byzantium, he did so on the grounds of his loyalty to the memory of Amalasuintha. Since at the end of his life, he hearkened back with pride to his achievements under Theoderic, his defection cannot have owed anything to the "Roman" claims of Justinian. Whether or not Tuluin actually had his eyes on the throne, his career background and his office in a time of uncertain security make it likely that he was one of the party urging a military upbringing for the young king.[48]

Brought up in Theoderic's early reign, Tuluin had started his life surrounded by the ideology of *civilitas*. Paradoxically, at the time when Tuluin himself achieved the supreme command, the main contradiction to, and support of, *civilitas*, the military-civilian office of the king himself, no longer existed. It had split. Athalaric carried the magisterial and quasi-imperial attributes of the Italian *rex*, Tuluin its military duties.

---

[46] PA Tuluin.

[47] PA Tuluin, *Anonyma 2; PLRE2 Tuluin; Wolfram, *Goths*, pp. 335–7; Ensslin, "Patricius," pp. 246–7; on the title, above, see ch. 3, p. 92 with n. 29.

[48] He would thus have been one of PA Anonymi 11, 12, 13, the "three Goths" of Procopius; also Wolfram, *Goths*, p. 336, and Ensslin, "Patricius," pp. 245–6 (with reservations).

But we find Tuluin urging the government to keep this military-civilian office alive, against Amalasuintha, who preferred that her son be raised far from the army. Athalaric's government began by sending out letters suffused with revived *civilitas* rhetoric, except for the letter to the army.[49] It was presumably felt that *civilitas* no longer appealed to the military commanders. Such a development is in line with the royal government's increasing stress on the sacrality and history of the Amal family, along with its peculiar association with the army and that army's elect claims as a *gens*. This ideology also required that the (Amal) ruler be the commander of the army.[50]

Tuluin, then, did not support *civilitas* in the sense of a functional division between soldiers and civilians in Italy, led by a soldier-civilian king. He himself, as *maior domus regiae*, had served in the king's closest circle, a *consilium* composed of people of all backgrounds, including men with military-civilian offices.[51] We cannot say anything about Tuluin's attitude toward the word "Goth," but it is obvious that he represented the increasing authority of the army in the governance of Italy.[52]

Tuluin's career and behavior match those of Cyprian, even though Cyprian came from an Italian family and was called a "Roman" by the king. Cyprian bought into the attributes of "Goth" under Theoderic; Tuluin had two of them already: his name and his profession. Both men rose through the army and personal service to the king, both men achieved their highest office after the Boethius affair, and both men disappear from history after the crisis involving Athalaric's education, in which both seem to have been involved. On the embassy to Justinian, Cyprian's relative Opilio defended Amalasuintha's murderer Theodahad, and Tuluin's replacement Liberius stuck by Amalasuintha.

Other military parvenus accepted and benefited from Theoderic's bellicose post-*civilitas* ideology. This was naturally especially the case with individuals who had exclusively military careers. One such family was that of Witigis, whom Procopius says was of "obscure birth;" his uncle and nephew were both soldiers. Like Tuluin and Cyprian, he first came to prominence fighting in the Sirmium war of 504–5. Much later, he became *spatharius* and adviser to Athalaric, swordbearer, which

---

[49] Ch. 2 above, pp. 71–2.

[50] Ch. 2 above, pp. 66–75.

[51] *Var.* 5.41.3 on Cyprian's advice to the king, "which used to be given in the former *consistoria*;" other members of this *consilium* appear to have been the *maiores domus regiae* PA **A**rigernus, **B**edeulfus, **G**udila 1 and **W**acca. Of these, **A**rigernus and **G**udila 1 held both military and civilian offices; **W**acca was a civilian.

[52] On this phenomenon in general in the fifth- and sixth-century West, epitomized by the title and the *officium* of Ricimer, Theoderic and Tuluin (*patricius praesentalis, officium nostrum*), see Sinnigen, "Administrative shifts of competence in Ostrogothic Italy," pp. 456–67.

might suggest that he too was part of the pro-military party; he certainly appears immediately afterward as the army's answer to Theodahad. He fought again at Sirmium in the late 520s, and was eventually appointed to the high position *armiger*, commander of the bodyguard, to Theodahad, and was leading Gothic forces at Rome when he ordered Theodahad's murder in 536.[53]

Witigis was a soldier of military family who accepted Theoderic's late ideology of the supremacy of the Gothic *gens* as an army, as his royal rhetoric shows. Witigis had not benefited early on; Theoderic allotted him no reward for his fighting at Sirmium in 504/5.[54] Witigis only rose to prominence at the accession of Athalaric, at a time when the army received the only letter that did not use *civilitas* rhetoric of all the major constituencies of Italy. When Witigis himself became king, as we have seen, the letters of the *Variae* and the panegyric of Cassiodorus propagated the image of the Goths as a people under arms who owed their fame solely to their valor in war, not to their acceptance of the *prudentia Romanorum* or even the *sanguis Amalorum*.[55] Witigis stressed the military vocation of Goths over the sacrality of Amal blood, despite his service to three Amal kings, two of them in intimate positions. He did away with Theodahad, and his forcible marriage to Matasuentha smacks of political exigency rather than a mystical respect for the Amal line.[56]

Of course, the reception of the *civilitas* and *bellicositas* ideologies was often confused. Soldiers and civilians fought for their prerogatives. Costula and Daila petitioned Theoderic to have *onera servilia* removed, on the basis that Goths ought to possess *libertas*. The king ordered their commander to see that the two men recovered their *libertas*, probably freedom from taxation in this case.[57] At precisely the same time, the king was propagating *civilitas* ideology in Pannonia, where he stated that *antiqui barbari* who had married Roman wives had to assume the burdens that came with the land.[58] These soldiers may have given up their military duties, but such a distinction may have been more obvious in Ravenna than in the towns and garrisons of the kingdom. Even the

---

[53] PA *Witigis; relatives: Ulitheus, Uraïas. On *armiger*, see Wolfram, *Goths*, p. 351; Moorhead, *Theoderic*, p. 101; PLRE3: 1383.

[54] Cassiodorus, *Oratio* 2, p. 476, lines 6–9, with PLRE3: 1383.

[55] Ch. 2, pp. 77–8.

[56] Wolfram (*Goths*, p. 343) implicitly connects the marriage to the necessity of Amal leadership of the Goths. Matasuentha herself felt differently: PA *Matasuentha. Heather ("Theoderic," pp. 165–73) rightly sees the issue of succession as a matter of "practical leadership ability" and not as the fully inculcated respect for a dynasty.

[57] PA Costula and Daila; *Var.* 5.30.

[58] *Var.* 5.14.6.

king does not inquire whether Costula and Daila ought legally to be paying taxes; to them it must have seemed that soldiers ought not to bear such humiliating burdens whatever the circumstances. It is the same mentality that led to the constant conflicts and seizures of property between Gothic and Roman *consortes*.[59]

Nonetheless, the rise of parvenus to both military and civilian positions exposed the obvious conflict between functional *civilitas* and reality. Nor was the mystical ideology of Amal superiority maintained by Theoderic universally recognized. Theoderic himself suspected not only Boethius and John, but also the military plots of Odoin in 500 and Pitzia in 514. Witigis murdered Theodahad by the hand of a soldier named Optaris who himself held a grudge against the Amal king; as we have seen, Amalasuintha had reason to fear the claims of Tuluin.[60]

What, in fact, united people called Goths, when a soldier like Starcedius could obtain a discharge for a *vita otiosa*? He lost his donative, but went from being a mere *vir strenuus* to being a *vir spectabilis*, and the enjoyment of the senatorial virtue of *otium*. While he apparently settled down to the life of a comfortable landowner, other parvenus rose to dizzying heights. Tancila combined the garrison commandership of Como with its civil governance. Triwila went from *saio* to *praepositus cubiculi*, was addressed as *domnus* by Ennodius, obtained the ear of Theoderic, and may have obtained yet higher office in the affair over Athalaric's education, in which he too seems to have been involved.[61]

"Increasing social differentiation" was splitting apart military men labeled Goths.[62] In their new lives, the parvenus moved in the widest circles of power. The Arian Triwila was a correspondent of Ennodius but also a friend of Theoderic's Catholic physician Helpidius, who in turn knew Caesarius of Arles, Avitus of Vienne and later Procopius. Tuluin, despite his purely military background, acquired land near the monastery of Lucullanum, the center of the Catholic intellectual circle of Boethius, Dionysius Exiguus and Pope John I – hardly the place we would expect to find the commander-in-chief of the Gothic army in Italy.[63]

But on all levels, soldiers settled down and learned local loyalties and

---

[59] See above, ch. 2, and Goffart, *Barbarians and Romans*, pp. 91–9. The ruling classes in Frankish Gaul probably developed a similar mindset about paying and collecting taxes or rent: Heinrich Dannenbauer, "Die Rechtsstellung der Gallorömer im Frankischenreich," in Dannenbauer, *Grundlagen der mittelalterlichen Welt* (Stuttgart, 1958), pp. 102–20.

[60] PA Odoin, Pitzia, Optaris.

[61] PA Starcedius, Tancila, Triwila.

[62] Moorhead, *Theoderic*, pp. 100–101.

[63] PA Triwila, Tuluin, PLRE2 Helpidius 6.

patronage outside their allegiance to the king and army.[64] The *dromonarii* Witterit, Andreas and Secundus all owned land near Ravenna. Gundila was a landowner and church patron at Nepi; so perhaps was Tzalico. Ursus, probably *dux Norici*, paid for splendid mosaics in the Catholic church of Teurnia in Carinthia. Theoderic's *maior domus regiae* Gudila made euergetic restorations and an inscription at Faenza. One family with both Latin and Germanic names stayed in Como over three generations and patronized the local saint and Catholic church.[65] Inscriptions do not often specify profession; if they did, we would be able to see many more soldiers engaged in local life. The process of localization becomes clearer in the Gothic Wars, but it was well underway by the first decade of the sixth century.

It is easy to see how institutional or ethnographic loyalties and identities – soldier, Goth – could be eroded both by the process of a successful career and by the growth of local patronage and ties of property and family. Such erosion motivated Theoderic's later bellicose ideology and the crisis over Athalaric's education when the military commanders asserted their authority and identity in the strongest terms. In the late 520s, although reconquest was not yet in the air, the notion of a single Mediterranean Empire certainly was. The kingdom of Italy was also under threat from Franks and Vandals. None of this need have posed a problem to the army except that Theoderic's ideology had already been claiming for years that the army was a separate, distinct community within Italian society – and except that Justinian's ideology would propose exactly the same thing in different terms. The Gothic army could not become merely the army of Italy while these two ideologies and the outside threats existed.

How could the *exercitus Gothorum* continue to exist when its members were indistinguishable from the other inhabitants of Italy, except by profession? The problem of defining soldiers had bothered the fifth-century emperors, with their constant plea to keep the military and civil spheres separate,[66] and the Burgundian kings, whose system of military

---

[64] General references: *barbari* acquiring *praedia* in Italy after 489 (*Var.* 1.14); *antiqui barbari* in Pannonia acquiring Roman wives and taxpaying land (*Var.* 5.14.6); building houses in the *castellum* of Verruca (*Var.* 3.48); Goths of Picenum and Tuscia to pay tax on any land that they own (*Var.* 4.14).

[65] PA Andreas, Secundus, Witterit; on Gundila and Tzalico, see above, p. 150 with n. 4, and Gundila, Anonyma 5, Anonymi 39+ (with family); Ursus; Gudila 1; on family see Guntelda (with Basilius and Guntio).

[66] Note especially *Nov. Iust.* 116; amplifying CJ 12.35.15–16, of Leo I: neither *milites* or *foederati* are to own land requiring them to pay *utilitates*. They did, of course, own land anyway, but see below on the greater restrictions on Byzantine soldiers than on Gothic soldiers, with accompanying consequences for the Gothic Wars.

provisioning and salary was under threat from assimilation, intermarriage and the sale of *sortes*.[67] The kind of assimilation that we see in Ostrogothic Italy threatened the same process: if soldiers owned land and paid taxes, the very military fabric could break down.

Meanwhile, right up until the Gothic Wars, civilians in Italy continued to believe in Theoderic's Roman Empire. One urban senator, Salventius, described his brother Traianus's service as a provincial governor as *"servans imperium"* in April 533, while Justinian's armies were preparing for their invasion of Africa. The brother had been born under Theoderic and died under Athalaric.[68] Such senators could not yet imagine that Italy and Rome needed to be "restored" to the Roman Empire. Justinian's ideology did not penetrate all levels even of the senatorial aristocracy. These men had benefited from high office under the Ostrogothic kings; Salventius had been appointed urban prefect by Athalaric in that year. If some senators had good reason to welcome Justinian's invasion, there were many who did not. This was all the more true at less exalted levels of Italian society, upon whom the Gothic Wars fell like a bomb.

SOLDIERS, CIVILIANS AND IDEOLOGY DURING THE GOTHIC WARS, 535–554

Ideology on both sides conspired to make the Goths an army again during the Gothic Wars, so it is particularly relevant that it is during this period that we can most clearly see Goths or soldiers with local or regional identities. Sometimes these local ties express themselves in the institutional behavior of the army as a whole. But this institution was itself split by status and region. It was impossible to lift Goths out of civilian life, "cleanly intercepting" their ties of marriage, property or religion in the manner that emperors and kings may have done at their whim when they required soldiers from generals or rents due to landowners.

In Italy between 535 and 554, the Italian civilian population suffered continuously from the demands on their allegiance by the armies of Justinian and of the Gothic kings. But this civilian population was not, of course, as disconnected from the Gothic army as Procopius's rhetoric would have us believe. Through Procopius's description we can clearly see the tribulations of people and groups of people like Gundila, whose

---

[67] Amory, "The meaning and purpose of ethnic terminology," pp. 24–6; Amory, "Names, ethnic identity and community," pp. 26–8.
[68] ICUR no. 1031, set up by Praetextatus Salventius Verecundus Traianus *vir clarissimus et spectabilis* on 22 April 533; PLRE3 Traianus 1.

non-military associations and allegiances conflicted with the identities demanded by the Byzantine and Gothic generals.

Some historians argue that Italian sympathies generally lay with the Byzantines, and against the Goths, part of the "perceived unity of the sub-Roman world."[69] Aside from the inconsistency and constant change in perceptions of such unity,[70] the evidence does not support this view. Who were the civilians? Many senators and the leaders of the Catholic church supported Justinian's invasion, at least once it had occurred. But even here there were divergences, and Vigilius and his bishops came to regret that support. Further down on the social scale, Italians desperately tried to fend for themselves as armies warred over their heads, devastated their lands and slaughtered their families. Support for either side was dictated partly by the proximity of one army or the other, partly by belief in ideology and partly by familial and regional ties to soldiers of either side.

Much as Procopius would have us believe that two alien armies sought to woo the Italian population, the truth was that many smaller military bands, Gothic and Byzantine, were preying alternately upon the civilian population. More than this, both military groups had ties to the civilian population – both, since members of the Italian ("Gothic") army rapidly defected to the Byzantine ("Roman") side, and vice-versa. The changing allegiances of the Gothic Wars reveal the civilian population's closer ties to a city or region of Italy than to those of the competing armies.

Totila reminded the people of Rome of the good rule of Theoderic. Belisarius and Narses told them that as Romans they belonged to the Empire and the rule of the Catholic Roman emperor Justinian in Constantinople. Vigilius told them that they were properly the Catholic citizens of a Roman Empire that Gothic, Arian barbarians were attempting to destroy. But in what predicament did this place the senator Flavius Maximus, married to an Amal princess – or the Gothic garrisons of the Cottian Alps, settled there for two generations with wives and children? Neither the revived *civilitas* ideology of Totila, nor

---

[69] Moorhead, "Italian loyalties during Justinian's Gothic war," p. 596. Although E. A. Thompson (in "The Byzantine conquest of Italy: public opinion," in Thompson [ed.], *Romans and Barbarians*, pp. 92–109), recognized desertions and the changing sympathies of cities like Naples, he saw the identities of the three groups as sharply defined (although he recognizes desertions), and thus his analysis concludes that "the Italians were basically pro-Byzantine," apparently on the basis that Totila's war-dance could not appeal to Romans (p. 108). Revealingly, he elsewhere includes civilian Italians among "the Byzantines" (p. 104). Altogether, despite occasional skepticism, Thompson falls into the trap of taking Procopius's narrative at face-value.

[70] Ch. 4 discusses some of these perceptions; ch. 6 discusses the overlapping, not always congruent, perceptions of a Christian Empire and a Catholic *congregatio fidelium*.

the ideology of the Gothic *gens* promoted by Witigis and (negatively) by Justinian, nor the *renovatio* ideology of Justinian, could adequately regroup the population of Italy into opposing sides. The result was one of the most drawn-out and horrifying wars of the early Middle Ages.

Political allegiance and profession counted for more than kinship in Justinian's world-view. With some exceptions, like the case of Gundila, we can see few individuals during the Gothic Wars outside the gaze of Procopius. But his language and his personal beliefs can escape the bounds of Justinianic ideology. When this happens individuals appear whose kinship does not match their political allegiance, or actually appears to *change* when their political allegiance changes; more frequently, local and professional loyalties do not match Procopius's stated political allegiance.

Kinship and "compatriotism" have a problematic relationship in Procopius.[71] Soldiers defected to either side continually during the wars, and are thenceforth called "Goths" or "Romans." True, the "Roman army," we learn rapidly, is a mixed bunch comprising *barbaroi* or people with ethnographic *gens*-names, or people given regional names chiefly from the Balkans, such as "Thracian" or "Illyrian."[72] But as we shall see, not only do the names indicating political allegiance change according to circumstance, but also the very individual *gens*-names.

As for the Goths, Procopius always configures them as a homogeneous military group, despite the large number of defections to their side, and even when he initially allots the defectors another identity. Ten Hunnic soldiers deserted from the Byzantine army in Libya and escaped to Campania just before the Byzantine invasion of Italy.[73] "Romans and Moors" deserted to the Gothic side in Bruttium in 546.[74]

---

[71] This will be addressed below. *Katharoi* usually refers to allegiance, "compatriots," those who are loyal, *xungeneis* to "kinsmen," often the same people, e.g. BGI(5).13.17; but Herodian and his Isaurians become not only "kinsmen" but "born kinsmen" upon defecting to the Goths: *xungeneis gegenemenoi*, 3(7).21.16. Agathias claims that Ragnaris was neither *katharos* nor *xungenes* to the Goths. In fact, these concepts were completely confused. See further below, and PA Herodianus, Ragnaris.

[72] On the composition of Justinian's armies, John L. Teall, "The barbarians in Justinian's armies," *Speculum* 40 (1965), 294–325, a detailed discussion that however presumes discrete ethnic identities in ethnographic group-names ("essentially a question of ethnic composition," p. 295); Teall tries to differentiate between subjects and non-subjects of the emperor, but as he admits, these legal (as opposed to political) distinctions counted for less and less (296–7). His argument (297–312) that Justinian's armies went from being largely Roman to being "truly imperial, composed of peoples far more diverse in origin" is unsupported. In fact, they went from being largely *Eastern*, recruited from the diversity of groups in the original provinces under Justinian's domination, to being more *Mediterranean*, as Justinian's armies absorbed the armies of the kingdoms that they conquered.

[73] PA Anonymi 23–32.

[74] PA Anonymi 35+.

But every individual soldier on the Gothic side is called a "Goth" if his identity is mentioned at all. In Procopius's description, certain defectors even gain "kinship" along with "compatriotism." No civilians can ever be Goths. This is classical ethnogeography in action. It did not describe the most important allegiances and identities of many of the soldiers involved.

Institutional and regional loyalty: the first phase of the Gothic Wars, 535–540

A number of cases of changing allegiance and identity occurred at the end of the first phase of the Gothic Wars, just before Belisarius's capture of Ravenna in 540. Defection could change identity in the eyes of Procopius, but the defecting Goths ran the risk of giving up their family and property in Italy to go with Justinian's armies to wherever they were posted. In exchange, they became "Romans."

At the Byzantine siege of Urbino, the Goths surrendered on condition "that they should become subjects of the emperor, on terms of complete equality with the Roman army;"[75] that is, that they should join Justinian's army, always called "Romans" by Procopius. At the siege of Petra, the Goths surrendered on condition that they become subjects of the emperor and obedient to Belisarius.[76] The Byzantine troops led most of them away, "putting them on a basis of complete equality with themselves," leaving the rest with their wives and children and a small garrison of "Romans."[77] The Gothic garrison of Fiesole, and those of Treviso and other fortresses in the Veneto, were similarly absorbed into the Byzantine armies.[78] "All the Goths settled in Dalmatia and Liburnia" joined the Byzantine forces even earlier, in 536–7, after the defeat of their commander.[79] The Gothic commander Pitzas surrendered himself and "the Goths of Samnium" to Belisarius in 537, and received the command of the region.[80]

At the siege of Osimo, the Goths surrendered to Belisarius, and, after some wrangling over what would become of their property, they "mingled with the emperor's army," becoming "subjects of the emperor."[81] This passage describes the same process as the others. It

[75] Procopius, BG 2(6).19.17.
[76] Ibid. 2(6).11.19; Dewing 3: 385 misleadingly translates *douloi* as "slaves" of the emperor, and *katekooi* as "subject to" Belisarius.
[77] Procopius, BG 2(6).11.20.
[78] Ibid. 2(6).27.25–6; 2(6).29.40–1.
[79] PA Anonymi 34+; their commander, Gripas, fled back to Ravenna with some of his troops.
[80] PA Pitzas.
[81] Procopius, BG 2(6).27.31–4, perhaps including their commander, PA Visandus 2.

reveals Goths becoming Romans in two ways: by service in the Roman (Byzantine) army, and by accepting the emperor as ruler. In older parlance, they became Roman citizens. Of course, Goths and Italians had been considered Roman citizens of the *res publica* under Theoderic, but under Justinianic ideology, citizenship was being restored through the Byzantine reconquest of Italy. Roman citizenship now entailed acknowledging the direct rule of Constantinople; the name "Roman" did not change, but the definition of the name and its consequent implied allegiance had.

These passages show not only that it was easy to change ethnographic identity, but also that these Goths had local ties. The men of the garrison of Petra were clearly local, and some of them were able to remain with their families. The soldiers of the Osimo garrison worried what would become of their property there. Perhaps they made arrangements similar to those of Gundila, who began his travails at about this time, and had lost his property in the same way. Of course, not all garrisons were composed exclusively of local soldiers; unsurprisingly, the Goths defending Ravenna during Witigis's last stand did not all live there. But instead of being pressed into the Byzantine army, the soldiers in Ravenna were sent "home" after Belisarius's capture of the city in 540.[82] Probably the Byzantine generals assumed that the war was more or less over, so that the soldiers need not be pressed into immediate service. They returned to their families and lands, wherever they might be.

This conflict between local ties and political allegiance is clearest in the garrisons of the Cottian Alps in 539–40, where "the noblest of the Goths resided ... together with their wives and children."[83] The Gothic commander Sisigis submitted to Belisarius, joining his forces to those of the Byzantine general. Uraïas, Witigis's uncle, then besieged the defector Sisigis. But, after another Byzantine general had enslaved local women and children, "most" of Uraïas's men detached themselves from his army and joined the Byzantine forces, for these men were "natives" of the fortresses.[84]

These local garrisons had been established in the Cottian Alps since before 508, when Theoderic addressed a letter to "all the Goths and Romans living in Dertona," a fortress there.[85] The king instructed these "Goths and Romans" to build themselves houses within the fort for

---

[82] Ibid. 2(6).29.35–6.
[83] Ibid. 2(6).28.29; the meaning of *aristoi* here is unclear: see pp. 159, 161–2, above on "nobility" among the Goths. This seems to be a formulaic phrase of Procopius's for establishing that individuals are worthy opponents.
[84] Ibid. 2(6).28.28–35; PA Sisigis, Uraïas.
[85] *Var.* 1.17; on the date, Krautschick, *Cassiodor*, pp. 64, 73.

protection. Close relations between soldiers and civilians in the fort, doubtless including intermarriage, thus dated back thirty years, if not more,[86] from the defection of the soldiers of Sisigis and Uraïas, frightened for their families and their property. In fact, we hear of no Italians or civilians in the tale of Procopius, simply of soldiers and soldiers' families.[87]

These surrenders and negotiations allowed soldiers to preserve not only their freedom but also their local positions and ties. Witigis is said to have warned his soldiers in Ravenna that they would be "enslaved" if they lost to the Byzantines;[88] although we must discount the actual speech as the concoction of Procopius, with its classicizing verbiage and evocations of a Tacitean barbarian *libertas*, there is no question that in some sense this slavery was true. Goths left at a camp in Picenum were enslaved by the troops of Ildiger.[89] Such slavery may have involved actual servitude, but even if it allowed the soldiers their professions, they were certainly no longer in control of their destiny. Captured Vandal garrisons had been sent to the far Eastern frontier by Justinian in the 530s. The army of Ostrogothic Italy, unused to postings that would carry them so far away, wished to preserve their extra-institutional ties and belongings.

The Byzantine army itself suffered from the conflict between its duties and the non-military ties of its members. Long-distance postings, years of service in a foreign land, were the lot of the diverse Byzantine soldiers in Italy – as the soldiers of the Gothic side realized. Ultimately, even if Goths defected with special conditions, they would be liable to being "cleanly intercepted" and removed to Justinian's next project. Not all Byzantine soldiers were willing to put up with this, despite their supposed common identity as Romans. Procopius many times specifies that a Byzantine soldier was a "barbarian," a "Hun," a "Goth by birth" or a "Thracian." These identities could be more important than the catch-all term "Roman" by which Procopius refers to them. Unpaid Illyrian soldiers under Belisarius in the early 540s withdrew homeward of their own accord, since their relatives there were suffering from "Hunnic" depredations. Justinian forgave them, as no doubt he had to in order to retain them in his army.[90]

Local ties, as much as ideology, determined the stubbornness of the

---

[86] Procopius, BG2(6).28.29 confirms this: "garrisoned, as had been the custom for many years . . ."
[87] On the possibility that rural civilians could become low-grade soldiers on demand, see below, pp. 183–4.
[88] Procopius, BG 1(5).29.3–12.
[89] Ibid. 2(6).18.1.
[90] Ibid. 3(7).11.13–16.

remnants of the Gothic forces who refused to surrender to Justinian in 540. Rather than accept rule from and service under the emperor at Constantinople, they offered the kingship – or perhaps the defunct Western imperial throne – to Belisarius![91] The Gothic army wanted not so much a "Gothic" king as a local government, based in Italy, rather than rule from the East. Even Witigis was ready to abdicate for Belisarius in order to achieve this end.[92] But the Byzantines were as good at exploiting the family ties of Gothic leaders as they were of soldiers. After Hildebad made a second offer of the kingship to Belisarius, the general abducted the king's own children to Constantinople, with, however, no effect in this case.[93]

The Gothic army had little reason to trust that their individual kings and leaders would preserve the effective autonomy of Italy and the continuance of the army as a regional institution. Almost without exception the kings had proved amenable to offers of honorable and comfortable retirement in Constantinople (such as Gelimer of the Vandals had already received). Both Amalasuintha and Theodahad secretly negotiated for a surrender and a move to the Eastern capital; Theodahad may have suffered the vengeance of the army partly for this reason.[94] By 540, every surviving Amal was on the Byzantine side; Matasuentha actively attempted to betray her husband Witigis.[95] Witigis himself was the only king who succeeded in getting to Byzantium. For the cost of a humiliating defeat and capture, he received the patriciate and doubtless retired wealthy like Gelimer. Totila was on the verge of surrendering when he was offered the kingship; Hildebad and Eraric were each ready to give up what they saw as a lost cause in 540 and 541.[96]

Institutional and regional loyalty, as much as any belief in the Gothic *gens*, determined the longing of the Gothic army for its continued existence outside the Byzantine army. Not all its leaders abandoned it. Witigis's uncle Uraïas showed himself staunch twice, first during the affair of the Cottian Alps, and then again after the fall of Ravenna, when he refused the kingship but stayed on as a Gothic commander. Even Uraïas did not put too much faith in the power of the name Goth. After the extinction of hopes that Belisarius would accept the kingship, he championed the cause of Hildebad on the grounds that Hildebad's uncle

---

[91] Ibid. 2(6).29.17–28; 2(6).30.1–30.
[92] Ibid. 2(6).29.21.
[93] PA *Hildebadus.
[94] PA *Amalasuintha, *Theodahadus.
[95] PA Amalafridas, Ebremud, *Matasuentha, possibly *Amalaberga, *Theodegisclus and *Theodenantha, as well as *Anonyma 4 (sister of Amalfridas).
[96] PA *Witigis, *Totila, *Hildebadus, *Erarichus.

Theudis, the king of Spain, would come to assist the Goths of Italy. Now Theudis was an Italian Goth who had been placed on the Visigothic throne by Theoderic after his conquest of the Visigothic kingdom; in the 540s, Theudis was still ruling Spain. But it was not to be expected that Theudis would come to assist the Goths of Italy because they were all Goths together, or even all Ostrogoths. Uraïas thought that Theudis might enter the war on their side because of his ties of kinship to *Hildebad*.[97] Even in this he was mistaken; although Hildebad's own nephew Totila continued family rule in Italy for the next decade or more, Theudis remaind resolutely neutral.[98]

Among Italian civilians, despite some senatorial and ecclesiastical support for Justinian, more civilians supported the Goths at a local level in the first phase of the Wars than Procopius's polarized depiction suggests. After all, some of them were related to soldiers, including Flavius Maximus, the senator who married an Amal princess.[99] Although Belisarius took the cities of Sicily with no difficulty,[100] he seems to have received the surrender of cities in Rhegium only because those cities were not fortified.[101]

By the time that Belisarius reached Naples, he faced outright opposition from the civilian inhabitants, not just the Gothic garrison there. One man attempted to convince Belisarius that it was not worth his time to take the city. Only after being bribed did he and another man go back to recommend to the Neapolitans that they surrender, saying that they would suffer if they did not. Another pair of Neapolitans, named Pastor and Asclepiodotus, firmly supported the Gothic side, as did the Jews of Naples, who must have realized that they fared better under the religious tolerance of the Gothic kings than they would under Justinian. Against the arguments of the first messengers, they convinced the citizens of Naples not to give up the city to the Byzantines, arguing that the revenge of the Gothic army would eventually fall upon them.

The Neapolitans decided not to surrender and sent word to Theodahad begging his assistance; the Jews even manned the walls against the Byzantine forces. Belisarius eventually took the city, with great slaughter of the civilian population, which took its own revenge against

---

[97] Procopius, BG2(6).30.15.

[98] PA *Theudis.

[99] Flavius Maximus: see PLRE2 Maximus 20 and PA *Anonyma 3.

[100] Procopius, BG 1(5).5.12–19.

[101] Ibid. 1(5).8.1–3. Procopius also states of the people in Rhegium: "Because of their hostility toward the Goths, they were, as was natural, greatly dissatisfied with their present government;" since he next immediately describes the surrender of the troops there of PA Ebremud, who was married to Theodahad's daughter, we should take this highly ideological statement with a grain of salt.

Pastor and Asclepiodotus for their advice. Despite the rhetoric of Procopius and the excuses of both sides,[102] it is clear that a substantial proportion of the inhabitants of Naples had little sympathy for the claims of the Byzantine emperor, and were willing to run considerable risks in opposing his army.[103]

The episode also reveals that the Gothic garrison and the civilian inhabitants of Naples shared the same predicament. The first Neapolitan sent to Belisarius brings up the dilemma of the Gothic garrison, which would be forced to fight: the guard of "barbarians" whom the Neapolitans have as "masters" – this, of course, in a speech invented by Procopius – would themselves suffer if they surrendered, for their wives, children and property were in the hands of Theodahad. Belisarius in return offered the garrison the chance to join his army or to return to their homes as they wished.[104] While the speeches are typically Procopian, the plea for the garrison and Belisarius's offer ring true in light of the evidence for local ties of soldiers examined above. This garrison did not happen to be local to Naples, but neither were its members' loyalties exclusive to the Gothic army; they had family and possessions to lose elsewhere if they chose wrongly. The civilians of Naples, this passage suggests, were able to empathize with their garrison. The Neapolitan civilians believed that the soldiers were defending the city against attack, as indeed they had been doing for the previous thirty-five years. But both the civilians and the soldiers were put in the intolerable position of predicting the immediate future of the war.

Belisarius next moved on to Rome. There, as we shall see, the alleged treachery of Pope Silverius demonstrates not his pro-Gothic sympathies but his attempt to keep the papacy independent of both secular powers. But the accusations show that it was possible for people to believe in a fifth column during the Gothic siege of Rome. Belisarius also exiled some of the senators on the same suspicion, including Flavius Maximus.[105] In both cases his actions seem odd; Silverius owed his appointment to Theodahad, who had been murdered by Witigis, while Max-

---

[102] Belisarius blames any potential carnage upon the uncontrollable barbarians in his army.

[103] Procopius, BG 1(5).8.5–45, 9.1, 9.8–30, 10.1–48. The *Liber Pontificalis*, at this point contemporary and pro-Byzantine, confirms both the Gothic sympathies of the Neapolitans and the subsequent slaughter of civilians (LP Silverius §3, 1: 290). On the date of this first part of the life of Silverius, see Paul Hildebrand, "Die Absetzung des Papstes Silverius (537)," *Historisches Jahrbuch* 42 (1922), 216–17; Duchesne LP 1: xxxix–xli. Thompson, in "The Byzantine conquest of Italy: public opinion," pp. 101–2, is sensible on this incident, although his use of Jordanes, *Rom.* 370–1 does not support his case for unanimous Neapolitan opposition very well (Goths and *rebelling* Romans were killed).

[104] Procopius, BG1(5).8.7–9, 16.

[105] Ibid. 1(5).25.13–15.

imus was Theodahad's relative by marriage. Belisarius acted as if the Italian population was already polarized into supporters of the Goths or the Byzantines, when in fact previous divisions still existed. Meanwhile, the defections of Belisarius's own soldiers to the Gothic side cannot have provided much comfort to the besieged civilians of Rome.[106]

Initially, in fact, the senators and the people thought Belisarius's decision to defend the city rash, and feared the vengeance of the Gothic army.[107] Belisarius is said to have written to the emperor that the Italians held their own safety more lightly than their loyalty to the Empire, but Procopius's own narrative does not bear out this ideological statement.[108] The inhabitants of Rome, particularly the senators, resorted to divination and interpretation of oracles in order to predict their fate.[109] Belisarius rotated guards at the gates in fear of treachery.[110]

In the end, the citizens of Rome supported Belisarius because they had no choice. The Gothic garrison had abandoned them at the approach of the Byzantine troops; after the long siege, during which civilians also manned the walls, there was no question that Witigis's soldiers would take revenge if they took the city. After the deposition of Silverius, moreover, the new pope, Vigilius, owed his election and his safety to Belisarius and Justinian; we have seen that he actively promoted the Roman cause. Meanwhile, according to Procopius, both Belisarius and Witigis attempted to sway the loyalties of the citizens of Rome, the one by telling them that they were being restored to the Roman Empire, the other by reminding them of the many years of safety and prosperity under the Gothic kings. But clearly, in the end, it was exigency of the moment, not ideology, that determined the allegiance of the city of Rome in 536–7.

Meanwhile in the north, tensions were running high and allegiances *had* to be chosen. The other Byzantine troops were attacking Milan and Liguria, where the civilians under bishop Datius, later an ally of Vigilius, at first welcomed them. But even the Milanese wavered in their support for the Byzantines in 538.[111] It did not avail them. Particularly enraged over the treachery of the Milanese, the Gothic army massacred thousands of civilians, as well as Italians who took up civilian office under the Byzantines. First they slaughtered Fidelis, formerly

[106] PA Anonymi 15+.
[107] Procopius, BG 1(5).14.16–17, 20.5–20.
[108] Ibid. 1(5).24.10, 25.19–25.
[109] Ibid. 1(5).24.22–37.
[110] Ibid. 1(5).25.15–16.
[111] Ibid. 2(6).21.11.

Athalaric's quaestor, then praetorian prefect under Belisarius. Then they murdered his successor in the prefecture, Reparatus.[112] They spared the Byzantine garrison at Milan, but not the Milanese: their anger was for the treacherous Italians, not the invaders.[113]

By this time, the Italian civilians began to recognize their essential helplessness in the face of the two armies. Procopius declares that when Belisarius entered Rome, "Rome became subject to the Romans again after a space of sixty years,"[114] that is, for the first time since 476, the turning-point envisaged by Justinian's *renovatio* ideology. The reality was different. In 539 was proposed the contract between Justinian and Witigis to divide Italy in half.[115] Here indeed was the political collapse of the Roman Empire brought home with a vengeance. No longer even in theory could Rome be thought the *caput mundi* or Italy the *sedes civilitatis*; suddenly men from the East were telling the Italians that they had actually lived in barbarism all these years.

And how did people called "Goth" feel? Did they act like foreigners, or, to use a familiar late Roman equation, like professional soldiers? To a certain extent, they did identify with profession: they blended easily with the Byzantine army when there was no choice but surrender. But the army reacted to the treachery of the Ligurians with ruthless vengeance. These soldiers, born and bred in Theoderic's Italy, had been told repeatedly by the government that they and the provincials were mutually and providentially interdependent, a match sanctioned by law and ethnographic inevitability. These Goths, Italians by upbringing and circumstance, regarded the betrayal by the provincials of Liguria, whom they had just previously been defending against Burgundians and Franks, as absolutely intolerable. For those of the Gothic army who were married into the families of provincials and owned land in those provinces, giving up Italy was not an easy option.

Kinship and compatriotism in the second phase of the Gothic Wars: 541–554

The wavering loyalty of Italians on either side during the short first phase of the Gothic Wars barely hints at the extraordinary changes of allegiance that were to occur during the long second phase. Over the course of a nineteen-year war, old allegiances to *civilitas*, to the idea of a Western Roman Empire, to a Catholic Mediterranean Empire, became irrelevant or evolved into new and different ties. As regions changed

---

[112] Ibid. 2(6).21.39–42.
[113] Ibid. 2(6).21.29.
[114] Ibid. 1(5).14.14.
[115] Ibid. 2(6).29.1–2.

hands and the sides became progressively more vicious in their retaliation against perceived treachery, people put their faith in religion, family and city. As Justinianic ideology more and more shrilly proclaimed the restoration of the Roman Empire, Italy was torn to shreds, and we can already see the outlines of fractured political allegiance to come: the Ravenna corridor, the disaffected (later Lombard) North, the localized papacy with the broadest claims to religious overlordship.

One ultimate effect of the long war was to re-form people labeled "Goths" into an army – or to reconfigure the Italian army as "the Goths" – a group that ballooned and dwindled according to its success. Totila assuredly desired more than this, and it is a shame that we can only view this extraordinary figure through Procopius, aside from his coins and a few other references. But although Totila revived Theoderic's ideology of *civilitas* in order to fight the claims of Justinian's *renovatio*, the king was ultimately reduced to military tactics, alternately rewarding and punishing the Italian civilians.[116]

The implementation of Justinian's demanding taxation in Italy in 540 made Italians, and even Byzantine soldiers, aware that the interests of Italy and those of Constantinople need not coincide. The first financial administrator, Alexander the Logothete, was nicknamed "Clippers" for his meanness and perseverance. Procopius alleges that he not only managed to alienate the Italian civilians (here called "Italians," not "Romans"), but also Byzantine soldiers stationed in Italy. Alexander extracted unpaid taxes owed to the royal (that is, Gothic) government, and made soldiers unwilling to fight by paying them poorly and by taking them to court over fiscal property that they had seized in the course of the war. People could not see where the taxes were going.[117]

The result of this quasi-colonial rule from Constantinople was civilian and military defection to the Gothic army holding out in Transpadane

---

[116] See PA ★Totila. Here Procopius remains our main guide, but his biases change. In Books 3 and 4 of the Gothic Wars, Procopius's sympathies switched from Belisarius, whose personal life he thought a disgrace, to Totila, whom he admired very much. Although Procopius's history remains fully suffused with ethnographic commonplaces, Justinianic *renovatio* ideology and, most of all, the demands of his classicizing genre, the author's own dissent with the conduct of the wars peers through. This complexity of opinion makes Procopius harder, not easier, to use as a source for the behavior of people in Italy, since it becomes more difficult to tell what his biases are in a particular passage. Needless to say, the Constantinopolitan Greek-speaking author did not favor Gothic rule in Italy, no matter how much he admired Totila. Rather, he could use the virtues of Totila and the mistakes and corruption of the Byzantine generals as a platform from which to criticize Byzantine policy in Italy. Just as in Tacitus's virtue-based ethnography of the *Germani*, which emphasized Roman failings by idealizing the barbarians, Procopius's reversal of traditional expectations does not make his description any the less ideological or tendentious. We must tread with care.

[117] Procopius, BG 3(7).1.28–33; Dewing 4: 161 quaintly translates *Psalidios*, from *psalis*, "scissors," as "Snips."

Italy in 540–1. Hildebad "gathered about him all the barbarians and as many of the Roman soldiers as were inclined to favor a revolution," to recover the rule of Italy for "the *genos* of the Goths," and "little by little all the inhabitants of Liguria and Venetia came over to his side."[118]

These defections also owed something to the departure of Belisarius and his refusal of the kingship, upon which they followed directly. Apparently the Byzantine soldiers themselves did not mind the idea of their leader assuming the rule of Italy. Such assumption of effective kingship by warlords with their *doryphoroi* occurred in the fifth century; the *doryphoroi* could only benefit from the rise of their leader. No longer could they be reassigned elsewhere by a distant emperor, as Justinian in fact did with Belisarius's *doryphoroi* after the triumphant general arrived in Constantinople.[119] Moreover, in 542, Justinian reiterated earlier Eastern laws forbidding soldiers to own property.[120] Although these laws were never effectively enforced,[121] they can only have increased the fears of Italian soldiers that their local ties would be threatened in the Byzantine army.

Defections, of course, also followed the success of an army, and now Totila's army was in the ascent. After his first great victory against the Byzantines at Mugello in 542, he "showed great kindness to his prisoners, and thereby succeeded in winning their allegiance, and henceforth most of them voluntarily served under him against the Romans."[122] This is the beginning of Procopius's love affair with Totila, but whatever tactics the king used, there can be no question that Byzantines "mingled" with his army as Witigis's Goths had mingled with the Byzantine army in 538–9.

These defections gave people a new identity in Procopius's eyes. One of Belisarius's commanders, Herodianus, defected in 545, changing not only his allegiance ("compatriotism") but his identity ("kinship"), in the eyes of Procopius. Herodianus had been left with the delicate task of governing the garrison of Naples after the bloody capture of the city in 535. He accompanied Belisarius to Constantinople in 540. By 542, Herodianus was back in Italy, in charge of Spoleto, which he surrendered to the new king, Totila, in 545. Procopius, now in his anti-Belisarius phase, states that Herodianus deserted because he could no longer face Belisarius's extortionate demands for money.[123]

---

[118] Ibid. 3(7).1.25.
[119] See below, n. 145.
[120] *Nov. Iust.* 116; amplifying cj 12.35.15–16, of Leo I.
[121] Brown, *Gentlemen and Officers*, pp. 106–7.
[122] Procopius, BG 3(7).5.19.
[123] PA **Herodianus**.

Procopius did not originally describe Herodianus as a Goth by birth. He had Balkan associations: he first appears in Illyricum, and we later find him leading Thracian soldiers. Procopius groups him among "the commanders of the Roman army."[124] But after Herodianus surrendered Spoleto, Totila held him up as an example to the senators of Rome. Unlike them, Herodianus had proved himself friend and *kinsman* of the Goths.[125] Apparently, from Procopius's, and perhaps Totila's, point of view, changing allegiance could mean changing one's birth.

Herodianus had a Greek name and Balkan–Roman associations. But Procopius does not explain the behavior of other defectors with Germanic names, often called "barbarians" or "Goths" by birth, through any previous kinship with the Goths of Italy. One of Belisarius's *doryphoroi*, Gundulf, also called Indulf, was a "barbarian by birth" (with two Germanic names) and a "Roman." Indeed, at the time of his desertion, he was able to mingle with the people of Mouicurum, because he was "a Roman and a member of Belisarius' suite." After he defected to Totila in 548, Procopius calls him "one of the most notable of the Goths," but his barbarian birth is not given as the cause of his defection; he defected "for no good reason."[126]

Kinship, it seems, was a result of defection! Hence we find Totila, in his first speech to his men, addressing them as "my kinsmen." We have just learned from Procopius that this army included Byzantine soldiers who defected to Hildebad, as well as the Rugians who elected Eraric king. The Rugians only married their own and had children of unmixed blood. Kinship was an *expression* of political allegiance – for Procopius, the Byzantine observer. This might have been the view of Totila too, of course, but it is important to remember the use of this equation in classical ethnography. For Theoderic in his early years, kinship was *not* an expression of political allegiance.

If we followed Wolfram, we might see Totila's speech as evidence for kings promoting ethnogenesis. Ethnogenesis theory builds upon the widespread assumptions of classical ethnography in late antiquity. But that ethnography, as we have seen, was inconsistent and inconsistently accepted. The bellicose Gothic-*gens* ideology of Theoderic and Witigis used such equations indeed, but given that Totila did spread *civilitas* ideology again, and that this reference occurs in a speech of Procopius, and that it matched Justinian's theories, we can be sure that kinship-as-

---

[124] Procopius, BG 1(5).5.2–3; 3(7).6.10; 3(7).7.2.
[125] Ibid. 3(7).21.15–16; Hodgkin (*Italy and Her Invaders* 4: 499) is misleading on this speech.
[126] PA Gundulf/Indulf; quotations at Procopius, BG 3(7).35.23–5.

allegiance formed part of the Byzantine formula. By this time, competing with the statements of the Byzantine armies that the Italians owed kinship-allegiance to the "Romans" of Constantinople, the Gothic kings and their soldiers had little to gain by promoting such equations.

Such kinship, in Procopius's eyes, did not always spread to non-soldiers. His ideological stance did not often allow Italian civilians to become Goths: that would have undermined the whole cause of the Gothic Wars and Justinian's restoration. Totila's quaestor, Spinus, was a "Roman" who was loyal to Totila. But in Procopius's attributed speech, Spinus refers to Totila and the Gothic army as "we" and says "if we ever overcome that army," where "that army" has been defined earlier as "the Romans."[127] Of three other civilians associated with the Gothic army, all envoys, two similarly have Latin names. Two of them Procopius calls "Romans," but the third, although he had a Latin name, is called a "Goth."[128]

Procopius's own confusion shows how his ethnography inadequately described the identities of defectors, which even ethnographically speaking were more complicated than he suggests. Belisarius's *doryphoros* Bessas, steadfastly loyal, was, according to Procopius, descended from the Goths who did not follow Theoderic to Italy from the Balkans. As we have seen, he spoke a language comprehensible to the soldiers of Italy. But Jordanes says that Bessas was a descendant of the *genus* of "Sauromatae . . . quos Sarmates dicimus, et Cemandri, et quidam ex Hunnis." His name was Greek or Thracian, and appears to contain a reference to the ancient Thracian group called the *Bessi*, who did contribute a Byzantine defector to the Goths in 539. This defector of the *Bessi*, unlike the loyal "Goth" Bessas, or the disloyal "Roman" Herodianus, did have a Germanic name.[129]

In the early 540s, according to Procopius, there was massive civilian disaffection from the Byzantine side. The Byzantine army managed to alienate Italians by oppressing them, making them long for the "barbarians."[130] The Italians were suffering at the hands of both armies, says Procopius. Of course, this is partly based on his view that no Goth could be Italian. From the Byzantine army itself, the above-mentioned unpaid Illyrians withdrew homeward. The Byzantine army continued

---

[127] Procopius, BG 3(7).40.28 (the Goths are "we"); 3(7).40.22 ("If we ever overcome that [Roman] army"); 3(7).40.20 (Spinus called a "Roman"); PA Spinus.
[128] PA Caballarius ("Goth"), Stephanus, Anonymus 3.
[129] PA Bessas; Burcentius (of the *Bessi*), deserted at Osimo in 539.
[130] Procopius, BG 3(7).9.1–6.

to shrink as soldiers deserted from the army or defected to the Goths.[131] Totila captured city after city by surrender.[132]

The oppression of Byzantine soldiers and the exactions of Alexander, as well as the desertion of Byzantine troops from 541 to 544, all followed the first appearance of the bubonic plague in the Mediterranean in 541. Misery was everywhere, and these events combined to deliver Italy into the hands of Totila. Totila revived *civilitas* ideology in a letter to the senate in 544, also denouncing the Byzantines as "Greeks."[133] In his anxiety, Justinian sent Belisarius back to Italy in the same year with a message for the inhabitants of Ravenna. Addressing both Goths in Ravenna and "Roman" soldiers, Belisarius offered to right the wrongs committed by both sides. The result, however, was that "not one of the enemy came over to him, either Goth or Roman."[134]

As Italians flocked to Totila's side, Procopius's rhetoric breaks down interestingly. By his own definitions, how could there be "Goths" in Ravenna, a city controlled by the Byzantines? How could there be "Romans" who were not on the Byzantine side? The context makes it clear that these "Goths" and "Romans" were Italian soldiers and civilians who did not favor the Byzantine reconquest. In this brief moment of crisis, we can see groups in Italy more clearly, as they had been defined before the arrival of Justinianic ideology.

Procopius, and perhaps Belisarius himself, assumes in this speech that the addressees in Ravenna will be connected closely to the soldiers of Totila. "If any one of you, then, chances to have relatives or friends with the usurper Totila, let him summon these as quickly as possible, explaining the emperor's purpose."[135] Although the Byzantines had succeeded in the late 530s in wresting the Italian army away from its Italian allegiance, its Italian families and its Italian properties, the massive reverse desertions of the early 540s had recreated the earlier situation. Once more, the army of "Goths" was firmly tied to the civilian world of Italy, extending its connections of blood and friendship even into the Byzantine stronghold of Ravenna.

Of course, in the mid-540s, not all Italian civilians moved over to the Goths. But instead of supporting the Byzantines directly, they appear as representatives of their own cities and localities, like the Neapolitans in 535. A certain Marcianus, "a man of note among the Veneti," who

---

[131] Ibid. 3(7).10.1, 12.1–10.
[132] Ibid. 3(7).12.12 (Firmum and Ascalum), 12.13 (Spoleto, through Herodianus), 12.17–20 (Assisi, through the treachery of PA Ulifus).
[133] Ibid. 3(7).8.21, 9.10, 9.12.
[134] Ibid. 3(7).11.1–10; quotation at 10.
[135] Ibid. 3(7).11.7.

"lived in a fortress not far distant from the city of Verona," betrayed the city into the hands of the Byzantines. Procopius tells us that Marcianus supported the emperor's cause, but we learn that he managed to get a guard to leave a gate open because he had known the guard from childhood![136]

Both the civilian and the soldier came from the Veneto, near Verona; they were doing what they thought was best for their city as a Byzantine army of 12,000 marched toward it.[137] Verona was the first city captured by Theoderic in 489; it was the location of the Transpadane Goths who held out under Hildebad after the capture of Ravenna in 540; Theoderic's court had stayed there, and the city was still holding out against the Byzantines after the defeat of Totila in 552.[138] Verona, then, was a center of Gothic sympathies, no doubt through circumstance, but also through the sorts of life-long ties that bound the notable Marcianus to a guardsman at the city gate.

A parallel to the local loyalties of Marcianus occurs in the desperate antics of the civilian magnate Tullianus, "a Roman who possessed great power among the Brutii and Lucani." He was the son of Venantius, a name suggesting senatorial connections, but more likely, given Tullianus's local position, belonging to the provincial parvenu elite.[139] The forces of the Byzantine general John had just captured the cities of nearby Calabria in 545. Tullianus came before John, complaining of the treatment that the Brutii and Lucani had received from the emperor's army,[140] but also telling John just what he thought John would want to hear:

It was not, he said, by their own will that they [the Lucani and Brutii] had yielded to men who were both barbarians and Arians, but because they had been placed under most dire constraint by their opponents, and *had also* been treated with injustice by the emperor's soldiers.[141]

This passage mixes together Procopius's own ethnographic viewpoint, that of Justinian, with his criticisms of the emperor's army. But there

---

[136] Ibid. 3(7).3.6–8; Wolfram (in *Goths*, p. 516, n. 397) identifies him as a soldier with no evidence: see PA [**M**arcianus].

[137] Ibid. 3(7).3.4.

[138] Ibid. 2(6).29.41 (Hildebad in 540); 4(8).33.3–4 (holding out in 552); Moorhead, *Theoderic*, pp. 21–2, 219 (captured in 489, Theoderic's court there at the accusation of Boethius).

[139] Senatorial: PLRE2 Venantius 3, 5, Basilius 13, Opilio 5, Faustus 10, Faustus 11; provincial parvenu: PLRE2 Venantius 2 (son of Liberius and a relative of Ennodius), probably 4. The Greek name of Tullianus's brother Deopheron may also suggest a southern Italian origin for the family – it is not a common name anywhere in Western Europe, unlike, for example, the Greek names of martyrs that were Latinized and used everywhere.

[140] Procopius, BG 3(7).18.20.

[141] Ibid. 3(7).18.21, trans. Dewing 4: 309; emphasis mine.

is no need to doubt that Tullianus expressed exactly these sentiments, because it combines a genuine complaint with a mimicking of Justinianic reasons for taking Italy back from the Goths. Moreover, it demonstrates that local magnates could be the spokesmen for their regions, a phenomenon we have already observed among the Neapolitans and the Veneti. The injustice of the soldiers is the likely complaint, and the rhetoric of the speech, whether or not Tullianus believed it, shows the desire of the Lucani and Brutii to get on the right side when the Byzantines were in the area, and – especially important – to clear their names with the Byzantine army lest they suffer as traitors. They doubtless remembered the massacre of the Neapolitans some ten years earlier.

Significantly, Procopius then distinguishes between the identities and allegiances of Tullianus and John. He ends the passage: "And upon John's declaration that thereafter the *Italians* would receive every blessing from the army, Tullianus went with him. Consequently the soldiers no longer entertained any suspicion as regards the Italians . . ."[142] Just before, Tullianus and the army were both "Romans," but now the text admits that the supplicants were "Italian," and as such had something to fear from the Byzantine forces – just as those forces had good reason to distrust them.

Tullianus, however, spoke for himself, not for all the inhabitants of Lucani et Brutii. Totila, hearing of their treason, sent forces south. Tullianus assembled a peasant militia (*agroikoi*) from the region to defend a pass against the Goths. Disdaining to send his own men against such a force, Totila recruited other rustics from the same region to take the pass. At the same time, tenants and domestics of senators in the hands of Totila abandoned the Byzantine army, being promised the ownership of the lands that they tilled. In the end, the defeated Tullianus fled with the Byzantine commanders, and southern Italy was back in Totila's hands without his having to send any of his own soldiers there.

This event, which is quite famous in the literature, reveals the limited options of Italians lower down on the social scale than Tullianus. They could not simply flee as the magnate did, as the senators of Rome fled to Constantinople, and as Gothic kings and princesses left Italy for retirement, abandoning their armies to their fates. Similarly, when Totila offered the remnants of Byzantine forces in Rome in 550 the choice of joining his army or going home, only the two commanders went back to Constantinople as non-combatants.[143] That option was not

---

[142] Ibid. 3(7).18.22–3, emphasis mine.

[143] Ibid. 3(7).36.17–28: Totila offered them the option of keeping their own possessions and fighting with the Gothic army, "enjoying full and complete equality with the Goths"; Procopius declares that they were originally all for going to Byzantium, but due to fear of ambush, shame

available to ordinary soldiers. They required their profession in order to live. If they could not make their living fighting for Justinian, then they would make it fighting for Totila.

The ordinary Italian, just like the soldier Gundila, was tied to his land, if not by law, then at least by necessity. All of a sudden we discover here that tenants of southern Italy, "Italians," hence civilians, had been pressed into service in the Byzantine army, just as Tullianus pressed his own rustics into service for his own ends. For an appropriate reward – the ownership of land in the regions where they were tied to estates – these men were perfectly willing to abandon the Byzantine forces.

Not only region, but status and power, divided the Italians of what-ever background, just as it divided the Byzantines. Uraïas, the uncle of the king, could choose not to desert in the Cottian Alps; his men there with their families had no such choice. The army of Hildebad demanded Italian rule as their kings and royal family left for the East. Many of the senators of Italy could support Justinian's invasion with impunity; they had the offer of office and a home at Constantinople where they had widespread lands in any case. The men and women in the middle – the families of the Neapolitan magnates, of Marcianus, Tullianus and Gundila – could switch their allegiances if they operated with care and tried to satisfy the opposite side that they were now to be trusted. At the lowest levels of society, the tenant-farmers and urban inhabitants could only watch and hope, and seize what opportunities presented themselves.

The events in Lucani et Brutii also reveal that the army and civilian population were not divided in precisely the way that Theoderic's depiction would have led us to imagine. The facts are unclear, but warfare in the Mediterranean was increasingly emphasizing the primacy of professional horsemen.[144] Where did the infantry come from? The *agroikoi* of Tullianus, the tenants of the senators serving in the Byzantine and then the Gothic forces, may have supplied them.[145] Such ad hoc

and resentment against the emperor because they had not been paid, "they all mingled volunt-arily with the Gothic army." The two who left, Paulus and the Isaurian Mindes, "stated that they had children and wives in their native land, and apart from these they were unable to live."

[144] Delbrück, *History of the Art of War* 2: 408–9; Procopius, BP 1(I).1.8–16, on the mounted archers of his time compared with the footsoldiers of Homer: "There are those who . . . give no credit to modern improvements" (16); on the refusal of handbooks like that of Vegetius to acknowledge such changes, see, for example, Goffart, "The date and purpose of Vegetius' *De re militari*," p. 72 with n. 125 and references. On cavalry see also Bernard S. Bachrach, "Animals and warfare in early medieval Europe," in *L'Uomo di fronte al mondo animale nell'alto medioevo*, 2 vols., Settimane di Studio 31 (1985), 2: 710–11.

[145] Thus, I suggest, they were the *coloni*-soldiers of great landlords. Just as their taxes (paid to their masters rather than to tax-collectors) looked like rents, their military service could be in the

recruitment to the army was occurring among the farmers of southern Italy in 545. Tullianus used his own soldiers; Totila exercised the prerogatives of the imperial government in intercepting the soldiers of the senators who were in his power.

The very passage of events in this part of the Gothic Wars led to the growth of local loyalties. The swift transfer of a region like Lucani et Brutii from Gothic control to Byzantine control and back to the Goths meant that no Lucanus or Brutius could safely give his allegiance to either side, could identify himself as a "Goth" or a "Roman" without fear of retribution.

Such pressures did not let up. Tullianus's brother, who had the Greek name Deopheron, appears with Byzantine forces in a fortress near Rusciane in 548, pleading for his life and the safety of the people inside. Procopius calls him an "Italian;" he pleads to Totila alongside a Byzantine "Thracian" officer bearing the name Godilas – a name common among the "Goths" of Italy, one that may even have the word "Goth" within it.[146] "Seeing that their provisions had completely failed them and that they had no further hope of assistance from the Romans [Byzantines]," they begged Totila to "pardon them for their deeds." Totila spared their lives, but cut off the hands and genitals of the "Massagetic" commander of the fortress for disregarding a previous agreement. The Italians within lost all their property; the Byzantines were allowed to keep theirs on condition that they joined the Gothic army, as eighty of them did.[147]

Italian, Roman, Gothic, Thracian, Massagetic; Greek names and Germanic names: none of these evanescent things meant anything next

private army of a landlord, lower-ranking than his *bucellarii* or *doryphoroi*. On differentiation within private armies in the later Empire, see Whittaker, *Frontiers*, pp. 243–75, esp. 257–62, 272–5. On the rents of wealthy magnates, which the emperor might "cleanly intercept" (as taxes), see Walter Goffart, "From Roman taxation to medieval seigneurie: three notes," and "Old and new in Merovingian taxation," both in Goffart, *Rome's Fall and After*, pp. 167–231, esp. 188–9, 200–3, quotation at p. 200. Similarly, Justinian was able to redistribute Belisarius's *doryphoi* and their subsidiary *hypaspistai* to his palace officers and eunuchs: Procopius, SH 4.13. An example of "cleanly intercepting" *coloni*: a law of 409 threatens landowners who received defeated barbarian Sciri as their taxpaying *coloni* with punishment if the magnates did not surrender their new *coloni* to the emperor as soldiers when necessary: CT 5.6.3; N. D. Fustel de Coulanges, "Le colonat romain," in Fustel de Coulanges, *Recherches sur quelques problèmes d'histoire* (Paris, 1894), pp. 52–3. Similarly, *bucellarii* could be stationed at the house of a rich man, who would then be directed by the state to pay their *annona* directly: Whittaker, *Frontiers*, pp. 274–5. The whole question of private armies and *bucellarii* and their relationship to the army of the state requires re-examination along the lines of Goffart's study on tax and rent: the difference between public and private was not as clear as we sometimes believe.

[146] On Goudilas/Gudila, see above ch. 3, p. 100 with nn. 75–6.

[147] Procopius, BG 3(7).30.19–24; Deopheron called an "Italian" here and at 3(7).30.6, Goudilas called a "Thracian" at 3(7).30.6; "Italians" differentiated from the "Roman army" (the Byzantine army) at 3(7).30.6.

to the immediate threats that menaced everyone during the Wars. Everyone was out for himself and his property, attempting to avoid alliance with the wrong side and the dreadful punishments that followed mistakes. The best that one could do was to parrot the ideology of the side prevailing at the moment – and hope for the best.

Two groups with wider loyalties than region alone were the Catholic clergy and the Roman senatorial aristocracy. They both threw in their lot with the Byzantine reconquest early, and Totila never allowed them to forget it. The king lambasted the senators for their disloyalty in the face of the losses that he claimed they suffered under Justinian.[148] He took them and their families hostage. Not all of them may have supported the Byzantines so constantly, but without any regional identity other than the thrice-besieged city of Rome or the Roman Empire (however broadly configured), and as the chief targets of propaganda from both sides, those senators who remained in Italy constantly wavered. The hapless Flavius Maximus, suspected by Belisarius of collaborating with Witigis in the 530s, was finally forced to seek asylum from Totila in St. Peter's, and was eventually sent as a hostage to Campania, where Teia executed him in 552.[149] In Constantinople, Italian senators who had definitively sided with Justinian lobbied hard for the emperor to step up the War; these exiles could gain nothing from a Gothic victory.[150] Italians in the East with ecclesiastical connections, however, like Vigilius and Cassiodorus, were by this time chiefly caught up in the Three Chapters controversy and the fate of the pope in the hands of the emperor.[151]

In Procopius's narrative of the siege of the city of Rome in 546, just as everywhere else, the civilians were caught between a rock and a hard place. The inhabitants complain to the Byzantine generals that "they are regarded neither as Romans, as relatives or as political allies, but quite simply as enemies, an accusation which Bessas and Conon are forced to see is justified."[152] This was true not only of the plebs, but also of the aristocrats.

The fate of the claims of the Catholic church would be disappointment in the East from Justinian, and fragmentation and localization of the dioceses of Italy after the 540s.[153] Such fragmentation may already have been taking place. Totila's constant retaliation against Catholic

---

[148] Procopius, BG 3(7)21.12–16.
[149] PLRE2 Maximus 20.
[150] Cameron, *Procopius*, pp. 193–5.
[151] Ibid., p. 195, and ch. 6, below.
[152] Ibid., pp. 194–5.
[153] Below, ch. 6.

bishops, remembered and dramatized decades later by Gregory the Great, may owe something to the role of bishops as leaders of their cities, in a war that was mainly about capturing and surrendering cities.[154] If these bishops represented the interests of townspeople in negotiations with garrisons and besieging forces – as bishops had been doing in Italy since the mid-fifth century – then they were no longer representing the church as a whole, but their own localities.[155] It is not surprising that we do not see such activity in Procopius, since his classicizing genre forced him to minimize appearances of Christianity and Christian institutions in his work.[156]

The very behavior of Pope Vigilius in Rome in 544–5 demonstrates the localized role of the pope as bishop of Rome as much as his allegiance to the Byzantine army and the Catholic emperor. His inscriptions in the catacombs, and his additions to the Roman liturgy, are a manifestation of anti-Gothic and anti-Arian propaganda.[157] They also increased the prestige of the see of St. Peter and that of the *city* of Rome. The liturgical additions plead for the safety of the city of Rome from barbarian incursions, not for the safety of the Roman Empire.[158] The papal commission of Arator's *De actibus apostolorum*, proclaimed in public at this crucial moment for spreading propaganda, exalted the role of the papacy in the language of *Roma Aeterna*.[159] Such language did indeed feed into Justinian's reconquest ideology,[160] but it shows the local loyalties of the pope and Catholic clergy of Rome as much as their allegiance to the Byzantine forces. The use of *libertas* in the poem hearkens back not only to Justinian's use of *libertas* but Theoderic's. Secular rulers had been drawing on the inherited connotations of the

---

[154] Totila cut off the hands of a Catholic bishop whom he suspected of lying to him: Procopius, BG 3(7).9.20–1; he ordered the torture of the bishop of Perugia, Gregory the Great, *Dialogi* 3.13 (ed. Adalbert de Vogüé, 3 vols., Sources chrétiennes 251, 260, 265 [Paris, 1978–80]), PA Anonymus 19; Lanzoni 2: 445 on Gregory and Totila. The Perugia incident seems to have occurred after the Byzantines abandoned the city during a lengthy siege: Procopius, BG 3(7).35.2.

[155] On Bishop Epiphanius as a representative of Pavia and Liguria in the 470s and 480s, see ch. 6, below.

[156] Cameron, *Procopius*, pp. 113–33.

[157] The expulsion of Arian clergy from Rome in 543 by PA Iohannes 2, on suspicion of their sympathy with Totila (entirely plausible, of course) must have had support from Vigilius as well; see Anonymi 14+. This event occurred near the time of the addition of prayers for the safety of the city (see next note) and two years before the vandalism of the catacombs by Totila's troops, leading to Vigilius's ethnographically anti-Arian inscriptions (on which see ch. 4). On the anti-Gothic and pro-Justinianic behavior of Iohannes (John, the nephew of Vitalian), see below.

[158] Hope, *The Leonine Sacramentary*, pp. 82–3.

[159] Arator, *De actibus apostolorum* 2.1225–50, ed. Arthur Patch McKinlay, CSEL 72 (Vienna, 1951).

[160] Moorhead, "Italian loyalties during Justinian's Gothic war," pp. 591–2.

word long before Justinian's reconquest; it was only natural that the papacy should try to claim it for itself.

The pressures on clergy from both sides reduced them to spokesmen for their own communities and regions. Shortly Vigilius would be at odds with the emperor; he may already have been in dispute with Theodora at this time in the early 540s.[161] Similarly, bishop Datius of Milan, who cooperated with the Goths in the first phase of the Wars, tried to bring his city over to the Byzantines in 539 with the resulting carnage described above.[162] He ultimately ended up in Constantinople opposing Justinian at Vigilius's side, sending letters all over the West and emphasizing the orthodox belief of his own see in comparison to those of the East. In the end, of course, Milan would break off from Rome and Constantinople in the northern Italian schism of the late sixth century.[163]

Military defection was constant. Disruption rather than continuity marked membership of the Gothic army during the Wars. Few soldiers can have stayed Goths right to the end, as the army shrank and shrank in the defeats of Teia and finally Aligernus. Even in the 540s, virtually no one after the demise of Witigis's family can be traced back into Theoderic's days, with the exception of the family of Totila himself, which came into prominence with the appointment of Theudis as regent of Spain under Theoderic.[164]

The equation of allegiance with identity is confirmed for three commanders by the rare juxtaposition of another source with Procopius. Procopius calls Viliarid, Bleda and Ruderit "the three most warlike of the Goths;" Gregory the Great, fifty years later, referred to the same three men as "Totila's most loyal supporters."[165] Aside from this rare confirmation that Procopius was not making up the story of the Wars

---

[161] LP Vigilius §§3–4, 1: 296–7, suggests that Vigilius, like Silverius, tangled with Theodora over the reappointment of Anthimus to the patriarchate of Constantinople – though it must be emphasized that this life is much later than the first portion of that of Silverius: Hildebrand, "Die Absetzung des Papstes Silverius," pp. 221–3.

[162] Moorhead, "Italian loyalties during Justinian's Gothic war," p. 588; on the carnage, see above, pp. 174–5.

[163] Ch. 6 below, pp. 230–3.

[164] Another possible exception is Totila's commander PA Viliarid (also spelled Uliaris, Vuliarid), if he is identical to **W**ilarit 1 *and* **W**iliarius. If so, he would be the Wiliarit welcomed into the army by Theoderic as one of his *iuvenes*, and to the Wiliarius *vir inlustris, comes* who was leading forces in preparation for the aborted attack upon the Vandals in 526. He would have had a long and successful career extending from his youth in about 507 to his service at Naples in 533 or 534 and under Totila in 542. But the prefix Wilia-/Vilia-/Ulia- is extremely common in Ostrogothic Italy (the spellings vary), and it is impossible to make the connection with certitude.

[165] Procopius, BG 3(7).5.1; Gregory the Great, *Dialogi* 2.14; PA **B**leda, **R**uderit, Viliarid. On the last, see previous note.

as he went along, Gregory's grouping of the same three according to their *loyalty* again suggests that Procopius's Goths were defined by allegiance. Warlike they may have been; they were, after all, soldiers (like all Procopius's Goths), and, for both writers, barbarians (naturally bellicose for Procopius, as in classical ethnogeography). The two groupings in the two independent sources illuminates both Procopius's biases (the same, to some extent, as Gregory's) and the realities of the Gothic Wars hidden beneath these biases.

Allegiance determined one's future. Few commanders who had defected went back again to their original side: Herodianus and Gundulf supported the Goths right up until the end of the war. Soldiers defected back when the circumstances were right.[166] Some of the soldiers of Herodianus's garrison at Spoleto rejoined the Byzantine army under the influence of Martinianus, who, for a change, was a "Byzantine" (Constantinopolitan) by birth. Pretending to be a deserter to the Goths, Martinianus managed to get his wife and one of his two children back from Totila. Apparently Eastern soldiers could come to Italy with their families, leaving themselves open to the same sorts of blackmail that the Italian soldiers suffered from the Byzantine armies. In this case, Martinianus was able to regain his family without defecting, although one would not like to conjecture the fate of his other child after he betrayed Totila slightly later.[167]

Available ethnographic identities, however, could cast a shadow over allegiance. One of the most important and successful Byzantine commanders, John, the nephew of Vitalian, needed to escape the memory of his uncle's identity and allegiance. Vitalian came from the Balkans; some people defined him as a "Goth" in his struggle against Anastasius. Although Vitalian was a strict Chalcedonian, he was murdered on the orders of Justin and Justinian in 520 as an overpowerful threat to the throne.[168]

John was always associated with his uncle in people's minds; in Procopius, he is always called "John, the nephew of Vitalian," or even "the Vitalianic John."[169] His famous uncle could be classified as a Goth: John went out of his way to show that he was a Roman. According to Procopius, he showed *sklērotes*, "austerity," unmatched by any bar-

---

[166] Procopius, BG 3(7).26.10–14.
[167] Ibid. 3(7).23.1–7.
[168] On Vitalian, see ch. 4 above, pp. 127–30; PA Vitalianus 1; PLRE2 Vitalianus 2. On John, see PA Iohannes 2; PLRE3 Ioannes 46.
[169] See PLRE3: 652 for examples. Both Procopius and Agathias sometimes simply call John *ho Vitalianou*.

barian or common soldier.[170] It was a word denoting ancient Roman military and personal virtue. John did not accept Matasuentha's secret offer of marriage,[171] and he never considered defecting or negotiating with the Goths, unlike his *doryphoros* Godilas.[172] Godilas, like John himself from the Balkans, was a "Thracian," and a member of John's large following of *barbaroi*, sometimes "Huns."[173] The various descriptions of John's following can be compared with the confused descriptions of his uncle's army.[174]

Though it is clear that John, closely associated with a "Goth" and an enemy of Justinian, went out of his way to disassociate himself from either category, he himself was not classifed as a Roman upon his death. Like his uncle and his bodyguard, his deepest connections were to the Balkans. His epitaph merely says that he was *provinciae Moesiae natus*.[175] His uncle was also remembered as a Moesian provincial by birth.[176]

A man of similarly mixed antecedents, and placed in a similarly delicate situation, was Totila's officer Ragnaris.[177] Procopius twice calls him *Gothos anēr* in 552, but when he reappeared leading a force of Goths two years later, Agathias calls him "a Hun from the tribe of the Bitigurs," and, implicitly correcting Procopius, "neither kinsmen nor compatriot" of the Goths.[178] Which observer was correct? At least two historians have thought that Agathias, who was on the spot in 554, was better informed. They define Ragnaris as a Hun.[179] But the key word is *observer*. Why would Procopius twice use the phrase *Gothos anēr*, which he habitually reserves for Goths "by kinship," if he had any doubt as to the man's identity? Agathias, on the other hand, denies even Ragnaris's allegiance to the Goths, although he admits that he was leading Goths in 554, and although we know that Ragnaris was serving under Totila in 552. But there is no need to choose between Procopius and Agathias, since a man could have several identities at once. The

---

[170] Procopius, BG 2(6).10.10.
[171] Rather, he married Justinian's cousin Justina, the daughter of Germanus, thus connecting himself not only with the imperial family but also, in the end, with Matasuentha, Germanus's second wife. But as Moorhead, *Justinian*, p. 102, points out, John's ambition ran high, and he moved carefully.
[172] See above, p. 184.
[173] PLRE3: 661.
[174] See above, ch. 4, pp. 128, 129.
[175] ICUR 2.1, no. 14.
[176] PLRE2: 1171.
[177] PA Ragnaris.
[178] Procopius, BG 4(8).26.4, 34.9; Agathias 2.13.3.
[179] Cameron, *Agathias*, pp. 42–3; PLRE3: 1076.

two identities in question each match the political exigencies of each period, 552 and 554.

Ragnaris was using his belief in his own kinship – or at least using the labels of ethnography – in order to take advantage of the most useful compatriotism of the moment. While in Totila's army in 552, he had to call himself a "Goth," but when he was holding out after Totila's defeat in 554, at a time when various bands of all different sides were criss-crossing Italy, it was more useful to choose the identity "a Hun of the Bitigurs," which did not automatically tie him to one of the major sides in the conflict (by this time consisting of Franks, Goths and Byzantines). He saw which way the wind was blowing. Just like Mundo, the Gepid prince who became a bandit, then a Goth and then a Roman,[180] Ragnaris chose the label most useful to him at the time. Perhaps he really did have ancestors known by these labels, or believed that he had. It does not really matter, and cannot have mattered, in the Italy of 554. Allegiance, in the end, outweighed other forms of identity. And allegiance, as in the case of Herodianus, ultimately determined kinship.

The examples of John and of Ragnaris again emphasize the extreme diversity of the opposing armies during the Gothic Wars, and the willingness of their members to take advantage of ethnographic ideology to advance their own careers. The murderer of Totila, the "Gepid" Asbadus, embodied this sort of opportunism. Procopius calls Asbadus a Gepid in Justinian's army. After the battle of Busta Gallorum in 552, Totila was fleeing with some of his closet followers. Asbadus followed them and attacked a man whom he thought was Totila. A "Gothic youth" shouted at him, "What is this, you dog? Are you rushing to smite your own master?", thus definitively identifying Totila to Asbadus.[181]

Why should the phrase "your master" have identified the king to a Byzantine soldier? It does not seem that Asbadus was a deserter from the Gothic side.[182] The answer is that ethnographic classification, and the political arrangements of the previous century, had defined "Gepids" as a subgroup of "Goths."[183] The Gepid prince Mundo became a "Goth" when he allied with Theoderic in 504–5. A contemporary Gepid prince bore the suggestive name Ustrigotthus. Procopius refers to the murderer of Hildebad, Velas, as "one among the Goths" but "a

---

[180] PA **M**undo.
[181] Procopius, BG 4(8).32.24.
[182] Ibid. 4(8).26.13.
[183] Jordanes, *Get.* 94.

Gepid by birth."[184] As a Gepid, Procopius expects the reader to understand, Asbadus was a "natural" subject of Totila. Kinship and allegiance
are again conflated.

But Asbadus was not only a firm supporter of the Byzantine army
in Italy – he went out of his way to emphasize his Romanity. His
metrical epitaph of 556 uses imperial victory ideology and Justinianic
renovatio ideology to depict him as one of the restorers of the Roman
Empire in Italy, not a Gepid who belonged under the sway of the
Gothic king. "In war, after the Gothic *gens* was expelled, you, as victor,
gave the Alps to Latium and the Empire." No *gens* had been "expelled,"
of course, and the Alps and his resting-place, Pavia, would shortly be
Lombard and independent of the Empire. Ironically, Asbadus's epitaph
would be preserved in a chronicle made for Queen Theodelinda of the
Lombards.[185] That chronicle in turn interpreted the *feritas Gothicae gentis*
for Lombard readers, ensuring that classical ethnographic topoi would
not die out in the early Middle Ages.[186]

Asbadus was a Catholic soldier fighting for the Roman emperor, or
a Gepid barbarian who betrayed his Gothic king, depending on how
you want to look at him. Men were hard-pressed to live up to names
and labels. Thus, even in the first phase of the Gothic Wars, we have
the spectacle of a "Goth" with the Latin name Asinarius and leading
"Suevic" troops, battling the "Roman" Mauricius, whose father bore
the Germanic name Mundo.[187] Mundo, like another "Roman" commander, Vitalian, could himself be seen as a "Goth" from Constantinople and the East.[188] Vitalian's nephew John tried to escape his father's
associations by cultivating an image of republican austerity, while his
epitaph declares that he was by birth of the province of Moesia.

Procopius's perspective plays a role in these descriptions, but this
perspective was itself partly a manifestation of Justinianic ethnographic
ideology, which commanders in Italy spread in their justification of the
reconquest. Asbadus, called a Gepid by Procopius, defiantly called himself restorer of the Roman rule in Italy. He cannot have been deaf to
the rhetoric of Roman restoration spread by Belisarius and Narses, nor
ignorant of other men called Gepids, like Mundo and Ustrigotthus.
When necessary, identities like Gepid could be useful: the soldier Goar,
captured by the Byzantines, escaped with the Lombard prince Ildigisal

[184] PA **M**undo, **U**strigotthus, **V**elas.
[185] *Auct. Havn. Extr.* 2; cf. 14, 24 on Theodelinda.
[186] Ibid. 1.
[187] PA **A**sinarius, **M**auricius.
[188] PA **M**undo, **V**italianus 1.

to the land of the Gepids – though he himself, according to Procopius, was a *Gothos anēr*.[189]

In the end, however, the label Goth no longer served anyone's interests in Italy.[190] Ragnaris, who might have been a candidate for preserving the label, was now called a Hun. After 554, only one man is called a Goth, and that by a source centuries later. The last Goth in Italy, Widin *comes Gothorum*, joined with a Frankish war-leader to rebel against Narses at some point in the 550s or the very early 560s. Widin's origins are unclear, and the late attestation of his label "Goth" may be a red herring. But we know that northern Italy suffered from endless chevauchées or warbands from this period through to the end of the century. Their leaders were men with strange names and stranger identities: Osso, who led *Romanus suus exercitus* in the 590s, or Nordulfus, who is said to have led a group of Lombards, but "restoring cities to the Roman Empire."[191] If he actually existed, Widin was no doubt similar, an opportunistic leader like them, like Ragnaris or like the last Gothic leader Aligernus, who had joined the Byzantine army against the Franks in 554.[192] Widin's epithet "Goth" would then perhaps have been left over from service under one of the last Gothic kings. It seems likely that he was a powerful professional mercenary with followers, who was attempting to find work without submerging himself within the Byzantine army.

CONCLUSION

Military and civilian reactions to the label "Goth" and "Roman" were complex and evolved constantly as the ideologies defining these labels themselves evolved. For Cyprian, a "Roman" by birth, but a member of the army, it was to his advantage to adopt "Gothic" ways. For Asbadus, a "Gepid" by birth, it was useful to attempt to be as "Roman" as possible, parroting the rhetoric of Justinian in defense of his career. But the Roman defined by Theoderic in 526, and the Roman defined by Justinian in 556, were entirely different from one another: the one was a representative of peaceful civilian life, learning and the cultivation

---

[189] PA Goar.
[190] There are no Goths in Italy after the Gothic Wars, with one possible exception: PA **Wililiwa** (613/641, but the reading "Guta" in the papyrus is a hazardous emendation). The individuals referred to as "living by the law of the Goths" in the eighth and ninth centuries (e.g. Schiaparelli, *Codice diplomatico longobardo* nos. 38, 228) were making *professiones iuris*, not statements of identity. On this (later) development, see Amory, "The meaning and purpose of ethnic terminology," pp. 19–23, contra for example, Theodor Mommsen, "OGS," NA 14: 535.
[191] PA **Osso**. See Brown, *Gentlemen and Officers*, p. 73; PLRE3: 958; cf. also PLRE3 Adobin.
[192] PA ***Aligernus**, the brother of the last Gothic king, Teia.

of law; the other was a virtuous soldier regaining lands from barbaric *gentes*. Both images of the Roman were ancient. Theoderic and Justinian simply chose different images at different times, and the resultant ideologies could change people's behavior accordingly.

That ethnographic ideologies were simplifying and schematic is shown by the multitude of cultural traits and even of ethnographic labels that an individual could possess and from which he or she could choose in order to define himself or herself most profitably at a given moment. The Gothic language spoken by soldiers served to differentiate soldiers under Theoderic, and by learning it, Cyprian made himself praiseworthy in the eyes of the king. But in the Gothic Wars, when that same language could betray "kinship" to the wrong side, people could use Latin instead to show their "allegiance" to the right side. When necessary, the civilians of Lucani et Brutii could become soldiers – on either side. When necessary, an individual could convert to Catholicism and smoothly switch to patronizing Catholic churches in the town where he owned his property. Names could not differentiate Byzantine from Gothic soldiers during the Gothic Wars, since Germanic, Greek, Thracian and Celtic names existed among both armies alongside Latin ones. Similarly, Italian civilians could have names of both Germanic and Graeco-Latin origins. Ethnographic labels were fully available for use, if one had the right associations, believed that one had the right associations or could convince people that one had the right associations. The Roman John, nephew of a Goth; the Goth and Bitigur-Hun Ragnaris; the Gepid-Goth-Hun Mundo who ended serving the Roman emperor: all these people could choose labels and loyalties that served their purposes best at a given moment.[193]

In the end, at all levels of Italian society, the Wars themselves ensured that locality and regional ties would prove to be the safest badge of identity, and certainly the strongest in economic and emotional terms. John himself reverted to being a Moesian at his death. The Goths who were "natives" of the Cottian Alps were willing to give up any allegiance to the Gothic king in order to preserve their family and property there. The Transpadane Goths in 540 bargained for an Italy autonomous of Constantinople. The Lucani et Brutii, the Neapolitans and the Veneti offered their allegiance and their military service as pragmatically as possible to the Gothic or Byzantine armies in order to preserve their lands, friends and families intact.

---

[193] For a perhaps parallel situation in Merovingian Gaul, see Geary, "Ethnicity as a situational construct in the early Middle Ages," pp. 15–26; but are we really justified in calling this kind of behavior "ethnicity"?

The Gothic army of Theoderic, which entered Italy in 489, put down local roots rapidly through its absorption of the previous Italian troops, intermarriage, the purchase of property, and the institutional involvement of the army in every area of civilian life. Despite the attempts of Theoderic in his later years to create an ancient Gothic past, people called Goths in Italy had already become too identified with the land to be removable from it. The *exercitus Gothorum* had become the *exercitus Italiae*, as Justinian's armies found upon their arrival.[194] Not only was the label "Goth" changeable and shirkable, but political and social circumstances had mingled Theoderic's settlers and Italian natives, people labeled Goth and people labeled Roman, much more thoroughly than had been the case in the Byzantine reconquest of Africa. What impact had the ideologies of the Catholic church on these developments?

---

[194] This chapter thus proposes an entirely different reading of the evidence from Heather, "Theoderic," pp. 172–3, who sees "Theoderic's original Gothic powerbase" as the lasting military force in the Wars: an equation that only works if one can assume that the term "Goth" was stable and the group "Goths" unchanging and fixed. The evidence suggests the opposite.

Chapter 6

CATHOLIC COMMUNITIES AND
CHRISTIAN EMPIRE

In the maelstrom of allegiances and identities competing in sixth-century Italy, religious affiliation played not a small role. The plight of Gundila only hints at the impact that struggles over belief had upon the individual. Contrary to most studies, however, religious affiliation failed to match neatly political constituency, let alone the labels "Goth" or "Roman."

The Catholic church, in particular, has too frequently been presented as a monolithic citadel first forced to collude with Theoderic in opposition to a heretical emperor, then happily reconciled with the East against the Arian rulers and their supposedly Arian followers. In fact, popes disagreed with their predecessors, struggled with kings and emperors throughout the lifetime of the Gothic kingdom, faced internal and external ecclesiastical quarrels over faith, and never led a unified political theology, let alone a unified attitude toward the label "Goth" or even Arian belief. This chapter and the next examine this chaotic situation in detail, and set the context of ecclesiastical politics and religious heterodoxy into a cultural framework that was constantly affected by secular politics, but which never mirrored secular factions.

The question of Arianism is pungent. How did evolving ideals of Catholic community affect attitudes toward the Arian king and his followers (of whatever belief)? The sixth-century papacy inherited mutually contradictory Christian conceptions of community with which it struggled to define its claims to supremacy.[1] Catholics cohabited the Italian peninsula not only with Arians and the new settlers, but with the ancient vestiges of a divided Christianity. Manichaeans, Pelagians and Novatians continued to maintain congregations, even within the

---

[1] For surveys of the sixth-century ecclesiasical history, see Louis Duchesne, *L'Eglise au VIe siècle* (Paris, 1925) and Erich Caspar, *Geschichte des Papsttums von den Anfängen bis zur Höhe der Weltherrschaft* 2, *Das Papsttum unter byzantinischer Herrschaft* (Tübingen, 1933), with the revisions of Ernest Stein, "La période byzantine de la papauté," *Catholic Historical Review* 21 (1935), 129–63. More recent literature appears in the notes below, but no single work has yet supplanted Caspar or Duchesne.

city of Rome.[2] The papacy needed to assert its authority not only over the schismatic Easterners and its Western suffragans, but also over its neighbors on its very doorstep.

Nascent papal supremacism and Augustinian universality conflicted naturally with a more ancient ecclesiastical ideal: the Eusebian notion of a Christian Roman Empire led by a sacral emperor, the vicar of Christ. Eusebianism remained triumphant in the East, but the West possessed a single patriarch – the pope – with pretensions to supremacy over all other patriarchs, and the West had seen the rapid fragmentation and disappearance of effective imperial control by the 460s and 470s. Simultaneously, monophysitism led to a growing break between the Eastern and Western churches, confirmed by the Emperor Zeno's proclamation of the Henotikon, a compromise with the monophysites, in 482. The papal response to the Henotikon was excommunication of Acacius, patriarch of Constantinople, in 484, the beginning of the Acacian schism (484–519).[3]

THE INITIAL CATHOLIC RESPONSE TO THE OSTROGOTHIC SETTLEMENT, 489–498

The decade after Theoderic's arrival in Italy began with famine and tumult and ended with the beginning of the Laurentian schism and the king's triumphant visit to Rome. During this period, a mere ten to twenty years after the removal of the last Western emperor and the loss of the last Gallic provinces, one might particularly expect to find aggressive traditional anti-barbarian attitudes and nostalgia for the Empire. But although the sources are particularly scanty and difficult for these years, they reveal no conception of a disappearance of the Western Empire. Stranger still, ecclesiastical sources such as the papal letters reveal virtually no reaction to the Arianism of the new ruler and many of his followers.[4] Their views on Constantinople, on the other hand, relate only to the monophysite heresy and the Acacian schism. The sources do not yet connect the issue of ecclesiastical union with

---

[2] See below, pp. 198, 199–200. Ch. 7 discusses the indigenous Arian community already existing in Italy when Theoderic arrived.

[3] On papal supremacy, Augustinianism, and Eusebianism in the West versus Eusebianism in the East, see ch. 1.

[4] On papal attitudes toward Arianism, see the summary in Moorhead, *Theoderic*, pp. 89–97, esp. 91. I modify Moorhead's conclusions in the sections below (indicated in the notes). Georg Pfeilschrifter's book on Theoderic's relations with the church has been superseded by subsequent research, all indicated in the notes, although it is still cited frequently as the only monograph on the subject: *Der Ostgotenkönig Theoderich der Grosse und die katholische Kirche*, Kirchengeschichtliche Studien 3 (Münster, 1896).

the East with political union, despite the undoubted conceptual fusion of religion and governance in people's minds. The inescapable conclusion is that the church in the 490s either favored Theoderic's rule and viewed political division as desirable or saw no inherent break with Byzantium. The Italians had already lived for thirteen years under the rule of a previous Arian general, Odoacer. Although he spread no recorded ethnographic propaganda, and did not conceive of his following as a single people, his conciliatory, neutral church policy resembled that of Theoderic.[5]

Much of this picture of an Italy unaware of any momentous change in the arrival of the Ostrogoths emerges from the prolific writing of Pope Gelasius I (492–6). He was not only one of the most influential architects of papal doctrinal supremacy but also one particularly concerned with the secular, that is, imperial, role in ecclesiastical governance.[6] He did not ignore Theoderic, but in the pope's vision of the Catholic church, the king stood outside the "community of belief." Unlike the emperor, he did not interfere with dogma, and as an Arian, he had no claim to the pope's interest.[7] Gelasius was able to ignore the king's religion because Theoderic was *not* the emperor, despite his pretensions. Thus Theoderic had no possible claims over ecclesiastical governance from the papal theoretical point of view, whatever his heretical affiliation. To Gelasius, Odoacer and Theoderic were *magistri militum*, imperially appointed generals like Ricimer and Gundobad before them. Their religious beliefs were doubtless a matter of concern, but had nothing like the cataclysmic effect of a heretical Roman emperor.

It may seem incredible that Gelasius spent more time and energy fighting distant monophysitism than the Arian heresy right on his doorstep. But the beliefs of a new, local and possibly temporary[8] ruler must have seemed insignificant in the pope's powerful vision of a single Cath-

---

[5] On Odoacer, see Sundwall, *Abhandlungen*, pp. 178–85; Moorhead, *Theoderic*, pp. 9–11; on Odoacer's following, see Ian Wood, "Ethnicity and the ethnogenesis of the Burgundians," in *Typen der Ethnogenese* 1: 63.

[6] Ullmann, *Gelasius I.*, pp. 172–216.

[7] Ibid., pp. 220–1. Ullmann also adduces an alleged cultural divide between pope and king (pp. 217–18), which I dismiss above (ch. 4, n. 152, and *passim*), throughout this book. It helps Ullmann's theory of a cultural divide that he rejects many of the letters between Gelasius and Theoderic as forgeries, a notion without any basis (see below, n. 22). Much of Ullmann's difficulty comes from his imagining that Theoderic brought an entire Arian people into Italy. When we realize that there had been Arians in Italy since the days of Ambrose and before, and that many of Theoderic's following were Catholic, as the king's mother was, this difficulty vanishes. On the Arian church in Italy, see below, ch. 7.

[8] Ibid., p. 218. From a legitimist, imperially oriented standpoint, the Goths were still an army of occupation under Gelasius; Theoderic only finally received imperial recognition in 497, one year after Gelasius's death.

olic "ecclesiological society," governed by ecclesiastical *auctoritas* and imperial *potestas*.[9] The Arians had split off from the orthodox, in Gelasius's mind, in 325; they were a minor branch and one, we must remember, that had already existed in Odoacer's Italy and before. Theoderic was not introducing a brand-new heresy. The emperors who had just promoted the Henotikon, however, were Catholics who wished to be in communion with Rome. In his traditional role as referee over opposing doctrines, moreover, the emperor could dangerously influence the entire Catholic community – for Gelasius, superficially conservative in the foundations of his political outlook, defined Christian society in Roman terms,[10] and the imperial danger was thus greater and more immediate.

Although Gelasius did write two treatises against Arianism (unfortunately lost), most of his letters rail against imperial monophysitism and related secular encroachments on papal authority. In his single-mindedness, Gelasius can even imply a "hierarchy of heresies," some more dangerous than others. In a religious world far more fragmented into communities than in his ideal, the pope confronted not only monophysitism and Arianism, but also a famous reappearance of Pelagianism in Italy, the much-feared and ineradicable Manichaeanism, and the celebration of the pagan Lupercalia in the senatorial palaces of the Esquiline Hill.[11] Pagan observances may have continued in Rome long after Gelasius's death.[12] In a letter to an African bishop, the pope could point out that although the Catholic church in Africa was suffering from the "saeventium barbarorum feralia iura," the situation in Constantinople

---

[9] Gelasius, JK 632 = *ep*. "Famuli vestrae pietatis" (Thiel 12, pp. 349–58) to Anastasius I; Caspar, *Papsttum* 2: 65–71; Ullmann, *Gelasius*, pp. 198–212 (using the phrase "ecclesiological society"), but note that Stein argues that the concepts are mere antitheses of rhetoric, "La période byzantine de la papauté," p. 135. Ullmann has rebutted Stein's arguments without, apparently, being aware of them.

[10] Gelasius, JK 632, tries to influence Anastasius by equating the "nomen Romanum" with the "nomen Christianum;" see §§1–2 (Thiel, p. 350), §4 (Thiel, pp. 352–3), but compare his use of these terms in his letter on the Lupercalia (see below, n. 11), and Ullmann, *Gelasius*, pp. 163, 212–16. Despite Gelasius's innovations, he always insisted firmly on the observance of ancient law and on the evil of novelty, e.g. JK 664 = *ep*. "Valde mirati sumus" (Thiel 26, pp. 392–422) §1, p. 393; JK 714 (Löwenfeld 19, p. 10).

[11] Pelagianism: Gelasius, JK 621, 626, 627 (Thiel 4–6, pp. 321–35) to bishops of Picenum and Dalmatia; JK 627 = *Tractatus* 5, *Adversus Pelagianam haeresim* (Thiel, pp. 571–98); cf. also *Notitia epistolae non extantium* 2, 18–19 (Thiel, pp. 608, 612–13). Manichaeanism: LP Gelasius §1, 1: 255, and on the reputation of Manichaeanism, Bury, HLRE 1:378–9, 2: 364–5. Lupercalia: Gelasius, JK 672 = *Tractatus* 6, *Ad Andromachum senatorem* (hereafter *Tractatus adversus Lupercalia*) (Thiel, pp. 598–607); this last probably a cultural rather than a pious survival.

[12] Procopius, BG 1(5).24.28–31 (A.D. 536) apparently a true story, judging from the fragments of a Latin Sybilline oracle preserved in the midst of Procopius's Greek; see further Chadwick, *Boethius*, pp. 14–16.

was just as bad: "Have you not noticed that in the East, as in Africa, the Antichrist has been striving to conquer Jesus?"[13]

Despite his rhetoric, Gelasius did not equate barbarians with heretics. For example, in the midst of the "tempest of continuing wars" tearing apart Italy in 493, the pope wrote to the Dardanian bishops to warn them about monophysitism, which he compares, as an evil, to Arianism.[14] But although two Arian barbarians, Odoacer and Theoderic, were carrying on the war in question, Gelasius never connects them with the danger of sect. In fact, he only uses ethnography with accusations of heresy against the *Greeks* – "apud Graecos, quibus multas haereses abundare non dubium est."[15]

The letter to the Dardanian bishops is astonishingly anti-Greek and anti-monophysite at the precise moment when we would expect the pope to wax anti-barbarian and anti-Arian. Gelasius's ecclesiastical policy concentrated on the threat from the East; he dismissed the danger of the Arian heresy because of his overall sense of ecclesiological providence, not because of ethnic alienation, or the chaos of a long, devastating war.[16]

This is not to say that Gelasius never complains about *barbari*. But he uses the word either as a rote tool for traditional rhetorical antithesis, or else as a merely descriptive term referring to the new inhabitants of Italy.[17] "Barbarorum feritas" carries traditional rhetorical overtones,[18] but more typical is his weary reference to farms "quae vel a barbaris vel a Romanis inconvenienter invasa sunt."[19] In another letter of 493, to the bishops of Picenum, Gelasius laments the "barbarian incursions" then devastating that province. This proves to be a comparison for the even more awful religious deviations of the region, caused by the aged Pelagian Seneca. A lengthy refutation of Pelagianism follows.[20] The pope did not find the wars insignificant, of course. They were causing a deficiency in qualified clergy.[21]

---

[13] Gelasius, JK 628 = *ep.* "Cum tuae dilectionis" (Thiel 9, pp. 339–41) §3, p. 340.

[14] Gelasius, JK 623 = *ep.* "Ubi primum respirare" (Thiel 7, pp. 335–7): "continuorum tempestas bellorum . . . vel in illis provinciis vel in istis," §1, p. 335; Arianism, §§2–3, pp. 336–7.

[15] Ibid. §2, p. 336; similarly, §3, p. 336.

[16] Without any evidence, Ullmann adduces ethnic alienation to the chaotic situation, *Gelasius*, pp. 217–18.

[17] An exception is possibly the description of Odoacer as "barbarus haereticus" (below, p. 200 with n. 23), but even here the point is to emphasize just how badly the emperor Zeno has behaved in contrast.

[18] It caused the "provinciae [Thusciae] vastitatem," Gelasius, JK 706 = *ep.* "Praecepta canonum" (Thiel, *frag.* 9, p. 488).

[19] Gelasius, JK 685 = *ep.* "Ad cumulum vero" (Thiel, *frag.* 35, pp. 501–2).

[20] Gelasius, JK 621 = *ep.* "Barbaricis hactenus" (Thiel 6, pp. 325–35).

[21] Gelasius, JK 636 = *Gelasianum Decretum* (Thiel, pp. 360–79), §1, p. 362.

This complex background of worldly chaos and a welter of competing sects within Italy, and a pope who felt called to yet wider issues, sets the stage for Gelasius's useful contacts with Theoderic.[22] Although the pope, like his successors, could not have approved of an Arian ruler, he sought a *modus vivendi* with him. For Gelasius, this *modus* consisted of a series of hectoring letters similar in tone to his letters to the emperor: under no circumstances could clergy be subject to any kind of secular control. Theoderic acceded to the pope's demands, and Gelasius clearly found the ecclesiastically neutral barbarian rulers more malleable than the emperors. He compared Odoacer, "barbarus haereticus regnum Italiae tunc tenens," favorably to the interfering emperor Zeno.[23]

True, it is hardly surprising that Gelasius always referred to the reigning Theoderic in the most favorable terms, "vir praecellentissimus filius meus Theodoricus rex."[24] On the other hand, Theoderic and he saw eye-to-eye on the jurisdiction of clergy, and the pope knew about and exploited elements of *civilitas* ideology.[25] Moreover, Theoderic's mother Ereleuva was Catholic, and Gelasius enlisted her support in his petitions to the king.[26]

Theoderic's anomalously neutral position regarding the church, when combined with his actual secular power, was an opportunity for a pragmatic pontiff like Gelasius.[27] Theoderic may have been willing to jeopardize Anastasius's recognition of his rule in Italy by refusing the emperor's request to force the pope to approve the Henotikon. The king's position then led to the dual embassies of Festus and Faustus to Constantinople, Roman senators pleading for the pope and for the Gothic king simultaneously.[28]

---

[22] Ullmann's wholesale rejection of Gelasius's letters to Theoderic (*Gelasius*, p. 218, n.3 and pp. 225–6), corroborating his otherwise baseless theory that the pope would have no contact with an Arian or a barbarian ruler (pp. 217–18), is based on his judgment of the *Collectio Britannica* as a highly suspect collection of later medieval forgeries. But JK 721, 723 and 743, which do not come from this source, refer to the king in respectful terms and imply that the pope was already having contact with him. Moreover, JK 650, which does come from the *Collectio*, contains a wealth of circumstantial detail that is difficult to lay at the door of a tenth-century canon lawyer. If there are problems with the letters of Leo VI in this collection, I see no reason to extend them to those of Gelasius, generally accepted by other historians. Ullmann, despite his lucid interpretation of Gelasius's policies generally, is ignorant of Theoderic's strong interest in Catholicism, and, astonishingly, seems to think that Cassiodorus was an Arian (p. 221).

[23] Gelasius, JK 664 = *ep.* "Valde mirati sumus," §11, p. 409: Odoacer had wisely stayed out of the papal election of 483.

[24] Gelasius, JK 743 = *ep.* "Felix et Petrus" (Thiel, fr. 13, p. 490).

[25] Above, ch. 2, pp. 82–4.

[26] Gelasius, JK 683 = *ep.* "Qui pro victu" (Thiel, p. 502); JK 721 = *ep.* "Felicem et Petrum" (Ewald 46, pp. 521–2). Various other members of Theoderic's family were probably Catholic: see ch. 7, below, pp. 268–9.

[27] Moorhead, *Theoderic*, p. 92.

[28] Noble, "Theoderic and the papacy;" Wolfram, *Goths*, p. 284.

Gelasius's use of "filius meus" for Theoderic is odd because it implies the spiritual fatherhood of a bishop over a member of his flock. In his writings, Gelasius imagined the ideal secular ruler as a *filius* of the apostolic succession, a "structural member of the church."[29] Theoderic's flexibility on ecclesiastical matters, and his refusal to push a doctrine on the pope, must have made him considerably easier for the autocratic Gelasius to accept – despite his heretical beliefs – than the stubborn Anastasius I.[30]

A conservative lawyer, a man dedicated to a single Christian polity, and a stern opponent of heresy including Arianism, Pope Gelasius makes a strange candidate for a friend of Theoderic's rule. His example should immediately make us beware of using older systems of thought to explicate the events of the late fifth century. People were changing their behavior in line with the political times, even if their language might sometimes recall an earlier way of life. Gelasius's description of a Christian Empire governed by Roman law can sound like the fourth-century ideal of Constantine and Eusebius. In reality, influenced by Augustine,[31] he could envisage an entire Christian world governed ultimately by the pope, a *congregatio fidelium* under a new sacral *ius publicum*. He paved the way for the later medieval development of papal authority, canon law and the concept of Christendom.[32] In this world view, as in that of Augustine, the *nomen Romanorum*, though the source of much good, is essentially pagan and has thus "been brought to various extremes."[33]

Despite their intransigence over doctrine, the Western bishops had become accustomed to mediating with Arian military rulers. Men like St. Severinus and Avitus of Vienne were experts at it; so was an Italian contemporary of Gelasius, Epiphanius of Pavia.[34] Epiphanius represented his constituency – in this case, the Ligurian region – to Arian kings. The ability of saintly bishops to influence savage rulers is a topos in hagiography, but one may reflect the ability of realistic ecclesiastical politicians to throw aside their prejudices and to communicate effectively, probably on a regular and friendly level.[35]

---

[29] Ullmann, *Gelasius*, p. 202.
[30] One must wonder how long Gelasius would have survived under a ruler like Justinian.
[31] Ullmann, *Gelasius*, p. 163: especially the *City of God*.
[32] Ibid., pp. 213–16.
[33] Gelasius, JK 672 = *Tractatus contra Lupercalia* §14, p. 607.
[34] On this work of Ennodius, see above, ch. 4; here I try to separate Ennodius's views from the behavior of Epiphanius.
[35] Note the gap between Eugippius's distaste for the Rugian kings and the apparent reality of his hero Severinus's willingness to work with them: R. A. Markus, "The end of the Roman Empire: a note on Eugippius, *Vita Sancti Severini*, 20," *Nottingham Medieval Studies* 26 (1982), 2–3. Avitus of Vienne was close enough to the Arian Gundobad to write letters for him and engage in frequent theological discussion: Ian Wood, "Avitus of Vienne: religion and culture

Epiphanius negotiated with Euric, Gundobad, Odoacer and Theoderic over the ransom of northern Italian captives, and with Odoacer and Theoderic about the remission of Ligurian taxes.[36] Epiphanius did not restrict himself to interceding and representing local interests before barbarian rulers. During the earlier war between the emperor Anthemius and the barbarian general Ricimer, Epiphanius pleaded similarly on both sides for peace. Ennodius puts into the bishop's mouth a speech to Anthemius showing him how he can shame the "ferocissimus Geta," Ricimer, by taming his own *iracundia*.[37] Ennodius here invokes the classical association of internal imbalance with the ferocity of the external barbarian,[38] putting Anthemius and Ricimer on the same moral level, that is, beneath Epiphanius.[39] The text places blame equally on the barbarian *patricius* and the Greek emperor. The resulting *concordia*, an episcopal speciality,[40] is purely the doing of the bishop and of his personal merit as man of God.

The ideal of a Christian universe governed by the Church, not necessarily contiguous with the former Roman Empire, and an accompanying willingness to work closely with whatever secular authorities existed, inform the behavior and attitudes of churchmen throughout the life of Ostrogothic Italy. These ideals evolved, however. While in the 490s Gelasius and Epiphanius accommodate and work with a new and doubtless unpleasant reality, a man like Ennodius positively welcomes the Ostrogothic regime and celebrates it continuously. Still later, when the alternative of secular rule from a reconciled Eastern Empire became available after 519, the traditional ideal of a Mediterranean Christian Empire reappeared in Italy along with a renewed anti-Arianism. Such changes to some extent explain the behavior of John I and Vigilius. These popes faced rivals who clung to the Ostrogothic

in the Auvergne and the Rhône valley, 470–530," D.Phil. dissertation, Oxford, 1979, pp. 91, 161–2. Hagiographical topos: for example, Gregory the Great, *Dialogi* 2.14–15, ed. Adalbert de Vogüé, Sources Chrétiennes 251, 260, 265 (Paris, 1978–80) on St. Benedict and Totila, and more positively, on relations between St. Hilarus of Galliata (near Ravenna), and Theoderic, the *Vita Hilari Galeatensis*, ed. Daniel Papebroch, Acta Sanctorum, Maii 3 (Antwerp, 1680), pp. 474D–F: one receives the impression that Theoderic was Catholic. On the probable contemporaneity of this work, see Giovanni Lucchesi, "Ellero," in *Bibliotheca Sanctorum* 4 (Rome, 1964), cols. 1140–41.

[36] Ennodius, *Vita Epifani* §§85–94 (Euric), §§141–70 (Gundobad), §§111–17 (Odoacer and Theoderic, about captives), §§106–7 (Odoacer, about taxes), §§182–9 (Theoderic, about taxes): Ennodius, *Opera*, ed. Friedrich Vogel, MGH: AA 7 (Berlin, 1885).

[37] Ennodius, *Vita Epifani* §§51–74, at §64.

[38] Dauge, *Le barbare*, pp. 436–9, 534–6, 622–3, 806–10.

[39] Beat Näf, "Das Zeitbewuβtsein des Ennodius und der Untergang Roms," p. 118, notes that Epiphanius stands above both parties.

[40] Ennodius, *Vita Epifani*, §74; on *concordia*, see Peter Brown, *The Cult of the Saints: Its Rise and Function in Latin Christianity* (Chicago, 1981), passim.

modus vivendi, and in the ultimate failure of Vigilius's ecclesiastical negotiations in the 540s and 550s, we see the nascent recognition that Western Latin Christianity was fundamentally different from that of the Eastern churches. In this last period, less exalted ecclesiastical sources looked back at Theoderic's early reign as a golden age for the church.

NEUTRAL GROUND: ATTITUDES TOWARD THEODERIC'S
KINGSHIP DURING THE LAURENTIAN AND ACACIAN SCHISMS,
498–514

The Catholic church in Italy was riven by two schisms at this time, the Acacian with Constantinople (484–519) and the Laurentian within Rome (498–506). However, later sources would see the period as a golden age because Theoderic's government took a diplomatic stance toward Catholic ecclesiastical politics, unlike the king's policy in the 520s, and unlike the subsequent programs of Justinian. This golden age began with the king's triumphant entry into Rome to celebrate his *tricennalia* in the year 500. The contemporary churchman Ferrandus, a Catholic refugee from the Arian persecutors in Africa, described Theoderic's honors to St. Peter in the most glowing terms.[41] The author of the *Anonymus Valesianus* in the 540s must have had a very similar contemporary source, judging by his description.[42]

At the time of Theoderic's entry into Rome, the king had just helped to resolve the beginnings of the Laurentian schism.[43] In 498, factions of the senate and clergy had elected two popes, Symmachus and Laurentius. In the end, after synods confirming Symmachus's legitimacy, and several years of struggle and riots during cohabitation of the city of Rome, Laurentius agreed to step down and accept the bishopric of Nocera. Enormous scholarly effort has gone into attempting to define the factional interests involved: Decii versus Anicii, the senate versus the plebs, Blues versus Greens, those favoring compromise over the Acacian schism with the East versus those who did not – i.e. probyzantines versus antibyzantines, and *tituli* priests versus deacons.[44]

---

[41] Ferrandus, *Vita Fulgentii* 13.27, PL 65:130–1 (Paris, 1847); see further Moorhead, *Theoderic*, pp. 60–3.

[42] AV 65–7.

[43] The best summary of the events of the Laurentian schism is Moorhead, *Theoderic*, pp. 114–39, but one should beware aspects of his interpretation based on long-term factions.

[44] Decii versus Anicii: Giuseppe Zecchini, "I 'gesta de Xysti purgatione' e le fazioni aristocratiche a Roma alla metà del V secolo," *Rivista di storia della Chiesa in Italia* 34 (1980), 61, 74; senate versus plebs and Blues versus Greens: Charles Pietri, "Le sénat, le peuple chrétien et les parties du cirque à Rome sous le pape Symmaque (498–514)," *Mélanges d'archéologie et d'histoire de l'École Française de Rome* 78 (1966), 123–39; probyzantines versus antibyzantines: John Moorhead,

It is impossible to equate any of these factions, whatever their principal motivations, with pro- or anti-Gothic interests – whether in the
political sense of supporting Theoderic's regime, or in the socio-cultural
sense of sympathy to the settlement of Theoderic's followers. No source
makes any such equation. The documents of either side reveal sympathy
or antipathy toward the king based exclusively on his favoring or disfav-
oring that side.[45] To draw a huge circle equating the fanatically pro-
Symmachan Ennodius, for example, with a largely non-senatorial group
favoring Theoderic's rule, is to ignore the fact that it is the Symmachan
Liber Pontificalis, and not the *Laurentian Fragment*, that calls the king a
heretic. It is to ignore Ennodius's frantic attempts to make connections
with well-placed senators of all persuasions, even if after the schism.
Ennodius's views on the papacy derived from his doctrine, and from
his relationship to his patron Faustus Niger. One cannot prove that
they had anything to do with his favorable views of the king. Theoderic,
in fact, helped to promote reconciliation with the East.[46]

Both the *Laurentian Fragment* and the Symmachan Acts of the Synods
of 499 and 502 show that the grounds of the schism were the church's
right to alienate ecclesiastical property, with larger overtones of the
question of secular control over the church and the sole authority of a
consecrated pope.[47] If either side had another hidden program relating
to the Acacian schism, why do the sources not talk about it? It is no
secret that Pope Anastasius II favored reconciliation of the schism, and
that Symmachus, a protégé of Gelasius, did not, and that therefore Symmachus reviled Anastasius. Such connections doubtless defined interest
groups holding common beliefs within the ecclesiastical community at
Rome, but they do not allow us to attribute goals to the schismatic

---

"The Laurentian schism: East and West in the Roman church," pp. 125–36; *tituli* priests versus
deacons: Peter Llewellyn, "The Roman church during the Laurentian schism: priests and senators," *Church History* 45 (1976), 417–27; Llewellyn, "The roman clergy during the Laurentian
schism (498–506): a preliminary analysis," pp. 245–75. Henry Chadwick synthesizes the diverse
explanations in *Boethius: The Consolations of Music, Logic, Theology and Philosophy* (Oxford, 1981),
pp. 30–41.
[45] Ennodius, one the chief spokesmen for Symmachus, is careful to treat the king as being above
the schism, whatever his decision; *Op.* 235 (*ep.* 5.13 to Hormisdas, early 506), "when fear was
standing forth in us and we were hanging uncertainly in doubtful estimation of the merits of
the clemency of the pious king . . ."
[46] Noble, "Theoderic and the papacy;" and see below.
[47] LF, p. 44: "Accusatur etiam ab universo clero Romano quod contra decretum a suis decessoribus
observatum ecclesiastica dilapidasse praedia et per hoc anathematis se vinculis inretisset" (adding
to the accusations of the pope's immorality); *Acta synhodi a. CCCCXCVIIII* §7, p. 405, lines
22–7; *Acta synhodi a. DII* §3, pp. 444–5, §12, p. 450. Moorhead discusses this aspect of the
schism, but believes it to have been less important than senatorial factions and attitudes toward
the East, without, to my mind, proving his point: *Theoderic*, pp. 135–8.

factions not stated in the comparatively abundant evidence relating to the schism.[48]

It is anachronistic to divide Italian secular politics, let alone ecclesiastical affairs, into one group of people that supported Constantinople and another that supported Ravenna. Many senators believed that the Italian *res publica* remained part of a larger Roman *res publica*. It took time for an awareness of any break with the past to affect people's political allegiances. They had to cope with the tiny demands of the moment. Only we can see a teleologically big picture leading to Justinian's reconquest of Italy in the 530s and 540s.

Nothing about attitudes toward the Goths – or even about the king's political status – thus emerges from the Laurentian schism, except Theoderic's delicacy in Catholic ecclesiastical matters and his success in wooing support from the church. Pope Symmachus himself, unsurprisingly, held views on the Christian community similar to those of Gelasius. Comparing himself (in a letter to the emperor Anastasius) to Ambrose advising Gratian, Symmachus also uses a "hierarchy of heresies": "You say that I am a Manichaean. But am I a Eutychian [monophysite], or a defender of Eutychians, whose *furor* greatly outdoes the error of the Manichaeans?"[49] This is an extraordinary statement for a Catholic bishop.

Symmachus was, of course, aware that he lived under an Arian monarch, not the Roman emperor, but he used his orthodoxy under these difficult conditions as a stick with which to beat the hapless emperor: "Si mihi, imperator, apud exteros reges, eosque totius divinitatis ignaros, pro fide catholica dicendum foret, quidquid eius veritati rationique congrueret, etiam praetenta morte perorarem." The pope goes on to compare the emperor's sympathetic hearing to the ambassadors of barbarian peoples, and castigates him for not giving a similar hearing to the "voice of the apostolic bishop."[50] Symmachus, of course, must have deliberately used rhetoric that he thought would strike a chord with the emperor, but there is no reason not to consider these his actual beliefs. It was not good to labor under an Arian king; it would be worse to do so under a monophysite emperor. Elsewhere, the pope sent his condolences to the Catholic bishops exiled from Africa by the

---

[48] Thus Sundwall, *Abhandlungen*, p. 191, would like to make Zeno's negative reply to the mission of Festus in 490 "probably, in fact, by agreement with the emperor," a statement for which there is no evidence whatsoever, apart from Sundwall's assumptions about what a Roman senator *would* think at the time, and about Festus's supposedly probyzantine position ten years later in the Laurentian schism.

[49] Symmachus, JK 761 = *ep.* "Ad augustae memoriae" (Thiel 10, pp. 700–8) §6, p. 702.

[50] Ibid., §1, p. 700.

Arian Vandal kings: he must have realized that his own position was incomparably superior to theirs.[51]

The deacon Ennodius, Symmachus's great defender and occasional amanuensis, was a more enthusiastic supporter of the Ostrogothic regime than the pope. Although his *Panegyricus* certainly told Theoderic's government what it wanted to hear, these views are echoed so exactly in a letter to Caesarius of Arles, of 512, that Ennodius must have absorbed them himself. He closes his letter by begging Christ to give the "clementissimus rex" a heir of his own blood, "so that the good features of such a man should not grow old in one age."[52] As a churchman, Ennodius had few qualms about the king's Arianism. Ennodius was chosen by Hormisdas "cum consilio regis" for the pope's first embassy to Constantinople in 514;[53] perhaps he served doubly as royal and papal legate, like earlier embassies. Although Ennodius's epitaph of 521 credits him with some ultimate influence on the resolution of the Acacian schism,[54] it mentions neither his views on Arianism, nor his panegyric to the king. In 521, of course, the ecclesiastical climate was quite different from what it had been in 512.

BALANCING THE *PIUS PRINCEPS ROMANAE REIPUBLICAE*
AGAINST PAPAL *AUCTORITAS*: PAPAL POLITICS UNDER
HORMISDAS, 514–523

If the first part of Theoderic's rule was a "golden age" for Ennodius, the second part was, in some quarters, the beginning of an "age of hope."[55] It was the beginning of the age of Justin and Justinian, a time of intellectual and theological ferment. The new emperor and his nephew brought hope for reunion of the divided churches, for renewal of a single orthodox realm, and eventually, for the political reunion of the two halves of the Roman Empire. These ideas were necessarily associated with each other in both Eastern and Western ecclesiology and notions of the state. But they emerge slowly and incoherently. Ecclesiastical reunion did not have to imply reconquest yet, for the popes, the

---

[51] Symmachus, JK 762 = *ep.* "Lucrum forsitan" (Thiel 11, pp. 708–9).

[52] Ennodius, *Op.* 458 (*ep.* 9.30), §10, p. 319 (unaddressed, titled "In Christi signo"). The rest of this letter mirrors the Panegyric closely; see Näf, "Das Zeitbewußtsein des Ennodius und der Untergang Roms," p. 108 with n. 27. In his edition of Ennodius, Vogel originally thought that the addressee was Pope Symmachus, which would be suggestive indeed, but changed his mind: Friedrich Vogel, "Chronologische Untersuchungen zu Ennodius," *Neues Archiv* 23 (1898), 54, accepted by Sundwall, *Abhandlungen*, p. 69.

[53] LP Hormisdas §2, 1:269.

[54] *Epitaphium Ennodi*, in Ennodius, ed. Vogel, p. lviii.

[55] R. A. Markus, *The End of Ancient Christianity* (Cambridge, 1990), p. 218.

senators or the emperors. In the meantime, the other provinces of the West continued to excite the interest of the papacy.

The political context of the papal imperial letters in the *Collectio Avellana* is important. The 510s in Italy were the years when Theoderic began to recruit support from the parvenu aristocracy rather than from the old families of Rome, causing the possible alienation of part of the senate. In the East, the monophysite Anastasius I was under political and doctrinal siege from the Byzantine Catholic general Vitalian, who led his army to the walls of Constantinople twice, in 513 and 514. After Anastasius's death in 518, his successor Justin I, under the influence of his nephew Justinian, established good relations with the pope, temporarily making the dangerous Vitalian an ally, and in 519 healed the Acacian schism with the agreement of Theoderic. It should have been a bumper year for the Ostrogothic king. Immediately afterwards, he made both of Boethius's young sons consuls, an unheard-of honor, and Boethius himself *magister officiorum*. Any rift between the king and the senate was apparently mended.

Against this background of shifting loyalties we must situate the letters of the *Avellana*, which talk in the grandest terms about re-establishing a Christian empire. They contain two superficially similar viewpoints that would eventually produce much strife between the papacy and the imperial throne. On the one hand, Hormisdas, the former deacon and firm supporter of Symmachus, continued to propagate Gelasian ideals of a theocratic Christian society. On the other hand, Justinian had already begun to set forth his notion of a rejuvenated Roman Empire ruled by Christian autocrats and universally subscribing to a single Christian doctrine. Today we can see that the papal compromises on the limits of the Catholic community, and the authoritarian role of the pope within it, could never be acceptable to Justinian. Similarly, the emperor's eventual claim not only to arbitrate but also to determine orthodoxy would clash with the dearest convictions of the post-Leonian and Gelasian popes.[56]

---

[56] The seeds of disagreement between the papacy and Justinian are visible only to us in this delicate exchange of letters of the 510s, as each side groped for ways of describing the ideal Christian community without offending each other or outside forces like Ravenna. In fact, of course, the churches of the East and of Rome had already diverged quite a distance since one emperor had ruled them both. The popes had governed the Western churches without secular interference ever since Honorius's decree against the Pelagians in 418. They had not been forced to develop the Eastern forms of ecclesiastical resistance, where bishops and monks could use subtle means such as stirring up the populace about doctrine or conspiring with imperial consorts for influence over the appointment of the patriarch. These essential gaps in mutual understanding contribute to explaining the conflicts that arose between Justinian and the popes from 530 onwards. They had already determined the respective visions of Empire propagated by each

Hormisdas, like his predecessors, did not look exclusively toward the East. The pope walked the tightrope between the ideal of a Mediterranean imperial Christianity and that of papal authority in the West.[57] It is the survival of his letters in the *Avellana* that makes him look obsessed with the monophysite controversy. In this mental framework, he commissioned Dionysius Exiguus to translate the canons of the Greek church into Latin. In the process, Dionysius created a new, Western interpretation of ecclesiastical law. Dionysius's canons rapidly penetrated Gaul and Spain, with the papal assistance of the vicariate of Arles.[58] They tried to bring the pope's Western suffragans, already developing their own canons, under papal authority in a Mediterranean Christian community. Similarly, Hormisdas inspired Avitus of Vienne to hold the important Council of Epaon in 517.[59] The pope ensured that his Western suffragans received information relating to the Acacian schism, and simultaneously flexed his authority in deciding the long-standing dispute over jurisdiction between the sees of Arles and Vienne.[60]

Hormisdas envisaged a universal church under papal control, including the Empire in the East and the barbarian kingdoms in the West, but neither region was under his effective authority. He could, however, draw his Western suffragans onto his side in the fight against the "Greek" monophysites,[61] a policy that would eventually have great consequences in the hands of later popes. He had the luxury of playing

---

side in the 510s. See further Caspar, *Papsttum* 2. On Eastern methods of episcopal resistance, see Brown, *Power and Persuasion*, pp. 71–117.

[57] As usual, the Balkans had for long provided an area for dispute, in this case with the claims of the patriarch of Constantinople, an issue in which Justinian would take much interest. See Charles Pietri, "La géographie de l'Illyricum ecclésiastique et ses relations avec l'Eglise de Rome (Ve–VIe siècles)," in *Villes et peuplement dans l'Illyricum protobyzantin*, pp. 30–62. Sundwall discusses Gelasius's advances toward the Illyrian bishops during Theoderic's negotiations with the East in 496–7: *Abhandlungen*, p. 199 with n. 2.

[58] Paul Fournier and Gabriel Le Bras, *Histoire des collections canoniques en Occident depuis les Fausses Décrétales jusqu'au Décret de Gratien*, 2 vols. (Paris, 1931–2), I: 49–50, 78.

[59] Wood, "Avitus of Vienne," pp. 226–7.

[60] Avitus, *ep.* 41 to Hormisdas; Hormisdas, JK 784 = *ep.* "Qui de his" (Thiel 22, pp. 783–6) to Avitus (on both the Acacian schism and on the Gallic dispute); see also Hormisdas, JK 777 = *ep.* "Justum est" (Thiel 9, pp. 758–61) to Caesarius of Arles, and JK 788 = *ep.* "Inter ea quae" (Thiel 26, pp. 793–6), to the bishops of Spain. Nevertheless, it can be no accident that increased papal interest in Provence and Spain directly followed Theoderic's conquest of the two regions. On relations between Hormisdas and Provence and Spain, see further Knut Schäferdiek, *Die Kirche in den Reichen der Westgoten und Suewen bis zur Errichtung der westgotischen katholischen Staatskirche* (Berlin, 1967), pp. 68–81.

[61] Thus Avitus, *ep.* 41, p. 70, lines 3–5, tells Hormisdas "His adicitur, quod diversorum fida relatione comperimus de reconciliatione vel concordia ecclesiae Romanae iactitare se Graeciam," a Latin- and Western-oriented view that, as we shall see, did not resemble much of either papal or Eastern rhetoric at the time of the actual reconciliation.

with this idea because he lived in the neutral middle ground of Theoderic's Italy, unlike his unfortunate successor Vigilius.

The emperor Anastasius had less ambitious goals than his successors. A monophysite perfectly happy to live under the compromise of the Henotikon, and a man prudent in matters of money, he did not want to alienate whole eastern provinces by insisting on the strict observance of Chalcedon. Such *laissez-faire*-ism may also have informed his attitudes toward the West, as his peculiar letter to the Roman senate suggests. This antiquarianizing document of 516 apparently attempts to recall the ancient relationship between the senate and emperor, without, however, antagonizing Theoderic. It is addressed to the "proconsuls, consuls, praetors, tribunes of the plebs and the senate," and continues with the ancient formula: "Si vos liberique vestri valetis, bene est: ego exercitusque meus valemus." In his list of cognomina, the emperor retains Alamannicus, Francicus and Sarmaticus, but omits Gothicus.[62] So far from asserting his rights in Italy,[63] Anastasius seems to be pleading that ecclesiastical authority be devolved in Italy like civil authority. He urges the senate to try to influence the king and pope – using the correct titulature for each – for the purposes of "harmony" between "uterque publicae res," even though "multa pars reipublicae vestrae" opposes it. If his unstated goal (universal consent to the Henotikon) is achieved, "utriusque reipublicae membra sperata sanitate salventur."[64]

The letter argues for the peaceful coexistence of two or more Christian heterodoxies, parallel to the political coexistence in a Roman province of a king "to whom the power and care of ruling you have been committed."[65] It thus invokes Theoderic's own conception of his kingdom, as a separate but Roman sphere, independent in policy but part of

---

[62] Emperor Anastasius I, *ep.* "Si vos liberique" (*Avellana* 113 = Thiel, pp. 765–6). The Byzantines were well aware of the effect that victory cognomina could have on barbarian kings: Agathias, *Historiae* 1.4 (Theudebert enraged by Justinian's use of "Francicus"); note Ennodius's resentment of Anastasius's use of "Alamannicus," above, ch. 4, p. 115 with n. 40.

[63] Past commentators have interpreted this letter as an attempt to woo the senate away from the king with archaicizing speech, but do not note the omission of Gothicus (used in Anastasius's other letters) and the subsequent respectful remarks about the king; e.g., Robin Macpherson, *Rome in Involution: Cassiodorus' Variae in their Literary and Historical Setting*, Uniwersytet im. Adama Mickiewicza w Pozananiu, Seria Filologia Kasyczna 14 (Poznan, 1989), p. 70; Francis Dvornik, *Early Christian and Byzantine Political Philosophy: Origins and Background*, 2 vols., Dumbarton Oaks Studies 9 (Washington, 1966), 2: 814 (seeing a subtle insistence on the delegation of imperial power to both king and pope).

[64] Emperor Anastasius I, *ep.* "Si vos liberique," p. 756.

[65] Ibid.: "excelsum regem, cui regendi vos potestas et sollicitudo commissa est." Dvornik, *Early Christian and Byzantine Political Philosophy* 2: 814, notes the parallel between the twin portfolios of king and pope under the emperor.

the civilized world.[66] Even the language is similar to that of Cassiodorus, playing with Roman legal concepts like *libertas* and *publica utilitas*. The notion of two *res publicae* also appears in Theoderic's letters to Anastasius of 507–8 and 510, so it was evidently common ground between the two rulers.[67] Witigis's wife Gudeliva was to resurrect it to no effect in a letter to Theodora in 535, after the situation had changed completely, partly due to the events of the 510s.[68] Finally, religious toleration was a pillar of Theoderic's policy as well, if couched in different terms for different reasons.[69]

The reply of the senate demonstrates how out of date Anastasius was. Unlike the classicizing imperial letter, it is composed in good late antique style, obsequious to every possible authority. It concedes the rule of "utraque republica" to the emperor, but gives due respect to "dominus noster invictissimus rex Theodoricus filius vester" as ruler of Italy.[70] The emperor tried to treat the senate as an independent political institution; it replied as a body fully under the thumb of the pope. The letter, unlike that of the emperor, is studded with scriptural citations and resembles the pope's letter of the same time in its attention to *scandalum*.[71] It studiously ignores any appeal to coexistence of religious beliefs: the possibility does not exist.

This sort of single-minded blindness of purpose characterizes much of Hormisdas's policy, and indeed his epistolary style, which is simple, patristic and concerned with purely spiritual and ecclesiastical issues. In his mild, firm way the pope presses for the only logical end to the schism: the East must give way. He does not indulge in long conceits, secular parallels and hyperbolic language like Gelasius (who repeatedly uses words like "destabilis" and "execrabilis"); he avoids referring to the king, and tries to avoid secular issues in general. This serious religiosity would serve him well in ending the schism, because it enabled him – with one exception – to discuss an ideal Christian realm in spiritual terms that did not apparently conflict with the goals of either Justinian or Theoderic.

Similarly, there is no reason to see in Justinian's early correspondence any early Reconquest ideology: the emperor-elect apparently wanted ecclesiastical reunion but not political – or else did not yet see the kingdom of Italy as divided from the Empire. For example, in one of

---

[66] See above, ch. 2, pp. 53, 55–6, 58–9.
[67] *Var.* 1.1, 2.1; on the dates, see Krautschick, *Cassiodor*, pp. 51, 57 with n. 5.
[68] *Var.* 10.21.2; on the date, see Krautschick, *Cassiodor*, p. 93.
[69] See ch. 2, n. 12, and pp. 60, 80–1 with n. 196, above.
[70] *Rescriptum senatus urbis Romae ad Anastasium Augustum* (*Avellana* 114 = Thiel, pp. 768–70), §§1–2, pp. 768–9.
[71] Ibid.; cf. Hormisdas, JK 779 = *ep.* "Sollicitari animum" (*Avellana* 114 = Thiel 13, p. 767), §2, p. 767.

his first letters to the pope, Justinian reiterates both his own and his uncle's desire for reconciliation, and mentions that he has also ordered that the *invictissimus rex* be informed of the events in the *religionis negotium*.[72] This was doubtless a pragmatic move in an uncertain time, but both the emperors and the pope took care to keep in step with the king during their negotiations. In fact, the evidence indicates that Theoderic himself wanted to hasten reconciliation among the Catholics, and that both sides viewed him as a useful tool.[73]

However, in the long subsequent series of letters effecting the unification of the Eastern and Western churches, Theoderic and the kingdom of Italy drop out of the discussion entirely. Understandably, people focused on the earth-shattering event of ecclesiastical reconciliation after more than a generation of schism, but the rhetoric used for unifying the Catholic world, consciously or unconsciously, seems to anticipate the conditions for unifying the Roman world. The two worlds may still have seemed largely contiguous from the vantage-point of the Mediterranean, of course, but it was just at this time that Eastern sources start to talk about the West as "lost,"[74] and some of this sense of a broken realm may have affected the rhetoric about the churches. The difference is that these letters seem to imagine that effecting ecclesiastical reunion will automatically bring about political reunion.

Nascent reconquest rhetoric appears in a letter of John, patriarch of Constantinople, to Hormisdas in April 519, the year of Eutharic's consulship and Cassiodorus's *Chronicon*. The letter opens by praising Justin as "pious emperor of the *Romana respublica*," and continues excitedly, "evidently perceiving that both churches both of old and new Rome to be one, and correctly defining one seat of them both, I recognize an indivisible union and our harmonious agreement in the integrity of judgment." John closes by again praising Justin as "universo mundo clementissimum et Christianissimum principem."[75]

In the face of fervor like this – we are back to one *res publica*! – Anastasius's careful language looks pale, and the route to Justinianic ideology appears clear. But while John's language found echoes at the

---

[72] Justinian, *ep.* "Desiderabile tempus" (*Avellana* 147 = Thiel, pp. 833–4), p. 834.

[73] On Hormisdas and the king, LP Hormisdas §§2 and 5 (1:269–70), though note that Duchesne rejects the second consultation (at LP 1: 273, n. 15). Vitalian had approached the king earlier: Eduard Schwartz, *Publizistische Sammlungen*, p. 251 (Schwartz's explanation of the rapprochement between Vitalian and Theoderic on the basis of an alleged ethnic tie should be rejected: see above, ch. 4).

[74] Krautschick, "Zwei Aspekte," pp. 363–71; further on this issue, see ch. 4, above.

[75] John, patriarch of Constantinople, *ep.* "Quando Deus propria" (*Avellana* 161 = Thiel, pp. 862–4).

imperial palace,[76] Hormisdas was characteristically more restrained. The pope stresses mere "ecclesiastica pax" and "ecclesiarum redintegratio" in a series of letters from slightly earlier.[77] One should nevertheless remember that quantity of repeated phrases may be insignificant, since these all came out of the papal chancery very close to one another, suggesting mass-production of letters at a busy time.

More significant is Hormisdas's series of letters from July 519, responding to the Constantinopolitan celebration of reunion. Perhaps treading a delicate diplomatic line vis-à-vis Theoderic,[78] he restrains his enthusiasm in seven of the letters dated 9 July,[79] but in the eighth, to the emperor Justin, the papal rhetoric goes sky-high. God gave to Justin the "Orientis imperium" for the fulfillment of the divine will, supporting both Justin's rule and the solid, unconquered strength of his *respublica*. The pope compares the emperor to David.[80] Such a parallel leads the pope into a prediction of Justin's victories over the *gentes*:

> Bellabis tu quidem divino tutus auxilio, excellentissime princeps, et tuae reipublicae iugo ferocissimarum gentium colla submittes . . . Enimvero ceterorum natura proeliorum distincta gentibus, regionibus terminata . . . hunc omnibus regionis imputabis triumphum.[81]

This is the only appearance of imperial victory rhetoric – of the type that Ennodius applied to Theoderic – in Hormisdas's surviving writings. It is striking that it should appear at the moment of a reunion of churches. Traditional notions could exercise a strong subconscious pull.

---

[76] Emperor Justin I, *ep.* "Scias effectum" (*Avellana* 160 = Thiel, pp. 861–2), written on the same day (22 April 519) as that of John.

[77] Hormisdas, JK 807 = *ep.* "Ecclesiarum pax" (*Avellana* 156 = Thiel, p. 844); JK 812 = *ep.* "Bonae voluntatis" (*Avellana* 157 = Thiel, p. 848); JK 814 = *ep.* "Ea quae caritas" (*Avellana* 151 = Thiel, pp. 849), of January–February 519, to the empress Euphemia, to Anastasia and Palmatia, and to John, patriarch of Constantinople, respectively.

[78] Sundwall, *Abhandlungen*, pp. 232–3.

[79] Hormisdas, JK 820 = *ep.* "Consideranti mihi" (*Avellana* 169 = Thiel 80, pp. 879–81); JK 821 = *ep.* "Benedicimus ineffabile" (*Avellana* 176 = Thiel 81, pp. 881–2); JK 822 = *ep.* "Cum necesse fuerit" (*Avellana* 177 = Thiel 82, p. 882); JK 823 = *ep.* "Ita devotionis" (*Avellana* 174 = Thiel 83, pp. 882–3); JK 824 = *ep.* "Litteris amplitudinis" (*Avellana* 179 = Thiel 85, pp. 883–4); JK 825 = *ep.* "Postquam Deus noster" (*Avellana* 180 = Thiel 84, p. 883); JK 827 = *ep.* "De his, quae acta" (*Avellana* 170 = Thiel 87, pp. 884–5). All the letters are to people in Constantinople, including Justinian and John, patriarch of Constantinople.

[80] Hormisdas, JK 819 = *ep.* "Lectis clementiae" (*Avellana* 168 = Thiel 79, pp. 877–9), §§1–2, pp. 877–8.

[81] Ibid., §3, p. 878: "Indeed, you will fight safely with divine help, most excellent emperor, and you will bow down the necks of the ferocious *gentes* to your *res publica* . . . And when the situation of distinct *gentes* and regions of other battles has ended, you will display this triumph to the whole world." The *iugum* metaphor also appears in Justinian's reconquest rhetoric: above, ch. 4, p. 143.

Even to a level-headed theologian like Hormisdas,[82] the ideal Christian realm could suddenly seem within reach when the Roman Emperor behaved properly.

Elsewhere, Hormisdas restricted his effusions to quiet joy over the joining of the churches, even in the accompanying letter to the emperor's nephew Justinian.[83] Was his explosion in the letter to Justin a momentary loss of control? Or was he telling the emperor what the emperor wanted to hear? It is not possible to say, but since subsequent letters in the *Avellana* rapidly sink into the morass of the Theopaschite controversy, there was little room left for such expressions on either side.

Whatever the lingering attractions of Eusebian caesaropapism, at least one section of the Roman clergy, probably including Hormisdas himself, tended to see the resolution of the Acacian schism as a triumph for the West and papacy over the East. Hormisdas's metrical epitaph was composed by his son Silverius, who seems from his subsequent activity as pope to have shared his father's outlook.[84] The language of the poem neatly shows the complex interaction of a Christian Empire and a Catholic, papal West. The epitaph addresses the deceased Hormisdas: "You have healed the body of the *patria*, lacerated by schism, restoring torn-off members to their rightful places: in the pious Empire, conquered Greece gave way to you, rejoicing that it had regained its lost faith."[85] The subsequent mention of Hormisdas's helpful activity on behalf of the Catholic bishops in Africa, repressed by the Arian Vandal kings there, shows that Arianism – at least in its intolerant African form – remained a strong concern as well.[86]

For Hormisdas and Silverius in 523, the *orbis* remains equivalent to the *patria* and the *imperium*, and it is a naturally Christian (*pius*) realm. But there is no mention of the emperor, and the East is reduced to

---

[82] At the end of the letter, the pope abruptly comes back down to earth, reminding the emperor in plain language to make sure that the churches of Antioch and Alexandria stay in line: ibid., §4, p. 879.

[83] Moorhead, *Theoderic*, p. 199, compares Patriarch John's emphasis on the role of the emperor with the more restrained views of Hormisdas, without, however, noticing the pope's outburst to Justin in JK 819.

[84] See below, pp. 226–7.

[85] Silverius, *Epitaphium Hormisdae pontificis*, ed. Angelo Silvagni, *Inscriptiones christianae urbis Romae*, n.s. 2, no. 4150: "sanasti patriae laceratum scismate corpus/restituens propriis membra revulsa locis/imperio devicta pio tibi Graecia cessit/amissam gaudens se reparasse fidem." "Imperio pio" could also be translated in the dative in apposition to "tibi," producing "conquered Greece gave way to your pious power." The attribution of *imperium* to Hormisdas, given that it is Greece (i.e., the emperor) who is giving way, could then be significant for contemporary papal claims.

[86] Ibid.: "Africa laetatur multos captiva per annos/pontifices precibus promuerisse tuis . . ."

Graecia. The Mediterranean is still the center of the Christian world, but this center lies with the pope at Rome, not the emperor at Constantinople. The epitaph foresees a happy future for the reunited church, but it is not quite the future envisaged by Justinian and the Eastern patriarchs. This dislocation of the ideal of the geography of belief and its rightful center, determined already by several generations of different ecclesiastical developments in East and West, would shortly grow into major differences between the papacy and Constantinople. It would take the Gothic Wars for the consequences of these differences to become obvious.

While the pope generally emphasized only a reunion of churches, and not of *respublicae*, other forces in the Italian church were beginning to find problems with the Arian heresy of the Ostrogothic ruler. The first edition of the *Liber Pontificalis*, composed probably by a bureaucrat in the papal chancery,[87] a contemporary of the pontificate of Hormisdas (514–21),[88] is the earliest surviving Italian source to call Theoderic a heretic.[89] The life of Symmachus portrays the embattled pope as standing between *Theodoricus hereticus* and *Anastasius euthicianus* – the sole force for good in the world. Although the king is then said to make the "iudicium aequitatis" in choosing the principle of first-come-first-served in deciding between the rival popes of 499, he becomes *hereticus* again after his behavior in 502.[90] In the subsequent life of Hormisdas, however, probably written in the early years of John I (521–5), the king loses the epithet *hereticus* and it is applied to the emperor Anastasius.

Various views on Arianism existed at the same time in Catholic circles: one could ignore it, as the pope generally did,[91] or condemn it at various times, as did the anonymous author or authors of the first *Liber Pontificalis*. The author of the *Laurentian Fragment*, who wrote

---

[87] I accept the arguments of Thomas F. X. Noble, "A new look at the *Liber Pontificalis*," *Archivum Historiae Pontificiae* 23 (1985), 354–5, against Duchesne, LP 1: clxii–clxiii (arguing for production in the papal *vestiarium*).

[88] Duchesne, LP 1: xlvii–xlviii; Cyrille Vogel, LP 3: 7–9; Cyrille Vogel, "Le 'Liber Pontificalis' dans l'édition de Louis Duchesne: état de la question," in *Monseigneur Duchesne et son temps*, Collection de l'Ecole Française de Rome 23 (Rome, 1975), pp. 103–4. I accept Duchesne's unified first edition over the two earlier recensions hypothesized by Vielliard, and accepted by Llewellyn, "The Roman church during the Laurentian schism: priests and senators," pp. 417–18.

[89] Moorhead, *Theoderic*, pp. 92–3.

[90] LP¹ Symmachus, 1: 97.

[91] Hormisdas, of course, did not approve of Arianism, and did not shrink from mentioning it in a list of condemned heresies: JK 862 = *Decretale in urbe Roma* (Thiel 125, pp. 931–8), cap. 3 (= §4), p. 933, undated.

between 514 and 518,[92] scorned the picture of Symmachus as trapped between two heretical stools, seeing the Acacian schism as "pointless" and chaffing the pope for not celebrating Easter "cum universitate."[93] This text never describes the king as a heretic. Appeals to the king had helped to bolster Laurentius's position, of course. Nevertheless, it was also by royal fiat that the schism was ended in favor of Symmachus; the text chooses to blame this mistake on the *insinuatio* of Symmachus and Dioscorus.[94] For whatever reason, the Fragment did not think to use the king's beliefs against him, even when he did not operate in favor of its subject Laurentius, while the Symmachan *Liber Pontificalis* did employ the slanderous epithet "heretic."

Clearly, one could choose one's imputation of heresy for various effects. One clergyman's letter of 519 or 520 answers the senator Faustus Niger's questions about the Theopaschite formula by comparing it to Arianism.[95] This was not the usual means of fighting the Theopaschite formula – if extraordinarily penetrating in some ways[96] – but it shows that supporters of Hormisdas would stop at nothing to halt a doctrine that was considered to water down Chalcedon. Nonetheless, the body of the letter makes it clear that monophysitism was the author's first concern, even if he invoked Arian associations to make Theopaschitism appear doubly horrifying.

The reappearance of Arianism as a contemporary evil in 519 to 520 has an ominous ring, however. At this very moment, the powerful Arian and Catholic churches in Ravenna were locked in a bloody struggle. It was the first outbreak of such conflict in Theoderic's reign. The initial dispute was provoked by a disagreement on the rights of the Jews of Ravenna over one of their synagogues. The Italian Catholic clergy had a tradition of intolerance toward the Jews that stretched back to Ambrose; the Arians, as represented by the king, probably supported general tolerance because it was in their own interests as a minority religion. That Theoderic's new heir, the Arian Eutharic, chose to support the Jewish cause, must have increased the friction.

Eutharic, in his consulship of 519 the symbol of Theoderic's role in

---

[92] Duchesne, LP I: xlvii.

[93] LF, p. 44.

[94] Ibid., p. 46.

[95] Trifolius, *Epistola ad beatum Faustum senatorem contra Ioannem Scytham monachum*, ed. Eduard Schwartz, *Publizistische Sammlungen*, pp. 115–16: "Ista doctrina de fonte Arii prodivit"; "Quid est dicere unum de trinitate passum nisi ostendere alterum de trinitate inpassibilem sicut Arrius?"

[96] Cf. Friedrich Loofs, *Leontius von Byzanz und die gleichnamigen Schriftsteller der griechischen Kirche*, Texte und Untersuchungen 3.1–2 (Leipzig, 1887), p. 255: the Theopaschite formula really addressed issues of the Trinity rather than of Christology.

the reconciliation of the Catholic church, attracted the rage of the Ravenna Catholics. As an Arian, "contra fidem catholicam inimicus,"[97] upholding the rights of yet a third religious community, the Jews, he was actually following his father-in-law's footsteps. But in the fervor following the Catholic triumph in the Mediterranean, and accompanying all the rhetoric of that year about a single belief, such partisanship seems to have infuriated some Italian Catholics. Their horizons, and ambitions, had momentarily seemed wider.

This incident is only described in the *Anonymus Valesianus*, a source from years later, and one that admittedly forgets to mention the healing of the Acacian schism. Although probably an isolated local event, it is difficult not to connect the Ravenna disturbance with the changes in outlook that the reunion could produce even in as sober-minded a churchman as Hormisdas. Theoderic had campaigned for the rights of Jews over burned synagogues years before. He issued a law protecting these rights, and enforced that law subsequently.[98] There was nothing new in the Ravenna incident except that it happened in 519 and that the consul Eutharic took charge of it. Eutharic was consul, of course, as a result of the reunion of churches. The level of reaction recorded by the *Anonymus Valesianus* can only be explained through this connection – or through the benefit of hindsight.

THE IMMEDIATE CATHOLIC RESPONSE TO THEODERIC'S PERSECUTION OF POPE JOHN I AND BOETHIUS, 523–533

Immediately after the reunion of the churches, Theoderic appointed the Graecophile Boethius's sons consuls, Boethius himself *magister officiorum*. Boethius's close friend John became pope. Shortly afterwards, Theoderic turned against both of them with unprecedented fury.[99]

The chief effect of the persecution of Boethius and John was to show Catholics how fragile their position could be in a land ruled by an Arian monarch. The incident helped to make options much clearer. Later, the papacy and Justinian's generals would use the story of the persecutions as an instrument with which to draw reluctant Italian provincials to their side in the Wars.[100] At the time, the reverberations of the rhetoric of reunion continued to be slight.

---

[97] AV 80.
[98] See ch. 2, pp. 60, 81 with n. 196.
[99] See chs. 2 and 4.
[100] Procopius depicts Theoderic's attack on Boethius and Symmachus as the only injustice that this legitimate (in Byzantine eyes) Gothic king had perpetrated: BG 1(5).1.33–9; cf. the story of Rusticiana, Boethius's widow and Symmachus's daughter, under Totila, 3(7).20.26–31

It is wrong to connect Theoderic's sudden turn against Pope John I in 523 with the Ravenna incident of 519, as the later *Anonymus Valesianus* does.[101] But the king's change in policy did have something to do with the reunion of churches. Both John and Boethius belonged to an intellectual circle with interests in Greek philosophy and theology, with long-term contacts in Constantinople.

In both cases, it seems to have been the potential consequences of the Catholic Roman Empire evoked in the letters of 519 that frightened the king. While Boethius was accused of political treason, John was judged guilty of somehow abetting persecution of Arians in the East, even though he had traveled there to plead with the emperor to halt persecution.[102] Justin and Justinian had decided to enforce long dormant imperial laws against Arians as part of their general commitment to a single orthodox belief in their realm.[103] Theoderic must have perceived that it was but a short step from such a commitment to enforcing such consistency everywhere in the Empire or former Empire; it was just at this time that Marcellinus was writing his Chronicle containing the first statement that the Western Empire had been lost and never recovered in 476. Since Theoderic's power was founded on the consensus that he ruled in a Roman realm that was in fact independent, such conceptions threatened the security of his rule, particularly if anyone within Italy decided to accept them. Since these conceptions emerged quite naturally out of the reunion with churches, and the recent reminder that the king was not of the Catholic (hence Roman) faith, it was inevitable that Italians would encounter them.

In retaliation, Theoderic persecuted the men whom he saw, rightly or wrongly, as stirring up unrest. For Boethius, who like Hormisdas and Silverius had been subtly influenced by the resolution of the Acacian schism, the rhetoric of Empire sat easily in his imagined Mediterranean Catholic community.[104]

Theoderic had long been an expert at maintaining balance and con-

---

(a generous woman who had suffered from Theoderic and was slandered by Totila's soldiers as a possible traitor). The second edition of LP, which depicts Theoderic as particularly wicked for his behavior towards John, was probably produced in the time of Vigilius, whose views on Goths it mirrors (see below).

[101] AV 85–93.

[102] If John the Deacon who wrote to Ennodius's relative and ambassador of Theoderic, Senarius, was actually the same as John I (Schanz-Hosius, p. 595), then it is noteworthy that his comments on Arians include none of the strong language of Symmachus or Agapetus: *Epistula ad Senarium* 9, PL 59: 404 (Paris, 1847).

[103] They enforced old laws against the Arians; new ones did not appear until Justinian's sole rule in 527: Pierre Goubert, "Autour du voyage à Byzance du pape S. Jean I," *Orientalia Christiana Periodica* 24 (1958), 351–2.

[104] For whom Graecia was one part of the *res publica*: above, pp. 213–14.

sensus: why did the stories of the informers strike a chord? The foundations of his own philosophy of Roman government and barbarian military virtue were being eroded by the new Catholic solidarity. It is precisely at this time that Theoderic began to propagate a new image of the Goths as a bellicose *gens* elected not for their comprehension of Roman wisdom, but for the alleged splendor and antiquity of the Amal dynasty and its separate traditions.

The king himself increased tension by causing the deaths of two respected senators of powerful family and the pope at the same time. There had been nothing inevitably inimical to Theoderic about the actions of Boethius, John or even the emperor. Reconquest was not yet in the air. Looking back from the 540s, the *Anonymus Valesianus*, Procopius and the second edition of the *Liber Pontificalis* saw the executions as a watershed in Theoderic's reign. These views descended to Gregory the Great[105] and thence to modern interpreters of the events.

Nevertheless, if the situation changed for some people in the confusing events leading to the fall of Boethius, there is no question that many, perhaps most Catholics, remained loyal to the Ostrogothic monarchy. Cassiodorus, Cyprian and Opilio – the latter a signatory to the Council of Orange – positively benefited from Boethius's downfall, and so did members of the Decii and Theoderic's chosen new pope, Felix IV. The doctrinal opinions of Cassiodorus and Opilio were important enough to Pope John II in 532 that he consulted them on his definitions of faith.[106] The Catholic deacon and doctor Helpidius continued serving Theoderic right up to the king's death, when Theoderic told him about his feelings of guilt over the Boethius affair.[107] It is inaccurate to say Boethius's "death was seen by *contemporaries* as a crucial incident in a conflict between Gothic Italy and the East Roman Empire."[108] In fact, this view comes from the 540s, from Procopius, the *Anonymus Valesianus* and the second edition of the *Liber Pontificalis*, produced under very different political and ecclesiastical circumstances. People in the 520s, in Italy as in the East, had mixed reactions to Boethius's down-

---

[105] Gregory the Great, *Dialogi* 4.30. Gregory seems to have realized that the evil of Theoderic was not necessarily obvious at the time; he got the story from a friend whose father-in-law, on being informed of Theoderic's death, replied, "God forbid: we left him alive at our departure from Rome!"

[106] See below, pp. 222–3.

[107] PLRE2 Helpidius 6, p. 537. The doctor may have spread the story (attributed to him by Procopius) partly in order to exculpate the king.

[108] Chadwick, *Boethius*, p. 68, emphasis added.

fall.[109] Too many people failed to concur with his view of the world.[110]

In fact, despite the imprisonment and ill-treatment of a pope, the evidence shows no immediate backlash against the regime. The Ravenna government became diplomatic after the death of Theoderic in August 526, and Athalaric directed conciliatory letters reviving *civilitas* ideology to all the political constituencies of Italy. However, his first letter to the Gothic army was quite different, stressing its bellicose virtues rather than the uplifting qualities of Roman law. The new government thus continued the trend begun by Theoderic at least six years earlier.[111]

Boethius was not a catalyst but a symptom. Whatever the efforts of Athalaric's government, the choices of allegiance for people who preferred an independent "Ostrogothic" Italy were beginning to dwindle. Whereas the Catholic church had re-established contacts with the East and the reviving notion of a Christian Empire, alienating the king, the king and his government were promoting *civilitas* less and less and defining the Goths more and more as an independent *gens* defined by their inherited warlike nature, without reference to the Roman past. After the attack on John I, anti-Arianism was no longer a moot point.

Until the life of John I, the author or authors of the first edition of the *Liber Pontificalis* had continued to reserve negative comments for Theoderic according to context. Thus, while Theoderic can alternately be a heretic or a just ruler in the life of Symmachus, in the life of Hormisdas, probably composed just after that pope's death in 522,[112] Theoderic twice helps the negotiations to end the Acacian schism, and the text makes no reference to his beliefs.[113]

---

[109] Another possible enemy of Boethius was the poet Maximian, panegyricist of Theodahad, depending on how one interprets his third Elegy on Boethius's philandering. Danuta Shanzer, in "Ennodius, Boethius and the date and interpretation of Maximianus' *Elegia* III," *Rivista di filologia e di istruzione classica* 111 (1983), 194–5, argues that Maximian was hostile to Boethius; she sees Maximian as writing later in the century and appears to be unaware of the Theodahad poem now attributed to Maximian (*Poesos Saeculi Sexti Fragmenta* 3, on which, see ch. 2, n. 169, above). Barnish, in "Maximian, Cassiodorus, Boethius, Theodahad," pp. 21–8, argues that Maximian's poem is the work of a "sceptical admirer, even of a critical friend" (p. 27). On other possible enemies, see John Moorhead ("Boethius and Romans in Ostrogothic service," *Historia* 27, 604–12) who argues that Boethius was entirely alienated from Cassiodorus, Ennodius and the rest of the king's courtiers, partly on the basis of another poem ridiculing Boethius (Ennodius, *Op.* 339/*Carm.* 2.132) and partly on the basis of supposed disagreement over the Laurentian schism, in which, however, the views of Cassiodorus and Boethius remain unknown.

[110] For some examples, see ch. 4 above.

[111] See ch. 2, pp. 70–2, above.

[112] The date must be after Hormisdas's death but before the imprisonment of John, hence 522 or 523.

[113] LP[1] Hormisdas, 1: 101.

As we shall see, the second edition of the *Liber Pontificalis*, compiled in the 540s, rewrote the life of Hormisdas to imply the imminent return of a Catholic empire against the heretics. The author of 522 still wrote in the Gelasian mindset of papal supremacy. He may describe Justin I as the "the orthodox Augustus,"[114] but he sees the reunion of churches as merely "reconciling the Greeks, who were held under an anathema."[115] The emperor Anastasius, not Theoderic, receives the epithet "hereticus."[116]

In the first-edition life of John I, composed after the pope's murder in about 525, Theoderic has become evil, but not quite the demon that he will become in the second edition. The king is "Arrianus," but "hereticus" only once, and the areas concerned are "the Greek parts" and "Italy," conceived as separate political entities.[117] There is less emphasis on the honors accorded to the pope by the emperor than there is to be in the later version. Only in the second edition will the life of John resemble a *Passio* commemorating a martyr. True, in the first edition the emperor decides to grant grace to Eastern Arians "propter sanguinem Romanorum," but since this phrase occurs in the same sentence describing senators "urbis Romae,"[118] it is difficult to know how much weight to give it as evidence for a conception of a Catholic Roman Empire.

No other evidence from directly after the fall of John I depicts any resistance or hostility to the king or the Goths based on religion. It is surprising that the death of John I did not have more immediate consequences in changing recorded attitudes toward the monarchy. But we only possess one side of the story. John, like Symmachus a consecrated pope, might have had enemies of his own.

Historians have, indeed, connected the contested double election of Boniface II and Dioscorus in 530 to a rift leading back to the Boethius affair.[119] But this schism, like the Laurentian schism, was again a local controversy in the city of Rome.[120] The participants show no evidence

---

[114] Ibid., 1: 102.

[115] Ibid., 1: 99.

[116] Ibid., 1: 101.

[117] LP¹ John I, 1:105: ". . . ut redderentur ecclesias hereticis in partes Greciarum; quod si non fuerit factum, omnem Italiam ad gladium perderet."

[118] Ibid.

[119] Chadwick, *Boethius*, pp. 64–5; Caspar, *Papsttum* 2: 195; Duchesne, "La succession du pape Félix IV," pp. 241–2.

[120] The schism of 530: LP Boniface II §§1–4, 1:281; LP Agapetus I §1, 1:287, and the three documents discovered by Amelli in Verona in 1881, *Praeceptum Felicis papae morientis*, *Senatusconsultum ann. 530* and *Libellus quem dederunt presbyteri 60*, ed. Eduard Schwartz, 1914, reprinted in PLS 3: 1280–2 (Paris, 1963). As Caspar pointed out as long ago as the 1930s, none of the evidence makes any reference to the Gothic government at Ravenna or to the imperial government at Constantinople: *Papsttum* 2: 767–8; cf. 195–6. But the scholarship on the dispute has

of being pro- or anti-Ostrogothic, or even pro- or anti-Byzantine.[121] It is impossible to identify the level of senatorial support enjoyed by each side, or even what their larger goals might have been.

To judge from their few letters, Felix IV and Boniface II were primarily concerned with semi-Pelagianism in Gaul, condemned at the Council of Orange in 529. High noblemen from Theoderic's court, including Boethius's enemy Opilio and the prefect Liberius, attended and subscribed this council; Ravenna apparently approved of such Western interests.[122] The gap left by these popes in the *Collectio Avellana*, which is concerned with the entire Mediterranean Christian community, shows that they did not address broader issues, perhaps with the fate of John I in mind. The *Avellana* would have included any of their letters on these subjects if there had been any.

EARLY FRICTIONS: THE PAPACY AND JUSTINIAN AT THE TIME OF THE BYZANTINE RECONQUEST OF THE WEST, 533–537

Evidence of papal interest in the East first reappears with the pontificate of John II (532–5), who was assaulted by congratulatory letters from both Ravenna and Constantinople.[123] The letter from Justinian in 533 contains a *professio fidei* coupled with many expressions of support for the apostolic see. He does not omit a statement about the consubstantiality of the Trinity, although he does not define this as anti-Arian. Nevertheless, Justinian was already promulgating anti-Arian legislation in Africa and Constantinople, and the pope could not have missed the

mainly tried to identify such references to larger political allegiance: see Harnack, "Der erste deutsche Papst," pp. 24–42; Stein, *Bas Empire* 2: 329–30, 331–2; Stein, "La période byzantine de la papauté," p. 141, criticizing Harnack's conclusions; and Duchesne, "La succession du pape Félix IV," pp. 239–66. See further pp. 203–5 above, on the shakiness of the factions defined by these writers. Llewellyn makes a good case for seeing the Boniface–Dioscorus conflict as yet another dispute between the Roman deacons and *tituli*-priests (see below, n. 140), but elsewhere uses the evidence to place the "clergy of Rome . . . firmly on the imperial side," *Rome in the Dark Ages*, p. 49.

[121] The one reference to larger secular politics is in Felix's deathbed nomination of Boniface as his successor: "domnis et filiis nostris regnantibus" (*Praeceptum Felicis papae morientis*, col. 1280), interpreted as "king and emperor" by Harnack, "Der erste deutsche Papst," p. 28, n. 1, and as "Amalasuntha and Athalaric" by Caspar, *Papsttum* 2: 194, n. 6. The interpretation of the latter seems more in line with previous papal practice, but in neither case need the reference offer any clue to political allegiance or sympathies.

[122] Felix IV, JK 875 = *ep. fr.* "Cum enim" (PL 62: 91–2), esp. col. 92B–C; Boniface II, JK 881 = *ep.* "Per filium nostrum" (PL 65: 31–4); *Acta Concilii Arausionensis*, ed. F. Maassen, Concilia Aevi Merowingici, MGH: Concilia 1 (Hanover, 1893), pp. 53–4. Unsurprisingly, the letter of Boniface contains Augustinian language: Harnack, "Der erste deutsche Papst," p. 37 with nn. 2–3.

[123] Athalaric and Cassiodorus: *Variae* 9.15.

implications. Unlike the discreet Anastasius I, the emperor included the cognomen "Gothicus" in his titulature.[124]

John replied cautiously to Justinian's overtures, but more from alarm at the emperor's claims over doctrine than from fear of offending Ravenna. The pope talks only of *religionis unitas* and *pax ecclesiae*,[125] and delicately maintains an Ambrosian policy on imperial meddling in matters of faith.[126] Nevertheless, he approves Justinian's edict condemning Nestor, Eutyches and Apollinaris, and agrees to insert a version of the Theopaschite formula into the Credo. Whatever the ecclesiastical significance of this apparent concession to the emperor, John says nothing about a Christian empire or about Arianism.[127]

Meanwhile, in 534, the pope was careful to recruit support for his behavior toward Constantinople from a group of powerful Catholic parvenu-senators, all apparently associated with Athalaric's court.[128] They include Cassiodorus, then praetorian prefect, Liberius, praetorian prefect of Gaul, Opilio the enemy of Boethius and ex-*comes sacrarum largitionum*, Fidelis, ex-quaestor and eventual successor of Cassiodorus as prefect, and Avienus, ex-praetorian prefect and probably *caput senatus*.[129]

Although some of these men had been long-time servants of the Amals, John addresses them in their capacity as representatives of the *senatus*:[130] he was not so much concerned about alienating the king as he was of alienating the most powerful Catholics. Maintaining a distinction between the king and his senatorial servants would have been superfluous twenty years earlier. But since we know that many of these same men would shortly decamp to Constantinople, and since John does not men-

---

[124] Emperor Justinian I, *ep.* "Reddentes honorem" (*Avellana*, ed. Guenther, pp. 322–5 = pp. 344–7; PL 66: 14–17). Trinity: col. 15C. Titulature: only survives in the 536 copy of this letter within a letter of Agapetus (Guenther, p. 344), but the original 533 version also omits the entire prologue; it is unlikely that the pope would have changed the titulature later.

[125] John II, JK 884 = *ep.* "Inter claras sapientiae" (*Avellana* 84 = PL 66:17–20), col. 18A.

[126] Caspar, *Papsttum* 2: 218–19.

[127] Stein, "La période byzantine du papauté," pp. 141–2, warns against reducing this incident to a conflict over caesaropapism.

[128] John II, JK 885 = *ep.* "Olim quidem" (*Avellana* = PL 66: 20–4), to "illustribus ac magnificis viris Avieno, Senatori, Liberio, Severino, Fideli, Avito, Opilioni, Joanni, Silverio, Clementiano et Ampelio," dated to between 4 March and 7 April 534 (JK) or before 24 March 534 (PLRE 3 s.n. Ampelius 1).

[129] As the senior surviving consul; PLRE2 s.n. Avienus 2, p. 193.

[130] John II, JK 885 = *ep.* "Olim quidem," col. 20B. Hermann Usener noted that the pope thus allowed the senate an integral role in interpreting doctrine, but, imprecisely, saw this group as Athalaric's consistory, "Das Verhältnis des römischen Senats zur Kirche in der Ostgothenzeit," 1877, reprinted in Usener, *Kleine Schriften* 4 (Leipzig, 1913), p. 152 with n. 125. Caspar, *Papsttum* 2: 219 with n. 4 argued from a grammatical point that the pope was merely telling the senate about the church's decision, not granting them the right to participate; Eduard Schwartz rightly accepted Usener's reading of the questionable sentence, in *Acta Conciliorum Oecumenicorum* 4.2: xxviii.

tion the king, it seems reasonable to conclude that such changes were in the air. Justinian's army was in Africa, even if Athalaric was still alive and the emperor did not yet have a pretext for reclaiming Italy. Worse, the emperor's legates were in Ravenna, interfering with royal policy. Amalasuintha had triumphed against Tuluin's faction two years earlier, but in the process had briefly begged asylum of the emperor.[131] The political classes were not yet sure what would happen, but the situation cannot have looked good for the Ostrogothic monarchy.

In his attempts to define a credo welcome to all sides, the pope envisages a Mediterranean Catholic community, referring to the emperor as "Justinianus imperator filius noster," and the senators as "Christianissimi filii."[132] The Arian rulers of Italy were not to have a say in this Catholic doctrinal matter. Nevertheless, it is going too far to use these letters as evidence that the pope sympathized politically with Justinian, and that these senators opposed too close a dependency on Byzantium.[133] It is also difficult to read political viewpoints into the senators' apparent support for the near-Nestorian Acoemetan or sleepless monks, opposed by Justinian and John II.[134] Religious difference was not yet political difference: the rhetoric involved does not approach that of the letters of 519, at a time when such changes were far less conceivable.

Justinian's armies conquered Africa in the following year. In May 535, over 200 bishops at a council of Carthage, now renamed Justiniana, wrote to John II to ask his opinion on how to receive Arian bishops and laymen back into the Catholic church.[135] The incentives for conversion were strong. Justinian was shortly to promulgate a novel forbidding all Arian rites in Africa, followed by a series of increasingly restrictive edicts.[136]

The African letter put the pope in a delicate position. Theodahad had just succeeded to the throne, without imperial recognition. Justinian had just taken the liberty of issuing a law allowing 100 years' prescription to the church of Rome, the first law addressed to Italy issued by an emperor in over sixty years.[137] One month after the bishops wrote their letter, Belisarius's ships were to sail for Catania. The African bishops had chosen this moment to announce triumphantly to the pope

---

[131] Wolfram, *Goths*, pp. 336–8.
[132] John II, JK 885 = *ep.* "Olim quidem," cols. 20C, 24A.
[133] As argued by Sundwall, *Abhandlungen*, p. 276, and Norman H. Baynes, "Justinian and Amalasuntha," 1925, reprinted in Baynes, *Byzantine Studies*, p. 223.
[134] As does Sundwall, *Abhandlungen*, p. 276 with n. 3.
[135] Reparatus, Florentinianus, Datianus et al., *ep.* "Optimam consuetudinem" (*Avellana* 85 = Guenther, pp. 328–30), dated to "around May" by Guenther, p. 328.
[136] *Nov. Iust.* 37, 45.
[137] *Nov. Iust.* 9.

their first synod since the end of the "violenta captivitas" of the whole African church by the "tyrannus Huniricus," and to rejoice that Justinian had made Carthage his own city.[138]

John was preserved from answering their dangerous question by his death, but his successor Agapetus I (535–6) wrote back, without any apparent qualm, on 9 September 535. In his reply he rejoices at the prosperities brought to the African bishops, and hence, tacitly, at Justinian's conquest of Africa. Suggestively, he quotes Luke 1: 71: "liberavit nos ab inimicis nostris et de manu omnium, qui nos oderunt." He uses the term *Arriani* and describes the sect in the harshest terms: "illius pestilentiae labe pollutos." He orders that Arian bishops converted to Catholicism must not be allowed to continue in their former office.[139]

Agapetus represents a new papal viewpoint. In his vocal dislike of Arianism, and in view of the larger political arena available, he implies that he was willing to work closely with the emperor to build a new Christian polity. On the other hand, his insistence on papal authority and Chalcedonian orthodoxy would eventually lead him into disagreement with Justinian.

Unlike John II, Agapetus was a strong-minded pope who did not mind telling anyone what he thought. He forcibly destroyed evidence of earlier division among the clergy of Rome by burning the documents of anathema of the anti-pope Dioscorus, extorted by Boniface II in 530.[140] He hated Arianism, and unlike every pope since Gelasius, expressed himself on the subject in the strongest terms. He evidently had no qualms about offending Theodahad, although he traveled to Constantinople ostensibly as the king's legate. During his visit to the East, he happened to discover that Theodora had successfully managed to get the monophysite Anthimus, bishop of Trebizond, elected patriarch of Constantinople. Without further ado he excommunicated Anthimus and convinced the emperor to exile him.

At first, the pope's vision of a Catholic realm appeared to match the emperor's. He expressed admiration for Justinian in high terms, and

---

[138] Reparatus et al., *ep.* "Optimam consuetudinem," §1, p. 328.

[139] Agapetus I, JK 892 = *ep.* "Iamdudum quidem" (*Avellana* 86 = Guenther, pp. 330–2).

[140] LP Agapetus I §1, 1:287, apparently the first act of his reign. Note that although the LP connects the proceedings with a negative view of Boniface, Agapetus himself may well have simply been trying to reconcile both sides of the battered clergy, particularly since he was an archdeacon and his predecessor John II had been the first priest and non-deacon elected for a century, whereas Boniface himself had been a deacon extracting promises from priests; on Boniface and John, see Llewellyn, "The Roman clergy during the Laurentian schism: a preliminary analysis," p. 248 with n. 9. Whatever Agapetus's aims were, Harnack ("Der erste deutsche Papst," p. 36) considered his action "a misstep such as few popes have made" for damaging the reputation of a consecrated predecessor.

praised him for favoring a united Catholic religion everywhere, equating Justinian's empire with the kingdom of God: "ubicumque vestrum propagatur imperium regnum mox incipiat proficere sempiternum."[141] But Agapetus nonetheless continued to criticize Justinian. He did not approve of the emperor's mildness toward former Arian bishops in Africa.[142] In subsequent letters, he told Justinian that he admired the profession of faith that the emperor had sent to John II, but that he did not think that it was proper for laymen to teach theology.[143] He had to stand up to the emperor to defend his removal of the patriarch Anthimus, which he did with zeal, remarking acidly, "I desired to come to the most Christian Emperor Justinian, but I found Diocletian."[144] It is not surprising that Agapetus's later letters are entirely occupied by the Anthimus incident.[145] Like other popes who decided to throw in their lot with Justinian, he found that disagreeing with the emperor led to protracted conflict.

Whatever Agapetus's original ideals, the lower clergy at Rome remembered him chiefly for his ability to stand up to Justinian, rather than for his zeal against Arianism. The life of Agapetus in the *Liber Pontificalis* is a rhetorical demonstration not only of the primacy of the Roman see among the patriarchates, but also of the supremacy of the pope over the emperor in ecclesiastical matters. It refers to Amalasuintha and Theodahad, but does not call them heretics.[146] Justinian receives the epithet "piissimus" only because he gives way to the pope. Agapetus is depicted as saying to the emperor, "Nevertheless, so that you will know that you are insufficient in the Christian religion, let your bishop [Anthimus] confess two natures in Christ." The defeated emperor thankfully prostrates himself before Agapetus.[147]

Friction between pope and emperor appeared, in other words, as soon as the two attempted to put the ideal of a Catholic Empire into practice. After Agapetus, Justinian began his reconquest of Italy, and he stopped giving way to popes on matters of doctrine. The split in loyalties that so many scholars have wanted to see in the papal disputes of

---

[141] Agapetus I, JK 894 = *ep.* "Licet de sacerdotii" (*Avellana* 88 = Guenther, pp. 333–8), §5, pp. 334–5.

[142] Ibid., §6, p. 335.

[143] *Avellana*, pp. 344–7.

[144] LP Agapetus I §3, quoted by Llewellyn, *Rome in the Dark Ages*, p. 55.

[145] Stein, *Bas-Empire* 2: 382–5; cf. Agapetus's other letters in the *Avellana*.

[146] This omission must immediately call into question the later claim of Liberatus of Carthage, that Agapetus obeyed Theodahad only after the king threatened to put the senators of Rome to the sword; Liberatus, *Breviarium causae Nestorianorum et Eutychianorum*, ed. Eduard Schwartz, Acta Conciliorum Oecumenicorum 2.5, Concilium Universale Chalcedonense 5 (Berlin, 1936), §21, p. 135.

[147] LP Agapetus I §§2–5, 1:287–8.

499, 502 and 530 appears unequivocally in the sources for the sad pontificate of Silverius (536–7). The clergy of Rome was divided between those who preferred the status quo of Ostrogothic rule, and those who wanted to ally themselves with Byzantium.

The Gothic Wars had just begun, while Agapetus was staying at Constantinople. No longer could Italians imagine themselves in a new world that was somehow part of the Roman Empire and Mediterranean civilization but was also ruled by an emperor-like king who led a barbarian army. At the start of Silverius's pontificate in 536, people all over Italy were being forced to choose their loyalties. For the first time, in the life of Agapetus, the *Liber Pontificalis* calls the king not just *rex* but *rex Gothorum*.[148] The epithet may record the dawning realization that political power resided with two groups, the Goths and the Greeks, and that Italy, the ancient Roman heartland, had no will of its own.

Silverius was elected while Justinian and Theodora had a more malleable candidate in mind, Vigilius. By early 536, Belisarius's troops were in Rome, and Witigis was besieging it with the Gothic army outside. Theodora wrote to the new pope, demanding that he reinstate the deposed monophysite patriarch Anthimus. Silverius's response to this imperial pressure was difficult: should he support an Arian king or an autocratic emperor with a monophysite wife and millions of monophysite subjects? The hostile first part of Pope Silverius's life in the *Liber Pontificalis* claims that Theodahad appointed him in return for cash. The truth may have been rather that Silverius opposed the emperor than that he supported the Goths. The pope would not obey Theodora's orders; he refused to "recall a heretic condemned in his iniquity."[149] Of course, Silverius had more solid reasons to oppose the emperor: Theodora was patroness of the apocrisiarius Vigilius, who hoped finally to achieve the papal throne.[150]

Whatever the truth of the subsequent accusations that Silverius was ready to surrender the besieged city of Rome to Witigis's army in 537 (and it is difficult to see why, if he were a protégé of Theodahad, he would be sympathetic to his assassin),[151] it seems clear that Vigilius was operating against Silverius with Theodora, Belisarius and probably Jus-

---

[148] Ibid., §2, 1: 287.

[149] Silverius, JK 900* (lost, recorded in LP Silverius §6, 1: 292).

[150] LP Silverius §7, 1: 292. This source is biased toward Silverius, but see also the next two notes.

[151] LP Silverius §§7–8, 1: 292–3 (Vigilius turns the empress against Silverius, who orders Belisarius to confect some reason to depose him); Procopius, BG 1(5).11.26; 1(5).14.4; 1(5).25. 13 (presenting the pope as an ambiguous figure who falls under suspicion); SH 1.14, 27 (presenting the pope as victim of Theodora); Liberatus, *Breviarium* §22, pp. 136–7 (Vigilius bribes Belisarius to arrest Silverius!).

tinian.[152] Silverius's wariness of Constantinople at such a delicate time was doubtless enough to convict him with the suspicious emperor.[153] It is not surprising that Vigilius first appears as a dedicated supporter of Justinian's Christian Empire, and a firm opponent of Arian barbarians. The balance of power rested with Vigilius, and Silverius was removed from his see by Belisarius and exiled to a small island.

The question of loyalties may not have been obvious at the time. It made sense for Vigilius to throw in his lot with Theodora (aside from the dangers of her monophysite sympathies), since it would be easy to incriminate Silverius. Then the apocrisiarius could continue to build papal power with the help of the emperor and his reconquest ideology (or so Vigilius thought). But it may not have been so clear to Silverius whom he should support. He did not approve of Justinian or Theodora, but the Gothic ruler, Theodahad, whose legitimacy was questionable anyway, was soon killed. Witigis had fewer reasonable claims than Theodahad. Both, of course, were Arian. Silverius may not have taken a position. But in the Italy of 536, not taking a position was perilous. Silverius, the son of Hormisdas, may have been a more old-fashioned pope, who would have been more at home in the Acacius-divided church.[154] A pope in the mould of the early sixth-century pontiffs would have found life easier in the delicate balance of Theoderic's status quo than in the enforced harmony of Justinian's empire.

POPE VIGILIUS, THE THREE CHAPTERS CONTROVERSY AND THE EMERGENCE OF THE WESTERN CATHOLIC CHURCH, 538–555

Although Vigilius's backing came from Constantinople, his first concerns were with Arianism and his suffragans in the West. He immedi-

---

[152] Duchesne, "Vigile et Pélage," p. 373. Even Procopius, the only source not to incriminate Vigilius directly, immediately continues ". . . a little later Belisarius appointed another man, Vigilius by name . . ." (BG 1[5].25.13). One gets a similar impression even from the pro-Vigilius LP Vigilius §1 and §6, 1: 296 and 298, although this may have been confected much later by an author sympathetic to Silverius (Hildebrand, "Die Absetzung des Papstes Silverius," pp. 221–3).

[153] Since Procopius, who must have met him, presents Silverius both as the object of a special exhortation by Witigis to remember Theoderic (BG 1[5].11.26), and also as the loudest voice begging the citizens to allow Belisarius's army into Rome (1[5].14.4), Silverius's loyalty to the emperor clearly looked suspect at the time. Procopius himself does not venture a viewpoint on his guilt (1[5].25.13: hypopsias . . . gegenēmenēs, "suspicions arose"); if the historian's depiction in the *Secret History* presents him as a victim, we must remember the function of that work as invective, one-sided in its own way.

[154] Llewellyn's characterization of Silverius as "son of the Gothic sympathizer Pope Hormisdas," *Rome in the Dark Ages*, p. 59, misses all the complexity of the allegiances of both Hormisdas and Silverius. But he is right to class the two popes as similar. Hormisdas was lucky enough

ately took steps to ensure that his relations with the bishops and Catholic rulers in the West would be good. He wrote to Caesarius of Arles, praising the Catholic Frankish king Theudebert,[155] and to Profuturus of Braga, with instructions on readmitting Arians, of whom he said "plurimis in gentibus iniquitas illa subrexit." He made it even clearer than Agapetus that Arianism was for barbarians.[156] The *Liber Pontificalis* later claimed that he led the defeated Witigis into the basilica Iuliae at Rome and gave him the sacrament, certainly a new relationship between a pope and an Ostrogothic king.[157]

Vigilius did not foresee that his Constantinopolitan support would eventually conflict with his concern for a strong church in the West. Although Vigilius would urge the bishops of Gaul, from the safety of Sicily in 545–6, to work for peace between the Catholic Frankish king Childebert I and Justinian,[158] it never occurred to him to do the same between the emperor and the Arian Totila, despite the ravages of the wars in Italy. Vigilius's aims were simple: to keep the Franks from allying with the Goths, to support all Catholic monarchs, and to bring the bishops of the West around to his ecclesiastical and theological policies. In 550, by which time Vigilius was at Constantinople, he wrote to Aurelianus of Arles to beg him to ask Childebert to write to Totila "and his Goths," asking them not to disturb the properties of the Catholic church if they took Rome. Vigilius fears Totila's "lex aliena," that is, his Arianism, but trusts Childebert because he is a Catholic king "quem Christianitatis studio venerationem integram sedi apostolicae, cui nos Deus praeesse voluit, cognovimus exhibere."[159]

Vigilius's dislike of Arianism emerges clearly from these letters: he had no interest in compromising. But his interest in the Catholic West, and in his apostolic vicar of Arles, points to another important facet of his policy: he maintained his influence in the Western churches. Only at the beginning of his pontificate was he able to use such influence in the service of a Justinianic Catholic Empire, working for peace between the emperor and Childebert.

---

to be living at the time of Theoderic's tolerance; Silverius was unlucky enough to come to power at the precise moment when Justinian's tolerance ran out.

[155] Vigilius, JK 906 = *ep.* "Si pro observatione" (*Arelat.* 38 = PL 69: 21): "gloriosus filius noster rex Theodebertus," from March 538.

[156] Vigilius, JK 907 = *ep.* "Directas ad nos" (PL 69: 15–19), from June 538.

[157] LP Vigilius §1, 1:296. Duchesne doubts that the event took place, though allows that it was possible "à la rigueur," LP 1: 300, n. 3.

[158] Vigilius, JK 913 = *ep.* "Sicut nos" (*Arelat.* 41 = PL 69: 27–8); JK 914 = *ep.* "Quantium nos divina" (*Arelat.* 40 = PL 69: 29–30); JK 915 = *ep.* "Licet fraternitati" (*Arelat.* 42 = PL 69: 29); JK 918 = *ep.* "Administrationem" (*Arelat.* 44 = PL 69: 37–9); JK 919 = *ep.* "Admonet nos loci" (*Arelat.* 43 = PL 69: 39–40).

[159] Vigilius, JK 925 = *ep.* "Fraternitatis vestrae litteras" (*Arelat.* 45 = PL 69: 40–3), col. 42.

Other clerics in the Italy of the Gothic Wars shared Vigilius's pro-Eastern viewpoint. The second edition of the *Liber Pontificalis*, produced under his pontificate,[160] rewrote the lives of Symmachus, Hormisdas and John I to portray Theoderic as a good man undone by his Arianism. The epithet "hereticus," attached to the king in the first-edition life of Symmachus, now vanishes from that section. The life of John I, on the other hand, becomes a reverent evocation of a martyr-pope venerated by the Catholic emperor and hence reviled by the Arian king.[161] The new text adds a section, true or not, describing Justin as being crowned by John. The emperor was "gaudio repletus est, quia meruit temporibus suis vicarium beati Petri apostoli videre in regno suo."[162] An exactly parallel rhetorical picture of the fall of the Arian king and the rise of the Catholic emperor appears in the *Anonymus Valesianus*,[163] produced in Ravenna at the same time, possibly by a cleric, and certainly by someone with a strong interest in the church.[164]

While the *Anonymus Valesianus* blames the king only for his Arianism, and has nothing to say against the Goths per se,[165] Vigilius himself classified the Goths as barbarians. In a series of inscriptions left in the catacombs of Rome at the time of Totila's siege in 545, and in a series of masses inserted in the Roman liturgy at the same time, Vigilius made use of traditional ethnographic terms like "Getae" and stereotypes of ferocious, heathen barbarian behavior. Such use of classicizing ethnography was a deliberate gambit in parallel with Justinian's propaganda against the Goths as a naturally hostile and Arian people, but for Vigilius, trained in classical rhetoric, such language must also have come naturally.[166]

But everything was already changing between Justinian and Vigilius;

---

[160] Duchesne, LP 1: ccxxxi, Vogel, "Le 'Liber Pontificalis,'" p. 107: the second edition was completed before the Byzantine government finally took power in Italy, so before 552, but after the death of Silverius, hence in Vigilius's pontificate.

[161] Symmachus: LP Symmachus §1, 1: 260 (compare with LP¹ Symmachus, 1: 97 with n. 1), §4, 1: 260 (compare with LP¹ Symmachus, 1: 97 with n. 23). On John I, for example, note LP John I §1, 1: 275, "Theoderici regis et Iustini Augusti christiani" (omitted in LP¹ John I, 1: 105 with n. 2), §2, 1: 275 "hereticus rex" ("Theodoricus arrianus" in LP¹ John I, 1: 105 with n. 11), §4, 1: 275, "liberata est Italia a rege Theodorico heretico" (omitted in LP¹ John I, 1: 105 with n. 26).

[162] LP John I §4, 1: 275 (omitted in LP¹ John I, 1: 105 with n. 27).

[163] AV 65–7 (Theoderic "beato Petro devotissimus ac si catholicus" in 500, has good relations with Symmachus); 82–94 (urged on by the Arian Eutharic, turns against the senate and the pope). At 91, Justin receives John I "ac si beato Petro," perhaps an echo of the earlier phrase applied to Theoderic.

[164] Barnish, "The *Anonymus Valesianus* II as a source for the last years of Theoderic," pp. 577–8.

[165] Ibid., p. 578.

[166] On Justinian's reconquest rhetoric and Vigilius's inscriptions, see ch. 4, above.

Justinian had got word of the idea[167] that the monophysites might reconcile themselves to Chalcedon if the church condemned the works and person of Theodore of Mopsuestia, and some of the works of Ibas of Edessa and Theodoret of Cyr. They were men explicitly or implicitly approved by the Council of Chalcedon and the Tome of Leo. Without consulting the pope or the bishops, Justinian promptly issued an edict in 544 damning them in three sections, an arrangement which lent its name to the Three Chapters controversy.

Vigilius changed his mind repeatedly on the Three Chapters controversy between 546 and 554.[168] But his correspondence with the Western bishops during his years in Constantinople document both his disenchantment with a Justinianic Christian community, and his attempt to build a new church on Western and Latin foundations. This redefinition of the geography of belief struck a chord with some clergy in Italy, particularly in the north, where the cities of Milan and Aquileia would continue in schism with Rome and Constantinople for some years after the Council of Constantinople in 553. It had repercussions in Illyricum and Africa as well.[169]

The real reason that a break was inevitable between Vigilius and Justinian, of course, was that Justinian had monophysite subjects to worry about.[170] Neither the pope nor the Western bishops would suffer the emperor to dictate ecclesiastical policy that seemed to water down Chalcedon, with its guarantee of papal authority. At the height of Vigilius's difficulties, when the pope was a prisoner in the church of St. Euphemia in Chalcedon in 552, the emperor had stopped any communication between the pope and the Western bishops. Justinian did not want Vigilius's new views against the condemnation of the Three Chapters to be known in the West, nor did he want the pope to be swayed by the similar views current in Gaul and Italy.[171]

Nevertheless, Vigilius managed to inform his suffragans in the West about his predicament and the evils of the emperor. Significantly he uses geographical-linguistic terminology to suggest an inherent division in the Mediterranean world. "African," "Illyrian" and "Gallic" bishops, all "Latini," joined him in condemning Justinian's supporter Theodore

---

[167] Liberatus claimed that Theodore Askidas told him that he regretted that he had ever come up with the idea: *Breviarium*, §24, p. 140.

[168] On the Three Chapters controversy, see Eduard Schwartz, *Zur Kirchenpolitik Iustinians*, Sitzungsberichte der bayerischen Akademie der Wissenschaften, philosophisch-historische Abteilung 1940.2 (Munich, 1940); Caspar, *Papsttum* 2: 230–90; Duchesne, "Vigile et Pélage," pp. 369–440; and Stein, *Bas-Empire* 2: 632–83.

[169] Stein, *Bas-Empire* 2: 676–83.

[170] Frend, "The monophysites," pp. 339–65, esp. 364–5.

[171] Caspar, *Papsttum* 2: 265.

of Caesarea, and thirteen Italian bishops also supported the pope.[172] This letter is part of the remains of a pro-Western "Aktenbundel" sent to Vigilius's ally, the bishop of Arles. The dossier fortuitously survives in a manuscript from Rheims, later in the Phillipps collection. It originally contained an emotive description of Vigilius's sad mistreatment at the hands of the emperor, during which an altar had fallen on him as Justinian's soldiers were dragging him by his beard from the basilica of St. Peter in Ormisda in Constantinople.[173] The portfolio sent to Gaul also contained a supportive and propagandistic letter from the clergy of Milan to the Frankish legates on their way from Gaul to Constantinople, written toward the end of 551. After its certification by the pope, it was to be returned to Aurelianus in Arles.[174]

This "letter of the Milanese clergy" indulges in none of the quasi-Eusebian rhetoric of a Christian Empire that permeates Vigilius's early correspondence and the documents of the reunion of churches thirty years earlier. Rather, it opens with an Augustinian statement of divine providence: grace operates through all peoples, "in omnibus gentibus," and the afterworld is more important than the current world. There follows a depiction of division between the African, Illyrian and Dalmatian bishops on the one hand, and "the Greeks" on the other. The former will not agree to condemn the Three Chapters, and Vigilius tells Justinian that he will not do it without their support, that is, the support of his suffragan bishops in the West. After the Africans arrive in Constantinople they are abused and eventually exiled; the *praefectus Africae* puts new bishops into their sees. The "Greek bishops," however, follow the *voluntas principis* in condemning the Three Chapters.[175] After the pope's excommunication of Justinian's supporters and his flight from the palace in July 551, Datius of Milan strongly supports the pope's actions, speaking for all the bishops of the pope's provinces, "id est Galliae Burgundiae Spaniae Liguriae Aemiliae atque Venetiae," "also als Wortführer der gesamten europäisch-abendländischen Kirche."[176]

The letter of the Milanese clergy, which opposes the *civitas regia*,

---

[172] Vigilius, JK 930 = *ep.* "Res est quidem" (Schwartz 2, pp. 10–15), pp. 10, 14; see Caspar, *Papsttum*, 2: 264.

[173] The MS is now Berlin, MS 84, edited and discussed by Eduard Schwartz, *Vigiliusbriefe*, Sitzungsberichte der bayerischen Akademie der Wissenschaften 1940 (Munich, 1940), esp. p. 31.

[174] *Epistola legatariis* = *ep.* "Ita se in omnibus gentibus" (Schwartz 4, pp. 18–25). The circumstances of the production of this letter are extremely complex: see Caspar, *Papsttum*, 2: 265, n. 3; Schwartz, *Vigiliusbriefe*, pp. 27–8, 30–1.

[175] *Ep.* "Ita se in omnibus gentibus," pp. 18–20.

[176] Ibid., p. 21; Caspar, *Papsttum* 2: 264.

Constantinople, to the *sedes apostolica*, Rome,[177] documents the maturity of the notion that the papal Catholic Western provinces could aspire to more than a Christian Empire. Their community, destined to include *omnes gentes*, was fundamentally different from the Eastern, imperial-run and thus secular-controlled "Greek" church. The Greeks could be part of the Christian world if they chose, but as just another *gens*, not as the divinely chosen center of state Christianity. The irony of their position must have been obvious to Italians writing from the midst of the wars between Totila and Narses. Reparatus of Carthage – the same bishop who had written so joyfully to John II fifteen years earlier about the end of Arian repression and the beginnings of Justinian's rule in Africa – had been summarily deposed by the emperor on a flimsy pretext upon his arrival in Constantinople to support the pope.[178] The letter dwells on the interference with the African sees by a mere imperial official.[179] All this clearly horrified the Italian bishops, and was meant to horrify the Gallic bishops – as it must have done, given their usual independence in theological matters.

Not all Italy supported the pope either in his opposition to Justinian or in his eventual capitulation to the emperor. Justinian had been court- ing the bishops of Ravenna from shortly after Belisarius's conquest of the city in 540. He bestowed the title *archiepiscopus* on Bishop Maxim- ian, and used the bishop of the city as a spearhead in his doctrinal initiative to condemn the Three Chapters. Subsequently, the newly metropolitan bishops of Ravenna attempted to consecrate malleable candidates for the schismatic sees of the north who continued to oppose Justinian's edict and Vigilius's eventual capitulation in 553.[180]

While the patriarch of Aquileia was at loggerheads with both Rav- enna and with the popes, the bishops of Ravenna, the reinstated imperial capital of Italy, began an enduring rivalry with the popes at Rome and their traditions of independence from imperial authority.[181] Although the papacy and the bishop of Ravenna cooperated for a while

---

[177] *Ep.* "Ita se in omnibus gentibus," p. 23.
[178] Ibid., p. 20: Justinian alleged that Reparatus had committed treason in the time of Aerobindus and the tyrant Guntharit. But Reparatus was only arrested when he came to Constantinople to support Vigilius, six years later.
[179] Ibid., p. 21.
[180] R. A. Markus, "Carthage – Prima Justiniana – Ravenna: an aspect of Justinian's *Kirchenpolitik*," *Byzantion* 49 (1979), 292–9.
[181] Culminating in the emperor Constans II's grant of *autocephalia* to Ravenna in 666, ecclesiastical independence from Rome; T. S. Brown, "The church of Ravenna and the imperial adminis- tration in the seventh century," *English Historical Review* 94 (1979), 11–13; see also pp. 15–17 for the parallel with Maximian and Vigilius.

after 554, this harmony was necessarily fragile.[182] Meanwhile, the imperial government countered the schismatic see of Aquileia not only with the new empowerment of the Ravenna bishops but by installing a patriarchate at Grado, leading the patriarch of Aquileia to denounce the violence of the "Greeks."[183]

Only in the short run did the imperial government prevail. Vigilius had given way and condemned the Three Chapters at the Council of Constantinople in 553. He died on his return to Rome. Neither Vigilius nor his immediate successors managed to avoid opposition to the forced agreement with the emperor from the other Western sees in northern Italy and Gaul.

The providential Roman Empire no longer served the same purpose for the papacy. In the 550s, the notion that barbarians were Arians no longer held water: only the Visigoths remained of the major Arian barbarian groups. Even the rulers of the Lombards, despite subsequent papal propaganda, were both Catholics and Arians, and probably benefited from the schism dividing the north of Italy from the papacy and from Ravenna after 553.[184]

The reformulation of the past, in divided ecclesiastical Italy as in the governmental Constantinople, forced a re-imagination of the construction of the universe. Vigilius's pontificate was a "fundamental caesura" in church history – inseparably the caesura of Justinian's momentous reign.[185] This time of synthesis marked the beginning of the consolidation of the notion that the pope led a distinctively Western and Latin Christian community.[186] Vigilius inscribed his vacillations in church his-

---

[182] R. A. Markus, "Ravenna and Rome, 554–604," *Byzantion* 51 (1981), 566–78.

[183] Brown, *Gentlemen and Officers*, p. 146.

[184] Steven C. Fanning, "Lombard Arianism reconsidered," *Speculum* 56 (1981), 241–58; Georg Hauptfeld, "Zur langobardischen Eroberung Italiens: Das Heer und die Bischöfe," *Mitteilungen des Instituts für Österreichische Geschichtsforschung* 91 (1983), 37–94, esp. 93–4.

[185] It was a "un temps de synthèse, de réportoriage et d'établissment de collections: codification de droit romain, *Liber Pontificalis*, *Liber diurnus*, *Libellis Missarum* de Vérone": Vogel, "Le 'Liber Pontificalis,' " p. 107, n. 19.

[186] Needless to say, papal supremacy was not accepted by all the popes' suffragans, but the idea of a Latin Christianity had come to maturation, particularly in Africa, where many bishops, and later many provinces, opposed the popes' claims to authority rather than symbolic primacy. On the consciousness of Latin Christianity in Africa, see R. A. Markus, "Reflections on religious dissent in North Africa in the Byzantine period," in *Schism, Heresy and Religious Protest*, ed. Derek Baker, Studies in Church History 9 (Cambridge, 1972), pp. 140–9, esp. pp. 146–8 on Facundus of Hermiane and his *pietas et constantia ecclesiae Latinorum*, articulated against Justinian in the Three Chapters. On African opposition to papal supremacy (greater in Numidia than Carthage), see pp. 148–9 and Markus, "Country bishops in Byzantine Africa," in *The Church in Town and Countryside*, ed. Derek Baker, Studies in Church History 18 (Cambridge, 1979), pp. 1–15, esp. 10–15.

tory, ensuring that never again would a pope make the mistake of willingly conceding the emperor a measure of authority in church doctrine. The ecclesiastical developments parallel the increasing categorization of Greeks as aliens within Italy.[187]

In the meantime, tact was the order of the day. Vigilius's successor, the more successfully flexible Pelagius I (556–61), who had once written in defense of the condemned Chapters, upheld his predecessor's decision to anathematize them in the face of repeated queries from Gaul, rephrasing the events of the letter of the Milanese clergy and using the neutral geographical term *Oriens* instead of the suggestive linguistic *Graeci*.[188] Pelagius restricted his activities to rebuilding Italy, admitting Arians whom Justinian's legislation for Italy strongly encouraged to become Catholic, and maintaining his contacts in Gaul. In the 590s, Gregory the Great maintained a careful respect for the emperor,[189] governed the city of Rome and the papal estates,[190] and talked about the "four" ecumenical councils.[191] Gregory sent missionaries to Anglo-Saxon England, and although he continued to consider himself a citizen of the Roman Empire, the horizons of the papacy were far broader.[192] Aquileia and Milan remained in schism with the pope for giving in to the emperor, and the heritage of Vigilius's imprisonment was to reverberate in the subsequent history of the papacy and its eventual, final turn to the West in 800.

CONCLUSION

Secular notions of community impinged necessarily on religious ones. As political states were growing smaller, the Christian community was

---

[187] Brown, *Gentlemen and Officers*, pp. 144–7. See also ch. 4 above.

[188] Pelagius I, JK 978 = *ep.* "Quomodo ergo me" (Gassò and Batlle 19, pp. 55–61), esp. §7, p. 57: *Oriens*, Illyricum and Africa have all accepted the condemnation of the Three Chapters; why should any other regions hold out? On Pelagius's conciliatory policy toward Justinian, see Stein, *Bas-Empire* 2: 669–75, and Duchesne, "Vigile et Pélage," pp. 420–40.

[189] R. A. Markus, "Gregory the Great's Europe," *Transactions of the Royal Historical Society*, 5th ser. 31 (1981), 29–34.

[190] J. Richards, *Consul of God: The Life and Times of Gregory the Great* (London, 1980), pp. 85–139.

[191] Thus ignoring Constantinople II (553), which ratified Justinian's edict on the Three Chapters; GR 1.24; 3.10; G. R. Evans, *The Thought of Gregory the Great* (Cambridge, 1986), p. 141.

[192] Markus, "Gregory the Great's Europe," pp. 21–36, esp. 24–8, 29, 33–6. I part from Markus in seeing Gregory's cosmology as less Byzantinocentric. We must recall Gregory's entirely anomalous background and career in dicussing his political views: he was of senatorial Roman family, and had served in Constantinople as papal *apocrisiarius*; although he certainly perpetuated traditional ethnographic topoi about the barbarians and the Roman world, it is impossible to see him as typical. His activity in Britain and Francia shows that he could escape Byzantino-centrism in any case, as his heavily Augustinian beliefs might suggest; see Markus, *The End of Ancient Christianity*, pp. 227–8, where he posits an altogether less secular world for Gregory

growing larger. The Western church did not disassociate religion from politics. To put it in the most simplistic terms, it moved from the pagan concept of a religion defined by the state to the Augustinian notion of a state defined by religion. During this process Italian churchmen could express themselves in terms of classical political geography or according to more relevant categorisations. Within Italy itself, the *pius princeps Romanae reipublicae*[193] could, by the end of the period, also be seen as a *Graecus*.

Simultaneously, smaller Christian communities, the see and *civitas*, persisted beneath the big labels of *imperium Christianum* or *congregatio fidelium*. Epiphanius represented his region, Liguria, and his city, Pavia. More complicatedly, Ennodius fought for the pope in the Laurentian and Acacian schisms, but identified with Italy and the Western Roman Empire. His day-to-day activity was firmly concentrated on Pavia and Milan. In Arles, Caesarius attempted to impose a local Christian identity on the various larger and smaller communities that competed for the allegiance of the citizens.[194]

The transformation of Western Christian mental geography was a result not only of the disintegration of the late Roman Empire as a Mediterranean polity but also of the slightly later recognition of that disintegration. As with secular notions of community, this recognition dawned at different times in Constantinople and in Italy, and in different groups of people in each place.

The Eusebian ideal of a Christian Empire, and Catholic distaste for Arianism, dictated some papal policy in sixth-century Italy. But the popes in general showed themselves more willing to work closely with the Ostrogothic kings than one might expect in return for their ecclesiastical neutrality. More surprisingly, they seem to have considered Arianism the lesser evil when compared with monophysitism. So Catholic ideals affected perceptions of the Goths, but the Goths were less important to the Catholics than one might at first believe. Such explicit examination of the problem is essential in order to lay to rest traditional assumptions of how clergymen and Catholic senators made their political decisions and placed their allegiances. Who, in fact, were their Arian opponents?

than in his other articles – and a world in which the issue of secularity confronted by Augustine had largely vanished.

[193] John, patriarch of Constantinople, *ep.* "Quando Deus propria," p. 863.

[194] William E. Klingshirn, *Caesarius of Arles: The Making of a Christian Community in Late Antique Gaul* (Cambridge, 1994), pp. 171–200, esp. 171–81.

Chapter 7

INDIVIDUAL REACTIONS TO IDEOLOGY III:
ARIANS AND CATHOLICS

Why did the Arian church under Theoderic call itself the "church of Gothic belief"? Historians have believed that Arianism appealed to the Goths because it helped them to preserve their group identity.[1] No cultural trait has been seen as more fundamental to the definition of an Italian Goth than Arian belief. In the end, according to this interpretation, Ostrogothic Italy could not survive as a kingdom because, unlike Frankish Gaul, the heretical faith of the settlers slowed assimilation and promoted conflict.[2] "[Theoderic's] Arianism was a national identity-card for the Goths." "We may suspect that for the Goths an essential feature of their Arianism was simply that it was not the faith of the Romans." "Wherever in Italy there was any substantial Gothic garrison, the Arians had their own church buildings." "Vero *punctum dolens* nei rapporti fra Goti e Romani era la diversità di confessione: Teoderico, con la maggioranza del suo seguito, era ariano."[3]

These statements are questionable. They rest on the following assumptions, each of which would need to be proven: Goths and Romans are easily definable as peoples; one people has only one religion; belonging to a people determines one's religion; and that religion is the same as the religion of the king or the emperor.

These historians understand Arianism as the religion of the Goths because it was the religion of Theoderic, yet members of Theoderic's family were Catholics. They see Arianism as the Achilles' heel of Theoderic's policy of reconciliation between the churches of East and West. His Arian followers and Catholic Italians could never be formed into one society – particularly when the Catholic Justinian was hoping to reconquer Italy. But Italian Catholic views on the relative dangers

---

[1] See ch. 1, n. 72; Wolfram, *Goths*, p. 85; Russell, *The Germanization of Early Medieval Christianity*, pp. 139–40 (who cites more references for this view, which he supports).

[2] Repeated in many textbooks, and expressed, for example, by Wolfram, "Gotisches Königtum und römisches Kaisertum," pp. 25–6. If restricted to the religion of the *kings*, this interpretation would carry more weight.

[3] Quotations from Chadwick, *Boethius*, p. 3; Moorhead, *Theoderic*, p. 94; Chadwick, *Boethius*, p. 59; Scardigli, *Lingua e storia*, p. 163, respectively.

of Arianism and monophysitism were complex,[4] and reconquest ideology took years to develop after Justin's accession. These historians imply that Arianism was the religion of the Gothic army – on the basis of Arian church buildings in Ravenna and Rome, Italy's two biggest cities. They believe that the supposed use by the church of a comprehensible vernacular tongue spoken by Theoderic's followers enabled the continuing popularity of Arianism among people called Goths.

The traditional interpretation has much power because of the terms *ecclesia legis Gothorum* or merely *ecclesia Gothica*. The Arian liturgy was written in a Germanic language that we call Gothic, and the churches used Ulfilas's fourth-century translation of the scriptures into this language, with its accompanying alphabet. There are Germanic names among Arian clergy, but none among Catholic clergy. Theoderic and all the subsequent Gothic kings were Arian believers. How could this church be anything other than a uniting cultural and communal symbol of Gothic identity?

But such an interpretation of the Gothic Arian church ignores the Latin Arian heritage that continued to survive in sixth-century Italy. How did the *ecclesia legis Gothorum* fit into the evolution of Latin Arian ecclesiology?

ARIAN CHURCHES IN THE FIFTH-CENTURY WEST

The mechanism by which the Arian churches of Italy in the late 300s became the Gothic church of Italy in the early 500s has never seemed very clear. Historians have dimly acknowledged that Arian clergymen and texts are attested in mid-fifth-century Italy. But it has proved impossible to get away from the idea that the Goths somehow "reintroduced" Arianism in 489, bringing back into the Empire a sect that had been completely eradicated there.[5]

In this view, Ulfilas carried Arianism out of the Empire to the Goths in the 330s, Arianism disappeared from the Empire after the Council of Constantinople in 380, and then the unfortunately Arian Goths, having spread their faith to other barbarians, carried it back into the Empire, "ut ibi primum fides Romano imperio frangeretur ubi fracta

---

[4] See ch. 6, above.

[5] See, for example, Robert E. McNally, " 'Christus' in the pseudo-Isidorian 'Liber de ortu et obitu patriarchum'," *Traditio* 21 (1965), 167; and Moorhead, *Theoderic*, p. 90. Aside from the evidence for Latin Arianism in fifth-century Italy, discussed below, there was the Arianism of Ricimer and Odoacer, generally ignored or explained by their "barbarianness." They would of course have required places of worship and priests to administer the sacraments. Theoderic's Goths are invariably identified as "Arians," as though religion was only a group phenomenon, not a regional phenomenon (e.g. Moorhead, *Theoderic*, pp. 54, 89).

est Deo," as the staunchly anti-Arian and anti-barbarian St. Ambrose put it in the fourth century.[6] The notion originates in Ambrose's polemic, and has been perpetuated by Germanic philologists and historians who privilege the influence of Ulfilas over Latin and Greek Arian traditions.[7]

In fact, Arian belief and Arian clergy never vanished from the Empire. In certain regions it was stronger than in others, and one of these regions was the Balkans, whence came Theoderic. Another region where Arianism survived was Italy, whither Theoderic went.[8] During the fourth and fifth centuries, both regions produced scholars who used the writings and memory of Ulfilas and his conversion of groups called Goths beyond the Danube in the early fourth century.

Arianism in the fourth century was not the homogeneous heresy that its opponents wanted it to be. There were various schools of thought that denied the equality of substance and divinity in the Father and the Son, but in different degrees and in different ways.[9] Moreover, there were Greek and Latin Arian writings. Both Greek and Latin Arians were interested in Ulfilas's project of translating the Scriptures into the Gothic tongue, which he did in the regions where Greek met Latin in the Roman Empire: the Balkans.

Ulfilas seems to have represented a moderate form of Arian belief theologically,[10] but there is no question that in his translation of the Bible, he drew on cultural traditions that were neither Latin nor Greek. Wolfram has convincingly argued, from Ulfilas's translations of various words, and from his omission of the warlike Book of Kings, that Ulfilas's Bible served a cultural community very unlike that of Mediterranean Christianity.[11] Through a few other fourth-century texts, such

---

[6] Ambrose, *De fide* 2.16.139, PL 16: 527–698 (Paris, 1845). The work, was, of course, addressed to the emperor Gratian. On the significance of such dogma, see Michel Meslin, *Les Ariens d'Occident, 335–430*, Patristica Sorbonensia 8 (Paris, 1967), pp. 97–8. Sadly, we no longer possess the Arian response to this section of *De fide* in the fragmentary *Contra de fide* of Palladius of Ratiara, which would have cast much light on the developing Arian ecclesiology of the late 300s.

[7] Ambrose's words are cited as fact by Zeiller, *Les origines chrétiennes dans les provinces danubiennes*, pp. 342–3 with n. 5; on such views, see Meslin, *Les Ariens d'Occident*, p. 92 with n. 198.

[8] These were the strongholds of Western Arianism in the fourth and early fifth centuries. See Meslin, *Les Ariens d'Occident*, map after p. 416.

[9] For summaries, see Thompson, *The Visigoths in the Time of Ulfila*, pp. xix–xxi; Heather and Matthews, *The Goths in the Fourth Century*, pp. 135–41.

[10] Ibid.

[11] Herwig Wolfram, "Gotische Studien I: Das Richtertum Athanarichs," *Mitteilungen des Instituts für Österreichische Geschichtsforschung* 83 (1975), 1–32; Wolfram, "Gotische Studien II: Die terwingische Stammesverfassung und das Bibelgotisch (1)," ibid., pp. 289–324; Wolfram, "Gotische Studien III: Die terwingisch Stammesverfassung und das Bibelgotisch (2)," *Mitteilungen des Insti-*

as the *Passio Sabae*, we gain a precious window into this community: the frontier world of a group or groups on the Danube calling themselves Goths in the fourth century.

The particular Danube culture that influenced Ulfilas's translation did not survive, although his Bible itself spread throughout the Mediterranean in educated circles and in Arian communities. The distinction between *thiudans* and *reiks*, between sacral king and military leader, is never attested in any of the barbarian groups who came into the Roman Empire. Any other associated culture either vanished or evolved. The spoken Germanic language of the fourth-century Danube, partly frozen in the written language Gothic Bible, may have continued to be spoken on the Danube in the sixth century. Something possibly like it, Theoderic's *lingua nostra*, seems still to have been spoken in sixth-century Italy, but by so few people and in such a Latin-dominated society that its impact on culture and identity is not measurable.

Ulfilas's Bible, and in fact all written Gothic except for two lines, comes down to us from manuscripts produced in Ostrogothic Italy, some with royal patronage. But the text of that Bible had evolved yet further in the transmission from its original form in the fourth-century Balkans. Its original form already showed strong traces of Greek influence in vocabulary and syntax.[12] It subsequently suffered further Greek influence in stages of transmission between Ulfilas and the Italian manuscripts.[13] In its sixth-century form, Latin word-order changed it further.

The original fourth-century translation was extremely literal. Every Greek word was represented by a Gothic word, even particles peculiar to Greek such as *men* and *an*, as well as rigid Greek word-order. The result was often unidiomatic or meaningless.[14] This in itself was not unusual in ancient translation,[15] except that since Gothic had never been written down before, Ulfilas was effectively creating not only an alphabet, but a written language. His word-for-word translation created a language far removed from any common parlance when it was written.

---

tuts für Österreichische Geschichtsforschung 84 (1976), 239–61; Wolfram, *History of the Goths*, pp. 89–116; see further Heather and Matthews, *The Goths in the Fourth Century*, pp. 103–31; Thompson, *The Visigoths in the Time of Ulfila*, pp. 64–77, 94–119 (the latter to be used with some care).

[12] Heather and Matthews, *The Goths in the Fourth Century*, pp. 158–9; Philip Baldi, *An Introduction to the Indo-European Languages* (Carbondale, Ill., 1983), p. 135.

[13] M. J. Hunter, "The Gothic Bible," in *The Cambridge History of the Bible* 2, ed. G. W. H. Lampe (Cambridge, 1969), pp. 352–3.

[14] Ibid., p. 342.

[15] Ibid., p. 343; another example of extreme literalness is the Septuagint.

By the time that we encounter it in Italy, it has achieved a very strange form indeed.[16] How did the text evolve?

The Gothic Bible, despite its non-Mediterranean origins, exercised an outsize influence on the evolution of scriptural texts in Western Europe. In a world that as yet possessed no consensus on what constituted the correct form and translation of the Scriptures, but where few people could understand the original Hebrew and Greek, all versions of the text of the Bible were prized. Eventually, of course, Jerome's Vulgate would come to dominate the field in the West, but it did not achieve that domination until the end of the eighth century or later. In the fifth and sixth centuries, a huge variety of bibles and translations were current.

Two of the five Gothic biblical fragments are bilingual Gothic–Latin texts of the Gospels.[17] In one of these, preserved in the *Codex Brixianus*, there is clear evidence that the Gothic influenced the Latin.[18] But, astonishingly, that Gothic text already contains a number of readings derived from the Vetus Latina, which are also evident in the most famous manuscript of the Gothic bible, the *Codex Argenteus*.[19] The *Argenteus* also shows sporadic readings from the Africana, the African recension of the Vetus Latina. Since the Africana manuscript itself survives in Italy, and since most manuscripts of the Vetus Latina come from northern Italy and southern Gaul, centers of Arian belief in the late fifth and early sixth centuries, it seems likely that the Gothic text became Latinized in the course of reciprocal transmission of scriptural textual readings in the fifth-century Western Mediterranean.

The Latin-influenced Gothic Bible as it existed in Ostrogothic Italy was thus the product of a learned fifth-century Mediterranean Latin world, both Arian and Catholic, that exchanged versions of biblical translations. In the course of these transmissions, the Gothic text influenced the Latin text in its turn, scattering Graecisms in manuscripts of the Vetus Latina. Such scholarship resembles that of Jerome, who, though more

---

[16] Copying of texts does not, of course, prove that language of the texts is a spoken language comprehensible to everyone, as Mastrelli, in "I Goti e il gotico," assumes: "Da questa intensa attività culturale risulta quindi evidente che la traduzione del visigoto Ulfila doveva essere immediatamente comprensibile agli stessi Ostrogoti," p. 277. The activity in itself need only prove that it was comprehensible to the copyists, a learned group.

[17] For full shelfmarks and *Codices Latini Antiquiores* numbers of original Gothic and Latin Arian MSS, see Jan-Olof Tjäder, "Der Codex argenteus in Uppsala und der Buchmeister Viliaric in Ravenna," *Studia Gotica: Die eisenzeitlichen Verbindungen zwischen Schweden und Südosteuropa, Vorträge beim Gotensymposion im Statens Historiska Museum Stockholm 1970*, Kungl. Vitterhets Historie och Antikvitets Akademiens handlingar, Antikvariska serien 25 (Stockholm, 1972), pp. 159–61, nn. 6–8, 30.

[18] Ibid., p. 350; Heather and Matthews, *The Goths in the Fourth Century*, pp. 172–3.

[19] Hunter, "The Gothic Bible," p. 348. On the scribe of the *Argenteus* see below, pp. 255–6.

learned than any of the people producing the Western pre-Vulgate texts, similarly corresponded with people throughout the Mediterranean in producing his Latin Vulgate. Two of these people, interestingly, were a pair of Catholic "Goths" in Rome called Sunnia and Fretela, clergymen who wrote seeking Jerome's advice in the early fifth century. They do not mention the Gothic text; they were interested in the relationship of a Gallican Psalter to the Greek and Hebrew texts.[20] Sunnia and Fretela, although "Goths" by some criterion (perhaps they had been in the following of Alaric, or had emigrated from beyond the Danube?) were not Arians and were not interested in Gothic texts, but they are representatives of the broad, learned circles of biblical textual criticism current in the Mediterranean in the fifth century.

Not only Gothic-speakers, but Latin- and Greek-speakers, read and used the Gothic text. Not only Arians, but Catholics, had spread and changed Ulfilas's translation of the Bible. There is no question that communities of Arians in the fifth-century West could use the Gothic Bible, whether they considered themselves Goths or not, and whether they considered their Arian religion a Gothic church or not.

The Gothic Arian churches of sixth-century Italy looked back to the fourth-century Ulfilas through Gothic texts and Latin sermons and commentaries produced in the intervening fifth century. These Latin-speaking fourth- and fifth-century Arians have been fully studied by Michel Meslin, in a book whose importance for the evolution of sixth-century Arianism has not yet been recognized.[21] For the works of these men, significantly, are preserved in the same sixth-century Italian manuscripts that preserve fragments of written Gothic. In other words, it is impossible to understand the meaning of written Gothic, and the *ecclesia Gothica* in Italy, without also understanding the Latin Arian heritage of the fifth-century West.

Latin and Greek Arian texts from the fifth century were the first to create the image of Ulfilas as apostle of the Goths, as, indeed, a "Moses." The closest thing to a contemporary description that we possess, a letter by the Arian bishop Auxentius of Durostorum, written soon after 381, saw Ulfilas as "an inhabitant of the Roman Empire winning converts for the Roman faith, rather than a Goth and an Apostle of the Goths."[22] Ulfilas's own beliefs about the relationship

---

[20] Ibid., p. 351; Thompson, *The Visigoths in the Time of Ulfila*, p. 139.

[21] Meslin, *Les Ariens d'Occident*; its importance has not been recognized, for example, by Heather and Matthews (*The Goths in the Fourth Century*), who cite from it but take little account of the consequences of its argument for an understanding of Ulfilas and Arianism in the Balkans.

[22] Thompson, *The Visigoths in the Time of Ulfila*, p. 120. Similarly, the fifth-century Greek Arian historian Philostorgius described Ulfilas as the "Moses of our time;" *Historia Ecclesiastica* 2.5,

between Arianism and the name "Goth" are unknown, but this much is certain: he was descended from people born within the Roman Empire, he spread Arian Christianity at a time when Arian Christianity was the faith of the Roman Emperors Constantius II and Valens, and in no way could he have considered his own religion as a special or minority form of Christianity restricted to people speaking a Germanic tongue on the Danube and calling themselves Goths.[23]

In other words, the restricted identification of Arianism with the name Goth had to postdate Ulfilas. It could only come about after Arianism had been officially and finally condemned as a heresy by the Roman government. Translating the Scriptures into a new language does not automatically create a new Christian community; the Bible had already been translated into Syriac and Coptic. If those Syriac and Coptic Scriptures would eventually become the biblical texts used by the Jacobite and monophysite churches, no one could have predicted this in the fourth century, nor would the translators have thought it desirable that their theological beliefs would eventually be restricted to the Christian believers of a certain region. And even after it occurred, those churches were sufficiently numerous in their membership to continue to claim universality and orthodoxy; the head of the Jacobite church is, after all, still called the Katholikos today.

The collection of Latin Arian sermons surviving in Verona MS LI (49) is now known to have been produced by a number of writers in fifth-century Italy. Although originally attributed to the Catholic Maximus of Turin, and then reattributed to an Arian bishop Maximinus who had a disputation with Augustine in the late 420s, Roger Gryson has shown that only some of the texts can have been written by Maximinus.[24] They were copied in Italy, around the year 500, in Verona.[25]

These and related Italian Latin texts preserve the memory of Ulfilas and his evangelism. In Maximinus's commentary on the Council of Aquileia, where Ambrose defeated Arian bishops, the Italian Arian

trans. Heather and Matthews, *The Goths in the Fourth Century*, p. 145 – though Philostorgius, unlike the more contemporary Auxentius, also saw him as going outside the Empire to convert the Goths.

[23] Wolfram, *Goths*, p. 78, wants to see Ulfilas as resolving "*in Christo* the ethnic difference between Goths and Romans," on the basis of Maximinus, *Dissertatio* 34 (55) (that Auxentius was raised by Ulfilas as a disciple); this seems to me unfounded and anachronistic; a sort of Augustinian viewpoint at best.

[24] Roger Gryson, "Les citations scriptuaires des oeuvres attribuées à l'évêque arien Maximinus," *Revue bénédictine* 88 (1978), 45–80; Roger Gryson, *Le recueil arien de Vérone*, Instrumenta Patristica 13 (The Hague, 1982), pp. 21–8.

[25] Gryson, *Recueil arien*, pp. 67–70; the collection is edited by Roger Gryson, *Collectio Arianae Veronensis*, Scripta arriana latina I, CCSL 87 (Turnhout, 1982), 1–145.

bishop points out that at least his church had spread the faith to the barbarians. The text compares the conversion of the Goths – the *gens Gothorum* – to the election of the Israelites. Other texts record the persecution of the fourth-century groups called Goths by the *iudex Gothorum*.[26]

The Latin Arian commentary on the council of Aquileia was produced in Italy around the 440s, exactly midway between the conciliar condemnation of Arianism in 381 and the copying of the text in Ostrogothic Verona in 500.[27] Already Latin-speaking Arians were using the Ulfilan heritage of the Balkans, and were speaking with pride of Ulfilas and his conversion of Goths there. One of these bishops, possibly Maximinus himself, ministered to Arian communities on the Danube.[28]

The Italian and Balkan Arian communities were not yet called *ecclesia Gothica* in the fifth century. Indeed, the author of one Latin Arian text, probably preserved in sixth-century Italy,[29] refers to having just lived "sub tyrannis et gentium dominatione."[30] The same author criticizes the people amongst whom he lives for their devotion to war, calling them *barbarae gentes*.[31] This has led one historian to call this author "un Germain de l'Empire, un Germain civilisé ou dégermanisé," and another to deny entirely that he could have been a barbarian or sympathetic to barbarians.[32] Such conclusions pay no attention to the uses of ethnographic language and rhetoric. Tyrants and bellicosity were always associated with *gentes* and *barbari*, and these terms provided stock imagery with which to criticize them from a Christian point of view. What impact the use of such imagery may have had on the attitude of the authors toward the ethnographic group-name *Gothi* is unknown, but like Theoderic himself, this text does not explicitly associate that group-name with the evils of barbaric behavior. The example of Theoderic shows, of course, that someone calling himself a Goth could

[26] Maximinus, *Dissertatio* §23, ed. Roger Gryson, *Scripta arriana latina* I, CCSL 87 (Turnhout, 1982), p. 160 (Ulfilas); ibid., §35, p. 164 (*gens Gothorum* and Israelites); §§36–7, pp. 164–5 (persecution); *Palladi Ratiarensis fragmenta*, ibid., p. 195.

[27] On the date, see Gryson, *Scripta arriana latina*, pp. xxi–xxii; Heather and Matthews, pp. 145–6.

[28] This bishop was the author of the *Opus imperfectum in Matthaeum*, a Latin work, edited in PG 56: 611–946, with the corrections of Meslin, *Les Ariens d'Occident*, pp. 181–2. On the author's Danube connections, see Zeiller, *Les origines chrétiennes dans les provinces danubiennes*, pp. 477–8, and J. van Banning, *Opus imperfectum in Matthaeum: praefatio*, CCSL 87B (Turnhout, 1988), pp. v–vi. On the authorship of the text, see Meslin, ibid., pp. 163–80 (opting for Maximinus); van Banning, pp. v–vi (opting for an Arian bishop or priest in the Balkans, in the second or third quarter of the fifth century).

[29] van Banning, *Opus imperfectum*, p. xvi: the best MSS survive from Bobbio.

[30] *Opus imperfectum*, col. 767.

[31] Ibid., col. 626.

[32] Zeiller, *Les origines chrétiennes dans les provinces danubiennes*, p. 478, and Meslin, *Les Ariens d'Occident*, pp. 92, 97–8, 173, respectively; similarly, van Banning, pp. v–vi (not a Goth).

denigrate *barbari* and even *exterae gentes* without considering himself to denigrate Goths. Theoderic's is an early sixth-century perspective, a use of the language that could only come about once a corporate group calling itself *Gothi* was in control of a Roman province, considering itself to assist in the governance of the Roman Empire. In the mid-fifth century, the evolution of *Gothi* as a positive term in literary texts had not fully come about. What is important is that the author did not associate Arian (correct) belief with barbarians, but with Christians; indeed, he castigates Catholics for converting barbarians indiscriminately, thus giving warlike people the false name of Christian.[33]

The famous early fifth-century calendar written in Gothic does associate Arian martyrs with the Goths – distinguishing them from non-Gothic Arian martyrs. In doing so, it competed with texts associating Catholic martyrs with the Goths – for the claims of Maximinus and Philostorgius that Ulfilas was the Moses of the Goths were propagandistic.[34] There had also been several Catholic missionaries to the Goths of Ulfilas, some his contemporaries.[35] Texts like the Greek *Passio* of the Catholic Goth Saba, who died in *Gothia*, were eagerly promoted by anti-Arians such as Basil of Caesaraea.[36] An Arian Greek *Passio* on martyrs burned in a church was used in the Gothic calendar, which talks of martyrs not in *Gothia* but in *Gutthiudai*, "land of the Gothic people" or merely "the Gothic people."[37] Needless to say, the Arian "martyrs of the Goths" were not the same as the Catholic "martyrs of the Goths." The calendar also lists two Arians who were not classed as Goths, the emperor Constantine (probably a mistake for Constantius II) and Dorotheus the patriarch of Constantinople, as well as the apostles Philip and Andrew and the "old women of Beroea" in Thrace, who may have died under the Licinian persecutions and whose cult would

---

[33] *Opus imperfectum*, col. 824, comparing the traducing of Christ to the gentiles, in an extended conceit, to the indiscriminate conversion of barbarians (Christ = *verbum veritatis*). The "impious *sacerdotes*" who thus create false Christians are *haeretici*, elsewhere defined principally as *homoousiani* (Catholics): col. 903. The concern with the *nomen Christianum*, and the notion of a Christian church as an elect group within society, are typically dissenting fourth-century ideas on the role of Christianity in a Christian Empire; this text attests the transformation of some Arian groups into a minority persecuted church, on which see below, p. 245; further pp. 262–3.

[34] On Philostorgius, see above, n. 22.

[35] Goddas, Eutyches, Saba, possibly Nicetas and Theophilus; Audius, a lone schismatic alienated from both sides, also made converts: Thompson, *The Visigoths in the Time of Ulfila*, pp. 82, 95, 161–5. On the pro-Catholic activity of Vetranio, bishop of Tomi in Scythia, and Soranus the *dux Scythiae*, see Wolfram, *Goths*, p. 83.

[36] Heather and Matthews, *The Goths in the Fourth Century*, pp. 103–27.

[37] "Gothic land:" Wolfram, *History of the Goths*, p. 22; Heather and Matthews, *The Goths in the Fourth Century*, p. 129, where "Gutthiadai" is clearly a misprint or a mistake in transliteration from the Gothic letters on the facing page, p. 128.

then have been taken over by Arians in the Balkans.[38] The calendar draws on both Greek and Gothic Arian tradition, but may have itself originally been translated from Greek, like Ulfilas's Bible, together with which it was eventually preserved in Ostrogothic Italy.[39]

The gap between Latin and Gothic Arian texts of the 440s or so, and the *ecclesia Gothica* of the early 500s, is more difficult to fill. But Arian communities did not vanish from the Balkans or from Italy between 440 and 489. Theologically speaking, Arian conceptions of a limited Christian community were appropriate for preserving a minority belief. Like the Novatians, the Donatists or the Pelagians, who managed to preserve small groups of believers in a sea of Catholicism, fifth-century Arians denied the primacy of the see of Rome and considered themselves a Church of Saints, an elect group amidst gentiles and unbelievers.[40] While Eastern Eusebianism and Western Augustinianism respectively encouraged the wide definitions of a Christian Empire and of a world of Catholics encompassing a *civitas dei* of unknowable extent, the Arians continued to propagate the older image of a persecuted and limited church – which they had in fact become after 381.[41]

Byzantine writers would later see this period as one of barbarian evangelization, part of the constant Byzantine definition of Arianism as a barbarous religion – the standard smear going back to Ambrose. Jordanes linked the spread of Arianism to the Gothic tongue: "Omnem ubique linguae eius nationem ad culturam huius sectae invitavere."[42] The production of Latin sermons in the Balkans shows that Jordanes's explanation cannot be correct, even if the influence of Ambrose remains strong enough that modern historians often cannot see Arianism as anything other than the religion of barbarians within the Empire.[43] Of

---

[38] Gothic Calendar, ed. and trans. Heather and Matthews, in *The Goths in the Fourth Century*, pp. 128–30; on Constantius II and the old women of Beroea, see ibid., p. 130, nn. 63, 66.

[39] Ibid., p. 129.

[40] Meslin, *Les Ariens d'Occident*, pp. 339–52, esp. 348–52. On Pelagians, Novatianists and Donatists, see Peter Brown, "Pelagius and his supporters: aims and environment," 1968, reprinted in Brown, *Religion and Society in the Age of Saint Augustine* (London, 1972), pp. 183–207, esp. 200–1: "the Christianity of discontinuity."

[41] On Eusebian and Augustinian definitions of the community of the faithful, see above, ch. 1, nn. 38–9; and ch. 6.

[42] Jordanes, *Get.* 25.

[43] Thompson, *The Visigoths in the Time of Ulfila*, p. 128: "And so long as the Western Empire lasted – and in some cases even longer – the barbarians inside its frontiers kept themselves distinct from the Romans by adhering to a form of Christianity (Arianism) which was clearly marked off from the official Roman religion . . ." Thompson is thus led into uncharacteristically unsupported (and unannotated) statements such as "Moreover, when the Burgundians in 516 and the Visigoths in 589 became officially Catholic, the victory of Catholicism was regarded by many of the barbarians themselves as a defeat for the barbarian element in the population of Burgundy and Spain" (ibid.), a view for which there is no evidence whatsoever.

course, the Germanic language of some Arian texts, the history of the conversion of Goths by Ulfilas, and the martyrdoms of Arians among groups called Goths in the fourth century, still recorded in the fifth century, must all have appealed to people who lived near the original events, many of whom may still have spoken a Germanic tongue themselves and may have laid claim to the name Goth. But this is speculation. We cannot see this process clearly. The one Arian leader from the Balkans at this time whose views we can see is Theoderic, and he never connected his Arian belief with the Goths. The only thing that we can assume is that Theoderic, some of his family, and some of his followers were Arian because they came from the Balkans, where Arians still maintained a strong presence, as in Italy.[44]

Meanwhile, in late fifth-century Italy, there is patchy evidence for Arian continuity. The *magistri militum* Ricimer, Gundobad and Odoacer were Arians,[45] and they presumably had clergy to administer the sacraments and churches in which to worship: some at least of the six or seven Arian churches in Ravenna pre-dated Theoderic.[46] At some point between 459 and 472, Ricimer decorated, but did not found, an Arian church at Rome, today Sant'Agata dei Goti.[47] Another Arian church, on the Via Merulana, later San Severino, is of unknown date.[48] Fourth-

---

[44] It is impossible to use the tangled arguments of E. A. Thompson, "Christianity and the northern barbarians," in *The Conflict Between Paganism and Christianity in the Fourth Century*, ed. Arnaldo Momigliano (Oxford, 1963), pp. 72–6, esp. 73, that "Gothic" missionaries from Constantinople converted the "Ostrogoths" (from paganism!) in Pannonia between 456–72, so bedeviled are they by assumptions since proved questionable: that the Ostrogoths and the Visigoths were peoples with static membership, that the groups who bore those names in the early sixth century can be identified with the Tervingi and Greuthungi of the fourth century, and that the Ostrogoths under Attila (so-called only by Jordanes) were identical with the people who followed Theoderic into Italy, that one people could only have one religion, that Arian texts, let alone Gothic-language Arian texts, were only handed down by Goths, and so on. Some people might find it unconvincing, moreover, to attribute paganism to Attila's Goths on the basis of Orosius's claim that the Goths of Radagaisus in 406 practised human sacrifice.

[45] PLRE2: 525, 793, 945.

[46] On these church buildings, see Jacques Zeiller, "Etude sur l'arianisme en Italie à l'époque ostrogothique et à l'époque lombarde," *Mélanges d'archéologie et d'histoire de l'Ecole Française de Rome* 25 (1905), 128–30. Deichmann, *Ravenna* 1: 43–7. Zeiller (p. 130) claims that an Arian church was erected in Verona in the time of Odoacer, but gives no reference.

[47] ICUR 2, no. 127: FLA·RICIMER·VI·MAG·UVTRIVSQ·MILITIAE·EXCONS·ORD·PRO VOTO·SVO ADORNAVIT, discussed by Jacques Zeiller, "Les églises ariennes de Rome à l'époque de la domination gothique," *Mélanges d'archéologie et d'histoire de l'Ecole Française de Rome* 24 (1904), 19–20. The inscription may date from between 470 and 472 since a bronze dagger with Ricimer's name and the date 470 was also found in the church. Although this might suggest simply that he was buried there, intramural burials were very rare at this period: Zeiller, ibid., p. 20.

[48] Zeiller, "Les églises ariennes," pp. 23–5; Carlo Cecchelli, "L'Arianesimo e le chiese ariane d'Italia," in *Le chiese nei regni dell'Europa occidentale e i loro rapporti con Roma sino all'800*, Settimane di Studio 7 (Spoleto, 1960), 757, 765–7.

century Arian church buildings existed in Aquileia and Milan, and there is no reason to suppose that they went out of use.[49] A fifth-century Arian church building probably existed in Grado, and possibly also in Spoleto and Split.[50] Meanwhile, Ulfilas's Gothic Bible continued to be used, changed and transmitted, and someone was preserving the early- and mid-fifth-century Latin Arian texts. There is no reason to assume that Arianism was eradicated in Italy between 440 and 489.

The mid-fifth-century Latin Arian texts were still used in sixth-century Italy; in fact only one Gothic non-liturgical non-scriptural text survives at all, and its use also seems to have been purely ceremonial.[51] Since Ulfilas is said to have produced sermons in Gothic for Gothic speakers in the fourth century,[52] it is surely significant that only Latin sermons survive from the sixth century.

Sermons, didactic texts, are the most important part of the liturgy for communication. Arranged according to the great feasts, they are the place where the service departs from the ceremonial and engages in direct and topical communication with the congregation.[53] It is, of course, possible that Gothic sermons were preserved or produced in sixth-century Italy. But Latin ones survive, and given that the vast majority, if not all, of attested people otherwise called Goths, including all speakers of the spoken Gothic language in sixth century Italy, did speak Latin, we can assume that Latin sermons were used in sixth-century Gothic Arian churches.

ARIAN GOTHIC AND LATIN LITURGICAL TEXTS IN
LATIN-SPEAKING ITALY

The preservation and use of Ulfilas's Gothic Bible by Arian Italians must be related to their use of the term *ecclesia legis Gothorum*. But what

---

[49] Cecchelli, "L'Arianesimo e le chiese ariane," pp. 757–9 (Aquileia), 761–4 (Milan).

[50] Ibid., pp. 759–60 (Grado); 772–3 (Spoleto, San Salvatore); Dyggve, *History of Salonitan Christianity*, pp. 56–7 and 66, n. 34 (a fairly hazardous argument for an Arian cemetery in Split), and Wolfram, *Goths*, pp. 326, 520 with n. 460 (again, hazardous arguments for Split). Further on Split, where the vast cemetery of Manastirine was certainly Catholic, see PA Ariver with references there. But the two inscriptions referring to an *ecclesia katholiké* in Split (one from 382 and the other from the fifth century: Dyggve, ibid.) certainly suggests that there was also an Arian *ecclesia* there before Theoderic's arrival in Italy, as does a reference to a conflict between Arians and Catholics after the death of the emperor-bishop Glycerius in 480 (Cecchelli, "L'arianesimo e le chiese ariane," p. 760).

[51] The *Skeireins*: see below, pp. 248–9.

[52] Thompson, *The Visigoths in the Time of Ulfila*, p. 116.

[53] This is to simplify an enormously complex issue on the role of communication in liturgy. On language and communication in late antiquity in an ecclesiastical context, see Banniard, *Viva Voce*, pp. 11–63; on sermons in the liturgy, pp. 92–104 (Augustinian Africa), and pp. 148–72 (homilies of Gregory the Great). Banniard (pp. 38–9) distinguishes between three levels of

did Ulfilas's Gothic language mean to them? It seems to have been an archaic, ceremonial language used in the ritual parts of the mass, and in certain other ceremonial occasions for the church. Like Hebrew among the medieval Jews, or Latin in the modern Catholic church before Vatican II, Ulfilas's Gothic became a mystical, learned tongue used to emphasize the distinction of the church within society, and to delineate the separation of clergy and laity.[54] The artificiality of Ulfilas's translation may have divided clergy from laity even in the fourth century, when the language of his Bible was still closely related to some spoken Germanic tongue.[55]

The one Gothic text that might depart from this model is the *Skeireins*, a commentary on the Gospel of St. John originally produced, like Ulfilas's Bible, in the fourth-century Balkans.[56] Like almost all our surviving Gothic texts, it was indeed copied in Ostrogothic Italy.[57] Furthermore, cadence and pause marks in the manuscript show that it was read aloud in church, like the Gothic Bible.[58]

However, a commentary is not a sermon. The *Skeireins* is probably a translation from a Greek original, and its own contamination by Greek and Latin places it in the same confused textual transmission and language as the Gothic Bible.[59] It was another text inherited from the

---

liturgy used to communicate: first, readings from scripture, then sermons composed for the circumstance of the day or the time of year, and finally improvisation of oral sermons or homilies on the spot. Above all, sermons are the most important locus in which to identify communication between celebrant and congregation (p. 47). I am most grateful to Yitzhak Hen for his advice in this matter; needless to say, he is not responsible for any errors in my interpretation of the role of Latin sermons in Gothic liturgy.

[54] The parallel with Hebrew, is, of course, not exact, since the Diaspora Jewish communities taught Hebrew to men who did not become rabbis; nor is the rabbinical system parallel to Christian clergy. But not all Jewish men, and few women, learned Hebrew. Like Latin in the late medieval and modern Catholic church, Hebrew remained incomprehensible to some part of the congregation. See further Stefan C. Reif, "Aspects of medieval Jewish literacy," in *The Uses of Literacy*, pp. 150–4: in Cairo in the central Middle Ages, literacy in Hebrew was very widespread among Jewish men. Old Church Slavonic is not a parallel: it varied according to the vernacular of the region, whereas in Italian Arian churches the communicative part of the liturgy was in Latin.

[55] Because Ulfilas's Gothic was so different from any everyday fourth-century language, Peter Heather rightly remarks, "Gothic literacy in this form was probably largely the preserve of, and may have . . . empowered, a priestly class" ("Literacy and power in the migration period," pp. 178–9).

[56] *The Gothic Commentary on the Gospel of John: skeireins ai waggeljons thairh iohannen*, ed. and trans. William Holmes Bennett, Modern Language Association of America Monograph 21 (New York, 1960).

[57] Bennett in ibid., pp. 8–9, although the Danube and the south of France are not excluded for the provenance of the manuscript. If it was produced on the Danube, it would be unique among surviving early sixth-century MSS.

[58] Bennett in ibid., pp. 29–30.

[59] Ibid., pp. 41–2, 134–5.

fourth-century Ulfilan past, and as such commanded the same sort of reverence as the texts of the Gothic Bible with which it was probably transmitted. Its language, phonology, morphology and syntax show that the *Skeireins* was as artificial a creation as the Bible,[60] and that it was no closer to a living language than the other written Gothic liturgical texts.

The sixth-century Gothic manuscripts indicate bilingualism in written Gothic and Latin, not only in the contaminated texts that they contain, but also in their codicology and palaeography. Two of the manuscripts of the Gothic Bible were preserved in bilingual Gothic–Latin editions. As we have seen, the Gothic and Latin texts had contaminated each other. The preface to one of these bilingual editions survives, preserved in the *Codex Brixianus*. It attests not only bilingualism, but the primacy of Latin – for the preface is written in Latin. The author explains that in his desire to achieve a perfect translation, he has annotated doubtful translations in the Gothic with *vulthres*, "which in the Latin language means 'adnotatio,' " to explain the use of certain Gothic words for certain Latin or Greek words. We do not, of course, know when this author was writing; he might have been one and the same as the scribe of the sixth-century manuscript, or he might have written at any time in the previous century. In either case he was one of the scholars responsible for the production of biblical texts. None of these learned annotations survives, but his *vulthres* may have even been interpolated into the biblical text itself, contaminating the confused text further.[61]

More relevant for the issue of sixth-century ceremonial practice are the Gothic glosses on the Arian Latin sermons contained in the Veronensis. These glosses consist of single words in Gothic, designed to lead the reader from the relevant liturgical text (the Veronensis is mostly composed of sermons for great feasts) to the relevant book of the Gothic Bible.

These glosses thus presume a bilingual clerical readership. They do not translate or clarify the texts.[62] They also show that the Latin sermons themselves were meant to be used in liturgies that also included the Gothic Bible, and possibly other Gothic ceremonial texts such as the

---

[60] Ibid., pp. 134–5.
[61] Preface to the *Codex Brixianus*, ed. W. Streitberg, *Die Gotische Bibel*, 2 vols. (Heidelberg, 1908–10), 1: xlii–xliii; trans. with notes by Heather and Matthews, *The Goths in the Fourth Century*, pp. 169–73; interpolation of *vulthres*, p. 172. Hunter, in "The Gothic Bible," pp. 350–1, dates the composition of the preface to the time of the production of the sixth-century manuscript, but gives no grounds for so doing.
[62] Gryson, *Le recueil arien*, p. 80; Gryson, *Scripta arriana latina*, pp. xxi–xxii.

Skeireins, as we know from breathing and cadence marks on those manuscripts.

The Gothic glosses on the sermons are almost certainly the work of contemporaries of the sixth-century copies of the text. Although almost all the glosses on the Veronensis are placed on the fifth-century Latin sermons discussed above, one gloss was placed on a fragment of Augustine's anti-Arian *De trinitate*, originally in this collection and since removed.[63] The annotator saw the text as being part of the series of Arian homilies, which it originally followed in the manuscript. No contemporary of Augustine's, and certainly not Augustine's Arian opponent Maximinus, the author of some of the sermons, could have made this mistake. It seems reasonable to conclude that the glosses themselves were made around the time that the Veronensis was produced, near the year 500.[64]

These fifth-century Italian Latin texts, which themselves used the memory of the conversion of the Goths, actually became part of the liturgy of the *ecclesia Gothica* in sixth-century Italy, the part of liturgy that was designed to communicate with the Arian laity. An Arian community in Italy that praised Ulfilas and saw the conversion of the Goths as its great achievement was transformed into "the church of the Goths." If the type of transformation is thus evident, the mechanics of the transformation remain unclear. We cannot say whether Arians in Italy before Theoderic's arrival welcomed a group called Goths, whose leader and some of whose members were Arian, and thus merged itself into that group, or whether contacts between Italy and Balkan Arians had persisted over the previous fifty years since the time of Maximinus. But the circulation of Gothic texts in Italy and the West during those fifty years certainly suggests the latter: persistent contacts and the gradual evolution of the Italian–Balkan Arian church into the "church of the Goths."

The Latin Arian tradition thus absorbed the work and deeds of Ulfilas, and as Arianism became a minority religion, raised that memory to the status of its defining identity as a community. The liturgical, textual and palaeographical evidence alone attests this phenomenon. The notion that Theoderic and his followers reintroduced an Arian belief into Italy which they and they alone identified as "Gothic"

[63] B. Pagnin, "Il codice Giustiniani Recanati in onciale del sesto secolo ed il passo del 'De Trinitate' di S. Agostino in esso contenuto," *Atti e Memorie dell'Accademia Patavina di scienze, lettere ed arti* 90.3 (1977–8), 171–82; Gryson, *Le recueil arien*, p. 79.
[64] Gryson, *Le recueil arien*, p. 79.

cannot be the case – nor does any contemporary source state that it was the case. Arianism always existed in Italy; Arian churchmen gradually made the Arian Gothic heritage their own, and the process was underway before Theoderic came to Italy.

THE GOTHIC SUBSCRIPTIONS IN THE RAVENNA PAPYRI

Further evidence for the ossification and the ceremonial use of the written Gothic language comes from two extraordinary Ravenna papyri, which show that Arian clerics could still write in the Gothic language. Scholars have assumed that the Gothic subscriptions in the two papyri are proof that Gothic was a living language,[65] and that laymen could write Gothic.[66] This was not the case. This interpretation does not dovetail with philological evidence showing that the contaminated and archaic Gothic of Ulfilas's Bible was far from any spoken tongue, or with the evidence for learned clerical bilingualism and the use of Latin in the sermons of the Arian churches of Italy. Above all, it does not take account of the awkward, formulaic form of the Gothic subscriptions themselves.

Much confusion has emerged from the Gothic subscriptions to the Ravenna papyri. In interpreting a document from 551, it is simply meaningless to use the linguistic origin of names as an automatic key to the label Goth or Roman. Nevertheless, Tjäder interprets the personal names of the clergy as follows: "The clergy consists, as one sees, of 19 persons, of whom 15 are obviously Goths [because they have Germanic names, one presumes]. The other four – Vitalianus, Petrus, Paulus and Benenatus – have Latin names, and Petrus and Paulus, who can write for themselves, also sign in Latin; in my opinion these two are Romans, while no conclusion is possible for Vitalianus and Benenatus."[67] From another document, Tjäder concludes that a possible writer of Gothic named Latinus "ist also ein Gote, der seinen ursprünglichen gotischen Namen abgeworfen hat."[68] Kampers asserts with no evidence that no Roman took a Germanic name in Italy – a meaningless statement unless "Roman" has been proved to be a stable, immutable category in the first place – and thus judges that the Christian non-

---

[65] For example, Bruno Luiselli, "Cassiodoro e la storia dei Goti," in *Passaggio dal mondo antico al medio evo da Teodosio a San Gregorio Magno,* Atti dei Convegni Lincei 45 (Rome, 1980), p. 230.
[66] See discussion at PA Latinus, Anonymus 1.
[67] Tjäder 2: 95; my translation; similarly, Scardigli, "Sprache und Kultur," p. 294.
[68] Tjäder 2: 260, n. 31.

Germanic names in this papyrus "einen vielleicht ursprünglich geführten germanischen Namen verdrängen können."[69]

Two Ravenna papyri contain definite written Gothic, one of them long since lost, but preserved in a seventeenth-century transcription.[70] The more important one, *PItal* 34, records the sale of swamplands belonging to the *ecclesia legis Gothorum sanctae Anastasiae* at Ravenna in 551. It is witnessed by the *universus clerus* of the church; four of nineteen subscribers signed with a sentence in Gothic. The less important one, also the one that was lost long ago, is *PDip* 118,[71] which records the purchase of four-twelfths of a farm by one man from another, both apparently deacons, perhaps near Faenza. One of the two men signed with a sentence in Gothic.

Latin is the language of both documents – and the language understood by all the participants. But although they understood Latin, not all the clergy of the church of St. Anastasia were literate. Of the ten who could write for themselves, six signed in Latin, and the illiterate remainder put their marks on prepared Latin statements. There is no question that these men signed in Latin because they could not write Gothic, rather than the reverse.[72]

The four Gothic subscriptions on the document of St. Anastasia are formulaic and almost exactly the same. They all run: "I, X, have subscribed in my own hand, and we have received 60 *skilliggans* [i.e., "shillings," *solidi*]; and earlier, as security, we received, with the deacon who stands for all of us, and with our colleagues, 120 *skilliggans* as the value of this swampland."[73] The other three subscriptions differ only in very rare variations in orthography and in one haplography.[74] Only their names and offices are different: *papa* (priest), *diakon* (deacon), and *bokareis* (*spodeus*). It almost looks as if they were copying from the same template, or using a formula that had always been used.

---

[69] Kampers, "Anmerkungen," p. 146 (on the "Romans" and Germanic names, see also p. 143). I postpone the issue of the meaning of names until after we have established the meaning of written Gothic. It has been sufficiently shown that a personal name can be, but need not be, a clue to identity, and that all such relationships are complex.

[70] *PItal* 34 and *PDip* 118 = *PItal* 8; referred to by Germanic philologists as the *Documentum Neapolitanum* and the *Documentum Aretinum*, from the places in whose archives the manuscripts first came to light. But both documents were produced in sixth-century Ravenna, and these names are so misleading as to suggest that they should be dropped.

[71] Now re-edited, from the seventeenth-century printed edition, by Tjäder as *PItal*† 8, but still, confusingly, referred to by him as "Pap. Marini 118," so I will use both forms together.

[72] Tjäder 2: 95, n. 43.

[73] This translation from *PItal* 34.88–91, the subscription of Optarit/Ufitahari, using the translation of Tjäder 2: 101 and his understanding of *mith diakuna alamoda unsaramma* at 2: 96–7.

[74] Tjäder 2: 274, n. 33.

In contrast, the six Latin subscriptions differ among themselves greatly. Compare:

Ego Petrus, subdiaconus aclisie gotice sancte Anastasie, uic in solutum cessionis venditionisque et documentum padulis suprascriptorum cum omnibus ad se pertinentibus, a me vel suprascriptis collivertis vel conministris meis factum vobi, suprascripto Petro viro reverendo defensori, conparatori, ad omnia suprascripta relegi, consensis et suscribsi, et testes, ut suscriberent, pariter conrogavimus, et pretium centu octoginta solidos, id est centum viginti per cautione antea accepisse profitemur, et nunc de presenti alios sexaginta solidos percipimus . . .

Ego Paulus, clericus eclesie legis Gothorum sanctae Anastasie, huic documentum a nobis factum suscribsi, et pretium auri solidos cento octuginta, hoc est cento viginti per cautione antea accepimus et nunc de preesenti alius sexaginta solidos de presenti percipisse videmur pro padules suprascriptas.[75]

Not only orthography, but vocabulary, sentence structure and content divide the Latin subscriptions. To be sure, they all contain certain legal formulae. But they have also been influenced by the habit or choice of the man in question.

The Latin subscriptions, in other words, look like a living, spoken language, the natural tongue of the men who wrote them. The Gothic subscriptions look like a formula copied out of a book. That is not to say that the Gothic subscribers did not understand what they were writing – that was against the law, and there is no need to assume it. As the use of sermons in Latin and the archaicisms in the Gothic Bible imply, it may simply be that what they were writing was a dead, learned language, an alphabet and vocabulary that had to be learned out of books, like school exercises in Latin today.[76] For those who could write and understand Gothic – we must recall that this meant learning an alphabet in addition to a language – the *ecclesia Gothica* of Ravenna provided a formula in which to do it.

Why did the four clerics sign in Gothic? Gothic was the sacred language of the Arian church in Italy, and transactions of church property were sacred business. In subsequent centuries in Italy, Latin subscriptions may have become formulaic and endowed with a mystical aura. Subscriptions had validated documents under Roman law. Once early

---

[75] *PItal* 34.98–105, 108–115. Tjäder's expansions and emendations are not indicated.

[76] Or at best we could imagine a half-living language like Latin in the Catholic church of the modern period until recently; it was passed on by erudites and initiates as a learned language, which, however, was still learned as a second language and actually spoken only by a minority of Catholic clergy.

medieval societies recognized private instruments, as would occur by
the seventh century in Gaul and Italy, the church lent all its weight to
ensure that holiness suffused these documents of which they were so
often the beneficiaries.[77] The chrismon and the *sanctio*, if not yet the
invocation to Christ, date from this time. We do not yet find such
things in sixth-century Ravenna, but already witnesses are signing with
the *signum crucis*.[78]

That these transactions had particular importance to the Arian church
is suggested by the preservation of the documents by the Catholic
church of Ravenna.[79] As the Arian clergy in Byzantine Ravenna in 551
must have been aware, the emperor would shortly enforce laws against
the Arian churches in Italy and transfer all their properties to the Catholic church.[80] In this way these documents found their way into the
archiepiscopal archive of Ravenna, which is how we possess them
today. The purchaser of the swamplands from St. Anastasia was the
defensor ecclesiae Petrus, certainly a Catholic clergyman.[81] This was a delicate time for the Arian church, condemned soon to lose its patrimony.
It thus had all the more reason for infusing such transactions with as
solemn a sense of its own importance and of its own peculiar traditions
as possible. These traditions included the Gothic language, with its
sacral associations with the Gothic version of the Bible used in their
church.

One such quasi-sacred element in the Gothic formulaic subscriptions
could be the phrase *mith diakuna alamoda unsaramma*. Scardigli and
Tjäder understand this, probably correctly, as "with our deacon representing us," representing the *universus clerus*, a sort of translation of
"singuli et in solido invicem nos innodantes" in some of the Latin
subscriptions.[82] But why a deacon? Is this a piece of Gothic church
tradition in Italy that has otherwise missed us?

Strangely, given the reference to a *diakuna alamoda*, the other lost
papyrus contains a subscription by a deacon Alamud, referred to in the

[77] On the sacrality of writing, see Armando Petrucci, "Aspetti simbolici delle testimonianze
scritte," in *Simboli e simbologia nell'alto medioevo*, Settimane di Studio 23, 2 vols. (Spoleto, 1976),
2: 813–44; on subscriptions, see Paola Supino Martini, "Le sottoscrizione lucchese," *Bulletino
dell'istituto storico italiano* 98 (1992), 87–108. On the transition from *Actenwesen* to *Urkundenwesen*,
from Roman legal acts to medieval physical sacrality of instruments, see Peter Classen, *Kaiserreskript und Königsurkunden: Diplomatische Studien zum Problem der Kontinuität zwischen Altertum und
Mittelalter*, 1956 (reprint, Thessalonica, 1977).
[78] *PItal* 34.92, 106, 130–5.
[79] Tjäder 1: 17–23.
[80] On the *reconciliatio* of Arian church property to the Catholic church in Ravenna, see Tjäder 1:
180–1. A Catholic document recording the possessions acquired in this way is *PItal* 2.
[81] Tjäder 2: 93; Scardigli, *Sprache und Kultur*, pp. 282–3.
[82] Tjäder 2: 96–7.

Gothic subscription by the other deacon as *dkn Alamoda*. This subscription, by a deacon named Gudilibus, seems less formulaic than the ones in the document of St. Anastasia. It even goes so far as to translate the name of the farm, *Casa Caballaria*, into the Gothic form *Hugsis Kaballarja*.[83] This Alamud seems to be a real person, but, oddly enough, he does not subscribe the document, even though he purchased the farm. The difficulty remains for philologists to disentangle, but it is at least notable that the subscriptions to these documents, prepared thirteen years apart and in different places, contain the same mysterious phrase.[84] Again, it may have had formulaic or sacred meaning. Alamud and Gudilibus were deacons, Arian clergy, like all other attested writers of Gothic.[85]

The very spelling and choice of Germanic personal names in the subscriptions attests the special meaning of the written Gothic language to these clerics. The clerics signing in Gothic transliterated the spellings of their names into Gothic, and one cleric with both a Latin and a Germanic name chose to use his Germanic name in his subscription, even though he subscribed in Latin here, and elsewhere signed a subscription with his Latin name.[86]

It is further likely that one of these four subscribers in Gothic copied

---

[83] *PDip* 118 = *PItal*† 8.45–50.

[84] See further PA **O**ptarit, **A**lamaud. Kampers, "Anmerkungen," pp. 147–9, partly undermines the arguments of Scardigli and Tjäder, and would again like to see a real deacon Alamud somehow involved in *PItal* 34, but admits that it cannot be explained why that deacon is then only mentioned in the subscriptions in Gothic, not in the subscriptions in Latin, and why he does not subscribe to the document.

[85] *PDip* 118 = *PItal* 8.48; *PItal* 34.94. In re-editing J.-Baptista Doni's edition from the seventeenth century, Tjäder argues that *Gudileb-us diaconus* in Doni was a misexpansion of *Gudilib u d*, "Gudilibus *vir devotus*." That is to say, Tjäder argues that he was a layman who knew Gothic. But in his Gothic subscription, Gudilibus calls himself and Alamud *dkn*, which must be an abbreviation for *diakon*, attested in the other papyrus. Tjäder 2: 42 admits this difficulty but does not propose a way around it. In fact, Tjäder is only conjecturing that Doni misexpanded a "d," on the basis of line 18, where Doni wrote "d" but no "u" and put no case-ending on "Alamud": *PDip* 118 = *PItal* 8.17–18: "a Lamud d" in Doni's version, and "Alamud [v.]d. (?)" in Tjäder's. The space indicated in Doni's version surely further indicates that he was not expanding a "d," but a much longer word that he could not decipher here – which elsewhere was clearly *diaconus*. I think that we can safely take Doni's reading *diaconus* in the Latin sections as correct on the basis of *d(ia)k(o)n* in the Gothic subscription, and disregard the missing "u" at line 18, where Doni may indeed have overlooked one letter in his transcription. See further PA **A**lamud, **G**udilibus.

[86] Names announced in Latin forms: *PItal* 34.82–5; subscribed in Germanic forms: *PItal* 34.88, 94, 126, 136, Willienant (for Minnulus) at 116, his other subscription (as Minnulus) at *PItal*† 10 (the same man: Tjäder 2: 83), Igila (for Danihel) at 119; Gudilibus throughout *PDip* 118 = *PItal*† 8, e.g. lines 16, 46, but Gudilub or Gudilib at his Gothic subscription, line 47. On the transliterations, see also Kampers, "Anmerkungen," p. 145.

the greatest Gothic biblical codex of all, the *Codex Argenteus*.[87] Written in silver and gold letters on purple parchment, this Uppsala manuscript was probably commissioned by one of the Gothic kings at Ravenna. It is extraordinary that we can directly trace one of the five Gothic biblical fragments to one of the six individuals with attested knowledge of written Gothic. It could be coincidence. But since only a minority even of the Arian clergy in Ravenna appear to have been able to write Gothic, the connection between Wiliarit *bokareis* and the *Codex Argenteus* further suggests that the language was the purview of an extremely small number of scholars.

The Gothic subscriptions do not even mention the *ecclesia legis Gothorum*, unlike all the Latin subscriptions. The written Gothic language in itself specified the Arian church sufficiently. Like the liturgical evidence, the Gothic subscriptions demonstrate the restricted knowledge of written Gothic – restricted to Arian clergy, and only to some of them – as well as the formulaic, archaic nature of this written language, and possibly also its sacral properties.

They also show that the Arian clergy in Italy could use this language to emphasize their difference from the rest of a Latin-speaking and Latin-writing society. Within the Gothic church of St. Anastasia, knowledge of written Gothic was restricted to the higher clergy, the priests and the deacons (and not all of the deacons), along with one scribe. The evidence of the subscriptions reinforces the picture given by the biblical and liturgical texts, that written Gothic was not used in the world of the Arian laity except when it was necessary to impress or overawe them, at masses and at solemn transactions involving the church or its members.[88]

THE ARIAN CHURCH AND THE CATHOLIC CHURCH IN ITALY

The history that allowed the Arian church to take the name Goth is clear. But why did it take the name Goth, aside from pride in the Arian

---

[87] Uppsala, University Library Cod. DG.1 (not in *Codices Latini Antiquiores*); the same scribe, PA Wiliarit 4 or "Viliaric magister antiquarius," may also have written the Latin Florence Orosius, Biblioteca Laurenziana 65.1 = CLA 3.298: Tjäder, "Der Codex argenteus in Uppsala und der Buchmeister Viliaric in Ravenna," pp. 143–64. On the *Argenteus* and the sacrality of writing, see Petrucci, "Aspetti simbolici," p. 836.

[88] Tjäder identified two other laymen who wrote in Gothic besides Gudilibus (who was actually a deacon). His evidence is to my mind entirely unconvincing, but must be noted, since it comes from the greatest authority on Latin papyri. See PA Latinus, Anonymus 1 and discussion there. In both cases, if they *did* know how to write Gothic, there is reason to suspect that they might have been former Arian clergy who converted to Catholicism, losing their clerical office in the process. But Tjäder's case is shaky. Of course, some laymen may have sufficiently close association with the church to learn the written Gothic language, just as some Carolingian

conversion of Goths and the memory of Ulfilas? After all, there was no need for Arians to use the Gothic Bible if they spoke Latin, although it should be pointed out that the Gothic glosses and the copying of the Bible do not prove that the Gothic Bible was used to the exclusion of all other bibles in Arian churches in sixth-century Italy. Nor was there a need to emphasize the memory of Ulfilas over that of other illustrious Arians of the past who were not associated with groups called Goths.

The Italian Arians assumed the name Goth in two contemporary contexts, political and cultural. The Catholic church claimed hegemony over all Christians; it was not content merely to be a majority church, and its theology did not allow it to be one. The secular rulers of Italy, Arian patrons back to the days of Ricimer, offered the Arian church a means to combat this hegemony – not with a hegemony of its own, as in Vandal Africa, but with a declaration of its right to exist, and its special identity in the Catholic-defined Christian Empire current in papal thought from Leo the Great to Gelasius. Furthermore, ethnographic ideology, spread both by the Catholic church (sporadically) and by Theoderic (once he got into power) offered a form of identity with which the Arian church was already associated: the name Goth and its various histories and meanings.

A decisive step was Theoderic's accession to rule over Italy. No minority church had a right to expect such largesse as he gave the Arian church. The king was deeply religious, and in the tradition of the Roman emperors, he made his religiosity known to his church through rich material gifts. Anyone who has visited Ravenna will have seen the splendid mosaics of Sant'Apollinare Nuovo and the Baptistery of the Arians. At least four other Arian church buildings existed in Ravenna; two of them were founded by Theoderic as well. The king commissioned magnificent manuscripts of the Gothic Bible. He endowed the church with land, and even ensured that some of its clergy received tax revenues as salary.[89] Most importantly, he instituted a policy of religious toleration that ensured the survival of a faith that certainly counted only a tiny minority of Italians as believers.[90]

---

noblemen learned how to write classicizing Latin. From these two questionable examples, however, one cannot argue that laymen apparently unassociated with the Gothic church knew how to write Gothic.

[89] Endowments: PA Unscila. Salary: PA Butila. Tax *professiones* transferred to the Arian church: *Var.* 1.26.3.

[90] On Theoderic's religious toleration, see ch. 2 above. On Theoderic's generosity to his church, see Wolfram, *Goths*, pp. 325–6; Moorhead, *Theoderic*, p. 94. My arguments on the relationship of Theoderic to the Arian church are an exact reversal of those of Hans von Schubert, "Arianismus," in *Reallexikon der germanischen Altertumskunde* 1, ed. Johannes Hoops, (1st edn, Strasbourg,

Theoderic, however, did not actively give the name Goth to his church.[91] No evidence whatsoever, including the inscription recording the foundation of Sant'Apollinare Nuovo,[92] indicates that he thought of his religion as the religion of the Goths.[93] In his ideology of social consensus, such an equation did not make any sense, and, as he must have realized, would have been political foolishness. His overtures to the papacy, his delicate behavior in the two Catholic schisms, perhaps also a decree prohibiting conversions to Arianism but allowing conversions to Catholicism, show that Theoderic was deeply concerned about the danger of alienating Catholics in his realm.[94] Of course, some scholars believe that he eventually did succeed in alienating them, at the very end of his reign. But damaging as the Boethius–John affair was, many Catholics stuck by the king.[95] Theoderic had gone out of his way to ensure that his religion would not divide his kingdom. A later Catholic source sums up Theoderic's policy virtually in his own terms,

---

1911–13), 120–1; Schubert, *Das älteste germanische Christentum oder der sogenannte "Arianismus" der Germanen* (Tübingen, 1909).

[91] He merely referred to "our religion": Moorhead, *Theoderic*, p. 92.

[92] F-S 181: Theodericus rex hanc ecclesiam a fundamentis in nomine domini nostri Iesu Christi fecit. (The church only gained its dedication to St. Apollinaris in the ninth century, after a four-century Catholic interlude as Sanctus Martinus in caelo aureo.)

[93] *Ecclesia nostra* in *Var.* 1.26.3, and *religio nostra* (compared with *religio vestra*) in a letter to the Catholic bishops in the Laurentian schism, *Anagnosticum regis*, p. 425, lines 16–18, the latter noted by Moorhead, *Theoderic*, p. 92. I do not think *noster* here can have the same force as *exercitus noster*, *Gothi nostri*, *miles noster*, which all refer to the army and have overtones explicitly laid out in *civilitas* rhetoric, which Arianism certainly does not. In specific cases, Theoderic spoke even more neutrally: in a letter to an Arian bishop, Theoderic was able to refer to *ecclesia vestra*, and, in another mentioning an Arian bishop, refers to the *ecclesia vir venerabilis Unscilae antistes* (*Var.* 2.18.2; 2.26.2, the latter the *ecclesia nostra* mentioned above).

[94] Moorhead, *Theoderic*, pp. 91–3, 95–6. During the autumn of 501, just after his letter accompanying the *maiores domus* to Rome in the Laurentian schism, Theoderic sent an *anagnosticum*, a dictated note, to the people, clergy and senate: *Anagnosticum regis = Acta synodi a. DI 5*, pp. 425–6; on its authorship, see Mommsen in *Acta synodi*, p. 417. Theoderic promises that he will not interfere; and in his own words ("haec cum diceret, ita proposuit similitudinem," runs the note; what follows, unlike the preceding part, is in short sentences, with no metaphor, resembling spoken language: ibid., p. 425, lines 23–6), points to the example of Aspar, who said that he would not make himself emperor, in order not to set a bad example. The text seems to suggest Aspar as a parallel for secular interference in ecclesiastical affairs, such as the restraint of the praetorian prefect Basilius in the papal election of 483, remembered by the synod of a year later. (*Acta synodi a. DII* §3, pp. 44–5.) Surely the answer is that Aspar, like Theoderic, was an Arian. The king thus raises the issue of his religion with infinite delicacy, under the guise of a promise that secular authorities would not interfere. The Catholic emperors had taken sides in ecclesiastical disputes, but as viceroys of God, they might claim such rights; Theoderic assumed no such privileges. (The comparison of Theoderic with Aspar has nothing to do with their "barbarianness": Aspar's son took the imperial-sounding name Iulius Patricius when he became Caesar, and promised to convert from Arianism to Catholicism should he become Augustus: PLRE2 Patricius 15.) On Aspar and Leo I after the death of Marcian, see Bury, HLREI: 314.

[95] Above, ch. 6.

clearly separating his ethnographic ideology from his personal religious beliefs:

Sic gubernavit duas gentes in uno, Romanorum et Gothorum, dum ipse quidem Arrianae sectae esset, tamen nihil contra religionem catholicam temptans.[96]

Theoderic must have realized that not all the people that he called Goths were Arians, and that he ran the risk of alienating his own following and his own army by implying that the two terms were congruent. The king's mother, and several other members of his family, were Catholic.[97] Some, if not most, of his following upon his arrival in Italy had surely been Catholics in the Balkans, even more numerous there than the believers in the Arian faith.[98] Absorption, recruitment, intermarriage and conversion would have diluted any Arian majority that may have existed. When we can see the religion of soldiers in Italy, we can see at least seven Catholic soldiers – and only three Arian soldiers, one of whom converted to Catholicism.[99]

Theoderic as leader of the army, the *exercitus Gothorum*, is thus not to be equated with Theoderic the Arian patron. For the king, *Gothus* meant first a soldier in his own following, and much later a member of an elect *gens* privileged by his own (Arian and Catholic) dynasty. In neither equation does *Gothus* mean or imply an Arian believer.

The assumption of the name *ecclesia Gothica*, though not unconnected with Theoderic's belief, looks like a unilateral move on the part of Arian churches in Italy, a move just as much related to their belief in the Ulfilan past and the sacrality of Gothic texts as to the advantages that Theoderic's generosity brought to them. It is thus precisely the opposite of Vandal Africa, where royal patronage and active persecution of Catholics gave the name *ecclesia Vandalorum* to the African Arian

---

[96] AV 60, and this in a source that later once uses the word *Romani* to mean "Catholics," on which, see below, pp. 267–8.

[97] See below, pp. 268–9.

[98] Zeiller, *Les origines chrétiennes des provinces danubiennes*, pp. 344–76. One must not exclude Bonosians, Nestorians or monophysites among Theoderic's following either.

[99] Catholic soldiers: PA **A**ra, Cyprianus, Ursus, **A**nonymi 20+, **A**malafridas, Gundila (converted from Arianism), probably also **R**omulus, Valentinianus. Given the association of Germanic names with soldiers, we can expect that many of the Catholics with Germanic names in PA III, table 8 were soldiers. Arian soldiers: **T**eia (military post uncertain), Triwila (also civilian), Gundila (converted to Catholicism); but the relatives of the post-Amal Arian Gothic kings listed at PA III, table 6 may indicate more Arians among soldiers than are certainly attested. The story of **R**iggo, Viliarid, **B**leda and **R**uderit in Gregory the Great suggests that they were Arian, but on Gregory's depictions of soldiers on the Gothic side in the Gothic Wars, see above, ch. 5, n. 154. On Arian soldiers, see also below, p. 272.

church[100] – while the cultural heritage of Arian Gothic texts and Ulfilas bestowed the name Gothic on their liturgy, as in Burgundy.[101]

At the time that the Arian church claimed the name Goth, the Catholic church under Gelasius was laying claim to the name Roman – and also laying claim to all Christians within the Roman Empire. Simultaneously, another trend within the papal church was to lay claim to the entire world as a potential Christian community. If the name "Goth" limited the claims of the Arian church, the name "Catholic" – universal – underlined the unlimited potential for correct belief and papal power that the Catholic church had inherited from Augustine, Prosper and Leo.

So long as political circumstances and the Acacian schism ensured toleration of Arians in Italy, the Italian Catholic hierarchy pursued a policy of pretending that such heterodoxy did not exist. By ignoring Arianism as a problem, it also arrogantly assumed that all Arians would become Catholic. When the Catholic church does admit that heterodoxy exists, it speaks of it in strictly doctrinal terms. Catholics usually refer to Arianism by such coyly neutral phrases as *alter communio* or *lex aliena*. Texts overtly hostile to Arianism use *Arrianus* or *hereticus*.[102]

In other words, until Vigilius, no Italian Catholic text allows that

---

[100] *Année épigraphique* (1968), no. 638: "Victorinus episcopus in pace Vandalorum;" Catholic ideologues called them "Arians" but identified the Arian church with the Vandal kings and their courtiers: Victor Vitensis, *Historia persecutionis* 1.23; 1.43; 2.8. A new study of Arianism in Vandal Africa might illuminate the ways in which provinces exercised their own influence on the development of their cultural history. The fierceness of the Vandal persecution of Catholics may have its roots in the fierceness of Christian division in Africa as much as in any culture carried by the Vandal kings themselves. Had not the Arian church learned its lessons from the strictly coercive and repressive Catholic church of Augustine, itself a legacy of the persecutions of the time of Cyprian and of the Donatists? On the rigor of African Christianity, see Markus, *Saeculum*, pp. 127–53; Markus, "Religious dissent in north Africa," pp. 146–9.

[101] On a Gothic language among African Arians, see ch. 3, n. 110, above. On Burgundy, see *Passio Sancti Sigismundi Regis* 4, ed. Bruno Krusch, MGH: SRM 2 (Hanover, 1888), p. 335, which calls Arianism "lex Gotica;" parallel noted by Moorhead, *Theoderic*, p. 95, n. 139, without reference to liturgy. This development may well be related to the Mediterranean circulation of Gothic liturgical texts discussed above. Burgundy had a greater number of ostentatious Catholics in its royal family than did Ostrogothic Italy, which perhaps made it difficult for the Arian church to aquire the name *ecclesia Burgundionum*; at any rate, the use of "Gothic" for the Arian faith there surely again shows the influence of the Ulfilan textual and historical heritage. On Catholics in the Burgundian royal family, see Ian Wood, "Avitus of Vienne: religion and culture in the Auvergne and the Rhône valley, 470–550," Diss., Oxford, 1980, pp. 150–2 (Chlotild, Crona, Theudelinda, Caratena and Sigismund, perhaps also Chilperic I and Gundioc; Theudelinda, Caratena and Sigismund all founded churches).

[102] *Alter communio*: Gelasius, JK 650 = *ep.* "Si conscientia" (Loewenfeld, *ep. in.* 9, p. 6). *Lex aliena*: Avitus, *ep.* 38. *Arrianus, hereticus*: LP and AV: see ch. 3 for references and for discussion of the nuances of hostility in these words.

Arriani are *Gothi*.[103] To allow such an identification would not only
have contradicted the ideology of Theoderic, the Goth qua Goth, but
would also have helped to exclude conversions to Catholicism by individuals labeled Goth by other criteria, such as military service. Since
the Catholic church assuredly desired Arian conversions to Catholicism,
it was not in its interest to associate the heresy with any group in Italy
whose members might convert, or with any group that already included
people who were demonstrably Catholic, such as Theoderic's mother.

It was the Byzantines, influenced by equations such as that of
Ambrose, who claimed that *Gotthoi* were *Arrianoi*. Justinian, like
Ambrose, employed classical ethnogeography and imperial victory
ideology to associate heresy with barbarians, who had therefore to be
conquered. Justinianic ideology, unlike Theoderican ideology, saw all
the inhabitants of the Empire as properly Roman and properly Catholic.
Such equations helped to justify the reconquest of Italy, and both Procopius and Justinian's generals used them in the Gothic Wars. So did
Pope Vigilius, who initially supported the reconquest and the notion
of a Catholic Christian Empire led by emperor and pope in tandem.
The equation of *Gotthoi* with *Arrianoi* by Justinian and Vigilius was
political, and could only occur in Italy once there was a chance of
forcing Arians to convert.[104] Revealingly, after the Wars were over, and
there were no more "Goths" in Italy, the Justinianic *reconciliatio* of Arian
church lands knew them as *ecclesiae Arrianorum*.[105]

The refusal of Theoderic and of Italian Catholics to equate the Arian
church with the Goths shows that the Arian church itself made that
identification, as the Arian texts suggest. But the generous patronage
of Theoderic, and the wide claims on Christianity made by Italian Catholics, provided new reasons for the Arian church to take on the name
Goth besides its reverence for the memory of Ulfilas.

---

[103] A single possible exception: Ferrandus, *ep. dogmatica* 1, col. 24, on Eugippius's theological
opponent, whom Ferrandus calls *arrianus comes Gothorum*. But we do not know whether Eugippius made this equation, or Ferrandus, who was then probably in exile in Sardinia from the
African Arian persecutions, and who was a member of a church that ideologically equated
Arianism with barbarians. Moreover, the force of *Gothorum* here is unknown: we must surely
translate "Arian count of the Goths," but "count of the Goths" could merely mean "army
officer" or even "military judge" (as in *Var.* 7.3). See further PA **Anonymus** 38.

[104] CT 1.5.12.17, from 527, exempting *Gothi foederati* from the severity of the new laws against
Arianism. Needless to say, there were Arians in the East who were not Goths, as even Justinianic propagandists such as Cyril of Scythopolis suggest (*Vita Sabae* 72 [176.4–5]: also Gepids
and Vandals, and Justinian's army included "Gepids"). We should probably see this law as
allowing *de facto* religious toleration of soldiers; Justinian's rhetoric does not allow him to equate
Arians with Romans (i.e. his subjects).

[105] *PItal* 2.32, from Ravenna in 560.

How was this minority church to identify itself? It called its own believers *Christiani* and Catholics "heretics" or "homoousians." But as an institution within Catholic Italian society, the name Goth provided many advantages. The church thus identified itself with the personal patronage and power of the king, and his ideology of Goths as a virtuous people, both under *civilitas* and in post-*civilitas* rhetoric. It distinguished itself, in an easy opposition inherited from classical ethnography, from the claims of the "Roman" church. It also denied that other title of its opponents, the "Catholic" church. As a minority Church of Saints, the Arians made no attempt at defining the universality of the world as Christians or as potential Christians; such notions were Augustinian in any case. It had long given up pretensions to being the church of the Roman Empire.

The name Goth allowed the Arian church in Italy to leave universalist pretensions and responsibilities, to the Catholics, while lending the Arians the prestige of Ulfilas and, paradoxically, of his evangelism, along with the prestige of Theoderic. The Arian assumption of the name Goth also played into the ethnographic-theogonistic heritage of Judaeo-Christian scripture, much used by persecuted religious groups in late antiquity. If Ulfilas was a Moses, then he led a chosen people, a people elected by God for right belief in a sea of gentiles. Such notions were hogwash to Augustine but informed conceptions of religious community among minority sects like the Novatians, and even continued to influence the Eusebian identification of "Roman" with "Christian" in the Eastern Empire. The tendency of some barbarian groups to adopt this language in the process of ethnogenesis (or ethnonym-genesis) provided further models. Theoderic's post-*civilitas* rhetoric suggests that the Goths were a chosen people. The Franks would eventually think in the same terms, on the basis of Clovis's conversion to Catholicism.

Rather than taking over a name of undisputed meaning, the Arian church lent new meaning to that name, by defining its own *congregatio fidelium*. The Arian church added to the complexity of the label "Goth" in sixth-century Italy the heritage of Ulfilan Christianity and its associated texts, along with the history of persecuted Arianism in the Roman Empire, and its associated texts. To some extent, the church was successful in claiming the name.[106] After the Byzantine invasion, of course, enemies of Arianism were happy to identify Arians as Goths – as a smear, in the sense of Ambrose and Justinian. The Gothic Wars ensured that the fate of the Arian church would be bound up with the

---

[106] Thus in doctrinally neutral texts like the Ravenna papyri we find the only non-Arian references to an *ecclesia Gothica*. This does not mean, of course, that all people who used the term believed that all Arians were Goths, any more than people necessarily believed that all soldiers were Goths.

fate of the Gothic kings, not only because of their Arianism, but because of their religious toleration, the opposite of the policy of Justinian. The equation passed down from the Gothic Wars to the Middle Ages.[107]

PERSONAL NAMES AND RELIGIOUS AFFILIATION AMONG ARIANS AND CATHOLICS

How did personal names reflect religion? For Christians, names could be a statement of belief. By the early sixth century, there existed a fund of ostentatiously "Christian" names from which to draw. The Bible provided the names of the prophets and the apostles. The history of the church contributed the names of martyrs and of other saints. Then there were "speaking names," like Clemens, Inportunus and Adeodatus, which expressed Christian humility, hopes, virtues or the patronage of the Lord.[108]

Even among committed Christians, however, the other meanings of names continued to influence naming practices, particularly familial, professional and prestigious meanings. Families with any pride of descent maintained a pool of names held by members of both sides of the family. Among the senatorial aristocracy, which continued to use multiple names for individuals, familial names were the rule. Professional names and *signa* or supernomina could indicate membership in burial clubs and fraternities, a practice perhaps encouraged by the heritability of professions in the late Roman Empire.[109] The praenomen or agnomen Flavius could be used by servants of the emperor, civilian and military, to the extent that it took on the meaning of rank grade, the so-called "Flaviate." Finally, names could indicate prestige. The number of people called Theodosius among all classes increases dramatically after the accession to power of the Theodosian dynasty.[110] People might use Germanic names enclosing the word "Goth," or derived from the Amal family and its dynastic propaganda.[111]

---

[107] Gregory the Great's *Dialogi* played a role in transmitting this equation, although even Gregory admits that there was a Catholic monk called a "Goth": PA Anonymus 21. Even this monk is naive and stupid.

[108] Danilo Mazzoleni, "Names, personal," in *The Encyclopedia of the Early Church*, ed. Angelo di Berardino, 1982, trans. Adrian Walford, 2 vols. (Cambridge, 1992), 2: 580. Mazzoleni's statement that "Christians (unlike Jews) attached no special importance to the eytmology of personal names" is immediately contradicted by the evidence that he presents, and it seems that the statement must be meant to refer to the church of the first three centuries and not subsequently – unless he means "etymology" specifically to refer to the scientific inquiry into the origin of words, rather than to "the meaning of words."

[109] On *signa*, professions and burial clubs, see Kajanto, *Supernomina*, pp. 17–18, 49–52 (only rarely burial clubs, against traditional scholarship on the subject).

[110] Compare PLRE1 s.n. Theodosius with PLRE2 and PLRE3 s.n. Theodosius.

[111] See ch. 3 above, pp. 99–100, though never enclosing the element "Amala" outside the Amal family.

Moreover, although sources usually only record one name, many people must have carried more. Indeed, it is difficult to know even when multiple names are recorded whether we have the full lot or not. We only know the full name of Flavius Triadius Marianus Michaelius Gabrielius Constantinus Theodorus Martyrius Iulianus Athanasius – honorary *magister militum* and honorary consul, *patricius, dux et augustalis Thebaidis* in the late 560s – because it is recorded in an Egyptian papryrus; elsewhere it is curtailed.[112] Athanasius's full name combines Christian names (of two or three sorts) with family names, as well as with the Flaviate and with the prestigious name of the emperor Constantine.

In senatorial families, the common name in use was the last name in the series. In other families, an appropriate single name might be used in circumstances appropriate for the meaning of the name, as we shall see, making it difficult to identify people whose multiple names may not be attested together. Bishops and priests, who in Italy seem to have jettisoned claims to family,[113] are never listed with more than one name, though they may have continued to possess such names.

The names of Catholic clergy in Ostrogothic Italy are extremely well attested, and none of them is Germanic. From synodal subscriptions, episcopal lists, inscriptions, letters and ecclesiastical histories are attested the names of hundreds of Catholic clergymen in Italy in the period from 489 to 554. Not one Catholic clergyman is attested with a Germanic name in this period, although they existed elsewhere.[114] The first

---

[112] PLRE3 Athanasius 3.

[113] As opposed to Gaul, where bishops went out of their way to publicize their noble birth and senatorial descent, on which see Heinzelmann, *Bischofsherrschaft*, *passim*; there is no evidence whatsoever to show such sentiments in Italy. See Lanzoni, *passim*, for metrical epitaphs of Italian bishops, which, unlike the Gallic ones, never refer to secular birth. Senators in Gaul looked to the ecclesiastical office when their access to imperial and curule dignities declined due to political changes; in Italy, such access remained open throughout the lifetime of the Ostrogothic kingdom, and in any case the senate maintained an institutional role in the church of the city of Rome. The result was that aristocrats entered the church in Italy for different reasons, and doubtless left more opportunities for ecclesiastical careers to non-senators. Brown, *Gentlemen and Officers*, pp. 181–4, suggests that because Italian senators never succeeded in dominating the bishoprics, senatorial families vanished from the Italian aristocracy. Further study of the differences between the Gallic and Italian episcopates would be useful.

[114] For example, the early sixth-century Albiso of Langres. They are not common in Gaul, perhaps due to similar distaste for Germanic–Gothic languages, but also perhaps because of the senatorial monopoly of the episcopate: see Amory, "Names, ethnic identity and community," pp. 24–5. The patriarch of Constantinople in 489, directly after the unfortunate Acacius, bore the illustrious Germanic name Fravitas, the name of the "Gothic" Flavius Fravitta, *magister militum per Orientem* between 395 and 400; see Cameron and Long, *Barbarians and Politics at the Court of Arcadius*, p. 252 (suggesting that the patriarch was the son or grandson of the *magister militum*). The patriarch was remembered favorably in late fifth-century Byzantium (Zosimus, *Historia Nova* 4.56, 5.20–2), and although Zosimus may have been a pagan, he was also anti-barbarian. Even in Vandal Africa, Fulgentius of Ruspe corresponded with an Abragila *presbyter.* Schanz-Hosius, pp. 578–80, no. a4.

Catholic bishop with a Germanic name appears in Vercelli in the early seventh century.[115] Some lower Catholic clergy with Germanic names appear at some point in the sixth century, most of them probably in the second half,[116] and the first to be definitely dated is the *lector* Amara of the church of Grado in 579, whose wife and daughters bore the Graeco-Latin names Antonia, Haelia and Mellita.[117]

The Catholic clergy may have *avoided* taking or using Germanic names, since two popes had fathers with Germanic names, since Germanic names were used elsewhere, and since Arian clergy *are* attested with Germanic names.[118] Popes are virtually the only clergy about whom we have any evidence as to family. That two out of fourteen sixth-century popes had fathers with Germanic names makes it reasonable to suggest that many more clergy who did not rise as high had Germanic names in their families. The proportion 2:14 is far larger than the proportion of Germanic names to Latin names attested in the whole period, including inscriptions, and far larger than the proportion of people in Theoderic's following to native Italians.

Catholic clergy could possess more than one name and could change

---

[115] Berardus of Vercelli, date uncertain, but several bishops after 541/556, so well after the end of Ostrogothic rule; Lanzoni 2: 1041–2: Berardus "è il primo nome teutonico certo, che s'incontra nelle liste episcopali d'Italia, dopo mezzo secolo di dominazione longobarda." Another possibility might be Fredianus or Frigidianus of Lucca, but his name is probably the Latin Frigidianus, dated to the Gothic Wars or the early Lombard period, and atttested in Gregory's *Dialogi*: Lanzoni 1: 590–2. Germanic names only attested in later medieval episcopal lists turn out to be obvious later interpolations matching the names of ninth- and tenth-century incumbents, e.g. Seufridus of Piacenza (supposedly 532, but a Seufridus held the see in 865 and Sigefredus in the tenth or eleventh centuries); similarly, Distaldus, Dodo, Francus and Sebaldus of Acqui; Adelbertus of Genoa; and Arimbertus, Lotarius, and Valfrancus of Belluno, respectively discussed by Lanzoni 2: 818, 829, 840, 906. Aside from much later evidence for the use of such names, and their even later attestation, none of these names is once attested in Ostrogothic Italy, although they became common in the Carolingian period and subsequently.

[116] See PA **A**cio and **B**erevulfus (date of the latter not certain, but if early sixth-century, probably an Arian priest for the reasons given here), and PA III, table 14. The late fifth century **G**uttus might be a Germanic name, but not with any certainty, and in any case he died only an acolyte. The date of **S**arabonus presbyter is uncertain, and it may be significant that his name seems to be an incoherent confusion of Latin and Germanic elements (q.v.). If contemporaries did not know whether Guttus or Sarabonus were Germanic names (as we do not), then there would have been less pressure for them to change them. The only possible exception is **T**ransmundus, who may have been *praepositus basilicae sancti Petri*. But whether he held this office is unclear from the fragmentary inscription, and the rank of the office in the clerical hierarchy is unknown; even if he did hold it, it could have been a lay position. The very shakiness of all this evidence, in light of the huge sample of names of Catholic clergy from the period, is telling.

[117] PA **A**mara 2, Antonia, Haelia, Mellita, thus thirteen years after the final defeat of the Gothic army, and at the very least nine years after Justinian's legislation banning the (Gothic) Arian church in Italy.

[118] Popes with fathers who had Germanic names: PA **B**onifatius (II) (father **S**igibuldus), **P**elagius (II), (father **U**nigildus). Arian bishops: PA **G**udila 2, **U**nimundus. Arian clergy: PA III, table 7.

their names. Pope John II was originally known as Mercurius. He took
the name John upon his consecration. It was, of course, the name of
an apostle, as well as that of the pope who had recently died in Theoderic's prison, John I. John II retained Mercurius as a *cognomen*.[119] That
name had obvious pagan connotations,[120] and was presumably considered inappropriate for the leader of the Catholic church. Since a
bishop of Castiglione in Latium bore the name Mercurius in the 490s
and in 501,[121] perhaps John had inherited it as a family name.[122]

Like John II, the two popes whose fathers had Germanic names,
Boniface II and Pelagius II, may have been conscious of the meaning
of names in their careers. It is notable that they both bore the names
of previous popes. The practice of popes taking new names upon consecration had not yet become general, and would not for some centuries
to come.[123] But the names of illustrious popes, many of whom became
saints after their deaths, were perhaps given to children destined for the
church, or used by pious families.

Another piece of evidence for the awareness of the meaning of names
among Catholic clergy is the use of the agnomen Caelius, a quasititle
used by the pope, certain bishops in Italy, and by certain priests in the
church of the city of Rome.[124] Its use was inconsistent,[125] but it seems
to have derived from the Caelian Hill at Rome, and to have indicated

---

[119] LP John II §1, 2: 285: Ioannes qui et Mercurius. An inscription in San Petro in Vincoli records
the name and title PAPA·N·IOHANNE COGNOME(N)TO MERCURIO EX SCE ECCL·
ROM· PREBYTERIS ORDINATO. Two other inscriptions, from the basilica of San Cle-
mente where John had been presbyter, were erected by MERCURIUS PB, one to Pope
Hormisdas two decades earlier. All these inscriptions: LP 2: 285, n. 1. It is clear that John was
called Mercurius before his consecration, and that after his consecration he retained the name
Mercurius.

[120] Although in Acts 14:12, Paul takes the name Mercurius. The Acts were the section of the
Bible dearest to the hearts of papal supremacists, and were shortly to be commissioned in epic
verse from Arator by Vigilius. It is just possible that Mercurius could have Christian connotations as a name in sixth-century Italy. Note an Apollo *v.d.* buried at Rome, interpreted by
Antonio Ferrua as "vir dei" rather than "vir devotus," ICUR n.s. 8, no. 22979, with comments
at p. 343. But note also that the fourth-century Arian bishop of Milan, Auxentius, changed
his name from Mercurinus (Wolfram, *Goths*, p. 78).

[121] Lanzoni I: 131.

[122] John was born in the city of Rome (LP John II §1, 1: 285 with n. 1), but this was close enough
to Castiglione for a relationship not to be ruled out.

[123] Felix III, Anastasius II, Felix IV and John III are the other examples from the period.

[124] *Acta synhodi a. CCCCXCVIIII*, pp. 405–6, nos. 1–4 (pope and bishops), pp. 410–11 (priests);
only the first in order of precedence receive the agnomen. Pope Felix III is attested as "Celius
Felix" by Agnellus, who was using an original document at this point: Agnellus, *Liber Pontificalis
Ravennatis* 60, p. 321, lines 12–13. On the original document, see Agnellus 60, p. 319, line 9.

[125] Used in the acts of the synod of Rome of 499, but not in those of 502. The announcement
of the clergymen attending the synod of 499, unlike the subscriptions to the acts, omits the
name Caelius: p. 399, nos. 1–3; p. 491, nos. 1–2.

high prestige and close ties to the papacy.[126] Mommsen suggests that it was the ecclesiastical equivalent of the Flaviate.[127]

That "Caelius" indicated prestige and closeness to the pope seems indisputable, but it may have had a further meaning intended to distinguish its users from Arian clergy. Both Aurelianus and Ecclesius of Ravenna, bishops in the late 510s and the early 520s respectively, used the agnomen Caelius. In the texts in which this survives, the two bishops also distinguished their church as the *ecclesia catholica*.[128] *Catholica* was not only a standard claim of universality, but a way to distinguish their church from the Arian church of Ravenna,[129] which, as we have seen, was wealthy and basking in the patronage of Theoderic. The very building projects of the two churches competed visibly across the center of the city of Ravenna, the Catholics on the west, the Arians on the east.[130] In 519–20, Arian–Catholic disputes fractured the populace of Ravenna down the middle, and Theoderic's court was implicated, at least in the mind of one later source.[131] Shortly thereafter, Ecclesius himself was sent to Constantinople by Theoderic in the entourage of the ill-fated Pope John I.[132] What better way for the Catholic bishops to assert their identity and their primacy, faced with the "Gothic" claims of the Arian church of Ravenna, than to use the name Caelius, with its links to the pope and the traditions of the city and church of Rome?

Such ideology does not seem far from equating "Catholics" with "Romans," of course, and it is easy to fall into the trap of assuming that the use of Latin names supported such an equation. In fact, the association was probably as much about the papacy as about the Empire. The Augustinian popes and Italian Catholics had a complex attitude toward the name "Roman." The city of Rome was as important to Catholic ideology as the Empire and the emperors of Rome, and it would shortly become far more important to the popes than either the Empire or the emperors. When we see texts like the *Anonymus*

---

[126] Note also a deacon or subdeacon of Rome with the suggestively geographical name Caelius Sabinus, ICUR n.s. 4, no. 11170, from the year 519.

[127] Mommsen, index to Cassiodorus, p. 490 s.v., with n. 1.

[128] Lanzoni 2: 757.

[129] Tjäder 2: 351 s.v. *ecclesia*; *Anneé épigraphique* 1988, no. 30: "Ypatius Galata praesb amicus bonoru sancte aeclesiae catholice Ravennat," probably late fifth century, found in the basilica of San Marco at Rome (p. 15). In Africa, where Catholics had to differentiate themselves also from Donatists, the label *ecclesia catholica* or *fides catholica* occurs even more frequently, e.g. *Revue des publications épigraphiques* 1916, nos. 81–3, 85; 1922, no. 25; 1924, no. 27; *Année épigraphique* 1968, no. 636; ILCV 1590A ("Peregrinus presuiter religionis katolice . . .").

[130] Deichmann, *Ravenna* 1:43–7.

[131] AV 81–2, on which see Moorhead, *Theoderic*, pp. 98–9.

[132] AV 90.

Valesianus, produced in the 540s or so, referring to the Catholics of Ravenna as "Romans,"[133] this may be a reflection of Justinianic ideology. But it could also stem from the association of Catholicism with the primacy of the see of Rome and the prestige of the popes.

The *Liber Pontificalis* uses *Romanus* in a strictly urban, *stadtrömisch* sense. Popes who are *natione Romanus* are so called because they were actually born in the city of Rome, as the parallel phrases *natione Sardus*, *natione Tuscus*, *natione Campanus* for other popes show, along with the further geographical details given with these general statements of origin.[134] The popes themselves used the wider, Eusebian connotations of *Romanus* as well, of course.[135] But the appeal of this formula lay partly in their close association with the ancient capital of the Roman Empire, and it is unclear how far these aspects of papal ideology trickled down within the Catholic hierarchy, let alone the mass of Catholic believers. Like "Goth," "Roman" had come to have many meanings.

Boniface II and Pelagius II, or their families, rejected the Germanic names of their fathers for Catholic clerical sons. This behavior mirrors the general awareness of Christian names among the popes and the Catholic clergy. We can see it more clearly in the naming behavior of Catholic laity, where the multiple names of individuals, and the names carried in their families, are more frequently attested.

The most prestigious conversion to (or baptism in) Catholicism, with accompanying adoption of a Graeco-Latin name, was Theoderic's mother Ereleuva:

Mater, Ereriliva dicta Gothica, catholica quidem erat, quae in baptismo Eusebia dicta.[136]

The Gothic name Ereleuva became the Catholic name Eusebia.[137] There are few clearer indications of the Catholic attitude toward Germanic names.[138] Ereleuva became a serious Catholic, as her correspon-

---

[133] AV 82, *omnis populus Romanus* referring back to *Christiani* of 81.

[134] *Natione Romanus*: LP Felix III §1, 1: 252; Anastasius II §1, 1:258, Boniface II §1, 1: 281, etc.; *natione Sardus*: Hilarus §1, 2: 242; Symmachus §1, 1: 260; *natione Tuscus*: Leo I §1, 1: 238; John I §1, 1: 275; *natione Campanus*: Hormisdas §1, 1: 269; Silverius §1, 1: 290. Further geographical specifications: John II §1, 1: 285: *natione Romanus, ex patre Proiecto, de Caeliomonte*; Hormisdas §1, 1: 269: *natione Campanus, ex patre Iusto, de civitate Frisinone*. See Duchesne in LP 1: 272, n. 1; 1: 282–3, nn. 1, 14.

[135] See ch. 6 above.

[136] AV 58. *Quae* is transmitted as *qui*, which Adams, in *The Text and Language*, pp. 32–3, argues can be used to refer to a feminine antecendent at this period.

[137] On the spelling of her name, see PA *Ereleuva.

[138] There is the faint possibility that Ereleuva was converted from paganism, not Arianism, as baptism might perhaps suggest: Moorhead, *Theoderic*, pp. 89–90. This paganism would not

dence with Pope Gelasius and a reference by Ennodius demonstrate.[139]
Other Catholics assuredly existed in Theoderic's family,[140] but the
only other dual name attested in a probable Catholic is that of his
daughter Ostrogotho Areagni, who married the Catholic Sigismund,
king of Burgundy. Her names make a statement of both Ostrogothic
and imperial allegiance. Areagni was an imperial name from the ancestry
of the Burgundian kings, the empress Ariadne, wife of Zeno and then
Anastasius I. The empress Ariadne was also a friend of Theoderic's sister,
and was known as a devout Catholic who venerated African refugees
from Arian persecution. Thus the Greek name Areagni (Ariadne) may
reflect a baptism in or conversion to Catholicism appropriate for a
daughter who married a Catholic monarch.[141]
There are three other examples of Catholics with dual names. A
Catholic church assistant named Livania also had the Christian vituperative name Simplex. A certain Gundeberga also bore the name Nonnica, probably meaning "nun." The brother of a Catholic woman in

have been the unattested "Germanic" religion imagined by Bierbrauer, cited by Moorhead,
on the basis of eagle brooches and suchlike: "Aspetti archeologici di Goti," p. 450 (imagining
that a Germanic pagan past was revealed in syncretism with Arianism via eagle brooches);
Moorhead, *Theoderic*, p. 89 with n. 108 (tentatively). It would have been a rural Roman or
Hellenizing religion, presumably like that from which the Sardinian pope Symmachus had
been baptized, Duchesne in LP 1: 263, n. 1, *ex paganitate*, (decades before he became pope,
one assumes). On the other hand, with no evidence whatsoever for paganism in Italy or the
Balkans at this time, outside the antiquarian habits of the senators of the city of Rome, it is
probably safer to regard Ereleuva's baptism as being from Arianism. Despite the rulings of
canon law on this point, rebaptism for Arians seems to have been common. Or else, given
Ereleuva's age (born in the 430s at the latest), she may have been waiting for adult baptism,
as was the custom among uncommitted Christians in the time of Augustine. Finally, there is
the possibility that she had been baptized a Catholic at birth, receiving one name from her
family, one name from the Catholic church; a conversion is not required. We badly need a
new study of baptism, rebaptism and the practice of baptismal names, attested also, for example,
in Belisarius's rebaptism and renaming of his adopted son Theodosius (from Arianism ["Euno-
mianism"]: PLRE3 Theodosius 8; Procopius, SH 1.15–16); the recent book by Peter Cramer,
Baptism and Change in the Early Middle Ages c. 200–c.1150 (Cambridge, 1993), ignores the subject,
and, indeed, seems notably weak on the "early" Middle Ages as opposed to the Carolingian
period and the twelfth century, despite the claims of its title; cf. the review by Carol Harrison,
Early Medieval Europe 3 (1994), 78–9.

[139] PA ★Ereleuva.

[140] Certain: PA Amalafridas, ★Matasuentha, ★Anonyma 3 (the latter two possibly through conversion upon marrying Catholic husbands); probable: ★Audefleda (the sister of the Catholic
Clovis), ★Trasimundus; possible: ★Amalaberga, ★Anonyma 4, perhaps even Ostrogotho's
mother ★Anonyma 1; on their Catholicism or possible Catholicism, see their individual entries
in the PA.

[141] PA ★Ostrogotho, with the lengthy and complex argument there. The empress Ariadne venerated Catholic refugees from Arian persecutions in Africa: Victor Vitensis, *Historia* 3.30. There
are many similar political name changes among imperial families of the East at this time (Aspar–
Iulius Patricius, Basiliscus–Leo, Tarasicodissa–Zeno, Lupicina–Euphemia, Tiberius–Constantine). "Areagni" is a frequent Latin spelling of the empress's name this time, e.g. in AV,
Jordanes and Victor Tonnennensis (references at ★Ostrogotho).

Ravenna in 553, in a family otherwise bearing Germanic names, bore the Germanic name Ademunt alongside the Christian apostolic name Andreas.[142]

Of forty-six possible Catholics with Germanic names, twenty-five had Graeco-Latin names in their families. But in virtually every case where we have more than one attested member of a Catholic family that includes Germanic names, that family also has Graeco-Latin names.[143] This situation may reflect competition between Catholic Christian names and family names as much as intermarriage; that is to say, Arian–Catholic assimilation as much as settler–native intermarriage. Elsewhere in Europe, there is similar evidence for dual or changed names for Catholics with Germanic names in their families.[144]

The naming behavior of Arians was entirely different. For Arian believers, Germanic and Graeco-Latin names coexisted as a *Christian* fund of names upon which to draw. The fragment of the Gothic calendar of saints and martyrs, produced in the early fifth century is, of course, preserved in a sixth-century manuscript along with parts of the Gothic Bible. The Graeco-Latin and biblical names in the Calendar were transliterated into written Gothic, but the Calendar itself may have been translated from a Greek original anyway.[145] It contains the Germanic names Frithareikeis, Werekan and Batwin, "among the many martyrs in *Gutthiudai*." It also contains the Graeco-Latin and biblical names Kustanteinus (Constantine), Daurithaius (Dorotheus, patriarch of

---

[142] PA **S**implex nomine Livania, **G**undeberga quae et Nonnica, **A**demunt qui et Andreas, with discussions there.

[143] PA III, tables 8 and 11: the only possible exception is the family of PA <Fravi>ta, which included one woman with the name **M**ustila and may have included another with the name **M**ustela, the former spelling of which implies a Germanic name, the latter a Latin or at any rate non-Germanic name; see further Mustila, Mustela. On families attested, see PA Totals (94 per cent have both Gothic and Roman criteria of identity). Further examples, possibly from after 554, of Catholic families with both Germanic and Graeco-Latin names, include the family of **A**mara 2 (with **A**ntonina, **H**aelia and **M**ellita) and Gainus of Parenzo, whose wife may have been called Renata (see under **A**cio; Brown, *Gentlemen and Officers*, p. 260 s.n. Gainas). These are from 579 and after 560 (Grado and Parenzo) respectively, but the families may have been living in Italy under Ostrogothic rule. Due to the question of their presence in Italy 489–554, they are not included in PA III, tables 8 and 11.

[144] In Gaul in the 540s, the daughter of Ansemundus of Vienne, Remila *vocabulo* Eugenia, had taken a name particularly suitable for a nun; she was to be abbess of a new monastery; see the *Donatio Ansemundi*, ed. Patrick Amory, *Francia* 20.1 (1993), 163–83, and Amory, "Names, ethnic identity and community," pp. 27–8 with nn. 186–9.

[145] Heather and Matthews, *The Goths in the Fourth Century*, p. 129. The Calendar's transmission of Gothic names may not be consistent anyway, to judge from the spellings of Batwin (Bathouses) and Werekan (Werkas) in the Gothic Martyrology (a), p. 126 – although that is a Greek text as it stands. *PItal* 34 also suggests that Germanic onomastic orthography was particularly inconsistent. Only one piece of evidence shows transliteration of Graeco-Latin into Gothic in sixth-century Italy: the *Kaballarja* (Caballaria) of *PDip* 118, on which, see above.

Constantinople), Filippaus (the apostle Philip) and Andriins (the apostle Andrew).[146] A lay martyr in fourth-century *Gothia* already possessed the biblical name Silas.[147]

The Ravenna papyri show us Arian clergy with Germanic, Graeco-Latin and biblical names.[148] These names can be Christian or family names. The two deacons of 538 had Germanic names.[149] Of the nineteen attested clergy of St. Anastasia, fifteen had Germanic names,[150] one of these also a biblical name,[151] and one also a Latin name.[152] Four had Latin names only. Of the five Latin names, three are Christian,[153] and two probably familial.[154] The father of the cleric called Minnulus and also Willienant bore the Christian theophorous name Christodorus.[155]

Since the five other Arian clerics attested in Italy all bore Germanic names,[156] it is clear that members of the Gothic church preferred Germanic names to Graeco-Latin or biblical ones, but could use the latter as well, even in the same individual, thus laying claim to extra-Gothic Christian (and Greek or Latin Arian Christian) tradition. As we saw above, these clerics were aware of the Gothic–Arian connotations of Germanic names, transliterating their names into Gothic, or choosing to sign with their Germanic names even when they subscribed in Latin. The attitude of Catholic clergy toward Germanic names could have influenced their behavior on this point. But although Arian clergy preferred Germanic names, they had no need to reject Graeco-Latin or biblical ones, many of which existed in their Christian tradition as well. They did not need to make as much a point of names, and the three clergymen who are announced by Graeco-Latin names and also sign with them perhaps had only these names.[157]

---

[146] Gothic Calendar, pp. 128–9. See also PLRE2 Patricius 15. On the possible meanings of *Gutthiu-dai* (*Gothia*), see above, p. 244 with n. 37.

[147] Ed. H. Delehaye, "Saints de Thrace et de Mésie," *Analecta Bollandiana* 31 (1912), 279 = Heather and Matthews, trans., Gothic Martyrology (a), p. 126.

[148] On the following, see PA III, table 7.

[149] PA Alamud, Gudilibus.

[150] PA Amalatheus, Costila, Danihel/Igila, Gudelivus 2, Guderit, Hosbut, Minnulus/Willienant, Mirica, Optarit, Sindila, Suniefridus, Theudila, Wiliarit 3, Wiliarit 4, •••la.

[151] PA Danihel/Igila.

[152] PA Minnulus/Willienant.

[153] PA Benenatus, Paulus, Petrus.

[154] PA Minnulus (also called Willienant), Vitalianus.

[155] PA Christodorus.

[156] PA Berevulfus, Butila, Gudila 2, Unimundus, Unscila.

[157] Contra Kampers, "Anmerkungen," p. 146; although Petrus and Paulus *could have* replaced "original Germanic names," perhaps also Benenatus, there is no reason to think this about Vitalianus and Minnulus. In fact, there is no evidence to suggest that any of them changed their names – it is perfectly possible to imagine Arian Christians christening their children Petrus and Paulus!

Of Arian laymen, one, a cousin of two Arian clergymen in Ravenna, bore the Graeco-Latin saint's name Anastasia, to whom her cousin's Arian church in Ravenna was dedicated, and who was the center of an Arian cult in Constantinople.[158] With this one exception, the attested sixteen Arian laymen had Germanic names. But eleven of these were members of royal families. Three of the other five were soldiers, among whom, as we have seen, Germanic names were common for different reasons.[159] The prominent possession of Latin names among Arian clergy implies that they were probably even more common among Arian laity.

We know that names were meaningful from general behavior. The anonymous Arian text produced in the Balkans in the 440s clearly associates the choice of Germanic names with soldiers.[160] No Germanic names appear among the Catholic clergy of Italy. The Gothic clergy of St. Anastasia chose to sign with their Gothic names, not their Latin ones. None of the Gothic subscriptions to that document refers to the *ecclesia legis Gothorum* mentioned by the Latin subscriptions: the very Germanic language of the Gothic subscriptions specified the Arian church sufficiently. Later Catholic possessors of the Arian Latin sermon collection of Verona rubbed out the Gothic glosses. The very language and lettering of Gothic carried connotations of Arianism;[161] in fact, this written language had had no other connotation or function at all in Ostrogothic Italy. For Catholic clergy and some believers, this taint carried over to Germanic names. There may have been many more people among the Catholic clergy who were considered Goths, or who counted Goths in their families, than is visible from the evidence of names, and we again see reactions to ideologies of identity and community when people changed their personal names.

RELIGIOUS FAITH AND OTHER CRITERIA OF GOTHIC IDENTITY

Soldiers, defined as Goths by Theoderic, included as many Catholics as Arians, so far as our evidence goes.[162] Many of these had Latin names;

---

[158] PA **Anastasia**; Kampers, "Anmerkungen," p. 146, though, against Kampers, she could have had this name from birth: there is no reason to postulate a change from an unattested Germanic name. I am unconvinced by Kampers's suggestion, that **Agata**, daughter of **Gattila**, was an Arian due to the existence of a church in Rome and a village near Benevento both called Sant'Agata dei Goti (resting on arguments of Zeiller), on which, see **Agata**.

[159] PA III, table 6. If Gregory the Great correctly depicted **Riggo**, **Viliarid**, **Ruderit** and **Bleda** as heretics – only implied by their behavior in the hagiography, not explicitly stated – then we can add four more soldiers. But his depiction is suspect for reasons stated above, n. 107.

[160] See above, ch. 3.

[161] Gryson, *Le recueil arien*, pp. 70–1.

[162] See n. 99, above.

the above argument suggests that they might have been changed from Germanic names, or selected in lieu of Germanic names from the family fund of names, but they may also have always had Latin names.

Although changing one's name to a Graeco-Latin name, or adding a new name, might indicate a change in faith, plenty of Catholics retained their Germanic names despite their Arian connotations. This was true in circles very close to the king, in his palace on the Arian side of Ravenna with its attached Arian palace church, today Sant'Apollinare Nuovo. The Catholicism of advisors like Cassiodorus, Liberius and Cyprian is not in doubt. But we also find the Catholic Seda, eunuch and *cubicularius regis Theoderici*, buried in the Catholic cathedral at Ravenna.[163] We must assume that members of the royal family who were Catholic, like Ereleuva, walked across town to worship, unless there was an undiscovered Catholic chapel also attached to the palace.

Other Catholics with Germanic names included Ennodius's correspondents Alico and the Roman senator Meribaudus, who may have inherited his name from the fifth-century panegyricist of Aetius.[164] A number of Catholics with Germanic names were buried in the churches of Rome.[165] Others were buried at Catholic churches in Split,[166] in Milan,[167] Modena,[168] Potenza,[169] Catania,[170] and, with local patronage over three generations, at Como.[171]

People with Germanic names made donations to the Catholic church in Ravenna,[172] moved in circles with powerful Catholics,[173] and witnessed documents of sale.[174] In the Gothic Wars, we can generally only see the Catholicism of soldiers on the Byzantine side, who are attested in other sources besides Procopius, but of these, two with Germanic

---

[163] PA Liberius, Cyprianus, Seda; cf. also Ennodius's relative Senarius, whose name is probably Germanic, an ambassador of Theoderic and a Catholic.

[164] PA Alico, Meribaudus.

[165] PA Mustila and her husband <Fravi>ta, also their possible daughter Mustela, in St. Peter's; Dumilda at San Paolo-fuori-le-mura.

[166] PA Ariver.

[167] PA Manifrit.

[168] PA Gundeberga quae et Nonnica.

[169] PA Simplex nomine Livania.

[170] PA Iohannes I, son of Ustarric.

[171] PA Guntelda, Basilius and Guntio.

[172] PA Hildevara, Ranilo and Felithanc.

[173] PA Thulgilo, whose sale of land was witnessed by the Catholic banker Iulianus, who built the churches of San Vitale, San Apollinare in Classe and San Michaele in Africisco, on whom see PLRE3 Iulianus 7.

[174] PA Eusebius-Riccitanc.

names and Italian connections were devout Catholics.[175] Gundila, once
he converted to Catholicism, does not seem to have changed his name,
but he became a Catholic church patron in his city of Nepi.[176]

The various other examples of mixtures of Latin and Germanic names
within families may or may not indicate religious affiliation, just as they
may or may not indicate military profession.[177] Names alone cannot
identify a Goth or a Roman, just as Arianism alone, or military profession alone, cannot identify a Goth or Roman.[178] Once more, the
evidence suggests that the words Goth and Roman were ideological
constructs defined differently at different times.

Even the spoken Gothic language, which may still have had some
recognizable relationship to the written language used in Gothic liturgy,
is attributed only to Catholics (outside the royal family). The Gothic-
speaking Byzantine general Bessas was probably a moderate monophysite.[179] The family of Cyprian were devout Catholics.[180]

Arianism looms large in the sources because of ideology and because
royal patronage ensured that its architecture and manuscripts would
remain conspicuous. Despite its impact on the use of personal names,
it seems likely that most people who were considered Goths, like most
people in Italy, were or became Catholics.

CONCLUSION

In people of both faiths, changing one's name or adding a new name
shows the influence of competing ethnographic ideologies in the most
complex way. Catholics rejected Arian names because the Arian church

---

[175] PA **A**malafridas and **A**sbadus; on the Italian connections of Asbadus, see also ch. 5 above (he
might have served on the Gothic side at one point).

[176] PA **G**undila and ch. 5 above.

[177] PA III, table 11; most of these, though not all, are also listed by Kampers, "Anmerkungen,"
p. 144.

[178] The statement of Kampers, "Anmerkungen," p. 143, that Goths took Roman names but
Romans did not take Gothic names (similarly Moorhead, *Theoderic*, p. 86) is obviously nonsense
if names are already their criterion used to identify "Goths" and "Romans," and is contradicted
by his own statement that "name-giving among the Ostrogoths was . . . influenced by the late
antique world [namely giving Greek and Latin names]" (p. 147). As we have seen, giving
names and changing names could be strategic responses to ideology. If Ustarric was the father
of Iohannes, but Basilius was the father of Guntio, who was the Goth and who was the
Roman?

[179] If he was the Bessas *comes* who received a letter from Jacob of Sarug before 521, as seems
likely: PA **B**essas, PLRE2 Bessas; on Jacob's doctrines, see J. Gribomont, "Jacob of Sarug," in
Encyclopedia of the Early Church 1: 429.

[180] PA **C**yprianus, **O**pilio, **A**nonymi 20+, deduced from the behavior of Opilio, which seems safe;
even hostile sources do not call Cyprian an Arian.

had gathered to itself a religious heritage associated with the name Goth and an archaic Germanic language. The religious meaning of names competed additionally with the other meanings of names: professional, familial and prestigious. Only Catholic clergy placed primary importance on religious names. Among other people, and even within families, names were given for both religious and secular reasons.

Although ethnographic ideologies influenced religious behavior, they did not succeed in making everyone alter their behavior according to those ideologies. Even in the Arian church itself, the term Goth does not acquire the full personal meaning that it does in the ideologies of Theoderic and Justinian. As a group, the clergy of St. Anastasia belongs to the *ecclesia legis Gothorum* or the *ecclesia Gothica*. But this church is not a "church of Goths," but a "church of the Gothic belief." The final emphasis is on the inherited Ulfilan and Arian tradition, summed up by the phrase *lex Gothorum*.

No individual is called *Gothus* just because he was an Arian, even the clergymen of St. Anastasia for whom the word Goth and its religious connotations were so important. By the same token, no one called himself *Romanus* only because he was a Catholic believer. The words can in some cases indicate religious groups, but do not descend to the level of individual consciousness, so far as our evidence goes, and our Catholic evidence is full indeed.

The name Goth appealed to the Arian church in Italy as a means of preserving its identity. This statement is an exact reversal of the traditional interpretation of the "church of Goths." The story of the transformation of Italian Arians into the *ecclesia legis Gothorum*, with its preservation of the first written Germanic texts, is extraordinary. It demonstrates the power of ethnographic names, and the diversity of culture within the Roman Empire that we are rarely privileged to see. The ideology deployed by the Arian Gothic churches of Italy allowed them to define their community by history and current circumstances in opposition to the overpowering claims of the majority Catholic church in Italy. In doing so, it influenced the behavior of the Catholic church and Catholic believers, as well as the behavior of members of its own faith.

That the Arian church did not go beyond a religious community may be a result of its own ecclesiology. For more than a century, Arianism had been a minority persecuted faith, with an exalted idea of itself as an elect community. There was the early example of Ulfilas, but he operated in a time when Arianism was the religion of Roman emperors. The Arian church in Italy did not evangelize, and indeed, Theoderic seems to have discouraged any evangelism that it wanted to do.

Finally, the failure of the Arian Gothic church to grow beyond a religious community shows the power of other affiliations in Italy among people called Goths. There were always strong incentives to convert to the faith of the majority, or to stay in that faith if one was born into it. The Arian religious definition of Goth remained another of the overlapping circles within which Italians could live.

Chapter 8

THE ORIGIN OF THE GOTHS AND BALKAN MILITARY CULTURE

If the term "Goth" in Italy was a claim or an ideological label for a disparate collection of changing individuals, who were the "Goths" who crossed the Isonzo to arrive in Italy in 489? Was there an original Balkan-based ethnic or cultural grouping characterized by the traits later considered "Gothic" under Theoderic and Justinian? What was this group, which may have had more internal cohesion than the various communities called *Gothi* in the subsequent decades of Italian history?

Although we know too little about the Theoderican Goths of the Balkans to judge them as we can the Goths of Italy, the grouping of 489 is not likely to have possessed a discrete ethnicity in the sense of consciousness of common descent. Like most of his Goths, Theoderic grew up in imperial provinces, and he seems to have recruited followers in Pannonia and Moesia just as he later did in Italy. The prosopography of Italian Goths shows diversity from the 490s onward. Theoderic's Gothic ideology would not emphasize descent until thirty years later, in the 520s.

What about culture? If many of the cultural traits associated with *Gothi* in ethnographic texts are drawn from the classicizing discourse of ethnography, such as ferocity or illiteracy, others were clearly present in Theoderic's followers upon their arrival in Italy. These include the occasional use of a Germanic language, of personal names of Germanic origin, occasional belief in the Arian heresy to which Theoderic subscribed, and the military profession.

None of these traits was in itself new or unfamiliar to Italians, as we have seen.[1] Unfortunately, the philological construct "Germanic culture" has encouraged historians to imagine these traits as originally part of one, unified culture or civilization, assumed to have existed in pristine form long ago, and now broken down by contact with the Roman Empire.[2] But in southern Europe, Germanic language and Arian belief

---

[1] Germanic tongue: ch. 3; Arian heresy: ch. 7. For a discussion of other cultural traits frequently, and wrongly, considered "Gothic" by modern commentators, see appendix 4 below.

[2] See appendix 2 below.

can more profitably be seen as part of the diversity within the Empire itself, and on its fringes, here specifically the frontier culture of Balkan warbands.

The two unifying and peculiar characteristics of Theoderic's Goths in 489 were their military profession and their immediate regional origin: the Balkan provinces of the Roman Empire. The frontier armies of the fifth- and sixth-century Balkans produced a powerful aristocracy of their own, and this aristocracy evolved within a varied frontier milieu that included Germanic, Latin and Greek, bilingualism, hybrid personal names, floating ethnographic labels and religious heterodoxy.

Cultural traits associated with the Balkan military milieu drifted throughout the Mediterranean with the widespread service of these soldiers in the Roman army and their own movements and migrations, first during the reigns of the non-military Theodosian emperors at Constantinople (395–450), and then during a period during which every emperor came from the military, and most from Balkan military families (450–582, 602–10). Chapter 5 discussed the striking similarities between the Gothic and Byzantine armies during the Gothic Wars that already existed prior to the defections in both directions. These similarities reflect not only the similarities in the life of professional soldiers in the late Roman Mediterranean, but also the Balkan history and background of many of those soldiers. This regional and professional context sheds much light on the fortunes of Theoderic and the label "Goth" in Italy, as well as the ideological contests in which Italy and Constantinople later found themselves.

THE BALKAN MILITARY IN THE FIFTH AND SIXTH CENTURIES

The Balkan frontier military milieu from which Theoderic's Goths arrived in Italy was as diverse as the fifth- and sixth-century Balkan provinces themselves. We have seen that Vitalian, Mundo, Bessas and the Scythian monks displayed the same kind of blurry ethnographic identity that we see later in Ostrogothic Italy. In the exceedingly powerful and exceedingly mixed regional professional group of Balkan soldiers, dividing people into static collectivities of "barbarians," "Goths" or "Romans" is even less useful than in Italy. We need to know why people called people "Romans" or "barbarians," and why individuals might want to claim one name or the other. The demands of elite culture in Constantinople and the Hellenistic cities of the Mediterranean coast forced all kinds of difficult changes and adjustments, most spectacularly, as I shall suggest, in the case of Justinian and Jordanes.

The Balkans were a liminal region, being both the geographical obstruction and the connection between East and West, between Mediterranean and *barbaricum*. Names and languages were particularly mixed. We find Germanic–Greek hybrid names, and families with both Germanic and Greek names.[3] A fourth or fifth-century Moesian family used both Germanic and Latin names; the father served in a regular unit of the Roman army.[4] There are bilingual Greek and Latin inscriptions.[5] Beneath all this move Thracian and Illyrian substrata, attested in personal names if not language; Illyrian may have survived in isolated areas to produce modern Albanian.[6]

Multiple allegiances and identities reflect the variety of languages and names among the Balkan soldiers who began to dominate the Eastern Roman armies from the late fifth and early sixth centuries. These provinces suffered decades of invasion, civil war and rebellion,[7] resulting in the destruction of cities and the construction of fortified villages.[8] The historic economic links of Thrace with Constantinople were severed. Thracian peasants might ally with "barbarian" warbands. The Balkans provided private armies for the Byzantine generals who came from those regions, men whose loyalty to their leader followed local and

---

[3] Hybrid: PLRE3 Gibastes, from Axiopolis (Scythia), with a daughter named Anthusa; Gibastes may have been *comes et dux Scythiae*, probably in the sixth century. Mixed in families: PLRE3 Alziola *numerarius*, with daughter Bizantia, in sixth-century Thrace.

[4] *Année épigraphique* 1976, no. 617: In hoc tumulum est positus Terentius filius Gaione annorum uiginti cinque militans inter sagittarios iuniores (with comments at p. 174, from Tomi in Scythia).

[5] PLRE2 Euphrasius 2 = *ILCV* 117, from Split; CIL 3.2657 and 1032 from Dalmatia, dating from 435, with Zeiller, *Les origines chrétiennes dans le province romaine de Dalmatie*, Bibliothèque de l'Ecole des Hautes Etudes: Sciences historiques et philologiques 155 [Paris, 1906], p. 145; CIL 3.9534 from Dalmatia, dating from the sixth century (with ibid., p. 158).

[6] Dimiter Detschew, *Die thrakischen Sprachreste*, Österreichische Akademie der Wissenschaften, philosophisch-historische Klasse: Schriften der Balkankommission, Linguistische Abteilung 14 (Vienna, 1957); Anton Mayer, *Die Sprache der alten Illyrier* 1, *Einleitung, Wörterbuch der illyrischen Sprachreste*, Österreichische Akademie der Wissenschaften, philosophisch-historische Klasse: Schriften der Balkankommission, Linguistische Abteilung 15 (Vienna, 1957). On Albanian, see John Wilkes, *The Illyrians* (Oxford, 1992), pp. 278–80 (the current language, whatever its origins, contains borrowings from Latin and Slavic).

[7] Paul Lemerle, "Invasions et migrations dans les Balkans depuis la fin de l'époque romaine jusqu'au VIIIe siècle;" *Revue Historique* 211 (1954), 265–308; *Villes et peuplement dans l'Illyricum protobyzantin*, Collection de l'Ecole Française de Rome 77 (Rome, 1984). Illyricum, of course, was the focus of wars between East and West from the time of Stilicho to that of Theoderic; from the 400s, parts of it were effectively independent of either Ravenna or Constantinople, under Attila, Nepos, Marcellinus of Salona, Theoderic, Thraustila and Mundo. On Illyricum's anomalous position in the late Roman polity, see Emilienne Demougeot, "Le partage des provinces de l'Illyricum entre la *pars Occidentis* et la *pars Orientis*, de la tétrarchie au règne de Théodoric," in *La géographie administrative et politique d'Alexandre à Mahomet* (Leiden, 1981), pp. 229–53, and Stein, "Untersuchungen zur spätrömischen Verwaltungsgeschichte," pp. 347–80.

[8] V. Velkov, "Les campagnes et la population rurale en Thrace au IVe–VIe siècles," *Byzantinobulgarica* 1(1962), 31–66.

economic loyalties as much as ethnographic group-names.[9] Centralizing imperial authority had retreated from the Balkans, if only in the social sense: "Son territoire n'y est pas encore amputé, mais sa société, celle que nous étudions, n'y est plus tout à fait elle-même, surtout après 550."[10] In this milieu, available allegiances and identities included groups called *Romani*, *Gothi*, *Gepidae*, *Langobardi*, *foederati*, the following of Vitalian, the following of Attila (*Attilani*), or simply, perhaps, *antiqui barbari*; any of these might indicate imperial military service whether directly or via an effectively private army; only Attila's confederation was explicitly opposed to the emperor, and its remnants actively sought imperial service.[11]

As in Italy, a survey of individuals illuminates the choices available. Two of the most well-known late fifth-century Balkan soldiers, with the same Germanic name, were Theoderic Strabo (a Latin nickname) and Theoderic the Amal, who both led groups claiming the name "Goth" in the 470s. The origin of each is far from clear.[12] But whatever the later claims in Jordanes about their dynastic histories extending back through the confederation of Attila to the famous Gothic leaders of the late fourth century, both these men owed their immediate power to their command over soldiers and the imperial patronage, titulature and employment which both of them constantly struggled to attain. Both could or would claim relationships to the fifth-century Roman military aristocracy.[13]

The two Theoderics competed with similar warlords who led groups with or without ethnographic names. A certain Bigelis is called *Getarum rex* by Jordanes; he was killed by Leo's *magister militum* Ardabur probably

---

[9] Evelyne Patlagean, *Pauvreté économique et pauvreté sociale à Byzance, 4e–7e siècles*, Civilisations et Sociétés 48 (Paris, 1977), pp. 303–5, especially on economic reasons for Thracian support for Vitalian.

[10] Patlagean, *Pauvreté économique et pauvreté sociale*, p. 307.

[11] On Vitalian, see ch. 4, to which add the discussion of his nephew John in ch. 5; on *Attilani*, see PA Mundo; on two or more groups called *Gothi* in the late 400s, see below; on *antiqui barbari* (perhaps simply a description of taxable status), *Var.* 5.14.6, see Šašel, "Antiqui Barbari," pp. 125–36 and the discussion at ch. 3, n. 34.

[12] The two Theoderics were not related, despite Wolfram's arguments on this front (unless Wolfram means that Theoderic the Amal later argued that he was related to Strabo in order to gain legitimacy over Strabo's following): on this, and on the confused origins of these groups in general, see Heather, *Goths and Romans*, pp. 240–71, esp. pp. 251–3, the most sensible discussion of these events.

[13] On the importance of Roman titulature for legitimacy, see Wolfram, "Gotische Königtum und römisches Kaisertum," pp. 1–28 (the importance of *gens* and dynastic claims diminishes to vanishing point if Jordanes is left out of the equation: on Jordanes, see below); on the relationship between the *reges* and the military aristocracy, see Demandt, "Magister militum," cols. 785–6.

in the late 460s.[14] Jordanes makes no attempt to fit him into the history of his other groups called Goths or into the history of the Amals.[15] If he really did claim the name Goth, then he was simply another warlord out for himself. At the same time, in 471, a *comes rei militaris* in Thrace named Ostrys, a follower of Aspar, attempted to avenge his master's murder and attacked the palace; he then ravaged Thrace.[16] A later Eastern source calls him a "Goth."[17]

Soldiers of more unambivalently "Byzantine" allegiance strikingly resemble the Gothic Balkan leaders, and many of them have Germanic names similar to those found in Ostrogothic Italy. The Byzantine officers Blivila and Froila came from the same settlement in Illyricum as Bessas, who, as we have seen, was described very differently by Procopius and Jordanes.[18] Blivila became *dux Libyae Pentapolis*.[19] A Tancus *comes* was killed in the Balkans fighting for the Byzantines against the Bulgars in 499;[20] the name is Germanic and occurs in at least two names in Ostrogothic Italy.[21] We have examined some of the Thracian commanders on the Byzantine side in the Gothic Wars in chapter 6. In Thrace itself, Germanic names continued in use by Byzantine forces, some of them, like Gudilas or Godilas, Guduin, and Rhecitangus, ones used by "Goths" in Ostrogothic Italy.[22]

The identities of these men were unclear to observers. One of Anastasius's commanders in the Isaurian war is called Apsical, a non-Germanic name, but a "Goth" according to John of Antioch. Two *magistri militum per Thracias* with the Germanic names Arnegisclus and Anagastes were father and son, serving in the office in the 440s and 460s respectively. Again, Byzantine sources call them Goths. Anagastes revolted against Leo I in 469–70 and seized "Roman" fortresses in Thrace.[23] But a contemporary source describes both Anagastes and Ostrys as "Roman generals" who were fighting enemies called Goths.[24] When Anagastes revolted, another contemporary source describes him

[14] Jordanes, *Rom.* 336.
[15] Heather, *Goths and Romans*, pp. 14, 20, 251.
[16] PLRE2 Ostrys.
[17] John Malalas, *Chronographia* 371.
[18] PA Bessas.
[19] PLRE2 Blivila, Froila.
[20] PLRE2 Tancus.
[21] PA Tanca, Tancila.
[22] PLRE3 Godilas 1 and 2, Guduin, Rhecitangus, all in Thrace; on the names cf. PA Gudila 1–4, Gundila, Rhecimundus.
[23] PLRE2 Apsical, Arnegisclus, Anagastes.
[24] Priscus, fr. 49.

as "Scythian," often a synonym for "Hun" in this particular text,[25] but Anagastes is associated with a *tyrannus Gothus* named Ullibos in another contemporary text.[26]

The linguistic origin of personal names did not necessarily match allegiance, just as in the Gothic Wars. One of Theoderic's commanders in Epirus in 479, according to Malchus "the greatest of the generals under him," bore the Greek name Soas.[27] A *comes* of Theoderic's father Thiudimir during his invasion of Illyricum in 473 bore the Persian name Astat.[28] Just as in Italy, personal name-changes and naming strategies could reflect the power of ethnographic group-names – and could be irrelevant to it.

Ancient personal and ethnographic names could no longer easily explain Balkan regional culture or political allegiance. This situation is epitomized by the powerful family of Armatus and Odoacer. Stefan Krautschick has demonstrated that Odoacer's family was closely related to that of the Eastern usurper Basiliscus, who took the Eastern throne in 476.[29] Odoacer is called a Scirian, a Rugian, a Goth or a Thuringian in sources; his father is called a Hun, his mother a Scirian.[30] Odoacer's father Edeco was associated first with the Huns under Attila, and then with a group called *Sciri*, an ethnographic name that appears intermittently in fifth-century sources. While Odoacer went off to lead a Saxon warband in Gaul in the late 460s, his brother Onoulphus went to Constantinople to fight with Armatus, *magister militum per Thracias* in 469. Armatus gave him money and advanced him in his career.[31]

Krautschick has established that Armatus was brother of Onoulphus and Odoacer.[32] Since Armatus was nephew of the usurper Basiliscus,

---

[25] John of Antioch, fr. 205.

[26] PLRE2 Ullibos.

[27] PLRE2 Soas; Malchus, fr. 20, p. 441, lines 111–12.

[28] PLRE2 Astat.

[29] Krautschick, "Zwei Aspekte," pp. 344–51; cf. Moorhead, *Theoderic*, pp. 9–10 with n. 10.

[30] Wood, "Ethnicity and ethnogenesis," p. 63, sensibly argues that he therefore did not have one identity; Krautschick, "Zwei Aspekte," pp. 344–5, argues that his father was a Hun and his mother a Scirian, and therefore would omit Rugian, Goth and Thuringian as "assertions influenced by other factors" (though Malchus, fr. 13 is unambiguous on the father's connection with the Thuringians) but, as Wood implies, it is exactly the variety of such assertions that are important. There is no reason to assume, moreover, that either Edeco or Odoacer's mother were restricted only to the identities described here; aside from their possible political associations with groups bearing other names, what were the identities of *their* parents?

[31] Krautschick, "Zwei Aspekte," pp. 344–51; PLRE2 Armatus, Onoulphus (on titles).

[32] Krautschick, "Zwei Aspekte," pp. 349–50 with n. 39. Krautschick's argument requires radical changes at PLRE2 Armatus and Onoulphus. The previous emended reading of the relevant fragment of John of Antioch (209.1) suggested that Onoulphus was the murderer of Armatus rather than his brother, thus amplifying Malchus, fr. 9.4. The emendation of John of Antioch is unnecessary because the fragment is perfectly clear, and there is no reason why Onoulphus could not have been both brother and murderer of Armatus. Blockley, in *The Fragmentary*

Odoacer himself was nephew of the man who seized the imperial throne in the same year that he seized the throne of Italy – not, apparently, with any mutual conspiracy.[33] After the fall of Basiliscus, Armatus was made *magister militum per Illyricum*. Zeno accused him of being in league with Theoderic Strabo and cutting off the hands of the "Romans" of Thrace.[34] But he was later remembered for his adultery and his habit of dressing up like Achilles and "parading around the hippodrome of his house;" the people of Constantinople called him "Pyrrhus."[35] Unlike his uncle Basiliscus, Armatus was not known as a barbarian, nor does his alleged behavior suggest that he wished to be known as one. These men were full members of the late Roman military aristocracy, a group that was showing increasing tendencies to build their own careers around their own forces, from Stilicho and Boniface through Aetius and Aspar.[36]

The inadequacy of sources to describe the identities of Odoacer, Armatus and Basiliscus, and the mixture of Latin and Germanic names in the family, is hardly surprising, since the military aristocracy and the imperial dynasties had been intermarrying with families bearing Germanic names since the fourth century.[37] Basiliscus himself had been *magister militum per Thracias* before his nephew Armatus. One contemporary source calls Basiliscus *barbaros*, and explains the term by his military career: *hēmeis barbaroi ontes kai eis arma anastrephomenoi*.[38] Krautschick takes the phrase to be proof of Armatus's relationship with Odoacer. This may be so, but for this outside observer, the "barbarianness" of Basiliscus's relatives need only have been an aspect of Basiliscus's Balkan military origins.

The family of Odoacer and Basiliscus epitomizes both the militarization of the term barbarian, discussed in chapter 1, and the confusion regarding the identity of people from the Balkans, discussed in chapter 4. Vitalian, Mundo and Bessas are other examples of this phenomenon. Just as Eastern observers could make neither head nor tail of the identity of Vitalian and his followers, Odoacer and his family receive a number

---

Classicising Historians, 1: 50, 165, n. 12, attributes the fragment to Priscus (= fr. 64.1), retaining the traditional emendation.

[33] Krautschick, "Zwei Aspekte," pp. 352–5; Moorhead, *Theoderic*, p. 9, n. 10, suspects conspiracy.

[34] Malchus, fr. 15, lines 15–20.

[35] *Suda* A3970 (Blockley, *The Fragmentary Classicising Historians*, 2: 476, quotation translated at 477); on adultery, see Candidus, fr. 1, lines 60–6.

[36] Krautschick, "Zwei Aspekte," pp. 349–55.

[37] Demandt, "The osmosis of the late Roman and Germanic aristocracies," pp. 76–86.

[38] *V. Dan. Styl.* 84, on which see Krautschick, "Zwei Aspekte," p. 350; the implications of *barbaros* are rejected by PLRE2: 212, which did not yet know of the family connections between Onoulphus and Odoacer and Basiliscus and Armatus.

of ethnographic names, one just the generic "barbarian," even though that member became Eastern emperor (retrospectively, a usurper). Odoacer's subsequent kingdom in Italy never succeeded in acquiring a single ethnographic term either; he was merely *rex gentium*. Had he survived longer, he might have used ethnographic ideology to recreate his followers, or indeed the entire population of his kingdom, into one group.[39] A notice in Cassiodorus's *Chronicon* might suggest that Odoacer's army were becoming one group just before their defeat – he calls them a *gens*. But this word means "army" here, as it would everywhere else.[40]

It was from this military frontier milieu that Theoderic and his followers appeared, a group more firmly attached to an ethnographic name than any other, but sharing characteristics of heterodoxical naming traditions and religious belief with other Balkan war-leaders. Odoacer was an Arian believer with a Germanic name. Basiliscus was a monophysite,[41] but perhaps took his Latin name as a symbol of his conversion from Arianism. Arians could not become emperors in the late fifth century, as Aspar and Theoderic realized.[42] Aspar's son was named Iulius Patricius, and he was proclaimed Caesar by Leo I in 470. Aspar had to promise the bishops that Patricius would become a Catholic before he became emperor;[43] his name doubtless also reflects his father's plans for him.

Not only the military aristocracy, but all the Eastern emperors from Marcian to Tiberius II, came from frontier military regions, either from Isauria or the Balkans, and chiefly the latter. When we recall that the Western Empire was under the control of military generalissimos from about the same period, the appearance of military emperors in the East at this time takes on new meaning. The accession of the pious and unmilitary Arcadius and Honorius to the throne as children in 395, and the continued rule of empresses through the reigns of Theodosius II and Valentinian III through 450 and 455 in East and West respectively, denoted the emergence of a new kind of emperor. All the fourth-century emperors had been soldiers who actively led their troops, with the brief exceptions of Gratian and Valentinian II. It is possible that the unmilitary rule of the House of Theodosius represented the triumph

---

[39] Wood, "Ethnicity and ethnogenesis of the Burgundians," p. 63.

[40] Cassiodorus, *Chronicon* 1320 (s.a. 489): after Theoderic's entry into Italy, "Odovacar ad Isontium pugnam parans victus *cum tota gente* fugatus est."

[41] PLRE2 Basiliscus 2.

[42] Aspar: see PLRE2 Patricius 15. Theoderic: *Anagnosticum regis*, p. 425, lines 21–5, with discussion at ch. 2, above.

[43] PLRE2 Patricius 15.

of anti-militaristic forces at court; it certainly represented the triumph of the quiescent monarchy.[44] After 450 in the East, the army – or a part of it – took over the throne once more. The dominance of the Balkan military at Constantinople had repercussions which we cannot examine here, one of which may have been the long-lasting use of Latin as an official language in the East.

Thus Marcian was an Illyrian or Thracian from the Balkans, Leo I was a "Bessian" born in Thrace, Basiliscus is first attested in the Balkans and called a "barbarian," Zeno and the usurper Leontius were Isaurian soldiers (the latter once called Thracian also!), and Anastasius was from Dyrrachium in Nova Epirus in Illyricum,[45] where Theoderic was to rule for several years.[46] Anastasius was the least military of them, but began his career among the weapon-bearing palace *silentiarii*.[47] Zeno saw fit to change his original Isaurian name Tarasicodissa to the Greek Zeno, made famous by another Isaurian soldier.[48]

The family of Justin I and Justinian was, of course, of obscure military origin; Justin was born in Naissus in Dacia, which according to Priscus was almost entirely depopulated by "the enemy" (Attila's Huns), at a date that must have been near the time of his birth. Justinian was born at Tauresium in Illyricum. Both began in posts as palace guardsmen. They had military relatives in Thrace, one with the Thracian name Boraides. After their election, they took part in the murder of a rival military leader from the Balkans, Vitalian.[49] Justin II, brought up in the palace, did not begin life as a soldier, but he too was born in Thrace.[50] But his successor Tiberius II was a native of Thrace and began as *comes excubitorum*, just like Justin I; his daughter Charito had a Germanic name. Tiberius added the imperial name Constantine to his name when he became emperor.[51]

At the end of the sixth century, the conflict between Maurice and

---

[44] Wolfram, "Gotisches Königtum und Römisches Kaisertum," pp. 13–14 (the "domestication of the emperorship," quoting H. G. Beck), adducing the bureaucratization and centralization of the administration and the importance of residence in Constantinople to retain power. Goffart, "Rome, Constantinople and the barbarians," pp. 18–24: whether or not one agrees with his argument for a dismantling of Empire, his characterization of the Theodosian dynasty, "pious youths," and their military policy, is accurate. Similarly, with remarks on the importance of Constantinople, Goffart, "An empire unmade," pp. 37, 41–2.

[45] PLRE2 Marcianus 8, Leo 6, Basiliscus 2, Zenon 7, Leontius 17, Anastasius 4.

[46] Heather, *Goths and Romans*, pp. 292–3, 296, 299.

[47] PLRE2 Anastasius 4; on *silentiarii*, see PA **R**omulus.

[48] PLRE2 Zenon 7.

[49] PLRE2 Iustinus 4, Iustinianus 7; relatives: PLRE3 Iustinus 4; Boraides; on Naissus: Priscus, fr. 11.2, lines 51–2.

[50] PLRE3 Iustinus 5.

[51] PLRE3 Tiberius 1, Charito.

Phocas demonstrates the solidarity of Balkan soldiers. The series of military emperors had finally came to an end with Maurice, a *chartularius* from Cappadocia, but his reign did not satisfy the Balkan army. Maurice did indeed become *magister militum per Orientem*, but he had had no previous military experience.

Phocas first appears leading a deputation from the Thracian army to complain about the treatment that they had received from Maurice. He subsequently led another one which also failed in its demands. In the end, the Thracian army revolted and proclaimed Phocas emperor; Phocas himself was eventually overthrown by the Armenian or Cappadocian soldier Heraclius.[52] Subsequently the Balkans moved out of the sphere of Byzantine dominance and produced no emperors for centuries. Some scanty evidence suggests that collaboration and assimilation between the already varied indigenous population and the Slav and Avar populations aided the process of final Balkan alienation from Constantinople.[53]

The Balkan military emperors ensured that Balkan soldiers received preferment in the ranks. During the Gothic Wars, most of the commanders were Thracian, Illyrian or associated with the Balkans: Belisarius, John the nephew of Vitalian, Constantinus, Valerianus, Bessas, Herodianus, and Germanus (the nephew of Justin I and the husband of Matasuentha); only Narses was Persoarmenian.[54] A common first

---

[52] PLRE3 Mauricius 4 (pp. 856–7 on his career background); Phocas 7; Heraclius 4.

[53] The situation is, of course, far more complicated, notably because of the shaky imperial finances and the incessant warfare caused by the Avars, the Slavs and other groups: see Michael Whitby, *The Emperor Maurice and His Historian: Theophylact Simocatta on Persian and Balkan Warfare* (Oxford, 1988), pp. 138–91. Phocas as emperor was forced to draw many of his troops over to the Persian border; his policies are obscured by the anti-Phocaian propaganda of Heraclius and his successors. After 602, the obscurity of the seventh-century sources famously draws a curtain over Balkan events, and any ethnogenesis that took place there among natives of various identities and the Avars and Slavs in particular can only be deduced from subsequent events. Any parallels with other ethnographic group-names would not be with the unsuccessful Goths but with the Franks in northern Gaul or the Angles and Saxons in lowland Britain, both of whom lent their names to the local populations via processes that still wait to be elucidated. Note that the Avars were a heterogeneous political federation including Utrigurs, Cotrigurs, Gepids and doubtless people formerly of other identities (Whitby, p. 80; on the complex processes of Avar status and professionally based ethnogenesis, see Pohl, *Die Awaren*, pp. 215–25), a group deploying loose political and military strategies similar to those of the Hunnic federation (Whitby, p. 84), whereas the Slavs were diverse and disunited small groups (pp. 82–3). Note also that "Roman" and "barbarian" settlements become archeologically indistinguishable (pp. 136–7) and that "Romans" collaborated with "barbarians" against the emperors (p. 185). The imperial oppositional rhetoric of Theophylact Simocatta, the *Miracula Sancti Demetrii* and the later works of Constantine Porphyrogenitus conceal processes of assimilation, collaboration, multiple identities and general confused loyalties in the seventh-century Balkans just as official sources do for the earlier period.

[54] PLRE3 Belisarius, Ioannes 46, Constantinus 3, Valerianus 1, Bessas, Herodianus, Narses 1, PLRE2 Germanus 4.

high office for ambitious military men was *magister militum per Illyricum* or *per Thracias*, many of whom had non-Graeco-Latin names, perhaps Hunnic, such as Calluc, or non-Roman ethnographic epithets, such as John "the Scythian."[55] We constantly hear of Byzantine soldiers from Illyricum, Thrace or Isauria,[56] and occasionally of commanders being sent to raise soldiers from those regions.[57] The huge retinues of *doryphoroi* and the composition of the Byzantine army in Italy are often described as both barbarians and Romans, regular troops and *foederati* (in the sixth-century sense), but they frequently included large numbers from Thrace and from Isauria.[58]

The army was as diverse as the Eastern Empire itself – and as diverse as the Balkans. Of the Byzantine officers in Italy, about a third had Germanic names, slightly under half had Graeco-Latin names, and the rest names of other origin.[59] The name of Belisarius himself may well be Thracian linguistically,[60] and some spellings of it confuse it with a Germanic name.[61] The son-in-law of Belisarius had the Germanic name Ildiger. Belisarius also adopted a son from Thrace named Theodosius, who was an Arian. The general baptized him a Catholic; there can be no doubt that Theodosius only then received the name of the great anti-Arian emperor.[62]

The uncertainty of identity, and the lack of cultural differentiation, spread across frontiers into regions never claimed as "Roman." A member of Justinian's household named Chilbudius was *magister militum per Thracias* in the early 530s. Later an individual whom Procopius calls "one of the Antes" claimed Chilbudius's name when he was captured by the Slavs, in order to convince them that he was an important person who might be ransomed. The real Chilbudius is always called a "general of the Romans," not an Ante, and Narses was able to identify the imposter despite his excellent Latin and his imitation of Chilbudius's "personal peculiarities."[63] But the Slavs were unable to tell the differ-

---

[55] PLRE3 Calluc, Iohannes 34 Scytha.
[56] e.g., Procopius, BG2(6).11.5.
[57] e.g., ibid., 1(5).7.26; 3(7).10.1–2; 3(7).12.4.
[58] e.g., ibid., 1(5).5.2–4; 3(7).6.10.
[59] PA III, table 2, commentary.
[60] PLRE3: 182.
[61] ICUR I, no. 1057 "Wilisarius," no. 1062 "Velesarius."
[62] PLRE3 Ildiger, Theodosius 8; Procopius, SH 1.15–16, calls him a "Eunomian," which could be taken as evidence that Arians in the Balkans were still split among several groups (Eunomius of Cyzicus led a splinter-group of radical Arians in the 360s), but I prefer to take the word "Eunomian" here as merely an instance of the inexactitude of Procopius in Christian matters; either way, Theodosius was an Arian.
[63] Procopius, BG 3(7).14.7–36; PLRE2 Chilbudius 1 and 2.

ence. The name Chilbudius is Germanic, but it had no bearing on the case, even in Procopius's ethnography-influenced account.

We have seen that it suited Mundo and Asbadus to claim different ethnographic names at different times. The same went for these other people. The false Chilbudius needed to be a Roman when he was captured by the Slavs; presumably there were no people called "Antae" who were prestigious or powerful enough to demand to be ransomed. The ostentatiously Roman Iulius Patricius, the son of Aspar, needed to have a Latin name and to be a Catholic in order to become emperor. The same may have been true of Basiliscus, who had Arians with Germanic names in his family, and Tiberius II, who amplified his already imperial name with the addition of Constantine.

But all these Balkan military men, Roman though some of them appeared, had murkier sides to them. Justinian had a godson named Ascum, variously called a "Hun" or a "Bulgar," whom he sponsored at baptism. Ascum became *magister militum per Illyricum*.[64] Belisarius had Arians and a man with a Germanic name in his own family. Basiliscus and Armatus were related to Onoulphus and Odoacer. The emperor Zeno adopted Theoderic as his *filius per arma*, but his predecessor Marcian had been related by marriage to Ricimer, and, through his wife's family, to the fourth-century barbarian officers Bauto and Richomer.[65] Of course, Zeno himself could have been seen as a barbarian, since he was an Isaurian, and he may have been aware of this, since he changed his barbarous name to a Greek one.

A certain anxiety pervades the attempts of some of these men to be seen as Romans, as we saw in the case of John, the nephew of Vitalian, or in Asbadus. This did not end with the sixth century. A "Sueve" named Droctulfus, brought up among the Lombards, was a Catholic and deserted to the Byzantines, served in Italy and Thrace, was commended by Gregory the Great, went to Africa and ended his days in Ravenna, where his epitaph praised him for opposing his own people, the Lombards, and for supporting his *patria* of Ravenna and the Roman commonwealth:

Hic et amans semper Romana et publica signa, vastator genti adfuit ipse suae. Contempsit caros, dum nos amat ille, parentes, hanc patriam reputans esse Ravenna suam.

His house at Ravenna later became the episcopal palace, and he was remembered with respect.[66]

---

[64] PLRE3 Ascum; Stein, *Bas-Empire* 2: 307.
[65] Demandt, "The osmosis of late Roman and Germanic aristocracies," table after p. 86.
[66] PLRE3 Droctulfus 1.

The family of Justinian himself is the best example of this sort of anxiety. As Tony Honoré argues in his lengthy and instructive comparison of Justinian to Stalin, the emperor was a provincial who came to a seat of power and learning, Constantinople, where he had to prove that he was fit to be emperor of Rome. His repeated attempts to impose an antiquated *Romanitas* on his policy – which was actually extremely innovative – are a manifestation of the worries of the arriviste. He was to be the Roman emperor par excellence, and his interminable emphasis on the Roman past, the renewal of Roman power, and the glory of the Empire as displayed in himself, may go to the heart of a provincial military man who was uncomfortable in the learned Greek circles of the capital.

Justinian faced some jeering at his origins. Procopius, retailing gossip from the capital, tells us that Justin's wife Lupicina was considered a "slave" and a "rustic," and that people thought her a "barbarian." Justinian himself, we hear, was like a barbarian in his speech, his dress and his thinking. His speech was uncouth and rough. None of this need have been true, and given that it occurs in Procopius's work of invective, the *Secret History*, it most likely is not true. The point is not that Lupicina and Justinian actually did behave like barbarians, but that Procopius could accuse the Roman emperor and his family of behaving like barbarians, and that this could be connected with their Illyrian origins.[67]

Justinian's renaming his Illyrian birthplace as Justiniana thus appears defensive. Similarly, in a law pretending to restore the past and actually innovating, he created the classicizing office of *quaestor exercitus* for the Aegean islands and the provinces of Scythia and Moesia, referring to them as *regiones a barbaris infestatae*.[68] In a law addressed to the bishop of his birthplace, Justinian granted him special privileges, and ordered him to repel the evil of the Bonosians from Aquis in Dacia, and bring that region back to the orthodox faith.[69]

In his attempt to bridge East and West, Justinian actively supported the compromise theology of the "Scythian monks," Balkan clergymen who could be seen by their compatriot Dionysius as natives of a land of barbarians. Not merely their theology, but their very names and family connections with Vitalian raised flickers of suspicion in the Egyptian papal ambassador Dioscorus and in the Campanian pope Hormisdas. The theology of the Scythian monks, like their ethnographic

---

[67] Procopius, SH 6.17; 9. 47 (Lupicina); 14.2–3, cf. 6.1–3 (Justinian).

[68] *Nov. Iust.* 41; 50: *eis choras hypo barbariōn enochloumenas* in the original Greek of the first law; *a provinciae barbaris inquietatae* in the original Latin of the second.

[69] *Nov. Iust.* 11, esp. §5.

name and their geographical location, came from a tradition of Balkan ecclesiastical communities that tried to connect the Greek and Latin churches in a literal sense.[70]

The Balkans were a problem. Observers were unsure whether or not Vitalian was a barbarian, and whether or not his troops were barbarians. Justinian solved this problem by ensuring that he was more Roman and more Catholic than anyone else.[71] He redefined the word Roman, being careful to use ancient rhetoric in his decriptions, and his very name implied that he embodied Roman law, the key element of Roman superiority in ethnographic thought.[72]

In this context, Justinian and Theoderic begin to look very similar. They were both military men from military families in the Balkans, and they both journeyed from the margins of the Empire to one of its two historical and ideological centers. Both received a classical education early enough in life to make a deep impression. They were both fascinated by the Roman past and the classifications of classical ethnography. Both claimed to uphold the ancient rule of Roman law while changing it through and through.

The difference is how they described their origins. This description itself affected their policy greatly. Theoderic saw himself as a Goth, and took pride in the Goths – if chiefly for their superiority to other *gentes* in their acceptance of Roman *prudentia*. Justinian saw himself as a Roman, and thus loudly proclaimed himself superior to the *gentes* with which Balkan inhabitants were forever being confused by outsiders. Theoderic undertook a *modus vivendi* in order to reconcile opposed groups within his diverse kingdom; Justinian attempted to impose homogeneity from above in order to reconcile opposed groups in his empire. In the end, even Justinian was forced to try to conciliate the monophysites.

Their origins were in fact strikingly similar: the Balkan military milieu of disrupted frontier provinces. Both men were concerned not only with Roman law, but with military valor. Theoderic connected his military success with the military successes of groups called Goths and

---

[70] See ch. 4, above.

[71] Stein, *Bas Empire* 2: 276: "Ce fils d'incultes provinciaux professe avec ferveur l'amour de l'Antiquité que, sans cesse, il s'efforce, à tort et à travers, de faire revivre, et qu'il appelle, dans une de ses lois, 'exempte de faute'..." and 2: 279: "Comme tous les empereurs, il avait naturellement au plus haut degré le souci de l'unité de l'Eglise; catholique de naissance et latin au plus profond de son coeur ... mais en pratique, Justinien, se croyant, même dans le domaine spirituel, supérieur à tous les évêques y compris le pape, n'admettait pas cette primauté [of the papacy]."

[72] On the importance of his name (which also, of course, referred to his adoption by Justin), see Honoré, *Tribonian*, pp. 16–17.

of his family who had led such groups for two generations at least; Justinian connected his success with the ancient military traditions of the Roman emperors. But the armies of both men fought in the same way, with the same weapons and the same tactics. Both armies contained men of various religious beliefs, men with Latin, Germanic and other names, men who spoke a mutually comprehensible military slang. Soldiers from each army during the Gothic Wars were able to transfer their loyalties smoothly from one to the other under necessity. The only difference was that Byzantine soldiers were forced to serve all over the Mediterranean, and were, when they first arrived in Italy, an occupying foreign power, while the soldiers of the Gothic army had put down local ties in Italy. This difference was dictated by the different sizes of the kingdom of Italy and of Justinian's Empire, not by a cultural difference between Theoderic's Goths and Justinian's Romans.

ETHNOGRAPHY AND THE BALKANS: JORDANES

The crucial text that historians have used to prove the existence of a consciousness of a Gothic culture and history, and thus of the existence or creation of a Gothic ethnicity, is the *Getica* of Jordanes. This singular text may actually be an unusual voice speaking from the Balkan military milieu of the fifth and sixth centuries, passed through the web of classical ethnographic discourse.

We saw in chapter 4 that traditional ethnogeographic terminology had great difficulty in describing the identity and allegiance of a man like Vitalian. Jordanes represents an attempt to reconcile ethnogeography with this situation at a crucial political juncture for the Balkan provincial Justinian. The work of Jordanes exemplifies the widening gap between ethnographic description and the newly visible diversity of the former Roman Empire.

I have placed Jordanes at the end of this book, rather than at the beginning, for three reasons. First, he wrote at the end of the Gothic Wars, in 550 or 551; as a text, the *Getica* properly belongs at the end of any history of the Goths in Italy. Second, his work has attracted so much controversy over its purpose, its authorship, and its sources, that it seemed to me useful to attempt a new survey of Ostrogothic Italy that looked at every other source first, and then compared the text of Jordanes with the picture thus brought to light. Third, whatever older material he contains, Jordanes was an inhabitant of Constantinople writing in the early 550s. There is no evidence that he ever visited Italy, and given the disputes over his sources, I think that he cannot be treated as the starting-point for a history of the Ostrogothic kingdom. He must come last, at least until the perplexities surrounding his work are resolved.

The four potential levels of importance of Jordanes come from his claim that he was summarizing the lost *Gothic History* of Cassiodorus, commissioned by Theoderic.[73] If he summarized it faithfully, then we might possess in him a chain going back to the oral traditions of the Goths themselves. If Jordanes actually preserves no oral traditions, then he might still preserve what Theoderic wanted the Italians to believe were oral traditions. If Jordanes actually preserves none of Theoderic's ideology, then he might still preserve Cassiodorus's work, writing as a contemporary of Theoderic and Athalaric. If he actually preserves none of Cassiodorus's work, then he might still preserve precious material on what it meant to be a Goth, since Jordanes describes himself as a Goth.

The various disputes on Jordanes have been described in chapter 1. Briefly, Walter Goffart argues that Jordanes must be viewed as a Byzantine writer in Constantinople, and that he was a court propagandist for Justinian.[74] Herwig Wolfram argues that Jordanes preserves Cassiodorus's *History* intact, and that the *Getica* shows that Theoderic believed in and propagated an *origo Gothica*, an origin myth utilizing the claims of the Amal dynasty in order to build his heterogeneous "Goths" into a people, *the* Goths, connected with the prestigious histories of every group called Goth in the past.[75]

I accept neither of these views. Goffart's literary reading of the *Getica* as an allegorical love-story between (feminine) Goths and (masculine) Romans, written by a pseudonymous author for the emperor, forces the text and does not convince. Heather has pointed out that Goffart's proposed allegory is so oblique that its use as propaganda would be difficult, and its very propagation a problem.[76] Wolfram's *origo Gothica* ignores the textual problems of a work that cannot be proved to be the faithful rendering of Cassiodorus, and he easily elides the four levels of possible transmission listed above.[77] Moreover, as Heather and Goffart point out, the *Getica* only glorifies the Amals to a certain extent; it spends much time on other matters, including the Visigothic dynasty of the Balthi, and Justinian's ultimate triumph over the Goths.

---

[73] Jordanes, *Get.* 1–2. We know about the *Gothic History* from Cassiodorus, *Var. praef.* no. 1, §11; *Var.* 9.25.3–6; *Ordo generis Cassiodororum*, lines 21–2.

[74] Goffart, *Narrators*, pp. 20–111.

[75] Wolfram, *Goths*, pp. 3–18 and *passim*; "Einleitung," 19–31.

[76] Heather, *Goths and Romans*, pp. 38–52.

[77] Goffart, *Narrators*, pp. 58–62; Heather, *Goths and Romans*, pp. 50–1.

It does not look like a piece of Theoderican ideology, even though it may contain some remnants of such ideology.[78]

Given the thorny problems of textual transmission, I would like to follow the lead offered by Walter Goffart and especially Brian Croke, who study Jordanes as an East Roman historian in his own right. What is the cultural context of Jordanes's work?

The *Getica* draws on a type of writing popular in sixth-century Constantinople: ethnogeography. Like Tacitus and Pliny and the ethnographic excursuses in Procopius, it begins with the essential geographic survey of the world.[79] It ties in elements of classical mythology and non-classical theogony (descent from gods, the Amazons),[80] and employs stereotypes of the barbarians (stupidity, bellicosity),[81] Judaeo-Christian biblical models,[82] as well as the virtue-based ethnography of Tacitus (the Goths as primitive but unspoilt). It weaves a story about a *gens* around the providential history of the Roman Empire.[83]

Most notably, the *Getica* combines the history of various groups from the same region, the Black Sea – Scythians, Getae and various groups called Goths – using the so-called doctrine of transference; that is, geographical places continuously produce the same peoples with different names.[84] An important corollary to this is that places and peoples become indistinguishable from one another, so that one proceeds smoothly from Scythia to Scythians to Goths, or the reverse. The *Getica*

[78] Goffart, *Narrators*, pp. 62–8; Heather, *Goths and Romans*, pp. 46–7, 51–61 (moderating Goffart's position, but not going so far as Wolfram); on Heather's literal reading of some of Wolfram's statements, see Wolfram, review of Heather, pp. 257–8.
[79] Tacitus, *Germania* 1.1: "Germania omnis a Gallis Raetisque et Pannoniis Rheno et Danuvio fluminibus, a Sarmatis Dacisque mutuo metu aut montibus separatur;" Jordanes, *Getica* 4: "Maiores nostri, ut refert Orosius, totius terrae circulum Oceani limbo circumseptum triquadrum statuerunt eiusque tres partes Asiam, Eoropam et Africam vocaverunt," a direct quotation from Orosius; the text goes on to describe the geography of the world from Julius Honorius, Orosius, Pomponius Mela, and Strabo. Pliny began his *Natural History* with a description of the world and astronomy, and progressed on to time, the relation of climate to *gens*, various natural wonders, and only then began to describe *situs, gentes, maria, oppida, portus, montes, flumina, mensurae, populi qui sunt aut qui fuerunt Baeticae, Hispaniae citerioris, Narbonensis provinciae*, etc. (*Nat. Hist.* 1, table of contents for Books 2–3). Geography and the physical world was an essential preamble for the description of *gentes* in ethnogeography; Jordanes falls into this tradition.
[80] Theogony: *Get.* 79–81 (using Germanic names); Amazons: *Get.* 44–56, 107.
[81] e.g. *Get.* 259: after Attila's death, his sons discuss how to divide up the empire, suggesting that each son should receive a "warlike king and his people" (*bellicosi reges cum populis*).
[82] The Magog story, tied into the Scythians via Josephus: *Get.* 28–9.
[83] Wolfram, "Gothic history," p. 311; Wolfram, *Goths*, p. 4; against Wolfram, a history of an extra-imperial *gens* was not an innovation: Goffart, *Narrators*, pp. 36–7.
[84] Scythia: *Get.* 27–39; Getae: 40–2, 58, etc. On Goths, Scythians and Getae, see Wolfram, *Goths*, p. 44 (an ancient equivalence by this time), but *Scytha* could also mean "Hun" or "inhabitant of the province of Scythia" in the sixth-century East.

thus contains dozens of detailed and apparently inconsequential geographies of the Balkans.

If we attach the *Getica* to the *Romana*, as Jordanes explicitly says that we must,[85] we can then see it as a form of ethnographic excursus in itself, an excursus from the *Romana*.[86] The *Romana* contained much on the Goths. A geographical and ethnographic digression explaining the origin, customs and history of a barbarian *gens* was completely in the tradition of classicizing histories. Such digressions appear in Ammianus, Procopius and Agathias. Jordanes was certainly familiar with Ammianus, whom he uses as a source for the *Getica*.[87]

The *Romana*, of course, is no classicizing history. It is a dry, annalistic compendium in the tradition of Eusebius, Jerome and their fifth-century Latin continuations. Such chronicles are exemplified in the East by the chronicle of Marcellinus Comes and its continuation, with which both the *Romana* and the *Getica* stand in some relation. It also contains similarities to the Greek chronicles of John Malalas and the *Chronicon Paschale*.[88]

Neither is the *Getica* a classicizing ethnography. It is certainly something new in the whole of its form, as opposed to its details. We possess no contemporary text like it — though as we shall see, one may have been produced.[89] The other "barbarian histories" with which it has been grouped in fact share no similarities with it whatsoever.[90] It can be compared neither with Tacitus's satirical *Germania*, which manifestly observes, or rather represents, the *Germani* from the perspective of an outsider, nor yet with the *Origo gentis Romanae*, an insider's view (written by a "Roman" for "Romans"), but a mere epitome of the Aeneas story, probably condensed for bored aristocrats in the late fourth century.[91]

The *Getica* is a compendium of various ethnographic commonplaces,

---

[85] Jordanes, *Rom.* 4, with Goffart, *Narrators*, p. 107, dismissed by Heather, p. 48, n. 39 as "assertion," but it seems to me to be amply supported by Goffart's arguments at p. 21, n. 6, and Heather himself acknowledges the pro-Justinianic force of the two works combined at p. 51.

[86] We can thus see the *Getica* as an outsized carbuncle on the *Romana* – *iungens aliud volumen de origine actusque Getice gentis*: *Rom.* 4.

[87] Mommsen, in Jordanes, pp. xxxiii–iv.

[88] On the relationship between the *Romana* and other chronicles including the *Getica* (far from resolved), see Croke, "a.d. 476, the manufacture of a turning point," pp. 81–119; Croke, "Cassiodorus and the *Getica* of Jordanes," pp. 117–34; Johann Weißensteiner, "Cassiodor/Jordanes als Geschichtsschreiber," n. 12.

[89] See below, pp. 304–5, on the lost *Isaurica* of Capito.

[90] Goffart, *Narrators*, *passim*.

[91] It is thus difficult to see the *Getica* as falling into a literary tradition of *origines gentium* from which it differs greatly, contra Wolfram: see Goffart, *Narrators*, pp. 36–7 with n. 73. Goffart proposes Josephus as a more likely parallel (p. 87, n. 322).

forms and techniques, drawing on a large body of sources. These include various works of history, which themselves contained ethnography, as well as most of the key works of classical ethnogeography: Strabo, Pomponius Mela, Tacitus, Ptolemy, and geographical maps – though not, surprisingly, Pliny.[92] Other works, like Dexippus and Priscus, may also have contained ethnographic rhetorical constructs: the fragments of Priscus that survive certainly do so.[93]

Here we must digress to examine the question of the preservation of oral "Gothic" tradition in the *Getica*. It is a mistake to think that any of the material in the *Getica* comes from oral tradition, as the text presents it. At the very least this depends on how one defines oral tradition. The search for orality in the *Getica* has been so fierce that some scholars have concluded that whenever Jordanes uses the phrase "Ablabius storicus refert," he is retailing oral traditions, and concealing his use under the name of an otherwise unattested historian of the Goths, Ablabius.[94]

"Oral" is a loaded word. Peter Heather argues that the *Getica* is orally influenced because it anachronistically groups the Goths of the past into Visigoths and Ostrogoths, western and eastern Goths.[95] This was, of course, the situation in the 550s, when Jordanes was writing; Visigothic Spain was west of Ostrogothic Italy, so Jordanes or his sources grouped all the groups called Goths in the past who were recorded as antecedents of the Goths of Italy and Spain under these names. But is this oral "history"? *Need* we think of Goths going round and telling tales or singing songs of Goths in the past, at dinners or around campfires, and regrouping them according to their present-day geographical locations? The answer is clearly negative. Such notions could have been "orally" available in Constantinople, as commonplaces, court gossip, learned deductions or the stories brought back by travelers and soldiers from the West.

We have no authority and no necessity to explain such an anachronism by recourse to "oral history," with all its connotations of ideas and memories otherwise unavailable to contemporaries. True oral history can be detected in two ways: when an author declares that he is setting it down, and when the form of the text itself suggests non-literate speech,

---

[92] Mommsen, in Jordanes, pp. xxxii–iv.

[93] Priscus, fr. 11.2, lines 406–510: the famous story of the Roman who defected to the barbarians, which Priscus uses to criticize imperial policy in a Tacitan/Themistian sense, and also to demonstrate the ultimate superiority of Roman law when correctly implemented. Note also his depiction of Attila as a violent and abusive man (ibid., lines 171–88), calling him "the barbarian."

[94] Scardigli, *Sprache und Kultur*, pp. 282–3.

[95] Heather, *Goths and Romans*, pp. 63–7.

through archaic vocabulary, sudden ascent into metrical forms, or the use of formulae such as complex stereotypes.[96] None of the latter appears in the *Getica*, nor has anyone been able to point to any. Jordanes twice refers to *fabulae*, once to dismiss them, once to retail the genealogy of the Amals, which certainly comes from Cassiodorus, and once to *carmina*; all three instances are connected with literary sources.[97] Cassiodorus himself, describing his *History*, implies that he had to do his research in books because the ancestry of the Goths was *not* preserved in song.[98]

Importantly, the only orality that any philologist has been able to find in the *Getica* suggests the oral transmission of Mediterranean classical ethnography, something very different from songs around campfires. In the section where Jordanes recounts the peoples supposedly ruled by Ermanaric in the fourth century, the list of names occurs in the same geographical order as they do in Ptolemy. The forms of the names, however, suggest that they have been transliterated from Greek into a Germanic language, and then again into Latin.[99]

The notion that a text as learned and abstruse as Ptolemy could have been read and passed down among Germanic-speaking people is difficult to absorb. But there is no inherent reason why it should not have been the case. When we can see the views of barbarian kings, such as Theoderic himself, we can see a keen interest in the classifications of ethnography. For anyone who wished to identify himself with a non-Roman *gens*, as Wolfram has pointed out, only ethnography offered

---

[96] Jan Vansina, *Oral Tradition: A Study in Historical Methodology*, 1961, trans. H. M. Wright (1965; reprint, Harmondsworth, 1973), pp. 1–18, 67–74, 109–10 and *passim*; Ruth Finnegan, "Oral tradition and historical evidence," *History and Theory* 9 (1970), 195–201. A well-known, if contested, example of oral tradition in an early medieval source is to be found in certain sixth-century annals in the *Anglo-Saxon Chronicle* containing allegedly archaic language, first noted by Henry Sweet, "Some of the sources of the *Anglo-Saxon Chronicle*," *Englische Studien* 2 (1879), 310–12. The whole work is now seen as a much later literary preparation in the ninth-century court of Alfred: Patrick Sims-Williams, "The settlement of England in Bede and the *Chronicle*," *Anglo-Saxon England* 12 (1983), 1–43; David Dumville, "The West Saxon Genealogical Regnal List and the chronology of early Wessex," *Peritia* 4 (1985), 21–67. Here at least we are dealing with traditions set down in the language through which they were supposedly communicated!

[97] Jordanes, *Get.* 38, with Goffart, *Narrators*, pp. 93–4, connecting these "silly fables" with court gossip, since both Procopius and Jordanes mention the Goths and Britain; *Get.* 77 on the genealogy of the Amals, and *Get.* 28 on Filimer, a story that Jordanes accepts, but only through the medium of the historian Ablabius, on which see Heather, *Goths and Romans*, pp. 61–2. Each of the three *fabuluae* is connected with a literary source: Britain with Procopius, the genealogy with Cassiodorus, the Filimer story with Ablabius.

[98] Goffart, *Narrators*, pp. 78–9.

[99] Jordanes, *Get.* 116 with Irma Korkkanen, *The Peoples of Hermanaric: Jordanes, "Getica" 116*, Annales Academiae Scientiarum Fennicae, ser. b, 187 (Helsinki, 1975), pp. 48–73.

written material with which to construct a history.[100] Written history was the prerogative of the Roman Empire and Roman observers. In this context we can understand the possibility that the Germanic word *Ostrogothi* is a transliteration of Latin *Austrogothi*, itself a Latin compound of the Germanic word *Gothi*.[101]

This is not to claim that no non-literate group had oral traditions of its own; this question we cannot answer. But when orality is in close proximity to literate societies, it survives only with difficulty as an integrated and living tradition.[102] Can we really begin to examine elements of the *Getica* as an autonomous *Wandersage* like the ones found in Africa by anthropologists, when the *Wandersage* of the Goths was committed to writing by someone who knew the stories of Aeneas and Moses, about a group of people who knew the stories of Aeneas and Moses? No attested barbarian group was ever far away from the overwhelming literacy of the Roman Empire, and there is good reason to assert that all the barbarian groups that we know from the fourth, fifth and sixth centuries were in constant contact with the Roman Empire.[103]

If any oral tradition did exist among groups within the Roman Empire, that tradition had to exist in constant dialogue with literate tradition. Moreover, any oral tradition that did exist would be precipi- tously weakened by its permanent adjacency to a form of memory –

---

[100] Wolfram, *Goths*, pp. 3–4, still believing the Roman filtration of non-Roman tradition pre- served important parts of that tradition. But *Get.* 116 suggests that Roman tradition became non-Roman tradition and then once more Roman tradition.

[101] See above, ch. 1, pp. 37–8.

[102] Vansina, *Oral Tradition*, p. 3; Jack Goody, "Introduction," in *Literacy in Traditional Societies*, ed. Jack Goody (Cambridge, 1968), pp. 4–10. See further Rosamond McKitterick, "The writ- ten word and oral communication: Rome's legacy to the Franks," in *Germania Latina*, ed. R. North and T. Hofstra (Groningen, 1992), pp. 87–110, for evidence on oral and written contact in a later and more northerly society.

[103] The situation in northern Europe was entirely different, of course, and there is reason to believe that some kind of oral culture existed in northern Germany, Scandinavia and probably also in England between 400 and 1000; this culture assimilated elements from the south (coins in Sutton Hoo, the alphabet in runes, classical heroes and southern barbarian rulers in *Widsith*, and even the memory of Theoderic as a great warrior on the Rökstein). The existence of this much assimilation of written culture in lands hundreds of miles from the Empire suggests how much greater the assimilation was on the frontiers and within the Empire itself. On the culture of northern Europe during this period, see Karl Hauck, "Text und Bild in einer oralen Kultur," pp. 510–99, with references (particularly to his monumental series of articles on gold bracteates). The skeptical may wonder about our ability to define religion and particularly paganism from an evidentiary base chiefly composed of imagery, and some commentators clearly take Hauck's theses too far, e.g. Lotte Hedeager, "Kingdoms, ethnicity and material culture: Denmark in a European perspective," in *The Age of Sutton Hoo*, ed. Martin Carver (Woodbridge, 1992), pp. 279–300.

written texts – that are far more permanent and far less subject to change and contamination than the contents of the human mind.[104]

The barbarian groups, with their secretaries and notaries and interpreters, their letters demanding tribute, their codicils of office, their treaties and their enrollment on imperial tax registers, their acquisition of land and their members' involvement in law-courts, were as inundated by the avalanche of papyrus as any other inhabitants of the Empire. In every city that the Balkan Goths entered – Dyrrachium, Novae or Serdica – they were surrounded by the euergetic mass of civic inscription, the power of the Roman word and the Roman emperor inscribed into stone. This is not to mention the education of kings and royal families, and doubtless other aristocrats, and the pervasive influence of the church, which in the school of Ulfilas managed to create an entire written language and a scholarship devoted to the arcanities of Scriptural translation and commentaries. How could an autonomous oral tradition survive in such a milieu?

The *Getica* indeed preserves or records non-Latin group-names and place-names, just as classical ethnography had always done.[105] But it is difficult, if not impossible, to prove that it contains extra-Roman traditions in the sense of discrete and untainted traditions from *outside* the frontiers, and it is certainly impossible to prove whether anyone accepted any such tradition.

In fact, the profoundly literary and ethnographic content of the *Getica* is typical of the intellectual and ideological ferment of Constantinople in the early 550s, when old historical genres were being transformed and new ones developing. As Brian Croke has demonstrated, Jordanes moved in a section of this world. He was secretary to an eastern general, where he learned at first hand about the Roman army and its enemies in the Balkans. Croke summarizes, "Jordanes' commissioned works suggest an experienced army official moving in the outer reaches of the military and court circles in the capital and generally sharing its horizons and viewpoint."[106]

This assessment of Jordanes as Byzantine military official is surely correct. There is yet more nuance. Jordanes, a *native* of the Balkans, was bilingual in Greek and a specifically Moesian Latin. His grandfather

[104] Goody, "Introduction," pp. 4–10.
[105] Pliny, *Nat. Hist.* 4.14.99–101, preserves the non-Latin names of the "Burgodiones, Varinnae, Charini, Gutones": does this mean that Pliny was preserving oral tradition? Wolfram, "Origo et religio," pp. 19–38, argues that the preservation of such names demonstrates that the *Getica* preserved extra-Roman tradition, and that people must have believed in such tradition. But Korkkanen's analysis (above, n. 99) suggests that this tradition transmitted classical ethnographic literature, not orality.
[106] Croke, "Cassiodorus and the *Getica* of Jordanes," p. 134.

had also been secretary to a Balkan general – as had been Marcellinus Comes and Procopius.[107] Though the text suggests that Jordanes could have counted more diverse ancestry had he so wished,[108] he was happy to call himself a Goth, as long as he could distance himself from Arianism![109] Similarly, he could write about Goths favorably while applauding Justinian's victory over them. He thus differs from Procopius, who in his more classicizing style must support Mediterranean superiority unequivocally even when he admires individuals like Totila. Procopius, of course, came from Caesarea in Palestine and moved in learned classicizing circles in Constantinople;[110] Jordanes came from the Balkans and moved in military and religious circles. Without necessarily postulating any differences in belief or faction, their respective origins and genres meant that Jordanes could write about the Empire and a *gens* with which he was closely associated in different terms from those of Procopius.

But although Jordanes's text is clearly unusual, it does partake of a larger narrative current in Justinian's Constantinople – that of a fallen Empire in the stages of rebirth and regeneration.[111] A formal parallel to Jordanes is Marcellinus Comes, another Balkan Latin military historian who moved to Constantinople. It is in Marcellinus that the year 476 first appears as a historical turning point, alongside the suggestion that by the 520s the Western provinces had been lost to the Roman Empire through the stupidity of the generals and the fierceness of the barbarians. This notice is the first appearance of Justinian's *renovatio* and reconquest ideology, and it coincided with Justinian's accession to the throne in 527.[112] Jordanes picks up Marcellinus's notice about 476 and repeats it almost verbatim in both the *Romana* and the *Getica*.

Roman ethnography had often had an ideological intent: to clarify, in effect to schematize, imperial history in a providential geographical framework. We have seen a sixth-century Byzantine revival of this in Procopius's introduction to his *Wars*, where he justifies Justinian's reconquests through a Mediterranean-centered geographic survey.[113]

---

[107] Ibid., pp. 118–34.

[108] Goffart, *Narrators*, pp. 42–7, is insightful on this issue; Croke, "Cassiodorus and the *Getica* of Jordanes," p. 119–20 (on Jordanes's languages, also implying that he knew some form of Gothic – but there is no evidence for this).

[109] Croke, "Cassiodorus and the *Getica* of Jordanes," p. 125.

[110] Cameron, *Procopius*, pp. 5–18.

[111] See esp. Maas, *John Lydus and the Roman Past*, on *renovatio* in sixth-century Constantinople.

[112] Croke, "A.D. 476: the manufacture of a turning point," pp. 115–19; Krautschick, "Zwei Aspekte," pp. 358–67 with n. 114.

[113] Procopius, BV 1(3).2.2–6, discussed above, ch. 4, pp. 141–2. Elements of this passage are similar to notions of Jordanes (or vice-versa); see ch. 4, n. 181.

Similarly, the very structure of the *Getica* lays a heavy ethnogeographic emphasis on the Goths' attachment to the Balkans, a region which, as we have seen, had powerful resonances in sixth-century Byzantium. Although the Goths are said to originate in the island of Scandza, the work begins with an Exodus-like journey from Scandza to a region that Jordanes calls "Scythia."[114] Scandza is then forgotten about: Scythia is the great focus of the text. Jordanes describes this Scythia as the Goths' "aptissimae sedes," their rightful homeland, in a phrase that will recur.[115] The geography of this region is given in great detail repeatedly throughout the *Getica*, in no fewer than seven passages spread evenly throughout the work.[116] Scythia consists of lands on both sides of the Danube, that is, both within and without the Roman Empire, which the Goths themselves are said to predate.

Jordanes's "Scythia," though initially equivalent to the large Herodotean area north of the Danube, comes to mean the Balkan Roman provinces of Pannonia and Moesia, to some extent also Illyricum, Dacia and Thrace.[117] It is in these lands, the future imperial Balkan provinces, that the Goths go on to learn philosophy and wisdom from the neighbouring Greeks.[118] Eventually, their law and government can be compared with that of the neighbouring Romans.[119] They add these Mediterranean traits to their native barbarian virtue of military valor to produce a people who are *meant* to be living in the Balkans. As Goffart has noted, Jordanes then allots the Balkan Goths the most praise when they are in service to the Roman army.[120]

The central paradox of the *Getica* is its praise for the Goths, even when they are in revolt against the Empire, alongside its firm support for the central imperial system epitomized by the strong emperors Con-

---

[114] *Get.* 16–24 (Scandza, a climato-geographical description buttressed by Ptolemy and Mela); 25–9 (exodus from Scandza to Scythia, significantly using Josephus and the biblical story of Magog).

[115] *Get.* 27; 281; cf. 246, and note the notion of everyone returning to their *propriae sedes* at 110–12, after the Gothic devastations of the mid-third century.

[116] *Get.* 30–8 (overview of Scythian places and *gentes* mixed up and tied together, including Moesia, Dacia, Thrace, Illyricum and Pannnonia); 58–60 (Moesia); 73–5 (Dacia); 82–3 (referring back to 30–8); 93 (Marcianopolis in Moesia); 116–20 (the *gentes* along the Danube, mirroring Ptolemy, on which see n. 99, above); 178 (rivers of Scythia crossed by Attila); 263–71 (settlement of various *gentes* after the death of Attila, in Dacia, Pannonia, Scythia minor, Moesia and other regions in the Balkans).

[117] See references in previous note; *Get.* 82–3, on the division of the Goths into Ostrogoths and Visigoths, specifically refers to the portion of "Scythia" comprised of the Roman provinces of Moesia, Thrace, Dacia and Scythia minor.

[118] *Get.* 39–66 inserts the Goths into pre-Roman Mediterranean history, making them equivalent to Getae and Scythians in classical sources; wisdom learned from the Greeks at 39–42.

[119] *Get.* 67–72, under King Dicineus. The sentiment echoes *civilitas* ideology, which, however, does not appear in the section on Theoderic.

[120] Goffart, *Narrators*, pp. 62–8.

stantine, Theodosius and Justinian. This tension between imperial center and periphery is resolved through the use of an outside agent, namely, the Huns. The golden age of the Goths in Scythia, culminating with the rule of Hermanaric in the 360s, is terminated by the advent of this cruel, savage people, who are depicted as an unstoppable natural force.[121] The Huns bring the first part of the *Getica* to a close by dividing the Goths (unnaturally) into two groups, Ostrogoths and Visigoths, and by driving the latter into the Empire and precipitating the battle of Adrianople in 378.[122] The mismanagement of their reception into the Empire by Valens also plays an important role, however. The Romans are partly to blame for the subsequent disasters, the Eastern theme of the importance of 476 thus appearing earlier in history, and preparing us for its rectification by Justinian in the present day.[123]

The next part of the work, covering the period from 378 to 451, follows the fortunes of the Visigoths under the Balt kings and the Ostrogoths under the Amal kings in the conflicts between the Huns and Rome. The Visigoths are unable to gain adequate support or treaty from the vacillating emperors; the result is constant devastation of the Western provinces. The Ostrogoths are brought into the Empire as a subject army in Attila's confederation. This section ends with a lengthy set-piece on the Battle of the Catalaunian Fields in Gaul in 451, when the Romans, allied with the Visigoths, defeat the Hunnic confederation, which eventually dissolves, freeing the Ostrogoths to seek employment, once more, in the Scythian provinces.[124]

These repeated devastations lead up to the fall of the Western Empire in 476, a crucial turning-point in the *Getica*.[125] Here Jordanes suddenly announces that he has been explaining the history of the Goths from their origin in their "original Scythian homeland" to the present-day complexity of Ostrogoths and Visigoths.[126] This passage heads another major section on the Balkans containing more ethnography and geography.[127] The Balkans in turn set the stage for the invitation by Zeno to

---

[121] Golden age: *Get.* 116–20; appearance of Huns, *gens omni ferocitate atrocior*, 121–8.

[122] *Get.* 129–38.

[123] *Get.* 132–3 (Valens an Arian heretic); 146–51 (death of Theodosius *amator pacis generis Gothorum*); 152–8 (mismanagement of Honorius clearly underlined).

[124] *Get.* 159–224. The expansive section on the Battle of the Catalaunian Fields may use another source; it is marked by lengthy rhetorical passages and manufactured speeches to troops.

[125] *Get.* 242–3, very similar to Marcellinus Comes, tracing the Empire from Augustus to Augustulus.

[126] Jordanes, *Get.* 246, echoing *Get.* 82, which has prepared us for this development: the two passages occur at roughly one-third and two-thirds of the way through the text. The passage also mirrors *Rom.* 86. Weißensteiner, "Cassiodor/Jordanes als Geschichtsschreiber," n. 12, sees this passage as Jordanes's stated purpose.

[127] *Get.* 259–71.

Theoderic to lead his Ostrogothic troops from the Balkans to Italy to regain Rome for his rule.[128] Theoderic's Italy is then covered in about four pages of the printed edition, including the Gothic Wars, and the prediction of Justinian and Belisarius's glorious triumph over the Ostrogoths and the restoration of the Empire entire.[129]

This sprawling, digressive story swings around three narrative pivots that keep the reader focused on two ethnogeographic arguments. The first argument is that the Goths are destined to live in Scythia, whence they are driven by the Huns and imperial incompetence, and the second argument is that the Roman Emperor Justinian will destroy the Mediterranean kingdoms that they have built. The first pivot is *Getica* 79–83, which gives the genealogy of the Amals from Gapt to Germanus, and refers forwards and backwards, to the forthcoming destruction of the kingdom of the Amals at the end of the book, and to the long geography of Scythia at the beginning of the book.[130] The second pivot is the end of Hermanaric's golden age and the arrival of the Huns in Scythia at *Getica* 121–8, a parody of the exodus of the Goths themselves from Scandza. The third pivot is *Getica* 242–51, following the fall of the Huns: the description of the year 476, the repetition of part of the Amal genealogy from Hermanaric through Germanus, and the return to the ill-fated Ostrogoths who will leave their *antiquae Scythicae sedes* under the impact of the dissolution of the Hunnic kingdom. The following Balkan geographies and the mismanagement of Zeno prepare us for the establishment of Theoderic's kingdom in Italy, and its destruction by Justinian.

The Balkan geographies of the *Getica* serve Justinianic ideology. By easily tracing back two enemies – the Visigoths and the Ostrogoths, against whom Justinian's armies were fighting – to a Balkan origin, the *Getica* effectively restores an earlier order from an imperial and ethnographic point of view. At the same time it explains and justifies the obvious diversity of peoples within a section of the Empire. The Goths become an honorable but mobile *gens* with an *origo* and a destiny in Pannonia and Thrace, but who are now occupying Spain and Italy to the detriment of the Empire. Ideally they should live at peace, serving the Balkan armies under the Roman emperor.

Jordanes need not have been working for Justinian explicitly in order to espouse or propagate the Eastern ideology of reconquest and renewal. As recent studies have demonstrated for Procopius, Agathias and John Lydus, works produced in Justinianic Constantinople were impercep-

---

[128] *Get.* 272–88.

[129] *Get.* 289–314. Note that this passage does not predict the end of the Goths, merely the end of their independent rule outside the emperor's authority.

[130] *Get.* 81, 82–3.

tibly suffused by the emperor's powerful ideology and propaganda, publicized assiduously over the previous quarter-century.[131] Nor did Justinian invent *renovatio* ideology and the revival of ethnogeography out of
his own head. These were ideas floating around the capital, if with
strong government support. Constantinopolitans could oppose specific
policies of the emperor, as did Jordanes, Procopius and Lydus, while
firmly supporting his *Weltanschauung*, itself a product of a culture in
which they participated.[132]

When we further place Jordanes as a Latin speaker in a Greek world,
as a military man in the capital, and as a Balkan provincial in the East,
the notion that his views could reflect Justinian's seems less odd. Political circumstances, moreover, suggest that this was the only option for
a writer at the time. Jordanes's mysterious patrons, Vigilius and Castal-
ius, are allotted the honorifics due to Byzantines of extremely high
position. After Justinian's political purges, it is unlikely that there were
any men in the capital who retained their position without at least
publicly supporting the emperor.[133] It was the year 550 or 551; the
Gothic Wars were still continuing, and the emperor and pope were
embroiled in the Three Chapters Controversy. It was at this time that
Justinian went to great lengths to prevent the captive pope Vigilius
from communicating with his suffragans in the West, for fear that the
pope would influence them or that they would influence the pope.[134]
Correct thinking was the only possible thinking, at least in public.

The *Getica* is thus not propaganda, but the product of men influenced
by propaganda. "Histories are not good vehicles for propaganda," says
Peter Heather, who compares their potential impact unfavorably with
that of panegyric.[135] But histories can reflect propaganda. Their interests
will be directed partly by the interests that the powerful think is healthy
for their subjects to have. There is no reason to think that Jordanes
thought of the conquest of Italy as anything other than a good thing,
despite his pro-Amal remarks.

The Balkans loom large in the *Getica*, a history written at a time
when the emperor and many of his highest servants were Balkan prov-

---

[131] Cameron, *Procopius*, pp. 19–32; Maas, *John Lydus*, pp. 83–96 and *passim*.

[132] Heather's assertion, *Goths and Romans*, p. 43, that Jordanes occasionally criticizes Justinian's
policies and therefore cannot support Justinianic ideology, will not stand. The parallels with
Procopius are obvious, and in fact Jordanes's criticisms strikingly mirror those of Procopius,
esp. *Get.* 364, 366 (Justinian's victories over internal enemies are not as glorious as Belisarius's
triumph over the Vandals).

[133] Honoré, *Tribonian*, pp. 22–3, on Justinian's ruthlessness toward ideological enemies.

[134] On this, see above, chs. 1 and 6.

[135] Heather, *Goths and Romans*, pp. 42–3; in contrast, at pp. 60–1 he argues that Cassiodorus's
original history reflected Amal propaganda.

incial elites transplanted to the cultural centers of the Mediterranean. The geographical and ethnographic tendentiousness of the text may document the strain in resolving these regional pecularities with Roman imperial and ideological norms. The defensiveness of the Balkan emperor himself about his homeland, and about his own Romanity, suggests that Jordanes indeed spoke for circles in the court.

Jordanes's ethnography of the major non-Roman group to which Balkan inhabitants were constantly presumed to belong, namely the Goths, sets that group in its proper place as an ancient extra-Roman *gens* within the Empire, and explains the multiplicity of names that that group seemed to have had, all associated with the Balkans: Scythians, Getae, Goths, Visigoths, Ostrogoths, even Huns. It makes the Balkans an epicenter of political events for the previous 2,000 years of history. It justifies Justinian's wars even while it admires a worthy enemy, and explains how that enemy came to possess large portions of the former Empire.

There is a single, possible, almost contemporary parallel for Jordanes's work. It is the lost *Isaurica* of the Lycian historian Capito, now attested only by citations in the *Ethnika* of Stephanus of Byzantium, and in the *Suidas*. About forty years before Jordanes, this Capito wrote a history of the Isaurians, another important military and "barbarian" group within the Roman Empire, and one with a distant past, coming from a region, like the Balkans, that produced the military emperors of the period.[136] Like the *Getica*, the *Isaurica* contained a host of ethnographic detail.[137] Like Jordanes, Capito also produced a work of Roman history, in this case, a translation of Eutropius, one of Jordanes's sources for the *Romana*.[138] Like Jordanes, Capito came from the region where his subjects lived, a region in which official sources describe provincials as the victims of Isaurian banditry – just as the provincials of the Balkans were supposed to have been the victims of the Goths.[139] Like Jordanes,

---

[136] Full references on Capito at ch. 4, n. 159, above. See PLRE2 Capito. On the Isaurians as barbarians, see Goffart, "Rome, Constantinople and the barbarians," p. 4, and Goffart, "The theme of *the* barbarian invasions," p. 113 with n. 7 (the group or its name had existed for centuries). On the Balkan and Isaurian emperors and usurpers, see above.

[137] The many references to the *Isaurica* in the *Ethnika* of Stephanus of Byzantium demonstrates the quantity of geographic and ethnographic detail to be found in the former. See *Ethnika* 260, 379, 456 and 591 for *ethnika* reported by Capito; 58, 75, 83–4, 129, 225, 368, 409, 444, 457, 525, 589, 591, 702 for geographical cities, *choria* and *phrouria* reported by Capito. All these are, of course, cities and regions of Lycia, Cappadocia and Isauria and their inhabitants grouped by *ethnika*: Capito's opinion of the Isaurians remains largely invisible, but see n. 140, below.

[138] Edition of Capito's translation cited above, ch. 4, n. 159; on Eutropius in the *Romana*: see Mommsen in Jordanes, pp. xxv–vi.

[139] On the Isaurians and banditry, see Jones, LRE I: 25, 116 and esp. 192; McCormick, *Eternal Victory*, p. 256; and above, ch. 1, n. 71; on official depictions of the Isaurians, see Goffart,

Capito could sympathize with the rebellious subjects of his work, but seems to have supported the Empire in which he lived.[140] The Balkans and Isauria were two regions where we have reason to believe that in fact provincials could cooperate with "bandits" or "barbarians."[141] We cannot know for certain, but it seems likely that the *Getica* and the *Isaurica* emerged from similar circumstances. The *Isaurica* is the only other known history of a barbarian group within the Roman Empire, and it was produced in the East toward the same period, at a time when interest in classical ethnography and the political importance of Goths and Isaurians ensured that such works would find an audience.

Although ethnographic discourse, historical genre and regional politics explain some of the peculiarities of the *Getica*, they leave open Jordanes's relationship to Cassiodorus. Any use of the *Getica* as evidence for a genuine Gothic ethnicity and culture must rest on the question of oral tradition (which, I have argued, it is impossible to isolate in the work) and its relationship to Theoderic's own propaganda as transmitted in Cassiodorus's lost *Gothic History*.

Did the *Getica* transmit Theoderican ideology unattested elsewhere? Despite its Justinianic tone, the *Getica* clearly contains elements of Cassiodorus's history, and thus of Theoderic's propaganda. Since Theoderic and Cassiodorus were also heavily influenced by classical ethnography, it makes sense that the text could preserve such elements. The work as a whole, if not in its detail, looks to me Justinianic, as it does to Goffart. But it is easy to see why Theoderic in his later years, combating the assimilation of his army at home and the claims of Justinianic *renovatio* ideology abroad, would also have wanted to establish a history of the Goths as a mobile people.

As we saw in chapter 2, the writing of Cassiodorus's *Gothic History* coincided with Theoderic's late propagation of a view of the Goths as

---

"Rome, Constantinople and the barbarians," p. 4. On depictions of the Goths in the Balkans, see above ch. 4 (Justinian); note also Zeno's allegations against Armatus and Theoderic Strabo, above.

[140] Sympathy for rebellious Isaurians: Capito described Conon of Psimatha in Isauria as a "wise man" (Stephanus, *Ethnika* 702); this Conon was a military man who became bishop of Apamea under the Isaurian Zeno, but then later became a general in the Isaurian rebellion against Anastasius in the early 490s: PLRE2 Conon 4. Support of the Empire: few more ideological statements of Roman imperial expansion and authority exist than Capito's other interest, Eutropius's *Breviarium*, dedicated to Valens "Gothicus" and beginning with a classic statement of victory ideology: Eutropius described the conquest of Isauria under P. Servilius Vatia, who received the victory cognomen "Isauricus": *Breviarium*, ed. Carlo Santini (Stuttgart, 1979), *praef.* and 1.1.1–2; 6.3 and 6.5. The parallel with the early Roman victories over the Goths, reported approvingly by Jordanes at *Rom.* 288–90, is clear: Goths and Isaurians belonged under Roman rule.

[141] Whittaker, *Frontiers*, pp. 192–3; on bandits, see also PA Mundo.

an elect *gens* led by Amal dynasty. Some of this clearly survives in the *Getica*, although the emphasis on the Amals has been submerged, as Goffart points out. The Amals are still mentioned in important places, in Jordanes's *genealogia Ostragatharum* and at the very end of the text, but they hardly pervade the entire ethnography of the Goths. No text that ends with such a eulogy to Justinian, and that contains so little on the Amals, can be identical to the text that Cassiodorus says he produced in his letter to the senate.

It does not in fact matter for this argument whether or not Jordanes preserves Cassiodorus. Although Jordanes cannot have preserved "the sense intact if not the words," as he himself claims,[142] he could have preserved the "words intact," and given them an entirely new meaning. Doubtful though it seems, Johann Weißensteiner has announced that he will present an argument that every sentence in Jordanes can be traced stylistically to Cassiodorus.[143] This need not invalidate arguments about the effect of the work as a whole. The selective choice of sentences and sections can always produce a new work. Since Jordanes also says that he added new material, I think that we must conclude that we have, essentially, a new work, a Justinianic work, whether Cassiodorus participated in its final redaction or not.

There is finally the matter of ethnogenesis. Herwig Wolfram sees the Amal-dynastic material in the *Getica* as evidence for the creation of the Gothic *gens*, an ethnogenesis. We know that Theoderic was creating a Gothic Amal past in the 520s.[144] The elements that Jordanes took from Cassiodorus surely include the Amal genealogy extending back to the eponymous Ostrogotha, parts of which are also attested in the late *Variae*, as we saw in chapter 2.

But we cannot use merely the propagation of ideology as evidence for an ethnogenesis of the Goths in Italy. We need to see people receiving and reacting to that ideology. The analysis of individual behavior in the previous chapters demonstrates that if any such reception occurred, it was restricted to the increasing encroachment of the army on civil affairs, culminating in the conflict over Athalaric's education. *Civilitas* ideology and professional notions of a Gothic army proved more enduring than Theoderic's dynastic claims, as the actions of Totila and Witigis respectively demonstrate. The notion of a Gothic *gens* providentially chosen by the leadership of the Amals finds little resonance in the individual behavior of people labeled Goth in Italy.

---

[142] Jordanes, *Get.* 2.
[143] Announced by Weißensteiner, "Cassiodor/Jordanes als Geschichtsschreiber."
[144] See ch. 2, above.

Very shortly after the composition of Cassiodorus's *Gothic History*, Witigis would reject the Amals, Justinian would invade Italy, and Vigilius would begin to identify Goths as Arian heretics. Witigis emphasized the military *virtus* of the Goths over royal sacrality. The pressing needs of the moment competed fiercely with any attractions that Theoderic's late ideology might offer to people called Goths, or that it might offer to people who might call themselves Goths in certain circumstances. The people who benefited from the king in his later years and from his successors, Cyprian, Opilio, Tuluin, Witigis, Cassiodorus and Liberius, had all left Italy or vanished from history by the year 540. Flavius Maximus, the senator who married into the Amal family, suffered woefully from both sides during the Wars. The Goths who were left had little reason to thank the treacherous Amals, much as they might revere the memory of Theoderic himself.

There was no time for an ethnogenesis to occur, and political circumstances, combined with the increasing multiple allegiances and local ties of people who could be called Goths, militate against the possibility that any such ethnogenesis did occur. When we add to this evidence the argument that the *Getica* of Jordanes is a product of the meeting between Byzantine Constantinople and Balkan military culture, and can only imperfectly reflect the text of Cassiodorus in the 520s, let alone the propaganda of Theoderic, the value of Jordanes for Gothic ethnogenesis seems slight indeed.

The *Getica* of Jordanes may well preserve elements of Theoderic's dynastic ideology via Cassiodorus, but it has much more to tell us than just that. The work of Jordanes represents an attempt to reconcile ethnogeography with the disappearance of a Mediterranean-wide political and cultural unity. He wrote at a crucial political juncture for his compatriot, the Balkan provincial Justinian, and the many Balkan advisers and soldiers with which the emperor surrounded himself. The Balkan military context suggests that Jordanes's history is a sixth-century Byzantine history, an attempt to remake the past using old tools. Amidst chaotic regional change, the eruption of ethnography in Eastern texts, such as those of Jordanes and Capito, can be seen as an attempt to stabilize and explain such confusion, in a language inherited from centuries earlier and itself evolving into something new.

THE WIDER CONTEXT: BARBARIANS IN THE WEST

The Balkan military context suggests that the history of Ostrogothic Italy is the history of collapsing frontiers, the merging of margin and center, the workings of social, political and ideological change caused by the availability of new identities clashing with the claims of ancient and well-established notions of power and hegemony. Such confusion eroded existing boundaries of identity, replacing the dichotomy "citizen–barbarian" with the dichotomies "civilian–soldier" or "Thracian–Constantinopolitan."

Nevertheless, historians have paid more attention to the similarities between the Goths and the other barbarians in the West than to those between the Goths and the Byzantine armies, between Theoderic and Justinian. Some of these similarities were real. The East Germanic language-family, the ties of kinship and marriage among royal families, and particularly the Arian religion common among all these royal families, suggest that a Balkan origin cannot be the only explanation for the cohesiveness of Theoderic's original Goths in 489.

Here I can only briefly suggest that barbarian similarities owe less to Germanic culture and ethnicity than to an intermarried military aristocracy that included the imperial dynasties, and to elements of frontier culture that spread throughout the Mediterranean with mobile armies – whether "Roman" or "barbarian" – in the fifth century. In fact, the differences in the evolution of the various barbarian groups of the West are as striking as the similarities, and these differences emerge not only from the varying origins of the barbarian groups but also from the differences between the provinces through which they moved and eventually settled. New studies of the various groups and provinces involved could refine this picture of varied evolution and experience.

The Ostrogoths are frequently compared with the Vandals, whose royal family was also Arian. The Arian heresy existed in Africa before the arrival of the Vandals; after their arrival, the church there achieved the name *ecclesia Vandalorum* – an apparent parallel to the *ecclesia legis Gothorum*. But unlike in Italy, the Vandal kings believed that "Vandal" ought to be equivalent to "Arian," and used persecution to make Arianism a state religion. Again in contrast with Italy, the persecuted Catholic hierarchy explicitly made the equation between "Vandal" and "Arian," even though there were people called "Vandals" who were also Catholics. Arianism became so important to the Vandal identity that despite the relaxation of persecution by the later kings, Vandal soldiers refused to become assimilated into Justinian's armies because of their Arianism.[145] No religious scruples stopped soldiers of the Gothic army from joining the Byzantine side in Italy, where even among the Arian church hierarchy the word "Goth" could designate "Arian."

Provinces exercised their own influence on the development of their

---

[145] Kaegi, "Arianism and the Byzantine army in Africa," pp. 23–53.

cultural history. The fierceness of the Vandal persecution of Catholics may have its roots in the fierceness of Christian division in Africa as much as in any culture carried by the Vandal kings themselves. Had not the Arian church learned its lessons from the strictly coercive and repressive Catholic church of Augustine, itself a legacy of the persecutions of the time of Cyprian and of the Donatists? The rigorous African form of Latin Christianity survived the downfall of the Vandal kings. After the 530s, the African bishops took the lead in opposing the Three Chapters edicts of the emperor, and Numidian opposition to the pope continued into the 590s. Fierce religious localism, smeared as "Donatism" by its opponents, continued into the late 500s.[146]

Arianism was not widespread in the rest of the Roman West at the beginning of the fifth century, and in southern Gaul and in Spain, the kings of the Burgundians and the Visigoths, and some of their followers, may have effectively reintroduced the heresy, or introduced it for the first time. Like the family of Theoderic, the Burgundian royal family counted several Catholics among its ranks, one of whom, Sigismund, became king in 516.[147] In Burgundy, there is no evidence whatsoever for an identification of the ethnographic name "Burgundian" with the Arianism of some of the kings. In fact, in Burgundy, "Arian" seems to have had associations with "Goth," as in Italy.[148] This evidence suggests that Arianism in Gaul and Spain, unlike in Italy, was a new introduction that took its association with the name Goth from the Visigothic kings, from the influence of the Gothic Arian church of Italy, and, of course, from the probable use of Gothic texts such as Ulfilas's Bible, which seems to have undergone textual criticism and transmission in these regions in the fifth century.

There is evidence for persecution or conflict in the Visigothic kingdom, but it did not become fierce until the reign of Leovigild (555–68). In Visigothic Spain, "Goth" does seem to have become equivalent to "Arian" because "Roman was used as a synonym for "Catholic." But a Catholic Gallic writer such as Avitus of Vienne went out of his way to avoid ethnographic terminology at the same time that his own kings, Gundobad and Sigismund, were propagating such terminology in

---

[146] On African ecclesiology and dissent, and on repression and the need for unity as embodied in the thought transmitted by Cyprian, Augustine and (paradoxically) the Donatists, see Markus, *Saeculum*, pp. 127–53; and Markus, "Reflections on religious dissent in north Africa," pp. 146–9.

[147] Wood, "Avitus of Vienne," pp. 150–1: Catholics in the Burgundian royal family include Sigismund, Chlothilde, Crona, Theudelinda, Caratene, and probably also the early rulers Gundioc and Chilperic I.

[148] Amory, "Names, ethnic identity, and community," p. 15 with n. 94.

their law-codes.[149] The Catholic clergy of Burgundy had either dropped ethnogeography completely, which would make sense in light of the influence of Augustinianism on Avitus of Vienne, or saw no need to use it. The notion of a Eusebian Christian Empire, still so seductive to the popes and some Italian Catholics, exercised little attraction for the clergy of Gaul.[150]

Service in the imperial armies, and a heritage in the theological diversity of the Balkans, offers an alternative explanation for Arianism among the southern European barbarian groups. In whatever way Arianism spread in the late Roman and post-Roman West, it was favored among soldiers, which mirrors the general use of Germanic names among soldiers all over the Mediterranean. The Eastern Roman emperors up to Justinian found it convenient to make exceptions to the laws against Arianism for their own armies, where the religion was apparently popular. Among these same armies, Germanic names were widespread from the early or mid-fifth century onwards. They might be attached to people called "Goths" (Gainas or Aspar) or to people called "Romans" (Venilus, the son of Vitalian, or Areobindus).

Similarly a language called "Gothic" was spoken by at least one Byzantine soldier, Bessas – called by one source a Goth, by another a mixture of various other ethnographic names. I have already suggested that this language was some sort of Mediterranean military cant if it had any real existence as a language at all. It may simply have been a soldier's koiné, Latin in origin, but so penetrated by vocabulary from other languages, including Germanic ones, to have been seen as a different tongue by some contemporaries.

All these cultural features saw different evolutions and different destinies in the former Roman provinces. In northern Gaul, Germanic names and Catholicism spread to all parts of society. In southern Gaul and in Spain, senatorial bishops retained their family names but eventually adopted Germanic names as well, while military *comites* with Germanic names who adopted Catholicism might also take non-Germanic names into their families.[151] In Africa, Arianism continued to exist not only alongside Catholicism, but also alongside other forms of religious dissent, just as Latin and Germanic names existed alongside Punic and Berber names. Latin names existed among the Arian clergy of Africa,

---

[149] Ibid., pp. 13–14; Amory, "Ethnographic rhetoric, political allegiance and aristocratic attitudes," pp. 447–8.

[150] See above, ch. 6, on Gallic ecclesiological developments in the context of the overtures of the papacy and the Eastern church, particularly the Three Chapters Controversy, by which time there was no question of respecting the emperor's role in making doctrine.

[151] Amory, "Names, ethnic identity and comunity," pp. 27–8.

who under certain circumstances might pretend that they only spoke their Germanic liturgical language, written Gothic.

Of course, a Balkan origin cannot explain why the Arian religion was also associated with the Vandal kings and some members of the Burgundian royal family, whose histories carried their dynasties back to the Rhine or the Alps or the regions just beyond. We do not know how these families, and some of their followers, became converted, since we know little about any groups bearing these names before they founded kingdoms. Perhaps Arianism was passed on during the fourth and fifth centuries via evangelism along the Danube frontier and thence to communities on the Rhine or in the interior of Germany. But it would be odd if the Vandals and Burgundians succeeded in carrying the Arian religion *out* of Germany, leaving no traces behind. Or perhaps some members of these groups received it from service in the Roman army, the Burgundians under Constantius or Aetius, the Vandals with Boniface (all three, however, Catholics), or perhaps from contact with Alaric's Visigoths. We simply do not know how Arianism spread in these Western regions, and we should beware of connecting it with any culture other than Ulfila's Bible, a Balkan production.

The truth is probably related to the diverse geographical origins of groups calling themselves Vandals. The Vandals, Alans and Sueves who invaded Gaul by crossing the Rhine at the end of 406 had not all originated in Germany. Jerome tells us that they contained *Pannoniani provinciales* among their ranks – provincials, that is, from his own province. We have seen that Pannonia, like other Balkan provinces, was home to Arian communities. Although the armed groups of 406 were just then moving across the Rhine, evidently some of their members had come there from elsewhere, in the Balkans. The evidence does not permit a firm conclusion, but it is striking that upon their first appearance in history, the strongly Arian Vandals are allotted a connection with the Balkans.

The Byzantine Empire retained the diversity of the Roman Empire for as long as it retained lands over all the Mediterranean. In the East alone, different sorts of monophysitism contended with Catholicism (Chalcedonian orthodoxy) and Nestorianism. Among the aristocracy, Germanic, Greek, Latin, Egyptian and Syrian names were all common, and, of course, Syriac and Coptic were spoken in addition to Greek and Latin. The close identification of the Empire with orthodox Christianity and the Greek language could only really begin after the mid-seventh century, when it finally lost Africa, Egypt and most of the Balkans. At all times we must keep the diversity of the Empire itself firmly in mind. Any similarities among the barbarian groups must be set in the imperial context in which they all lived and by which they were all influenced.

CONCLUSION

Any cultural traits in Italy associated with Goths were in fact widespread across the Mediterranean. They were originally part of a Balkan frontier world of soldiers and warbands in the occasional service of the Roman emperor. In the late fifth and early sixth centuries, this varied milieu threw up a series of Eastern emperors, and also, I argue, Theoderic himself. The Eastern emperors had decided to lay claim to the name "Roman," Theoderic to the name "Goth." His choice was doubtless dictated by the names claimed by his ancestors, but was also one of political, military and religious expedience.

It was difficult for outsiders to tell who were Romans and who were Goths, so regional had become the Balkan military milieu. Personal names, religious affiliation, profession and place of birth offered no reliable guide. Nor did the group-name of the people led by a general: if Vitalian led Huns, was he himself a Hun? If Odoacer led Sciri, was he himself a Scirian? One could always fall back on the word *barbaros*, but since that word had come to mean "soldier" anyway, one ran the risk of tautology. Since so many successful soldiers were Balkan, the tautology expressed a semantic reality.

The issue of Balkan identity would not have been important had it not been for the pressing issue of political allegiance. Constantinople was within attacking distance of these chronically disrupted provinces, as both Theoderic and Vitalian well knew. The Eastern emperors could not afford any threat to their power with Persia rising again in the East. As Isauria and Thrace offered usurpers and rebels, the emperors found themselves returning to imperial victory ideology as a means of ensuring their continued hegemony within their realm.

With the emperor claiming the name "Roman" so nearby, it was incumbent upon rebel military leaders in the Balkans to define themselves and their followers, for the purpose of political cohesion. Simply calling oneself "Roman" if one was in revolt could lead to the dangers of failed usurpation, the fate of Basiliscus and Vitalian. But ethnographic group-names, available culturally in the region anyway through the history there of groups with those names, and also, as I have suggested, through the general knowledge of classical ethnography, offered alternative means of identifying oneself and mobilizing support. *Gothi* could be in revolt with the emperor if they were *foederati*, simply demanding food and employment, not the replacement of the emperor himself.

Basiliscus chose usurpation; his nephew Odoacer chose a more subtle and less dangerous route: rule, not reign. He sent the imperial regalia from Italy to the discomfited Zeno, assuring the emperor that he would govern in his name.

The existence of these group-names, and of people claiming these group-names, demonstrates nothing about distinctive cultural traits, let alone ethnic identity. The various warbands in the Balkans were not mutually distinguishable from one another except insofar as they claimed different names, and these names changed. Even when one of these warbands moved to Italy, the *Gothi* of Theoderic, they brought nothing new – Arianism, Germanic names and military dress having been there before – and their rapid assimilation of Odoacer's Italian soldiers ensured that the group could retain no distinctive homogeneity anyway.

In 550 or 551, one member of this Balkan milieu, Jordanes, set down a schematized history of one of the most popular group-names claimed in the Balkans, at a time when the Balkan military emperor was going to great extremes to homogenize his empire and to prove that he was a Roman. What Jordanes's personal motivations were, or those of his patrons, we cannot say. It is hardly surprising, given his Balkan origins and those of many soldiers around the palace, that he and his patron could be associated with the Goths. But the effect of such a work, produced at such a time and in such a place, was to publicize the reassuring maxims of classical ethnography. "So much for the origin of the Goths and the nobility of the Amals and the deeds of strong men. This praiseworthy family has given way to the even more praiseworthy prince, and has surrendered to a stronger leader, and their fame will never be silenced in any century or in any age; for the *victor et triumphator* the Emperor Justinian, and the consul Belisarius, will be called the victors over the Vandals of Africa and of the Goths." The eventual failure of Justinian and his successors to retain the allegiance of Africa and Italy and finally, after Phocas, the Balkans, was partly a result of the inadequacy of imperial ideology to draw together the varied elites of new frontiers into a single homogeneous cultural, religious and political culture determined by Constantinople.

CONCLUSION

Ethnographic discourse did not merely describe society: it attempted to order and reorder it. This reordering succeeded in creating something different from ethnicity: political opportunities that vanished as soon as they appeared. The many uses of ethnographic discourse in fifth- and sixth-century Italy evolved over periods of time, and conflicted with each other and with non-ethnographic ways of imagining community. The words "Goth" and "Roman," redefinable as they were, could never fully describe or reorder a society far more complex than a division into two groups. Although some people attempted to fit themselves into the historically received categories of Goth and Roman in different ways at different times, in the end neither of these categories succeeded in constructing a meaningful or permanent community. Rather, they succeeded in changing individual behavior briefly, introducing new routes to political power for the ambitious, and destroying the lives of those who could not take advantage of them.

In Ostrogothic Italy, the words of the powerful weighed heavily on people's necks. Ideology did not float away, unnoticed, into the air. Everyone was surrounded by the marks and pressures of officialdom, the demands of the priest, the magistrate, the tax collector and the general. A lengthy ceremony surrounded even the request to enter the judge's office to present a petition.[1] At the end of a case judged in his favor, a relieved *curialis* said "limitless thanks" and the court notary duly set down his words in the record.[2] Gundila and his heirs spent year after year in petitions to Belisarius, the pope, the Arian bishop of Rome, and an urban magistrate, in order to hold on to their property.

Ideology forced changes in behavior, but did not always implant ethnographic allegiances in people's minds. Even after the Byzantine conquest of Italy, not all the emperor's new subjects used the ethnographic rhetoric of Pelagius II and Gregory the Great. A papyrus document issued in Ravenna in the year 553 refers to the wars as *tempus hoc*

---

[1] *PItal* 21.3–10.
[2] *PDip* 107: "Vigilius dixit infinitas gratias."

314

barbarici. For the scribe of this document, barbarity referred not to the governance of Italy under the Goths, but rather, unsurprisingly, to the long devastation of Italy by the wars between the emperor's generals and the Gothic kings.[3] This is as close as we can get to a written statement of Italian views of the wars. The woman making this donation to the Catholic church of Ravenna bore a Germanic name, as did her father and her husband. Her brother bore both a Germanic and a Latin name.[4] Justinian's ideology, resonant though it might be in certain circles, could not adequately categorize such a family.[5]

Classical ethnography did not have the same meaning or goals as our ethnography, just as sixth-century historical writing is only superficially similar to our historical writing. Modern observers have taken Procopius and Jordanes for impartial observers of events, not men who wrote in a literary genre that contemporaries confused with panegyric.[6] Some scholars continue to believe that Jordanes wrote a history of the Goths because someone had a romantic interest in the history of his own people. But the *Getica* is clearly more than just a history – or a romance. The recreation of the past under current political auspices was a pre-occupation of the age of Theoderic and Justinian, and Jordanes was no exception.

While classical ethnogeography petrified as a system, inappropriate for the political realities of the late antique Mediterranean, it continued to exert an influence on anyone brought up with a traditional education. Even Augustine, who did more than any other writer to demolish the continuing importance of ethnography as an explicative discourse, was unable fully to shrug off the assumptions that had surrounded him as he grew up. Barbarians will become Christians, but as he famously remarked in a different context, "not yet." It was left to later ecclesiastical writers to take the logic of Augustine's arguments to their conclusion, and to take practical steps to expand the Christian community beyond the Roman polity.

---

[3] *PItal* 13.11; on *barbaricum* meaning "war," cf. *Liber diurnus* 86: "sive pacis sive barbarici temporis;" further, Tjäder 1: 444, n. 5.

[4] PA **R**anilo, Felithanc, **A**derit, **A**demunt qui et Andreas.

[5] It is further noteworthy that the late sixth- or early seventh-century Italian commentary on the *Codex Iustinianus*, the *Summa Perusina*, changes the word *barbari* to *gentes* or *inimici*: 4.24.6 (*ad inimicus*); 4.40.2; 4.41.1; 4.63.2 (*gentes inimicae*); 8.50.9: ed. Friderico Patetta, *Bulletino dell'Istituto di diritto Romano* 12 (1900); on the date, Patetta, pp. lxii–lxv (probably first half of the seventh century); Brown, *Gentlemen and Officers*, p. 105 (probably second half of the sixth century). The *Summa* was produced in Byzantine Italy, probably in or near Rome (Patetta, p. xliv); it contrasts notably with the ethnographic rhetoric of some contemporary popes (PA **P**elagius II and Gregory the Great, both notable for their classicizing fulminations against the barbaric Lombards).

[6] MacCormack, "Latin prose panegyrics," pp. 151–4.

The obvious decline of ethnogeography as a useful way of under-standing the world did not lead to its disappearance, but rather either to its artificial revival (under Justinian) or to the selective use of its literary and artistic elements for purposes far removed from its original conception (under Theoderic).

Both Theoderic and Justinian laid claim to ancient names and their associated ethnographic culture, propagating ideologies designed to extend their own hegemony in the name of restoring the past. Individuals who did not fit into these schematized formulations of social community and Mediterranean history could choose to modify their behavior in order to take advantage of a group-name or to disassociate themselves from it. Armatus, the relative of Odoacer and the "bar-barian" Basiliscus, and an associate of Theoderic Strabo, identified himself with Achilles and the classical ideal of a warrior. Cyprian, a "Roman" from an established Italian provincial family, identified him-self with the Goths and the Gothic language. Both were reacting to prevailing ideology of how Romans or barbarians should behave. Such reactions to ideology were not uncommon. Merovingians who wanted to remove themselves from the complexities and danger of their family politics had themselves tonsured, removing the visible sign of their Merovingian status, and taking on the safe identity of a Christian monk. The name-changes and naming strategies of profession and religion explored in chapters 3, 5 and 7 are related phenomena.

We cannot say to what extent these vagaries of behavior were "rational choices." For an Italian Catholic soldier of the early sixth century, a Germanic name carried a complex mixture of associations: military glory, family, the taint of heretical belief. Armatus, a native of the Balkans and the Aegean culture-province, could have looked nat-urally back to Homeric heroes as models of behavior, a past inextricably connected to the military Balkans and the disrupted Roman provinces of his own time. Material gain offered pressing reasons to alter one's behavior or to choose different names, but this behavior and these names came from a common past that only we can divide into categor-ies like "Graeco-Roman" or "Germanic." For fifth- and sixth-century Mediterranean men and women, classical education and its associated ethnographic categories was only one element of a common culture that included a vast diversity of ways of behaving. On this culture, the restricting ideologies of Justinian and Theoderic made an impact, but that impact was scattered and diffuse, producing a variety of individual reactions themselves rooted in the enduring allegiances of profession and region.

It should be absolutely clear that in Ostrogothic Italy, ethnography had the same obscure relationship to real communities as historical writing and panegyric had to real events. Each could describe, and each could influence, the way the world was supposed to be. The influence of ethnography did not create community, it created political opportunity. These opportunities could rapidly turn into disadvantages, since those in power kept rewriting the rules of the game.

Ethnicity itself is in constant evolution, and ethnic groups constantly change in membership. But our changing groups of *Gothi* and *Romani* cannot usefully be described as ethnic groups. Although *gens* and *natio* contain etymological connotations of descent, no one in Ostrogothic Italy attaches a belief in common descent to the words *Gothi* or *Romani*. Theoderic's *maiores* are the Roman emperors, the praiseworthy creators of the good institutions of *antiquitas*.

A modern comparison shows the hopelessness of selecting ethnicity as an explanation of group behavior in sixth-century Italy. In Krajina in Croatia, several armed bands have been fighting over their rights to rule the land. But in no way is this situation similar to the Gothic Wars. It is impossible to imagine defeated Croatian soldiers smoothly integrating themselves into Serbian armies, as Gothic soldiers did in the Byzantine armies. More than political allegiance is at stake in Krajina, since the different sides have the myth of ethnicity and the myth of "race" to propel their fighting. Only one group of people can win, and the other people must not only lose, but they must physically disappear. The Goths disappeared in Italy not because they were forced to leave the country, but because the indefinite name Goth lost every advantage that it had ever held, and became a positive disadvantage. People still lived in Italy who had been known as Goths, such as Aligernus and his men, but by changing their allegiance they changed their identity. Such an evanescent identity cannot be called ethnic, unless we wish to make ethnicity such a flexible term as to be almost meaningless.

The chief forces of group cohesion in Ostrogothic Italy were neither ethnic nor based on the group-names of classical ethnography. They were region and profession. The administrative structures of the realm allowed rapid advancement for the ambitious, particularly within the army. The circumstances of the settlement, and the generality of cultural traits called "Gothic" within the Mediterranean, allowed rapid and easy assimilation for the followers of Theoderic, and ensured that a number of identities remained available for anyone who could be called a Goth at any time.

Economics and history ensured that profession and region remained primary forms of identity. The late emperors laid down law after law requiring sons to take the professions of their fathers, *curiales* to take on their inherited responsibility, *coloni* to stay on the land that their parents had cultivated. These laws were ineffective, as their repeated promulgation shows, but the main escape-route from the straitjacket of region and profession was the imperial service, whether the army or the bureaucracy. The other option was to defect to usurpers or "barbarians" (or both), or to become a bandit.[7]

In the fifth century, all these escape-routes, including the army and the bureaucracy, had themselves become regionalized, the former in various provinces, the latter in Ravenna or Constantinople. The bureaucracy had always maintained a strong professional identity at its lower levels. The earlier barbarian groups had rarely moved through more than one diocese in a generation, with the possible exception of Alaric's Goths, a group that itself was constantly changing in membership. By the late fifth century each barbarian group-name within the Empire was associated firmly with one place, one *regnum*, with the exception of the disrupted Balkans.

From the late fifth century, Italian cities, which inherited the remnants of euergetic traditions of the past, commanded the primary loyalties of citizens who stayed there. Their economic activity was increasingly limited to their regions. Trans-Mediterranean trade continued in some luxury products. But for most cities, the chief focus of economic activity was among the *possessores* and the estates cultivated in the hinterland of the city. This had always to some extent been the case.[8]

Available political horizons had shrunk also, from a Mediterranean-wide arena to that of the peninsula of Italy and the adjacent regions conquered by Theoderic. Provincial families still provided sons for the *cursus honorum* of the palace and the bureaucracy, but this palace and bureaucracy were now firmly fixed in Italy. All these limitations on

---

[7] These seem to me to have been the main causes of mobility of population in the Mediterranean, although in the East there was a drain of country-dwellers into cities in the fifth and early sixth centuries. The removal of towns from valley sites to hilltops shows the effects of disruption; it does not prove that the bulk of population shifted hugely in the period. This topic demands further study. See Patlagean, *Pauvreté économique et pauvreté sociale*, pp. 301–40.

[8] A huge subject, to which I hope that the picture of community in Italy presented in this volume may contribute; see, among others, Bryan Ward-Perkins, "The towns of northern Italy: rebirth or renewal?" in *The Rebirth of Towns in the West, A.D. 700–1050*, ed. Richard Hodges and B. Hobley, CBA Research Report 68 (Oxford, 1988); S. J. B. Barnish, "Pigs, plebeians and *potentes*: Rome's economic hinterland, c. 350–600 A.D.," *Papers of the British School at Rome* 55 (1987), 157–85. On contemporary developments in Byzantium (delayed but similar), see Patlagean, *Pauvreté économique et pauvreté sociale*, pp. 156–235, esp. 156–81, drawing in Christian and cultural causes for the changes. Chris Wickham, "Marx, Sherlock Holmes and late Roman commerce," 1988, reprinted in Wickham, *Land and Power*, pp. 77–98, argues that Mediterranean long-distance trade depended on the existence of the imperial political structure.

regional and professional activity affected the ways in which people thought about community.

Gens and *natio* could indicate regions, of which Ostrogothic Italy contained many. The sixth-century popes were *natione Tuscus, natione Romanus* (the city of Rome) or *natione Campanus.* Two sisters buried in Rome in 442 were called "natione Galla" on their epitaph.[9] The epitaph of a man buried in Rome between 530 and 533 declared that he was "quem tellus genuit Italica, natus Picens."[10] A tutor at Rome used the rhetoric of the past to praise the city that had given him his livelihood, but he had come from Dacia, remembered his *patria* there and had a mother with a Thracian or Illyrian name.[11] We also find a Iohannis Alicensis from Halycias in Sicily,[12] and the family of a *comes* at Aquileia who were all "natione Itali, cives Aquilienses."[13] With the rare exceptions of the defensive declarations of Droctulfus, Asbadus and John the nephew of Vitalian, inscriptions, the most personal material that we have, never even associate the deceased with Goths or Romans. Not one inscription ever makes an unequivocal statement of Gothic or Roman identity.

Professional and regional labels were strangely intermixed. Italy contained not only taxpaying Veneti and Bruttii, but also Gravassiani and Pontonates who complained that excessive tribute had been imposed on them.[14] A former Italian *populus,* the Capillati, became a term for the soldiers of Italy.[15] The Breones of the Alps were a geographical group known to classical ethnography, but treated by Theoderic as uncontrollable barbarian soldiers.[16] Subdivisions of the Italian Gothic army, such as Rugians and Gepids, may have represented regiments who indeed preserved separate identities along with their ancient

---

[9] ICUR n.s. 8, no. 20819.

[10] ICUR n.s. 6, no. 15785, a *vir spectabilis*, with the comments of Antonio Ferrua, p. 58.

[11] ILCV 740: Dacia quem genuit suscepit inclita Roma, maerorem patriae tantum luctusque remisit (*inclita Roma* clearly referring to the city in which he was buried, but using language associated with victory ideology), quoting Vergil; his father's name was Alexander and his mother's name Dioclia. Similar layers of rhetorical identity appear in an edict of Glycerius (a.d. 473), to his praetorian prefect (who bore the Germanic name Himelco), which condemns simony in the name of avoiding misfortune for the *Romana gens*, but refers to cities of Italy as the *patriae* of their *cives*, ed. Gustav Haenel, *Corpus legum ab imperatoribus Romanis ante Iustinianum latarum, quae extra constitutionum codices supersunt* (Leipzig, 1857), p. 260. *Patria* means "homeland" for a man returning to his property, in *Var.* 3.46.4.

[12] ICUR n.s. 2, no. 4179.

[13] ILCV 284.

[14] *Var.* 4.38.

[15] Above, ch. 3, n. 43; below, appendix 4, pp. 345–6.

[16] Wolfram, "Ethnogenese im Donau- und Ostalpenraum," pp. 118–22; see further PA Servatus and the rhetoric of *Var.* 1.11.

group-names. But they were all soldiers, all Goths from the viewpoint of Theoderic and Justinian.

These Goths had become regional in a larger sense: they were by three definitions the army of Italy.[17] For Procopius, Italy contained Romans and Goths, or Romans (Byzantines), Italians and Goths. But in his geographical survey, the Italians consisted of a variety of undistinguished provincial groups and *gentes*: Calabrians, Apulians, Samnites, Piceni, Bruttii, Lucani, Veneti, Ligurians and Albani, the Tuscan peoples, Carnii and Norici. Beyond these were Siscii and Suevi, Dacians and Pannonians – and all these groups were ruled by the Goths.[18] His own text demonstrates how the soldier-Goths were also members of these various groups.

On top of these local allegiances, the changing and competing ideologies of secular and ecclesiastical institutions offered the history-laden names of classical ethnography as forms of cohesion. Paradoxically, the propagation of ethnographic ideology fostered not cohesion, but disruption. The competition of ideologies of community culminated in the twenty-years devastation of Italy that we call the Gothic Wars, during which individuals – who at their hearts held allegiance to their families, properties and professions – were forced constantly to choose changing higher loyalties, and to suffer for their choices. By the year 600, Italy was divided, but not between Goths and Romans. Both groups had effectively disappeared.

[17] In the two ideologies of Theoderic, and in that of Justinian.
[18] Procopius, BG I(5)15.20–30.

Appendix 1

THE INQUIRY INTO GUNDILA'S PROPERTY:
A TRANSLATION AND CHRONOLOGY

TRANSLATION OF *PItal* **49** (*inquest of 557: two attached documents*)

. . . and that it should be returned by the abbot Anastasius, and that he should possess it . . . Afterwards, he came with his sons, fully converted from his sin [*malus*] . . . [I swear,] by the four evangelists that these things, which I have said . . .

[*End of earlier document. In a different hand:*]

In the thirty-first year of the reign of our lord Justinian, ever Augustus, and in the sixteenth year after the consulate of Basilius, in the fifth indiction [A.D. 557], on the third of June. I have written this at the request of Sitza, *vir honestus*, [?*com* . . .] . . . [1]

. . . that he [Sitza] had been invited by the order of Adeodatus, *vir spectabilis*, *vicarius urbis emininentissimi praefecti*, before Andreas, *vir strenuus, executor* . . . [and the] representative of the monastery of St. Aelia . . . and St. Stephanus, so that . . . he should say what he knew, by the holy evangelists . . . [and] whence he knew it.

[SITZA:] ". . . Gundila [wished to be] converted by [Vig]ilius, and in our faith [*lex nostra*] he converted him . . . They had occupied it . . . [*or* the Goths had occupied it . . . by Tzalico[2]], and whatever he was able to find. Once he had converted, he made a donation to the church of St. Maria in Nepi with his wife and his sons."

[ANDREAS:] Andreas, *vir strenuus, executor*, asked him, "And how do you know this, and how old are you?"

[SITZA:] To which responded the aforementioned Sitza, "I am sixty years old, and more . . ."

[?SITZA:] " . . . Then, after he had been converted, he went to Rome and asked the pope and the bishop of the Goths and they gave him the order that

---

[1] On Sitza's status, see Tjäder 2: 299, n. 7 (perhaps *inluster*), and PA Sitza.

[2] Tjäder does not hazard a translation of lines 15–16, "a̲to̲ti [. . ..] o̲ccupav̲erunt ill[. . ..]c[. . . . . .]a̲sa̲lent[..] in [. . . . .] // c̲one" (underlined letters indicate uncertain readings), but does suggest that the first "t" in "toti" can just as well be a "g," to produce "Goti," while the space at the end of line 15 could easily hold "Tzali-", to add up with line 16 to produce "Tzalicone," ablative. Moreover, the readings "Goths" and "Tzalico" would work well with the claim of Tzalico's sons to have already received the property, further on in the document: Tjäder 2: 300, n. 12. See also discussion, below.

he should receive his property, and he did receive it. After he [had] received it, after some time came the sons of Tzalico *comes*, and they similarly occupied those portions saying that it had been a donative. Also after several years came the *patricius* Belisarius . . . he asked the *patricius* Belisarius, saying, 'why, after I have converted, have the sons of Tzalico *comes* come, . . . ri and Gudila, and occupied my property?' [Belisarius replied], '. . . my son." And he handed over those portions . . . [?]

[?SITZA:] "Afterwards he announced it to the pope, and said that a good thing would be done, if. . . And the pope soon became furious, and made out an order and sent it to . . . that abbot, and made him return the portions, so that he [Gundila] should possess them . . . [?And I swear that what I have said . . .]"

[Later document breaks off here]

CHRONOLOGY

This translation and interpretation owes much to Tjäder 2: 194–9, 298–302, to whose skill and ingenuity I am fully indebted. Indeed, if one looks at the reproduction of this important but well-used and obscure document at Tjäder 3, plates 153–4, one might be tempted to call Tjäder's work an act of heroism.

My interpretation, building on Tjäder's, can be found under PA Gundila; see further chapter 5. I make only two new points: taking *donativa* as a technical, military term rather than merely as "gift," and placing Gundila's reversal of fortune in the context of the taking of Etruria by Totila's troops in the early 540s, among whom we must then count the *comes* Tzalico and his sons.

Absolute chronology

Terminus post quem: 537/8, Vigilius's consecration as pope
Terminus ante quem: 557, the date of the inquest
Events implied: 537/8–40, 544–6, Belisarius and Vigilius both
                        in Italy
                        c. 539–40, Byzantine army in Nepi
                        c. 541–4, Gothic army in Nepi
                        ?545–6, Byzantine army again in Nepi?
                        552, Gothic army in Nepi

Relative chronology

Several periods are envisaged:

1. Gundila loses his property for the first time, and converts to Catholicism under Vigilius to regain it.

2. "After some time," Tzalico *comes* or his sons occupied the property, "saying that it was a donative."

3. "After several years," Gundila approached Belisarius and Vigilius to regain his property, and got it. Part of it was still in the hands of Tzalico's sons, part of it in the hands of the monasteries.

4. An inquiry into the events took place at an uncertain time (the opening fragment). Perhaps one of the documents relating to Periods 1, 2 or 3. There were probably several of these.[3]

5. In 557, this inquiry took place, reopening the question under the adjudication of the *vicarius* of Rome (since Nepi was in the suburbicarian region), with a court officer (*executor*), a representative of one or both monasteries, and this witness, Sitza, who is clearly sympathetic to Gundila. The dispute appears to be between Gundila or his heirs, and the monasteries, but given the fragmentary state of the papyrus, we cannot close out the possible presence of the sons of Tzalico or of his heirs.

Period 1 must be between 538 and 541, at a time when the Byzantine army was in control of Etruria (it was retaken by Totila in 541/2) and also while Vigilius was still in Rome (he became pope in 537, left for Constantinople in 545, and never returned to the city). It must be "several years" before Period 3, which we can pinpoint to 544/5 or 546 (see below). As Tjäder points out, it must be after March 538, when Witigis lifted his siege of Rome, during which Vigilius had become pope.[4]

Period 2 cannot be immediately after Period 1 (but see below), since Gundila needs to have reclaimed his property, converted to Catholicism, visited Rome, returned to Nepi, and made a donation to the church of St. Maria. We may conjecture that it was in 541 or 542, when the army of Totila had swept down over the centre of Italy and retaken the cities of Etruria.[5] At this time, Tzalico and his sons were given Gundila's property or part of it.

Period 3 must be in 544/5, "after several years," when Belisarius returned to Italy for the first time since he left in early 540, and while Vigilius was still in Rome.[6] But it could be as late as 546, if we assume that Vigilius communicated with Belisarius from Sicily, where he stayed until January 547. Late in 545, Belisarius contemplated occupying cities

---

[3] At least two, probably more: Tjäder 2: 195, 197.

[4] Tjäder 2: 196.

[5] On this campaign, see Hodgkin, *Italy and Her Invaders* 4: 396–8; on Totila's further conquests in the region in early 545: see ibid., 462–3. Tzalico and his sons could have received the property as late as this.

[6] Tjäder 2: 196.

near Rome from which to help the besieged city, perhaps including Nepi, but does not seem to have put his plan into effect.[7] It is thus difficult to see how Belisarius could have "come" to Gundila, unless the two met elsewhere; Belisarius may merely have conveyed Gundila's request to the pope (see below).

Period 4, the earlier inquiry, could be a record made at the time of the events of Period 1 or 3, and brought by one of the parties to the dispute in 557.

Period 5 is 3 June 557, when the case was brought to the court of the *vicarius urbis*. (The documents may have all been brought together, in the form that we now have them, even later.)

However, if the alternative reading of "the Goths had occupied it . . . by Tzalico" is correct (see n. 2, above), its placement in the narrative makes Period 2 follow Period 1 very shortly. In this case, we must condense the narrative at its outset: Gundila converted in 540/1, but by the time he returned to Nepi from Rome, the city was already in the hands of Totila's army, and Gundila's property already in the hands of Tzalico. In Period 3, Tzalico's sons were then occupying it in the name of their father or as his heirs. Although Tzalico's family lost the property in Period 4, they may have subsequently regained it, since by 552 Nepi was again in the hands of the Goths.[8]

We also cannot exclude the possibility that it was Tzalico and his sons who gave some of Gundila's property to the monasteries. This would obviate the need to place Belisarius in Nepi in 544/5 or 546, and would explain why Belisarius passed Gundila's petition on to Vigilius, and why Vigilius wrote to the abbot (presumably the Anastasius mentioned in line 1). A donation by Tzalico's family might also explain why Vigilius was "furious." The pope owed his election to Belisarius, the commander of the Byzantine army, and as we saw in chapter 6, he was not only anti-Arian, but anti-Goth. Still in his phase of supporting Justinian's Christian Empire, Vigilius can have had little sympathy with Catholics who served under the banner of Totila, or any act of his clergy that annoyed Belisarius.

This interpretation allows the power of the Catholic church to continue in Nepi but does not require an unattested recapture of the city by Byzantine forces in the mid-540s. Since Nepi was in Gothic hands in 552, it may have been so steadily from the early 540s. On the other hand, the possible reference to Belisarius handing over "those portions" implies that he handed over the portions belonging to Tzalico and his

---

[7] Procopius, BG 3(7).13.13; Jordanes, *Rom.* 380.
[8] Procopius, BG 4(8).34.16.

sons, and conveyed the request to the pope that the portions belonging to the monasteries be given back to Gundila. This interpretation would definitely make Tzalico and his sons the Catholic patrons of the monasteries, but would again require Belisarius or his armies to have briefly reoccupied Nepi in the mid-540s.

Either way, it is important to note that the chronology and the history of Nepi in the Wars do not allow Tzalico or his sons to have received the property from Belisarius, despite the implications of Gundila's petition to the general. Tzalico or his sons must have received the *donativa* when the Gothic army was in control of Etruria, between 541 and 544, when Belisarius was out of Italy, and therefore from the Gothic king or one of his officers.

The interpretation that places Tzalico and his sons under Totila fits with the demands on allegiance of the ethnographic ideology of both sides, and with the constant stress on Gundila's conversion to Catholicism. If the alternative reading of line 15 *Gothi occupaverunt . . . Tzalicone* is correct, it gives further support to this interpretation of the events. True, its placement in the narrative is odd; we must then understand Sitza's return to the story after being asked about his age as a slight back-tracking and repetition of what he had already said. But such a repetition seems necessary in any case, since Sitza also restates that Gundila converted and received back his property. After the abrupt and apparently irrelevant interruption of the court officer, Sitza seems to want to emphasize his point that Gundila was the rightful owner by right of his conversion and the judgment of the pope, which doubtless would have carried weight in a suit against the monasteries.

To avoid any confusion, it must be stressed that there is no chance that the *reconciliatio* of Gundila had anything to do with Justinian's order that the Arian churches of Italy be *reconciliatae* to the Catholic church. The emperor made the decree enforcing *reconciliatio* in 555. Vigilius died in that year, and Belisarius did not come back to Italy after 545. The only possible chronologies are the ones given above.

Appendix 2

THE GERMANIC CULTURE CONSTRUCT: LANGUAGE, RELIGION, LAW, MATERIAL CULTURE

The distribution by their lord of due reward to the brave is straight out of heroic poetry, and Cassiodorus' Latin rhetoric surely hides a thoroughly Germanic event designed to preserve ties of lord and follower.[1]

The above quotation appears in a scholarly journal published in 1995, but it could just as well have appeared in 1895. The techniques are Victorian: "seeing through" a written text to the rude oral reality, ignoring late antique social models in favour of subsequent medieval social models, and appealing to a common sense ("surely") of European nationalist notions, based in the Victorian era on race, in the modern era on ethnicity.

Germanicist philological historiography uses presumed oral sources to trace a warlike, nomadic culture from Tacitus to *Beowulf*, from the Goths and Burgundians of the fifth century to the *Nibelungenlied* and Icelandic sagas of the thirteenth. It is alive and well.[2] The following is a necessary brief survey of recent research that re-evaluates the origin of cultural traits traditionally considered "Germanic," including language, religion, law and naming traditions. The related challenges to using archeological evidence as a key to ancient culture or ethnicity are discussed in appendix 3.

The language/culture-based antithesis "Roman–Germanic" is the philologist's translation of the ancient ethnographic antithesis "Roman–barbarian." It is no less simplifying or artificial than its classical equivalent. Today, the evidence demonstrating diversity within the Roman Empire itself militates against grouping together all the barbarian groups as a single cultural entity in the late antique Mediterranean. Any cultural similarities that did exist may derive from imperial service or residence

---

[1] Heather, "Theoderic," pp. 161–2, on *Var.* 5.26–7, the letter on the distribution of Theoderic's donative to the Gothic soldiers of Samnium and Picenum.

[2] Most recently, in the field of history: Luiselli, *Storia culturale dei rapporti tra mondo romano e mondo germanico* (1992), pp. 443–85; Russell, *The Germanization of Medieval Christianity* (1994), *passim*. In the field of linguistics: Winfred P. Lehmann, *Historical Linguistics* (3rd edn, London, 1992).

in certain frontier regions or provinces.[3] Still other cultural traits may derive from a larger Indo-European cultural framework, or may properly be allotted to a northern European oral culture that is poorly attested if at all in southern Europe.

Language need not determine peoples. The notion that it does appeared in the nineteenth-century German nationalist scholarship of Grimm, Dahn, Muellenhoff and their heirs,[4] when it faced a certain amount of scholarly opposition.[5] In the multilingual Roman Empire, language was not thought to be primary: Tacitus believed that the similarities between the languages of the Peucini and those of his *Germani* in no way proved that the Peucini were *Germani*.[6]

The assumptions of the Germanicists have led to ingenious and dangerous use of source materials. As Julius Goebel pointed out as long ago as 1937,

... for the earliest period, between the *Germania* of Tacitus and the first monuments of Frankish law, an artful but artificial reconstruction was achieved by making the sources of central Europe speak as of a time quite other than their own, and then by drawing heavily upon the much later Scandinavian materials because these were conceived as representing an ancient culture level, unspoiled by contact with the Roman world.[7]

Since oral culture by its nature does not survive in written texts, it is easy to invent it.[8] But it is highly unlikely that a discrete oral culture could survive within the literate Roman Empire without being deeply affected by the political structures of literacy and power. Oral and literate cultures exist in a dialogue with one another, and oral cultures existed in the Empire long before the appearance of the barbarian groups of late antiquity.[9]

---

[3] See ch. 8, above, for the suggestion that traits attached to Theoderic's Goths derived not from Germanic culture but from Balkan military origins.

[4] Goffart, *Barbarians and Romans*, pp. 3–34.

[5] E. A. Freeman, "Race and language," in Freeman, *Historical Essays* 3 (London, 1879), pp. 173–230, a fascinating piece of opposition to the first deductions of Indo–European scholarship.

[6] Tacitus, *Germania* 46.1. See further the section on ethnography in ch. 1 for a survey of other characteristics of peoples in ancient thought.

[7] Julius Goebel, *Felony and Misdemeanour: A Study in the History of Criminal Law* (1937; reprint, Philadelphia, 1976), pp. 3–4.

[8] e.g. Heather, *Goths and Romans*, p. 328, on the supposed culture of Theoderic's Goths in the Balkans: "Legal customs are likely to have played a critical role." Any such legal customs are completely unknown, however, and certainly did not exist among Theoderic's Goths in Italy (ch. 2, n. 24, above).

[9] See ch. 8, above. References to Theoderic in later German sources such as the ninth-century *Hildebrandslied* or the medieval legends of Dietrich von Bern, while certainly indicative of his fame in Western Europe, thus need not demonstrate "the impact made by Theoderic on the *Germanic peoples of his day*" (emphasis mine), as Moorhead, *Theoderic*, p. 173, suggests. (Similarly,

Since language is only a possible marker of ethnicity, not a necessary determinant of it, anthropologists today warn historians to beware the "Pseudo-Völker" of linguistics.[10] These warnings continue to go unheeded. Linguistics textbooks routinely assume that a language denotes an ethnic group.[11] The Goths of Italy in particular are frequently allotted a distinct culture and ethnicity on the basis of language.[12]

Pagan "Germanic" religion is unattested within the borders of the Roman Empire,[13] so Germanicists have attempted to explain Arianism as a particularly "Germanic" form of Christianity.[14] The possibility that Arianism was a regional phenomenon, like the possibility that barbarian warlike behavior was a professional phenomenon, has largely passed unnoticed, even by scholars who condemn such social explanations of theology, e.g. E. A. Thompson: "Arianism was not a centralized or interprovincial organization: it remained a number of essentially separate, local and independent churches, and hence was more suited organizationally to a people who wished to preserve their identity inside the Roman Empire." This same evidence could surely show that Arian ecclesiastical organization was suited to regional and local churches within the Roman Empire.[15] On the persistent forgetfulness about Latin Arianism by modern historians of the barbarian kingdoms, see chapter 7 above.

The notion of early Germanic oral law, an edifice based largely on the

---

Luiselli, *Storia culturale*, pp. 716–17; also J. M. Wallace-Hadrill, *Early Germanic Kingship in England and On the Continent* [Oxford, 1971], p. 9.) Poetry written in Germanic languages and apparently oral in origin, such as *Widsith*, could also contain references to famous classical heroes such as Julius Caesar. The existence of oral culture is not in doubt: the existence of an entirely discrete Germanic-language-only oral culture, honoring a Germanic past, is.

[10] Mühlmann, "Ethnogonie," pp. 15–16. On ethnicity and markers, see ch. 1 above.

[11] Baldi, *An Introduction to the Indo-European Languages*, pp. 124–5: the linguistic terms such as "language family," "genealogical classification" and "common ancestry," which go back to Germanophone nineteenth-century scholarship (pp. 3–23), may encourage such assumptions. Lehmann, *Historical Linguistics*, emphasizes the greater complexities of dialects, frontiers and language change, but not bilingualism or multilingualism, for which one must go to more specialized studies.

[12] e.g. Heather, *Goths and Romans*, pp. 327–8. On the difficulties of understanding the boundary-making significance of the spoken and written Gothic languages – even the extent of their survival is not ascertained – within the multilingual provinces of the Balkans and Italy, see chs. 3 and 7 above. See these same chapters on the meaning of Germanic personal names in Italy. See appendix 3, below, on the difficulty of using place-name research in Italy to determine the breadth and function of any Germanic tongue; further, ch. 3 above.

[13] See the discussion of eagle brooches in appendix 3, below, with nn. 37–9. On "Germanic" paganism, see the works of Karl Hauck, cited at n. 20, below.

[14] Note the rebuttals of E. A. Thompson, *The Visigoths in the Time of Ulfila* (Oxford, 1966), p. 109, and of Manlio Simonetti, "L'incidenza dell'arianesimo nel rapporto fra romani e barbari," in *Passaggio dal mondo antico al medio evo*, p. 373 with n. 25.

[15] Thompson, *The Visigoths in the Time of Ulfila*, p. 110.

monumental work of Heinrich Brunner, whose *Deutsche Rechtsgeschichte* appeared in 1906, has been exploded. We now know that many of the similar elements found in the first law-codes issued by barbarian kings in the fifth century drew heavily on late Roman ("vulgar") law, either the constitutions of the later emperors, or from local and provincial custom, themselves orally transmitted.[16] On the fallacy of Gothic "customary law" in sixth-century Italy, see chapter 2, n. 24, above.

On place-names see appendix 3, below. On the various meanings of personal names whether Latin, Germanic or something else, see chapters 3 and 7 above.

Similarities that did exist between cultural traits attested among barbarian groups may also have been part of the much larger Indo-European cultural framework that contributed to archaic social and political structures in Greece and Rome, not to mention Babylon and India. The Laws of Hammurabi, for instance, from *c.* 1800 B.C., contain a system of monetary compensation for different sorts of personal injuries very similar to those found in the *Lex Salica* or the law-code of Aethelbehrt of Kent.[17] Karl Ferdinand Werner warns against the provincialism of historians, who too often think that the details of their subject are unique to the time and place of their own interest, a condition created by "national histories." For example, supposedly Germanic bipartite naming customs in fact existed among all the Indo-European languages, and in fact outside the Indo-European language family as well.[18] The broad spread of such institutions and culture without accompanying consciousness of kinship or community should warn us

[16] Crucial here are the works of Ernst Levy, *West Roman Vulgar Law: The Law of Property* (Philadelphia, 1951), of Jean Gaudemet, "A propos du 'droit vulgaire'," 1963, reprinted in *Etudes de droit romain* 1 (Camerino, 1979), and of Franz Wieacker, *Recht und Gesellschaft in der Spätantike* (Stuttgart, 1964). More recently, see the important article by Ian Wood, "Disputes in late fifth- and sixth-century Gaul: some problems," in *The Settlement of Disputes in Early Medieval Europe* (Cambridge, 1986), and the suggested evolution from classical law to late Roman law and the "barbarian" legal collections in Amory, "The meaning and purpose of ethnic terminology," pp. 15–19. See also next note, below.

[17] *Laws of Hammurabi* 196–214, in *The Babylonian Laws*, ed. and trans. G. R. Driver and John C. Miles, 2 vols., 1952–5 (2nd edn, Oxford, 1960), 2: 77–9; see similarly Wolfram's observation about the cognate words for "sacral-king" in Biblical Gothic, Burgundian and Latin: *thiudans-hendinos-ribunus*, *Goths*, pp. 94–5. On Indo-European mythology and institutions, see, e.g., Georges Dumézil, *Mitra-Varuna: An Essay on Two Indo-European Representations of Sovereignty*, 1948, trans. Derek Colman (New York, 1988), a study that probably goes too far in the reverse direction: Arnaldo Momigliano, "Introduction to a discussion of Georges Dumézil," 1983, reprinted in *Studies on Modern Scholarship*, ed. G. W. Bowersock and T. J. Cornell (Berkeley, 1994), pp. 286–301.

[18] "Liens de parenté et noms de personne: un problème historique et méthodologique," in *Famille et parenté dans l'occident médiéval*, Actes du colloque de Paris (6–8. juin 1974), Collection de l'Ecole Française de Rome 30 (Rome, 1977), pp. 16–18. Further on "Germanic" naming traditions, see ch. 3 above.

against using language-families as anything more or less than language-families.

So far we have only discussed traits attested in southern Europe in late antiquity: a more extreme practice of philological historiography is to take traits attested in northern Europe in the Middle Ages and to assume that they were carried by groups such as the Goths and the Vandals. A vestigial Germanic spoken-tongue, Germanic names and Arian Gothic liturgy in Italy do not prove the existence of northern European traits such as paganism, blood-feud, monetary composition for wounds, or wergeld. Not one of these phenomena is attested in Ostrogothic Italy.[19] If they had ever existed among previous Danubian groups called Goths, they died out before they could come to the attention of the written record. The chances are that they never did exist in the Balkans or on the Danube frontier, and that they were cultural traits specific to northwestern Europe.[20]

Disciplinary boundaries and the boundaries of periodization ensure that many of the assumptions of philological historiography continue to thrive in the scholarship of the barbarian groups. The border between antiquity and the Middle Ages is geographical as much as chronological. Classicists study Sidonius Apollinaris, while medievalists study Clovis. The Goths of Italy are already in the Middle Ages, but Boethius and Cassiodorus are the last of the Romans. When these assumptions of period-driven common behavior are attached to mobile barbarian

---

[19] The attempts of historians to see elements of blood-feud in Theoderic Strabo's opposition to Leo I on the basis of his relationship to Aspar, or Theoderic the Great's words to Odoacer as he killed him, "This is what you did to mine" (Moorhead, *Theoderic*, p. 26 with n. 102), seem to me absurd. Revenge is common to many cultures, including Mediterranean cultures. The institutionally recognized responsibility of family in settling disputes by sword or composition is not. Nor is the latter attested in southern Europe. Heather, *Goths and Romans*, p. 255, is sensible on the motivations behind Strabo's opposition to Leo: "Apart from a simple desire for revenge, Aspar's murder removed the Thracian Goths' principal guarantee of court patronage, and threatened their special status." On the supposed existence of a non-Mediterranean paganism in the fifth-century Balkans or Italy, see appendix 4.

[20] This difference between Northwest and Southeast is yet another indication of the weakness of the Germanic paradigm for understanding late antique culture. The relationship of certain of these cultural elements, such as a Germanic language and personal names, with cultures of illiterate northern Europe, need demonstrate no more than general cultural diffusion and geographical distribution throughout Europe. Culture flowed in both directions, of course. On the northern European oral culture see Karl Hauck, "Von einer spätantiker Randkultur zum karolingischen Europa," *Frühmittelalterliche Studien* 1 (1967), 3–93; and Hauck, "Text und Bild in einer oralen Kultur: Antworten auf die zeugniskritische Frage nach der Erreichbarkeit mündlicher Überlieferung im frühen Mittelalter (Zur Ikonologie der Goldbrakteaten 25)," *Frühmittelalterliche Studien* 17 (1983), 510–99. Identifying this northern European culture, if it really existed as a unity, with the culture of Balkan military warbands and calling it "Germanic," is a generalization that does an injustice to both worlds and ignores the influence of Graeco-Roman literacy on each. See further the discussion of orality in Jordanes, above, and of Hauck's theories at ch. 8, n. 103, above.

groups, the groups themselves carry their traditional periods with them on their backs for modern scholars. The separate discipline of Byzantine history, into which the Eastern Mediterranean becomes haplessly isolated with Anastasius and Justinian, means that study of the fifth- and sixth-century Mediterranean is further fractured.

When scholars raised in these different disciplines talk to one another, as is happening more frequently, they realize that the boundaries between their subjects are nowhere near as firm as they had thought. Late antique specialists now think of Sidonius as an opportunist episcopal aristocrat; medievalists think of Clovis as an intelligent and possibly educated ruler who used the Gallo-Roman bishops as tools to further his power. It is no accident that the first steps forward in this boundary-breaking have occurred in the study of Gaul, where the traditional boundaries first meet both temporally and geographically.[21] When we carry these insights forward to the experience of Goths in Italy, and to the various groups identified in the sixth-century Balkans, the boundaries between Theoderic and Justinian themselves break down, as this book argues.[22]

Germanic languages may well have survived in the sixth-century Mediterranean,[23] but their power to define groups remains unstudied except as an a priori assumption derived from the philologists. A re-examination of literary references and naming traditions in the context of linguistic theories of bilingualism and multilingualism may demonstrate other functions of language in the period, in particular associations with religion, profession and status. I believe that more close studies of Mediterranean elites from whatever background will show that the existence of Germanic language-families entailed no necessary equivalent larger cultural family within the fifth- and sixth-century world.

---

[21] Notable are the works of Ian Wood, for example *The Merovingian Kingdoms 470–751* (London, 1994), the collection of essays in John Drinkwater and Hugh Elton, *Fifth-Century Gaul: A Crisis of Identity?* (Cambridge, 1992), and the work of other scholars too numerous to mention here.

[22] See ch. 8.

[23] Astonishingly, the question requires more detailed study from linguists; see Markey, "Germanic in the Mediterranean," pp. 51–71.

Appendix 3

ARCHEOLOGICAL AND TOPONYMIC
RESEARCH ON OSTROGOTHIC ITALY

Archeology and toponymic study could ideally provide interesting perspectives on the strength of local and familial identity in Ostrogothic Italy. Unfortunately, the limited synthesis of archeological evidence that has been undertaken to date is almost entirely the work of one man – Volker Bierbrauer, a German archeologist working in the obsolete ethnic-ascription tradition (on which see below). Most influential is his *Die Ostgotischen Grab- und Schatzfunde in Italien*,[1] a book cited in every work on Ostrogothic history published since. In article after article, Bierbrauer continues to reiterate his basic theory: that the material culture that he calls "Ostrogothic," such as brooches, fibulae and pottery, exactly mirrors the migration story told by Jordanes.[2] A newer book by Michel Kazanski perpetuates Bierbrauer's claims to identify the migration of the Goths through a trail of artifacts from Scandinavia to southern Europe.[3] Kazanski himself admits that his evidence does not show consistent presence of the same grave-goods in male graves, only in female graves. Thus even within their own ethnic-ascription theory, the theses of Kazanski and Bierbrauer are fragile. As it is, site reports on excavations from within Italy, scanty for this period anyway, are conditioned by the expectation that the results will reveal something about the ethnic affiliation of the people who lived on or were buried at the site. This expectation has theoretical holes.

---

[1] Biblioteca degli studi medievali 7 (Spoleto, 1975). On the ethnic-ascription tradition (the *Siedlungsarchäologie* of Kosinna and the *kulturgeschichtlich* archeology of postwar Germanophone archeology), see below.

[2] See most recently Bierbrauer, "Aspetti archeologici di Goti, Alamanni e Longobardi," in *Magistra barbaritas*, pp. 445–508; Bierbrauer reaffirmed his interpretation yet again in 1992, fitting more and more evidence from his finds into his strict narrative: "Die Goten vom 1.–7. Jahrhundert n. Chr.: Siedelgebiete und Wanderbewegungen auf Grund archäologischer Quellen," *Teoderico il Grande e i Goti d'Italia*, Atti del XIII congresso internazionale sull'alto medioevo, Milan, 5 November 1992 (Spoleto, 1993), and in 1994, "Archeologia e storia dei Goti dal I al IV secolo" and "Archeologia degli Ostrogoti in Italia," both in *I Goti*, Catalogue of the Exhibition at Milan, Palazzo Reale, 28 January–8 May 1994 (Milan, 1994), pp. 22–107, 170–213.

[3] Michel Kazanski, *Les Goths (Ier–VIIe siècles après J.-C.)* (Paris, 1991); its assumptions are criticized in a review by Bernard S. Bachrach, *Francia* 20.1 (1993), 256.

The scantiness and wrongheadedness of the archeology also vitiates the study of place-names in sixth-century Italy. There is no doubt that some Italian place-names are of Germanic linguistic origin. Their presence could ideally shed some light on the strength of the Gothic language and the location of settlers speaking that language. Unfortunately, both archeologists and place-name scholars in Italy have used the conclusions of the other discipline as a base on which to found their claims that a place-name, or an excavated settlement, was Gothic.

This situation has led to the standard declaration in textbooks that Theoderic's soldiers were settled in the Po Valley and in northern Italy, since more (undatable) Germanic place-names are found there. Archeologists excavate in northern Italy – not necessarily at places with Germanic names – and uncover artifacts that they class as "Gothic." But it turns out that the classification of these place-names as Gothic, rather than of other Germanic origin, is arbitrary, and determined by the long-standing archeological claim that the north of Italy was the focus of Germanic settlement. Many of the place-names may well be Lombard, Frankish or even Ottonian in origin.[4] Recent work shows that toponyms cannot be attributed to Gothic or Lombard on purely linguistic evidence; one must adduce archeological evidence as well. But the archeological conclusions are partly based on "Gothic" place-names in these regions, so both arguments are founded on quicksand.[5]

Unlike in Britain,[6] there is no modern study of the earliest dates of attestation of Germanic place-names in Italy, followed by a linguistic analysis of their constituent roots, a desideratum that even Bierbrauer laments, if for the wrong reasons.[7] Not that this would necessarily help: it is impossible to use etymology alone to infer the original date of a place-name: it can suggest a date with no more precision than +/−150 years.[8] In Ostrogothic Italy we require a date within a period of some 65 years, so other criteria must also be used. All the Germanic place-names that do exist in Italy are only attached to small settlements, and it is noteworthy that no sixth-century source refers to a single one. If

[4] Carlo Alberto Mastrelli, "Lexical loans and Gothic onomastics: an updating," XIII Congresso sull'alto medioevo, Milan, 3 November 1992.
[5] Gothic garrisons in north: most recently reiterated by Heather, "Theoderic," p. 156 with map.
[6] On dating and attestation techniques used by place-name study in Britain, see Margaret Gelling, "Towards a chronology for English place-names," in *Anglo-Saxon Settlements*, ed. Della Hooke (Oxford, 1988), pp. 59–76.
[7] "Aspetti archeologici dei Goti," p. 489, n. 7.
[8] D. P. Blok, *Ortsnamen*, Typologie des sources du moyen âge occidental 54 (Turnhout, 1988), 21–5, esp. 23 with n. 10.

they had indeed become established, surely at least one would appear in a papyrus, an inscription, in the *Variae* or even in Procopius.[9] Further on place-names and Germanic language in sixth-century Italy, see chapter 3.

THE ARCHEOLOGY OF LATE ANTIQUITY AND THE ETHNIC-ASCRIPTION TRADITION

The archeology of late antiquity does little to support the notion of distinct cultural or ethnic groups in the midst of a larger homogeneity, despite the efforts of more than a century of German scholarship to insert material culture into such shakily attested historical frameworks. In assembling vast quantities of artifacts, settlement types and burial customs, dividing them into typologies, and then assigning each typology to a historically attested "people" – groups historically attested, of course, by Graeco-Latin ethnographic sources – Germanophone archeologists still effectively remain influenced by the *Siedlungsarchäologie* of Gustaf Kossinna, whose most important book was published in 1911.[10] In postwar *kulturgeschichtlich* archeology, Europe's common past of chequered *cultures*, which were brought or created by *peoples*, determined its particular social structures and therefore material remains. Kossinna envisaged these material-culture groups as the products of different races (*Völker*);[11] today they may be conceived as ethnic groups, but the theory is the same, minus the racial value-judgments.

Anglophone archeologists have long since shown that tying distinctive material remains to historically attested groups is hazardous in the extreme, since ethnicity (as we have seen) need not manifest itself in any single historical trait, including material culture, since material culture can travel without whole peoples (via trade, gift-exchange, fashion, diffusion and intermarriage) and since ethnographic description need

---

[9] We must also face the possibility that a place could bear both a Latin and a Germanic name, such as the *Casa Caballaria* in *PDip* 118 = *PItal* 8, also called *Hugsis Kaballarja* in that document, but see my argument in ch. 7, p. 255, above, that this was a piece of antiquarianizing ceremony on the part of an Arian deacon who was displaying his knowledge of the written Gothic language.

[10] Ian Hodder, "Archaeological theory in contemporary European societies," and Heinrich Härke, "All quiet on the Western front? Paradigms, methods and approaches in West German archaeology," both in *Archaeological Theory in Europe: The Last Three Decades*, ed. Ian Hodder (London, 1991), pp. 1–4, 188–90; Samson, "Translator's introduction," in Fehring, *Archaeology of Medieval Germany*, pp. xvi–xvii; on Kossinna, see Bruce G. Trigger, *A History of Archaeological Thought* (London, 1989), pp. 163–7.

[11] Trigger, *A History of Archaeological Thought*, p. 165.

not reflect reality of communities of any sort, let alone ethnic communities, let alone material cultures.[12]

The inherent flaws in the ethnic-ascription methodology of Kosinna and his heirs become obvious when these criticisms are applied. In the *kulturgeschichtlich* method, if a certain type of belt-buckle dating from the sixth century is found in the Rhône valley, then it must have belonged to the Burgundians, a group attested as living in that region at that time. If iron and bone combs are found in the Baltic regions in the second century and in the Carpathians in the late third century, they must have been brought by the Goths, a group described by Jordanes as having migrated between these two regions between these two periods.[13]

Combs play a strangely significant role in nationalist archeology, which shows no sign of dying out in Europe or elswhere. During last-minute Israeli excavations near Jericho before the withdrawal of their troops in 1993, one archeologist announced that a comb found in one cave "must have belonged to a refugee who fled to the caves during the Jewish revolt against the Romans in the first century A.D." Angry Palestinian scholars retorted, "We have lived here for 5,000 years. The archeology is our identity."[14] The notion that the comb could have belonged to someone who did not consider himself or herself a Jew or a Palestinian, or that a comb might not be a certain clue to ethnic identity, occurred to scholars of neither side.

Such ethno-cultural use of archeology remains particularly influential among non-archeologists. The intimidating alienness of the massive

---

[12] Timothy Champion, "Theoretical archaeology in Britain," in *Archaeological Theory*, pp. 129–60; on Anglo-American developments, see Trigger, *History*, pp. 289–369: the issue was raised in the 1960s and 1970s (pp. 383–4) and even by Gordon Childe as early as 1930 (p. 244). Ian Hodder first made the definitive case against the automatic attestation of ethnicity in material culture in *The Spatial Organization of Culture* (London, 1978), pp. 3–28, and in his *Symbols in Action: Ethnoarchaeological Studies in Material Culture* (Cambridge, 1982); the results for early medieval archeology have been restricted to Anglo-Saxon studies, e.g. C. J. Arnold, *Roman Britain to Saxon England: An Archaeological Study* (London, 1984).

Continental historians have been more receptive to this revolution in theory than have been Continental archeologists: see Walter Pohl, *Die Awaren: Ein Steppenvolk im Mitteleuropa 567–822 n. Chr.* (Munich, 1988), p. 219, and "Conceptions of ethnicity in early medieval studies," *Archaeologia Polona* 29 (1991), 47–8.

[13] Burgundian belt-buckles: Rudolf Moosbrugger-Leu, *Die frühmittelalterliche Gürtelbeschläge der Schweiz: Ein Beitrag zur Geschichte der Besidlung der Schweiz durch die Burgunder und Alamannen* (Basel, 1967), a deliberate organization of archeological artifacts in order to analyze the barbarian *Besiedlung* of the region. Gothic combs: e.g. Bierbrauer, "Archeologia e storia dei Goti," pp. 22–107, *passim*.

[14] Sarah Helm, "Palestinian fury at Israeli 'relic looting'," *Independent on Sunday*, 28 November 1993, p. 14.

fibulae and brooches illustrated in textbooks, the huge quantity of meticulously catalogued material evidence from undocumented northern Europe, is dangerously overwhelming to the non-specialist.[15] The thick, weighty catalogues that emerge from Germany and Italy every two years or so, richly illustrated with color plates on heavy paper, entitled *Die Hunnen, Die Alamannen* or *I Longobardi*, continue to flood our minds with information and imagery organized around a mental construction dating from Kosinna's book of 1911, a mental construction equating cultural traits with fixed racial communities of great antiquity. Brought up amidst the preconceptions and periodizations discussed in the Introduction, we text-trained historians too easily accept the analyses of Continental archeologists with their well-worn "ethnic" divisions of the European world.

The work of Continental archeologists working in the ethnic ascription tradition has, unhappily, penetrated various works by Anglophone historians. Peter Heather and John Matthews hesitatingly suggest that ethnic identity need not be evidenced in find-types, but finally accept the powerful archeological image of the Sîntana de Mureş/Černakov culture as the result of the impact of the Goths on the third- and fourth-century regions north of the Danube delta.[16] In fact, we do not know who these groups called "Goths" were, and their importance to the region is attested only by distant Graeco-Latin observers working within the framework of classical ethnographic rhetoric and imperial ideology.

Archeologically attested cultures are not simple, mass, unitary phenomena. They are structures composed of many complex elements. A group of artifacts, settlement-types or burial-types classed as a material culture can be left by a status-group, a regional group, a professional group or a religious group, assuming the classification of items was correct in the first place. Did the classifiers observe similarities properly and base these similarities on excavations and field surveys adequate in number and distribution to provide data for the entire area in question? Even assuming that such steps were followed, several material cultures can exist in one society, and a given individual can partake in several of them at once. Although there must be some relation between the

[15] On the effect of removing finds from their cultural context and analyzing them (or illustrating them) in such splendid isolation, see Härke, "All quiet on the Western front?" pp. 203–4 ("stamp-collecting"); p. 187 on the deserved fame of the German catalogues. See the bold layout of the illustrations in *Magistra Barbaritas*, pp. 451–66, 475–81 (an Italian publication with German archeological contributions).

[16] Heather and Matthews, *The Goths in the Fourth Century*, pp. 94–5. The equation of the Sinta de Mures Culture with the Goths also appears in Whittaker, *Frontiers*, pp. 176 (caption to fig. 43), 183.

spatial distribution of material culture and the activities of a past society, that correlation may not be immediately recoverable, and is probably neither simple in itself nor identical in type for every material culture attested in a given area.[17]

[17] Ian Hodder, *The Spatial Organisation of Culture*, pp. 3–28.

Appendix 4

DRESS, HAIRSTYLE AND MILITARY
CUSTOMS

Most of the cultural traits generally designated as Gothic are more correctly associated with the sixth-century Mediterranean military: Germanic names, some sort of Germanic language, the profession of soldier, a Balkan background, allegiance to a military king.[1] Adherence to the Arian heresy, not a prerogative of soldiers, was not specific to people who might be called Goths under other ideologies.[2]

It is therefore worth examining the few other specious "Gothic," "barbarian" or "Germanic" cultural traits that historians have identified in sixth-century Italy. Long hair, beards, certain kinds of jewelry, military dress and military customs were not specific to people called *Gothi*. The evidence of pictures and the topoi used by texts ought to have made it obvious by now that such traits had become widespread not only in Italy, but throughout the Empire and its successor-states.

It is the Germanic culture construct, together with the classicizing picture presented by ethnographically influenced texts, that has prevented us from integating beards and long hair properly into the diverse professional and regional picture of the late Roman world. The frontier culture of Balkan warbands spread throughout the Mediterranean with the army whether that army paid allegiance to the emperors or not. Long hair was becoming an Empire-wide trait of military prestige at the same time that Germanic words were penetrating the koiné of imperial soldiers across the Mediterranean.[3]

BEARDS

An occasional topos in sixth-century literary sources is that beards were a barbarian attribute. Ennodius chaffs an acquaintance in an epigram for combining a Gothic beard with a Roman cloak.[4] Procopius says

---

[1] Above, chs. 3 and 8.
[2] Above, ch. 7.
[3] On the "Gothic" language and its diffusion among both "Gothic" and "Byzantine" soldiers, see ch. 3; on Balkan military culture, see ch. 8.
[4] Ennodius, *Opp.* 182a–c (*Carm.* 2.57–9).

that circus partisans in Constantinople wore Hunnic hairstyles and Persian beards and moustaches, along with other distinguishing clothes.[5] Cassiodorus, combining two ethnographic commonplaces, derived the word *barbarus* from *barba* (beard) and *rus* (countryside), "because the barbarous person has never lived in the city, but is known to have dwelt always like a wild beast in the country."[6] A clean-shaven face had long been associated with Roman men,[7] and in statues and in the reliefs depicting imperial victory over barbarians, the triumphant emperor is clean-shaven and the submissive barbarians have beards.[8]

Nevertheless, Boethius's father, the consul of 487, wears a beard in his ivory consular diptych. So does Felix, consul in 428, and unnamed consuls from Rome in the 430s and 480s.[9] Various emperors from the fourth century onward are depicted with beards on their coins.[10] Bishop Maximian of Ravenna, the supporter of Justinian and opponent of the Arians, wears a beard in the famous mosaic of Justinian's court in San Vitale, as does a military man on the emperor's right, possibly Belisarius. Justinian himself, in this picture, appears to have a rather elegant short beard and moustache,[11] and Malalas states that Justinian was bearded.[12]

Theoderic, on the other hand, is once portrayed with a moustache, and once as clean-shaven.[13] Athalaric is clean-shaven (although only fourteen when depicted).[14] Theodahad has a moustache on his coins.[15]

---

[5] Procopius, SH 7.8–10; cf. Agathias 5.14.4.

[6] *Expositio Psalmorum* 113.1 (trans. P. G. Walsh).

[7] Pliny, *Nat. Hist.* 7.59.211 (though the Romans began shaving late, in 300 B.C.).

[8] Clean-shaven emperors triumphing over barbarians with beards in, for example, the Barberini Diptych, reproduced in MacCormack, *Art and Ceremony*, plate 22.

[9] Richard Delbrueck, *Die Consulardiptychen und verwandte Denkmäler*, Studien zur spätantiken Kunstgeschichte 2, 2 vols., text and plates (Berlin, 1929): plates 7, 3, 37, 40, respectively.

[10] Most famously Julian (because he was a philosopher), but also the usurpers Eugenius and John, as well as Theodosius II; Hodgkin, *Italy and Her Invaders* 1, plate after p. 12, no. 5; plate after p. 276.

[11] Illustrated for example in John Beckwith, *Early Christian and Byzantine Art* (1970, 2nd edn, 1979; reprint, Harmondsworth, 1990), p. 114.

[12] John Malalas, *Chronographia* 425. The tenth-century Byzantine notion that Maurice shaved his chin "in the Roman fashion" says more about tenth-century ideas of Romanity than sixth-century attitudes toward facial hair; cited by Michael Whitby, *The Emperor Maurice and His Historian: Theophylact Simocatta on Persian and Balkan Warfare* (Oxford, 1988), p. 3, on Leo Grammaticus.

[13] Moustache: the Senigalla medallion, Deichmann, *Ravenna* 1, fig. 12; clean-shaven: mosaic portrait in Sant' Apollinare Nuovo, illustrated at F-S, NF, plate 3 after p. 59, and in Deichmann, *Ravenna* 1, figs. 187–8 (mislabeled "Justinian" in the nineteenth century, a label here accepted by Deichmann); on the identity of this portrait with Theoderic, see F-S, text at no. 37, p. 27, and Deichmann, *Ravenna* 2:122, 174.

[14] Delbrueck, *Consulardiptychen*, plate 32, with comments at pp. 148–9.

[15] Hodgkin, *Italy and Her Invaders* 3, plate facing p. 649, no. 4. Odoacer is also depicted with a moustache, no. 1, but Teia as clean-shaven, no. 9; it is difficult to know whether these are

Witigis appears to be clean-shaven, and Totila to have a moustache, on their coins, but it is unclear whether these coins were representational, and if they were, whether they represented the kings or the emperors in whose name they were still nominally issued. Coins issued by the same king sometimes depict a clean-shaven face, sometimes one with a moustache.[16]

Beards had also long been associated with Hellenic philosophers, of course,[17] but by late antiquity they were also beginning to be associated with Christ and the Apostles. All the Evangelists were portrayed with long, flowing beards and moustaches in the presbyterium of San Vitale.[18] The sixth-century Rossano Gospels, written in silver on purple parchment, like the *Codex Argenteus*, depict Christ with a beard appearing before Pilate, who is similarly bearded.[19] Cyril of Scythopolis, no friend of barbarians, makes it clear that beards were valued as attributes in sixth-century Palestine, even for saints. After a fire burned off the beard of St. Sabas,

> he used to give thanks to God for the removal of his beard, reckoning it to be a divine providence, so that he should be humbled and not take pride in the hair of his beard.[20]

In late antique beards, as in so much else, we modern observers have chosen to accept the stereotyped classifications of classical ethnography over the casual revelations of a Palestinian monk or the evidence of our own eyes in mosaics and illustration.

The association of beards with "barbarians" was a classicizing topos, and did not reflect reality in the sixth-century Mediterranean. In the Martialan epigram of Ennodius, "Gothic beard" was a commonplace, much as Americans say "French fries," although fried potatoes are not exclusively French, or even French in origin. Ennodius's poem is an

---

portraits, and if they are, whether they represent the king or the emperor; Theodahad seems to be fairly certainly a portrait.

[16] Philip Grierson and Mark Blackburn, *Medieval European Coinage, With a Catalogue of the Coins in the Fitzwilliam Museum, Cambridge* 1, *The Early Middle Ages (5th–10th Centuries)* (Cambridge, 1986), plate 9, nos. 151–2 (Witigis, in the name of Justinian), nos. 153–5 (Totila, in the name of Anastasius I! thus recalling the former imperial legitimacy of the Ostrogothic monarchy during Justinian's invasions). Contrasting depictions of the face on Witigis's coins: nos. 151, 152.

[17] Balsdon, *Romans and Aliens*, p. 216.

[18] Deichmann, *Ravenna* 1, figs. 228–9, 231, 276 on left (Matthew); the caption at 228–31 wrongly lists the order of names, which should run "John, Mark, angel of Matthew, Luke" (cf. figs. 276–7).

[19] Kurt Weitzmann, *Late Antique and Early Christian Book Illumination* (New York, 1977), plates 30–1, probably produced for an emperor, in Antioch or Jerusalem, pp. 17, 20–1.

[20] Cyril of Scythopolis, *Vita Sabae* 107.5–9; trans. R. M. Price, *Cyril of Scythopolis: the Lives of the Monks of Palestine*, Cistercian Publications 114 (Kalamazoo, 1991), pp. 115–16.

extended play on the connotations of words or phrases that had out-grown their original meaning, as Ennodius, who had seen Theoderic and Boethius, surely knew.[21]

As for the "Hunnic hairstyles" and "Persian beards" of the circus factions, Alan Cameron argues convincingly that these were similar to tribal clothing worn by British teenagers and soccer hooligans, the uniforms of the young.[22] Procopius himself implies that such hairstyles had outgrown their non-Roman connotations: "the hair of their heads they cut off in front back to the temples, leaving the part behind to hang down to a very great length in a senseless fashion, just as the Massagetae do. Indeed for this reason, they *used to call* this the 'Hunnic' fashion."[23] Although Procopius ethnographically implies that "Massagetae" wear their hair this way, he reveals that the associated name for the fashion is no longer used; it is a typically Procopian antiquarian touch.

MILITARY DRESS: PHRYGIAN CAPS AND BARBARIAN JEWELRY

Procopius similarly castigates the "Hunnic" military dress and weapons carried by the circus faction members, and their criminal behavior in harrassing unarmed citizens. These bored, rich troublemakers of Constantinople[24] were echoing the behavior of the wealthy youth of the city of Rome in the early years of the fifth century. The emperors between 400 and 410 proclaimed decree after decree enforcing the sumptuary legislation, prohiting senators from wearing military cloaks (they ought to wear togas) and large decorated fibulae (symbols of specific imperial offices, especially military ones). In the early fifth century as in the mid-sixth, such clothing was described as "barbarian."

Soldiers could be distinguished in society because they were allowed to carry weapons, which were prohibited to civilians.[25] In fact, carrying a weapon in public was the only certain way that soldiers identified themselves in Roman society. Weapons were the uniform. Fibulae and buckles indicated rank.[26]

Just as people broke the laws prohibiting possession of weapons, more and more people wore military dress or something similar to it. Togas were restricted to Roman senators in any case, but illustrations in

---

[21] Riché, *Education and Culture*, p. 76 with n. 165, takes the poem literally.

[22] Alan Cameron, *Circus Factions: Blues and Greens at Rome and Byzantium* (Oxford, 1976), p. 76 with n. 10.

[23] Procopius, SH 7.10, trans. Dewing 6:79–81, emphasis mine.

[24] Procopius, SH 7.11–16.

[25] Above, ch. 3.

[26] M. C. Bishop and J. C. N. Coulston, *Roman Military Equipment From The Punic Wars To The Fall of Rome* (London, 1993), p. 196.

mosaics and manuscripts suggest that a short tunic with leggings and laced-up boots was common at all levels of society. In the ivory diptych of Orestes, consul in 530, Amalasuintha and Athalaric are portrayed in the upper corners. The consul wears, of course, a toga. But the king and his mother are wearing typical late antique dress.[27]

For Delbrueck, the editor of the diptychs, the military costume of the Gothic rulers was "national dress," moreover, "ein Symptom der seit 527 stark einsetzenden gotischen Forderungen an die römerfreund-liche Regierung der Amalasuntha."[28] Wolfram accepts Delbrueck's argument that Amalasuintha is wearing a "Phrygian cap," a memory or reference to ancient locations of the Goths, and Delbrueck describes her hair as "über der Stirnmitte in damals anscheinende unrömischer Weise gescheitelt," along with her earrings.[29] Wolfram argues that Amalasuintha's cap was "of the type worn by the queens of the Phrygians. The origins of the Ostrogoths had left traces not only in their tribal *memoria* but also in their insignia."[30]

But Athalaric's plain tunic is exactly the same as that of the Roman soldier, or indeed the emperor (as *triumphator*) in the Barbarini Diptych, or that of the soldiers behind Justinian in San Vitale.[31] Amalasuintha's cap need not be Phrygian — it is just a plain, slightly peaked cap with a round base. It resembles not women's dress, but men's — the caps or crowns worn by Theodahad and Totila on their coins, and (with the addition of the diadem) by Justinian, and thus indicates her regency.[32] Her earrings and jewelry resemble those of Theodora in San Vitale.[33] Culture could spread from the frontiers, and Amalasuintha's style of cap was perhaps Phrygian in origin — but there is no evidence that she, or Justinian, thought of such caps as Phrygian.

Similarly, in the eighth century, Paul the Deacon would look back at military figures in late sixth-century frescoes of soldiers and categorize them as "Lombards," because they wore tunics, leggings and sandals that laced up their calves.[34] But to judge from illustrations of the pro-

---

[27] Delbrueck, *Consulardiptychen*, plate 32.
[28] Ibid., p. 149, on plate 32.
[29] Delbrueck, ibid.; F-S, no. 39 with commentary at p. 28; Wolfram, *Goths*, p. 337.
[30] Wolfram, ibid. One is tempted to believe that he is making an extended ironic joke connecting the "Phrygian cap" of the French Revolution, used by Delbrueck as a convenient shorthand to describe the shape of Amalasuintha's headgear, with the classical Phrygians, by way of the Goths' legendary journey via the Bosporus. If so, the joke is perhaps oblique for non-Germanophone readers and is certainly entirely obscured in the English translation.
[31] MacCormack, *Art and Ceremony*, plates 22, 63.
[32] Deichmann, *Ravenna* 1, figs. 13–15. Note also Theoderic's hair on the Senigalla medallion, which is arranged in a similar shape; see n. 43, below.
[33] In MacCormack, *Art and Ceremony*, p. 62.
[34] Paul the Deacon, *Hist. Lang.*

genitor of the Romans, Aeneas, in the Vergilius Romanus,[35] and the depiction of Christ as soldier in the Catholic chapel of Sant'Andrea in Ravenna,[36] such clothing was standard for soldiers in late fifth and sixth centuries.

The sumptuary laws of the early fifth century represent a hopeless protest against a development that was already clearly well underway: the spread of military dress to the rest of society. The antiquarianizing descriptions of Procopius, and the confusion of Paul the Deacon, cannot hide the fact that distinctive dress alone could not differentiate barbarians from Romans. The association of military dress with barbarians may have emerged from the linguistic equation that made *barbarus* a synonym for "soldier" and *gens* a synonym for "a people under arms." If soldiers were barbarians, then military dress was barbarian dress. If such dress had originally come from regions on the Roman frontiers or altogether from outside the Empire, then it had infiltrated the very centers of Mediterranean by the first decade of the 400s, and not only among soldiers. Its actual cultural origins may have been from beyond the imperial frontiers, but as Procopius implies, describing such fashions as "Hunnic" was antiquarianizing. "Hunnic" is here a semantic and pejorative description, if it was common at all.

Cultural or ethnic distinctiveness is not easily assignable to the expressive but complex remnants of material culture. There is a style of extraordinarily beautiful cloisonné eagle brooch that appears in sixth-century Italy, similar to ones found in the Carpathians.[37] These eagle brooches are frequently identified with the arrival of Theoderic and his followers, and occasionally explained as a symbol of Germanic paganism or heroism.[38] Of course, no source or archeological site provides any evidence for Germanic paganism in Italy or the Balkans. More strikingly, the eagle had always been a symbol of Roman power and imperial victory. Eagles were still used as symbols of the emperors in the fourth century.[39] To take these brooches as non-Roman, let alone "Germanic"

[35] Weitzmann, *Late Antique and Early Christian Book Illumination*, plate 14 (Aeneas wearing leggings, tunic and cloak with brooch); cf. also Nestor and Patroclus in the Ilias Ambrosiana (late fifth century), plate 10.
[36] Claudio Marabini, *I mosaici di Ravenna* (Novara, 1981), illustration at p. 27 (tunic and laced-up sandals).
[37] Bierbrauer, *Die ostgotische Grab- und Schatzfunde*, plates 18–19, 26.
[38] Moorhead, *Theoderic*, p. 89 with n. 108 (with some reservation); Burns, *Ostrogoths*, pp. 49–50, 154–6.
[39] MacCormack, *Art and Ceremony*, pp. 136-7: eagles had been a Roman pagan symbol eventually connected with the imperial cult and the ascent of the emperor to heaven, by which they were taken into Christian art, e.g. the eagles in the twelve mosaics of PA Ursus and Ursina at Teurnia, on which, Peter F. Barton, *Die Frühzeit des Christentums in Österreich und Südostmitteleuropa bis 788*, Studien und Texte zur Kirchengeschichte und Geschichte 1st ser., 1.1 (Vienna, 1975),

or "pagan," is to assert an unprovable homogeneity of cultures on either side of a frontier that was not a line or an impermeable barrier, and to claim that the most famous symbol of the Roman Empire in fact proclaimed the distinctiveness of a group within that Empire.

LONG HAIR

Long hair has also been claimed as a Germanic trait retained by the kings of the barbarian tribes as a sign of their sacral right to rule. It too was actually an imperial trait, and was seen as such by the mid-fifth century, despite classicizing depictions to the contrary. Polemius Silvius, a friend of Eucherius of Lyons and writing after 449, connected Constantine's introduction of the imperial diadem with the imperial long hair, "which still continues today":

> vel Constantinus senior, qui Christianae religionis ministros privilegiis communiit, diadema capiti suo propter refluentes de fronte propria capillos (pro qua re saponis eiusdem cognomenti odorata confectio est, qua constringerentur), invenit; qui modus hodie custoditur.[40]

Polemius did not think of long hair as a Germanic or barbarian trait. Nor did he understand the use of soap as such. But soap has a better claim to being "Germanic" than long hair. The word *sapo* is Germanic linguistically, and first appears in Pliny and Martial.[41] The Romans of the Principate were revolted by the northern European use of animal fat, rather than oil, for washing one's body. Sidonius revives such notions in his famous remark, in a "satirical" poem, that Burgundians billeted in his house washed themselves with rancid butter.[42] Soap had, in fact, spread to the south of Europe long before, along with its name, and was no longer considered "barbarian" except in classicizing literary works like this one of Sidonius. If long hair also came from northern Europe, no one remembered that fact.

Illustrations prove that long hair was not restricted to barbarian kings – and that it was worn by emperors as well. Theoderic, indeed, only *seems* to be portrayed with long hair on the Senigallia Medallion, and he definitely has short hair in the mosaic in Sant'Apollinare

---

pp. 149–50: a combination of classical and Christian motifs (and not only classical or only Christian: p. 154). It should not be necessary to mention the eagle of St. John, depicted, e.g., on the roof of the chapel of Sant'Andrea in Ravenna (illustration in Marabini, *I mosaici*, p. 29).

[40] Polemius Silvius, *Breviarium temporum*, ed. Theodor Mommsen, MGH: AA 9 (Chronica Minora I), p. 547, lines 34–8.

[41] Lewis and Short, *A Latin Dictionary*, s.v.

[42] Sidonius, *Carm.* 10.

Nuovo.[43] Athalaric's slightly shorter hair in the diptych of Orestes is cut like Theoderic's in the medallion, but so is the hair of the consul, Orestes.[44] This rather odd bowl-haircut, similar to those of fifteenth-century European noblemen but longer in the back, seems to have been a widespread fashion in late antiquity.[45] Theodahad's hair in his coins, combed down over his forehead and rather long in the back, curling slightly around his neck, is identical to the hair of the emperors Constantine and his successors in their coins.[46] If the Merovingian kings were later known as *reges criniti* for their long hair, this may have been a result of their military service and relationship to the emperors rather than anything Germanic. Merovingian long hair may subsequently have gained new sacral or royal meaning, but that is a separate issue. We probably should connect the tradition with the symbols of Roman military office found in the grave of Childeric.[47]

Wolfram connects the use of the word *capillati* to denote soldiers or Goths in Italy with the barbarian royal custom of long hair, but also with the customs of the Roman army,[48] an artificial distinction given the memory of Constantine's hair. In fact, the word is first attested in an ethnographic and an Italian context, and is also associated with frontiers. Pliny describes the Capillati as a *populus* of the Cottian Alps in northern Italy.[49] He also called Transalpine Gaul "Long-haired Gaul," *Gallia Comata*.[50] According to Dio Chrysostom, in Thrace, the ancient Getic nobility and priests were called *pilleati*, "curly-haired." Jordanes connected the Getic name to the use of *capillati* among the Goths "today," part of his general ethnographic identification of Getae with

[43] Deichmann, *Ravenna* I, figs. 12 (medallion), 187–8 (short hair clearly part of the original mosaic, not its subsequent restoration); the curling at the bottom of the hair is the same in both pictures. The portrait in the medallion is difficult to evaluate, because the hair seems to begin so far above Theoderic's forehead that it does not, in fact, come down below his temples; it looks like a "helmet of hair," and gives the shape of his head the same appearance as other kings and emperors wearing helmets or crowns. (Deichmann, *Ravenna* I: 122, 174, hypothesizes the mosaic portrait originally portrayed Theoderic "mit Scheitelbandhelm der Goten" on his head, since the diadem and earrings appear to have been added later.) The portrait in the medallion is clearly meant to indicate hair, but the hair is not actually *long* so much as extended upwards.

[44] Delbrueck, *Consulardiptychen*, plate 32.

[45] e.g. the soldier facing the emperor in the Barberini Diptych, MacCormack, *Art and Ceremony*, plate 22, or the statue of an emperor believed to be Valentinian I, in ibid., plate 7.

[46] Theodahad: Grierson and Blackburn, *Medieval European Coinage* I, plate 8, nos. 142–4; Constantine and his successors, e.g. in Hodgkin, *Italy and Her Invaders* I, plate after p. 12, nos. 3–10 (through Valentinian II). This fashion seems to have continued through Valentinian III and Theodosius II (see ibid., plate after p. 276).

[47] On which, Whittaker, *Frontiers*, pp. 266–9; note the reconstructed illustration of the man, showing extremely long hair past his shoulders: pure fantasy.

[48] Wolfram, *Goths*, pp. 102–3, 301–2.

[49] Pliny, *Nat. Hist.* 3.5.47.

[50] Ibid. 4.17.105.

Goths.[51] Wolfram points out that the Gothic Bible borrows the Latin word to form *kapillon*, and hypothesizes that it means "getting a Roman type military haircut."[52]

 The sacrality and importance of long hair is obvious, but this collection of evidence suggests that long hair and curly hair had spread to military leaders from regional and military custom within the Roman Empire. The Capillati of Pliny's Italy and the *capillati* of Theoderic's Italy shared the trait of being groups within the Empire distinguishable by their hair. The custom may have spread through the Balkans in the intervening centuries, or may have been a general European trait of priests or soldiers. The certain attestation of the term *capillati* only in Italy or (through Jordanes) with Goths, who in Jordanes's time lived in Italy, suggests that we should posit regional and professional origins for the name, if not the custom. The occurrence of the name twice in ethnographic texts (Pliny and Jordanes) suggests that the equation "frontier"–"soldier"–"barbarian" is once more at work, lending the name of an ancient Italian tribe to the military *gens* of the Goths in Italy.

MILITARY CUSTOMS

In this military-imperial context we should see the supposedly Germanic custom of electing a king by raising him upon a shield. It was in fact the military part of the ceremony involved in the election of a Roman emperor, as Wolfram has noted.[53] Justin II was raised on a shield by four young men at his accession.[54] The custom, of course, went back to Claudius. When Witigis announced his election to the army by being raised upon a shield, *more maiorum*,[55] these *maiores* are clearly not only the Gothic kings, but the Western generalissimos and previously the Western emperors to whom the phrase *maiores*, "predecessors," refers in the *Variae* when used by the monarch.[56] It is an appeal

---

[51] Jordanes, *Getica* 40, 71–2.

[52] Wolfram, *Goths*, p. 103; "Gotische Studien I," p. 14; "Gotische Studien II," pp. 304, 307–8.

[53] Wolfram, "The shaping of the early medieval kingdom," p. 8, pointing out, however, that the emperor Julian was raised upon a shield by "Germanic 'barbarians;'" as so often, it is difficult to understand the force of the irony in Wolfram's statement.

[54] MacCormack, *Art and Ceremony*, p. 251: no reference to barbarians.

[55] *Var.* 10.31.1: *more maiorum scuto subposito regalem nobis contulisse praestante domino dignitatem.*

[56] *Var.* 5.14.7 (referring to the emperors) 6.18.4 (referring to Pompey), 7.9.2 and 7.10.2 (referring to the institutions of the Roman emperors and the Roman past), but note *Var.* 9.25.4, the announcement of Cassiodorus's *Gothic History* to the senate, where *maiores* refers to people who have retained memory of *prosapies nostra* in song: this, I argue in ch. 2, is part of Theoderic's late creation of a past worth remembering in such song. On the implications of this, see the

to the legitimacy established by past imperial and legal custom, a constant refrain in all texts of the period, and a particular concern of the Ostrogothic kings.

Dress, hair, jewelry and gesture were important in late antiquity. One's bearing and presence defined one's status and power, just as in eighteenth- and nineteenth-century England. But the consensus governing such elite behavior was breaking down in the fifth century, as Peter Brown has shown. Literary texts and imperial laws could imply that a common *paideia* and its defining social norms continued to exist as it always had, but in fact it was evolving. One aspect of this evolution was regional diffusion and reception of cultural traits, as elites became less mobile and trans-Mediterranean opportunity diminished.

Togas, short hair and clean-shaven faces no doubt continued to impress: they were the prerogatives of the wealthy. But they competed everywhere with different symbols of power: ostentatious weaponry, the military cloak, and the *gravitas* of a beard and an eagle brooch – or a cruciform brooch. Except in the very restricted circles of the senates of Rome and Constantinople, the army and the church were redefining the badges of status. Some of these badges came from the Balkans, but they spread all over the Mediterranean – to the extent that scholars argue over whether to identify images as those of emperors or of barbarian rulers.[57] Classicizing texts continue to pretend that such once outlandish frontier ways were still barbarian, but pictures and demotic sources tell a different story.

section on Jordanes, above, ch. 8. These uses of *maiores* are not to be confused with the *maiores domus regiae*, on whom see ch. 5, above.

[57] Such as the Florentine ivory of Amalasuintha – or is it of her aunt's friend, the empress Ariadne? Siena, "Sulle tracce della presenza gota in Italia," fig. 457 and p. 549 with n. 177.

A PROSOPOGRAPHY OF GOTHS IN ITALY, 489–554

METHOD AND PURPOSE

Few individuals from sixth-century Italy are called "Goth" or "Roman" outside the works of Procopius. In order to understand the force of the label "Goth," and by implication its occasional antithesis "Roman," this prosopography assembles every attested individual in Italy from the period of Ostrogothic rule who *could have been* classified as a "Goth" according to the various contemporary criteria identifying the group: a Germanic personal name (or one in the family), military service, Arian belief, membership in the Arian clergy, and knowledge of the Gothic language, and anyone related to people showing these characteristics (since classical ethnography assumes family ties among the people that it describes). The subsequent set of tables in Part III strains out these criteria to illustrate the extent to which they match up among different groups in Italian society at different dates.

This "prosopography of identity" thus serves a different function from traditional prosopography. It examines the ways in which individuals are not connected as much as the ways in which they are connected, within the limits of a community as defined by contemporary sources. Different groups inside and outside Italian society defined Goths in various ways: as Arian believers and clergymen, as soldiers, as *saiones* and military *comites*, as speakers of a Germanic language, and as the enemies of Justinian's armies in Italy. To what extent do these criteria coincide in an attested individual? The only control on these criteria, mostly attested from the sources, such as Cassiodorus and Procopius, that express ideologies drawing on ethnography, is when an individual explicitly calls him or herself a "Goth." This nearly never happens, and we must rely on the more doubtful labels of literary sources. Nonetheless, possible awareness of being a Goth may be visible in behavior. One clear result of the Ostrogothic settlement of 493 is the vast upsurge in Germanic names among the Italian population. Naming traditions are a complex subject, but they tend at all times, and particularly in late antiquity, to run in families. So the possession of a Germanic

348

name *may* be an indicator that the individual in question arrived in Italy with Theoderic, or was a descendant of such a person. When Germanic names coincide with the other criteria of identity like Arianism or military service, we may be able to see Theoderic's followers identifying themselves as "Goths," with the various ideological baggage that such an allegiance could carry in sixth-century Italy. When the criteria fail to match up, and when Germanic and Latin names appear in the same family, we may see disjunctures between ideology and reality. One must take account of the biases of the sources, of course; for example, the *Variae* tend to turn up soldiers with Germanic names, and office holders, without telling us their religion. This method is not perfect, and I do not use this surprisingly rich evidence as a quantitative sample. It is rather a portrait of individual attitudes and allegiances, which can be set against contemporary ideologies about community and state. This process may get us closer to the individual man or woman, whose views are crucial in determining the strength of ethnicity.

Out of 379 individuals, only 223, or 59 percent, are in the *Prosopography of the Later Roman Empire*; a few of these are listed in T. S. Brown, *Gentlemen and Officers*. This prosopography, however, adds new material in nearly all cases, since it takes identity as problematic. PLRE and Brown simply label a given individual "Goth," "Hun" or "Roman" – often without explaining why they are doing so. In addition, I occasionally modify or disagree with certain conclusions in both works, as well as occasional dates, and the vexed question of whether individuals with similar names are identical.

I must record my debt to both of these extremely well-researched and useful reference tools, without which this prosopography would not have been imaginable. My work, I hope, builds upon that of my predecessors to add some complexity to a sample which in both cases is a mere fragment of their work.

A note on the limits of the survey

This prosopography naturally spills over the chronological extent of the Ostrogothic kingdom at both ends, for two reasons. First, a wide net provides controlling evidence from Italy for the relationship between names, profession and religion from before the arrival of the Goths and after their political eclipse. Second, since human lifespans refuse to fit within historical periods, this approach should help to catch both those individuals who grew up in the Ostrogothic kingdom and survived the Gothic wars, and those who were already born when Theoderic arrived, and grew to maturity, perhaps learning to consider themselves Goths,

under Ostrogothic rule. Such messiness can only compound the selec-
tivity of the surviving evidence, of course, but it should also enrich this
corpus as a qualitative sample. Dates must be kept in mind, however:
see the separate lists at the end of the prosopography, which ensure
that early and late individuals are not included within separate categories
of behavior and allegiance attested during the lifespan of the Ostrogothic kingdom of Italy.

The survey also ranges beyond Italy both geographically and politically. It includes any Byzantine soldier in Italy whom Procopius calls
"Goth" (but not all Byzantine soldiers with Germanic names). It also
includes any individual from elsewhere who came to Italy, and whom
sources call "Goth" or "Scythian," such as Dionysius Exiguus and the
Scythian monks. This last group brings up the problem of relating antiquarianizing ethnographic labels to contemporary reality, an issue particularly complicated, in late antique eyes, in the Balkans. Since this
vagina gentium produced Theoderic and his followers, it is revealing to
examine the confused reports about the identities and allegiances of
individuals from Pannonia, Illyricum and Thrace, whom some sources
considered to be Goths (see **B**essas, **H**erodianus, **M**undo and
Vitalianus).

Individuals from (Visigothic) Spain are not included unless they
manifestly went from Italy to Spain after Theoderic's conquest of the
Visigothic kingdom (but see **V**eila).

Family members of any listed individual called a "Roman" are not
listed unless those family members themselves exhibit one or more of
the Gothic criteria (but see **O**pilio); I also exclude most of the relatives
of the selectively included individuals from outside Italy or the period.

ABBREVIATIONS AND CONVENTIONS

**Note: It is important to keep in mind the distinction between
parentheses and brackets (round brackets and square brackets)
in the sigla: the first indicates attribution of the criterion by
someone other than the individual; the second indicates a family
relationship to someone with the criteria listed.**

1a. Sigla for criteria of Gothic identity (left-hand column),
in capital letters:

N = Germanic **N**ame
J = Job is "Gothic" (soldier, *saio* or *comes civitatis* or *provinciae*)
S = Service on or active loyalty to the Gothic side, 535–54

A = Arian believer
† = Arian clergyman
G = knowledge of spoken or written **G**othic language(s)
D = Declaration of identity as "Goth"
[D] = Declaration of identity as "Goth" by someone else

( ) = Parentheses (round brackets) around sigla indicate that only a relative of the individual in question is attributed these "Gothic" characteristics.

——— separates "Gothic" from "Roman" criteria in same individual

1b. Sigla for criteria of Roman identity (opposite criteria) (left-hand column),
in lower-case letters:

n = Graeco-Latin or biblical name
j = "Roman job" (civilian layman, senator)
s = service on or active loyalty to Byzantine side, 535–54
c = Catholic believer
cc = Catholic **c**lergyman
l = Latin speaker or writer
d = declaration of identity as "Roman"
[d] = declaration of identity as "Roman" by someone else

( ) = Parentheses (round brackets) around sigla indicate that only a relative of the individual in question is attributed these "Roman" characteristics

Notes:
J and j: Women and minors take (J) or (j) from husbands or fathers.
G: Spoken and written "Gothic" had probably diverged, one to a military slang, the other an archaic clerical (Arian) language; see Chapters Three and Seven, above.
l: Latin speakers deduced from subscriptions to charters (indicating *comprehension* of Latin even when the subscriber does not sign in Latin, or was illiterate), description in source, addressees of letters in Latin, from language of parents, or from inscriptions, whether left by the family, or, often, composed by the individual before his death. It is likely that all but a tiny percentage could speak Latin – whatever other languages they might have had as well.
[D] and [d]: as part of the general confusion between identity and political allegiance, a "a leader of Goths" may or may not have been equivalent to "a Goth". Frequently thus [?D].

2. Cross-references

Gudelivus 1: A boldface letter at the beginning of the name directs attention to an individual listed in the main prosopography (I).

★**A**malaberga: A boldface asterisk directs attention to an individual listed in the ★royal prosopography (II).

Kings and queens are not listed with cross-referencing boldface in the main prosopography unless the text *specifically* refers to information found in the ★royal prosopography.

Traditional spellings for members of royal families are used unless a cross-reference is intended, thus: "instructed by Theoderic" but "niece of ★**T**heodericus."

Alternative spellings and dual names are fully cross-referenced unless the two entries would be contiguous.

3. Names and rank designations (central column)

a. Dual names

Given as attested, using the connecting wording, if any, when the two names are attached ("qui et," "dicta" or "nomine"), but with a slash ("/") when the names are only attested separately. Attached names may indicate that both names were used at the same time, while separate names may indicate a change of personal name. In cross-references:

- :two names attached by "qui et," etc., e.g. "Simplex-Livania"
/ :two names only attested separately, e.g. "Eusebius/Riccitanc"

b. Emended names
<> : Triangular brackets around part of the name indicate emendations.

c. Questionable Goths

?? :Two question marks before the name indicates that no criterion of Gothic identity is securely attested.

d. Goths who never lived under Ostrogothic rule in Italy

!! :Two exclamation points before the name indicates that the "Goth" lived outside the chronological limits 489–554, or lived in the Eastern Empire, or in Spain (with no evidence that he or she had come to Spain from Italy under the Ostrogothic kings), but matched one of the criteria of Gothic identity discussed in "Method and Purpose."

Note: Byzantine soldiers in Italy identified as "Goths," or as relatives of "Goths," do not receive exclamation points.

For dates after 554, family ties may indicate whether the individual in question came to Italy after 554. Discretion is used on uncertain dates.

e. Spurious Goths

[ ] :Square brackets around the name indicates either that scholars have identified the individual as "a Goth" with no evidence, or have wrongly attributed criteria to him or her that would make him or her a Goth in the framework of this prosopography, e.g. military service under Theoderic. (Not all examples have been listed. An attempt to include all the spurious Goths collected, e.g., by Fiebiger and Schmidt in the "Ostgoten" section of their *Inschriftensammlung* would overwhelm this prosopography. Note that a Germanic name and an *apparent* date from the sixth century is not sufficient for inclusion; for some of these undatable individuals, see section III, table 14.)

f. Fragmentary names

●●●: indicates that the name survives only in fragmentary form (equivalent to ". . ." in PLRE)

g. Rank designations

★Boldface with asterisk = kings, queens and most members of Ostrogothic royal families, listed in PAII (★royal prosopography)

Boldface = *inlustres* or higher ranks, including most *sublimes* and *nobiles*, and all *magnifici* and *gloriosi*

CAPITALS = *spectabiles*, and some *sublimes*

ITALIC CAPITALS = *clarissimi*

v.g. = *vir gloriosus*	
v.i. = *vir inlustris*	*i.f.* = *inlustris femina*
v.subl. = *vir sublimis*	*subl.f.* = *sublimis femina*
v.sp. = *vir spectabilis*	*sp.f.* = *spectabilis femina*
v.c. = *vir clarissimus*	*c.f.* = *clarissima femina*
v.d. = *vir devotus*	
v.h. = *vir honestus*	*h.f.* = *honesta femina*

These designations are always given according to the highest rank attained. In some cases they are only deduced from the office held. Note that possession of the illustrate or higher entitled the individual to membership in the senate. There is no reason to think that the attested senators **A**rigernus and **T**uluin were exceptions among people identified as Goths. Note that *saiones* were probably *viri devoti*: see Conti, *"Devotio."*

4. Offices (central column)

CSL = *comes sacrarum largitionum*
PPO = *praefectus praetorio*
MVM = *magister utriusque militiae*

comes = many offices: see Traube, index to Cassiodorus, pp. 523–4, Schmidt, "Die comites Gothorum," and Wolfram, *Goths*, pp. 290–5 (the title is discussed in the text whenever it appears)
dux = a military office, probably no longer strictly the leader of *limitanei* (frontier) forces (and possibly held alongside the title *comes*: see Wolfram, *Goths*, pp. 213, 291–2 with nn. 215–16)
doryphoros = "bodyguard," i.e. *bucellarius*, of Byzantine generals
archon and *strategos* = "general" in Procopius's classicizing language, occasionally equivalent to *dux*, *comes* or *MVM*

5. References to other prosopographies (central column)

PLRE2 = J. R. Martindale, *The Prosopography of the Later Roman Empire* 2, A.D. 395–527 (Cambridge, 1980).
PLRE3 = J.R. Martindale, *The Prosopography of the Later Roman Empire* 3, A.D. 527–641 (Cambridge, 1992).
B = T. S. Brown, *Gentlemen and Officers: Imperial Administration and Aristocratic Power in Byzantine Italy, A.D. 554–800* (Rome, 1984), "Prosopographical Index" at pp. 247–82.

Where the name and enumeration (but not necessarily the title) are *exactly* the same as my own, I use "(= PLRE2)" etc. Where they vary *at all*, I use "(= PLRE2 Gudila 2)" etc.

For full citation of other sources, see bibliography.

6. Dates when individual is attested (right-hand column)

b = born
d = died
/ = attested at some point between e.g. 523/526
– = attested for the period indicated, e.g. 541–57 (if these dates indicate the lifespan, it will say so in the text)

$VI^{in} = c.\ 500\text{--}25$ $VI^1 = c.\ 500\text{--}50$
$VI^{med} = c.\ 525\text{--}75$ $VI^2 = c.\ 550\text{--}600$
$VI^{ex} = c.\ 575\text{--}600$

Variae dates based on Krautschick, *Cassiodor*, with emendations as marked.

Opera of Ennodius dates based on Sundwall, *Abhandlungen*.

7. Other individuals mentioned in the text who are not Goths

See under. Certain individuals connected with Goths are occasionally cross-referenced with the words *see under.* see the text under the cross-reference for details of their careers and identities.

( ) : Parentheses (round brackets) are placed around certain names of non-Goths included in the tables in III, indicating that they are not listed in the prosopography, and do not count for purposes of determining proportions.

I. MAIN PROSOPOGRAPHY
(excludes members of royal families)

Criteria	Individual	Dates
?N	??!!Acio presbyter	VI^2

?n, c, cc, l — Name inscribed in the apse of the cathedral at Parenzo, which was built in the first half of the sixth century. He was therefore a Catholic clergyman with a Germanic name, but he probably lived after Ostrogothic rule in Italy. Included here despite the date due to his clerical position: inscriptions of laymen from the same location include the names Milricus, Benno, Teugantiius [*sic*], Engenalco, Richelda, Adelgarius, Burga, Gainus, and Amara; on the last name, cf. **A**mara 1 and 2, below. All listed at F-S NF no. 23; see also Rugo 2, nos. 97a, 102, 110 and 111; Mazzoleni nos. 38–44, 47–9, Gainus at *Inscriptiones Italiae* 10.2, no. 183.

?N: Mazzoleni, no. 38, p. 176, challenges its Germanic roots; Rugo 2:75 suggests that it could be a Greek cognomen. But derivation from the prefix "Agi-/Agio," common among the Lombards, seems the most likely explanation.

F-S NF no. 23.

N	Ademunt qui et Andreas (= PLRE3)	553

n, ?c, (l) — Illegitimate son of **A**derit, *v.g.*; sister of **R**anilo, whose Catholicism may relate to his dual Germanic and Latin name. *PItal* 13.21–2 (Ravenna).

N	**Aderit** vir gloriosus (= PLRE3)	VI[1]
——— (n), ?c, (l)	Father of both **A**demunt and **R**anilo. **R**anilo may have been Catholic. *PItal* 13.0–1, 19–20 (Ravenna).	d by 553

N, ?J	ADILA vir spectabilis, comes (= PLRE2 Adila 2)	507/511
——— ?j, l	Received a letter from Theoderic ordering him to give *tuitio* to the Sicilian possessions and people of the Catholic church of Milan.	

?J: The title could mean that he was *comes civitatis* or *provinciae*; *tuitio* implies that he was a soldier. PLRE2: 9 suggests that he had previously been a *saio* (cf. **D**uda 1 & 2, **G**uduin 1 and 2, **Q**uidila 1 and 2). Possibly identical with PLRE3 Adila 1, who had an agent named Italicus in Syria.
Var. 2.29.

N	**Adiud/Adiut** vir inlustris (= PLRE3)	557

One of the accusers of **G**udahals (cf. **G**underit 1 and **R**osemud). *PItal* 7.43, 58, 66, 78 (Rieti).

–	**[Aemilianus]** vir magnificus, magister militum (= PLRE2 Aemilianus 5, PLRE3 Aemilianus 3, B. Aemilianus)	558–60

Attested in a letter once attributed to Gelasius (in the 490s), which would have made him a military officer under Theoderic. But the letter has been securely reattributed to Pelagius I; he was thus a Byzantine *magister militum* in the late 550s. See Ewald, *Coll. Brit. Pel. ep.* 16, p. 542, n. 6; Pelagius I, JK 949 = *ep.* "Experientia tua" (Thiel, Gelasius I, *frag.* 3, p. 484).

(N) ——— n, l	Agata (= PLRE2)	*c.* 472– 512

Daughter of **G**attila comes. The dates represent her lifespan. The Graeco-Latin name Agatha was that of a saint allegedly popular among the Goths, with an Arian dedication in Rome: Zeiller, "Les églises ariennes," pp. 20–1 (without much proof); Kampers, "Anmerkungen," pp. 146–7, identifies Agata as an Arian on this basis. But Agatha was also revered by Catholics; cf. the "basilica sanctae Agathae in Caclano fundo," mentioned by Gelasius I, JK 681 = *ep.* "Dudum de sanctae" (Thiel, *frag.* 12, pp. 495–6). The dedication of the formerly Arian church in Rome to St. Agatha must date from Gregory the Great, who brought relics of Agatha into the church when he reconsecrated it to Catholicism; Zeiller, ibid., p. 21.
F-S 223; reproduction at Rugo 5, p. 168, plate 33.

N, ?J ——— ?j, l	AGILULPH ?comes Dalmatiae (= PLRE2 Agilulfus)	492/496

Gelasius I sent him a letter begging him to defend a small estate (*reculia*) in Dalmatia belonging to the Roman see. Gelasius asks him to take up the suggestions of Honorius, bishop of Split, and find the *conductores* (cf. the definition under **B**auto; here they had probably either seized the property or were refusing to remit their rents). No titles are mentioned in the fragmentary letter, but PLRE2: 34 plausibly suggests that he was *comes Dalmatiae*; this should mean that he commanded troops (see **O**suin, and Schmidt, "Die comites Gothorum," p. 130), hence ?J. Gelasius I, JK 686 = *ep.* "Precor autem" (Thiel, *frag.* 2, p. 484).

N, ?A, ?†, Alamud diaconus or ?vir devotus   538
G, ?D
—————— Bought $\frac{4}{12}$ of the *fundus* Casa Caballaria from **G**udilibus, recorded in a lost document possibly drawn up at Faenza. **G**udilibus signs in Gothic. Tjäder, p. 42, argues that J.-Baptista Doni's seventeenth-century reading of "Gudilebus diaconus" was a misexpansion of "Gudilib u d." This would certainly be plausible, except that Gudilibus calls himself "dkn" in his Gothic subscription – a problem, as Tjäder admits. Note the Gothic word "diakon" at *PItal* 34.9. Furthermore, the only other Gothic subscriptions attested are by clerics (though cf. **L**atinus). Tjäder is only *conjecturing* that Doni misexpanded a "d", on the basis of line 18, which has no "v." I think that we must accept "diaconus," with case endings on the names; see further **G**udilibus.
?A, ?† : A deacon associating with a deacon signing in Gothic was probably an Arian clergyman. (For a further complication relating to the name Alamud/Alamoda, see **O**ptarit.)
?D: If he was an Arian clergyman; see **D**anihel.
PDip 118 = *PItal* 8 (Tjäder 2: 43–5, re-editing from the eighteenth-century editions, the original being lost).

N, J, [?D] !!Alathort *MVM* per Thracias (= PLRE2 Alathar)   513–14
He was appointed *MVM* per Thracias by Anastasius after the death of the previous incumbent Cyrillus. He was defeated and captured by the then rebel **V**italianus 1. Alathort's name in Jordanes's form looks Germanic: Schönfeld, p. 11. John of Antioch (spelling the name "Alathar") calls him "Scythian," taken by Bury, HLRE 1: 449 and Stein, *Bas-Empire* 2: 180 to mean "Hun." But "Scythian" could also mean "Goth": cf. the confusions in the identities of **M**undo and **V**italianus 1, who were in the same place at the same time. Most probably in all their cases the language is struggling to describe something new and specifically Balkan. Jordanes, *Rom.* 358; Joh. Ant. fr. 214e6.

N, J, S, [D] Albilas, Gothic commander (= PLRE3)   537/539
Placed in command of the Orvieto garrison by **W**itigis (Procopius, BG 2.11.1) which apparently eventually fell to Belisarius's siege; called "a man especially esteemed among the Goths" by Procopius, BG 2.20.14.

N, S   Albis, envoy of Witigis (= PLRE3)   537
—————— Sent with other envoys by **W**itigis to Belisarius during the siege
j, l   of Rome. Procopius, BG 1.20.7.

N   *ALICO* ?vir clarissimus (= PLRE3)   505
————————   A Catholic friend of Ennodius, connected with a "venerabilis
c, 1   Amantius presbyter;" Ennodius wrote to him "pleading the
                   cause of the Church" in the Laurentian schism. Ennodius, *Op.*
                   118/*ep.* 4.2.

N   !!Aligernus (= B)   598
————————   Father-in-law of the son of Theodora: see **A**nonymus 5 and
(n), 1   **A**nonyma 3. He defrauded a widow out of her property. B:
                   "Goth?" Not to be confused with ★**A**ligernus, who led the last
                   Gothic forces in Italy in the 550s. GR 9.36 (Campania).

N, J   Aliulfus saio (= PLRE2)   526
————————   Theoderic ordered him to oversee collection of wood for build-
1   ing ships for the fleet to sail against Africa. *Var.* 5.20.

N, J, ?S,   Amalafridas, Byzantine commander, ?*MVM* (= PLRE3)   534,
[D]   Almost certainly a Catholic (note his friendship with the Frank- 540,
————————   ish queen St. Radegund, below). The son of Theoderic's   552,
s, c, 1   niece ★**A**malaberga and the Thuringian king Hermanifrid. He   ?567
                   and his mother escaped the Frankish conquest of Thuringia in
                   534, arriving at Ravenna. Called "Gothos anēr" by Procopius.
                   This evidence suggests that he felt more loyalty to his mother's
                   identity than to that of his father; perhaps he served with the
                   Gothic army under Witigis in besieged Ravenna (or earlier).
                   J: he was a soldier.
                   ?S: he may have been on the Gothic side before 540.
                   s: But after he came to Constantinople with the defeated
                   Witigis, in 540, he accepted a position in Justinian's army. He
                   commanded Byzantine troops sent to help the Lombards against
                   the Gepids in 552. Procopius, BG 4.25.11–14.
                   c: He was a childhood friend of the Frankish queen Radegund,
                   and may have visited her in Poitiers in 567; Venantius Fortun-
                   atus, *App. Carm.* 1.47–64, 65–6, 73–80, 95–100; 3.12–34; *Carm.*
                   8.1.23–4; on this evidence, see PLRE3: 51.

N, A, †, ?D   Amalatheus spodeus   551
————————   Scribe or producer of books at the Gothic Arian church of St.
1   Anastasia in Ravenna (on *spodeus*, in Gothic *bokareis*, bookseller
                   or scribe, see Tjäder 2: 95–6. Like **W**iliarit 4, he was probably
                   not a member of the clergy, but associated with the church as
                   a lay brother. His name is announced among the witnesses, but
                   his subscription does not appear below. It is probably cut off
                   with the bottom of the document (see Tjäder 2: 91, and 3, plate
                   121), appearing with that of **W**iliarit 4 after the clergy.
                   ?D: on this, and on the deed of sale that he witnessed, see
                   Danihel. *PItal* 34.85.

N, J   Amara 1 saio (= PLRE2 Amara)   507/511
————————   Abused his *tuitio* and power, apparently by extorting money;
1   **T**utizar *saio* was to force him to repay in double.
                   Mazzoleni, no. 35, p. 174, challenges the Germanic origin of

the name, citing attempts to trace it to Celtic or Hebrew. It also confused Wrede, pp. 119–20, who points out the name "Erpamara," belonging to a fourth-century figure in Jordanes. Perhaps the name was an early borrowing from Celtic or some other dialect; there are fourth- and fifth-century examples of it in Italy (Mazzoleni ibid.). Here it is associated with the *saiones*, not one of whom had a Graeco-Latin name; nor is it latinized with a masculine "-us" ending. Schönfeld, p. 17, was certain that it was Germanic.

Other examples found in Catholic churches (see **A**mara 2, and the undated Amara at Parenzo listed under **A**cio).

Var. 4.27.2, 4; 4.28.

N ——————— (n), c, cc, l	!!Amara 2 ?lector (= B Amara) Donated floor mosaics to cathedral of Grado. His wife was called **A**ntonina, and children **H**aelia and **M**ellita. The mosaic also includes the name of Haelias, bishop of Aquileia, so Amara was definitely a Catholic. On the name, see Amara 1. Inscription in *Notizie degli Scavi* (1928), 290 = Rugo 2, no. 52 (emending "lector"; against Rugo's transcription, all of the name Amara survives; see 2: 121, plate 52–52a).	579
(N), A, (†) ——————— n	Anastasia Cousin (*consubrina*) of **M**innulus/**W**illienant, thus probably the daughter of the sister of **C**hristodorus, both Arian clergymen. One of them benefited from her will at Ravenna, so she must have been Arian herself. The name Anastasia, moreover, was that of a Balkan saint revered by Arian churches in both Ravenna and Constantinople: Kampers, "Anmerkungen," p. 416. *PItal* 33.9	d by 541

Andreas = **A**derit

J, ?S ——————— n	Andreas praepositus dromonariorum (= PLRE3 Andreas 4) Chief of a regiment of *dromonarii*. He owned the *fundus Kalegaricus* near Faenza, and was dead by 539, when his name was mentioned in conjunction with **T**hulgilo's sale of a neighboring property. Other properties adjoining this one belonged to the *dromonarii* **S**ecundus and **W**itterit. J: The *dromonarii* were oarsmen and soldiers: note that **W**itterit was a *scutarius*; see *Var.* 5.16; and further Seeck, RE 5: 1716. They also had peacetime duties: *Var.* 2.31. ?S: If he was still alive at some point between 535 and 539, presumably he would have been serving under Theodahad and Witigis. *PItal* 30.15–16.	d by 539
N, J ——————— l	Anduit Former soldier who petitioned the king for help: due to his loss of eyesight, he had been enslaved by **G**udila 3 and **O**ppa. Theoderic assigned **N**eudis the task of making **G**udila 3 and	523/ 524/526

Oppa desist. Wolfram suggests that he was thus illegally deprived of the *libertas* of the Gothic army: *Goths*, p. 301 with n. 271.

Var. 5.29.

N, ?J
————
l

!!*ANILAS* comes (= B, PLRE3)   559
Received request from Pope Pelagius I to protect two churchmen; he was Catholic (the pope appeals to "ecclesiasticam unitatem"). Possibly *comes civitatis* in Tuscia Annonaria: PLRE3: 83 (rank presumably deduced from this title). JK 1026 = *EP.* "Petrum filium" (Gassò & Batlle 67, pp. 175–6)

N, J
————
c, l

!!*ANIO* comes castri Aprutiensis (= B, PLRE3)   598
Catholic: built an oratory & asked Gregory I to allow the bishop to dedicate it. GR 9.71. "Cannot be assigned to any particular people" (B, p. 73). Rank: PLRE3: 83 (presumably deduced from his title).

N, ?J
————
l

ANNA vir spectabilis, comes (= PLRE2)   507/511
Judged dispute over property, ordered to investigate a case against a presbyter Laurentius (whether Catholic or Arian is unknown).
Name: cf. F-S NF 51 (a sixth- or seventh-century example); it was homonymous with a Graeco-Latin feminine name: note PLRE3 Anna 1 and 2.
J: see **A**dila, and note that Anna exercised judicial functions. *Var.* 1.5; 4.18.

N, ?J

!!Ansila (= PLRE2 Ansila 2)   484/496
"Named by Dracontius as a person able to testify to a Vandal victory [presumably in Sicily] in the reign of . . . Gunthamund (a. 484–96);" hence "?Ostrogothic general," PLRE2: 93. Since, as PLRE2 points out, the Vandals were driven out of Sicily for good in 491, it seems just as possible that Ansila was a general under Odoacer as well as under Theoderic. The source, Dracontius, *Satisfactio* 211–14, is hardly explicit.

(N)
————
n, c, (cc), l

!!Antonina   579
The wife of **A**mara 2 (*lector*) and the mother of **H**aelia and Mellita. A Catholic. Mosaic in the cathedral of Grado. Rugo 2, no. 52.

N, J
————
c, l

Ara, dux regis Theoderici in Italia   510/526
While residing at Arles, he was said to have abused an archpriest of Nîmes. The archdeacon Johannes appeared to him in a dream, and, terrified and ashamed, Ara ordered the archpriest to be let free. The *dux* knelt before Johannes, and later ordered that he be made bishop of Nîmes; Gregory of Tours, *Gloria martyrum* 77. The story shows various hagiographic formulae, and it is unclear how a *dux* at Arles could order that a man be made bishop. Moreover, the events occur in the section theor-

etically allotted to St. Baudilius, but appear to concentrate the
holiness on the archdeacon Johannes, so even the literary context is odd – Gregory clearly did not have enough information
on his subject Baudilius. However, there is nothing unlikely
about Ara's name or office. The story implies that Ara was a
Catholic. Heinzelmann, "Gallische Prosopographie," p. 557,
accepts it as true.

[**Arborius**] vir subl. comes et vicedominus (= PLRE2 Arborius 2)   489
Taking the name from the old edition of the Latin papyri by
Marini as "Ardor," Mommsen classed him as "anscheinend
gothischer Nationalität": OGS, NA 14: 465 with n. 1. We now
know that the correct reading is "Arbori" – an example of a
left-facing "b": see *PItal* 10–11.I.11 with Tjäder 3, plate 55, line
11, and Tjäder 1: 98–101 on the letter B in late Roman cursive.

N
———   Ardica vir honestus   ?542
l   Witness of a sentencing document in Ravenna. *PItal* 43.35, 52.

             Ardor = Arborius

N, J   **Arigernus** vir inlustris, comes (= PLRE2)   502,
———   Member of the senate by 510, in which he participated actively; 510–511
j, l, [?d]   performed duties of a judge or police chief at Rome
             (Mommsen, OGS, NA 14: 514–15), perhaps holding the office
             of *comes urbis Romae* (Schmidt, "Die comites Gothorum," p.
             129). Earlier, in 502, as *maior domus regiae*, he had been a royal
             emissary in Rome to help mediate between the warring factions
             of the Laurentian schism, with **B**edeulfus and **G**udila 1; Arig-
             ernus was already *v.i.*, *comes* at the time, and thus probably the
             leader of the three.
             J: office of *comes*, military action in Gaul in 511. PLRE2: 141 also
             makes him Goth because of Cassiodorus's phrase describing him
             to the senate, "cives paene vester," and (not convincingly), his
             office of *maior domus*; see Mommsen, OGS, NA 14: 516, n. 1:
             we cannot see Theoderic's consistory as an ethnically specific
             phenomenon; similarly and further, Amory, "Military and
             civilian."
             [?d]: from "cives paene vester," the "paene," in the context,
             referring to his military service rather than his ethnographic
             affiliation – although of course these two concepts are associated
             in the *Variae*.
             Var. 3.36; 3.45; 4.16; 4.22; 4.23; 4.43; *Acta synhodorum*, pp. 422–
             3, 425, 429.

N
———   Ariver   VI[in]
(n), c, l   Inscription on a sarcophagus from the Catholic cemetery of
             Manastirine in Salona (Split). Ariver was son of Tro . . .
             Vonosus ("Ariver filius Tro . . . |Vonoso"). See Egger, at CIL
             3.9434 and idem, *Altchristliche Friedhof*, p. 103, no. 249, on the

filiation in the dative and on the probable date. Fiebiger, 2F, p. 12 with n. 1, makes him a "Goth in a Gothic city," following Schmidt, *Ostgermanen*, p. 383. Wolfram, *Goths*, p. 520, n. 460, sees the cemetery as Arian without any justification. The pieces of the sarcophagus were found in and very close to the Catholic church at the center of the cemetery: see Egger, ibid., with plan at p. 66.

F-S, 2F 12 = Egger, *Altchristliche Friedhof*, p. 103, no. 249.

N, J, ([D])	!!Aruth, Herul commander (= B, PLRE3) 552–4
(n), s, l	In the army of Narses, an "admirer of Roman ways," he married **A**nonyma 2, the daughter of **M**auricius, son of **M**undo (q.v. for ([D])). He joined the army of Narses just before Busta Gallorum, along with **A**sbadus of the Gepids. Procopius 4.32.24; Agathias 1.20.

N, J, ?S, [D] — s, c, l, d

Asbadus, Gepid soldier in the Byzantine army (= B Asbad, 549–52; PLRE3 Asbadus 2)   d 556

In the army of Narses in Italy; he was the killer of Totila, and was wounded by **S**cipuar. (Not identical to the Byzantine *candidatus* PLRE3 Asbadus 1, BG 3.38.4–6, 9, with PLRE3: 133, contra B, p. 253).

[D], ?S: when Asbadus rushed at Totila, **A**nonymus 4 shouted at him, "What is this, you dog? Are you rushing to smite your own master?" – a statement that, as Procopius expects the reader to understand, immediately identified Totila to Asbadus (Procopius, BG 4.32.24). The word for "master", i.e. *dominus*, is *despotēs*, used in the same sentence to indicate the relationship of Totila to the "Gothic youth." Therefore, Asbadus was recognized as a "natural" subject of Totila, which means either that he had been in Totila's army and had deserted to the Byzantines (unlikely given BG 4.26.13), or that we are expected to see Gepids as Goths (but cf. **V**elas), perhaps both. The latter is totally plausible: note Jordanes, *Rom.* 94, and see **M**undo, **U**strigotthus.

Nevertheless, Asbadus's metrical epitaph strongly emphasized his triumph over the Goths, using imperial victory ideology and elements of classical ethnography: "in war, the Gothic *gens* having been expelled, you, as victor, have given the Alps to Latium and the Empire." We may be seeing some ancient conflict between "Goths" and "Gepids" in these contrasting depictions of Asbadus.

c: The epitaph was left at the basilica of St. Nazarius in Pavia: he was therefore a Catholic.

d: implied by the rhetoric of the epitaph. Procopius, BG 4.26.13; 4.32.22–8; *Auct. Havn. Extr.* 200.1–3. Epitaph quoted at *Auct. Havn. Extr.* 200.2.

J, S

———————

n

Asinarius, Gothic commander (= PLRE3)   535–7
Fought and killed **Mauricius**, the son of **Mundus**, in 535/6; in
536/7, he gathered an army among the Suevi and joined **Uligisalus** and proceeded to Split to besiege it. The attempt by Schönfeld, p. 33, to make his name Germanic, must be rejected: he
sees it as Procopius's Hellenized spelling of an unattested
Gothic *Asinareis, derived from the attested Latin Asinarius, on
no basis other than Asinarius's affiliation with the Gothic army.
It is obviously simpler to accept that Asinarius had a Latin name.
Procopius, BG 1.7.1; 1.16.8, 12, 14–16.

N, [D]

———————

j, l

Athanarid Gothorum phylosophus   496/
One of the geographers at Theoderic's court in Ravenna,   497/507
along with **Heldebaldus** and **Marcomirus**, whose work was used
by the later Ravenna Cosmographer, e.g. 4.12/201. On date
and location, see Staab, "Ostrogothic geographers," pp. 30,
46–57.

–

[BACAUDA] vir spectabilis, tribunus voluptatum (= PLRE2   523/526
Bacauda 2)
Wolfram, *Goths*, p. 300, implies that he was a soldier. He was
not. *Var.* 5.25.

(N)

———————

n, c, l

Basilius (= PLRE3 Basilius 7)   VI
The son of **Guntelda**, the father of **Guntio**. Note how the Germanic root skipped a generation. Catholic: see **Guntelda**. Basilius's name was common among the senatorial clan of the Decii,
but also outside it (see PLRE2 and PLRE3 s.n.). From an inscription in Como. Date: see **Guntelda**. Rugo 5, no. 78.

N

———————

j, l

Bauto conductor domus regiae (= PLRE2)   508
Having been asked by **Julianus** *comes patrimonii* to decide a case
between Bauto and **Epiphanius** *chartarius*, Ennodius checked
Bauto's reference and found it confirmed, judging in Bauto's
favour. A *conductor* seems to have paid taxes as a tenant farmer
or lessee who did not actually till the soil himself: Goffart, *Barbarians and Romans*, p. 205, n. 61; cf. p. 135, n. 15. Bauto's
payment of taxes on his land does not necessarily make him *not*
J; he could have had a *sors* elsewhere. On the other hand, *conductor* seems to have been his primary function from Ennodius's
point of view, rather than, e.g., *miles* nor *comes*. For a *conductor
domus regiae* with the Latin name Moderatus, see Gelasius, JK
631 = *ep.* "Religionis probatur iniuria" (Loewenfeld, *ep. in.* 3,
p. 2) (from 493/4).
Ennodius, *Op.* 306/*ep.* 7.1.

N, ?J

———————

l

BEDEULFUS vir sublimis, maior domus regiae (= PLRE2)   502
He, **Arigernus** and **Gudila** 1 served as mediators of the king
between the factions of the Laurentian schism.
?J: see **Arigernus** on *maior domus*. *Acta synhodorum*, pp. 422, 425.

A, †, ?D   Benenatus ostiarius   551
————— Sexton of the Gothic church of St. Anastasia in Ravenna. On
n, l   the document, see **Danihel**. Possibly illiterate, since he only
signs with a cross at the end of the document – but so do all
the other *ostiarii*, so perhaps the lack of signature is just an indication of low status (contra Tjäder 2: 95).
?D: see **Danihel**. *PItal* 34.85, 135.

N, A, †, ?D   Berevulfus vir venerabilis, presbyter   VI
————— Dated by Fiebiger, presumably on palaeographical grounds, and
l   made an "Ostrogoth" on the basis of his name. If the inscription
is from the Ostrogothic period – and the man was seventy when
he died, so he surely lived through the Ostrogothic regime –
he was probably an Arian clergyman, due to the lack of Germanic names in any certainly Catholic clergy of the period of
Ostrogothic rule (see **Butila** and **Gudila 2**). The inscription
comes from Forum Iulii, now Iria, in Liguria.
?D: if an Arian clergyman; see **Danihel**.
F-S NF 48.

–   [**Bergantinus**] vir illustris, comes patrimonii, patricius (=   527–38
PLRE2)
Identified as a Goth by Mommsen, OGS, NA 14: 465, n. 1, on
unknown grounds. There is no reason to consider him one. On
his career see PLRE2: 225.

?N, J, [D],   **Bessas** archon/**Bessa** patricius, *MVM* (= PLRE2)   503
G   Origin: Thrace (Procopius, BG 1.5.3; 1.16.2), "a Goth by birth,   535–54
————— one of those who had dwelt in Thrace from of old, and had
c, s, l   not followed Theoderic when he led the Gothic nation thence
into Italy . . ." (trans. Dewing 3: 159); cf. BP 1.8.3 (on his earlier
experiences in Persia in 503 with **Godidisclus**). Wolfram seems
to make him into a possible Visigoth, *Goths*, p. 235 (namesake
near Toulouse), but then clearly calls him an Ostrogoth on p.
476, n. 531, noting the existence of the Thracian tribe of the
Bessi. All this is interesting in light of Jordanes's information,
speaking as if he knows Bessas or at least knows a lot about
him. Jordanes (*Get.* 265) makes Bessas a descendent of a *genus*
composed of "Sauromatae . . . quos Sarmates dicimus et Cemandri et quidam ex Hunnis" who settled at Castra Martis in
Dacia Ripensis. Jordanes's point, however, seems to be to
equate the ancient Greek Sauromatae with the Sarmatians, relating both to the Goths; see Wolfram, pp. 19, 28 with n. 87,
citing the amusing BG 4.5.6 which also equates Sauromatae with
Goths. According to Jordanes, also from this settlement were
two other Byzantine commanders who never came to Italy,
both of whom bore Germanic names, Blivila and Froila; see
further Maenchen-Helfen, *Huns*, p. 150; PLRE2 Blivila, Froila
("they were perhaps in fact Goths, like Bessas," p. 231).

Procopius mentions a Godidisclus whose family did not follow Theoderic to Italy (= PLRE3). For a member of the Bessi in Byzantine service who defected to the Goths, see **B**urcentius. Life: Bessas was a high Byzantine officer present for most of the Gothic Wars. Originally close to Belisarius, but then suspected of hostility by the general, who sent him away from Ravenna; later Bessas was put in charge of Italy after Belisarius's departure. Subsequently, he took part in Armenian, Lazican and Persian campaigns. *Patricius* in 551.

?N: The name could be Germanic or Thraco-Greek. Germanic: Schönfeld , p. 51, adducing the Frank Besso from *Chron. Caesaraug.* s.a. 531; Förstemann 1: 298, adducing a female Bessa of MGH: SRM 3: 589, with reservations. Thraco-Greek: *Griechische Eigennamen*, col. 287, noting the Thracian Bessi, and a reference of Plutarch (*Ser. num. vind.* 8) to a Paonian (the people northeast of the Bessi) called Bessos.

G: He spoke Gothic, BG1.10.10.

c: He received a letter from the moderate monophysite Jacob of Sarug: PLRE2: 226 (to Bessas *comes*: his name is very rare, and the title and date are correct; the identification seems safe).

Procopius, BP 1.8.3; BG 1.5.3; 1.16.2–3; 1.10; 1.16; 1.17; 1.18.35; 1.19.15; 1.23.13; 1.27.18; 2.1.3; 2.8.15; 2.29.29; 3 *passim*; 4.9; 4.11. *Cont. Marc.* ss.aa. 540.6, 542.3, 545.3. Jordanes, *Get.* 265.

N, J   BETANCUS comes (= PLRE2)   *c.* 512

Carried off as hostage a certain **A**vulus, a Gallic aristocrat, from Burgundian or Provençal regions, probably during Theoderic's invasion of Gaul in 508. Avitus of Vienne wrote a letter to Maximus, bishop of Pavia, requesting his aid in securing the return of the hostage home. The letter makes no reference to the Ostrogothic or Burgundian wars, simply mentioning *Galli* and *Italia* in Avitus's usual style. On the date, see PLRE2: 229. (Similarly involved in southern Gaul at the time: **I**bba, **M**ammo, **T**uluin, perhaps **L**iberius).

J: he was clearly a soldier, and his title of *comes* must therefore have been military.

Avitus, *ep.* 12.

(N)   Bilesarius   VI[med]

———— Husband of **S**ifilo, recorded in a Ravenna document of man-
n, ?j umission: they may have both been slaves; on this and the date, see **S**ifilo. *PItal* 9.14.

N, J, S, ?A, Bleda dux/archon (= PLRE3)   542
[D]   Sent with **V**iliarid and **R**uderit by Totila against the Byzantine army ensconced in Florence and led by Justinus, **B**essas, Cyprian and **I**ohannes 2. The Goths won; Bessas escaped wounded. Pro-

copius calls the three commanders "the most warlike of the Goths," hence [D]; Gregory the Great later referred to them as Totila's most loyal followers; *Dialogi* 2.14 (see further **R**iggo). *Cont. Marc.* s.a. 542 (calling him "Blidin," acc.); Procopius, BG 3.5.1 (calling him "Bledas").

N: the name could be Hunnic, since it was the name of Attila's older brother (PLRE2 Bleda), but linguistically it is apparently Germanic; see, contra PLRE3: 233, Maenchen-Helfen, *Huns*, pp. 387-8.

?A: see **R**iggo.

N ———————— (l)	**B**oherda (= PLRE3) Father of **O**dericus *vir clarissimus*, so possibly but not necessarily of high rank. Deceased at the time that Oderic witnessed the document of sale that mentions his father. *PItal* 36.65.	d by 575/591

N, J, [D]
————————
l

BOIO *vir spectabilis* (= PLRE2)   507/511
Instructed to return inheritance to his nephew or grandson (*nepos*) **W**iliarit 1, who is of age to fight in the army, and who is called a "Goth," implying that king thought of Boio as both a Goth and a soldier, hence J and [D]. Theoderic also refers to *iuvenes nostri*, the king's youths, the present and future soldiers of his army, but, possibly, in the cajoling, man-to-man tone of the letter, "your youths and mine," "we" both being Goths. "Valour makes maturity for the Goths" (*Var.* 1.38.2). (Note also Theoderic's possible reference to *tuitio*, the special duty normally given to *saiones*; Mommsen, in his edition of Cassiodorus, corrigenda to page 36.10, p. clxxxi; on *saiones* and *tuitio*, see Amory, "Military and civilian.") *Var.* 1.38.

(N)
————————
n, c, cc, l,
[d]

Bonifatius (Boniface II), pope   530-2
Son of **S**igibuldus, leading many historians rashly to call him a Goth or a German, e.g. Harnack, "Der erste deutsche Papst." Boniface had long been a deacon of the Roman church before he was nominated as pope by Felix IV.
[d]: The LP calls him "natione Romanus ex patre Sigibuldo": on the limited *stadtrömisch* meaning of this phrase, see **P**elagius II, below.
LP Boniface II, *Var.* 9.15, the Amelli documents (*PLS* 3: 1280-82), and Boniface II, JK 881 = *ep.* "Per filium nostrum" (*PL* 65: 31-4).

N
————————
j, s, l

Bonila praerogativarius   552-75
Officer of the Byzantine praetorian prefect of Italy. *PItal* 4–5.III.1 (Ravenna).

–

[**B**onosa]   564
Sold $\frac{1}{24}$ of a *fundus* near Ravenna in 564. Despite Tjäder 1: 509 s.n., the name is Latin. *PItal* 8.III.1.

Bonosus = **V**onosus

N, J   Brandila   523/
────────   Committed adultery with **Regina**, wife of **Patza**. Brandila was 524/526
(n), 1   the husband of **Procula**. Brandila was presumably a soldier, like
                  Patza, since his trial was entrusted to the *dux* **W**ilitancus. *Var.*
                  5.32–3.

N, J, S   Burcentius   539
────────   A Byzantine soldier on guard duty during the siege of Osimo,
s, 1   he turned traitor for money and worked as a messsenger for the
                  Goths. When he was caught (betrayed by **A**nonymus 6) his
                  former comrades burned him alive in front of the enemy.
                  Procopius says that he was of the "Besi," presumably the Bessi
                  of Thrace rather than the Vesi sc. Visigoths; note that the
                  Thracian **B**essas could be seen as a Goth, and that **H**erodianus,
                  who led troops from Thrace (Procopius, BG 3.1.1), also turned
                  traitor and joined the Goths (though allegedly due to the
                  pressure of blackmail from Belisarius: see **H**erodianus).
                  Burcentius's name is Germanic, and it is difficult not to imagine
                  some kind of connection here. But without further evidence it
                  is impossible even to hazard a [?D]. See also **M**undo and
                  Vitalianus on the confusions over the identity of soldiers from
                  the Balkans.
                  N: Detschew, p. 82, classifies the name as "Thracian," not for
                  linguistic reasons, but only because Procopius calls him one of
                  the "Besi" (on which see above). Note a Burdentius at ICUR
                  n.s., no. 14094.
                  Procopius, BG 2.26.3–5, 14–15, 2–6.

N, ?J, A,   Butila presbyter   507/511
†, ?D   His *sors* at Trent was relieved of taxation by a change in the
────────   state assessment books; that is, it now consisted of a payment
1   made directly to him without reference to the state or munici-
                  pality: see Goffart, *Barbarians and Romans*, pp. 77–9, 91. For
                  similar tranference of tax revenues to the Arian church, *Var.*
                  1.26.3.
                  ?J: he had a state allotment, and thus had possibly, although not
                  necessarily, been a member of Theoderic's army. Goffart
                  remarks, "Theoderic's cancellation of tax has no apparent con-
                  nection to Butila's being a priest" (p. 77, n. 39, continuing on
                  to p. 78), which is fair. It might simply have been a reward for
                  some other service.
                  A, †: his Germanic name strongly suggests that he belonged to
                  the Arian clergy; see **B**erevulfus and **G**udila 2.
                  ?D: see **D**anihel.
                  Var. 2.17.

S, [D]   Caballarius (= PLRE3)   541
────────   Sent as an envoy to Justinian by **E**raric. The name is Latin.
n, j, 1   Called a Goth. Procopius, BG 3.2.16.

?J   ??Candac ?saio (= PLRE2 Candac 2)   507/511
———————— Theoderic instructed him to give *tuitio* to Crispinianus, a task
l   normally assigned by the king to his *saiones*. Mommsen, index
               to Cassiodorus s.n., calls his name "Alan" since it was the same
               as that of a fifth-century Alan king; *Get.* 265–6.
               Name: cf. also Kandich, Avar envoy to Justin II; Menand. Prot.,
               fr. 5.1.
               Var. 1.37.

−   [CENSORIUS] vir spectabilis   VI[med]
               Epitaph at the cathedral of Trent, dating perhaps from 539, 554
               or 569. Wolfram, p. 516, n., 397, suggests that he was *comes*
               tractatus Italiae, but this is pure speculation. Cf. [Marcianus].
               Rogger, "Scavi e ricerche," pp. 20–2 with fig. 12 after p. 32.
               Missed by PLRE.

?N, (N), ?J,   Cessi/Cessis comes (= PLRE3 Cessis)   535/542
?S   Father-in-law of **G**hiveric/**G**iberit vir devotus, hence (N); the
               linguistic origin of Cessi's name is uncertain, as is the nomina-
               tive case from a genitive "Cessinis": Tjäder, 2: 347, opts for
               "Cessi," PLRE3 for "Cessis." Apparently still alive when the
               document was drawn up (no *quondam*). On the document, see
               Riccifrida.
               ?J, ?S: *comes* could be a military position: if it was, and he lived
               in Ravenna before 540, then he probably served the Gothic side
               in the Wars.
               PItal 43.51.

(N), A, †,   Christodorus presbyter   d by
?D   Father of **M**innulus/**W**illienant, hence (N), "presbyter legis sup- 541
———————— rascriptae [= ecclesiae Gotorum Ravennatis]," hence A and †.
n, (l)   Deceased at the time of Minnulus's sale of property. ?D: see
               Danihel.
               PItal 33.1, 10 (Classis and Ravenna).

J, S, [?D]   Coccas   552
———————— A Byzantine deserter, called "a Roman soldier" and "a man of
s, [d]   the Gothic army" by Procopius. Just before the battle of Busta
               Gallorum, Coccas challenged any Byzantine ("Roman") to
               single combat and was killed by the Armenian Anzalas. The
               name is not Germanic; it may be Thracian: Detschew, p. 251,
               s.n. Coca.
               Procopius, BG 4.31.12, 14–16.

J   **Colosseus** vir inlustris, comes Pannoniae Sirmiensis (= PLRE2) 507/
———————— Appointed to office in Pannonia and sent supplies there by **Sen-** 511,
n, l   arius; he had already had a long career, and was still in office ?511
               in ?511: on the date, Krautschick, *Cassiodor*, pp. 67–8, contra
               Mommsen (who opted for 509/510).
               J: *comites* of threatened frontier provinces are generally thought

to combine military and civil authority, e.g. Schmidt, "Die comites Gothorum," p. 130 (citing this letter; cf. **O**suin); Schmidt, Mommsen and Wolfram all make Colosseus a "Goth" due to his job: "Die comites Gothorum," p. 130; OGS, NA 14: 497, n. 3 (wrongly making his name Germanic as well); *Goths*, p. 321 ("a Goth with a non-Gothic name"). PLRE2: 305 thinks that Theoderic identifies Colosseus as a Goth, since the king instructs him to demonstrate the "Gothorum . . . iustitia" to the people of Pannonia. But this letter clearly imagines Colosseus as the representative of the Gothic king in Pannonia, and I doubt that we can derive any intentional identification of Colosseus himself from this statement. *Var.* 3.23-4; 4.13.

| N, A, †, ?D | Costila ostiarius | 551 |

N, A, †, ?D
——————
l

Costila ostiarius   551
Sexton of the Gothic church of St. Anastasia at Ravenna. On the document, see **D**anihel. Possibly illiterate (see **B**enenatus). Identified by Tjäder 2: 273, n. 30, with **C**ostula, on the grounds that they were both elderly; his argument does not carry sufficient weight.
?D: see **D**anihel.
PItal 34.84, 131.

N, J, [D]

Costula   523/526
He and **D**aila were said by Theoderic to "enjoy the liberty of our Goths," but both had been loaded with "onera servilia" by **G**uduin 2, and should have been freed from them.
J: service in the army. According to the Goffart thesis, they would have been forced to pay taxes. But on the ideological above. *Var.* 5.30.

N, ?J, [D]
——————
l

Cunigastus vir inlustris, ?comes (= PLRE2)   522/
Boethius complained that he and **T**riwila seized the property of 525, 527
the defenseless while at Theoderic's court, apparently including him among the avaricious *barbari* at court, hence [D]. Ironically, Cunigastus was ordered in 527 to hear a case over such a seizure: Constantius and Venerius complained that **T**anca had seized their farm and imposed conditions of servitude upon them. The names and situation imply two tax-paying Romans exploited by a tax-collecting Goth: Goffart, *Barbarians and Romans*, pp. 93–5; PLRE2: 330 simply calls them "two Romans" and "a Goth."
?J: Cases between Romans and Goths were to be heard by the *comes Gothorum* (*Var.* 7.3), that is, the military *comes civitatis*.
Var. 8.28; Boethius, *Consolatio* 1.4; *Var.* 8.28.

J, G
——————
n, j, ?c, (c), l, [d]

Cyprianus vir inlustris et magnificus, *CSL*, patricius, magister 504–27
officiorum (= PLRE2 Cyprianus 2)
He was considered to be a Roman during his lifetime; slightly later, the AV perhaps exhibits confusion over his identity: see below.

Presumably a Catholic like his brother **O**pilio. Father of
Anonymi 20+ (see also text below).

Not quite a parvenu (his father was *CSL* under Odoacer: see
PLRE2 Opilio 3), but a member of a family from the bureaucratic
elite, like Cassiodorus, who, unlike the senators of Rome, had
to display excellent qualities in order to come to the attention
of the king.

Unlike Cassiodorus, but like others in the Ostrogothic kingdom, Cyprianus came to prominence through military service.
He first appears in the Sirmium war of 504–5 (like ★**W**itigis).
Later, he made a habit of going on horse-rides with Theoderic
(*Var.* 5.40.4). He also served Theoderic in a civilian capacity,
working his way up through the palace administration via ?*tribunus et notarius, referendarius, comes sacrarum largitionum* and *magister officiorum* (details at PLRE2: 332–3), a *cursus* that further suggests a man of middling birth. Note the excuses made to the
senate about his appointment: *Var.* 8.22.2–3.

He spoke Gothic and Greek (*Var.* 5.40.5), and brought up his
children, **A**nonymi 20+, to speak Gothic and to become soldiers: *Var.* 8.21.6–7; 8.22.5.

Identity: Cassiodorus and the administration of Athalaric saw
him as "Romanae stirpis" (*Var.* 8.21.7); against this, his early
and close association with the army and with the Gothic language suggest that he wanted to be seen as a "Goth" under
civilitas ideology, or perhaps to have the best of both worlds.
There is some connection between his close association with
Gothic ideals and his enmity of Boethius, whom he delated to
Theoderic. But Boethius does not group him with the "barbarians" at court (*Consolatio* 1, prose 4). By the 540s, the AV
was able to imply that Boethius was a Roman and that his
enemy Cyprian was, perhaps, not (AV 85; the placement of the
section might also imply that Cyprian was an Arian, since at
this point in the narrative only Arians and Jews are on the side
of the king: this shows the perspective of a tendentious text; on
which see Barnish, "The *Anonymus Valesianus* II").

There is no question that we are viewing a clever opportunist
who saw a swift route to preferment at court, and who doubtless
resented the king's shift back in the 520s to promoting scions
of senatorial families over professionals like himself; Moorhead,
Theoderic, pp. 229–32. Cyprian became *CSL* shortly after the fall
of Boethius.

But to his parvenu or professional background must be added
his military interests. Boethius, like most senators, was unconnected with the army. Cyprian can possibly be placed among
the pro-military party who opposed the "Romanizing" education of Athalaric (see **A**nonymi 11, 12, 13) in the late 520s
(although he was already elderly in 527: *Var.* 8.21.2), a party to
which his brother **O**pilio also may have belonged; see further

Triwila, Tuluin, *Amalasuintha. Cyprian then exploited not only his professional connections in his rise, but also elements of Theoderic's *civilitas* ideology, to ally himself with the ("Gothic") army as well as the bureaucracy.

Var. 5.40; 5.41; 8.21; 8.22; AV 85; Boethius, *Consolatio* 1, prose 4.

N, J, [D]   Daila   523/526

He and Costula were said by Theoderic to "enjoy the liberty of our Goths;" see further Costula. *Var.* 5.30.

N, A, †, ?D   Danihel/Igila spodeus   551
————   *Spodeus* of the Gothic Arian church of St. Anastasia in Ravenna,
n, 1   possibly the Arian cathedral (Tjäder 2: 96). On "spodeus," see Amalatheus. There is no "qui et" for Danihel/Igila's pair of names: the identity rests on the signatures to the document following the announced list in order, which they do whenever the names are identical. The names vary when the subscribers sign in the Gothic language, but also occasionally, as in this case, when they sign in Latin: see the table at Tjäder 2: 95. *PItal* 34.83, 119.

This deed of sale, of swamplands belonging to St. Anastasia's, to the *defensor* Petrus, was witnessed and signed by many of the clergy of that church, and describes others who were present, including Amalatheus, Benenatus, Costila, Gudelivus 2, Guderit 1, Hosbut, Minnulus, Mirica, Optarit, Paulus, Petrus 2, Sindila, Suniefridus, Theudila, Vitalianus 2, Wiliarit 3, Wiliarit 4, and ●●●la. On the clergy and document, see Tjäder 2: 95–6, but beware his assumptions about the linguistic origin of names. See also the Gothic Arian presbyter Christodorus, father of Minnulus (both in *PItal* 33).

?D: The following discussion may apply to all Arian clerics from Ostrogothic Italy. The clergy of St. Anastasia, described as the *clerus universus* at 34.81, often calls its church "Gothic." Petrus signs as "aclisie gotice sancte Anastasie" at 34.98, Paulus 2 and Theudila as "eclesie legis Gothorum sanctae Anastasie" at 34.108, 122 respectively; none of the subscriptions in the Gothic language include any reference to Goths or a Gothic church; Christodorus is called "clericus legis Gothorum eclesiae Ravennatis" at 33.1; and note the similar description of Minnulus in the same document at 33.7–8, and his similar description of himself at 33.10. These ought to amount to clear-cut declarations of identity, but on the whole problem of the Arian church and its Gothic traits and pretensions, see ch. 7, above. Location of St. Anastasia: Lanzoni 2: 762 believed that the church of St. Anastasia became that of S. Teodoro, "presso la quale ammirasi il famoso *battistero degli ariani*"; Deichmann, *Ravenna*, is less certain that it can be located.

?N ??Danus famulus [regis] (= PLRE3) 533/
A sick young man in royal service, he was sent to Campania to 534/?
recover his health. Date: under Amalasuintha, Theodahad or 537
Witigis, probably one of the first two; Krautschick, *Cassiodor*,
pp. 96–7. *Var.* 11.10.
?N: Wrede, p. 133, classifies his name as a Latin version of
"Dane," hence Germanic. This remains open to question, but
the name is rare.

N, J, S, [D] Darida Gothorum comes (= PLRE3) *c.* 542
────── According to Gregory the Great, he was unable to cross the
l river Voltorno until he returned a stolen horse to the holy man
Libertinus. For similar use of "Goths" (almost always soldiers
serving under Totila), see **Riggo**, **Anonymus 18**, **Anonymus 19**.
Gregory the Great, *Dialogi* 1.2.

(N) Deutherius vir honestus 539
────── (N): son of **Thulgilo**, brother of **Domnica**. Witnessed his
n, j, c, l mother's sale of a property to a *vir strenuus* at Ravenna. He was
almost certainly a Catholic; see **Thulgilo**.
PItal 30.6, 22, 39–40, 73, 78, 85, 89, 94, 103–4.

?D ??Dionysius Exiguus 497–
────── The celebrated Catholic translator of Greek canon law lived at d 540
n, c, cc, l Rome from 497, and died in 540. He was a "Scythian" who
described himself as coming from a barbarian land, *ep.* "Novum
forsitan" (ACO 4.2: xi–xii), to the Scythian monks **Iohannes 3**
and **Leontius**. On the connotations of "Scythian" here, see ch.
4, above. There is little chance that any of these people were
viewed as Goths, but they are included to emphasize the difficulty of understanding this terminology.

(N) Domnica honesta femina 539
────── (N): daughter of **Thulgilo**, sister of **Deutherius** (q.v.); she wit-
n, j, c, l nessed her mother's sale of a property to a *vir strenuus* in Ravenna. She was almost certainly a Catholic; see **Thulgilo**.
PItal 30.5–6, 22, 39, 73, 77, 80, 85, 89, 94, 99, 103.

N Droctarius *c.* 525–
────── The dates indicate his lifespan. The inscription comes from 45
l Eporedia (Ivrea), in Liguria. F-S NF 43.

N, J Duda 1 saio (= PLRE2 Duda) 507/511
────── Ordered to ensure that some Campanian property of the pro-
l scribed *MVM* **Tufa** was rightfully put into the hands of the king
(*Var.* 4.32), told to supervise recovery of buried treasure (*Var.*
4.34), and placed in charge of returning property illegally seized
by the king's nephew **Theodahad** (*Var.* 4.39). Identified by
PLRE2: 381 with **Duda 2**, which seems plausible, on the basis
of **Adila**, but not proven.

N, J   DUDA 2 vir spectabilis, comes (= PLRE2 Duda)   507/511
———————   Ordered to try the case between **A**mara saio and Petrus *vir spect-*
1   *abilis*. Given the Germanic and Latin names of the litigators, and
          Amara's "Gothic job," this case could be seen as one between
          a "Roman" and a "Goth," a civilian and a soldier, implying
          that Duda was military *comes Gothorum* (*Var.* 7.3), probably *civit-*
          atis but possibly *provinciae*; cf. **A**dila and **C**olosseus. If the parallel
          with Adila is correct, then PLRE2: 381 may be right in ident-
          ifying Duda 1 with Duda 2, both having progressed from *saio*
          to (military) *comes*.
          Var. 4.28.

N, J   Dumerit saio (= PLRE2)   527
———————   Ordered by Athalaric to round up and punish "those of the
1   Goths and Romans who have plundered the *possessores* in Fav-
          entinum territorium;" he was given this mission alongside Flor-
          entianus *v.d.*, *comitianus* (= *comitiacus*). *Var.* 8.27.

N   Dumilda honestissima femina   *c.* 477–
———————   The dates indicate her lifespan. A Catholic: her epitaph was   531
(n), j, c, 1   placed in S. Paolo-fuori-le-mura, Rome. The mother of
          Theodosus, who was twelve at her death.
          F-S 223.

          Ebba = **I**bba dux.

N, J, S, **Ebremud** patricius (= PLRE3 Ebrimuth)   536
(D), [?D] Husband of Theodahad's daughter ★Theudenantha. He
———————   defected to Byzantium with troops from the Straits of Messina,
s   in early 536, after Belisarius had captured Sicily. Justinian
           rewarded him with the dignity of *patricius* and "many gifts of
           honour." Jordanes's context suggests that his desertion may have
           been connected to knowledge of the treachery of his father-in-
           law Theodahad, but this may have been the historian's hindsight
           at work. Procopius, BG 1.8.3 ("Ebrimous"); *Cont. Marc.* s.a. 536;
           Jordanes, *Rom.* 370, *Get.* 308–9 ("Evermud").
           (D): only because of his marriage to an Amal princess.
           [?D]: said to be leading Gothic forces by Procopius, BG 1.8.3;
           called "Theodahadi Gothorum regis gener" by Jordanes, *Rom.*
           370; similarly, *Get.* 308.

N, [?D] **Erdui** vir inlustris (= PLRE2 Erduic)   503
———————   Was he a Catholic? Mentioned with apparent approval in Enno-
?c, 1   dius's letter to the noblewoman Speciosa, "lux ecclesiae" and
           "ecclesiae decus." Unfortunately, Ennodius's prose is very dif-
           ficult to interpret here. He refers to Erdui as someone whom
           "you [Speciosa], an honor to the Church, have made me desire
           [to see]." PLRE2: 399–400 thinks that this means that Speciosa
           recommended Erdui highly to Ennodius. But the letter itself is
           an elaborately rhetorical apology to Speciosa: Ennodius has

come to Pavia bearing a message for Erdui from the bishop of
Milan; he hoped to see Speciosa before he delivered the message, but Erdui met him before he even reached the city, and
immediately offered his hospitality. So the line about desiring
to see Erdui could be a compliment to Speciosa: Ennodius
desired to see Erdui because this trip would enable him to see
Speciosa. If this interpretation is correct, it says nothing about
Erdui's religion one way or the other, and a bishop of Milan
might well have reason to communicate with an Arian if he
held a high secular office, as *vir inluster* implies. But note that
Ennodius's story does not quite ring true: why could he not
have gone to see Speciosa anyway, after seeing Erdui? It is of
course possible that the entire letter is an apology for not seeing
Speciosa *first*, but such extravagance is rare even in the annals
of late antique etiquette. Given this logic, it seems fair to infer
from the sentence about Speciosa and the message from the
bishop of Milan that Ennodius intended a typical rhetorical
device of the time: he wanted to see Erdui both because Speciosa had recommended him, and because journeying to Pavia
to see Erdui also enabled him to see Speciosa. Ennodius, *Op.*
36/*ep.* 2.3.

[?D]: PLRE2: 400 suggests that he was identical to **Herduic**. But
note that both names occur in Ennodius, and that PLRE2's spelling of "Erduic" is an emendation by Sirmond; Vogel's edition
of Ennodius, p. 36, apparatus. Two spellings by the same author
would not close out the possibility of the names referring to the
same person, since Latin spellings of Germanic names varied so
frequently. But Wrede, pp. 74–5, thinks the identification
unlikely, on philological grounds.

N

n, j, c, l

EUSEBIUS adiutor numerariorum scrinii canonum/*RICCIT-*   575–91
ANC vir clarissimus(= PLRE3 Eusebius 9 and PLRE 3 Riccitanc)
A Catholic: "manet ad" the church of St. Stefanus *maior* in Ravenna (see Tjäder 2: 279, n. 22). He witnessed the sale of a farm
near Rimini by Deusdedit *vir honestus* to **Hildigernus** *vir clarissimus* (*PItal* 36.35, 39, 63) between 575 and 591.
N: Tjäder 2: 278, n. 15, shows that Eusebius signed with an
unusual monogram, attached to an abbreviation for
"subscripsi," identical to that of Riccitanc *vir clarissimus*, son of
Montanus. Under this name, Riccitanc witnessed a charter at
Ravenna in 575: *PItal* 6.10–13. The handwriting is also
extremely similar (cf. Tjäder 3, plates 35, line 13, and 130, line
39). The placement of Eusebius's name in the witness list suggests that he was a *vir clarissimus*, as Riccitanc had been, although
in associating himself with the church, he does not state his
rank. This is convincing. Furthermore, Riccitanc's father had a
Latin name, so that his son might have received the two names
at birth or changed his name upon converting to Catholicism;

cf. Theoderic's mother *Ereleuva-Eusebia, or the nun Remila-Eugenia of the *Donatio Ansemundi*. PLRE3 does not notice Tjäder's argument.

Evermud = Ebremud patricius

Faffo = Rosemud

N
─────────
(n), c, l

Felithanc/Filithanc vir sublimis (= PLRE3)   553
A Catholic. Husband of Ranilo, he witnessed her donation to the church of Ravenna. Illiterate. Had he just converted? See Ranilo. *PItal* 13.52, 63, 66, 69, 73, 77, 80 (Ravenna).

Felix = Liberius

Felix = Valentinianus

N, ?J
─────────
c

!!Filimuth vir devotus (= B Filimuth 2)   591
Probably a retired soldier in Sicily, mentioned by Gregory the Great; GR 1.44. He had the same name as, but could not have been identical to, Filimuth, *strategos* of the Heruls in the Byzantine forces in Italy (= B Filimuth 1, PLRE3 Philemuth).

Filithanc = Felithanc

Flavius, Flavia *listed under second name*

N
─────────
(?n), c, l

<Fravi>ta (= PLRE2 . . .ta)   444 or
Husband of Mustila 1, named with her in inscription placed in   493
the crypt of St. Peter's, Rome, thus a Catholic. Unclear whether he or she was 48 years old, and unclear whether he was buried with her, or merely set up the inscription. The date: "Albinus v.c. con(s);" more probably 493 than 444. His name is emended by de Rossi, ICUR I: 402–3. See further ICUR n.s. 2, no. 4178, with the comments of Silvagni at 2: 33. (Note that the name is that of the Tervingi *MVM* Fravitta of 401. But it is also the emendation of de Rossi, so this similarity is not necessarily significant. Despite the fragility of de Rossi's emendation, a male name ending in "-ta" is almost certainly Germanic, and hence warrants inclusion here.)
ICUR I, no. 903 = ICUR n.s. 2, no. 4178.

N, (J), ?J,
(D)
─────────
(l)

Fredigernus (= PLRE3)   VI[1]
Father of *Teia and of *Aligernus. Note that his name is the same as that of the late fourth-century Tervingi chieftain Fritigern. Given the activities of his sons, he was probably, but not necessarily, a soldier. Agathias 1, praef. 31; 1.8.6; 1.20.1.

N, ?J
─────────
l

Fridibadus (= PLRE2)   507/511
Sent by Theoderic to "praeesse" over the provinces and *capillati* of Savia: his job seems to be that of provincial governor, bringing cattle-thieves and murderers to justice. PLRE2: 485 makes him *comes provinciae* from this description; Schmidt, "Die com-

ites Gothorum," p. 130, makes him a military *comes*. To the contrary, see Wolfram, *Goths*, p. 291 with n. 214: Savia already lay under the dual authority of the *comes* of Salona (a military *comes*) and a separate civil governor of Savia, and p. 320: Fridibadus was not sent in with the special title of *comes*, despite his authority over the *capillati*, whom Wolfram elsewhere equates with barbarians, or Goths, and the army (p. 302 with n. 274, citing this letter and *Var.* 3.24, *Get.* 72, ET 32, 34, 43, 145.3 and references). But note the discussion of *capillati* in appendix 4, above: another example of the typical attraction of an ethnographic group-name for a military unit. It seems most likely to me that Fridibadus was a military *comes civitatis* in the province, of which **O**suin held a larger military command: see further **O**suin and **S**everinus.

Var. 4.49.

N, J
—————
l

Frumarith saio (= PLRE2)
Ordered to ensure that a Venantius would pay money that he had promised as surety for a public debtor. *Var.* 2.13.

507/511

N
—————
(n), l

GATTILA comes (= PLRE2)
Named as father of **A**gata. His name on her epitaph in Milan probably, although not necessarily, implies that he set it up, and was therefore still alive in 512; assuming that he was at least about 20 at her birth in 472, his lifespan may extend back beyond about 452. Called "an Ostrogothic *comes*" by Kampers, "Anmerkungen," p. 147, on the basis of his name and the supposed Arianism of **A**gata (q.v.).
N: Wrede, p. 81, convincingly. Schönfeld, p. 103, thought that the name could have been either Germanic or Celtic.
F-S 223; reproduction at Rugo 5, p. 168, plate 33.

before *c.*
452–
after
512

N
—————
l

GEBERIC vir spectabilis (= PLRE2)
Ordered to restore illegally seized ecclesiastical property and to punish the offender. *Var.* 4.20.

507/511

N, J
—————
l

Gesila saio (= PLRE2)
Ordered to make the Goths of Picenum and Tuscia pay their "debitas functiones," i.e. taxes acquired with non-allotment land purchased by them (Goffart, *Barbarians and Romans*, p. 92), or simply to "undertake their public duties" (PLRE2: 510). *Var.* 4.20.

507/511

N
—————
j, l

Gevica inpulsor
The *inpulsor ordinatus*, apparently a substitute plaintiff, but possibly an *advocatus*, charged by a certain Marcellinus with conducting his case against Julianus, later *comes patrimonii*, a friend or relative (*adfinis*) of Ennodius (in Milan). The machinations of Marcellinus and Gevica were delaying the outcome. Ennodius asked Faustus Niger and Theoderic's relative ★**T**rasimundus

504

for assistance in speeding up the case. On Julianus, see PLRE2
Julianus 24. Ennodius, *Op.* 90/*ep.* 3.20.

N
——————
1

Ghiveric/Giberit vir devotus (= PLRE3 Giberit)   535/542
Son-in-law of Cessi; witnessed a document drawn up at Ravenna; on which see Riccifrida. He signs himself as "Ghiveric,"
and is listed as "Giberit." On the name, note also Geberic. *PItal*
43.26, 51.

N, J, S, [D]

Gibal archon (= PLRE3)   551
Procopius calls him one of "the most notable men of the
Goths" under Totila; cf. Gundulf and Scipuar, with whom he
was sent against Acona in Picenum. Later he was in command
of ships with Gundulf, who escaped, while Gibal himself was
captured. Procopius, BG 4.23.1, 12; 4.23.5–18.

Giberit = Ghiveric

N, J, S
——————
s

Gibimer archon (= PLRE3 Gibimer 1)   538
Witigis placed him in command of forces in the city of Chiusi
March 538. Around June, that garrison, and those of neighbouring cities, surrendered voluntarily to Belisarius, and were sent
to Naples and Sicily. Procopius mentions Gibimer in the same
sentence where he describes Witigis's other general Albilas as
"anēr Gothos;" it is unclear whether the omission of a similar
description for Gibimer is significant. Procopius, BG 2.11.1;
2.13.1–4.

N, J, [D]
——————
1

Gildila vir sublimis, comes Syracusanae civitatis (= PLRE2   526
Gildilas)
Ordered to repay taxes illegally exacted; and asked to reply to
accusations of abuse of power made by Sicilians. *Var.* 9.11; 9.14.
J: clearly a military *comes*; *Var.* 9.14.7–8 forbids him to judge
cases between two Romans without their consent (as is laid
down in the formula for that office, *Var.* 7.3.1); Schmidt, "Die
comites Gothorum," p. 129. Mommsen, OGS, NA14: 502, 503
with n. 4, combines the evidence of the formula and the second
letter to Gildila to show that the post was held by a Goth.
[D]: Athalaric advises him to show his integrity, since "Gothorum laus est civilitas custodita," implying that Gildila was himself a Goth.
Schmidt, "Die comites Gothorum," p. 129, assumed that Gildila
was a Goth anyway because of his Germanic name: "Gildila,
also ein Gote."

?N, J, S,
[D]

Goar (= PLRE3)   530s
Procopius calls him "Gothos anēr;" he was captured while   540s
fighting under Witigis in Dalmatia in 530s. He was taken to   551-2
Constantinople and later exiled to Antinoë in Egypt, under suspicion of treachery during the revival of the Gothic wars in the
540s. Later he was brought back to Constantinople, where he

played upon the sympathies of the Lombard hostage Ildigisal, and together they escaped, through Thrace and Illyricum, to the land of the Gepids. Procopius, BG 4.27.5–18.

?N: The name was borne by a king of the Alans in the fifth century, and is probably not Germanic: Schönfeld, p. 111.

N, [D]   Godidisclus (= PLRE2)   503
His family, like that of Bessas, were Goths who did not follow Theoderic from Thrace to Italy in the 480s. He went as a Byzantine officer to the Persian Wars with Bessas in 503. Procopius, BPI.8.3.

N, J, S   Gripas (= PLRE3)   535
Led the Gothic army with Asinarius in Dalmatia in 535. They   536/537
defeated and killed Mauricius, but were then repelled by his father Mundo. In 536/7, Gripas re-entered Dalmatia and took Split, but was defeated, fleeing back with his army to Ravenna from Constantianus, who thus "took possession of all Dalmatia and Liburnia, bringing over to his side all the Goths who were settled there" (trans. Dewing 3: 69) (= Anonymi 34+). Procopius, BG 1.7.1, 27–37; quotation at 1.7.36.

N   **Gudahals** vir inlustris (= B, PLRE3 Gunduhulus)   d by
Deceased husband of Gundihild, father of Landarit and Lenda-   557
rit. He was the object of the unspecified accusations of Adiud, Gunderit 1 and Rosemud. Mentioned in the document ensuring guardianship for Gundihild's children. PItal 7.4, 30, 43, and 57 (Rieti).

N   Gudelivus 1 (= PLRE2 Gudelivus)   508
─────   Ennodius sent him a note of congratulation on his success, prob-
j, 1   ably at Ravenna. He had apparently been appointed to some court office. See PLRE2: 521. Ennodius, Op. 295/ep 6.28.

N, A, †, ?D   Gudelivus 2 ostiarius   551
─────   Sexton at the Gothic Arian church of St. Anastasia in Ravenna.
1   Signed the deed of sale of lands to the *defensor* Petrus (see Danihel). Possibly illiterate (see Benenatus).
?D: see Danihel. PItal 34.84, 132.

                Gudelivus *see also* Gudilibus, ★Gudeliva

                Guderit *see also* Gunderit

N, A, †, ?D   Guderit 1 ostiarius   551
─────   Sexton at the Gothic Arian church of St. Anastasia in Ravenna.
1   On the deed of sale which he signed, see Danihel. Possibly illiterate (see Benenatus). Since Arian clergy could no longer hold church office after 554, he could be identical with Gunderit 1, 2 or 3, although probably not 1 due to difference in status, and not 3 if he was actually illiterate.
?D: see Danihel. PItal 34.84, 133.

N   Guderit 2 libertus   d by
——————————— The document confirming the inheritance of Stephanus, made 572
j   out by his guardian Gratianus, enumerates the goods of his
deceased freedman Guderit (*quondam libertus*), including various
furniture, cooking implements and "an old travelling jacket."
Burns's interpretation of this last, citing Tacitus, as a "short,
thick cloak worn by the Germans," (*History*, p. 134), is pure
fantasy. It is a *sagellum*, a perfectly normal late Latin word for a
cloak, the diminutive of *sagum* (Niermayer, *Lexicon*, p. 929 s.v.
sagellum; Lewis and Short, *Dictionary*, p. 1617, s.v. *sagum*). Guderit was not apparently identical with **Gunderit 2**, mentioned
later in the same document; B, p. 76, seems to confuse the two.
PItal 8.II.4, 11.

N   !!Guderit 3 (= B Guderit)   579
——————————— Catholic: donated mosaics to the cathedral of Grado, like **Amara**
c, 1   2 a year earlier. Recorded in an inscription: Rugo 2, no. 48–
9 = F-S 229. B, p. 76 (dating to "*c.* 580") makes him a "Goth,"
apparently on the basis of his Germanic name, one indeed borne
by people in Italy during the period of Ostrogothic rule (in
addition to the other **Guderits** above, see the **Gunderits** below).

Gudila *see also* **Gundila**

N, ?J   **Gudila** 1 vir sublimis, maior domus regiae/comes ordinis primi 502,
——————————— et curator rei publicae (= PLRE2 Gudila)   500s
?j, 1   He, **A**rigernus and **B**edeulfus served as mediators of the king
between the factions of the Laurentian schism.
?J: see **A**rigernus, and note the inscription below. *Acta synhodorum*, pp. 422, 425, 429. Mommsen, OGS, NA 14:514, identified
him with the Gudila *comes ordinis primi et curator rei publicae* who
is recorded on a Ravenna inscription as having restored a statue
on a marble base destroyed in an earthquake, in Faventia
(southwest of Ravenna), in the region of which he was the
highest administrative officer. F-S 182, with Fiebiger and
Schmidt's commentary, p. 94. Schmidt, "Die comites Gothorum," identifies Gudila and (without much evidence) all *comites
ordinis primi* as military *comites*. (Note PLRE2 Stephanus 21, who
seems to have followed the old imperial *cursus* from chief of the
agentes in rebus to *comes ordinis primi*.) In any case, the identification of Gudila *maior domus regis* with Gudila *comes*, followed
by PLRE2: 521, seems entirely plausible, given the former man's
close links with the king and the king's apparent trust in him,
and given that such restorations were highly Theoderican. The
inscription may have included a dedication to the king; PLRE2:
521. Mommsen, OGS, NA 14: 493, also identified him,
somewhat less plausibly, with **Gudila 3**, followed also by PLRE2:
521.

N, A, †, ?D   Gudila 2 episcopus   507/511
―――――――― Urged to investigate the decline in number of *curiales* in relation
1   to "your church" in Sarsenates. Becoming a member of the
clergy enabled *curiales* to escape their civic burdens of taxation;
it was occasionally against the law in the later Roman Empire.
Was this businesslike letter, envisaging a well-ensconced digni-
tary, addressed to a Catholic or to an Arian bishop? There are
no Germanic names among the clergy who attended the
Roman synods of 499 and 502, nor among any subsequent list
of Catholic bishops of the period. It seems entirely probable
that Gudila was an Arian bishop (similarly, see **Berevulfus** and
Butila).
?D: see **Danihel**. *Var.* 2.18.

N, ?J   Gudila 3 ?dux (= PLRE2 Gudila)   523/
―――――――― He and **Oppa** falsely asserted that the blind veteran **Anduit** was   524/526
1   their slave. Theoderic assigned **Neudis** the task of making the
two desist. Identified by Mommsen and PLRE2 with **Gudila** 1
(q.v.), which seems unlikely given the lack of any identifying
honorific attached to this Gudila, and by Tjäder with **Gundila**
(q.v.). Dux: suggested by the context of the letter; a military
position would mean a J. *Var.* 5.29.

N, ?J, ?S   Gudila 4 (= PLRE3 Gudila)   530s
―――――――― Son of **Tzalico** comes, brother of ●●●ri. He and his brother   540s
1   seized the property of **Gundila**. He might have come from   ?557
Nepi.
?J, ?S: see **Tzalico** and **Gundila** on the military position of his
father under Totila, which he may well have inherited.
PItal 49.26 (from 557).

Gudilas *see under* **Iohannes** 2

N, ?A, ?†,   Gudilibus diaconus or ?v.d.   538
G, ?D   Sold $\frac{4}{12}$ of the *fundus* Casa Caballaria to **Alamud**, as recorded in
―――――――― a document apparently drawn up at Faenza. He signs in the
1   Gothic language, with the abbreviation "dkn;" on Tjäder's
interpretation of the letters following his name as "vir devotus,"
see **Alamud**. Gudilibus translates the first part of the place-name
of the farm (*Casa*) into Gothic (*Hugsis*), on which see Tjäder,
"Note." All three witnesses to the deed had Latin names, one
a possible *vir devotus*, the other two illiterate. Tjäder emended
Gudilibus's name to Gudilib, taking the case-endings "-us" and
"-o" supplied by his seventeenth-century transcription as mis-
readings of the "v" in "v.d.," but there is no reason to doubt
case-endings; cf. **Gudelivus** 1 and 2; *★Gudeliva.
?D: see **Danihel**.
PDip 118 = *PItal* † 8.16, 46–7, 56, 59.

N, J   Gudinandus saio (= PLRE2)   526
―――――――― Ordered to hasten to get naval recruits to Ravenna (for the fleet
1   against Africa). *Var.* 5.19.

N, J	Gudisal saio (= PLRE2)	507/511
——	Ordered to make sure that none of the Goths or Romans in	
1	the city of Rome use the horses of the *cursus publicus* for private	
	purposes. *Var.* 4.47.	

N, J Guduin 1 saio (= PLRE2) 526
—— Told to summon the Goths of Picenum and Samnium to give
1 them their annual donatives (the traditional interpretation,
upheld by Stein, "Verwaltungsgeschichte," pp. 387–8, and followed by PLRE2: 521–2), or told to summon them to give them
their annual shares of tax-assessments (*millenae*) (Goffart, *Barbarians and Romans*, pp. 80–8). *Var.* 5.27.
Name: note PLRE3 Guduin 1 (commander in Thrace in 595 and
602) and Guduin 2 (*dux* at Naples in 603).
PLRE2: 522 suggests possible identification with Guduin 2.

N, J, [D] GUDUIN 2 vir spectabilis, dux (= PLRE2) 523/526
—— Told to observe justice and to remove the *onera servilia* that he
1 had imposed on Costula and Daila.
[D]: the implication that Goths should be tax-free is apparently
related by the letter to their service in the army; hence, the
label Goth should apply also to Guduin. PLRE2: 522 suggests
possible identification with Guduin 1 (then advancing from *saio*
to *dux*). *Var.* 5.30.
Name: see Guduin 1.

N Guiliarit *c.* 453–
—— He died in Capua in 533 at the age of eighty, leaving an inscrip- 533
1 tion, F-S 226.
The name was very common: note the various Wiliarits and
Wiliarics (similarly, F-S, p. 112).

N GUNDEBERGA qui et NONNICA spectabilis femina (= B, 526–70
—— PLRE3)
?n, c, ?cc, 1 The dates indicate her lifespan. Her epitaph was found on a
stone beneath two columns supporting the vault of the crypt of
the cathedral of Modena (Bormann in CIL 11: 169, at no. 941).
Fiebiger, NF, p. 30, states that "Nonnica" means "nun." See
ibid. on the use of "qui et" for a woman. B, p. 76, notes this
example in the tendency of people with Germanic names also
to adopt Latin or biblical ones. Perhaps this addditional name
came with Gundeberga's vocation. *Nonnaica* is eventually
attested to mean "of a nun" in Rudolf of Fulda: see *Novum
Glossarium*, vol. M–N, s.n. *Nonnica* (rather than *nonna*) is unique.
Nonetheless, although the Gallic Nonnichius (PLRE3 s.n.) may
look Germanic, it is probably also Latin (Heinzelmann, "Gallische Prosopographie" s.n. Nunechius; *Bischofsherrschaft*, p. 214
with n. 181.) People could, of course, hold two Germanic
names (cf. PLRE2 Gunthigis qui et Baza).
Since no Arian monasteries or monks or nuns are attested at all,
it seems likely that if she was a nun, she was a Catholic nun;

she might, however, have converted after Justinian's laws made such conversions attractive. See [Heper] on the oddness of a clergywoman keeping her rank designation.

The location of the epitaph suggests that she was a Catholic whether she was a nun or not.

B, p. 262, calls her a "Goth," presumably from the combination of her Germanic name and her year of birth.

F-S NF 45.

Gunderit *see also* Guderit

N	**Gunderit** 1 vir magnificus (= PLRE3 Gundirit)	557

One of the accusers of Gudahals, called both *vir magnificus* and *illustris vir*, but also, oddly, by the low-status designation *vir honestus*. *PItal* 7.44–5, 58, 67, 79 (Rieti).

N	Gunderit 2	before
———		564
1		

Gave $\frac{2}{12}$ of the farm of Savilianum, presumably near Ravenna, to the family of Stephanus, enumerated by Stephanus's guardian Gratianus in a document witnessed at Ravenna in 564. Apparently not the same as Guderit 2, mentioned in the previous paragraph. *PItal* 8.II.16.

N	Gunderit 3 exceptor curiae (= B Gunderit)	572
———		
j, 1		

Exceptor curiae at Ravenna, where he witnessed and wrote out the *gesta municipalia* document attesting the gift of half the farm of Bonus and Martyria to the church of Ravenna. *PItal* 14–15.1, 3, 7, 13.

N	**Gundihild**, inlustris femina (= B, PLRE3)	557
———		
1		

Widow of Gudahals, begged the *curia* of Rieti to provide guardianship for her two sons Landarit and Lendarit; they appointed a *vir honestus* named Flavianus, interpreted by B, p. 76, as the appointment of a Roman guardian over Gothic children. Oddly, like Gunderit 1, she is also once referred to as *honesta femina*. Also spelled Gundihil and Gundiildi in the document providing guardianship for the two boys. *PItal* 7.1–2, 4, 13–14, 16–20, 22, 25, 48, 65–6.

Gundila *see also* Gudila

N, ?J, ?S, A	Gundila	*c.* 540/
———		541 and
?s, c, (c), 1		544/

In Tjäder's interpretation, Gundila was an Arian who lost his property, probably as a result of Justinian's legislation during the Gothic Wars, in the 530s. He tried to get it back by turning Catholic, and was received into the Catholic communion by Vigilius. The pope and the bishop of the Goths (**Anonymus** 2) told him that he could take back his property; Gundila immediately made a gift of part of it to the church of St. Maria in Nepi, along with his wife and sons, **Anonyma** 5 and **Anonymi** 39+. (*c.* 540/541). But the brothers Gudila 4 and •••ri, the sons of Tzalico, seized the property, "saying that it was a *donativa.*" Gundila enlisted the support of Belisarius (544/545). Belisarius first put the property into ecclesiastical hands (the monasteries of St. Aelia and St. Stephanus), and then approached Vigilius, who ordered the monasteries to give it back to Gundila. In 557, an enquiry was ordered to find out exactly what had happened to the property of Gundila, now possibly dead. A record of this enquiry survives as a badly damaged papyrus, *PItal* 49. This interpretation: Tjäder 2: 195–6.

The circumstances are hardly clear, "eine merkwürdige Geschichte aus einer verworrenen Zeit" (Tjäder 2: 196). At least two questions arise out of Tjäder's interpretation: 1.) how could an Arian bishop have enabled the return of possessions confiscated by the Catholic imperial government, and 2.) how did the family of Tzalico come into possession of the property after Gundila had given part of it to St. Maria? The answer to the first may be that the Arian bishop simply certified that converted believers were no longer Arian. There are several possible answers to the second question. If the family of Tzalico was Catholic, it might have been awarded the confiscated possessions before Gundila converted, so that Gundila's gift to St. Maria was unrecognized (aided by lines 14–16, which seems to imply that someone had already occupied the property, probably Tzalico [". . . cone," with Tjäder 2: 300, n. 12]). Or perhaps the family of Tzalico seized the property illegally, aided by the confusion of the Gothic Wars going on at the time. But most likely, Tzalico's family received the property as members of the Gothic army, as the word *donativa* suggests (misleadingly translated by Tjäder as "Geschenk," 2: 199.24).

My interpretation, placing the events in the context of Etruria in the Gothic Wars, clears up the mystery of the whole process. Gundila, probably an Arian Gothic officer defeated in the first stages of the Gothic Wars, lost his property to the emperor. For whatever reason – perhaps an opportunity to serve under Belisarius – he was guaranteed his property back under condition of conversion to Catholicism. In the early 540s, however, Totila's armies swept through the region, and Totila reconfiscated the property, awarding it to Tzalico, a *comes*, and probably one of his officers, as a donative. After the final defeat of Totila, Gundila or his heirs claimed the property against the monasteries and possibly also against the sons of Tzalico (**Gudila 4** and ●●●ri), resulting a lengthy enquiry into the precise legal status of the property, an inquiry recorded in the papyrus that survives today.

Tjäder also suggests that Gundila was identical with **Gudila 3**, which would be highly unlikely, on the grounds of chronology, if Mommsen's identification of **Gudila 1** with **Gudila 3** was correct.

For further argument for my chronology and interpretation, see above, appendix 1, "The inquiry into Gundila's property: a translation and chronology."

Gunduhulus = Gudahals

N, J, S, [D] Gundulf/Indulf doryphoros, archon (= PLRE3 Indulf qui et   548–52
———————— Gundulf)
s, l, d   Originally a *doryphoros* of Belisarius, he was a man of "barbarian birth" who defected to Totila "for no good reason" (Procopius, BG 3.35.23) in 548. Totila sent him to Dalmatia, where he raided various towns.
[D]: Later (551), Totila sent him into Picenum with Gibal and Scipuar, and Procopius now calls him "one of the most notable men among the Goths," noting his former position with Belisarius (4.23.1). But he may not have been thought of as a Goth in his earlier incarnation, unless "barbarian birth" indicates such identification, since Procopius would surely have given this as a reason for his defection. In fact, earlier on (3.35.25), at the time of his desertion, Procopius says that he was able to mingle with the people of Mouicurum, "being a Roman and a member of Belisarius' suite" (trans. Dewing, 4: 465); PLRE3: 618 notes that "hate Rhōmaios" here refers to his recent support for the Roman (Byzantine) side. This characteristic confusion between allegiance and identity in Procopius is central to understanding Justinianic views of the Goths: see above, chs. 4 and 6, and cf., e.g., Herodianus, Ragnaris.
Gundulf was now in command of a fleet, and an *archon* – perhaps reason enough for his defection. At the end of the great naval battle, Gundulf, now called a *strategos*, escaped unobserved with eleven ships, landed, destroyed the ships, reported the disaster at Ancona, and fled onward to Osimo. After the battle of Mons Lactarius, he was among the thousand Goths who marched away from the negotiations with Narses and proceeded to Pavia and Transpadane Italy.
Name: Procopius notes that he was known as both Gundulf and Indulf, 4.23.2.
Procopius, BG 3.35.23–9; 4.23.1–3, 9–12, 38–40; 4.35.37.

N   Guntelda famula Christi (= PLRE3)   VI
———————— Mother of Basilius and grandmother of Guntio. Catholic: an
(n), c, l   original inscription from the church of S. Giuliano in Como, which, invoking the protection of St. Julianus, adjures "omnes Christiani" not to violate the tomb until the Day of Judgment. Date: the family lived in Italy for a long period within the sixth century (three generations), and therefore probably extends back to Ostrogothic domination; moreover, "Gun-/Gud-" names were very common in Ostrogothic Italy, and the inscrip-

tion, which is elaborate and names the patron saint, suggests
local patronage and power.
There is no reason to assume that Guntelda was a nun from
"famula Christi."
Rugo 5, no. 78.

N	Guntio (= PLRE3 Guntio 2)	VI

(n), c, l   The son of **B**asilius and the grandson of **G**untelda. Catholic.
On his religion and date, see **G**untelda. Inscription in Como:
Rugo 5, no. 78.

N	!!Gurdimer comes (= PLRE3)	559

?c, l   Probably a Catholic. Received a letter from Pope Pelagius I
instructing him to supervise some work in the fields. He was
apparently in or near Rome. PLRE3: 557 interprets this to mean
that "he was apparently a layman concerned with the management of papal lands," in which case it is difficult to understand
why he bore the title *comes*. PLRE3: 557 also makes him a *vir
clarissimus*. Pelagius I, JK 1034 = *ep.* "Ista prata" (Gassò and Batlle
76, p. 191).

?N	??Guttus acolyte	V^{ex}

?n, c, cc, l   Acolyte ("agolitus") of the church of Capua. A Catholic clergyman in minor orders.
?N: "Guttus" could mean "Gothus" or "Guta": Schönfeld, p.
120, and note all the names beginning with "Gud-" above, but
Diehl, ILCV 1253 adn. points out that it could represent
"Cottus" or "Cottius," given contemporary epigraphic
orthography. No Catholic clergymen of the period are attested
with Germanic names, but perhaps if his was Germanic, Guttus
would have changed it upon full ordination.
Rugo 4, no. 105 = ILCV 1253 = F-S 176.

(N)	!!Haelia	579

n, c, (cc), l   The daughter of **A**mara 2 (*lector*) and **A**ntonina, and sister of
Mellita. Mentioned in a mosaic in the cathedral of Grado. She
was thus a Catholic, and had the same name as Haelias, bishop
of Aquileia at the time and also mentioned in the mosaic. Rugo
2, no. 52.

N, [D]	Heldebaldus Gothorum phylosophus	496/

j, l   One of the geographers, with **A**thanarid and **M**arcomirus, at   497/507
Theoderic's court, whose work was used as a source by the
Ravenna Cosmographer; see **A**thanarid. Ravenna Cosmogra-
pher 4.42/301, etc.
Name: note the Ostrogothic king ★**H**ildebadus.

–	[Heper] comes vir inlustris [*sic*] diaconus	?VI

Called a "Goth" by de Rossi, ICUR 2: 312, n. 2, accepted as
such by F-S, p. 113. There is, however, no evidence for such
an identity; as de Rossi himself notes, the name is Hebrew.

(The office of *v.i. comes* need not be military either.) The inscription is also odd in listing the rank and (presumably) former secular office of a clergyman, and in placing office before rank designation.
F-S 227.

N, J, [D]   Herduic nobilissimus Gothus (= PLRE2)   504
Sent with **P**itzia comes to negotiate with the Gepid king Traseric at Sirmium. Ennodius's identification of him as a Goth may not be too important, since it occurs in a section of Ennodius's panegyric to Theoderic that emphasizes the special functions of the Goths as defenders of the *res publica*. On the other hand, these functions imply that Herduic was a military officer, hence J. PLRE2: 545–6 suggests that he was identical with **E**rdui, which is unlikely (q.v.). Ennodius, *Pan.* 62.

J, S, [D]   HERODIANUS archon (= PLRE3 Herodianus 1)   535–52
─────────   Byzantine commander of the infantry who eventually turned
s, l   traitor and joined the Goths. A native of Illyricum, **M**undo sent him to join the Byzantine forces in Africa in 535 (Procopius, BG 1.5.2–3). With Belisarius from the start of the Gothic Wars, he was left in charge of the Naples garrison after the siege of 535. Accompanied Belisarius to Constantinople after the fall of Witigis. He was sent back with a force of Thracian soldiers (3.6.10). In 542, Herodianus surrendered Spoleto to Totila, earning the king's praise, unlike the ungrateful senators of Rome: he had proved himself friend *and kinsman* of the Goths (Procopius, BG 3.21.15–16; Hodgkin, *Italy* 4 :499, is misleading on this speech). But Procopius elsewhere states that Herodianus deserted because he could no longer face the extortionate demands of Belisarius for money; SH 5.56. After Busta Gallorum, he was in command of Busta Gallorum with "Totila's brother" (4.34.19), actually ★**A**ligernus, the brother of ★**T**eia; cf. PLRE3: 595. On his possible *spectabilis* rank, PLRE3: 594.
Procopius, BG 1.5.3; 1.14.1; 2.16.21; 3.1.1; 3.6.10; 3.7.1–7; 3.12.16; 3.21.15–16; 3.23.3; 4.34.19; SH 5.56–8.

N   **Hildevara** inlustris femina (= B, PLRE2)   524
─────────   Catholic: made a donation to the Catholic church in Ravenna,
c, l   recorded by *PDip* 85 (now lost = *PItal*† 4; see Tjäder 1:53). B, pp. 76, 262, and PLRE2: 565 call her a "Goth," in the former presumably, in the latter definitely, on the basis of her Germanic name. For her alleged husband see [Iohannes].
PDip 85.

N   !!*HOLDIGERNUS* vir clarissimus (= B, PLRE3)   575/591
─────────   Purchased property near Rimini from Deusdedit *vir honestus*;
l   later mentioned in a document as a neighbor. Both documents drawn up at Ravenna. Called Hildigernus in the second document. *PItal* 36.8; 37.16.

(?N)   ??HONORATA clarissima et ?spectabilis femina (= PLRE3)   528–68
       The dates indicate her lifespan. She died and was buried in
n, c, 1   Albingaunum (Albenga) in the Cottian Alps in 568. She was
       the wife of **T**zitta 1 comes. On her rank and that of her hus-
       band, see PLRE3: 601–2. The inscription survived in an old
       monastery "detto della Doria": Rugo 5, p. 140. F-S 220.

N, A, †, ?D   Hosbut ostiarius   551
       Sexton at the Gothic Arian church of St. Anastasia in Ravenna,
1   Witnessed a document of sale with many other clergymen of
       that church (see **D**anihel). Possibly illiterate (see **B**enenatus).
       ?D: see **D**anihel. *PItal* 34.84, 134.

N, J, S, [D]   Hosdas archon (= PLRE3)   546
       "The most warlike of all the Goths," according to Procopius.
       He was burned to death in a siege tower by the road to Porto
       during Totila's first siege of Rome in 546. Procopius, BG
       3.19.20.

N, J, S,   Hunila dux Gothorum/Unilas archon (= PLRE3 Unilas)   537
[?D]   A commander of Witigis, sent with **P**issas (as Procopius
       recounts it) to take Perusia; his force was routed by Con-
       stantinus and suffered heavy losses. He was captured and sent
       to Rome. Jordanes's description of him as *dux Gothorum* may
       not count as a [D], since it need only refer to his military office.
       Jordanes, *Rom.* 374, *Get.* 311–12; Procopius, BG 1.16.5–7.

N, J   IBBA/Ebba vir sublimis, ?excomes, dux (= PLRE2)   508–13
       Commander under Theoderic. He defeated some Franks in 508
1   (Jordanes, *Get.* 302). In 511, Theoderic ordered him to maintain
       the rule of justice concerning the seizure of church property at
       Narbonne (*Var.* 4.17). He defeated Gesalicus, the bastard son of
       the Visigothic king Alaric II, twice at battles in 511 and 513
       (*Chron. Caesaraug.* s.a. 510; Isidore, *Historia Gothorum* 37–8, the
       last calling him "Ebba"). Jordanes refers to him as a *comes* (*Get.*
       302); other sources all call him *dux*. But it would have been
       unusual to progress from a *comitiva* to a *ducatus*; cf. Schmidt,
       "Die comites Gothorum," pp. 132–3. Also in the Gallic cam-
       paign were **B**etancus, **M**ammo, **T**uluin, perhaps Liberius.

       Igila = **D**anihel spodeus

       Indulf = **G**undulf doryphoros

–   [Iohannes]   524
       Said by Moorhead, *Theoderic*, p. 95, to be the husband of **H**ilde-
       vara, which if true, would make him an (N). But there is no
       indication that Iohannes, the first witness listed (and the only
       one surviving) in her donation, was the husband of Hildevara.
       Furthermore, he was only a *clarissimus*, whereas she was an
       illustris. *PDip* 85.21.

(N)   !!Iohannes 1   VI
————————   Son of **U**starric. His death at the age of three is recorded by an
n, (l)   inscription in Catania. F-S 234.

J, ([D])   **Iohannes** 2 *MVM* per Illyricum (= PLRE3 Ioannes 46)   537–?53
————————   The Byzantine general was nephew of the Thracian or Moesian
n, s, c, l, [d]   Flavius **V**italianus 1, whom some sources call a Goth. As with
                    his uncle, Iohannes's Balkan origins and associations were
                    remembered not only in his title, but in the record of his birth:
                    "provinciae Mysiae natus," ICUR 2.1, no. 14. His retinue of
                    doryphoroi in Italy included Thracians (as had his uncle's), one
                    whom, Gudilas, bore a name common among Italian Goths
                    (PLRE3 Godilas 2, but Procopius spells the name Goudilas; cf.
                    Gudila 1–4 and **G**undila, above). For another possible Thracian
                    with this same name, note PLRE3 Godilas 1, *MVM* ?per Thracias
                    in 528. Procopius notes elsewhere that Iohannes had barbarians
                    under his command: BG 3.18.29, but this may refer to docu-
                    mented Huns among his *doryphoroi* (PLRE3: 661).
                    Certainly a Catholic, like his uncle (see **A**nonymi 14+). Mata-
                    suentha offered herself in marriage to him after Witigis forcibly
                    took her as his wife (Procopius, BG 2.10.11). For details of
                    Iohannes's well-documented career during the Gothic Wars, see
                    PLRE3: 652–61.

[?D]   ??Iohannes 3 monachus Scytha   519–20
————————   One of the "Scythian monks" who advocated the Theopaschite
n, c, cc, l   formula; he and **L**eontius went to Rome in 520, when **D**iony-
                    ius Exiguus translated Cyril of Alexandria's letters to Successus
                    for them. Iohannes was therefore a Latin speaker.
                    [?D] **D**ionysius (q.v.) adverts to their common place of origin,
                    the Roman province of Scythia, as a "barbarian country;" on
                    the connotations of "Scythian," see above, ch. 4. He was also
                    a client of **V**italianus 1: Dioscorus, *ep.* "Verum est" (Avellana
                    216 = Thiel 75, pp. 868–71): "monachos de Scythia, qui de
                    domo magistri militum Vitaliani sunt" (§2, p. 869). Iohannes is
                    otherwise attested in Justinian, *ep.* "Propitia divinitate" (*Avellana*
                    187 = Thiel 78, pp. 875–7), and the works of the Scythian
                    monks, ed. F. Glorie, CCSL 85A; note especially his own work,
                    Responsio ad Hormisdam. He was not identical to the leader of
                    the Scythian monks, Iohannes Maxentius, an abbot, who did
                    not come to Rome: Glorie, pp. xl–xli, contra Schwartz. Glorie,
                    p. xli, makes Iohannes, like **L**eontius, a relative of **V**italianus 1,
                    presumably on the basis of Dioscorus's statement (above) that
                    they were both from his "household," but Dioscorus explicitly
                    says that **L**eontius was a relative. Further on the Scythian
                    monks, see **L**eontius.

                    Iulius = **V**alentinianus

N

1

LANDARIT clarissimus puer (= B, PLRE3)   557
Son of Gudahals and Gundihild, brother of Lendarit. The
guardian Flavianus *vir honestus* was appointed over him and his
brother by the *curia* of Rieti; see further Gundihild. *PItal* 7.66.

?G (if so:

?A, ?†, ?D)

n, j, c, 1

??Latinus vir honestus, possessor   539
A member of a college of *possessores* (with Tjäder 2: 260–1, n.
33), he witnessed the sale of Thulgilo. A Catholic? (see
Thulgilo).
?G: Tjäder 2: 260, n. 31, takes the one visible "c" before his
signature, and another now eradicated "c" attested in an earlier
edition, as evidence that he signed "[I]cc, Latinus . . ."; i.e.,
Gothic for "Ego, Latinus." Tjäder concludes that Latinus "ist
also ein Gote, der seinen ursprünglichen gotischen Namen
abgeworfen hat." B, p. 76, and Moorhead, *Theoderic*, p. 86 with
n. 88, follow Tjäder. But aside from the problem of the various
assumptions about what makes a Goth contained in Tjäder's
statement, it is not even certain that Tjäder interprets the missing letters correctly. Tjäder adduces as corroborative evidence
the signatures of the Gothic clergy of St. Anastasia's in P.34, 88,
94, 126, 136. But they all sign with "Ik," not "Icc." Furthermore, their entire subscriptions are in Gothic, whereas Latinus
continues the rest of his subscription in Latin. We are to believe
that one letter (and one lost letter) proves that the man knew
the Gothic language. Finally, Tjäder reveals his prejudices, infer-
ring that Latinus was a Goth because of his "bad spelling and
uneven and uncertain handwriting," traits possibly due to age,
bad education or his low rank of *possessor*, and traits *not* visible
in the signatures of the Gothic clergy of St. Anastasia's. This
would be, moreover, the only known example of a layman
writing in Gothic (although cf. Tjäder's conclusions on Alamud,
and perhaps those on Anonymus 1). The conclusions of the
leading scholar of late antique Italian papyri deserve consider-
ation, of course, but it seems here that Tjäder may well have
taken his conjectures too far.
Note that there is a Latin inscription from Mauretania beginning
with *Ic* for *Ego*; *Année épigraphique* 1966, no. 587.
?A, ?†: It is just possible, if Tjäder is right in his argument about
their knowledge of the Gothic language, that both Latinus and
the scribe of this contract, Anonymus 1, were Arian clergymen
who converted to Catholicism as it became apparent that Ravenna would fall to Justinian's forces; see further Anonymus 1.
PItal 30.102, 111; reproduction at Tjäder 3, plate 105, line 102,
far left.

N

1

LENDARIT clarissimus puer (= B, PLRE3)   557
Son of Gudahals and Gundihild, brother of Landarit. See further
Landarit, Gundihild. *PItal* 7.66.

N, J   Leodefridus saio (= PLRE2)   507/511
——————— Theoderic sent him to the Goths and Romans around the fort
l   of Verruca, near Trent, to supervise the construction of houses
for them to live in.
Var. 3. 48.

[?D], ([D])   Leontius monachus Scytha (= PLRE2 Leontius 26)   519–20
——————— One of the "Scythian monks" who advocated the Theopaschite
n, c, cc, l formula; he and Iohannes 3 went to Rome in 520, when
Dionysius Exiguus translated Cyril of Alexandria's letters to
Successus for them. Leontius was therefore a Latin speaker.
[?D]: Dionysius (q.v.) refers to their common place of origin,
the Roman province of Scythia, as a "barbarian country;" on
the connotations of "Scythian," see above, ch. 4.
([D]): Leontius was a relative of Vitalianus 1: Dioscorus, *ep.*
"Verum est" (Avellana 216 = Thiel 75, pp. 868–71): he "calls
himself a relative of the general;" cf. "monachos de Scythia, qui
de domo magistri militum Vitaliani sunt" (§2, p. 869). Leontius
is otherwise attested in Justinian, *ep.* "Propitia divinitate"
(*Avellana* 187 = Thiel 78, pp. 875–7), listing the other monks
as Iohannes 3, Achilles and Mauritius (the latter two not
included here because they are not attested as making the journey to Italy: but what people thought about the identities of
Leontius and Iohannes 3 probably applies to them too, as well
as to the abbot Iohannes Maxentius). See further the works of
the Scythian monks, ed. F. Glorie, CCSL 85A (Turnhout, 1978).
The confusion about people who come from the Balkans seems
to continue over the identity of the Scythian monks (cf. Bessas,
Mundo, Vitalianus 1), leading some modern scholars to call
them "Goths," e.g. Berthold Altaner, "Zum Schrifttum der
'skythischen' (gotischen) Mönche," pp. 489–506, an under-
standable assumption under the circumstances. Leontius was not
identical to the theologian Leontius of Byzantium; see Altaner,
"Der griechische Theologe Leontius," pp. 375–91, contra
Loofs, *Leontius von Byzanz*, pp. 223–317.

N, J, S   Leuderis archon (= PLRE3)   536–7
——————— Witigis set him in command of the garrison at Rome; he was
s   an elderly man of great discretion. After the fall of the city, he
remained behind, and Belisarius sent him to the emperor with
the keys to the city of Rome. Procopius, BG 1.11.26; 1.14.13,
15; 1.24.1. Name: cf. PLRE3 Leutharis (A.D. 553–4, called an
Alaman).

J   **Petrus Marcellinus Felix Liberius** vir inlustris et magnificus, *c.* 465–
——————— PPO Italiae, PPO Galliarum, patricius praesentalis (= PLRE2 after
n, j, c, l, [d] Liberius 3)   554
Like Senarius, he was related to Ennodius; like him and like
Cyprianus, he was came of minor aristocratic stock (distantly

related to Avienus, the consul of 502) and climbed to fame
through bureaucratic and military service; like **C**yprianus and
Opilio, he was assumed to have been a Roman.

He was a Catholic (see under **O**pilio). For his extraordinarily
long career, see PLRE2: 679–81.

J: As *PPO* Galliarum he was concerned with military matters
(*Var.* 11.1, esp. §16: *exercitualis vir . . . forma conspicuus, sed vulner-
ibus pulchior*, PLRE2: 679), so he may have been involved with
the conquest itself in 508 (cf. also **B**etancus, **M**ammo, **T**uluin);
he continued to have a military career under the Goths and
under Justinian, implying that he had early military experience
under Odoacer before he was appointed *PPO* (Italiae) by
Theoderic in 493. In 533, he received the military title *patricius
praesentalis*, doubtless commander-in-chief of the Gothic army,
and probably military viceroy with the minor *****A**thalaricus and
the female *****A**malasuintha; he continued to hold this title under
Athalaric's unmilitary successor *****T**heodahadus. On the meaning
of *patricius praesentalis*, see **T**uluin and Ensslin, "Patricius," esp.
pp. 248–9, with Wolfram, *Intitulatio* 1: 43–56. On the activities
of the military between 526 and 535, see **T**uluin, **A**nonymi 11,
12, 13, and *****A**malasuintha.

(Procopius's claim, that Liberius was "inexperienced in matters
of war," BG 3.39.7, does not explain why Justinian appointed
him to lead armies four times, let alone the evidence of his titles
and of his description in the *Variae*.)

Loyalties: although he remained loyal to Odoacer to the end,
he abandoned *****T**heodahadus on his embassy to Constantinople
for the king in 534 (unlike his fellow envoy **O**pilio), and hence-
forward served Justinian.

Family: his wife was PLRE2 Agretia, his son PLRE2 Venantius 2,
who received the title from *comes domesticorum vacans* Theoderic
as a means of conferring the illustrate upon him; it tells us
nothing of his son's choice of career (it need not have been
military).

Further see PLRE2: 677–81.

Livania = **S**implex

N
───
1

LIWIRIT vir spectabilis, comes (= PLRE2)   523/526

Received two letters from Theoderic jointly with Ampelius, *v.i.*
One contains instructions to look into allegations that people
were illegally selling Spanish corn earmarked for Africa (*Var.*
5.35). The second sends them to Spain to look into various
charges of corruption and administrative abuse, and to restore
order there (*Var.* 5.39). PLRE2: 686 states, "He was evidently a
Goth," without giving a reason, so presumably from the name.
Although Liwirit and Ampelius were to ensure that Goths in
cities were not unjustly loaded with servile burdens (5.39.15),
this need not mean that either one necessarily held a military

office. Krautschick, *Cassiodor*, p. 77, dates 5.39 to 526, without, however, giving his customary reference to an argument in the body of his text. Since 5.35 probably comes after it (since Liwirit and Ampelius are already in Spain), but before September 526 (both letters were written in the name of Theoderic), I revert to the general dating for letters in Book 5 of the *Variae*. *Var.* 5.35; 5.39.

| N, J, [?D] | MAMMO dux Gothorum (= PLRE2) | 509 |

A commander in Theoderic's reconquest of southern Gaul (cf. **Betancus**, **Ibba**, **Tuluin**, perhaps **Liberius**): "Mammo dux Gothorum partem Galliae depraedavit," Mar. Avent. s.a. 509. [?D]: as **Hunila**.

| N ———— c, l | Manifrit | VI^med |

Died at the age of 52, buried in Milan. His epitaph is in the church of S. Vincenzo di Galliano; he was a Catholic. The inscription is large and complex, with a huge cross down the center, an animal with another cross, and a palm tree. Rugo 5, no. 21 (5: 36 on date, attributing it to the era of the "regno goto").

| N ———— c, l | Manna vir devotus (= B, PLRE3) | 575 |

The son of the deceased **Nanderit**. Catholic: his will gave his entire property to the church of Ravenna. B, p. 75, asserts that he was a Goth who used both Romans and Goths as witnesses, all apparently based on the linguistic origin of names. The witnesses were Ioannes, Emilianus, Eusebius (signing with the Germanic name Riccitanc: see **Eusebius**), Theodosius, Andreas, Quiriacus and Petrus. The phrase *cives Romani* employed at line 3 is part of the formula for the manumission of slaves; see Tjäder 1: 420, n. 1. *PItal* 6.3, 8, 10, 14, 18.

| N, J ———— l | Mannila saio (= PLRE2) | 523/526 |

Ordered by Theoderic to impose penalties for misuse of the *cursus publicus*. See, similarly, **Gudisal** *saio*. *Var.* 5.5.

| N, ?J ———— l | **Marabadus** vir inlustris, comes (= PLRE2) | 510–11 |

Noted for his fairness. Theoderic sent him to Marseilles in 510 (*Var.* 3.34). In 511, he was told to decide, with Gemellus *vir spectabilis*, the lawsuit involving Liberius and Aetheria (*Var.* 4.12). Subsequently, the king told him to look into the matter further, since Liberius was claiming that the sentence passed on Aetheria was unfair (*Var.* 4.46).

?J: PLRE2: 706 conjectures that he was *comes Massiliae*, and Schmidt, "Die comites Gothorum," p. 130 with n. 8, sees him as one of a pair of military and civil counts placed over each of the cities of Provence, hence a military *comes*. Marabadus's judicial associate in the lawsuit, Gemellus, did indeed hold a civil office, the *vicarius praefectorum Galliarum* (PLRE2 Gemellus 2). Note further the reference to *incivilitas* in *Var.* 4.12.3, in a

letter filled with elements of Theoderic's *civilitas* rhetoric (esp.
4.12.1): this was a quality that the *comites Gothorum* were speci-
ally instituted to prevent (formula of office in *Var.* 7.3.2, on
hearing cases between Goths and Romans). Of course, *incivilitas*
in the letter to Marabadus could merely mean breaking the law,
but given the various other indicators, it seems to me to imply
that Marabadus was acting in the capacity of military *comes*, who
could hear a case between two Romans if they consented (*Var.*
9.14.7, with the comments of Schmidt, p. 129) – and note that
either or both Liberius and Aetheria could have been seen as
"Goths," despite their Latin names.
Var. 3.34; 4.12.

Marcellinus = Liberius

–	[Marcianus] (= PLRE3 Marcianus 4) A notable of Venetia, he betrayed the city of Verona to the Byzantines in 541/542 (under Totila). Wolfram, *Goths*, p. 516, n. 397, suggests that he and [Censorius] held some sort of mili- tary post, but the narrative of Procopius demonstrates, if any- thing, the opposite. A parallel to Marcianus is the civilian mag- nate Tullianus of the Brutii and Lucani (BG 3.18.20–3; 3.22.1–6). Procopius, BG 3.3.6–8.	541/542

J, S
─────
n

Marcias (= PLRE3)   536–7
Commanded a Gothic garrison in Gaul with some of the "noblest of the Gothic people," established there by Theodahad
during his abortive treaty with the Franks in 536. Summoned
back by Witigis to take part in the siege of Rome; since he
failed to arrive quickly enough, Witigis was forced to remain
temporarily at Ravenna. Eventually Marcias ended up commanding the Gothic forces at the Plain of Nero at Rome. Procopius, BG 1.13.15, 29; 1.16.7, 1.19.12; 1.29.2.
His name is Greek: *Griechische Eigennamen*, p. 863, citing this
example with others; *Greek Personal Names* 1: 298 (Cretan and
Cypriot examples, including one Jew). Schönfeld, p. 161, and
Wrede, p. 100, argue unconvincingly for a Hellenized Germanic name (cf. **A**sinarius). Note, however, the eighth-century
Frankish names "Marchio," etc., at Förstemann 1: 1095.

N, [D]
─────
j, l

Marcomirus Gothorum phylosophus   496/
One of the geographers at Theoderic's court used as a source 497/507
by the Ravenna Cosmographer, along with **A**thanarid and
Heldebaldus. For more details, see **A**thanarid. Ravenna Cosmographer 4.42/301, etc.

(N), J,
([D])
─────
n, s, [d]

Mauricius strategos (= PLRE3 Mauricius 1)   529–36
Byzantine general, son of **M**undo, father of **T**heudimundus and
Anonyma 2 (who married the Herul **A**ruth). Went with
Mundo to Constantinople to receive gifts from Justinian in 529.
In 532, took part in quelling the Nika riot, with **M**undo and

Belisarius. Died in Dalmatia in 536 repelling the assault of the Goths led by **Asinarius**, **Gripas** and **Uligasalus**; see **Gripas** and **Mundo**. PLRE3: 854 conjectures that he was an *MVM vacans*. For further details of his life and dates, see PLRE3: 854.
([D]): through his father **Mundo**.
Theoph., AA.MM. 6024, 6032; Joh. Malal. 450–1; Chron. Pasch. s.a. 532; Georgius Cedrenus, *Comp. Hist.* 1: 652; Procopius, BG 1.7.2–3, 12; 3.1.36, 4.26.13.

(?N)	??Maximinus	559

The husband of **Tucza** (q.v.), at Rieti. Pelagius I, JK 1021 = *ep.* "Tucza [a] filio veniens" (Gassò and Batlle 63, pp. 164–6).

Fl. Maximus *see under* ★Anonyma 3 (in royal prosopography)

N	Maza	507/511

Owned or laid claim to a farm (*fundus Mazenis*); appealed a judgment of **Anna** comes. *Var.* 1.5.

N, J, S, [?D]	Meligedius (= PLRE3)	552

Byzantine soldier; deserted to the Goths, later he planned to hand the city of Perugia over to Narses. In the ensuing fight between his men and those of his fellow commander **Ulifus**, the latter was killed, and the city was surrendered to the Romans. Procopius, BG 4.33.10–12.
[?D]: Procopius implies that certain other deserters, such as **Herodianus**, became Goths. Note that **Ulifus** had incentive of "promises" (bribes?) from Totila – but Procopius does not attribute such a motive to Meligedius, for what that is worth. **Ulifus**, too, served under Totila for eight years, and was loyal to him to the end.

(N)	!!Mellita	579

Daughter of **Amara** 2 (*lector*) and **Antonina**, sister of **Haelia**. A Catholic. Mosaic in the cathedral of Grado: Rugo 2, no. 52.

N	**Meribaudus** ?vir inlustris (= PLRE2)	511

Almost certainly a Catholic. He received a letter from Ennodius commending the Milanese student Ambrosius to him at Rome. Telling Meribaudus that he has the esteem of the best Ligurians, Ennodius requests his patronage and protection for the young man. Meribaudus was evidently highly eminent: the accompanying letters of recommendation were addressed to the exconsuls Faustus Niger and Petronius Probinus (who had previously been on opposite sides of the Laurentian schism). Such company raises the possibility that Meribaudus belonged to the family of the fifth-century senator and panegyricist of Aetius, Flavius Merobaudes (see also PLRE2: 756–7).
N: The name, although Germanic, is associated with "Franks" rather than "Goths" (the fourth-century Merobaudes was called

a Frank; note also the Salian ruler Merovech); Schönfeld, pp. 167, 284.

j: Given the other recipients of requests for letters of recommendation, it is likely that Meribaudus was a senator, thus *inlustris* (rather than *clarissimus*, as PLRE2: 756 has it).
Ennodius, *Op.* 425/*ep.* 9.3.

Merila = Mirica

N, A, †, ?D	Minnulus/Willienant spodeus, vir reverendus, clericus/lector	541
————	legis Gothorum ecclesiae	551
n, l	He was the son of Christodorus (also an Arian clergyman). In 541, Minnulus sold $\frac{2}{12}$ of the farm of *Domitianus* to the silk merchant Isacius (described as *vir reverendus clericus* and *lector*). In 551, he witnessed the sale of lands belonging to the Gothic Arian church of St. Anastasia in Ravenna (described as *spodeus*). On the second document and on *spodeus*, see **D**anihel. On the identification of the two Minnuli, see Tjäder 2: 83. On the identification of the Minnulus announced in the text and the Willienant who signs, Tjäder 2: 95. Like Danihel, Minnulus has both a Latin and Germanic name, and subscribes in Latin. ?D: see **D**anihel. *PItal* 33.1, 3, 6–8, 10 (A.D. 541); *PItal* 34.83, 116 (A.D. 551).	

N, A, †,	Mirica spodeus/Merila bokareis	551
G, ?D	*Spodeus* or *bokareis* at the Gothic Arian church of St. Anastasia	
————	in Ravenna; witnessed the document of sale of lands belonging	
l	to the church, with the rest of the clergy (on this document, and on *spodeus/bokareis*, see **D**anihel). Mirica is announced in Latin, and subscribes in Gothic; the different spellings do not seem to be significant. On the Gothic subscription, a formula also used by **O**ptarit, **S**uniefridus and **W**iliarit 4, see **O**ptarit. ?D: see **D**anihel. *PItal* 34.84, 126.	

(N)	*MONTANUS* vir clarissimus, notarius sacri vestearii (= PLRE3	540
————	Montanus)	d by
n, j, ?c, l	Probably a Catholic (see **E**usebius). Deceased father of Eusebius/Riccitanc *vir clarissimus*, mentioned when the son (signing as Riccitanc)˙witnessed the will of **M**anna. It seems probable that this Montanus was identical with the Montanus *vir clarissimus* who in 540 purchased property near Faventia from Domnicus vir honestus (*PItal* 43.I.12, II.6, III.4–6), and who was *notarius sacri vestearii*, evidently under Witigis. The dates fit, the ranks fit, the professions are similar, and both father and son were employed at Ravenna. Moreover, Tjäder 2: 262, n. 16, uses the identification ingeniously to explain a discrepancy in the description of Riccitanc's rank. The identification is not noticed by PLRE3: 895, which only discusses the Montanus of the 540s. *PItal* 6.39.	575

?N, J, S   Moras 1 (= PLRE3 Moras)   538–9
────────   Set over the garrison of Urbino by Witigis in 538 directly after
s   the failure of the siege of Rome. He had 2,000 men with him,
           "barbarians" (Procopius, BG 2.19.10). After Narses withdrew
           from the walls of Urbino, Belisarius treated with the garrison:
           they surrendered, and became free Roman subjects, retaining
           their profession of soldier, in the Byzantine army (2.19.17).
           ?N: Schönfeld, p. 169, argues that the name is Germanic, a Hel-
           lenized spelling of a Gothic *Maura. But this man and Moras
           2 are his only examples, from before the fourteenth century.
           On the other hand, it is not an attested Greek or Latin name,
           so Schönfeld's argument may stand. Wrede, pp. 104–5, sees it
           as a Gothicized version of the Latin name Maurus: it may just
           as well be a Hellenized version of that name (common at this
           date).
           Procopius, BG 2.11.2; 2.19.10.

?N, J, S   Moras 2 (= PLRE3 Moras)   552
           Commanded the Goths at Acherontia in the months before the
           battle of Busta Gallorum; along with **R**agnaris, he negotiated
           terms of surrender with Pacurius. **R**agnaris's negotiations did
           not work out. Moras is not mentioned again, but seems also to
           have withdrawn from negotiations, since Acherontia remained
           in Gothic hands (Procopius, BG 4.34.15, with PLRE3: 895). Prob-
           ably not identical with **M**oras 1, as PLRE3: 895 points out (still,
           however, putting the two men under the same entry).
           ?N: see **M**oras 1.
           Procopius, BG 4.26.4.

N, ?J   !!Mundilo senator scolae gentilium (= PLRE2)   V–VI
────────   Officer of the imperial or royal guard; he died in Florence at
1   the age of forty in the fifth or sixth century. He could thus have
           served under either Odoacer or Theoderic, or possibly under
           one of the last Western emperors. CIL 11.1708 = ILCV 562; see
           also **P**aulus 1 and **S**egetius.
           ?J: "Senator" was a late Roman military office; the *scola gentilium*
           had originally been recruited from among barbarians outside the
           Empire; after the time of Zeno, from within the Empire (*Der
           kleine Pauly*, s.v. schola). Procopius, SH 24.15–23; 26.8, and Aga-
           thias 5.15.1–6 say that they had declined into mere ceremonial
           units (but see Whitby and Whitby, *Chronicon Paschale*, p. 117,
           n. 351). This seems to have been true in the West as well, to
           judge from *Var.* 2.16.2, and Procopius SH 26.27–8 (at the
           imperial palaces of Rome; he does not talk about Ravenna),
           but as Barnish, *Cassiodorus: Variae*, p. 98, n. 4, points out, *Var.*
           1.10.1 and perhaps 6.6.1 imply that they still performed their
           function of defending the king (assuming that the *domestici* of the
           former shared the fate of the *scholares* of the latter). Moorhead,
           Theoderic, p. 254, however, accepts that they were now merely

an ornamental guard, their function usurped by the "Gothic army." The distinction is crucial: if the *scholares* continued to be soldiers, then they were Goths by Theoderic's definition. The unit still existed (or had been revived?) in seventh-century Ravenna: B. Anon. 29. Mundilo's Germanic name, and his service in a unit with traditional barbarian associations, is suggestive whether the unit was active or ceremonial.

Note that *Var.* 9.13. implies that *comites provinciae* had a retinue of *domestici*; for a military *comes provinciae*, see **O**suin.

Named regiments are unattested under the Ostrogoths: this need not have been true of the palace guardsmen.

N, J, [D]   **Mundo**/Mundus, leader of the Gepids, *MVM* per Illyricum   480s–
————————   (= PLRE2 Mundo, PLRE3 Mundus)   536
s   The dates indicate his lifespan. He had an extraordinary career of changing allegiances and identities in the Balkans, similar to that of **Vitalianus** 1. Son of a Gepid king, probably Giesmos, his uncle Trapstila claimed the throne of their kingdom near Sirmium in the 480s because Mundo was too young. On their way to Italy in 488, the Ostrogoths defeated the Gepids and killed Trapstila. His son Traseric, rather than Mundo, became the new king (Ennodius, *Pan.* 7.28–34; Paul Diac., *Rom.* 15.15; Jordanes, *Get.* 300). When Mundo came of age, around 500, he fled the Gepids and his cousin Traseric, establishing himself as the head of a group of "bandits" in Pannonia. His depredations caused the Byzantine government to send an army under the *MVM* per Illyricum Sabinianus, in 505 (Jordanes, *Get.* 300–1, Marc. com. s.a. 505). At this point, Theoderic's general **Pi**tzia advanced toward Sirmium, where Mundo joined his forces in order to defend himself against the Byzantines, who were defeated at Horreum Margi on the Morava (*Pan.* 12.60; Jordanes, *Rom.* 356 [not 387 as PLRE2: 768 says], *Get.* 300; Marc. com. s.a. 505). Mundo thus entered Ostrogothic service, but he now temporarily disappears from the sources, his realm subsumed in the Ostrogothic kingdom. In the 520s he reappears as a commander of Gepids and Heruls in Pannonia, and by 529 had gone over to the Byzantines, accepting the office of *MVM* per Illyricum (Joh. Malal. 451, Theoph. A.M. 6032, Georgius Cedrenus, *Comp. Hist.* 1: 652), winning battles against Slavs and Bulgars (see PLRE3: 903–4). In 531 he progressed to *MVM* per Orientem (Joh. Malal. 466), and shortly thereafter reassumed the office of *MVM* per Illyricum (Procopius, BP 1.24.41). In 532, he helped to quell the Nika riots at Constantinople, taking part in the massacre at the Hippodrome (Joh. Malal. 476; Chron. Pasch. s.a. 532, Theoph. A.M. 6024; Georgius Cedrenus, *Comp. Hist.*, 1: 647; Procopius, BP 1.24.41; Zach., HE 9.14). In 535, he went to Dalmatia at the outset of the Gothic Wars, where he took Split (Procopius, BG 1.5.2, 11). In repelling

the Gothic counterattack led by Asinarius, Gripas and Uligisalus in 536, his son Mauricius was killed. In grief and rage, Mundo defeated the Gothic forces, but lost his life himself in pursuing them (BG 1.7.1–5; *Rom.* 387). Procopius, who probably knew him, describes him as particularly loyal to Justinian (BG 1.5.2), who was, of course, his Illyrian compatriot.

PLRE2: 767–8 and 3: 903–5, doubts the identity of the two Mundos, based primarily on Jordanes's apparent statement that the first Mundo was of Hunnic descent. But leaving aside the problem of PLRE2's assumption that a person could only have a fixed, single identity, the certain continuity and consistency of events in Mundo's career shows that the bandit of the 500s was identical to the son of the Gepid king who served Byzantium in the 520s and 530s, as Croke demonstrates, "Mundo the Gepid," pp. 125–35; accepted also (without reference to Croke) by Wolfram, *Goths*, p. 339; Croke is rejected by PLRE3: 903, solely on the basis of the "Hun" and "Gepid" labels.

J: He entered Ostrogothic service as a military officer, hence a "Goth" under *civilitas* ideology – on the other hand, he began as a mere *foederatus* of the Goths: Ennodius, *Pan.* 12.63.

[D]: The references to Mundo's identity are instructively confused. Marcellinus comes, who probably knew him (Croke, "Mundo the Gepid," p. 132), calls him "Geta" (s.a. 505) a word he uses slightly later for Ostrogoths (s.a. 530). Procopius, who also probably knew him (ibid., p. 133), says that he was of barbarian descent (BG 1.5.2). Jordanes, on the other hand, says that the bandit Mundo was "formerly of the Attilani" (*Get.* 301), interpreted by PLRE3: 903 to mean that he was "of Hun descent," PLRE2: 767 "Mundo was a Hun," using this as evidence that he could not be identical to the later Mundo "Geta." But as Croke, ibid., p. 130, points out, "Attilani" could simply mean that he came from a group that was part of the Hunnic confederacy of Attila, which included both the Ostrogoths and the Gepids. Greek sources call him a Gepid or son of a king of the Gepids (Joh. Malal. 450, Theoph. A.M. 6032), or a Gepid and "king [*rhēx*] of Sirmium" (Georgius Cedrenus, *Comp. Hist.* 1: 652, lines 3–4); the context of Ennodius's description of him perhaps also implies that he was a Gepid: *Pan* 12. 60–4 (battles in the land of the Gepids).

Unfortunately, Croke goes on to use this evidence to establish Mundo's identity as "a Gepid by descent" (ibid., pp. 130–1), noting Jordanes's description of the "relationship" between the peoples of the Goths and the Gepids (*Get.* 94–5). This is plausible so far as it goes (see Ustrigotthus, perhaps Asbadus).

But Mundo's ancestors themselves may come from various groups calling themselves Huns, Goths or Gepids. If so, either he or others could choose one of his ancestor's identities to describe him, according to the needs of the moment, or the viewpoint of the observer.

Moreover, this variety of description seems to show that Mundo's identity changed in the eyes of observers according to his current or recent political allegiance. He was *de Attilanis* for Jordanes because he was embroiled in the mess left by the remnants of Attila's former followers in the Balkans, *Geta* for Marcellinus to indicate his former affiliation with either the Ostrogoths or the Gepids, *rex Gepidarum* to indicate his affiliation with the latter, and "of barbarian descent but loyal to the emperor," in the description of the classicizing Procopius, after he threw in his lot with the Byzantines. See further **V**italianus and the discussion of the changing meaning of "Scythia," "Scythians" and "Thrace" in ch. 4, above.

Father of **M**auricius, grandfather of **T**heudimundus and **A**nonyma 2.

?N ———— ?n, c, 1	??MUSTELA spectabilis femina (= PLRE3) The dates indicate her lifespan, taking in the whole period of legitimate Amal rule in Italy. She was a Catholic; her epitaph was placed in the Basilica S. Pancrati in Rome. On the name and a possible relationship, see **M**ustila. ICUR n.s. 2, no. 4287.	493–543
?N, (N) ———— ?n, c, 1	MUSTILA spectabilis femina (= PLRE2) A Catholic: buried in the Vatican crypt; husband of **F**ravita (q.v. on the inscription and date: more probably from 493 than 444). It would be extraordinary if she were the mother of **M**ustela, another Catholic, bearing the same name and rank, and also buried in a church at Rome. If so, Mustila might have died in childbirth. Like that of her husband, her name could be Germanic. Mus- is a Germanic personal name stem (Kauffmann, *Ergänzungsband*, p. 262), and Til-/-tila is a Gothic stem and suffix (Förstemann 1: 1394). But Mustela was a Latin name; note Astius Mustelus, an African of 526 (PLRE2: 769), and e/i confusions are common at this time. ICUR I, no. 903 = ICUR n.s. 2, no. 4178.	d 444 or 493
N ———— 1	Nasa (= B) Obstructed a share of an inheritance. The date is unclear in the fragmentary record of the dispute. It was presided by a *comes sacri stabuli* perhaps named Iohannes; see Tjäder 2: 307, nn. 1–2; PLRE3 Ioannes 48. This identification would place the document in the 550s (see PLRE3: 662), probably in Ravenna. Note B Iohannes 8, identifying him with Iohannes *patricius* in Venetia and Istria in 553–559 (B Iohannes 4, PLRE3 Ioannes 71); see further B, p. 46, n. 17. Now, however, Tjäder 2:307, n. 2, suggests identifying him with **I**ohannes 2 (= PLRE3 Ioannes 46), the nephew of **V**italianus 1, followed with hesitation by PLRE3: 662). (Note that PLRE3: 669 also suggests making the *patricius* of the 550s identical to **I**ohannes son of **V**italianus.) In any case, we are looking at the Byzantine, not the Ostrogothic, administration, with Tjäder 2: 307, n. 2.	VI^med

Name: although it also belonged to a Jew in Sicily in the 590s
(GR 5.32), it is Germanic, not Hebrew.
PItal 55.3.

N ――――― 1	**Nanderit** Deceased father of **Manna** *vir devotus*. Attested in **Manna**'s will. *PItal* 6.4, 8, 11, 15, 18, 22, 25.	d by 575

N, J   **Nanduin saio** (= PLRE2)   508
―――――   Instructed by Theoderic to have arms, horses and "all things
1   necessary" ready for the expedition to Gaul on 24 June 508;
       the letter is addressed to "all the Goths," i.e., the army. The
       text spells his name "Nandum" (accusative); see Mommsen,
       index to Cassiodorus, s.n., p. 497. *Var.* 1.24.

N, J   **Neudis** vir inlustris (= PLRE2)   523/
―――――   Ordered by Theoderic to make **Gudila** 3 and **Oppa** desist from   524/526
1   oppressing the blind veteran **Anduit**. He was thus probably a
       military officer (see **Anduit**, **Gudila** 3 and **Oppa**), "presumably
       a Gothic general" (Barnish, *Cassiodorus: Variae*, p. 86).
       Var. 5.29.

N   *NONNI* ?vir clarissimus, arcarius   after
       Genitive "Nonnitis." Tjäder 2: 295, n. 3, points to examples   510
       elsewhere of "Nonnito" and "Nonnita" (Germanic) He seems
       to have been an officer in the *arca* (treasury) of the praetorian
       prefecture. From a fragmentary papyrus listing documents kept
       in the archive of the *arcarii* of the praetorian prefecture in Rav-
       enna, probably prepared under Theoderic (Tjäder 2: 187–8).
       The *arcarii* were *viri clarissimi*, and held the office in pairs. Other
       such officers were called Petrus and Rusticus (ibid., 2: 188, n.
       20). Nonni was apparently not identical with the Nonnus listed
       slightly later in the same document (*PItal* 47–8.A.11); Nonnus
       is a Latin name. *PItal* 47–8.A.1.

       Nonnica = **Gundeberga**

N, J   ‼*OCCILA* vir magnificus, tribunus (= B, PLRE3)   599
―――――   Military tribune at Otranto, he received two letters from Gre-
c, 1   gory the Great, apparently appointed by the Byzantine exarch
       at Ravenna. See further PLRE3: 951, B, pp. 56–7 with nn. 34–
       5. GR 9.200; 9.205. B, p. 73, says that he "cannot be assigned
       to any particular people," apparently meaning that the name is
       not especially associated with any one barbarian group.

N   *ODERICUS/ODERIT* vir clarissimus (= B Odericus; PLRE3   575/591
―――――   Odericus)
1   Son of the deceased **Boherda**, he witnessed the sale of property
       of **Deusdedit** to **Holdigernus**. Signs as "Oderic" (with suspen-
       sion mark indicating "-us": see Tjäder 3, plate 130, line 45, at
       left; *PItal* 36.45), is listed as "Oderit" (*PItal* 36.65). B, p. 271,
       and PLRE3: 951 see the signature as "Odericus." The mark at

36.65 is interpreted by Tjäder as part of a "t" rather than a suspension mark over a "c." See Tjäder 3, plates 130, line 45, and 131, line 65, left-hand side in both cases.

N   Odoin comes (PLRE 2 Odoin)   500 or
Plotted against Theoderic and was beheaded at the Sessorian   504
Palace: AV 12.68–9 (implying that it occurred during Theoderic's tricennalia at Rome in 500); Mar. Avent. s.a. 500; *Auct.
Havn.* s.a. 504. Marius gives his name as Odoind; the *Auctarium*
as Odomus. PLRE2: 791 makes him *vir spectabilis*, presumably on
the basis of his title of *comes*. This last could indicate a military
comitiva, but there is no corroborating evidence.

(J), S, (G)   ??**Opilio** vir inlustris et magnificus, *CSL* (= PLRE2 Opilio 4)   VI^in
————   He was a Catholic: see below. Brother of **Cyprianus**, hence   −534
n, j, c, l, [d]   almost certainly considered a Roman: **Cyprianus** served as a
soldier and spoke Gothic, but was considered a Roman. Uncle
of **Anonymi** 20+. Unlike his brother, and despite his support
for the Ostrogothic kings, Opilio is not attested as having taken
on any criteria of Gothic identity himself.
A member of the parvenu bureaucratic and military aristocracy
(see **Cyprianus**; it included **Liberius**, **Valentinianus**, probably
Senarius, as well as Cassiodorus and Ennodius; connections with
the ancient senatorial clans did not necessarily ease their way),
his father Opilio was *CSL* under Odoacer, but failed to achieve
the "highest honours" (*Var.* 5.41.5). True, the junior Opilio is
described as "ex senatore natus," which is true by definition,
since his father received the illustrate through his office, but
without membership in a famous senatorial dynasty, Opilio's
route to office would not be automatic. Therefore he became
an *advocatus*, a traditional route toward palatine service, and got
a position at the palace through his brother. Like his brother,
Opilio informed against Boethius, and seems to have profited
from it (he and **Gaudentius** escaped an accusation of fraud
thereby; he became *CSL* after his brother).
Like his brother, he was closely associated with the kings.
Although he did not serve in the military, he performed various
functions unconnected with his civilian position. In 526, he
went to Liguria to announce the accession of Athalaric (*Var.*
8.16). Despite his association with the king at the time of the
murder of Boethius and Pope John I, Opilio was a devout Catholic. In 529, both he, and the *PPO Galliarum* and *patricius praesentalis* **Liberius**, subscribed to the Acts of the Council of
Orange against semi-Pelagianism, a deed that may have had political as well as theological significance. In 534, he and most of
the other prominent senators attached to Athalaric's court
received a letter from Pope John II explaining the papal opinion
on a recent *professio fidei* received from Justinian. But Opilio is
last attested from 534, when Theodahad sent him and **Liberius**

to plead the new king's case before Justinian: unlike Liberius, Opilio defended Theodahad.

Although he may have married into a senatorial clan (his wife was "Basilian," hence possibly a Decia, PLRE2: 888 – but possibly the family of the Basilius who informed on Boethius; see PLRE2 Basilius 10, p. 216, and further Moorhead, *Theoderic*, p. 227), and although he was a Catholic believer, his interests were clearly aligned with those of the Ostrogothic kings, like his brother. It would be useful to know whether his brother's military connections might place them both on the side of the pro-military party under Athalaric, but no judgment can be made (see further **Cyprianus** and **Anonymi** 11, 12, 13). *Var.* 8.16; 8.17; Rugo 1, no. 39; *Acta Concilii Arausionensis*, pp. 53–4; John II, JK 885 = *ep.* "Olim quidem" (*Avellana* = *PL* 66: 20–4); Procopius, BG 1.4.15 (described as a member of the Roman senate), 21, 23–5. He may have returned to Italy after his voyage to Constantinople, or later, if PLRE2: 808 correctly identifies ICUR 1.1114 as his epitaph (Rome, 546/566).

N, ?J   Oppa ?dux (= PLRE2)   523/
———   He and **Gudila** 3 falsely asserted that the blind veteran **Anduit** 524/526
l   was their slave. Theoderic assigned **Neudis** the task of making
               the two desist. Dux: suggested by the context of the letter; a
               military position would mean a J. *Var.* 5.29.

N, J, S, [D]   Optaris (= PLRE3)   536
               In December 536, **Witigis** sent him to kill **Theodahad** (against
               whom Optaris had a grudge in any case, according to Pro-
               copius). He murdered him "like a victim for sacrifice" on the
               road between Rome and Ravenna. On the name, cf. **Optarit**.
               [D]: Procopius calls him "anēr Gothos" (1.11.6).
               Procopius, 1.11.6–9.

N, A, †,   Optarit presbyter/Ufitahari papa   551
G, ?D   Presbyter and thus one of the highest–ranking clergyman of the
———   Gothic Arian church of St. Anastasia in Ravenna; on the docu-
l   ment that he subscribed with many other clergy, see **Danihel**.
               He subscribed in the Gothic language, using a formula repeated
               with little variation by **Suniefridus, Mirica** and **Wiliarit** 4. He
               is announced as Optarit (*PItal* 34.82), and subscribes as Ufitahari
               (*PItal* 34.88–91: "Ik Ufitahari, papa, ufm<el>da handau meinai,
               jah andnemum skilliggans .j., jah faurthis Thairh kawtsjon mith
               diakuna alamoda unsaramma jah mith gahlaiba[im] unsaraim
               andnemum skilliggans .rk. wairth thize s[aiwe]." Although
               "mith diakuna alamoda unsaramma" would normally translate
               "with our deacon Alamod," this expression seems to utilise a
               "fictional person" called Alamod, thus meaning, here, "with
               our deacon representing us all," having no reference to **Alamud**
               diaconus: Tjäder 2:96–7. (On the other hand, such an expla-
               nation should call into question the existence of **Alamud**, but

an examination of the document in which he appears seems to indicate that he is a real person there. This inconsistency needs resolution, since there must be some connection between the words "diakuna alamoda" here and "dkn Alamoda" at *PDip* 118 = *PItal* † 8.48. The problem requires further attention from the philologists.)
?D: see **Danihel**.
PItal 34.82, 88–9.

Oraio = **Uraïas**

N, J ———— [?d]	**!!Osso** vir gloriosus, ?*MVM* (= B, PLRE3) 590

Mentioned as leading "Romanus suus exercitus" in the Po valley in 590. This occurs in a letter from the exarch Romanus to the Frankish king Childebert II, which makes heavy use of reconquest rhetoric (mentioning cities "restored to the Roman Empire"); among the other generals mentioned in the letter occurs another with a Germanic name (Nordulf), who unlike Osso, was leading "his own Lombard followers" (PLRE3: 958). PLRE3: 958 says that Osso's "name was barbarian but he was a Roman military commander;" B, p. 73, n. 20, lists him among "Germanic *duces* and *magistri militum*," assuming him to be Lombard (p. 73, text), presumably on the basis of his name. *Epp. Austrasicae* 41.

N, J
————
1

Osuin vir inlustris, comes Dalmatiae et Saviae (= PLRE2)   510, 526
In 510, Theoderic appointed him *comes Dalmatiae*; *Var.* 1.40, 3.26 and 4.9 order him to obtain weapons for soldiers in Split. Since 3.26 is dated to 510 by Krautschick (*Cassiodor*, pp. 66, 75), I would hazard a guess that the other two letters date from near the same period. At the same time, **Fridibadus** was sent to the province to exercise judicial duties. Much later, in his old age, in 526, Athalaric appointed him to the same position again (*comes Dalmatiae et Saviae, Var.* 9.8; 9.9), which he perhaps held during the entire intervening period, in the same kind of relationship with **Severinus**.
J: Both **Severinus** and **Fridibadus** were thus military *comites* with judicial capacity, while **Osuin** was probably the commander of the frontier armies there. Schmidt argues that threatened frontier provinces like Dalmatia and Savia were governed by *comites* with a dual military and civil authority ("Die comites Gothorum," p. 130); see further Wolfram, "Ethnogenese," p. 112, n. 73: this seems to be confirmed by Osuin's instructions at his second appointment (9.8 and 9.9).
Var. 1.40; 3.26; 4.9; 9.8; 9.9.

N, ?D

Otratarit (= B)   575 or
Otratarit, at whose house a warehouse superintendent held before office (!). Quiriacus, *v.h.*, *orr(earius)*, "qui tenet stationem ad domo Otratarit" in Ravenna. This need not indicate that Otrat-

arit was alive – his house could simply have assumed his name. But the lack of "quondam" implies that he was still alive, and probably rented out space to Quiriacus. B, p. 271, calls Otratarit a "Goth," presumably on the basis of his Germanic name. ?D: The prefix "Otra" could just possibly be the prefix "Ostro" in "Ostrogoth"; note the soldier [O]traustaguta of ILCV 503, with Mommsen's emendation (adding the "O") at CIL 5.8740; against Mommsen's emendation, note Thraustila (Trapstila), the Gepid king, spelling as transmitted at Joh. Malal. 450. (Note also Ustrigotthus.) PItal 6.42.

N, J	Patza	523/
————	His wife **Regina** committed adultery with **Brandila** while Patza	524/526
(n), 1	was away on an expedition in Gaul. On the name, see **Pitzia**;	

cf. **Pitzas**, **Pissas**, **Pitio**; note the "**Batzas**" of *Cont. Marc. ss. aa.* 536, 538 (= PLRE3 Batzas 2). The letter implies that Patza was on military service, hence J. Wolfram's statement (*Goths*, p. 504, n. 238) that Patza is called *dux*, is not supported by the text of Cassiodorus. *Var.* 5.32; 5.33.

?J	??!!Paulus 1 primicerius scholae secundae (= PLRE3 Paulus 24)	415–80
————	He was an officer of the *scholares* in Rome; he died at age 65	or
n, 1	in the consulship "of Basilius" (either 480 or 541). Only if he	476–541

died in the latter consulship did he live under Ostrogothic rule. On the question of whether the *scholares*, palace guards, continued to fulfill a military function, see **Mundilo**; also note **Segetius**. ILCV 485b.

A, †, ?D	Paulus 2 clericus	551
————	One of the clergymen at the Gothic Arian church of St. Anasta-	
n, 1	sia who signed a deed of sale (see **Danihel**). Often, he and	

Petrus are judged to be "Romans," since they subscribed in Latin and had Latin names (Tjäder 2: 95, Wolfram, *Goths*, p. 325 with n. 459). Some clergymen with Gothic names, however, signed in Latin (**Minnulus/Willienant**, **Danihel/Igila**, **Theudila**), and other clergymen with Latin names (**Vitalianus 2**, **Benenatus**) who did not sign due to illiteracy, poor eyesight or low rank had Latin subscriptions written down for them. ?D: see **Danihel**. PItal 34.83, 108.

Pelagius diaconus, envoy *see under* PA III, table 4

(N)	Pelagius II, pope	579–90
————	The dates indicate his pontificate. His father's name was the	
n, c, cc, 1,	Germanic **Unigildus**: "natione Romanus, ex patre Unigildo."	
[d]	See, similarly, **Bonifatius** (Pope Boniface II).	

[d]: *natione Romanus* indicates that he was a native of the city of Rome (cf. John I, "natione Tuscus," etc., LP John I §1), but the potential for confusion between these two concepts is obvious.

Pelagius's father's Germanic name did not create any pan-Germanic identification for the pope, who loathed the Lombards from a perfectly Roman (or early Theoderican) perspective: B, p. 40; Pelagius II, JK 1052 = *ep.* "Omnia quidem" (ed. Hartmann, MGH Epp. 2: 440–1): "perfidia Langobardorum," "pericula totius Italiae Romanae omnia praesidio vacuatae videntur," "antequam nefandissimae gentis exercitus loca quae adhuc in republica detinentur." During his pontificate, Rome was being besieged and Italy devastated by the Lombards, so his rhetoric is hardly startling.

His parentage: LP Pelagius II §1.

Petia = **P**itzia

(N)	!!Petronia honesta femina	VI^{ex}–

(N) ———— n, j, l	!!Petronia honesta femina	VI[ex]–VII[in]

Wife of **P**itio *v.h.*, she sold $\frac{1}{12}$ of a farm to someone with her relative Maurus *vir reverendus*. Redated by Frösén to late sixth or early seventh century, after seeing the rediscovered original; PRainer Cent., p. 495. *PDip* 124 = *PItal* 10 = PRainer Cent. 166.9.

Petrus = **L**iberius

A, †, ?D ———— n, l	Petrus subdiaconus	551

One of the clergymen at the Gothic Arian church of St. Anastasia who signed a deed of sale (see **D**anihel). Often considered to be a "Roman" due to his Latin name and Latin subscription, but see **P**aulus 2.

?D: see **D**anihel. *PItal* 34.82, 98.

Petza, Petzamus = **P**itzia

?N, J, S ———— ?n .	Pissas archon (= PLRE3)	537

Witigis sent him and **H**unila against Constantinus *patricius* at Pergia in 537. He was defeated, captured and sent to Belisarius in Rome. Not identical to **P**itzas, who had defected to Belisarius the previous year. Procopius, BG 1.16.5–7. On the name, see **P**itzia; cf. **P**atza, **P**itzas, **P**itio; but "Pissas" is possibly a Greek name (*Griechische Eigennamen*, p. 1201, lists Pissa as a feminine name). Note also that a "Pissas" was said to be the father of the Lombard king Audoin: PLRE3:152 (from a ninth-century source).

N ———— (n), j, l	!!Pitio vir honestus	VI[ex]–VII[in]

Husband of **P**etronia *h.f.*, who sold $\frac{1}{12}$ of a farm to someone along with her relative Maurus *vir reverendus*. On the name, cf. **P**atza, **P**issas, **P**itzas, **P**itzia. Redated by Frösén to late sixth or early seventh century, after seeing the rediscovered original; PRainer Cent., p. 495. *PDip* 124 = *PItal* 10 = PRainer Cent. 166.9.

?N, J, S,   Pitzas (= PLRE2 Pitzias)   537
[D]   Surrendered himself and the Goths of Samnium to Belisarius in
───────   537. Belisarius allotted him a small force to help guard the
?n, s   region, which suggests that he was a soldier (as we would expect
               from his surrender). Procopius calls him "Gothos anēr." On
               the name, see **Pitzia**; cf. **Patza**, **Pissas** and **Pitio**. Procopius, BG
               1.15.1–2.
               PLRE2: 887 suggests that he was identical to the **Pitzia** of 504/
               505, attested in the 520s by *Var.* 5.29, rejecting the identification
               of the latter with the man killed by Theoderic in 514, but not
               noticing that the Pitzias of the *Variae* was already dead
               ("quondam" at *Var.* 5.29.3) in any case.

?N, J, [D]   **Pitzia** comes, nobilissimus Gothorum (= PLRE2 Petia and   504/
───────   Pitzias)   505–514
?n, l   In 504/505, sent by Theoderic to negotiate with Traseric and
               the Gepids near Sirmium; they fled and he seized the city. In
               505, he allied his army with that of **Mundo** in Dacia against the
               Byzantine army, defeating the forces of Sabinianus *MVM* per
               Illyricum, and securing the provinces of Pannonia, Savia and
               Dalmatia for Theoderic. Ennodius, *Pan.* 12.62–8; Jordanes, *Get.*
               300–1 (calling him Petza or Petzamus). Theoderic killed him
               by his own hand, at Milan, in 514; *Auct. Havn.* s.a. 514 (calling
               him Petia). Later, in the 520s, Theoderic apparently regretted
               his deed, holding up Pitzia's actions in the case of the blind
               soldier **Anduit** as an example to **Neudis**, and referring to him
               as deceased (*Var.* 5.29.2–3, calling him Pitzias: this interpretation
               follows Wolfram, *Goths*, p. 502, n. 223: but see below on the
               problem of identifying the victim of 514 with the deceased man
               of the 520s).
               ?N: Schroeder apud Mommsen, index to Cassiodorus, s.n., p.
               498, argues for a Germanicized Greek name (from Pythias), and
               Schönfeld, p. 128, says it is not Germanic. Indeed, the very
               similar **Pissas** may be Greek (q.v.). Schroeder's arguments, how-
               ever, do not take enough account of Jordanes's spellings "Petza"
               and "Petzamus;" note also **Pitio**, the Batzas of *Cont. Marc.* ss.aa.
               536, 538 (= PLRE3 Batzas 2, apparently a Germanic name, with
               Schönfeld, p. 47), and **Patza**, **Pitzas**: there seems to be some
               linguistic common ground here not totally explicable through
               a Greek origin.
               J: He was a high military officer. Wolfram, *Goths*, p. 291, con-
               jectures *dux* as well as *comes* (perhaps like **Ibba**: Wolfram thinks
               such dual titles were normal under Theoderic, expressing affili-
               ation with both the royal court or *comitatus*, and with army).
               [D]: Ennodius, praising him in his panegyric to Theoderic,
               places him and **Herduic** among the "nobilissimi Gothorum"
               (Jordanes calls him "inter primos electos").This phrase need not
               indicate some native Gothic nobility; cf. **Tuluin**.
               PLRE2: 886–7 does not think that this Pitzia was killed in 514,

seeing him as still alive in the 520s to judge the case of **A**nduit, and even suggesting that he was identical to the **P**itzas of the 530s (listing the victim of 514 separately under Petia: PLRE2: 861). For the identification of the first Pitzia with the Petia of 514: Mommsen, index to Cassiodorus, s.n., p. 498; Wolfram, *Goths*, p. 223, n. 502 (criticizing PLRE2 for missing Pitzia's death, but not noticing the separate entry under Petia). It does seem odd that the man killed in 514 could have had any say in the case of **A**nduit, unless the *Variae* letter of the 520s refers to an earlier case of at least nine years previously (although long court cases and repeated abuses of power were not uncommon in late antiquity); Wolfram's interpretation also requires that Pitzia was completely rehabilitated in the eyes of a penitent Theoderic (not out of character, if we believe Procopius on the king's regret over the deaths of Symmachus and Boethius). There is a summary of all this evidence, unnecessarily complicating matters, along with the suggestion that one of these men was also identical to **P**atza, and possibly to **P**itzas and **P**issas, at Krautschick, *Cassiodor*, p. 69, n. 3. Wolfram, *Goths*, p. 502, n. 223, suggests that **P**itzas was possibly a relative of **P**itzia, and comments "cf. . . . **P**atza." It seems most likely that the overpowerful general of 504/505 ended by suffering Theoderic's wrath in 514 (both *comites*, both attested as Petza/Petia – a spelling not attested at all for any of the others).

(N), (J)	Procula	523/
———	Wife of **B**randila: her husband committed adultery with **R**egina,	524/526
n, l	wife of **P**atza. **B**randila was apparently a soldier. *Var.* 5.32; see 5.33.	

N	Quiddila	VI
———	Name inscribed on a silver fibula found in Casteldavio, near	
l	Mantua: "[cross], QUIDDILA VIVAS IN DEO." Mowat, "Note sur des bijoux ornés," pp. 19, 21. Mowat identifies him with **Q**uidila 2, suggesting that this rich item was a gift from Theoderic or Athalaric, comparing it to the gifts of Roman emperors to military officers: pp. 20–3, and noting that the art is not "Germanic," but similar to other Italian jewelry of the time. (For some other Germanic names inscribed on fibulae, see PA III, table 14).	

N, J	Quidila 1 saio (= PLRE2 Quidila 2)	526
———	Sent by Athalaric to Sicily regarding complaints over increases	
l	in taxation. It is entirely possible that this Quidila was identical to **Q**uidila 2, being promoted to *comes* and *prior* directly after this mission – the dates, now more exactly established by Kraut-schick, *Cassiodor*, pp. 88, 89 (with nn. 2–3), 102–3, allow this conjecture not yet permitted to PLRE2: 932 (with Mommsen's dating, the two letters looked roughly contemporary). For a possible parallel advancement, see **G**uduin 1 and 2. *Var.* 9.10.	

N, J   Quidila 2 comes, prior Reatinorum et Nursinorum (= PLRE2   527

——————   Quidila 1)

1   Chosen as *prior* of the Goths at Rieti and Norcia by Theoderic,
              and finally appointed by Athalaric. He was the son of Sibia.
              Possibly identical to Quidila 1 or to Quiddila (qq.vv.).
              J: Although the letter places him above "vos," the addressees,
              viz. "all the Reatini and Nursini," the language of the letter
              makes it explicitly clear that it is addressed to the Goths in those
              regions. *Civilitas* rhetoric appears: "Nam quae necessitas ad iniu-
              sta compellat, cum vos et sortes alant propriae et munera nostra
              . . . ditificent? . . . quia vobis proficit, quod Romani quieti sunt,
              qui, dum aeraria nostra ditant, vestra donativa multiplicant"
              (*Var.* 8.26.3); Schmidt, "Die comites Gothorum," p. 132; Gof-
              fart, *Barbarians and Romans*, p. 83. As Schmidt points out, *prior*
              seems to be equivalent to a *tribunus provinciarum* (*Var.* 7.30), not
              a military officer, but a civil official with judicial duties, tied to
              the provincial administration. On the other hand, the language
              of the letter might seem to suppose something more similar to
              a military *comes*.
              Var. 8.26.

N, J, S, [D] Ragnaris (= PLRE3)   552–4
              A commander under Totila at Tarentum in 552, he opened
              negotiations with Pacurius (see Moras 2); later, after the battle
              of Busta Gallorum, he reneged on his agreement when he heard
              that Teias had become king; he tried to trick Pacurius, was
              defeated, and escaped to Acherontia. Two years later, he appears
              as leader of a contingent of Goths in southern Italy, apparently
              in 554, the spring following the capitulation of *Aligernus.
              Besieged by Narses, Ragnaris tried to entice him into a meeting;
              his trick backfired, and he was wounded by one of Narses's
              bodyguards and died two days later. Procopius, BG 4.26.4;
              4.34.9–15; Agathias 2.13.3; 2.14.2–5.
              [D]: Procopius calls him "Gothos aner" (BG 4.26.4; 4.34.9)
              whereas Agathias, implicitly correcting him, says that he was
              "neither kinsmen nor compatriot," although a leader, of the
              Goths, and in fact "Ounnikōn de to ethnos hoi Bitgores" – a
              Hun from the tribe of the Bitigurs (2.13.3); both agree that he
              was preeminent among the Goths. On the meaning of "kins-
              man," cf. Herodianus. Cameron, *Agathias*, pp. 42–3, implies
              that Agathias was better informed than Procopius; PLRE3: 1076
              likewise, seeing Ragnaris as simply "a Hun." Procopius's insist-
              ence on calling him a Goth may reveal more about his uses of
              such labels in the *Wars* than about contemporary Italy, but we
              should keep in mind – particularly since both historians were
              Byzantine and of similar outlook – the possibility that Ragnaris
              had more than one identity or allegiance, possibly by inherit-
              ance. The name is Germanic, for what that is worth. Cf.
              Mundo, Vitalianus 1.

| N | Ranihilda | 564 |

—————— Slave of the deceased Collictus, father of Stephanus. Ranihilda's

j   *cautio* and *pretium* were enumerated by Stephanus's guardian
Gratianus at Ravenna as part of the property that would come
to him when he became of age; cf. Guderit 2. *PItal* 8.II.4.

| N, A | Ranilda | 535 |

—————— Apparently persecuted by Theodahad for converting from

c   Arianism to Catholicism, but perhaps the reverse, at the behest
of Justinian; the text is very unclear.
Var. 10.26.

| N | **Ranilo** sublimis femina (= PLRE3) | 553 |

—————— A Catholic. She and her husband **Felithanc** donated property

(n), c, l   to the church of Ravenna in 553, recorded in a surviving
papyrus. She was the daughter of **Aderit** and the sister of **Adem-
unt-Andreas**. An invocation to "salutem invictissimi principis
obtestans Romanum gubernantis imperium" as a sort of sanctio
seems suggestive in a document dated so soon after Justinian's
final reconquest of Italy. It is a formula that finds use elsewhere,
e.g. *PItal* 8.I.12–13 (from 564); *PItal* 20.44–6 (from *c.* 600); cf.
Tjäder 1: 431, n. 22. The characteristic intertwining of emperor
and church might just suggest that Ranilo and her husband,
wealthy people of high rank, had recently converted in accord-
ance with the imperial laws and were making a timely gift to
prove their loyalty.
PItal 13.1, 19, 62, 65, 68, 72, 76, 69.

Reccifrida = **Riccifrida**

| (N), (J) | Regina | 523/ |

—————— The wife of **Patza**, she committed adultery with **Brandila**. *Var.* 524/526

n, l   5.33; cf. 5.32.

| N, J, S, | Rhecimundus (= PLRE3) | 546 |

[?D]   A Gothic commander under Totila. He was in charge of a force
of Goths, along with Romans and Moors who had deserted
(**Anonymi** 35+), at Bruttium. He was defeated by **Iohannes** 2.
[?D]: Procopius calls him a man of note *among* the Goths rather
than "Gothos aner" etc. The different phrasing may not be significant; cf. **Spinus**.
Procopius, BG 3.18.26–8.

| N | Riccifrida honesta femina (= PLRE3 Seccifrida) | ?542 |

—————— Husband of **Waduulfus**, they sued the shipbuilder **Leo** *v.h.* for

l   payment outstanding on the purchase of land. The document
recording the settlement was witnessed by **Ghiveric** and **Ardica**.
Riccifrida was apparently illiterate, like her husband (signing
with a cross, but the words "litteras nescientis" are not repeated
in her subscription: *PItal* 43.10–11). The name is also spelt
"Reccifrida" and "Ricchifrida." PLRE3: 1120 calls her "Seccif-

rida," presumably through misreading of late Roman cursive "r" as "s." *PItal* 43.5, 11, 16, 23, 29, 36, 43–4.

Riccitanc = **Eusebius**

N, J, S, ?A   **Riggo** spatharius (= PLRE3)   ?542
―――――――
l   The *spatharius* or sword-bearer of Totila, apparently one of several in the king's bodyguard (under Theoderic and Athalaric, *spatharius* was a high court office: this may or may not have changed under Totila; see **Unigis** and PLRE3: 1383 on Witigis). Gregory the Great relates a strange story that Totila decided to challenge the celebrated powers of St. Benedict by sending him Riggo dressed up as the king himself; Benedict saw through the error, and Totila came to him, prostrated himself, received advice and was thenceforth a less cruel ruler. The story gains some credibility from its association of **Bledas**, **Ruderit** and **Viliarid** (q.v.), otherwise attested as a group by Procopius (BG 3.5.1). ?A: Presumably Gregory means to imply that he was an Arian like his master Totila, since he was able to imagine playing such a trick on a saint.
Gregory the Great, *Dialogi* 2.14–15.

Roderic = **Ruderit**

J, S   *ROMULUS* vir clarissimus, silentiarius (= PLRE3 Romulus 1)   540
―――――――
n, ?c, l   *Silentiarius* under Witigis in Ravenna in 540, before the fall of the city to the Byzantines. He witnessed the deed of purchase of **Montanus**, another palace official.
J: *Silentiarii* in Constantinople were the ushers charged with keeping the silence in the presence of the emperor; they continued to have military duties and careers in the army (cf. PLRE2 Magnus 1; PLRE3 Adolius and Diomedes 1), doubtless necessary to enforce their will. Procopius, SH 26.28, explicitly says that *silentiarii* were no longer military in the West; he claims the same, wrongly, about the East at 24.15–23: on all this, see **Mundilo**.
?c: **Montanus** was probably a Catholic, hence also probably Romulus.
PItal 31.II.4.

N   **Rosemud** qui et Faffo (= PLRE3)   557
Along with **Adiud** and **Gunderit** 1, he brought unspecified charges against **Gudahals**. *PItal* 7.44, 58, 66–7, 79.

N, J, S, ?A,   **Ruderit** dux/Roderic archon/Rudericus comes (= PLRE3   542–6
[D]   Rudericus)
―――――――
l   In 542 Totila sent him with **Bleda** and **Viliarid** against the army of **Bessas**, **Justinus**, **Cyprianus** and **Iohannes** 2 at Florence: the Goths won; Bessas escaped wounded.
[D]: Procopius calls these three "the most warlike of the Goths;" see **Bleda**. Gregory the Great calls the three Totila's

most loyal supporters, all *comites*. Probably in this year (with PLRE3: 1097) occurred their visit with **R**iggo to see St. Benedict, as related by Gregory: *Dialogi* 2.14 (Rudericus comes). In 546, Ruderit was killed by the Byzantine commander Isaac at Porto. ?A: see **R**iggo.
Cont. Marc. s.a. 542, Procopius 3.5.1; 3.19.25–6, 34; Gregory the Great, *Dialogi* 2.14..

(?N)

―――――――

n, c, (cc), l

??!!Rusticiana honesta femina (= B Rusticiana 2, PLRE3 Rus- 591
ticiana 1)
A Catholic, since she was the daughter of a *defensor ecclesiae Romanae* called Felix; she married a Justinus, and later **T**zitta 2, a Byzantine soldier of the *numerus felicum Armeniarum*. She sold land near Rimini to a soldier (*adorator*) Iohannes in 591, in a document prepared in Classe at Ravenna. *PItal* 37.3, 27–8, 70, 74, 79, 85, 91, 98. On the possibly Gothic name of her second husband, see **T**zitta 2.

?N

―――――――

?n, c, cc, l

??!!Sarabonus presbyter   V/VI
He erected a monument to Fortunatus, bishop of Tusculanum. Hence Catholic. It is undated, but thought to be from the fifth or sixth century.
?N: The name is very odd indeed. "Sara-" is indeed a Germanic prefix (Förstemann 1: 1299–1301, with Kaufmann, p. 303), but "-bon" is only possibly a Germanic suffix, and may well be a Latin borrowing from Latin *bonus* (Kauffmann, pp. 67–8; see also F-S, p. 113). The name, whatever its date, may be a conscious or unconscious combination of Germanic and Latin name-elements. It would then be an example of "barbarolexis" (see Ruggieri, "*Teudisca lingua*," pp. 250–56; for an example in reverse, see ★**T**heodahadus–Theodatus). The name would be unique if it were *thought of* as Germanic and if it actually belonged to a Catholic clergyman of the first half of the sixth century. The certain and abundant evidence for Latin names among contemporary Catholic clergy should make us doubt either or both of these propositions.
F-S 227a.

N, J, S, [D]

Scipuar archon (= PLRE3)   551–2
Along with **G**ibal and **G**undulf, called by Procopius "the most notable among the Goths." He and the other two were appointed commander by Totila in order to capture Ancona in Picenum. Scipuar stayed at the siege while the other two went off to a naval battle. After the Gothic defeat at Sena Gallica, his army, presumably including its commander, retreated hastily to Osimo, leaving Ancona empty for the Byzantine forces under Valerian. In 552, Scipuar was with Totila in the king's last hours after Busta Gallorum, managing to wound his killer **A**sbadus. Procopius, BG 4.23.1, 12; 4.32.22–5.

Seccifrida = **R**iccifrida

J

n

Secundus dromonarius (= PLRE3)   d by

A soldier-oarsman; he owned a property (called Casanova) near 539
Faenza. On *dromonarii*, see **A**ndreas; see further **W**itterit (both
mentioned in the same document as owning farms in this
region). PLRE2: 1120 wrongly classifies him as *temonarius*, relying
on the outdated edition of Marini. See now Tjäder 2: 258, n.
9, and compare Tjäder 3, plate 100, line 14 at left ("[..]arii")
with line 16 at left ("dromunariorum").
PItal 30. 13–14.

N

j, c, l

Seda vir sublimis, ignucus et cubicularius regis Theoderici (=   *c.* 501–
PLRE2)   541
The dates indicate his lifespan. Inscription left on a beautifully
carved sarcophagus found in the Catholic cathedral of Ravenna
(Bormann at CIL 11: 64, no. 310). *Ignucus* = "eunuch;" eunuchs
traditionally served as *cubicularii*, who had an important court
role in Ravenna as in Constantinople (see F-S, p. 94). PLRE2:
987: "He presumably served under Thedoderic while in his
early twenties," i.e., in the early 520s.
Religion: it is certainly possible that the heavy sarcophagus was
removed to the Catholic cathedral at some later date, but given
the mention of the Arian Theoderic in the inscription, it seems
unlikely that anyone would have gone to the trouble to move
it. It was probably at the cathedral from the start, and Seda was
thus a Catholic, like many other servants of the king. On the
sarcophagus, see Dütschke, *Ravenna Studien*, p. 25 with fig. 8
(questioning, at p. 26, whether the sarcophagus had originally
been in the cathedral, since it mentions the "Arian Theoderic":
I think that this mention makes it more likely that the sarcophagus was originally there, in an era when Theoderic's name was
being acclaimed at papal synods and his portrait was on display
in the Catholic church of San Vitale [on which Deichmann,
Ravenna 2: 122, 174; Fiebiger in F-S NF no. 37, p. 27 with
plate 3 after p. 59], than that it was removed there at a later
time, after Theoderic had been vilified as an Arian oppressor:
on the chronological change in Catholic attitudes toward
Theoderic, see above, ch. 3). Deichmann, *Ravenna* 2.1: 127,
connects Seda with the "Gothic sphere" of the palace, calling
other officials "Roman"; this statement does nothing to clarify
Seda's role.
F-S 183.

N, ?J

l

!!Segetius [scholaris] (= PLRE2)   V–VI
Member of the imperial or royal guard, which may still have
served a non-ceremonial function; see further **M**undilo. Like
Mundilo, he belonged to the *schola gentilium*, and was buried in
Florence. CIL 11.1711 = ILCV 563.

?N

――――――――

?n, j, c,
(cc), l, ([d])

??**Senarius** vir inlustris, vir magnificus, comes patrimonii, 503–
?CRP, patricius (= PLRE2)   515/516
A relative of Ennodius, he was at Theoderic's court from an
early age. He served on twenty-five embassies to Byzantium
and to the barbarian kingdoms, probably as *patricius*. He received
many letters from Ennodius between 503 and 508. He became
comes patrimonii in 509 (*Var.* 4.3) and received three letters from
Theoderic while in office (*Var.* 4.7; 4.11; 4.13). He was a Catholic: in 515/516, he received a letter from Avitus of Vienne (*ep.*
39) inquiring about the papal legations to the East, and one from
a deacon John answering questions on baptismal liturgy (PL
59:399). This John was possibly later Pope John I
(Schanz-Hosius, p. 595). Senarius's letters from Ennodius are
particularly well-turned specimens of eloquence, perhaps calcu-
lated to appeal to a powerful connection who appreciated such
displays (Senarius's epitaph makes literary allusions to Virgil and
Horace, ed. Burmann/Mommsen, index to Cassiodorus, p.
499). He was friends with Faustus Niger, to judge from Ennodius's later letters on Christian issues (*Opp.* 273, 279, 310/*epp.*
6.8, 6.12, 7.5). See further *Opp.* 30, 78, 116, 160, 171, 241, 294,
383/*epp.* 1.23, 3.11, 3.34, 4.27, 4.33, 5.15, 6.27, 8.7.
Dates of his embassies: PLRE2: 988–9 places them between 493
and 509, presumably on the basis of *Var.* 4.3.2; 4.4.3 (appointing
him to the office of *comes patrimonii* in 509, referring to his work
as a legate); he might also have continued them later.
?N: Schönfeld, p. 202, saw the name as Germanic, similarly
Schroeder ap. Mommsen, index to Cassiodorus, p. 499 (from
"Siniharjis"); Wrede, p. 117, suggested a similar derivation, but
decided to accept Mommsen's statement that he was a Roman
(OGS, NA 14: 465, n. 1, not one of Mommsen's most perspi-
cacious moments – he also makes the *comes patrimonii* Bergan-
tinus a Goth, with no stated evidence to support either point).
The name is unattested elsewhere, but it could just possibly be
Celtic: Holder 2: 1465–7.

N

――――――――

l

Sendefara   *c.* 511–
The dates indicate her lifespan. She died in Tortona in northern 541
Italy. F-S 230.

J

――――――――

n, l

SERVATUS dux Raetiarum (= PLRE2)   507/511
Commanded frontier troops in the province of Raetia Secunda
under Theoderic. He was requested to investigate a claim that
some soldiers called "Breones" under his command were acting
against *civilitas* by seizing the slaves of a certain Moniarius. *Var.*
1.11.
J: Wolfram, *Goths*, pp. 316–17, makes him and his colleague in
Noricum, Ursus, "Romans" commanding local troops
(*limitanei*, including "federate" Breones) who "cannot have
been Goths," adducing as evidence that Servatus's soldiers

apparently "thought little of the Italian-Gothic *civilitas*." But the formula of the *ducatus Raetiarum*, cited by Wolfram himself (p. 502, n. 218), implies that Theoderic's government did indeed consider the Raetian troops to be Goths, in line with *civilitas* ideology (which the formula employs heavily): "ita tamen, ut milites tibi [sc. duci Raetiarum] commissi vivant cum provincialibus iure civili nec insolescat animus, qui se sentit armatum, quia clipeus ille exercitus nostri quietem debet praestare Romanis" (*Var.* 7.4.3). Such usage of *exercitus noster* opposite "Roman provincials" in the *Variae* always has the meaning "Gothic army" (see above, ch. 2; Wolfram, *Goths*, pp. 300–2). So Servatus commanded troops considered by the government to be Goths, and there is really no reason for doubting this aside from his Latin name (as Schmidt, "Die comites Gothorum," p. 130, realized); as for *incivilitas* among the Raetian troops, this was a problem all over Italy, as the *Variae* show repeatedly. The difference between Schmidt and Wolfram, who are both mistaken in their different ways, is that the former thought that Servatus was an "inherent" Goth (by descent) who happened to have a Latin name, while the latter thinks that he was a Roman in the Gothic army, whose troops were therefore not Goths. It does not occur to either that whatever Servatus's origins, his classification as a "Goth" despite his name is related to Theoderic's definitions of what constituted a Goth at that time, viz. service in his army.

On the Breones, see further Wolfram, *Goths*, p. 301; Wolfram, "Ethnogenese," pp. 118–22.

Sesi . . . = **S**esi. . . (under fragmentary names)

?J
———————
n, ?j, l

??**Severinus** vir inlustris et magnificus, ?comes (= PLRE2 Sever-   526
inus 4)

Ordered to go to Savia by Theoderic in 526 to reassess the tribute and to iron out disputes between the courts of the provincial governor (*iudex Romanus*) and that of the *comes Dalmatiae*. PLRE2: 1001 suggests that he was meant to act as a *peraequator*, but both his duties and his titulature suggest that he held a higher post. Very shortly afterward, Athalaric sent him and **O**suin to govern Dalmatia and Savia (not just Dalmatia, as PLRE2: 1001 states). In Mommsen's original dating, these letters would have been strewn between 523 and 527; but Krautschick, *Cassiodor*, p. 70, n. 1, p. 89, nn. 2–3, pp. 77, 103, now tentatively redates all three of them to 526, suggesting that Severinus never actually went to Savia, but was reappointed to the new position in Dalmatia shortly after Theoderic's death.

?J: In this interpretation, the elderly **O**suin, who had been *comes Dalmatiarum et Saviae* in *c*. 510, was reappointed to his post, by the new administration, and Severinus was sent to iron out troubles. Since Severinus's job involved easing tensions between

soldiers and civilians in these provinces, he was thus probably a
military *comes* and based in some city in the provinces indicated.
Only **O**suin is given the title *comes*, but such omissions are
common in the *Variae*. Earlier, **O**suin had held co-office with
Fridibadus, also sent out with judicial duties; they probably had
had the same arrangement (see further **O**suin). Neither **F**ridibadus nor **S**everinus was the *consularis provinciae Dalmatiae*, a mere
v.s. (one appointed in 523/526 was named Epiphanius: *Var.*
5.24; on the date, Krautschick, *Cassiodor*, p. 70, n. 1, against
Mommsen), between whom and the *comes* they were meant to
adjudicate cases.
Var. 5.14–15; 9.9; cf. 9.8.

N, (J) ———— (l)	Sibia (= PLRE2) Father of **Q**uidila 2 (who was possibly identical to **Q**uidila 1, q.v.). Mentioned in a letter of Athalaric in 527 (*Var.* 8.26), when he might still have been alive, since he is not described with *quondam*.	?527
N ———— (n), ?j	Sifilo (= B) Wife of **B**ilesarius, mentioned in a very fragmentary manumis- sion document from Ravenna. B, p. 76, conjectures that she (and thus presumably her husband) were slaves: the next surviv- ing fragment mentions "famuli." *PItal* 9.14, cf. line 15. Date: Tjäder 1: 248 (from the palaeography, but also from the possible connection with the reorganization of Ravenna church prop- erty directly after the Gothic Wars).	VI^{med,} shortly after 555
N ———— (n), c, (cc), (l), ([d])	Sigibuldus The father of Pope **B**onifatius II, hence probably Catholic. His Germanic name led Harnack to call Boniface "Der erste deutsche Papst," and has led to diverse speculation about Boni- face's pro-Gothic sympathies: see above, ch. 3. Note that Boni- face is described as a native of the city of Rome in LP (see **B**onifatius), and that the name Sigisvultus belonged to the powerful consul of 437 and *MVM* of the 440s (an Arian): see PLRE2 Sigisvultus, possibly a relative of Boniface's father (but almost certainly not identical, given the chronology). Note the similar combination of **U**nigildus and Pope **P**elagius II.	V²–VI¹
N, ?J ———— j, l	**Sigismer** vir inlustris, comes (= PLRE2 Sigismer 2) Administered an oath of loyalty to the senate of Rome upon Athalaric's succession in 526. *Var.* 8.2. The rank *vir inlustris* must have made him a member of the senate. But note that Athala- ric's letter to the senate does not explicitly associate him with that body, unlike other royal officials with Germanic names (see **A**rigernus), and he was clearly being sent from Ravenna to Rome to receive the oath there (*Var.* 8.2.9). ?J: Wolfram, *Goths*, p. 291, sees *viri inlustres comites* as military	526

comites with extended commands and responsibilities. This need not have been the case: see **Severinus** and **Sunhivadus**.

N	Simplex nomine Livania	*c.* 498–

———
n, ?c, l

A woman with two names, one Latin, one Germanic. She was 528 the assistant of the *ostiarius* Paulus at a church in Potentia, in Picenum. Was she a Catholic? Note the Arians with both non–Germanic and Germanic names in Ravenna: **D**anihel/Igila and **M**innulus/Willienant, etc, as well as the Arian clergyman **P**aulus 2. Either way, Fiebiger, F-S NF, p. 29, sees Simplex as a (Latin and actively Christian) name taken "im Kirchendienst." This is convincing: cf. Gundeberga qui et Nonnica. (Note that the Livania of PLRE2: 685, the addressee of a work of Pelagius in the early fifth century, was probably a deliberate error for "Iuliana.") F-S NF 42.

N, J, S

———
?s

Sinderith dux (= PLRE3)   535

Named by Jordanes as commander of the garrison of Syracuse when Belisarius took the city in the first major battle of the Gothic Wars (on the events, see Procopius, BG 1.5, and *Cont. Marc.* s.a. 535). The city was surrendered (BG 1.5.12), and Belisarius was applauded "by the army and by the Sicilians" (1.5.18) as he marched into the city, so Sinderith and his men might have favoured Byzantine rule – or they might simply have given up in the face of superior forces, as Jordanes (*Get.* 308) suggests. Jordanes, *Rom.* 369, *Get.* 308.

N, A, †. ?D

———
l

Sindila spodeus/Sinthila spodeus   551

Scribe or bookseller at the Gothic Arian church of St. Anastasia in Ravenna; witnessed deed of sale of land with many other clergy of the church. On *spodeus*, and further on the document, see **Danihel**. On Sindila's possible illiteracy, see **Benenatus**. ?D: see **Danihel**. *PItal* 34.84, 130.

N, J, [D]

———
s

Sisifridus (= PLRE3 Sisiphridos)   545

A Byzantine commander who, "though a Goth by birth, was exceedingly loyal to the Romans," according to Procopius. He commanded the garrison at Assisi in 545, and and held out against Totila at the time that **Herodianus** put Spoleto into the hands of the Goths. Sisifridus died in a sally from the besieged Assisi, and the inhabitants then surrendered the city to Totila. Procopius, BG 3.12.12–17.

N, J, S

———
s

Sisigis (= PLRE3)   539–540

Commanded the garrisons of the Cottian Alps under Witigis in 539; perhaps then a *comes provinciae*. He surrendered to Belisarius and encouraged other Gothic commanders to do likewise. When **Uraïas** arrived, he laid siege to the forces of Sisigis, now combined with the army of the Byzantine general Thomas. Sisigis and Thomas were rescued by the arrival of **Ioannes** 2, who captured the wives and children of men serving under

Uraïas, with the result that a large part of Uraïas's army defected
to the Byzantines – "for most of the men under his command
were natives of these very fortresses." This was at the time of
Belisarius's siege of Ravenna. Procopius, BG 2.28.30–35; translation Dewing, 4: 125.

N
———————
j, c, l

!!Sisivera honesta femina, liberta (= B)   *c.* 600
A Catholic. Freedwoman of the deceased **Theudifara**
("Theudifara patrona mea, quam mihi concessit ad confirman-
dam libertatem": *PItal* 20.23). Sisivera donated property to the
church of Ravenna. The witnesses were a diverse group of
people: B, p. 61. Both Tjäder 1: 344, 464, n. 27, and B, pp. 61,
76, 276, call her a "Goth" on the basis of her name (both citing
Förstemann 1: 1345–7). *PItal* 20.65, 70, 74, 78, 81, 86, 90, 93,
96, 100, 104, 108, 113.

N
———————
?j, c, l

Sitza ?vir honestus or ?comes   490s–
The dates indicate his lifespan. Gave evidence at the inquiry 557 or
into the extent of the property of **Gundila**, at Rome or Nepi, later
in 557. He was aged sixty years "or more" at the time (*PItal*
49.18–19). The words describing his rank and office are partly
obliterated in the papyrus, but they are not consistent with each
other. The "v.h." could be "v.i."; on the other hand, the
abbreviation or part–word "com" could be "con," so there is
room for conjecture either way (*PItal* 49.8; see Tjäder 2: 299,
n. 7). Perhaps he had been an officer on the Gothic side, now
forced to live as a mere *vir honestus*. On the name, note also
Tzitta 1 and 2, and the Byzantine *MVM* Sittas (= PLRE3 Sittas
1); see further **Tzitta** 1 for a discussion of its linguistic origin of
that name; Sitza is definitely Germanic.
c: He was a Catholic in 557 and had been for some time: *PItal*
49.14 ("lege nostra").
PItal 49.8, 18–19, *passim.*

Sona = **Suna**

S
———————
n, j, l [d]

Spinus [vir inlustris], QSP (= PLRE3)   550
The *quaestor* of Totila. A native of Spoleto, he fell into Byzantine hands in Catania. In order to escape the Byzantines, Spinus
promised them that he would persuade Totila to leave Sicily if
they released him. He duly convinced Totila to depart by telling
him about the planned Byzantine offensive from Dalmatia.
Spinus was exchanged for a senatorial Roman lady.
S: In general, during the Gothic Wars, belonging to one side
or the other gave an individual the label belonging to that side.
The unfortunate civilian Italians in the middle (confusingly also
called "Romans" sometimes, as the Byzantines are always called
in Procopius) were forced to change loyalties frequently out
of expediency, and their civilian status complicated things. But
Procopius specifically calls Spinus a "Roman": unlike **Herodi-**

anus and **A**sinarius, working for the Goths apparently did not
turn him into a Goth. They, of course, were both military officers, and according to both the old Theoderican ideology of
profession, and the new Justinianic ideology of allegiance, they
would have assumed the Gothic identity by joining the side of
the Gothic army. But with Spinus, simple loyalty to the Goths
was not enough for Procopius, although he has Spinus refer to
Totila and the Goths as "we" in a speech: 3.40.28, on which,
see above, ch. 6. And perhaps his venerable Roman administrative office triggered Procopius's use of "Roman."
Procopius, BG 3.40.20–9.

N, J   STARCEDIUS ?vir spectabilis (= PLRE2)   523/526
———
l   Obtained discharge from the army on request. Now more suited
for a *vita otiosa*, he could relax, but would lose his official donative. Although the references to the aristocratic ideal of *otium*
could be appropriate for a *spectabilis*, PLRE2: 1027 correctly
points out that the references to receiving a donative imply that
"v.s." in this letter could mean merely the soldierly rank of *vir
strenuus*. *Var.* 5.36.

S   Stephanus, envoy (= PLRE3 Stephanus 11)   550
———
n, j, l, [d]   Procopius calls him a "Roman." In 550, Totila sent him as an
envoy to Justinian, offering peace and an alliance (Justinian
rejected the offer). Cf. **C**aballarius and **S**pinus for other civilians
with Latin names in active service on the Gothic side (the
former called a "Goth," the latter a "Roman"). Note that Procopius identifies both **S**pinus and **A**nonymus 3 as "Romans,"
the latter possibly a senator, and former a *v.i.* due to his office;
perhaps the term indicated senatorial status as much as identity.
Procopius, BG 3.37.6–7.

N, ?J   **Suna** vir inlustris, comes (= PLRE2)   507/511
———
l   In office under Theoderic, who ordered him to rebuild the
walls of an unnamed *civitas* (*Var.* 2.7), and removed a case from
his court and placed it in the hands of Theodahad (*Var.* 3.15,
calling him "Sona").
?J: on his titulature, see **S**igismer; note also his position as a
judge, but this need not necessarily indicate that he was a military *comes*.
Var. 2.7; 3.15.

N, J   SUNHIVADUS vir spectabilis, [comes] (= PLRE2)   507/511
———
l   Long in the service of Theoderic, he was sent to govern the
province of Samnium (PLRE2: 1040 suggests that he was not
necessarily a provincial governor, but some sort of "special
commissioner").
J: He was to adjudicate cases between Goths and Romans, and
was thus a military *comes* ("*Gothorum*") (formula in *Var.* 7.3).
Not noted by Wolfram, *Goths*, p. 291 and nn. 212–13, who

would need him to be an *inlustris* to fit his theory about extended commands (see **Sigismer**). Schmidt, "Die comites Gothorum," p. 129, argues from this example that Sunhivadus was only a civil officer meant to adjudicate cases involving unmobilized Goths and in cases involving persons of both nations, but this seems to be conjecture, and is not supported by Schmidt's citation of *Var.* 7.1 (formula for a *comes provinciae*, a military office, and which does not mention Goths or Romans). *Var.* 3.13.

N, A, †, G, ?D ——— l	Suniefridus diaconus/Sunjaifrithas diakon Deacon at the Gothic Arian church of St. Anastasia's in Ravenna, subscribed the deed of sale of land with other clergymen: on the document, see **Danihel**. He subscribes in Gothic: the formula is not signicantly different from that of **Optarit**, **Mirica** or **Willienant** (so also Tjäder 2: 274, n. 33). ?D: see **Danihel**. *PItal* 34.82, 94–7.	551
N, ?J	Tanca Allegedly seized the property of Constantius and Venerius. Athalaric ordered **Cunigastus** to investigate the charges. See further **Cunigastus**. ?J: the circumstances suggest a tax-collecting soldier exploiting taxpaying civilians: see Goffart, *Barbarians and Romans*, ch. 3. *Var.* 8.28.	527
N ——— l	TANCILA vir sublimis/vir spectabilis, comes (= PLRE2) He was an officer at Theoderic's court in Ravenna in 503, when he informed Ennodius that the king would not be returning confiscated property to Lupicinus, the orphan son of Ennodius's sister Euprepia. Lupicinus had somehow lost it to **Torisa** (apparently acting on behalf of the king). Ennodius asked Faustus Niger to pursue the matter further, describing Tancila as a great admirer of the quaestor ("venerator vester"). By about 509, Tancila seems to have held an office at Como: a letter from the king instructed him to find a stolen bronze statue at Como; he could expend up to 100 solidi finding the culprit. Ennodius calls him *vir sublimis*; the *Variae vir spectabilis*. Schmidt, "Die comites Gothorum," p. 130, identifies him as the military *comes civitatis* of Como. Ennodius, *Op.* 60/*ep.* 2.23; *Var.* 2.35.	503–c. 509
N, J ——— l	Tata saio (= PLRE2) Theoderic sent him with archers to join **Wiliarius** comes so that "maius sumeret robur duplicatus exercitus," at the time of the preparations for war against Africa in 526. Tata is mentioned in a letter asking Abundantius *PPO* to supply "our youths," now exercising, but preparing for war, with *annonae* and ships. On *iuvenes nostri*, cf. **Wiliarit** 1 and **Anonymi** 20+. *Var.* 5.23.	526

N, A

1

TEIA/ZEIA vir sublimis, comes (= PLRE2)   494/495

Received two letters from Pope Gelasius I. In the first, Gelasius begs Teia (here spelled Zeia) to look into the case of Silvester and Faustianus, clerics and former slaves, who have been reclaimed by their master's widow or heiress, Theodora. He addresses Teia as "dilecte fili," a phrase that says nothing about Teia's Catholicism (Gelasius addressed Theoderic in the same way). Slightly later, the pope seems to have regretted asking the count to interfere in ecclesiastical politics. Gelasius, JK 728 = *ep.* "Christianis gratum semper" (Thiel 24, pp. 390–1). In the second letter, Gelasius politely but firmly urges Teia to withdraw his interference in the case of Eucharistus and Faustus, which Gelasius wanted to hear personally. Teia thought that the case belonged in the court of the local bishop of Volaterra. Now Gelasius addresses Teia three times with the formal "nobilitas tua," asking him to avoid meddling in church cases, particularly since there is no doubt that he is "alterius communionis," i.e. an Arian. The pope threatens to inform "domnum filium meum regem" if he does not desist. Anyone who lives in his kingdom should imitate the actions of the "rex magnificus," that is, in staying out of ecclesiastical affairs. Gelasius, JK 650 = *ep.* "Si conscientia" (Loewenfeld, *ep. in.* 9, pp. 5–6 [beginning of letter], Ewald, *Coll. Brit. Gel. ep.* 14, pp. 513–14 [end of letter], united as ETV 2). (PLRE2: 1057 fails to realize that the Loewenfeld letter is part of ETV 2, and so thinks that three letters survive from Gelasius to Teia rather than the actual two.) The order of events argues in favor of reversing the order of letters as suggested by JK (they place the Eucharistus affair before that of Silvester and Faustianus, but it seems unlikely that the pope would have asked Teia to interfere in church affairs after his condemnation of this in the Eucharistus affair). (The Eucharistus affair was wrapped up by the condemnation of Eucharistus, apparently by the pope – so Teia must have given way: Gelasius, JK 720 = *ep.* "Gelasius in synodo dixit" [Loewenfeld, *ep in.* 22, pp. 11–12]; JK 740 = *ep.* "Vobis enim" [Thiel, *frag.* 24, p. 498]; JK 741 = *ep.* "Volaterranae ecclesiae" [Thiel, *frag.* 23, pp. 496–7].)

He could simply have been *comes civitatis* of Volaterra, but this may have been identical with the job of military *comes* and garrison commander.

Teia shared a rare personal name with the Ostrogothic king *Teia.

N, [?D]

1

Theodagunda inlustris femina (= PLRE2)   511

Received a letter from Theoderic in 511 requesting her to ensure that her tenants were regulated in a manner appropriate to her birth and the royal authority. PLRE2: 1067 thus identifies her as an Amal. If true, Wolfram, *Goths*, pp. 374–5, has apparently missed her. Her name might support such a conjecture

(cf. Theodahad's daughter Theudenanda), although the suffix -*gunda*, for what it is worth, does not appear in attested Amal names. If an Amal, perhaps identical to **★Anonyma 2** or **3**, daughters of Theoderic.
[?D]: if PLRE2 is correct. *Var.* 4.37.

(N)
———
n, l
!!Theodora (= B Theodora 3)   598
Her son married the daughter of **Aligernus**; see **Anonymus 5** and **Anonyma 3**. She was the widow of **Javinus**, *defensor* of Sardinia. GR 9.36.

Theodorus, envoy *see under* PA III, table 3.

(N)
———
n, j, c, l
Theodosus ?honestus puer   519–
Twelve-year-old son of **Dumilda** *h.f.*, who died in 531; it is ?531
unclear whether he is buried with her, or whether he survived. He was doubtless Catholic like his mother. From an epitaph in Rome. F-S 225.

N
———
c
!!Theudifara   d by
She was *patrona* of the freedwoman **Sisivera**, probably in Rav- 600
enna. She had died by the time Sisivera made her donation in 600. *PItal* 20.23.

N, A, †, ?D
———
l
Theudila clericus   551
Clergyman at the Gothic Arian church of St. Anastasia in Ravenna. With the other clergymen, he witnessed a deed of sale of swamplands belonging to the church. For further details, and on ?D, see **Danihel**. *PItal* 34.122.

N, J, ([D])
———
(n), s
Theudimundus (= PLRE3 Theodimundus)   540/541
Barely escaped Hildebald's assault on Treviso. A youth at the time, he was apparently already a Byzantine soldier under the command of Vitalius *MVM* per Illyricum. He was the son of **Mauricius** and the grandson of **Mundo**, as well as the brother of **Anonyma 2**; his name seems to combine the Germanic prefix "Theudi-" with the Germanic name (and suffix) of his grandfather. But note that it was also the name of Theoderic's brother (= PLRE2 Theodimundus), active in the Balkans in 479. On his grandfather's identity, see **Mundo**. Procopius, BG 3.1.36.

N
———
(n), j, c, l
Thulgilo honesta femina   539
Almost certainly a Catholic, since **Iulianus** (see below) witnessed her document: Catholics and Arians had been at each other's throats in Ravenna in 519–20; there is no reason to suspect that tensions had eased when the city was under imminent threat from the devoutly Catholic and anti-Arian emperor.
Mother of **Deutherius** and **Domnica**, she sold land to the *vir strenuus* **Pelegrinus**, recorded in a document prepared at Ravenna. The name is also spelled "Tulgilo" in the document. She and her daughter were illiterate, while her son could write (*PItal* 30. 76–83). Witnesses included people with the names Serapion,

Opilio, Petrus, Iulianus (signing in Greek) and **Latinus**, all *viri honesti* or *strenui*; see the interesting discussion by Tjäder 2: 56, pointing to the connections with the palatial administration in Ravenna, and the presence of the "well-known banker and churchbuilder" Iulianus (= PLRE3 Iulianus 7), as well as identifying **Latinus** as a Goth (but see **Latinus**). On Iulianus, see further Deichmann, *Ravenna*. From just before the Byzantine capture of Ravenna in the Gothic Wars; the document is still completely "late Roman" in formula, rather than "Byzantine" (Tjäder 2: 56). *PItal* 30.5, 21, 39, 73, 76, 79–80, 85, 89, 94, 99, 103.

N	Torisa	503

He "and others" claimed property due to Ennodius's nephew Lupicinus, apparently on behalf of Theoderic, and **T**ancila had informed Ennodius that "it is very difficult to obtain restitution of anything once it has been claimed by our lord the king." For further details see **T**ancila. Torisa is mentioned in a letter of Ennodius to Faustus Niger seeking more help in the situation. Ennodius, *Op.* 60/*ep.* 2.23.

N	!!Totila milix de numero devoto	?
1		

His epitaph survived in Rome, and is undated. The "numerus devotus" is not otherwise attested (F-S, p. 111), if it is indeed the name of the regiment. Only included because of his rare name, also that of the Ostrogothic king ***T**otila. F–S 222.

Traguila = **T**riwila

N	Transmundus ?praepositus basilicae beati Petri	523
c, ?cc, 1		

A Catholic. An inscription describes him and Pope Hormisdas as conceding burial space within St. Peter's in Rome to Pe[trus] the ?*vicarius urbis Romae* (see PLRE2 Pe. . .) and his wife Iohanna. This inscription finishes, after a break, with the words "praep(o)s(i)t(o) bas(ili)c(ae) beati Petri [apostoli]," identified by de Rossi, Fiebiger and Schmidt with the Transmundus of the previous line. But Silvagni, ICUR n.s. 2:35 points out that there is room for another name between Transmundus and the title. In any event, Transmundus must have been some kind of clerical official. ICUR n.s. 2.4184 = F-S 190 (calling him an "Ostrogoth," p. 97). (Note the apparently Catholic Amal ***T**rasimundus [= PLRE2 Thrasimundus 2] mentioned by Ennodius, *Op.* 138.)

N	!!**Trasaric** *MVM* (?at Rome) (= B, PLRE3 Trasaric 2)	?589
?c		

Probably a Catholic. **W**iliaric is described as his *nepos* in an inscription at Sta. Prassede in Rome; it does not call Trasaric "quondam," so he may still have been alive in 589, with PLRE3: 1335. PLRE3 restrains itself from commenting on his ethnic allegiance; B, p. 279, hazards "Goth or Lombard." In this connection, it is worth noting that the name is also attested as that of a king of the Gepids (PLRE2 Trasericus, a relative of **Mundo**, above), as that of a Catholic patron in Gaul (PLRE3 Trasaricus 1), and as that of an Arian bishop associated with the Illyrian Gepids at the fall of their kingdom in *c.* 567 (Joh. Biclar. s.a. ?572; on the date see PLRE3 Cunimundus). ILCV 232.

N, J, S, [?D]	Tremo Gothorum dux (= PLRE3) Expelled from the *oppidum* of Aeternum by the Byzantine general Iohannes 2 on the latter's series of attacks in northern Italy in 538, which succeeded in drawing Witigis away from the siege of Rome. Tremo surrendered and prostrated himself before Iohannes. Oddly, Procopius does not recall this episode in his recounting of Iohannes's campaign in Samnium (described in terms of elegiac praise; BG 2.10.1–11). [?D]: as **Hunila.** *Cont. Marc.* s.a. 538.	538

N, J, A, [D], ?D
—————
j, l

Triwila saio/Triggua/Triwa praepositus cubiculi/Triguilla prae- 510–
positus/?Traguila (= PLRE2 Triwila)   523/
These names all seem to refer to the same person, who thus 525;
moved up the ladder from his office of *saio*. The evidence seems ?530s
to make him an Arian associate of the Catholic deacon and
physician to the king Helpidius (= PLRE2 Helpidius 6), of Ennodius, and possibly of Athalaric, and an enemy of Boethius.

As *saio* in 510, he (called "Triwila") and the *apparitor* Ferro-
cinctus were ordered to restore property seized illegally by the
PPO Faustus Niger (referred to as "that notorious plotter"). *Var.*
3.20 (probably from 510). In 511, he already seems to have risen
in office, since Ennodius in a letter to Helpidius refers to him as
"filius vester domnus Triggua." He and Helpidius were helping
Ennodius to buy a house in Milan; Moorhead suggests that this
dovetails with the evidence for Boethius's refusal to give Ennodius some property in Milan, and Ennodius's ill will toward
Boethius, to explain the enmity between Triwila and Boethius
(on which see below); "Boethius and Romans in Ostrogothic
service," p. 612, n. 47. Ennodius, *Op.* 445/*ep.* 9.21. In 519 or
shortly afterward, as *praepositus cubiculi* the Anonymus Valesianus
describes him (calling him "Triwa") as an Arian supporting
demands by Jews or royal action against Catholics, a disturbance
probably confined to Ravenna (see Barnish, "The *Anonymus
Valesianus* II"); AV 14.82. Between 523 and 525, Boethius
described him (calling him "Triguilla praepositus") in the *Consolatio* as someone whom he had frequently stopped from harm-
ing people while Boethius was *magister officiorum*. Boethius, *Consolatio* 1, prose 4. An extremely garbled story in Gregory of
Tours, *Historiae* 3.31 (on which see PLRE2: 1127; Moorhead,
Theoderic, pp. 228–9) claims that a "Traguila" was a slave who
was the lover of Amalasuintha; if Gregory actually means that
he was a friend of Athalaric, as seems likely from the context,
then Triwila might have been associated with the group of

Goths who resented the attempts to bring up Athalaric as an
effeminate "Roman" in the late 520s and early 530s (cf. Procopius, BG 1.2.1–1.4.27). Such attitudes would fit well with the
association of Triwila, as an enemy of Boethius, with another
enemy of Boethius, Cyprianus, a "Roman" who had become
"Gothicized" (cf. *Var.* 8.21, from 527). (See further Tuluin and
Anonymi 11, 12, 13.)

?D: If the interpretation of this last story is correct, Triwila
appears to have associated with people who were proud of being
"Goths," who associated the name with a certain behavior and
culture, and who publicized the fact.

[D]: Boethius included him and Cunigastus among the avaricious *barbari* whom he opposed at court. PLRE2: 1126 concludes, "He was certainly a Goth." He fills the traditional
requirements better than most of the other people discussed
here.

Tro . . . = **V**onosus

?N   ??Tucza/Tuizia   559
————   A Catholic. The wife of Maximinus, she left him and apparently
(n), c, ?cc, l   assumed the garb of a nun at Rieti. Whether or not she had
ecclesiastical authorization to do this is unclear. The letter may
be slightly corrupt: Gassò and Batlle, p. 165 n. These authors
(ibid., p. 164 n.) assume that the name is Gothic if spelled
Tucza. But it is not in Schönfeld, and bears some resemblance
to the apparently Iranian name Tutizar. Pelagius I, JK 1021 =
ep. "Tucza [a] filio veniens" (Gassò and Batlle 63, pp. 164–6).

J   ??**Tufa** *MVM* (= PLRE2)   489–93
————   A *magister militum* of Odoacer, he fell out with him and joined
?n   the invading army of Theoderic after the battle of Verona in
489. However, he turned traitor again and rejoined Odoacer
later in the year, betraying a number of Theoderic's officers to
his old master during his siege of Faventia (Faenza). Later, he
apparently left both Theoderic and Odoacer to join the Rugian
king Fredericus, with whom he fell out in 493 and who killed
him at a battle between Trent and Verona. Years later, Theoderic claimed a property of Tufa's on the basis of proscription;
see **D**uda 1.

His shifting loyalties may say something about his identity; he
is included here because of his brief allegiance to Theoderic.
?n: Schönfeld, pp. 242–3 saw his name as Latin; Wrede, p. 121
with n. 5, thought it unclassifiable.
Ennodius, *VEpif.* 111, *Pan.* 55; *Fast. Vind. Prior* s.a. 493; *Auct.
Havn.* s.a. 493; AV 11.51–2; *Var* 4.32.

Tuizia = **T**ucza

Tulgilo = **T**hulgilo

N, J, [D]   **Tuluin** [vir nobilis], patricius praesentalis (= PLRE2)   504–27
——————   Probably a parvenu careerist (see below), he married an Amal
j, l   princess (*Var.* 9.10.3; 9.9.7), *Anonyma 2 (in *royal
prosopography). Made *patricius praesentalis* upon the accession of
Athalaric. The title is not attested between the 490s and the
death of Theoderic, and presumably Tuluin replaced Theoderic
as commander-in-chief (both *magister militum* and *patricius*) of
the armed forces in Italy, since Athalaric was still a minor, and
Tuluin was hence viceroy of the emperor and effective co-ruler
with Amalasuintha (see Ensslin, "Patricius,", pp. 246–7; Wolfram, *Intitulatio* 1:47, *Goths*, p. 335). His career is described in
two long letters announcing his appointment. He was brought
up in the palace, and served in the expedition against Sirmium
and the Bulgars in 504–5 (hence under **Pitzia**); he became one
of Theoderic's closest advisers, and served as a *dux* in the
expedition to Gaul in 508 (hence with **Betancus**, **Ibba**, **Mammo**
and perhaps **Liberius**). He went again to Gaul during the war
with the Burgundians in 523–4, winning the Burgundian part
of Provence on the far side of the Durance for the Ostrogothic
kingdom. When Athalaric appointed him *patricius praesentalis*, he
was adlected into the senate of Rome: this implies that he now
received the illustrate for the first time, although his previous
service might have suggested that he had already become *v.i.*
comes. Significantly, given the viceregal overtones of his title,
Tuluin himself may have addressed the letter to the senate
announcing his appointment: see *Var.* rubrics to Book 8 (p.
229); with Mommsen, index to Cassiodorus, p. 501, and PLRE2:
1133. A property in the *castrum Lucullanum*, formerly owned
by the patrician Agnellus, and intended by Theoderic for the
referendarius Iohannes, was given by Athalaric to Tuluin, who in
527 gave it to Iohannes: it is interesting to see all this royal
activity in Lucullanum, probably the home of the deposed
emperor Romulus Augustulus, and according to some scholars,
the heart of philobyzantine (and anti-Gothic) political activity
in Italy (further on Lucullanum, Moorhead, *Theoderic*, pp. 208–
10). But it should be pointed out that Tuluin's command of the
army at the beginning of Athalaric's reign might suggest that he
was part of the "pro-army" or "pro-Goth" party to which **Triwila** may have belonged (q.v.), and further, that he was one of
the three notable Goths belonging to that party whom Amalasuintha exiled and killed (see **Anonymi** 11, 12, 13). Wolfram,
Intitulatio 1: 47, and *Goths*, p. 336, is certain that Tuluin was
part of the Amalasuintha party, allied with Theodahad, and
that he was one of the three noblemen killed by her; Ensslin,
"Patricius," pp. 245–6, 248, is less sure.
Status and birth: PLRE2: 1131 argues that he was of noble Gothic
birth, but this statement of Cassiodorus (*Gothorum nobilissima
stirpe gloriatur, Var.* 8.10.3) is probably as a *result* of his marriage

to the Amal princess *Anonyma 2, as noted by PLRE2, since
Tuluin is described by Cassiodorus in the previous letter as
iunctus Amalo generi, nobilissima tibi facta consocia (*Var.* 8.9.7), and
since his marriage is also alluded to in the letter that mentions
his *stirps* (*Var.* 8.10). He was thus probably a careerist who ended
by marrying into the royal family and taking the highest military
office of the realm. *Var.* 8.9; 8.10; 8.11.

J	Tutizar saio (= PLRE2)	507/511

He was instructed to force **Amara** *saio* to repay extorted money
in double. The name is perhaps Iranian, or at least Asiatic
(Schroeder apud Mommsen, index to Cassiodorus, p. 501,
citing a Massagetic *doryphoros* in Procopius); similarly, Schönfeld, p. 244 (Wrede, p. 119: "Sein Name bleibt völlig dunkel,"
suggesting an Alan origin). On the name, cf. also **Tucza**
(Tuizia).
Var. 4.27.

N, J, ?S	TZALICO comes (= PLRE3 Tzalicon[ius?])	530s or
		540s
l, ?c		?557

The father of **Gudila** 4 and • • •ri, mentioned in the document
of enquiry into the state of **Gundila**'s property in Nepi in 557.
He or his sons had occupied **Gundila**'s property in some way
when Belisarius was in Italy. For further details see **Gundila** and
above, appendix 1. He was perhaps still alive in 557 (absence
of "quondam," with PLRE3: 1347 – but the fragmentary state
of the document makes this uncertain). Note that only ". . .
cone" appears in lines 15–16: this probably refers to the same
person.
J, ?S: the title of *comes* and the fact that Tzalico or his sons had
received the property as a *donativa* in the 540s suggest strongly
that he was a military officer under Totila: for further details
see **Gundila**.
?c: if he donated some of **Gundila**'s property to monasteries of
Nepi; see above, appendix 1.
PItal 49.?15–16, 22, 25.

?N	??!!TZITTA 1 comes et tribunus (= B Tzittas 2, PLRE3	568
	Tzittanus)	
(n), 1		

Set up the epitaph for his wife **Honorata** in Albingaunum
(Albenga) in the Cottian Alps. PLRE3: 1348 identifies him as "*vir
spectabilis, comes* of the *civitas* of Albingaunum and *tribunus* of the
numerus stationed there." B, p. 57, n. 34, suggests that the military tribunate gave him the effective powers of a *comes* anyway,
so that the *comitiva* here referred to involved financial responsibilities. On the name see **Tzitta** 2. The two **Tzittas** and the
Sitza discussed here cannot possibly be identified with one
another. F-S 220.
Name: PLRE3: 1048 hypothesizes a nominative "Tzittanus"
from a genitive "Tzittani," but this last need not suppose a

nominative "-us," given that **T**zitta 2 has ablative "Tzitane" (*PItal* 37.5) (though with a genitive "Tzitani": *PItal* 37.71). On the name, note also **S**itza, as well as PLRE3 Sittas 1 and 2, **T**zittas 1 and 2, and **Z**ittas.

?N: The name could be Germanic (Schönfeld, p. 244) or Thracian (Detschew, pp. 452–3, 497), but there is no reason to think it Iranian or Armenian, as B suggests, pp. 66–7, n. 10 (commenting on an Italian *magister militum* of 600 = B (T)zitta 1, PLRE3 **Z**ittas), p. 75 with n. 32 (on this **T**zitta): his reference, Haussig, "Anfänge," merely cites the Sittas *MVM* per Armeniam, for whom no evidence states that he *came* from Armenia; see PLRE3 Sittas 1). That **T**zitta 2 was in the *numerus felicum Persoarmeniarum* need say nothing about the name, since ancient ethnic labels continued to attach to regiments that had long since become cosmopolitan, as B himself notes, pp. 66, 90. It is possible that the name was associated with Easterners, since there are no examples of it in Italy recorded before this period.

?N	??!!**T**zitta 2 vir devotus, miles numeri felicum Persoarmeniarum	591
(n), c, ?l	(= B **T**zitas 3, PLRE3 **T**zitas)	

Byzantine soldier in Ravenna, "the first case recorded of a soldier marrying locally and obtaining land" there (B, p. 69, n. 13), although we cannot doubt that this occurred in Ostrogothic Italy in general (see above, ch. 6). For an example of a soldier who held land near Ravenna, see **W**itterit. His wife **R**usticiana sold a farm near Rimini to a soldier **I**ohannes with his agreement; the document was prepared in Classe at Ravenna. A Catholic (see **R**usticiana). He was illiterate (*PItal* 37.71–2).

?l: Tjäder 2: 280, n. 4, conjectures that he spoke Greek, due to the name of his regiment and the presence of a subscription in Greek by one of the witnesses, noting that this regiment is attested only in this document.

Name and ?N: see **T**zitta 1.

PItal 37.5–6, 71, 74–5, 80, 86, 92, 98.

Ufitahari = **O**ptarit presbyter

Uliaris = **V**iliarid dux

N, S, [?D]	Ulias (= PLRE3)	537
?j		

Given as a hostage to the Byzantines in December 537, to guarantee the three-month truce during the siege of Rome. Procopius does not call him a "Goth" directly, simply saying that the Goths gave the Romans "Ulias, a man of no mean station." This could imply, as Mommsen suggested, that he was identical to **W**ilia 2 *v.i.* (q.v.), but this need not be the case.

?j: Hostages were not usually soldiers – though they could be. Procopius, BG 2.7.13.

N, J, S,
?[D]
———————
s

Ulifus (= PLRE3)   552

A Byzantine who deserted to the Goths in return for promises
from Totila, he murdered his garrison commander Cyprianus,
at Perugia in 544. Years later in 552, he was still commanding
the Gothic garrison at Perugia, with **Meligedius**. Meligedius
decided to surrender Perugia to the Byzantines, but Ulifus
would not go along. Ulifus was killed in the ensuing battle
between their supporters in the city; Meligedius surrendered the
town to Narses. Procopius, BG 3.12.18–20; 4.33.10–12; also
3.23.6 (not by name).
?[D]: See **Meligedius**.

N, J, S
———————
?s

Uligasalus archon (= PLRE3)   537–8

He was in command of the Gothic armies in Dalmatia with
Asinarius. He was defeated at Scardon and retreated to Burnus,
where he was joined by **A**sinarius. They proceeded to Split,
which they besieged (see further **A**sinarius). Later, Witigis put
him in charge of the garrison at Todi, which later surrendered
to Belisarius and was sent to Sicily and Naples (Uligasalus is
not mentioned in the surrender). BG 1.16.8, 12–13, 16; 2.11.2
(surrender of Todi at 2.13.2–4).

N, J, S, (D)
———————
(l)

Ulitheus (= PLRE3 Ulitheus 1)   538

The uncle of ★**W**itigis and thus great-uncle of Uraïas, he commanded a Gothic force in Picenum. Ulitheus was killed and his
army thoroughly defeated by **I**ohannes 2 in 538. Procopius, BG
2.10.2. On the name, note the presence of another Ulitheus
among the *doryphoroi* of the Byzantine *MVM* Gontharis in Africa
(= PLRE3 Ulitheus 2).
(D) and (l): through his relationship to the king.

N, ?J
———————
?j, l

UMBISUUS vir spectabilis (= PLRE2)   507/511

Sent with Saturninus to investigate claims that the Goths of
Adria would not pay their taxes to the *curiales*. With Goffart,
Barbarians and Romans, pp. 91–3, these Goths were soldiers who
had bought landed property, but who were avoiding paying
taxes (their usual tax-free status as holders of allotments of taxation encouraged this abuse, but liabilities of taxation were purchased along with taxed property). *Var.* 1.19.
?J: PLRE2: 1182: "He was evidently a German," apparently on
the basis of his name, but note PLRE2 Saturninus 5, p. 980:
"They presumably formed a two-man commission consisting of
one Roman and one Goth, such as Theoderic often used to
examine complaints and hold enquiries affecting the two communities." This seems plausible from the evidence of names,
but the letter, unusually for this subject at this time, contains
little that could be seen as *civilitas* rhetoric, aside from one reference to the rule of law.

N   Unigildus (= B)   VI^{med}
———————
(n), c, (cc),   Father of Pope **Pelagius** II. Possibly still alive at the time of his
(l), ([d])   son's election in 579, but the LP does not use *quondam* in the
    formula indicating parentage of the popes.
    LP Pelagius II §1.

N, J   **Unigis** [vir inlustris], spatharius (= PLRE2)   510
———   In 510, after the conquest of Provence, Theoderic instructed
l   him to ensure that escaped slaves were returned to their owners.
    The chaos of war had enabled all kinds of disorders, and the
    letter uses *civilitas* rhetoric to describe the Ostrogothic conquest:
    "We delight that those whom we defend by arms should live
    by Roman law" and "What profit is there with barbarian con-
    fusion removed, if people do not live by laws?" *Spatharius*,
    "sword-bearer," was a high-ranking military post at court, with
    PLRE2: 1182, allotting Unigis the illustrate. Witigis was also a
    spatharius, under Athalaric (PLRE3: 1383); see further **Riggo**. *Var.*
    3.43.

    Unilas = **Hunila**

N, A, †,   Unimundus episcopus [of Ravenna]   512/517
[?D], ?D   The Arian bishop of Ravenna "in the twenty-fourth year of
———   the reign of king Theoderic" (which could be 518, depending
?l   whether Agnellus, who was probably using an inscription (thus
    ?l), was calculating from 489 or 493). Unimundus built the
    church of St. Eusebius outside Ravenna "non longe a campo
    Coriandri" (it is unclear whether the original dedication was
    to St. Eusebius): Agnellus 86, p. 334.20–3. Agnellus calls him
    "Uvimundus" in another location (70, p. 326.26–7), the spelling
    accepted by Lanzoni 2: 756. Either name would be possible,
    but names beginning "Uni-" are attested from Ostrogothic
    Italy, and it seems likely that a copyist succumbed to the prob-
    lem of writing a "v" ("u") for an "n" rather than the other
    way round.
    [?D]: Agnellus mentions him in the section on the time when
    Justinian "omnes Gothorum ecclesias reconciliavit, quae
    Gothorum temporibus vel regis Theuderici constructae sunt"
    (86, p. 334.18–20), thus implying that Unimundus was himself
    a Goth. But this is a ninth-century source.
    ?D: see **Danihel**.
    Agnellus 70, 86.

N, A, †, ?D   Unscila vir venerabilis antistes   507/511
    Faustus Niger, then *PPO*, was ordered by Theoderic to ensure
    that Unscila's church should retain those things that Theoderic
    had long ago ("dudum") given it; the church is referred to as
    "ecclesia nostra." Therefore, Unscila was an Arian bishop. The
    force of "noster" here is unclear: it could merely refer to Theo-
    deric's endowment of it, and his membership in its denomi-

nation, or it could refer to the palace church in Ravenna. ?D: see **Danihel**.
Var. 1.26.

J, (D) ——— n, 1

Uraïas archon (= PLRE3 Uraïas) 538–40
Nephew of ★**Witigis**; q.v. on his humble family background. His wife was **Anonyma** 4. A general of the Goths. He besieged Milan in 538 and early 539, securing Liguria. He was summoned to reinforce Osimo by Witigis, but was blocked by a Byzantine force at Dertona (on the fate of Osimo, see further **Visandus** 2). Planned to come to the aid of Witigis at besieged Ravenna in 539, but was halted by desertions in the Cottian Alps, including the Gothic commander Sisigis (q.v.). He was with Hildebad in 540 in Transpadane Italy, probably in Pavia, when Belisarius captured Ravenna. He refused the kingship because, according to Procopius, of the "bad fortune of his family" (BG 2.11.12, interpreted too literally as his own [Gothic] belief by Wolfram, *Goths*, p. 350: cf. Cameron, *Procopius*, pp. 117–19 on Procopius's literary use of *tychē*). But whether his was good or bad fortune, Uraïas's prestige and wealth among the Goths seems to have outdone that of ★**Hildebadus** even after the latter was elected king, as Hildebad found out to his detriment after having Uraïas murdered (see esp. BG 3.1.39–49, and **Velas**). *Cont. Marc.* ss.aa. 538, 540; Procopius, BG 2.12.37; 2.18.19; 2.21.1; 2.22.6; 2.23.4; 2.24.20–22; 2.26.9; 2.28.31–5; 2.30.3–16; 3.1.37–49.
Name: called "Oraio" by *Cont. Marc.* (see an unconvincing argument for a Germanic origin from this spelling in Wrede, p. 105), but Orai in the second mention in the oldest MS, corrected by a later copyist to match the first mention: Mommsen, p. 106, apparatus to line 26.
But in Procopius's form, "Uraïas" looks very much like the biblical prophet "Uriah." "Uriah" occurs as "Urias" in Jer. 26:30; Oureias and Ourias in the Septuagint. The relation of Uraïas's name to the Arian religion or the written Gothic language is unknown, since these sections of the Gothic Bible have not survived. Old Testament names are rare but not unknown at this period; in this group, note **Andreas**, **Ademunt qui et Andreas**, and **Danihel**.
(D): through his relationship to the king.

(J) ——— n, c, 1

URSINA [spectabilis femina] *c.* 500/
The wife of Ursus in Noricum. See **Ursus** for further details. 510

J ——— n, c, 1

URSUS vir spectabilis, [dux Norici] *c.* 500/
A Catholic. He and his wife Ursina donated twelve pictorial 510
mosaics to the church in Teurnia (now St. Peter im Holz, in Carinthia), capital of Noricum Mediterraneum. On his probable office of *dux*: Heuberger, "Rätien," pp. 81–2; Wolfram, "Ethnogenese," pp. 112–14; idem, *Goths*, pp. 292–3 with n. 397,

suggesting parallels with **S**ervatus, [**C**ensorius] and [**M**arcianus]. There is no reason to make Ursus a "Roman" or a native of Noricum because he was a Catholic and had a Latin name, as Wolfram does (cf. **S**ervatus), and the idea that "Ursus" and "Ursina" were more common names in Noricum than elsewhere is false (they are found in Rome and all over Gaul: see indices to ICUR n.s., Le Blant, and RICG). Missed by PLRE2.
Date: Wolfram, "Ethnogenese," p. 114; Barton, *Frühzeit des Christentums*, p. 149.
ILCV 1879; reproduction at Egger, "Ausgrabungen in Kärnten," col. 167, fig. 83.

N, J, S, [D], ?D ⎯⎯⎯⎯⎯ ?l   **Usdrilas** archon (= PLRE3)   552
Totila's commander at Rimini, in the months before the battle of Busta Gallorum. He wrote an insolent letter to Valerianus and Narses at Ravenna; he was killed in a skirmish several days later.
[D]: Procopius calls him "Gothos anēr."
?D: If his letter is real, it makes arrogant claims for "the Goths," associating himself quite clearly with them; but Procopius frequently concocted these letters as evidence, on the model of Thucydides.
?l: if the letter actually existed, it was presumably written in Latin. BG 4.28.2–11; 4.29.3.

N, ?D   **Ustrigotthus** (= PLRE3)   548/
Son of the Gepid king Elemundus, when Turisindus stopped   549–52
him from succeeding to his father's throne, he fled to the Lombards, with whom the Gepids were then at war. (Note the similarity to the career of **M**undo.) Meanwhile, Turisindus had the Lombard pretender Ildigisal at his own court. Rather than risk the exchange of dangerous hostages, each king secretly murdered his own suppliant. Procopius, BG 4.27.19–29.
His name is "Ostrogothus" or "Ostrogotha," the name of one of Theoderic's legendary ancestors, already mentioned in writing by Cassiodorus in *Var.* 11.1.19, and soon to be described by Jordanes as sixth in descent from Gapt, the Amal progenitor; *Get.* 79: he attributes a story about Ostrogotha to Ablabius at *Get.* 82, so perhaps the legendary king was already famous in a third source. Moreover, Theoderic had named one of his daughters ★**O**strogotho; she married King Sigismund of the Burgundians. (For another possible example, see under **O**tratarit.) So it is not enough to dismiss Ustrigotthus as merely "a Gepidic personal name," as does Wolfram, *Goths*, p. 508, n. 261. The name makes some statement of loyalty or ancestry, which makes perfect sense when we recall that **M**undo, son of a Gepid king, could be described as a Goth, and that the Gepids could be seen as a Gothic subgroup (Jordanes, *Get.* 94; note also **A**sbadus; cf. **V**elas). Hence ?D.

N   ‼Ustarric   VI
——————   Father of Iohannes 1, he set up the epitaph for his son in
(n), 1   Catania. F-S 234.

                    Uvimundus = Unimundus

N, J, S   Vacimus archon (= PLRE3)   538
                    Commander of Gothic forces under Witigis, who sent him
                    against the forces of Conon at Ancona, first picking up the gar-
                    rison from nearby Osimo on the way. A bloody battle ensued.
                    On the Osimo battle, which possibly affected Vacimus, see
                    Visandus 2 – either commander could have perished or left
                    before the siege of Osimo in 539. Procopius, BG 2.13.5–15.

N, J, S, ?D   Vacis archon (= PLRE3)   537
——————   Commander of Gothic forces under Witigis, who sent him to
1   plead with the urban population of the city of Rome not to
                    desert the Goths, at the beginning of the siege of Rome. His
                    words drew no response. He was a "man of no mean station,"
                    but probaby not identical to the civilian Wacca (q.v.), contra
                    PLRE3: 1350.
                    ?D: if he actually spoke as Procopius implies; cf. Usdrilas.
                    Procopius, BG 1.18.39–41.

N, J, S, [D]   Valaris   541
                    A soldier under Totila, he challenged all the Romans at Faenza
                    to do single combat with him; slain by the Byzantine
                    (Armenian) soldier Artabazes. [D]: Procopius calls him "Gothos
                    anēr." Procopius, BG 3.4.21–8.

J   **Iulius Felix Valentinianus**, vir clarissimus ct [?inlustris], ex   452–519
——————   silentiario sacri palatii, ex comite consistorii, comes dom-
n, j, ?c, 1   esticorum (= PLRE2 Valentinianus 3)
                    He died in Rome at the age of 67 in 519. As PLRE2: 1138 points
                    out, he was only 24 at the accession of Odoacer, under whom
                    his first offices must thus have fallen. He was 41 when Theo-
                    deric took Ravenna, and continued to hold office (he was *comes
                    domesticorum* when he died). The office of *silentiarius* was military
                    (see Romulus), and although *comes domesticorum* was frequently
                    given as a *vacans* title to raise the holder to the illustrate (see
                    Var. 6.11; so here PLRE3: 1138), it may also have continued as
                    a real office alongside: see the discussion under Mundilo. A real
                    military post would make sense here, given Valentinianus's early
                    office among the palace *silentiarii*. Moreover, the inscription
                    does not actually say *inlustris*; F-S 187–8 emend "spectabilis."
                    His three names suggest high birth, but not necessarily the sena-
                    torial aristocracy; more likely the provincial elites who climbed
                    to success via the bureaucratic or military *cursus* (like Cyprianus
                    and Opilio, as well as Cassiodorus).
                    F-S 187–8.

Vandalarius = **V**isandus 1

N, J	!!VEILA comes (= PLRE2)	511

Killed at Barcelona in 511; PLRE2: 1152 conjectures that he was a Visigoth who opposed Gesalicus, the pretender to the Visigothic throne. But he could just as easily have been an official or a soldier of Theoderic, who now controlled Barcelona. *Chron. Caesaraug.* s.a. 511.

N, J, S, [?D]	Velas	540

A soldier under Hildebad, whom he killed, perhaps partially in revenge for the death of Uraïas, but also due to a personal slight. The incident shows some similarities to the death of ★Theodahadus (see **O**ptaris).
[?D]: Procopus calls him "one among the Goths" but "a Gepid by birth."
Procopius, BG 3.1.43–8.

N, J	Vera saio (= PLRE2)	523
—————— 1		

He was instructed to organize the transport of Gepid soldiers through the Veneto and Liguria to Gaul; 3 solidi were to be given to each *condama* so that they may buy, rather than plunder, supplies. *Var.* 5.10. On this letter, and the following one (*Var.* 5.11, to the Gepids themselves), see Goffart, "Three notes," pp. 178–9.

?A, ?†, ?D	??Victorinus vir venerabilis episcopus	526
—————— n, ?c, ?cc, l		

This bishop may have been an Arian. He received a letter from Athalaric containing earnest requests that Victorinus pray for him. They are not similar to the moralizing injunctions addressed to the Catholic clergy of Rome (*Var.* 8.24) or to Pope John II (*Var.* 9.15). This letter assumes such a personal tone that it almost sounds as if Victorinus is assumed to be of the same beliefs as the purported author of the letter (Athalaric, written for him by Cassiodorus, but doubtless under instruction from Amalasuintha and other advisors). On the other hand, it urges him to announce Athalaric's accession to the *provinciales* (probably in Gaul), which might suggest that he was Catholic, and it falls within the series of largely conciliatory letters to all constituencies in the kingdom issued by Athalaric's government shortly after his accession (on the others, see above, ch. 2). Since it follows the letter to the *provinciales* (of Gaul), and since this letter contains a reference to *provinciales*, it seems likely that Victorinus was based in Gaul; Provence and the Narbonnais, which had been largely in Visigothic and Ostrogothic hands since the 470s, must have contained many Arian clergymen. Nevertheless, the case remains open.
?D: if Arian; see **D**anihel. *Var.* 8.8.

Viliaric = **W**iliarit 4

N, J, S, ?A, Viliarid dux/Uliaris archon/Vuliarid comes (= PLRE3 Uliaris 2)   533/
[D]   One of the three "most warlike of the Goths" enumerated by   534–542
────────   Procopius, with **R**uderit and **B**leda. He was sent with them
1   against the Byzantine forces in Florence in 542, and won; see
              further **B**leda. Also mentioned in a group with the two other
              commanders by Gregory the Great (calling him "comes" and
              "Vuliarid"), as Totila's most loyal supporters; see further **R**iggo.
              Earlier, in 533/534, he had been the commander of Naples,
              when he received ten Huns who had deserted from the army
              in Libya (**A**nonymi 23–32). PLRE3: 1388 suggests that he was
              comes Neapolitanae civitatis at the time.
              ?A: see **R**iggo.
              Procopius, BG 1.3.15; 3.5.1; Marc. Com. s.a. 542, Gregory the
              Great, *Dialogi* 2.14. Very possibly identical to **W**iliarit 1 or **W**ili-
              arius, or both. Note that a *doryphoros* of Belisarius had the same
              name (= PLRE3 Uliaris 1).

N, J, S,   Visandus 1 Vandalarius (= PLRE3 Visandus 2)   537
[?D]   Nearly killed by Belisarius's forces during a sortie from Rome
              when it was under siege by Witigis. He was left for dead for
              three days, but survived and lived for a long time, famed among
              the Goths for his valour. Procopius, BG 1.18.29–33.
              [D]: Procopius calls him one "among the Goths;" on this
              phrase, see **V**elas. Note that the name Vandalarius belonged to
              Theoderic's grandfather, *Get.* 80, 251–2 On the possible over-
              tones of the use of such a name, see **U**strigotthus, but note that
              there is no proof that Vandalarius had received the same fame
              yet, since the *Getica* would not be published until 551. Wolfram
              interprets the name of Theoderic's grandfather as "conqueror
              of the Vandals," *Goths*, pp. 252, 305, 308 – "a byname . . .
              created by posterity"; for a different interpretation see Wrede,
              pp. 101–2. Visandus Vandalarius might have been identical to
              Visandus 2, but Procopius gives no such indication; similarly
              PLRE3: 1379 (nevertheless listing the two under the same entry).
              Name, cf. **W**andil.

N, J, S   Visandus 2 archon (= PLRE3 Visandus 2)   538–?53
────────   Commander of Gothic forces under Witigis. He was put in
?s   charge of the garrison of Osimo in Picenum in March 538. BG
              2.11.2.
              After a long and protracted siege in 539, the Osimo garrison
              would eventually surrender to Belisarius (BG 2.23–4; 2.26–7),
              becoming Roman subjects and mingling with the emperor's
              army (2.27.32–4). It is unclear whether Visandus was still among
              them. PLRE3: 1379 observes that **V**acimus had arrived with
              reinforcements later in 538 (BG 2.13.5), but neither commander
              is mentioned by name in the account of the siege. Probably not
              identical to **V**isandus 1 (q.v.).

(N), [D]   !!**Fl. Vitalianus** 1 vir magnificus et gloriosissimus, *MVM* per   503–20;
───────   Thracias 514–515, *MVM* praesentalis 518–520, cos.   520 (= d 520
n, c, 1   PLRE2 Vitalianus 2)
The dates represent the time from when he first attested (as a
young soldier) to his death. For his career, see PLRE2: 1171–6.
On the extreme confusions about his identity, see above, ch. 4.
It is Zacharias, HE 7.13, 8.2 ("Gothus vir") who calls him a
"Goth;" Marcellinus comes ss.aa. 514, 519 calls him "Scytha,"
a word that could mean "Goth," but usually means "Hun" for
Marcellinus. He was born either in lower Moesia or Thrace
(Joh. Ant. fr. 214e.1 [Zaldaba in Lower Moesia]; Joh. Malal.
402; Evagrius, HE 3.43). See the parallel confusions about the
identity and birth of **M**undo, another soldier active in the
Balkans near the same time.
(N): The son of Patriciolus; his children were called Cutzes,
Buzes and Venilus (the last name Germanic); uncle of **I**ohannes
2, and related to the Byzantine *comes* Stephanus (= PLRE2
Stephanus 22), and the "Scythian monk" Leontius. Schwartz,
Publizistische Sammlungen, accepted the statement of Zacharias at
face value, and made Vitalianus "ein reichsuntertäniger Gothe"
(p. 249 with n. 2), going so far as to translate "in partibus
Scythiae" in Anastasius's first letter to Hormisdas as "in der
Gothenprovinz" (p. 250), and implying a convergence of
interests among Theoderic, Vitalianus and the "skythischen,
d.h. gothischen Mönche" (pp. 261–2; cf. 249–51); similarly,
Wolfram, *Goths*, p. 328, describing the agreement between
Theoderic and his "former fellow-tribesman" Vitalianus. Too
many assumptions are being made here: see above, ch. 4.

A, †, ?D   Vitalianus 2 presbyter   551
───────   Priest at the Gothic Arian church of St. Anastasia in Ravenna,
n, 1   he joined other clergy in witnessing a document of sale of land
(see further **D**anihel). Vitalianus was one of two priests affiliated
with the church; the other was **O**ptarit. He did not sign in his
own hand due to failing eyesight.
?D: see **D**anihel. *PItal* 34.82, 94.

Vitterit = **W**itterit

(N)   Vonosus   VI^in
───────   From the Catholic cemetery of Manastirine in Salona (Split).
n, c, 1   He was the father of **A**river. His name may be "Tro. . . Vonosus" (i.e. "Bonosus"). Further on this inscription and the cemetery, see **A**river. Tjäder 1: 509 s.n. wrongly thinks that this is
a Germanic name (commenting on a Bonosa). F-S, 2F 12.

Vuliarid = **V**iliarid

N, S   Wacca maior domus (= PLRE3 Wacces)   534/535
───────   He was *maior domus* (?*palatii*) under Theodahad. Appointed to
j, 1   ensure that additional expense for the war against Justinian

would be fairly shared out. He is mentioned in a letter to the senate that revives *civilitas* rhetoric (on this letter, see above, ch. 2). Despite Wacca's military connection, he is clearly not a warrior: warriors should respect him because he helps them avoid death and obtain the necessary weapons. Therefore Mommsen's suggestion that he was identical to the general **V**acis (Mommsen, index to Cassiodorus, p. 501) is unconvincing – although **V**acis's alleged rhetoric at BG 1.18.40–41 strongly resembles that of Cassiodorus in the letter to the senate that mentions Wacca. PLRE3:1 397 suggests that they were possibly identical, but preserves their separate listings, which seems wise. *Var.* 10.18.

N ——— 1	Waduulfus vir devotus (= PLRE3)	?542

He and his wife **R**iccifrida sued a shipbuilder named Leo for a payment outstanding on a sale of land; a document witnessed by **A**rdica, **G**hiveric and others records the settlement. Apparently illiterate (see **R**iccifrida). *PItal* 43.5, 10, 15–16, 23, 29, 36, 43.

N, J, [D] ——— 1	Wandil (= PLRE2)	510

He was ordered to keep the peace in recently conquered Avignon. The phrase "qua resides" need not imply that he was an "Ostrogoth who had settled there" (so PLRE2: 1149) rather than a commander who had arrived recently; Krautschick's redating of the letter from 508 to 510 further weakens this notion of PLRE (*Cassiodor*, pp. 66 with n. 1, 75). He could be a *comes Gothorum*, i.e. a military *comes civitatis*, as PLRE2: 1149 suggests (so also Schmidt, "Die comites Gothorum," p. 130), but given the absence of the word *comes*, he could just as easily be another military officer. The letter does contain *civilitas* rhetoric: "Vivat noster exercitus civiliter cum Romanis." The association of Wandil with the army suggests J; the opposition of the army to the *Romani* suggests [D]. On the name, note the comments of Wolfram, *Goths*, p. 508, n. 261 (not entirely convincing here), and **V**isandus 1 Vandalarius. *Var.* 3.38.

N, J, ?S, [?D] ——— ?s	Widin "comes Gothorum" (= PLRE3)	?552 ?556 ?561

Possibly the last attested member of the Gothic army in Italy, but the source is late and the information difficult to decipher. According to Paul the Deacon, Widin *comes Gothorum* and a Frank called Amingus rebelled against Narses after the conquest of Italy. Widin was captured and sent to Constantinople; Amingus was put to the sword. PLRE3: 1403 dates this event to 561 on the evidence of Menand. *Prot.* fr. 3.1. But although both Menander and Paul clearly place the incident in northern Italy, near Verona, the apparent date in Menander may refer to another incident, and Mar. Avent. lists 556 as the date of the expulsion of the Franks from Italy; it is even possible that it was part of Narses's attempt to recapture Verona as early as 552,

when the Franks were involved in northern Italy (see Capo in
Paul. Diac., HL, p. 425, n. to lines 8–12). Paul's mention of the
Frankish commander Leutharis directly after the Widin story
might date it to before 554 (see PLRE3 Leutharis). The question
thus remains open whether Widin was a commander left independent after the defeat of the armies of Totila, of Teia, or of
Aligernus, or whether he joined the Byzantine forces (perhaps
with his following, hence *comes Gothorum* here, against which
see Capo, ibid.) and subsequently decided to join the Franks
against the Byzantines, as Paul's account suggests. PLRE3: 924
connects the event with "the reconquest of northern Italy from
the Goths and the Franks," which is certainly possible. Either
way, both the date and his identification as a leader of Goths
in northern Italy, suggest that he was in origin an Italian Goth,
not a Byzantine import. But one would like to know Paul's
source for the name: on the literary construction of this section
of HL, see Goffart, *Narrators*, pp. 388–90.
[?D]: as **H**unila.
Paul. Diac., HL 2.2.

N, ?J	Wilia 1 (= PLRE2)	507/511

N, ?J
———
?j, l

Wilia 1 (= PLRE2)   507/511
Theoderic instructed him and Domitianus to investigate claims
that "barbarians" had seized Roman estates ("praedia"), and to
restore those seized after Theoderic crossed the river Isonzo
(489). On the "pittacium delegatoris" and "praedia" of this
letter, see Goffart, *Barbarians and Romans*, p. 90, n. 63 (irrelevant
to allotments: these are actual estates, purchased with money).
The linguistic origins of their names perhaps suggest that he and
Domitianus were perhaps part of a one-Goth/one-Roman team
sent to look into sensitive matters (cf. **U**mbisuus). PLRE2: 1166–
7 suggests that he may have been identical to **W**ilia 2, which is
certainly possible. *Var.* 1.18.

N
———
j, l

Wilia 2 vir inlustris, comes patrimoniae (= PLRE2)   526
Shortly before Theoderic's death, the king ordered him to oversee collection of wood for shipbuilding for the fleet against the
Vandals (reiterated in the letter to **A**liulfus saio), and transport
of naval recruits (similarly to **G**udinandus saio). Later in 526,
after the accession of Athalaric, he brought the excesses of the
domestici to the attention of the new government, and was
instructed to correct the situation. He could have been identical
to **W**ilia 1 (PLRE2: 1167) or to **U**lias (Mommsen, index to
Cassiodorus, p. 501 [apparently mis-citing the reference to
Procopius, which ought to read "2.7.13"]). *Var.* 5.18; 5.19;
5.20; 9.13.

N
———
c, l

!!Wiliaric (= PLRE3)   d 589
A Catholic. *Nepos* of **T**rasaric *MVM*, buried in Rome in the
church of Sta. Prassede. ILCV 232.

Wiliarit *see also* **G**uiliarit, **V**ilarid, **W**iliaric, **W**iliarius

N, J, [D]   Wilarit 1 (= PLRE2)   507/511
—————   Nephew (*nepos*) of **B**oio *v.s.* Theoderic ordered his uncle to
(l)   restore his inheritance to Wiliarit, since he was of age to fight
in the army, referring to "iuvenes nostri" (on which see **T**ata,
and cf. **A**nonymi 20+). The king continues: "valor makes the
age of maturity for Goths," hence [D] (using *civilitas* ideology).
Var. 1.38.

Mommsen, index to Cassiodorus, p. 501, and PLRE2: 1167 both
suggest that he was identical to **V**iliarid, which is certainly possible. This might suggest that he was also identical to **W**iliarius,
having a career beginning as a young soldier in the 500s, becoming a military *v.i. comes* by 526, and one of the most famous
commanders of the Goths in the 540s during the Gothic Wars.

N   Wiliarit 2 eunuchus (= PLRE2)   *c.* 477–
—————   The dates indicate his lifespan. He was buried at Rome in early   532
j, ?c, l   532. PLRE2: 1167 suggests that he was palatine eunuch, presum-
ably at the imperial palaces at Rome, which were still kept up.
His epitaph was once at San Martino ai Monti (de Rossi at ICUR
I, no. 1028); if it were originally there, he was Catholic, like
Seda. ILCV 356.

N, A, †, ?D   Wiliarit 3 clericus   551
—————   Clergyman at the Gothic Arian church of St. Anastasia in Rav-
l   enna, he along with other clergy witnessed a deed of sale of land
(on which see **D**anihel). Like **V**italianus 2, he made a *signum* and
had someone else write out a subscription, due to the weakness
of his eyes.
?D: see **D**anihel. *PItal* 34.83, 106.

N, A, †,   Wiliarit 4 spodeus/Wiljarith bokareis/?Viliaric magister anti-   551
G, ?D   quarius
—————   Scribe or bookseller at the Gothic Arian church of St. Anastasia
l   in Ravenna, he, along with the clergy of that church, witnessed
a deed of sale of land (on the document, see **D**anihel). He was
a *spodeus* or (in Gothic) a *bokareis*, a bookseller or scribe. Since
his signature followed those of the lowly *ostiarii*, he was probably
not a member of the clergy, but was associated with the church
as a lay brother (Tjäder 2: 95), like **A**malatheus. Wiliarit subscribed in Gothic, using a formula for all intents and purposes
identical to that of **O**ptarit (q.v.), **M**irica and **S**uniefridus. He
may have been the "magister Viliaric antiquarius" who produced the manuscript of Orosius preserved in the Bibliotheca
Laurenziana in Florence, as well as the *Codex Brixianus*, *Codex
Vindobonensis* 847, and a sumptuous edition of the Gothic Bible,
written in silver letters on purple parchment, now surviving as
the *Codex Argenteus* in the University Library of Uppsala: see
Tjäder 2: 96 with n. 44, and idem, "Der Codex argenteus in

Uppsala and der Buchmeister Viliaric in Ravenna," pp. 144–64.
?D: see **Danihel**. *PItal* 34.85, 136–9.

N, J   **Wiliarius** vir inlustris, comes (= PLRE2)   526
With Theoderic's army in an unknown location, shortly before
the king's death in 526, during the preparations for war against
the Vandals. Theoderic instructed Abundantius *PPO* to provide
supplies and ships so that reinforcements could reach him. Possibly identical to **Viliarid** or **Wiliarit** 1 (q.v.). *Var.* 5.23.

N   Wilifara (= B)   *c.* 517–
————   The dates indicate her lifespan. Her epitaph was preserved at   57
1   Civitavecchia. B, p. 281, calls her "Goth," presumably on the
basis of her name.
F–S 231.

N, J   Wiligis saio (= PLRE2)   509
————   He was ordered to bring supplies from Ravenna to Liguria,
1   where the court was based during the war in Gaul, perhaps at
Pavia. *Var.* 2.20.

N, ?D   !!*WILILIWA* clarissima femina (= B Wiliwa)   613/641
————   In her Catholic donation she may call herself *Guta*, "Goth,"
c, 1   which would be unique among papyri and inscriptions of the
period. Of course, this papyrus is much later than any of the
others discussed here. On the other hand, Tjäder is completing
from a "g" followed by two nearly illegible characters that could
be a "u" and a "t." *PItal* 28.B5; Tjäder 1: 478, n. 3 ("die Lesung
ist nicht völlig sicher"); cf. Tjäder 3, plate 97, line 5, at right.
PItal 28.B5, 7 (spelled "Wililileva").

N, J   WILITANCUS dux (= PLRE2)   523/
————   He was ordered to conduct the trial of **Brandila** and **Procula** for   524/526
1   adultery, presumably a military court, since he held the office of
dux (a military setting is also suggested by the fact that the cuck-
olded **Patza**, husband of **Procula**, was a soldier). *Var.* 5.23.

    Willienant = **Minnulus**

N, J, ?S   WISIBADUS comes (= PLRE3)   535/536
————   Presumably *comes civitatis Ticinensis* (with PLRE3: 1407), he had
j, 1   long defended Pavia in times of war, and Theodahad now
offered him a peacetime position there – ironically enough,
right at the outset of the Gothic Wars. Wisibadus wanted to
delay taking up the post in order to get treatment for his gout.
He is not subsequently mentioned in Procopius. Described as
being of noble family. PLRE2: 1407 calls him "a Goth," presumably on the basis of his name and military position. *Var.* 10.29.

N   WITIGISCLUS vir spectabilis, censitor Siciliae provinciae (=   526
————   PLRE2)
j, 1   Athalaric's new government ordered him and the identically

titled Victor (= PLRE2 Victor 10) not to collect any excessive taxes in the fourth indiction and to repay an excess immediately. They were criticized for their slowness in coming to court when summoned first by Theoderic, and then by Athalaric. The latter also informed **Gildila** *comes Syracusanae civitatis* about the orders issued to the two. *Var.* 9.11; 9.12.

N, J, S   **Witterit** vir devotus, scutarius dromonariorum (= PLRE3)   538–9
Owned an estate ("fundus Salecto") in Faventia adjoining another estate, whose sale is recorded in a document witnessed at Ravenna in 539. He was presumably a soldier under Witigis, judging by his profession and the date. "Doubtless an Ostrogoth," concludes PLRE3: 1408. PLRE3 does not notice Tjäder's suggestion (2: 42, and 43 with n. f) that he was the same as a Vitterit recorded as owning a farm ("fundus Villa magna") adjoining that of **Gudilibus**: the references to *scutarii* and *dromonarii* in both cases, and the close dates, make the case convincing. On *dromonarii*, see **Andreas**; note also **Secundus**.
PItal 30.14; *PDip* 118 = *PItal* †8.4.

Zeia = **Teia**

Fragmentary names and anonymi (not including royal *anonymi*)

Not all *anonymi* are included. Multiple *anonymi* included for illustration

N, A,†, ?D   ●●●la, defensor   551
———   Clergyman of the Gothic Arian church of St. Anastasia in Rav-
l   enna, he witnessed the sale of lands to the *defensor* **Petrus** (on the document, see **Danihel**). It is strange, if it really is a name, as Tjäder 2: 274, n. 42 argues, contra Marini, that it is not announced with the rest at lines 82–5; see also Tjäder 2: 95. ?D: see **Danihel**. *PItal* 34.112.

?N,   (N),   ●●●ri
?J, ?S   Son of **Tzalico** comes, brother of **Gudila** 4. He and his brother   530s
———   seized the property of **Gundila**. He might have come from   540s
l   Nepi.   ?557
?J, ?S: see **Tzalico** and **Gundila** on the military position of his father, which he may well have inherited. *PItal* 49.25–6 (from 557).

    ●●●ta = <Fravi>ta

N   !!Sesi. . . cubicularius (= PLRE2)   V^{ex}–VI^{in}
———   A *cubicularius*, presumably in the palace, under one of the late
j, l   emperors or Odoacer or Theoderic. His epitaph was left at Aquileia. *Not. Scav.* (1928), p. 293, no. 13. On the name, note **Sisifridus**, **Sisigis**, **Sisivera**.

Tro. . . = **Vonosus**

?A, ?†, ?G,   ??Anonymus 1   539
?D   Scribe of a contract of sale. From his orthography, Tjäder 2: 57
—————   thinks it "very probable" that he was a Goth (i.e., someone
1   whose natural language of writing was Gothic). This would
likely make him a Gothic Arian clergyman: see **A**lamud, **G**udilibus and **O**ptarit, above, with references to other writers of
Gothic. But see also **L**atinus: although the contract includes two
people with Germanic names, and mentions three soldiers
(**T**hulgilo, **W**itterit, **A**ndreas, **S**ecundus), it is subscribed by the
banker Julianus Argentarius, the great builder of Catholic
churches in Ravenna. It is unlikely that his associates would
employ an Arian cleric as a scribe. Perhaps Anonymus 1 had
converted to Catholicism, as **G**undila did at about this time: he
would not retain a clerical position in his new faith, and would
have to find work elsewhere; since Arian clergy knew Latin as
well as (or even instead of) Gothic (see **D**anihel), this would be
an obvious choice of employment. In 539, of course, the Byzantine armies were at the gates of Ravenna, and Justinian's
religious policy was well known. But in any case, Tjäder's argument for Gothic orthography is not incontrovertible (*ae* for *e* is
common in sixth-century Latin).
?D: if Arian; see **D**anihel.
PItal 30.

A, †,   ?D,   Anonymus 2 episcopus Guthorum [Romae]   ?
[D]   He and Pope Vigilius ensured that **G**undila should receive his 540s
—————   property back after converting to Catholicism. On the problems
1   of this interpretation of a very fragmentary document, see
Gundila.
?D: see **D**anihel. *PItal* 49.20.

S, [?D]   **Anonymus 3** (= PLRE3 Anonymus 68)   537
—————   "A Roman of note among the Goths." Among the Gothic
[d], 1   envoys sent during Witigis's siege of Rome. These envoys are
otherwise referred to as "the Goths" or "the barbarians." A rare
example of Procopius admitting that being on the Gothic side
did not necessarily make one a Goth, and nonetheless included
here because of his usual practice. This man spoke to defend
Theoderic's rule and constitutional position in Italy. He might
have been a senator or a high bureaucrat: cf. **S**pinus. But PLRE3:
1439 translates "Rhōmaios anēr en Gothois dokimos" as "a
Roman, highly regarded among the Goths," thus making no
comment on his rank. The issue is whether to punctuate the
sentence so that "among the Goths" modifies the previous "a
Roman" or the subsequent adjective "esteemed," "notable."
Either interpretation is possible.
Procopius, BG 2.6.3–36.

J, S, [D]   Anonymus 4   552
Gothic youth who called **A**sbadus a dog for trying to smite his

own master (i.e. Totila), thus identifying the king to his killer. Procopius, BG 4.32.24.

(N)
———
(n), 1

!!Anonymus 5 598
Son of **Theodora**, married **Anonyma** 1, the daughter of **Aligernus**. GR 9.36.

J, S, [D]

Anonymus 6 539
Gothic soldier under **Witigis**. He was captured by the Byzantines during the siege of Osimo, and betrayed the traitor **Burcentius** to them. Procopius, 2.26.23–5.

A, †, ?D
———
1

Anonymi 7+ *c.* 494/
"Quidam clerici legis alienae" who delivered letters for Avitus 518 of Vienne from Helpidius, a Catholic deacon and physician to Theoderic. They must have been Arians; Avitus was shocked that Helpidius would use them as messengers. They may have been travelling to contact their fellow Arian clergymen in the Burgundian kingdom. Moorhead, *Theoderic*, pp. 167–8, comments that Helpidius found Arians no more "unclean" than Ennodius did.
?D: see **Danihel**. Avitus, *ep.* 38, line 8.

[D]
———
1

Anonymi 8, 9, 10 520s
"Three old men of the Goths," chosen by ★**Amalasuintha** to 530s instruct the young Athalaric, apparently in a classical education. The only men called "Goths" by Procopius who were apparently not soldiers. Procopius, BG 1.2.7.

[D], ?J

Anonymi 11, 12, 13 520s
"Three most notable Goths," seen by Amalasuintha as plotting 530s against her, and sent separately to far corners of Italy. From Procopius's context, they seem to be part of the group of Goths who opposed Athalaric's "Romanizing" upbringing, and wanted to see him trained in arms. Later, Amalasuintha killed them. Subsequently, she became afraid of retribution from their relatives, whom she had thus offended. These relatives later supported Thodahad against Amalasuintha after their marriage, enabling him to do away with her.
?J: if associated with the military, as seems likely. They might have included **Triwila** and **Tuluin** (qq.vv.), among others, but it is impossible to ascertain their identities (Wolfram, *Goths*, p. 336, definitely places Tuluin among them; see further references at **Tuluin**). It is suspicious that two groups of three Goths appear so rapidly in succession, in a section of Procopius that seems rather artificial and symmetrical (cf. **Anonymi** 8, 9, 10). Procopius, BG 1.2.10–17, 21–2, 25–6; 1.3.11; 1.4.13.

?S, A, †,
?D, [?D]

Anonymi 14+ 543
Arian clergymen in Rome (*tōn Areianōn tous hiereas*), expelled from the city in 543 by **Iohannes** 2, under suspicion of secretly helping ★**Totila**.

?S, [?D]: If they were actually helping ★Totila, then they favored the Gothic side during the Wars, making them Goths under Justinianic ideology.

?D: see **D**anihel. Procopius, BG 3.9.21.

J, S, [?D]	Anonymi 15+	537
s	Twenty-two Byzantine cavalry soldiers under the command of Innocentius who deserted to Witigis just before the siege of Rome. They were "barbarians by birth [genos] but soldiers of the Romans," according to Procopius, BG 1.17.17.	

[?D]: It is unclear whether Procopius intended to indicate by this comment that they deserted because they believed they shared a common cause with the Goths.

J, S	Anonymus 16	545/546
s	A Byzantine soldier under Innocentius during Totila's siege of Rome, he deserted to the Goths and revealed that they would be attacked from Portus. Procopius, BG 3.15.7.	

J, S, G	Anonymus 17	537/538
l	Gothic soldier under Witigis during his siege of Rome. Trapped in a pit with a Byzantine soldier, the two found that they got along together quite amicably, and pledged to one another that they would ensure that each would protect the other. When they were discovered by other Gothic soldiers, the Goth shouted up to them "in his native tongue" (de tē patriō glossē), tricking them into pulling both of them out. But it is very difficult to believe that mere knowledge of Gothic would convince the soldiers that he was "one of them," since various Gothic soldiers had deserted to the Byzantines, and since some Byzantines and Italians certainly knew Gothic in any case (**B**essas, **C**yprianus). It looks like a set-piece designed to deliver the lesson that the two sides could easily submerge their differences. See further ch. 6, above. Procopius, BG 2.1.11–20.	

J, S	Anonymus 18 spatharius	544/546
l	A *spatharius* of Totila. Bishop Cassius of Narnia drove demons out of him. This need not indicate that he was a Catholic. Gregory the Great, *Dial.* 3.6. Presumably not identical to **R**iggo, whom Gregory mentions by name elsewhere (q.v.). Date: PLRE3: 1087.	

J, S, ?A	Anonymus 19 comes (= PLRE Anonymus 70)	548–9
l	Commander of the Gothic troops who captured Perugia under Totila. He wrote to the king asking him what to do with bishop Herculanus and the population of the city. Totila told him to cut a long strip of skin off the bishop's back and then to kill him, and to put the population to the sword. The story, which describes a martyrdom and a miracle, and uses Gregory's perpetually naive caricature of Totila, may nonetheless contain an	

element of truth (cf. ★Totila for some of his documented cruel-
ties; Lanzoni 2: 445 on the king's long afterlife as the Italian
hagiographical stock evil ruler, interpreting this development,
however, as building on works of Gregory, who knew
eyewitnesses). Note also the story of **R**iggo. Date: PLRE3: 1439.
?A: the text presumably imagines that the Gothic leader was an
Arian, like his master, and was thus able to commit such wick-
edness against a Catholic bishop. It occurs in the book of the
Dialogi with the greatest number of stories about Arians.
Gregory the Great, *Dialogi* 3.13.

J, G	Anonymi 20–20a+	*c.* 510/
———————	Called "Romans" by Athalaric: see below.	512–527
(n), ?c, (c),	The sons of **C**yprianus, thus nephews of **O**pilio; there were at	
l, [d]	least two of them. They were mentioned in Athalaric's letters	

to Cyprian and to the senate in 527, when they were "in ipso
aetatis primordio adulescentiam transierunt," hence 14 or 15
years old (*Var.* 8.22.5). There were presumably only two or
three of them if they were all reaching manhood at the same
time.

J, G: Like their father, they were brought up to be soldiers, and
had been raised at the royal court. They also learned to speak
the Gothic language, as their father did: "Pueri stirpis Romanae
nostra lingua loquuntur" (*Var.* 8.21.7). See above, ch. 7 on the
association of the Gothic language with the army. On the military training of "iuvenes nostri," Gothic youths, note the archers in training under **T**ata, and Theoderic's letter regarding the
maturity of **W**iliarit 1: "Gothis aetatem legitimam virtus facit"
(*Var.* 1.38.2).

Given their upbringing, it is even possible that Cyprianus gave
the boys Germanic names.

?c, (c): They were presumably Catholic, like their uncle **O**pilio.
Var. 8.21.6–7; 8.22.5.

[D]	Anonymus 21	540s
———————	Gregory the Great tells a story of a monk attached to St. Bene-	
c, cc, l	dict, referred to as a Goth "poor in spirit, who had given up	

the world." The monk benefited from a miracle after he broke
a tool while working in the garden for the saint. Gregory the
Great, *Dial.* 2.6.

J	Anonymus 22 saio	507/511

Theoderic assigned an unnamed *saio* to Ecdicius *v.h.* for his
defensio when the latter received permission to collect a portion
of the *siliquaticum* (a tax). *Var.* 2.4.

J	Anonymi 23–32	533/534

Ten Hunnic soldiers who deserted from the Byzantine army in
Libya and escaped across the Mediterranean to Campania,
where they were welcomed by **V**iliarid in Naples, with the

blessing of ★**Amalasuintha**. On the date, see PLRE2: 1388 (s.n. Uliaris 2). Procopius, BG 1.3.15.

A, †, ?D	Anonymus 33 diaconus	493/526

A Catholic deacon under Theoderic, he apostatized to Arianism
c, ?cc, l   in order to obtain the approval of the king. But the king assailed
him, saying "if the guardians of the faith are not morally sound,
how can they act as guardians to men?" Story related by Theodore Lector; he was probably contemporary, but writing in the
East (and here and at 130.22 seems to have thought that Theoderic was a king in Africa). Moorhead, *Theoderic*, p. 93 states
that Theoderic killed the deacon; the Greek does not support
this interpretation ("apekephallomai" – "to attack"). ?D: see
Danihel. Theodore Lector, *Eccl. Hist.* 131.16–20.

J, S, [D]	Anonymi 34+	536/537

"All the Goths settled in Dalmatia and Liburnia," who joined
s   the forces of the Byzantine commander Constantianus after his
defeat of **G**ripas in 536/537 at Split. Procopius, BG 1.7.36 (trans.
Dewing 3: 69).

J, S	Anonymi 35+	546

Romans and Moors who deserted to the Gothic side in 546,
s, [d]   joining the command of Rhecimundus, at Bruttium. Procopius,
BG 3.18.26–8.

J	??Anonymus 36 ?saio	507/511

Theoderic ordered a certain Felix v.c. to restore property to his
defrauded relatives via *miles noster*, Traube, index to Cassiodorus
s.v. *miles*, p. 559, suggests that this man was a *saio*. *Var.* 1.7.

J, S, [D]	Anonymus 37	537

A soldier under Witigis in the Gothic Wars, "a man who was
of no mean station." He was pinned to a tree by a spear toward
the beginning of the siege of Rome. Procopius, BG 1.23.9–12.

?J, A, [D]	Anonymus 38 comes	500s or

Ferrandus Diaconus wrote a detailed letter against Arian the-   510s
?l   ology to Eugippius at his request, rebutting the propositions put
forth "ab arriano Gothorum comite."
?l: It thus seems likely that this man engaged in theological
debate with Eugippius, as did Arians and Catholics at the court
of Gundobad in Burgundy.
?J, [D]: *Comes Gothorum* is probably not technical in the sense
of *Var.* 7.3 (its only occurrence in the *Variae*, where it is a term
meaning "military *comes civitatis*," in the language of *civilitas*). It
is surely a reference either to the army or to the Arian community, or both.
Ferrandus, *ep. dogmatica* 1, col. 24.

(N), (A), ?A ——— c	Anonymi 39+ The children of **Gundila** and **Anonyma** 5. Together with their parents, they made a donation to the Catholic church of St. Maria in Nepi upon the conversion of their father to Catholicism. It is unclear whether they converted with him or whether they were already Catholics. Perhaps involved with the inquiry of 557; see above, ch. 6 and appendix 1. *PItal* 49.17.	540s ?557
[D]	Anonyma 1 A "mulier pauper de gente Gothica," she gave birth for four snakes, which was interpreted as a bad omen. In Ravenna. AV 14.84.	c. 520
(N), (J), ([D]) ——— (n), (s)	Anonyma 2 The daughter of **Mauricius** and granddaughter of **Mundo**, and the brother of **Theudimundus**. She married **Aruth**, leader of Heruls in the Byzantine army, who "admired Roman ways." Procopius, BG 4.26.13.	552
(N) ——— (n), 1	!!Anonyma 3 Daughter of **Aligernus**, married **Anonymus** 5, the son of Theodora. GR 9.36.	598
(J), (S) ——— (n)	Anonyma 4 The wife of **Uraïas**, she was a woman of great beauty and conspicuous magnificence of dress. She managed to offend ★**Anonyma** 5 (in ★royal prosopography), the wife of king ★**Hildebadus**, leading to her husband's death. There is no basis for describing her as an "an extremely wealthy Gothic lady," as does PLRE3: 1393. Procopius, BG 3.1.37–43.	541
(N), (A), ?A ——— c	Anonyma 5 The wife of **Gundila**. Upon his conversion to Catholicism, they and their children **Anonymi** 39+ made a donation to the church of St. Maria in Nepi. It is unclear whether she and her children converted with Gundila, or whether they were already Catholics. Perhaps involved with the inquiry of 557; see above, ch. 6 and appendix 1. *PItal* 49.17.	540s ?557

II. *ROYAL PROSOPOGRAPHY

Note: all Ostrogothic kings and queens, and children born into the Amal family while it retained power, are assumed to have identified themselves as Goths, hence D. Readers are referred to PLRE and other cited studies for fuller details of careers of rulers. Comments here touch only on issues of identity. Some Amal descendants in other royal families are not included. Some people related to, or married into, the royal families, are listed in the main prosopography; cross-references are provided here.

N, J, S, D   ***Aligernus** (= PLRE3)   552–4
——————
s, l   The last leader of the Ostrogoths in Italy, he never seems to have taken his brother's title of king, although he stubbornly guarded the royal *thesaurus* with **H**erodianus at Cumae, and held out against Narses for two years. (But see **W**idin: small bands of soldiers previously attached to the Gothic side probably continued to oppose Narses even after 554.)

The son of **F**redigernus (in main prosopography), and brother of *Teia.

Loyalties: Aligernus was guided by pragmatism, submitting to Narses in fear of the Franks, and battling the latter on the Byzantine side in 554. Procopius is ill-informed about Aligernus and the final stage of the Gothic War, wrongly claiming that he was the brother of *Totila, and that the last Goths either departed from Italy or withdrew beyond the Po to Pavia (BG 4.34.19; 4.35.36–8, not mentioning Aligernus by name; cf. Agathias 1.1.1; Wolfram, *Goths*, p. 534, n. 754). With Wolfram, *Goths*, pp. 361–2, Aligernus was one of a number of Gothic commanders (including **G**undulf/Indulf) who continued to resist Narses after Mons Lactarius, but who did not have sufficient men or support to resurrect the Gothic *gens*. Aligernus, guarding the royal insignia, and a relative of the previous king, would have been the natural choice, but he chose to join the Byzantines, like so many of his predecessors.

Name: note **A**ligernus in main prosopography.

Further on Aligernus, see PLRE3: 48.

N, D   ***Amalaberga** (= PLRE2)   *c.* 510–
——————
(c), l   Daughter of *Amalafrida, thus niece of *Theodericus and   *c.* 534 brother of *Theodahadus. She was married to Hermanifred, king of the Thuringians, by whom she bore **A**malafridas (in main prosopography) and a daughter who married Audoin, king of the Lombards (*Anonyma 4). In the accompanying letter, Cassiodorus describes her as so well educated that she would bring Italian civilization to Thuringia (*Var.* 4.1); despite the rhetorical overtones, there is no reason to discount her education.

Escaped to Ravenna in *c.* 534, after her husband's death during
the Frankish conquest of Thuringia. She brought her children
with her; her son may have served with the Gothic army (see
Amalafridas), and Procopius calls him "Gothos anēr" rather
than "Thuringian," so Amalaberga may have inculcated in her
children a sense of pride in their mother's heritage. Amalafridas
was almost certainly Catholic, being a close friend of St. Radegund of Poitiers; this unfortunately does not necessarily shed
any light on Amalaberga's religious beliefs. PLRE3: 63.

N, D
————
(c), 1

★Amalafrida (= PLRE2)
Sister of ★Theodericus, probably a friend of the empress Ariadne, wife of Zeno (Joh. Ant. fr. 214.8, with PLRE2: 63). Married first to ★Anonymus 1, who died in *c.* 500; their children
were ★Theodahadus and ★Amalaberga. She was the grandmother of Amalafridas. Married the Vandal king Thrasamund
in *c.* 500, fleeing from his relatives upon his death in 523 to
"barbarians" in Byzacium; subsequently captured and put in
prison, where she died, probably at some point in 526. See
above, ch. 2, on Theoderic's response, and Moorhead, *Theoderic*,
pp. 247–8, on the date of her death.
D: The reaction of the Vandals on the one hand, and of Theoderic on the other, show that she retained her Gothic identity
in Africa.
Further PLRE2: 63–4.

c. 487–
526

Fl. Amala Amalafrida Theodenanda = ★Theudenantha

Amalafridas = Amalafridas (in main prosopography)

N, D, A, G
————
(c), 1

★Amalasuintha regina (= PLRE2)
The dates indicate her lifespan (on her birthdate, see Wolfram,
Goths, p. 32). The daughter of ★Theodericus and ★Audefleda,
the husband of ★Eutharicus, and the mother of ★Athalaricus
and ★Matasuentha. She was not a soldier, despite the rhetoric
of *Var.* 11.1. She was well educated, and fluent in Latin, Greek
and Gothic (*Var.* 11.1.6). She insisted that her son ★Athalaricus
be brought up with a "Roman" education, according to Procopius, which roused opposition among certain Goths, apparently
more because of his consequent ignorance of warfare than his
ignorance of any Gothic culture: Procopius, BV 1.14.6; BG
1.2.4–4.31; see further Anonymi 8, 9, 10 and 11, 12, 13, and
Tuluin, with Wolfram, *Goths*, pp. 334–7. In fear of these men,
she requested political asylum from Constantinople at one point
(ibid., p. 336), later used as an excuse by Justinian for his
invasion of Italy. Gregory of Tours calls her an Arian and claims
that she poisoned her mother, in a particularly ill-informed section of the *Historiae* (3.31): see further ★Audefleda.
A: she was presumably an Arian like her father, or one of our
Catholic sources would inform otherwise. Further in general,
see PLRE 2: 65–6.

after
493–534

Areagni = *Ostrogotho/Areagni

N, ?J, A,   ***Athalaricus** rex (= PLRE2)   516/
D, ?G   The dates indicate his lifespan. This is his titulature as expressed 518–534
———   in the *Variae*, where it is probably incomplete (note *Var.*
(c), 1   11.1.14: "gloriosus rex;" see further *Theodericus). He almost
certainly did not hold *Theodericus's military titles: see Tuluin,
and Wolfram, *Goths*, p. 335. On his "Roman" and "Gothic"
upbringing, see *Amalasuintha. Son of Eutharicus and *Amalasuintha, grandson of *Theodericus, cousin of the Visigothic
king Amalaric.
A: John of Nikiu, *Chronicle* 88.56.
?J: He seems to have fallen in with soldiers as an adolescent,
but it is unlikely that he actually served as one. Tuluin and
Liberius seem to have served as commanders of the army during
his lifetime, so he may not even have been classed as military.
?G: His knowledge of the Gothic language is unknown; he was
at least initially given a Roman education, which was succeeded
by a "life of debauchery" among military men. Further see
PLRE2: 175–6.

N, ?A, (D)   ***Audefleda** (= PLRE2)   V^{ex}–VI^{in}
———   The wife of Theoderic and mother of *Amalasuintha; her pre-
(c), 1   decessor possibly only a concubine (*Anonyma 1). She was the
sister of Clovis, therefore a Frank by birth (AV 63: "de Francis").
It would be useful to know when she married Theoderic, in
order to determine her religion (since her brother converted to
Catholicism in 497 or 506). But it must have been before the
Laurentian schism began in 498 (from the order of events
around AV 63, which mentions the marriage). Moorhead, *Theoderic*, pp. 51–2, suggests 493 or shortly thereafter. The question
therefore remains open: she could even have arrived in Italy as
a pagan. Gregory of Tours states that she and her daughter were
Arians (*Hist.* 3.31), claiming that *Amalasuintha poisoned her
mother, in a story that is highly suspect (see further Triwila).
On other matters, see PLRE2: 185.

Baduila = *Totila

Ebremud = Ebremud (in main prosopography)

N, J, S, ?D   ***Erarichus** rex (= PLRE3)   541
———   Correct titulature unknown; cf. *Hildebadus.
s   Procopius calls him a Rugian, saying that the Goths accepted
him only reluctantly as king after the death of *Hildebadus.
?D: Was his choice as king then any indication of Gothic identity as well as a Rugian? Procopius states that the Rugians were
"indeed a Gothic nation" (*ethnos men eisi Gothikōn*) subsumed
under the Goths by Theoderic, but who maintained themselves
as a separate group through endogamous marriage.
Loyalties: aside from his official negotiations for an independent

Transpadane Italy under the Goths, he was also secretly arrang-
ing to betray his kingdom to Justinian in return for money and
the patriciate; cf. ★Amalasuintha, ★Theodahadus and ★Witigis.
He was found incompetent as a leader of the war, and suspected
of complicity in the murder of ★Hildebadus, leading to support
for the latter's relative ★Totila.

On his coins, see ★Hildebadus (cf. PLRE3: 447, implying that he
did not issue any). Further PLRE3: 447–8.

N, D		
n, c, l		

★**Ereleuva dicta Eusebia** regina (= PLRE2 Erelieva quae et   V¹ 492/
Eusebia)   496
The mother of ★Theodericus and concubine of Theodemer.   496–
The spelling of Gelasius, her contemporary, is to be preferred   ?506
to those of *AV* ("Ereriliva") and Jordanes ("Erelieva"); Gelasius
once calls her "Hereleuva," but his other usage, "Ereleuva,"
with the weight of the other sources, should favor a smooth
breathing at the start of the name. Gelasius uses the title *regina*,
and calls her "sublimitas tua."

She was a Catholic, and took the name "Eusebia" in baptism:
"Ereriliva dicta Gothica, catholica quidem erat, qui [sc. quae]
in baptismo Eusebia dicta," AV 59. (Note that Catholicism may
explain the similar pattern of the name of her granddaughter
★Ostrogotho Ariagni, q.v.) Probably for this reason, Ennodius
referred to her "sancta mater" (*Pan.* 42, with PLRE2: 400). She
also received letters from Pope Gelasius I seeking her influence
over the king in issues of ecclesiastical and secular jurisdiction
(though cf. Teia *comes*, an Arian correspondent of the pope).
On these letters, see above, chs. 2 and 6. On their authenticity,
contra Ullmann, see ch. 3. She is depicted as the addressee of
a speech from Theoderic, by Ennodius, *Pan.* 42–4, at the time
of the war for Italy in 489–93. Ennodius's reference does not
necessarily indicate that she was alive at the time of the *Panegyricus* (*c.* 506), but it is interesting that he does not use any
term such as "beatae recordationis" in mentioning her.

Gelasius, JK 683 = *ep.* "Qui pro victu" (Thiel, *frag.* 36, p. 502 =
ETV 4) (492/96, not 495 as PLRE2: 400 states); JK 721 = *ep.* "Fel-
icem et Petrum" (Ewald, *Coll. Brit. Gel. ep.* 46, pp. 521–2 =
ETV 5) (496); Ennodius, *Pan.* 42; AV 59; Jordanes, *Get.* 269.

Eusebia = ★Ereleuva

N, J, A, D		
n, j, (c), l		

★**Fl. Eutharicus Cilliga** consul (= PLRE2)   515 d
Married Theoderic's daughter ★Amalasuintha in 515, and was   by 526
consul with the emperor Justin in 519, when he was also
adopted as *filius per arma* by the emperor. He was probably designated as Theoderic's heir. He is described only by Jordanes as
a distant Amal relative living in Spain, interpreted probably
rightly by Wolfram as Theoderic's deliberate invention for the

purposes of dynastic credibility: *Goths*, pp. 32, 328. He died before Theoderic.

J: He was probably a soldier, as Jordanes's reference to his *virtus* suggests, although this was part of the ideal of a Gothic king under *civilitas*: see above, ch. 2. But it seems unlikely that Theoderic would have chosen someone as successor who could not lead the army, and Justin's adoption of Eutharic as "son in arms" also suggests that he was theoretically meant to serve the military interests of the Roman state, like his father-in-law, who had been adopted in the same way by the emperor Zeno.

A: Dual Germanic and Latin name notwithstanding, he was a staunch Arian. From the viewpoint of the 540s or so, he looked like "the enemy of the Catholic faith;" AV 14.80, probably over-interpreting local friction in Ravenna.

Further see Moorhead, *Theoderic*, pp. 201–2, and PLRE2: 438.

Flavius, Flavia *listed under second name*

Fredigernus = Fredigernus (in main prosopography)

Germanus *see under* ★**Matasuentha**

Germanus filius Germani *see under* ★**Matasuentha**

N, D
———
l, (c)

★**Gudeliva** regina (= PLRE2)   535
Wife of ★**Theodahadus**, presumably mother of ★**Theudegisclus** and ★**Theodenantha**. Wrote two letters on behalf of her husband to the empress Theodora in 535, written for her by Cassiodorus: *Var.* 10.21; 10.24. PLRE2: 520. On the name, note the **Gudelivus** 1 and 2.

Hereleuva = ★**Ereleuva**

N, J, S, D
———
l

★**Hildebadus** rex (= PLRE3 Ildibadus)   540–1
Spelling: Procopius indicates a smooth breathing, but both Latin sources add an "H."

He is the first king for whom we possess no documents from which to judge his titulature. Nephew of ★**Theudis**, uncle of ★**Totila**. Wife was ★**Anonyma** 5. Like ★**Witigis**, he seems to have come from a family that rose to prominence through military service (see ★**Theudis**). On the other hand, he was rich enough to own property sufficiently large to be mentioned by Pope Pelagius I (it had passed into the hands of the papal see: Pelagius I, JK 951 = *ep.* "Fraternitatem tuam" [Gassò and Batlle 14, pp. 44–6], §1, p. 44).

Loyalties: He was raised to the throne on the recommendation of Uraïas (in main prosopography) the nephew of his predecessor ★**Witigis**, (the Goths hoped for the support of his relative, the Visigothic king ★**Theudis**), by the Transpadane Goths who continued to resist after the fall of Ravenna. On their motivation and allegiance, see Wolfram, *Goths*, pp. 350–2 (but note my reservations on the *tychē* of Uraïas, q.v.). Hildebad's activities make it quite clear that he and his advisors represented the military interests of the *exercitus Italiae* as much as anything distinctively "Gothic": he offered to resign the kingship to Belisarius, and he recruited disaffected Byzantine soldiers (Procopius, BG 2.30.18–30; 3.1.1; 3.1.25–7). Belisarius refused his offer and took his children away to Constantinople. After this, Hildebad seems to have become determined to rule properly, capturing Treviso, and turning against his overpowerful supporter Uraïas, which may have led to his own death (see Uraïas and Velas).

Note also that he issued coins (Grierson and Blackburn, *Medieval European Coinage* 1: 37; cf. PLRE3: 614, which is somewhat misleading). PLRE3: 614–15

Ildibadus = *Hildebadus

N, S, D

———

(n), s, c, (c), l

*Matasuentha patricia (= PLRE3)   536–50
Daughter of *Amalasuintha and *Eutharicus, granddaughter of *Theodericus and sister of *Athalaricus. After the murders of her mother and cousin *Theodahadus, she was forced to marry *Witigis in 536, which may have led to her compromised loyalties during the Gothic Wars (Procopius, BG 2.10.11–12; 2.28.25–6), when she offered secret negotiations and marriage to the Catholic Iohannes 2 (2.10.11). Belisarius took her and her husband to Constantinople in 540. She must have become a Catholic, if she were not one already, by 549/550, when she married and bore a child to Germanus, a cousin of the emperor Justinian. The son was also named Germanus (on his possible subsequent career, PLRE3 Germanus 3 and Germanus 11). Jordanes describes this family as a union of "the family of the Anicii with the Amal line" (*Get.* 314); on this mysterious comment (no Anicii are known in Germanus's family), see Goffart, *Narrators*, p. 70 n. 249 with references. But note also the marriage of the Amal princess *Anonyma 3 to Flavius (Anicius) Maximus in 535: "*Getica*, 314 ... is perhaps based on a misunderstood report about this marriage" (Wolfram, *Goths*, p. 502, n. 222). Further see PLRE3: 851.

Fl. Maximus *see under* *Anonyma 3

Oraio = Uraïas (in main prosopography)

N, D

———

n, c, (c), l

*Ostrogotho/Areagni (= PLRE2 Areagni)   V^ex_–VI^in
"Areagni" in *AV* 63; "Ostrogotho" in Jord., *Get.* 297.
Daughter of *Theodericus by his first wife or concubine, *Anonyma 1; sister of *Theodegotha.
Probably a Catholic like her grandmother Ereleuva. Her dual Germanic and Latin names suggest baptism or conversion to Catholicism (like *Ereleuva-Eusebia, but note the Arian *Eutharicus Cilliga and Arian clergy like Minnulus-Willienant

and Danihel-Igila), and she married the Catholic king Sigimund
of the Burgundians. The name "Areagni," moreover, might be
a particularly illustrious choice from the non-Arian antecedents
of her husband's family: Sigismund's great-aunt Alypia (wife of
Ricimer) was sister-in-law to the empress Ariadne (also spelled
"Ariagni/e," at AV 39, Jordanes, *Rom.* 339, 349, and Victor of
Tunnuna s.a. 475.1), wife first of the emperor Zeno and then
of Anastasius, and the daughter of Leo and Verina. She was
known as a devout Catholic who venerated refugees from the
Arian persecution in Africa (Victor Vitensis, *Historia* 3.30). Such
a deliberate reference would have been useful to Theoderic as
well as to Gundobad and Sisigmund, who were all trying to
strengthen ties with Anastasius. Moreover, a sister of Theoderic
was a friend of the empress Ariadne: Joh. Ant. fr. 214.8
(perhaps ★Amalafrida) near the time when Ostrogotho/Areagni
must have been born (on the date, Wolfram, *Goths*, p. 32). On
the similarly Gothic or Amal ideological overtones of her name
Ostrogotho, see Ustrigotthus, Wolfram, *Goths*, p. 31, and
below. Note that AV63 states that Theoderic married her sister
★Theodegotha to Sigismund, and that Areagni was married to
Alaric II. Jordanes, *Get.* 297, is more explicit than AV, and Procopius, BG 1.12.22 also names ★Theodegotha as the wife of
Alaric, so it is usually assumed that AV has confused the names
in its single sentence devoted to the issue. But Wood, "Avitus
of Vienne," pp. 150–1, thinks that Sigismund's wife was
★Theodegotha, and that she was "definitely Arian," presumably
because of a reference by Avitus to a "foreign king" supporting
Arian bishops at the Burgundian court after 516 (Avitus, *ep.* 7,
cited by Wood, "Avitus of Vienne," p. 155), which would
make sense if Theoderic were supporting his daughter's religion.
But Theoderic did not require relatives in a region to uphold
the rights of Arians there, which were assuredly in danger after
the accession of the Catholic Sigismund: note Theoderic's reaction to the enforcement of anti-Arian laws in the East in 523.
Moorhead, *Theoderic*, p. 86 sees "Areagni" as appended to
Ostrogotho's name by mistake by AV, but offers no evidence
for this conclusion.

It seems to me entirely likely that Sigismund's wife was Catholic, and that therefore she was Ostrogotho/Areagni. She died
before *c.* 520. She had one son by Sigismund, called Sigeric (a
combination of Sigismund and Theoderic?), killed by his father
in 523.

Her other name, Ostrogotho, is a clear statement of political
identity: see Wolfram, *Goths*, p. 31; Ustrigotthus. (Note that
Wrede, pp. 65–6, sees Areagni as her real name, and the pair
to mean "die Ostgotin Areagni," thus distinguishing her from
the empress. I don't think that we can see AV making this dis-

tinction. Further see Ensslin, *Theoderich*, p. 88 with n. 5; Kampers, "Anmerkungen," p. 143.
PLRE2: 138–9.

N, J, S, D
————
1

*Teia rex (= PLRE3 Theia)   552
Alternate spellings: Thila, Thela, Theia, and Teïas (see PLRE3: 1224, opting for "Theia" from one of the alternatives found on his coins). Son of Fredigernus (listed in main prosopography), and older brother of *Aligernus.
Loyalties and geographical base: Teia briefly relaunched the Ostrogothic kingdom from Pavia in 552, as Hildebad had done twelve years earlier. He executed 300 well-born children from Italian cities, hostages taken by Totila. Similarly, he executed senators who had been evacuated to Campania by Totila and who tried to return to liberated Rome including Flavius Maximus, the husband of the Amal princess *Anonyma 2 (Procopius, BG 4.34.7), a hard-headed move in light of the mixed feelings of fear and confusion among the Gothic soldiers caused by the projected arrival of the partly Amal Germanus two years earlier. The battle of Mons Lactarius, according to Procopius, was provoked by Narses's attempt to take the Gothic *thesaurus* at Cumae; on this, see further *Aligernus. He wanted to draw the Franks into alliance. Procopius does not indicate that he wanted to negotiate with the Byzantines, unlike most of the other kings, but this omission may be due to the short length of time that he actually ruled.
See further PLRE3: 1224.

Theodagunda = Theodagunda (in main prosopography)

N, A, S, D
————
?n, j, s, (c),
1

*Theodahadus rex (= PLRE2)   507/
This is his titulature as expressed in the *Variae*, probably incom-   511–36
pletely (note *Var.* 11.13.16: "piissimus rex noster"; see further *Theodericus). Son of *Amalafrida by her first husband, thus brother of *Amalaberga and nephew of *Theodericus. He married *Gudeliva; their children were *Theudegisclus and *Theudenantha. An old man in 534, so he probably arrived in Italy with Theoderic.
N/?n: contemporary sources frequently call him "Theodatus," not a translation, but a form of "barbarolexis": it was unclear to his contemporaries whether his name was Germanic or Latin; cf. Sarabonus. Further on his name see Wrede, p. 90.
j: In 507/11, Theoderic refers to him as "senator." He was not a soldier, devoting his time to Latin scholarship and poetry, and, apparently, the amassing of land in Tuscany. His lack of military ability apparently led to his assassination.
Loyalties: He twice negotiated with Justinian to give up first his lands in Tuscany (533/534) and later his throne in exchange for a comfortable living in Constantinople. His apparent alliance

with the military Goths who were enemies of ★Amalasuintha thus looks opportunist: perhaps the queen saw him as a potential enemy, attempting to neutralize him through a sinecure king-ship in 534. This arrangement backfired on ★Amalasuintha, whom Theodahad exiled and later murdered. But Theodahad's own alliance with the military also backfired on himself. He faced growing resentment against his inaction during Belisarius's earliest campaigns, and probably against his secret negotiation with Byzantium. The result in 536 was his murder and the installation of ★Witigis as king.

Further see PLRE2: 1067–8; on Theodahad's scholarly activities, see Barnish, "Maximian, Cassiodorus, Boethius, Theodahad," pp. 28–32; Maximian, "Poesos quattuor" 3; on the vacillations of his reign, see Wolfram, *Goths*, 337–42.

N, A, D	★**Theodegotha** (= PLRE2)	V^ex^–VI^in

N, A, D
————
(c), 1

★**Theodegotha** (= PLRE2)   V^ex^–VI^in^
Daughter of ★Theodericus and ★Anonyma 1, sister of ★Ostro-gotho Ariagni. She married Alaric II of the Visigoths, and bore him Amalaric, a name that apparently combines the dynastic name of the Amals with the illustrious royal Visigothic name of Alaric (Wolfram, *Goths*, p. 244). She was almost certainly an Arian; her son Amalaric was an Arian and persecuted his Frank-ish, Catholic wife; see further PLRE2 Amalaricus, pp. 64–5. On the mistake of the AV in saying that she married Sigismund and that her sister married Alaric, see ★Ostrogotho. For references to Theodegotha, see further PLRE2: 1068.

N, J, A, G, D
————
j, (c), 1

★**Fl. Theodericus** rex, vir excellentissimus, exconsul, magister   ?454–
militum et patricius (= PLRE2 Theodericus 7)   526
The dates indicate his lifespan.
He expressed his own titulature in his letter to the senate of 506 as "Flavius Theodericus rex." He is never attested as "rex Gothorum" in the kingdom of Italy. All sources call him "rex." As for his rank, Gelasius calls him "magnificus," "excellentissi-mus," or "praecellentissimus"; Anastasius I and Justinian refer to him as "vir gloriosissimus" and "invictissimus" respectively. Inscriptions call him "dominus noster" and, on one occasion, "Augustus." Ennodius refers to him by every possible epithet (except "Augustus"), including *princeps*: see Vogel, index to Ennodius, p. 361; similarly, see Traube, index to Cassiodorus, pp. 580–1.
Theoderic's titles of "magister militum" and "patricius" are more complex. He was *MVM* praesentalis under Zeno twice (476/477–8 and 483–7) (the latter appointment described as *MVM* per Thracias by one later source: Theoph. A.M. 5977), and appointed *patricius* in 476/477. The latter title was an honour that one retained for life. Theoderic is usually con-sidered to have ruled over the Romans in Italy by virtue of his

title of *magister militum*, but he is not attested as reappointed to
the post after 487. Nonetheless, no other *magister militum* appears
in Italy until after the death of Theoderic, when **T**uluin appears
as *patricius praesentalis*, apparently combining the traditional
Western military titles of *patricius* and *MVM* praesentalis, to take
over the leadership of the Gothic army during the minority of
★**A**thalaricus (Wolfram, *Goths*, p. 335) (the non-military *patricii*
like **S**enarius are not significant; see Ensslin, "Patricius"). Since
Theoderic did replace Odoacer as ruler of Italy, and since
Odoacer also held the titles *magister militum* and *patricius*, like his
predecessors Ricimer, Gundobad and Orestes, it seems entirely
likely that the absence of these titles in Italy from 493 to 526
shows that Theoderic himself held them.
"Rex": never "rex Gothorum" in Italy, doubtless a purposeful
indication of Theoderic's absolute authority over everyone in
Italy, regardless of the barbarian origin of his title. Jordanes's
"Gothorum Romanorumque regnator" (*Get.* 295) is not a technical usage, but defines Theoderic's actual position. Theoderic
was adopted as *filius in arma* by the emperor Zeno at some point
before 478, and designated consul for the East in the year 488.
A: He was an Arian who tolerated and respected Catholicism, a
combination unusual enough to convince a Syriac monophysite
source that he converted to Catholicism on his deathbed
(Zacharias, HE 7.12) (cf. the similar story about Gundobad, king
of the Burgundians: Gregory of Tours, *Hist.* 2.34). This story
cannot possibly be true, or an Italian Catholic source would
mention it. But Theoderic's mother, ★**E**releuva, was a Catholic;
see further his wife ★**A**udefleda and his daughter ★**O**strogotho.
The king was a patron of the Arian church in Ravenna, building
and decorating churches there.
G: We must assume that he spoke Gothic, although there is no
direct evidence that he did. It seems very likely that he spoke
Greek too, having been educated in Constantinople from the
age of eight to the age of eighteen, and spending his youth and
early manhood in Thrace and Moesia, where there were many
Greek speakers.
Further see PLRE2: 1077–84; Moorhead, *Theoderic*.

N, D	★**Theudegisclus**	536
?s, 1		

Son of ★**T**heodahadus and ★**G**udeliva, sister of ★**T**heudenantha.
Mentioned only once, by Procopius, BG 1.11.10: ★**W**itigis
placed him under guard after the murder of his father, probably
in Rome. Aside from Theudegisclus's probable personal feelings
and claims to the throne, he might well have wanted to follow
the lead of his father and his brother-in-law Ebremud, as well
as his cousins ★**A**malasuintha and ★**M**atasuentha, in making
overtures to Byzantium.

N, D   ***Theudenantha** (= PLRE3 Theudenanthe)   535,

——————   Daughter of *Theodahadus and *Gudeliva, wife of Ebremud   ?536

?s, (s), 1   (in main prosopography), brother of *Theudegisclus. Mentioned only by Procopius, BG 1.8.3. But she may well be the
same as the "Fl. Amala Amalafrida Theodenanda" of ILCV 40,
who mourned the loss of a father and a child, probably in
Rome, in the mid-sixth century. The father would then be
*Theodahadus, killed in 536, with PLRE3: 1236. The inscription
was found in the church of S. Nicola in Genazzano, but almost
certainly had been brought there from Rome much later. See
further de Rossi, "Epigrafe d'una illustre," pp. 77–80. To PLRE's
comments, add that an inscription in verse might show interests
similar to those of her scholarly father. But since the Theodenanda of the inscription is only called *clarissima*, it is just possible
that she was not identical with Theudenantha, and was an
otherwise unattested member of the Amal family.

Her fate is unknown, but her husband Ebremud defected to
Byzantium   before   the   murder   of   his   father-in-law
*Theodahadus.

N, J, A, D   ***Theudis** rex ?Gothorum (*sc.* king of the Visigoths) (= PLRE2)   493/

——————   His titulature is unknown, but see *Chron. Caesaraug.* s.a. 544 (his   526–548

s   successor "regit Gotthos"): "rex Gothorum" may have been the
title in use in the Visigothic kingdom, unlike Italy.

Uncle of *Hildebad, thus great-uncle of *Totila.

He was an "Ostrogoth" in the sense that he came from Italy.
Like *Witigis, he seems to have worked his way up through
the army. He is first attested as *armiger* of Theoderic; he was sent
to command the army in Spain before 511, after Theoderic's
annexation of the Visigothic kingdom. He was made guardian
over Theoderic's grandson Amalaric (the son of *Theodegotha
and Alaric II), marrying a wealthy native non-Visigothic woman
(Procopius, BG 1.12.51, interpreted as "of noble Hispano-
Roman family" at PLRE2: 1112; more conservatively "Spanish"
at PLRE2 Anonyma 27). He was apparently the real ruler of Spain
during Amalaric's lifetime, with Theoderic's tacit consent. He
became actual king upon his ward's death in 531, reigning until
548.

A: called "haereticus, pacem tamen concessit ecclesiae" (Isidore,
HG 41), perhaps indicating that he followed the policy of his
patron Theoderic toward the Catholic churches in Spain –
which we would certainly expect while Spain remained part of
the Ostrogothic kingdom.

Further see PLRE2: 1112–13.

Thila = *Teia

Thrasimundus = *Trasimundus

N, J, S, A, ***Totila qui et Baduila** rex (= PLRE3)   541–52
D, ?G   Spelling and name: see PLRE3: 1328; the conjecture of Grierson
─────   and Blackburn, *Medieval European Coinage*, 1: 26, that "Totila"
1   was his familiar name and "Baduila" his official name, may be
            true, but almost all the sources besides his coinage call him
            "Totila," so I list him under this name.

His titulature, like that of his documented predecessors, included *rex* without further specification: see Grierson and Blackburn, *Medieval European Coinage* 1: 434–5 with plate 9, nos. 156–65; his rank designation and other titles are unknown.

Nephew of *Hildebadus, great-nephew of *Theudis; and *not* the brother of *Aligernus (with PLRE3: 1328, contra Procopius, BG 4.34.19).

Loyalties and motivation: upon the murder of his relative *Hildebadus in 541, he offered to surrender Treviso, where he commanded the garrison, to the Byzantine commander Constantianus. (Note that PLRE3: 1329 calls him perhaps *comes Gothorum*, implying military *comes civitatis* in the sense of *Var.* 7.3, a misleading description this far into the Gothic Wars: Totila was certainly garrison commander; whether he held additional duties is unknown.) Before the day fixed for the surrender, the Goths offered the kingship to Totila and killed *Erarichus on his demand. At this moment, he was clearly motivated by opportunity. Nevertheless, subsequently he displayed himself a politician of a high order, using the Gothic kingship to re-establish an independent Italian polity (on the following, see further Wolfram, *Goths*, pp. 353–61). He alternately attempted to terrify, and to enlist the support of, the indigenous Italian population. He wrote letters to the senate of Rome in 543, requesting their support; and managed to post placards in the besieged city announcing his overtures (Procopius, BG 3.9.20–1). In Naples and Campania he was generous to prisoners, but at Tibur in 544, he murdered them with deliberate cruelty. Similarly, he laid waste the city of Rome in 547. He captured a Catholic bishop named Valentinus and cut off both his hands when he suspected him of lying to him (BG 3.15.13–15). He attempted to arrange a marriage with a Frankish princess in ?549, and his elevation, like that of his uncle *Hildebadus, may have been connected with hopes of help from his great-uncle *Theudis in Spain. He was able to take Rome for a second time in 550, with the help of treachery, and deliberately settled the city with both Goths and Romans, celebrating games in the city. He continually negotiated with Justinian, and may have bribed the Slavs to attack Byzantine territory. During the war he urged farmers to continue cultivating their land, and continued to collect taxes from them for the upkeep of his army (BG 3.13.1; 3.22.30), as his predecessors had done. He drew several Byzantines over to his side: see **H**erodianus, **G**undulf, **U**lifus; see also BG 4.26.6. He encouraged Italian slaves and *coloni* to join his army in return for their freedom (on which see Wolfram, *Goths*, pp. 356–7). But with the arrival of ★**M**atasuentha's second husband Germanus, an Amal leader with senatorial and imperial connections, in 550, Totila faced a Justinianic takeover of his own propaganda, similarly spreading the notion of a revived independent Italy (ibid., p. 358).

A: He was an Arian: see **A**nonymi 14+, and Pope Vigilius, JK 925 = *ep.* "Fraternitatis vestrae litteras" (Arelat. 45 = PL 69:40–43), col. 42C: "lex aliena." He and his soldiers plundered the catacombs outside Rome during the siege of the city, leading Pope Vigilius to install a series of inscriptions mourning this sacrilege. Although Catholic soldiers were not above plundering churches, the catacombs were of such symbolic and historical importance for the Roman church that I think that we can see this as the activity of Arian believers. But it is not certain.

He prayed at St. Peter's in Rome, like Theoderic in 500; Procopius, BG 3.20.22. He venerated St. Benedict after the saint failed to be taken in by his deception (but this report is filled with hagiographic formulae), Gregory the Great, *Dialogi* 2.14–15, and see **R**iggo.

?G: His knowledge of Gothic is doubtful, since the source is shaky in the extreme. In the sixteenth century, the humanist Petrus Alcyonius wrote that a cardinal (the future Leo X) said that *he* had seen a work by an unknown Greek historian who recorded that Attila (*sic*) planned to start forcing people to speak Gothic in Italy. "Attila" has been taken as a misunderstanding of "Totila." Aside from the problem of the emendation, the source is unnamed, impossible to identify as any attested Byzantine historian, and at least three removes from us. Nor does the story sit well with the portrayal of Totila as imitator of Theoderic in Procopius. See Schmidt, "Das germanische Volkstum," pp. 433–4; Wattenbach and Levison, *Deutschlands Geschichtsquellen* 1: 78, n. 151.

References given here only for details absent in PLRE3. For a fuller description of his career, see PLRE3: 1328–33; Wolfram, *Goths*, pp. 353–61: a detailed study remains a major desideratum.

N, D	★**Trasimundus** vir inlustris (= PLRE2 T(h)rasimundus 2) 504–505
—————	A relative of ★**T**heodericus ("regiae stirpis germen"). Possibly
?c, l	Catholic (see below). In 504, Ennodius reported that Julianus (later *comes patrimonii*) had sent Thrasimundus a letter begging him to speed up his case (on which see **G**evica). Faustus Niger received a similar plea, and since Trasimundus is called "domnus" here (though possibly due only to his royal connections), he probably held some high office; Ennodius, *Op.* 90/*ep.* 3.20. In 505, Ennodius sent him a letter asking for some unspecified

favour (although he also implies that Trasimundus had invited him to write); *Op.* 138/*ep.* 4.10.

Possibly a Catholic: In this letter Ennodius addresses him as "*piissimus dominus*": "*pietas*" was an imperial characteristic, of course, and one that Ennodius had associated with Theoderic in his panegyric (*Pan.* 5, p. 204.2), but it is incredible to think that a Catholic clergyman could have associated piety with a mere relative of the king in a letter to him if that relative were an Arian. Vogel, index to Ennodius, p. 362, is surely wrong not to identify the Trasemundus of the first letter with the Trasimundus of the second, and also wrong to place him in Milan; PLRE2: 1117 correctly identifies the two as the same man (called "domnus" in the first letter, reference to his "claritas dominorum inserta natalibus" in the second).

Tuluin = **T**uluin (in main prosopography)

Ulitheus = **U**litheus (in main prosopography)

Uraïas = **U**raïas (in main prosopography)

N, J, S, A, D
———————
s, l

★Witigis rex (= PLRE3 Vitigis)   504–
This is his titulature in the *Variae*, where it is probably incom-   d 542
plete (see **★T**heodericus). Procopius states that he came from an obscure family (BG 1.11.5). He seems to have worked his way up to prominence via the army; his attested relatives are also soldiers (Uraïas, **U**litheus). Upon becoming king, he forcibly married the Amal princess **★M**atasuentha, for the purpose of legitimating his rule. (Note that other men in Italy whom Amal princesses married are similarly from an obscure military background, e.g. Ebremud, and probably Tuluin, despite Cassiodorus's statement about his noble birth, q.v.; a female example is perhaps **★G**udeliva. The exception is Fl. **M**aximus, a man of high senatorial birth.)

First came to prominence fighting the Gepids near Sirmium in 504; much later, he became spatharius to **★A**thalaricus (at any time during his reign; on spatharii, see further **U**nigis, **R**iggo): Witigis was also one of the king's advisors, presumably a member of the pro-military party at court (see **A**nonymi 11, 12, 13, as well as **★A**malasuintha). He repulsed a Gepid attempt to take back land near Sirmium, probably in the late 520s. He became the "armiger" of **★T**heodahadus, probably commander of his bodyguard. By 536, when Witigis was chosen king, he was a commander (*ductor:* Jordanes, *Get.* 309) of the Gothic army near Rome.

Loyalties: like other Ostrogothic monarchs, when things began to go badly, Witigis chose to negotiate for an honorable end to the war and a comfortable position for himself, earning the hostility of his soldiers (Procopius, BG 2.28.7–23; 2.29.1–3; 2.29.17). After his capture in Ravenna in 540, Belisarius treated him with honor, and upon his arrival in Constantinople he was made *patricius et comes*; he died there about two years after his arrival (probably in 542).

A: As with *Amalasuintha, a Catholic source would tell us if Witigis were Catholic.

Further PLRE3: 1382–6.

Royal *anonymi*

(D), ?D

———

(c), (l)

*Anonymus 1   d *c.* 500

First husband of *Amalafrida, the sister of *Theodericus. He was the father of *Theodahadus and of *Amalaberga, hence grandfather of Amalafridas, *Theudegisclus and *Theudenantha. He was presumably not one of Theoderic's many diplomatic family alliances, since Theodahad was already an adult by 507/511, so the marriage had probably taken place before Theoderic and his family came to Italy. He was therefore presumably someone from the Balkans, who probably identified himself as a Goth, and who probably had a Germanic name (since no Latin name appears among his children or his grandchildren). Given the possible dates, *Amalafrida might have married him upon her return to Theoderic from the retinue of the empress Ariadne in *c.* 487 (on this event see PLRE2: 63 and Wolfram, *Goths*, p. 278).

(D), ?D

———

(c)

*Anonyma 1   ?470s

Wife or concubine of *Theodericus before he married *Audefleda; mother of *Theodegotha and *Ostrogotho Ariagni. They were born in Moesia. See PLRE2: 1077.

D

*Anonyma 2   526

An Amal princess, possibly the daughter of *Theodericus, who married Tuluin (q.v.).

D

———

(n), (j), ?s,

c, l

*Anonyma 3   533–4

An Amal princess, possibly the daughter of *Theodericus. She married the exconsul and patrician Flavius Maximus, an Anicius: *Var.* 11.3; 12.3, before 533 or 534 (dates from Krautschick, *Cassiodor*, pp. 96, 99, contra Mommsen's date of 535, used by PLRE2: 748). She therefore must have been Catholic. It is unknown whether she accompanied Maximus in his subsequent vicissitudes during the Gothic Wars: he was suspected of collaborating with Witigis during the siege of Rome, sought asylum from Totila in St. Peter's, was sent by Totila to Campania, and was executed by Teia there in 552: see further PLRE2 Maximus 20. If she received a dowry of lands from a certain Marcianus, given by Theodahad, at the time of her marriage, then these were probably the lands later given by Justinian to Liberius in 554 (with PLRE2: 748–9). See further PLRE2 Maximus 20.

?D | ??**Anonyma** 4 | *c.* 540/
--- |
(s), (c), 1 | The daughter of **★A**malaberga and the Thuringian king 552
Hermanifred, she may or may not have identified herself as a
Goth (see further **★A**malafrida, and **A**malafridas, the latter in
main prosopography); sister of **A**malafridas, great-niece of
★Theodericus.

Betrothed to the Lombard king Audoin, probably at some point
during the dates indicated, by Justinian (with PLRE3: 152). She
was possibly identical with Rodelinda, the mother of the Lombard king Alboin. See further PLRE3 Audoin and PLRE3 Alboin.

(N), (J), | **★Anonyma** 5 | 541
(S), ?D | The wife of **★H**ildebadus. Offended by the airs and ostentatious
--- | wealth of **A**nonyma 4 (the wife of **U**raïas), she persuaded her
(l) | husband to have the latter murdered. Procopius, BG 3.1.37–43.

III. ANALYSIS OF NAMES AND INDIVIDUALS

Note: The proportions listed below as totals are not meant to imply statistical proportions of the population labeled "Goth" in fifth- and sixth-century Italy. The body of data is neither large nor broadly spread enough to allow such quantitative analysis. These proportions simply give an idea of possible margins of error incurred when using criteria such as Germanic names to identify probable identities, professions or allegiances of individuals.

Totals[1]

Individuals (including minimum number of *anonymi*):
379+ individuals listed total (40 from outside period or place)
339+ individuals from Italy 489–554 (17 with questionable criteria)
322+ individuals with definite criteria of Gothic identity, Italy 489–554[2]

Names (excluding all *anonymi*)
331 names listed (38 from outside period or place)
293 names from Italy 489–554 (15 with questionable criteria)
278 names with definite criteria of Gothic identity, Italy 489–554[3]

Definite criteria of Gothic identity (proportions only of definite examples in Italy 489–554, out of 278 names and 322+ individuals):

N^4: 229	Germanic names (82%)[4]	
J: 116	named soldiers (42%)	140+ individuals (44%)
S: 56	named people on Gothic side (20%)	68+ individuals (21%)
A: 40	named Arians including clergy (14%)	46+ individuals (14%)
†: 27	named Arian clergy (10%)	29+ individuals (9%)
G: 10	named Gothic speakers/writers (4%)	13+ individuals (4%)
D: 21	named declared Goths (8%) (**all royal**)	23+ individuals (7%)
[D]: 37	named declared Goths by others (13%)	51+ individuals (16%)

[1] The nine spurious Goths (names listed in square brackets) are not counted.
[2] Including 29 members of Ostrogothic royal families.
[3] Including 23 named members of Ostrogothic royal families.
[4] Counted as percentage of totals of *names* only, not *individuals*.

Definite criteria of Roman identity:

n^4: 45	Graeco-Latin or biblical names (16%)[5]	–
j: 36	named civilians and senators (13%)	39 individuals (12%)
s: 27	named people on Byzantine side (10%)	31+ individuals (10%)
c: 34	named Catholics incl. clergy (12%)	40+ individuals (12%)
cc: 4	named Catholic clergy (1%)	5 individuals (2%)
l: 200	named Latin speakers (72%)	215+ individuals (67%)
d: 1	named declared Roman (**Asbadus**) (0.4%)	1 individual (0.3%)
[d]: 11	named declared Romans by others (4%)	14+ individuals (4%)

Definite criteria of both Roman and Gothic identity in individual (proportions only of definite examples in Italy 489–554, out of 278 names and 322+individuals):

209	named individuals (75%)	227 individuals (71%)

Definite criteria of both Roman and Gothic identity in individuals in the same family (out of 99 attested individuals in families, definite examples in Italy 489–554):

93 individuals attested in families (94%)

Notes

The most important figures are those showing that 71% of individuals attested with criteria of Gothic identity are also attested with criteria of Roman identity, and that 94% of individuals with attested family members were from families encompassing both Gothic and Roman criteria.

The other overall figures and proportions mostly tell us about the limitations of the survey, which chose individuals on the basis of the first set of criteria, mostly Germanic names and military professions. Given these predominant traits, it is hardly surprising that there are virtually no Catholic clergy, who never have Germanic names and obviously could not be soldiers: there must be many "Goths" hiding behind the Graeco-Latin names of the synodal subscriptions. The low number of declarations of identity (all these D's are royal and are mostly

[5] Some individuals had both Graeco-Latin and Germanic names. Total of names is less than 100 per cent because several are Thracian, Armenian or of unknown origin.

implied rather than stated) is partly related to the sources (few individuals out of the entire population of Italy at the time call themselves Romans in any but the urban sense). The [D]s are, of course, more a key to the ideological viewpoint of the source than observations of anyone's own identity, but there are some exceptions to this rule in Procopius.

Nonetheless, there are several striking surprises. The extremely high proportion of Latin speakers is still not as high as it may have been, given the sources (it is virtually impossible to tell from Procopius whether someone spoke Latin), so nearly all the "Goths" in Italy probably spoke it.

The number of Catholics is also surprisingly high in a survey that set out to look for Arians. Even when we allow that Arians are less likely to appear in sources (inscriptions and dedications are difficult to assign to an Arian church; much easier to assign to a Catholic church), the vast majority of the Arian believers here were Arian clergy attached to a single church, and it is clear that Arians were probably in the minority even within the limits of this survey.

The figure of civilians is high in a survey that set out to look for soldiers, reminding us that there is no such thing as an ethnic group based solely on profession! Some of these civilians are attested through family ties to people with attested criteria of Gothic identity. But many of them have Germanic names themselves.

Finally, the figure for Graeco-Latin names is also surprisingly high in a survey that set out to look for Germanic names; this is more a result of family ties (probably intermarriage, but also possibly naming strategies) than of soldiers with Graeco-Latin names (see tables 1 and 2, below: but the proportion of the whole, 16%, is lower than the proportion of Graeco-Latin names among officers).

Limitations of source material (proportions out of 322 definite Goths and 379 possible Goths):

	Def. criteria		Possible	
Only from *Variae*:	67	(21%)	71	(19%)
Only from Ennodius:	9	(3%)	9	(2%)
Only from Procopius:	66	(21%)	66	(17%)
Only from a papyrus:	80	(25%)	83	(22%)
Only from an inscription:	29	(9%)	49	(13%)
Only from another source:	17	(5%)	31	(8%)
Only in 1 source, total:	266	(83%)	309	(82%)
In more than 1 source, total:	54	(17%)	70	(18%)

Most of the individuals appear only in the *Variae*, Procopius or a papyrus (a total of 65% of the definite examples), the last by far the best of these sources, since it usually allows us to see the individual acting directly, and since it does not represent one author's viewpoint.

Note that these sources tend to reveal only certain types of criteria. Cassiodorus usually shows us an N, J, l: a Latin-speaking soldier with a Germanic name. Procopius usually shows us a J, S, [D], a soldier fighting for the Gothic side whom he declares to be a "Goth." One can rarely identify a Catholic or an Arian from Cassiodorus, or a Latin speaker from Procopius. Procopius is almost completely silent about the religion of individuals, since Christianity did not lend itself to expression in classicizing terminology.

The intimate sources, papyri and inscriptions, present the reverse problem. They reveal Germanic names, Latin-speakers, Catholics and Arians but they rarely indicate whether the individual was thought of as a "Goth." One great exception to this rule is *PItal* 34, the deed of sale of the Gothic church of St. Anastasia in Ravenna. Military profession is also rarely obvious from these sources: it may hide behind the rank designation *vir devotus*, which could signify either a common soldier or anyone in the civil service.

Problems of chronological imbalance in survey (out of 322 and 379):

	Def. criteria		Possible	
Reign of Theoderic (489–526):	110	(34%)	123	(32%)
Up to Gothic Wars (526–35):	46	(14%)	50	(13%)
Gothic Wars (535–54):	136	(42%)	139	(37%)
After Gothic Wars (after 554):	21	(7%)	51	(13%)
Uncertain date from 489 to 554:	9	(3%)	16	(4%)

These figures are hardly surprising: they reflect the overwhelming imbalance of source material toward Cassiodorus, who best documents 507–11 and 523–6, and toward Procopius, who best documents 535–54. The papyri, which could have balanced these proportions somewhat, also fall chiefly in the period 535–54.

Introduction to tables of analysis

Only definite examples are used in most categories; questionable soldiers, officers and *saiones* are not listed unless there is little reasonable doubt; a wider range for *comites* and Catholics.

? = the individual is not certainly attributed the criterion necessary for inclusion in this category

?? = the individual is not certainly attributed any Gothic criterion (same usage as in prosopography)

!! = the individual probably or certainly did not live under Ostrogothic rule at any time (same usage as in prosopography)

() = the individual is not listed in the prosopography at all, but is included here for another reason

Only individuals who almost certainly lived during the time of Ostrogothic rule in Italy are usually listed, that is, from between 489 and 554. This time-span includes adults attested shortly after 554. Dates are simplified to a spread. See the prosopography for detail on dates.

Similarly, the various individuals listed in the main prosopography who were from the Balkans, or serving with the Byzantine army in Italy, are only included in Italian Gothic categories if they came to Italy and deserted to the Gothic side. Exception: the separate category for Byzantine soldiers identified as Goths, table 13.

Sources are given in full only if such listing illuminates something about the data in the category. See the prosopography for detail on sources.

Tables of analysis, with appropriate criteria necessary:

1. Ordinary soldiers of the Gothic army (J and sometimes S)
2. Officers and commanders of the Gothic army (J and sometimes S)
3. Envoys and civilians attached to Gothic side in Gothic Wars (S)
4. *Saiones* (J)
5a. Military *comites* (J)
5. Other *comites* (whether with Gothic criteria or not)
6. Arians (A)
7. Arian clergy (†)
8. Catholics, including clergy (c and cc)
9. Catholic clergy (cc)
10. Non-military laymen and laywomen (j)
11. Graeco-Latin and Germanic names in same family (N/n)
a. attested by marriage only
b. attested in one individual only
c. attested by marriage and descent
d. relationship unclear
e. Byzantines
12. Individuals with attested knowledge of Gothic language(s) (G)

13. Byzantine soldiers identified as Goths (s and [D], and S with or without [D])
14. Other Germanic names attested in Italy without dates

Table 1. *Ordinary soldiers of the Gothic army:*

Name	Source	Date
Anduit	*Variae*	523/526
Brandila (wife: Procula)	*Variae*	523/526
Costula	*Variae*	523/526
Daila	*Variae*	523/526
Patza (wife: Regina)	*Variae*	523/526
Starcedius	*Variae*	523/526
Goar	Procopius	530s–552
Anonymi 23–32 (deserter to Goths)	Procopius	533/534
Optaris	Procopius	536
Anonymi 34+ (deserter to Byz.)	Procopius	536/537
Visandus 1 Vandalarius	Procopius	537
Anonymi 15+ (deserter to Goths)	Procopius	537
Anonymus 37	Procopius	537
Anonymus 17	Procopius	537/538
Witterit	*PItal* 30, 8	538–9
Andreas	*PItal* 30	before 539
Secundus	*PItal* 30	before 539
Burcentius (deserter to Goths)	Procopius	539
Anonymus 6	Procopius	539
Vclas	Procopius	540
Valaris	Procopius	541
Anonymus 16 (deserter to Goths)	Procopius	545/546
Anonymi 35+ (deserter to Goths)	Procopius	546
Coccas (deserter to Goths)	Procopius	552
Meligedius (deserter to Goths)	Procopius	552
Ulifus (deserter to Goths)	Procopius	552
Anonymus 4	Procopius	552

All but Coccas, a deserter from the Byzantines, have Germanic or otherwise non–Graeco-Latin names. Our sources are, however, particularly limited in this category. Since the rank *vir devotus*, for example, could apply to both bureaucrats and soldiers, one would like to know which of the various *viri devoti* listed in the Ravenna papyri were soldiers. Many of these have Graeco-Latin names. Moreover, the apparent absence of named *numeri* in Ostrogothic Italy means that almost all soldiers are invisible in inscriptions. Note the greater distribution of Graeco-Latin names under officers and commanders: is this partly due to the greater variety of sources in that category? On the deserters, see table 13. Note that all the individual deserters listed here, except Coccas, are said to have deserted for money. Procopius describes the deserters Anonymi 23–32 as "Huns," Anonymi 15+ as "of barbarian race," and Anonymi 35+ as "Romans and Moors," qq.vv.

Table 2. *Officers and commanders at any time attested in the Gothic army*

Note: Ostrogothic kings are not listed. Any military offices attested are listed next to the name, but not Procopius's classicizing terms *archon* and *strategos*. Note that even the Latin terminology of *Cont. Marc.*, "comes Gothorum" and "dux Gothorum," may not be technical: PLRE3: 977. *Comites* not attested on active campaign or not explicitly called military officers are not included here, since *comes* could be a civil position; see below, tables 5–5a.

Name	Source	Date
Liberius	*Variae*, Ennodius, etc.	465–550s
Mundo	Ennodius, Jordanes, etc.	480s–536
Ursus dux	Inscr.	*c*. 500/510
Arigernus comes	Synods, *Variae*	502–11
Herduic	Ennodius	504
Pitzia comes	Ennodius, *Variae*, Jordanes, *Auct. Havn.*	504–14
Cyprianus	*Variae*, Boethius, AV	504–27
Tuluin patricius praesentalis	*Variae*	504–27
Boio	*Variae*	507/511
Colosseus comes	*Variae*	507/511
Duda 2 comes	*Variae*	507/511
Servatus dux	*Variae*	507/511
Wiliarit 1	*Variae*	507/511
Ibba ?excomes, dux	*Variae*, *Chron. Caesaraug.*, Jordanes	508–13
Isidore		
Mammo dux	Mar. Avent.	509
Unigis spatharius	*Variae*	510
Wandil	*Variae*	510
Ara dux	Gregory of Tours	510/526
Anonymi 20–20a+	*Variae*	*c*. 510/512–27
Betancus comes	Avitus	*c*. 512
Guduin 2 dux	*Variae*	523/526
Neudis	*Variae*	523/526
Wilitancus dux	*Variae*	523/526
Gildila comes	*Variae*	526
Wiliarius comes	*Variae*	526
Quidila 2 comes, prior	*Variae*	527
Viliarid dux or comes	Marc. comes, Procopius, Gregory the Great	533–42

Table 2. *(cont.)*

Name	Source	Date
Sinderith dux	Jordanes	535
Wisibadus	Procopius	535/536
Herodianus (deserter to Goths)	Procopius	535–52
Asinarius	Procopius	535–7
Gripas	Procopius	535/537
Ebremud	Procopius, Jordanes, *Cont. Marc.*	536
Optaris	Procopius	536
Leuderis	Procopius	536–7
Marcias	Procopius	536–7
Hunila	Procopius	537
Pissas	Procopius	537
Pitzas (deserter to Byzantines)	Procopius	537
Vacis	Procopius	537
Uligasalus	Procopius	537–8
Albilas	Procopius	537/539
Gibimer (deserter to Byzantines)	Procopius	538
Tremo dux	*Cont. Marc.*	538
Ulitheus	Procopius	538
Vacimus	Procopius	538
Moras 1	Procopius	538–9
Visandus 2	Procopius	538–?9
Uraïas	Procopius, *Cont. Marc.*	538–40
Sisigis	Procopius	539–40
Romulus	*PItal* 31	540
Riggo spatharius	Procopius, Gregory the Great	540s
Tzalico comes	*PItal* 49	540s
Darida comes	Gregory the Great	*c.* 542
Bleda dux	Procopius, Gregory the Great, *Cont. Marc.*	542
Ruderit dux or comes	Procopius, Gregory the Great, *Cont. Marc.*	542–6
Anonymus 18 spatharius	Gregory the Great	544/546
Hosdas	Procopius	546
Rhecimundus	Procopius	546
Anonymus 19 comes	Gregory the Great	548–9
Gundulf/Indulf	Procopius	548/552
Gibal	Procopius	551
Scipuar	Procopius	551–2
Moras 2	Procopius	552
Usdrilas	Procopius	552
Ragnaris	Procopius, Agathias	552–4
?Widin comes	Paul. Diac.	?550s/?560s

Out of 63 names, 12, or some 19%, are Graeco-Latin or biblical, one belonging to a Byzantine deserter (Herodianus), who may nonetheless be implicitly identified as a Goth by Procopius. For contrast, note that out of 105 names recorded as belonging to officers in the Byzantine army in Italy (including the deserters Mundo, Herodianus, Pitzia and Gundulf/Indulf, all listed above), 35 (33%), are Germanic, 51 (49%), are Graeco-Latin or biblical; and 19 (18%), are of some other origin (Iranian, Armenian, Thracian, Isaurian, etc.).

Table 3. *Envoys and other non-soldiers attached to Gothic side in Gothic Wars*

Name	Source	Date
Albis	Procopius	537
Ulias	Procopius	537
Anonymus 3	Procopius	537
Caballarius	Procopius	541
Spinus	Procopius	550
Stephanus	Procopius	550

Three are Latin names; Anonymus 3 is identified as a "Roman of note," perhaps a senator, by Procopius. Because they were clearly forced into service, I do not include PLRE3 Theodorus 14 (perhaps a senator, if identical to PLRE3 Theodorus 24) and the deacon Pelagius, whom Totila sent to Justinian after he took Rome in 546: if they betrayed Totila, he told them, he would be forced to raze Rome to the ground and kill members of the senate: Procopius, BG 3.21.18–19.

Table 4. *Saiones*

Name	Source	Date
Amara 1	*Variae*	507/511
??Candac	*Variae*	507/511
Duda 1	*Variae*	507/511
Frumarith	*Variae*	507/511
Gesila	*Variae*	507/511
Gudisal	*Variae*	507/511
Leodefridus	*Variae*	507/511
Tutizar	*Variae*	507/511
Anonymus 22	*Variae*	507/511
Wiligis	*Variae*	509

Table 4. *(cont.)*

Name	Source	Date
Triwila	*Variae*, Ennodius, Boethius, IAV, Gregory of Tours	510–?30s
Nanduin	*Variae*	508
Vera	*Variae*	523
Mannila	*Variae*	523/526
Aliulfus	*Variae*	526
Gudinandus	*Variae*	526
Guduin 1	*Variae*	526
Quidila 1	*Variae*	526
Tata	*Variae*	526
Dumerit	*Variae*	527

All names are of Germanic origin except those of Tutizar and Candac.

Table 5. *Military comites*

Note: the title *"comes"* applied to a variety of offices, and frequently is not defined more explicitly in the sources. The *comes "Gothorum"* described in *Var.* 7.3 was a military official with the right to judge cases between two Goths (soldiers) or between a Goth and a Roman (a soldier and a civilian); whether a *comes civitatis, comes provinciae* or a *comes* of a border region could also be a *comes "Gothorum"* is a vexed question; see further Traube, index to Cassiodorus, s.v. *comes rei militaris*. Given this uncertainty, I list both possible and definite military *comites*, and see also 5a.)

Name	Source	Date
?Agilulph	Gelasius	492/496
?Arigernus	Synods, *Variae*	502–11
?Gudila 1	Synods, Inscr.	502, 500s
?Adila	*Variae*	507/511
?Anna	*Variae*	507/511
Colosseus	*Variae*	507/511
Duda 2	*Variae*	507/511
?Fridibadus	*Variae*	507/511
?Suna	*Variae*	507/511
Sunhivadus	*Variae*	507/511
?Wandil	*Variae*	510
?Marabadus	*Variae*	510–11
?Osuin	*Variae*	510–26
?Cunigastus	*Variae*, Boethius	522/525–7
Gildila	*Variae*	526
Quidila 2	*Variae*	527

All names are Germanic except Colosseus and Severinus.

Table 5a. *Other comites prior to the Gothic Wars, as corrective to above, excluding comites explicitly defined as civil offices (e.g. CSL or comes patrimoniae)*

Note: parentheses indicate individuals not included in the prosopography; the source is then given more explicitly.

Name	Source	Date
Gattila comes	Inscr.	450s–after 512
(Petrus v.c. comes	ILCV 114, Capua	*c.* 485–549)
Teia vir subl., comes	Gelasius	494/495
(Hostilius comes	Gelasius, JK 644	494/495)
[Heper comes v.i. diaconus]	Inscr.	?VI
Odoinus comes	AV, Mar. Avent., Auct. Havn.	500 or 504
Tancila v.sp./v.subl., comes	Ennodius, *Variae*	503–*c.* 509
Pitzia comes	Ennodius, *Variae*, Jordanes, *Auct. Havn.*	504–14
(Stephanus v.sp. comes i. ord.	*Variae* 2.28	507/511)
(Simeonius v.c. comes	*Variae* 3.25	510)
(Amabilis v.d. comes	*Variae* 4.5	511)
Betancus comes	Avitus	*c.* 512
Liwirit vir spectabilis, comes	*Variae*	523/526
Wiliarius vir inlustris, comes	*Variae*	526
Sigimer vir inlustris, comes	*Variae*	526
Wisibadus comes	*Variae*	535/536
Cessi/Cessis comes	*PItal* 43	535/542

The names are still overwhelmingly Germanic, and there is little reason to connect Stephanus, Simeonius or Amabilis with a military *comitiva*. As for Petrus, note that no Germanic names are associated with a *v.c. comitiva*. Hostilius had joined some lower clergy "adversus ecclesiam," but this need not indicate a military position or Arian belief. Since most of the certain examples in table 5 were members of the illustrate, perhaps only Wiliarius could possibly be a military *comes* in this list. But the rank may have been different in different cities.

Table 6. *Arians* (add Arian clergymen from table 7)

Name	Source	Date
*Theodericus	AV, LP etc.	*c.* 457–526
?*Ereleuva (?later Catholic)	Gelasius, Ennodius, AV, Jordanes	492–506
*Theodegotha	AV	V^{ex}–VI^{in}
Anastasia	PItal 33	V^{ex}–*c.* 541
*Amalasuintha	Variae etc. (q.v.)	493–534
*Theudis	Isidore etc.	493/526–48
Anonymus 33 diaconus[6]	Theodore Lector	493/526
Teia comes	Gelasius	494/495
*Witigis	Vigilius	504–42
*Theodahadus	Variae etc. (q.v.)	507/511–36
Triwila	Variae, Ennodius, Boethius, AV, Gregory of Tours	510–?30s
*Eutharicus Cilliga	AV	515–?26
*Athalaricus	Variae etc. (q.v.)	516/518–34
?Viliarid	Gregory the Great, etc.	533–46
Ranilda (?later Catholic)	Variae	535
Gundila (later Catholic)	PItal 49	540–?57
*Totila	Procopius etc.	541–52
?Riggo	Gregory the Great	?542
?Bleda	Gregory the Great, etc.	542
?Ruderit	Gregory the Great, etc.	542–6
?Anonymus 19	Gregory the Great	548–9

This is a short list: it is much more difficult to identify Arians than it is to identify Catholics. All names Germanic, but see the Arian clergy in table 7. Of the five soldiers described by Gregory the Great in hagiographies, three are attested elsewhere; on their presumed Arianism, see **Riggo** and **Anonymus 19**. Note that all Ostrogothic kings and queens were Arians; it is more difficult to be certain about members of their families.

---

[6] Originally a Catholic deacon; just because he apostatized does not mean that he immediately became an Arian *clergyman*; the evidence of Catholic attitudes toward reverse conversions of Arian clergymen in fact suggests the opposite: see Agapetus I, JK 892 = *ep.* "Iamdudum quidem" (*Avell.* 86, pp. 330–2): Arian bishops in Africa who converted to Catholicism are not to be allowed to continue in their former *honores.*

Table 7. *Arian clergy*

Name	Source	Date
Anonymi 7+ clerici	Avitus	*c.* 494/518
Berevulfus presbyter	Inscr.	VI
Christodorus presbyter	PItal 33	VI[1]
Butila presbyter	Variae	507/511
Gudila 2 episcopus	Variae	507/511
Unscila antistes	Variae	507/511
Unimundus episcopus [Ravenna]	Agnellus	512/517
Alamud diaconus	PItal 8	538
Gudilibus diaconus	PItal 8	538
?Anonymus 1 [scribe]	PItal 30	539
Anonymus 2 episcopus Guthorum	PItal 49	?540s
Minnulus/Willienant spodeus	PItal 33, PItal 34	541–51
Anonymi 14+ hiereas	Procopius	543
Amalatheus spodeus	PItal 34	551
Benenatus ostiarius	PItal 34	551
Costila ostiarius	PItal 34	551
Danihel/Igila spodeus	PItal 34	551
Gudelivus 2 ostiarius	PItal 34	551
Guderit 1 ostiarius	PItal 34	551
Hosbut ostiarius	PItal 34	551
Mirica spodeus	PItal 34	551
Optarit presbyter	PItal 34	551
Paulus 2 clericus	PItal 34	551
Petrus subdiaconus	PItal 34	551
Sindila spodeus	PItal 34	551
Suniefridus diaconus	PItal 34	551
Theudila clericus	PItal 34	551
Vitalianus 2 presbyter	PItal 34	551
Wiliarit 3 clericus	PItal 34	551
Wiliarit 4 spodeus	PItal 34, MSS codices	551
• • •la, defensor	PItal 34	551

Out of 27 known names, seven are of biblical or Graeco-Latin origin; given the heavy balance of the evidence toward the clergy of the Ravenna church of St. Anastasia (those attested in *PItal* 34), this proportion may be meaningless. Eighteen of these names are from that church; four of those are of biblical or Graeco-Latin origin. Four out of these 18 subscribed in the Gothic language, all with Germanic names; see table 12, below.)

Table 8. *Catholics*

Key: ? = not definitely Catholic
?? = Catholic, but no definite Gothic criteria
(N/n) = Graeco-Latin and Germanic names in family

Name	Source	Date
Sigibuldus (N/n)	LP	V²–VI¹
\<Fravi\>ta	Inscr.	444 or 493
Mustila	Inscr.	444 or 493
Dumilda (N/n)	Inscr.	*c.* 477–531
Sitza	PItal 49	490s–557+
*Ereleuva–Eusebia (N/n) (?convert)	Gelasius, Ennodius, AV, Jordanes	492–506
Anonymus 33 (later Arian)	Theodore lector	493/526
??Mustela	Inscr.	493–543
??Dionysius Exiguus	Dionysius, etc.	497–540
?Simplex–Livania	Inscr.	*c.* 498–528
Ariver (N/n)	Inscr.	VIⁱⁿ
Vonosus (N/n)	Inscr.	VIⁱⁿ
?Aderit (N/n)	PItal 13	VI¹
Guntelda (N/n)	Inscr.	VI¹
Ursina	Inscr.	*c.* 500/510
Ursus	Inscr.	*c.* 500/510
Seda	Inscr.	*c.* 501–41
Bessas	Jacob of Sarug	503–54
?*Ostrogotho/Areagni (N/n)	AV, Jordanes, Procopius	500s–*c.* 520
?Erdui	Ennodius	503
?*Trasimundus	Ennodius	504–5
??Senarius (?N/n)	Variae, Ennodius, Avitus, Joh. Diac., Epitaph	503–15/16
Cyprianus	Variae, Boethius	504–27
Alico	Ennodius	505
Anonymi 20+	Variae	510/512–27
Ara	Gregory of Tours	510/526
Meribaudus	Ennodius	511
??Iohannes 3 (Scythian monk)	Hormisdas, etc.	519–20
Leontius (Scythian monk) (N/n)	Hormisdas, etc.	519–20
Theodosus (N/n)	Inscr.	519–?31
Transmundus	Inscr.	523
Hildevara	PItal 4	524
?Gundeberga–Nonnica	Inscr.	526–70
Pope Boniface II (N/n)	LP, etc.	530–2
*Anonyma 3 (N/n)	Variae	533–4
Amalafridas	Procopius, Fortunatus	534–?67
Randilda (?convert)	Variae	535
?*Matasuentha (convert) (N/n)	Procopius, etc.	536–550
?Deutherius (N/n)	PItal 30	539

Table 8. *(cont.)*

Name	Source	Date
?Domnica (N/n)	PItal 30	539
??Latinus	PItal 30	539
Thulgilo (N/n)	PItal 30	539
?Montanus (N/n)	PItal 6	540
Anonymus 21	Gregory the Great	540s
Basilius (N/n)	Inscr.	VI^{med}
Manifrit	Inscr.	VI^{med}
Unigildus (N/n)	LP	VI^{med}
Guntio (N/n)	Inscr.	VI^{med}/VI^2
Gundila (convert)	PItal 49	540–?57
Anonymi 39+ (?convert)	PItal 49	540–?57
Anonyma 5 (?convert)	PItal 49	540–?57
Asbadus	Auct. Havn.	549–56
?Ademunt–Andreas (N/n)	PItal 13	553
Felithanc (?convert) (N/n)	PItal 13	553
Ranilo (?convert) (N/n)	PItal 13	553
Eusebius/Riccitanc (N/n)	PItal 6, PItal 36	
(?convert)		575–91
Pope Pelagius II (N/n)	LP	579–90

Out of 40 named definite Catholics with some other definite attested criterion of Gothic identity, ten (25%) have solely Graeco-Latin names, or eleven (28%) if Mustila's name is Latin. Out of 46 named possible Catholics with some other definite attested criterion of Gothic identity, seventeen (37%) have Graeco-Latin names, and of these six (13%) have both Graeco-Latin and Germanic names, in one case, the Graeco-Latin name known to have been assumed upon baptism [Ereleuva-Eusebia]. Out of these 46, some 25 (54%) have both Graeco-Latin and Germanic names in their families – although one should note that the evidence favors such revelation among Catholic families, since surviving (Catholic) donations are our best source for names of family members overall. Hence also the apparent jump in mixed family nomenclature after the 520s, from which period more donations have survived. As one would expect, the number of Catholics will jump dramatically after 554. But for examples from before the Ostrogothic settlement, note Herila comes "in pace fidei Catholicae" (= PLRE2) in Rome from 462, Fl. Valila qui et Theodovius (= PLRE2), who founded a church near Tibur in 471, and bequeathed another to the see of Rome at his death in 483.

Table 9. *Catholic clergy*

Name	Source	Date
Anonymus 33 diaconus (later Arian)	Theodore Lector	493/526
?Transmundus ?praepositus basilicae sancti Petri	Inscr.	523
Leontius, "Scythian monk" relative of Vitalianus 1	Hormisdas, etc.	519–20
Pope Boniface II, father's name Sigibuldus	LP	530–2
Anonymus 21, monk and "Goth"	Gregory the Great	540s
Pope Pelagius II, father's name Unigildus	LP	579–90

Aside from Transmundus, who may not have been *praepositus*, and may only have held a lay position in the church, no Germanic name is definitely attested among the Catholic clergymen of Italy before Berardus of Vercelli, who lived at the very end of the sixth century. Neither is any Catholic clergyman attested as reading or speaking Gothic. Since none of the other criteria could possibly be attached to a Catholic clergyman (such as Arian belief, a military position, or one of the secular positions at court like *saio*), no Catholic clergymen of the period can easily be identified as a Goth. Name changes and unattested dual names may hide many people from families with Germanic names. Possible exceptions are as follows:

?Guttus   only an acolyte; name of uncertain origin

?Gundeberga-Nonnica   if a nun, probably a Catholic, taking Latin name

??Dionysius Exiguus   from "Scythia"

??Iohannes 3   "Scythian monk"

??!!Sarabonus   presbyter, but name origin and date uncertain

After the period here strictly defined, note also Tucza, who may have been a nun in 559; Amara 2, *lector* of the church of Grado in 579, whose wife and children bore Latin names, and Acio, a presbyter at Parenzo, probably from the second half of the sixth century – but whose name may be non-Germanic (q.v.).

Table 10. *Non-military laymen and laywomen*

Only fairly certain non-soldiers are included, e.g. *viri honesti*. All *comites* and *saiones* are listed separately above, whether they had military duties or not. Wives of soldiers are considered to be associated with the army. Clergy are listed separately above, tables 7 and 9.

Name	Source	Date
!!Sesi. . . cubicularius	Inscr.	V^{ex}–VI^{in}
Dumilda honestissima femina	Inscr.	*c.* 477–531
Wiliarit 2 eunuchus	Inscr.	*c.* 477–532
??Mustela spectabilis femina	Inscr.	493–543
Athanarid phylosophus	Ravenna Cosmographer	496/507
Heldebaldus phylosophus	Ravenna Cosmographer	496/507
Marcomirus phylosophus	Ravenna Cosmographer	496/507
Simplex-Livania, church asst.	Inscr.	498–501
Seda ignucus et cubicularius	Inscr.	*c.* 501–41
Opilio	*Variae*, etc.	VI^{in}–534
Gevica inpulsor	Ennodius	504
Umbisuus vir spectabilis	*Variae*	507/511
Wilia 1, [?civil servant]	*Variae*	507/511
Bauto conductor domus regiae	Ennodius	508
Gudelivus 1, [court official]	Ennodius	508
Nonni arcarius	*PItal* 47–8	after 510
Meribaudus [aristocrat]	Ennodius	511
Sendefara	Inscr.	511–41
Wilifara	Inscr.	517–57
Theodosus [honestus puer]	Inscr.	519–?31
Anonymi 8, 9, 10	Procopius	520s–30s
?Transmundus ?praepositus	Inscr.	523
Hildevara	*PItal*† 4	524
Witigisclus censitor Siciliae	*Variae*	526
Wacca maior domus	*Variae*	534/535
Deutherius vir honestus	*PItal* 30	539
Domnica honesta femina	*PItal* 30	539
??Latinus v.h., possessor	*PItal* 30	539
Thulgilo honesta femina	*PItal* 30	539
Montanus v.c., notarius	*PItal* 6, 43	540, d by 575
Caballarius, envoy	Procopius	541
Ardica vir honestus	*PItal* 43	?542
Riccifrida honesta femina	*PItal* 43	?542
Bilesarius, freedman	*PItal* 9	VI^{med}
Sifilo, freedwoman	*PItal* 9	VI^{med}
Spinus quaestor	Procopius	550
Bonila praerogativarius	*PItal* 4–5	552–75
Ranihilda, slave	*PItal* 8	564
Guderit 2 libertus	*PItal* 8	d by 572

All but eight of definite examples have Germanic names, but this group is generally only identifiable via names. The proportion is therefore meaningless. As to the proportion of laymen and laywomen versus military families, note that a greater survival rate of papyri and inscriptions, to offset the bulky evidence of Cassiodorus and Procopius, would have given us many more examples of laymen. Proportion of men to women here: 30 men to 11 women. But men are more likely to be attested than women, and we know much more about those men who are attested.

Table 11. *Graeco-Latin and Germanic names in the same family*

Note: The quasititular "Flavius" or "Flavia" is not considered.
Parents are listed first, followed by ":", then children; marriages indicated by "=".
Dates indicate implied attestation of family lifespan, i.e. a longer period than mere dates of attestation.

| *11a. Attested by marriage only* | |
Name	Date
Brandila=Procula	523/526
Patza=Regina	523/526
??Honorata=??Tzitta 1	528–68
*Anonyma 3[7]=(Flavius Maximus)	530s–?40s
Bilesarius=Sifilo	VI^{med}
??Maximinus=??Tucza	VI^{med}
!!Rusticiana=!!Tzitta 2	VI^2–591

| *11b. Attested only in one individual (see further examples under Table 11c)* | |
Name	Date
*Ereleuva–Eusebia	V^{med}–506
Ostrogotho/Areagni	500s–c. 520
Simplex–Livania	c. 498–528
*Eutharicus Cilliga	c. 515–d by 526
Gundeberga–Nonnica	526–570
Danihel/Igila	551

| *11c. Attested by marriage and descent* | |
Name	Date
Sigibuldus: Pope Boniface II	V^2–532
Gattila: Agata	V^2–512
Dumilda: Theodosus	c. 477–531
Vonosus: Ariver	V^{ex}–VI^{in}

[7] As an Amal princess and possible daughter of Theoderic, she must have had at least one Germanic name derived from Amal name elements.

!!Ustarric: !!Iohannes 1	VI
Guntelda: Basilius: Guntio	VI
*Witigis: Uraïas as (nephew)	VI¹
*Matasuentha=(Germanus): (Germanus minor)	c. 516-52
Thulgilo: Deutherius, Domnica	VI¹-539
Christodorus: Minnulus/Willienant, cousin Anastasia	VI¹-541
Aderit: Ademunt–Andreas, Ranilo=Felithanc	VI¹-553
Unigildus: Pope Pelagius II	VIᵐᵉᵈ
Amara=Antonina: Haelia, Mellita	VI¹/VIᵐᵉᵈ-579
Montanus: Eusebius/Riccitanc	VIᵐᵉᵈ-591

11d. Relationship unclear

Name	Date
??Senarius and (Ennodius)	503-516

11e. Byzantines

Name	Date
Mundo: Mauricius: Theudimundus	V²-VI¹
(Patriciolus): !!Vitalianus 1: (Cutzes), (Buzes), (Venilus)	V²-VI¹

The numbers are too small to allow generalization, but mixture of names by descent seems to increase through the sixth century; it will naturally pick up faster in the late sixth and early seventh centuries. Note how name elements skip one generation in the families of Guntelda and of Mundo. Note the following examples of name mixtures prior to the Ostrogothic settlement: Fl. Merobaudes *MVM* (= PLRE2), son-in-law of Fl. Astyrius, and possible ancestor of Meribaudus in main prosopography, above; Fl. Valila qui et Theodovius (= PLRE2).

Table 12. *Individuals with attested knowledge of Gothic language*

Note: (sp.) = spoken
(wr.) = written

Name	Source	Date
*Theodericus (sp.)	*Variae*	?454-526
*Amalasuintha (sp.)	*Variae*	493-534
Bessas patricius (sp.)	Procopius	503-54
Cyprianus patricius (sp.)	*Variae*	504-27
Anonymi 20+, his sons (sp.)	*Variae*	c. 510/512-27
?Anonymus 17, soldier (sp.)	Procopius	537-38
Alamud diaconus (wr.)	*PItal*† 8	538

Table 12. (cont.)

Name	Source	Date
Gudilibus diaconus (wr.)	PItal† 8	538
??Latinus possessor (?wr.)	PItal 30	539
??Anonymus 1, scribe (?wr.)	PItal 30	539
?*Totila rex (?sp./?wr.)	Unknown Greek historian	540–52
Mirica spodeus (wr.)	PItal 34	551
Optarit presbyter (wr.)	PItal 34	551
Suniefridus diaconus (wr.)	PItal 34	551
Wiliarit 4 spodeus (wr.)	PItal 34, MSS codices	551

The spoken and written languages called "Gothic" were probably very different: see above, chs. 3 and 7. Written use only displayed by Arian clerics; Latinus is very shaky (q.v. in main prosopography), and Anonymus 1, if indeed definite, may well have been a cleric; see above, ch. 7. Spoken use, outside the Amal family, only attributed to soldiers Cyprianus, Anonymi 20+ and Bessas; see further ch. 5. *Amalasuintha is similarly attributed knowledge of the language by Cassiodorus, who uses the same praise as he does for Cyprianus (viz. that she knew three languages). The strange passage about *Totila claims that he planned to force all Italy to learn the language in schools; aside from the distance of the source, this may be a garbled report about a plan to force the Arian religion on Italy, given the association of the Gothic tongue with the Arian churches. The story about Anonymus 17 is extremely unlikely (q.v.), although for purposes of credibility it does assume that the Gothic language was spoken by some people, somewhere; similarly the story about Bessas. It is important to notice that all the people on this list were at least bilingual, and some multilingual: Amalasuintha, Bessas, Cyprianus and probably Theoderic all knew Greek as well as Latin. The remainder all knew Latin.

Table 13. *Byzantine and other soldiers and officers identified as Goths (or as relatives of individuals identified as Goths in this period)*

Note: Includes Byzantine deserters with Germanic names. Any other identities, and instances of side-changing, noted below.

Name	Source	Date
Mundo (Gepid, Hun) (changed sides)	Ennodius, Joh. Malal., Theoph., Procopius, etc.	480s–536
Godidisclus (Thracian)	Procopius	503
Vitalianus 1 (Scythian, Goth)	Marc. comes, etc.	503–20
Bessas (Thracian)	Procopius, *Cont. Marc.*, Jordanes	503–54
Alathort (Thracian)	Joh. Ant., Jordanes	513–14
Mauricius	Procopius, etc.	529–36
Amalafridas	Procopius, Fortunatus	534–?67
Herodianus (Thracian) (deserter to Goths)	Procopius	535–52
Ebremud (deserter to Byz.)	Procopius, *Cont. Marc.*, Jordanes	536
Pitzas (deserter to Byz.)	Procopius	537
Anonymi 15+ ("barbarians")	Procopius (deserters to Goths)	537
Iohannes 2	Procopius, etc.	537–53
Moras 1 (deserter to Byzantines)	Procopius	538–9
Burcentius (Besi = Bessi or Vesi) (deserter to Goths)	Procopius	539
Sisigis (deserter to Byzantines)	Procopius	539–40
Theudimundus	Procopius	540/541
Sisifridus	Procopius	545
Anonymus 16	Procopius	545/546
Gundulf/Indulf (deserter to Goths)	Procopius	548–52
Ustrigotthus (Gepid + name)	Procopius	548–52
Asbadus (Gepid)	Procopius, *Auct. Havn.*	549–56
Coccas (deserter to Goths)	Procopius	552
Meligedius (deserter to Goths)	Procopius	552
Ulifus (deserter to Goths)	Procopius	552
Aruth (Herul)	Procopius, Agathias	552–4

Out of 23 named individuals, 16 (70%) have Germanic names. Vitalianus 1 on the one hand, and Mundo, Mauricius and Theudimundus on the other, come from families with both Germanic and Graeco-Latin names among their members. Of the 23 individuals, seven (30%) are identified as Thracian or were active in Thrace; when we add their relatives and the Gepids to this, we get 12 (52%). Note that four of these individuals are said to have deserted for money or other material reasons; these men are not explicitly identified as Goths (Herodianus, Burcentius, Meligedius and Ulifus; but see Herodianus in the main prosopography above for Procopius's implicit identification of him as a Goth). On Thrace and the Goths, note that PLRE3 Godilas 1 was *MVM* per Thracias in 528, and that PLRE3 Godilas 2, a Thracian *doryphoros* of Iohannes 2 in the Gothic Wars, both bore a name very common among the Italian Goths: see Gudila 1–4 and Gundila in the main prosopography, above. Other Byzantine officers active in the Balkans and bearing Germanic names included Baduarius dux Scythiae, Ascum *MVM* per Illyricum (identified as a "Hun" or a "Bulgar") and Chilbudius *MVM* per Thracias, all in PLRE3.

Table 14. *Other Germanic names attested in Italy possibly from this period*

Name	Source	Date
(Hegnolda)	F-S NF 84	?VI
(. . .ligerna *h.f.*)	F-S NF 47	?VI
(Taniilda) (on fibula)	Mowat, "Note," p. 24	?VI
(Aoderada) (on fibula)	Rugo 4, no. 66	VI
(Milricus, Benno, Teugantiius, Engenalco, Richelda, Adelgerius, Burga, Amara, Gainus: see under Acio; in Parenzo cathedral)		?VI^2
(Tilua pauper)	*PDip* 78.5	?VI^2
(Himnigilda) (on chalice)	Hessen et. al., *Tesoro*	VI
(Sivegerna) (on dish)	Hessen et. al., *Tesoro*	VI
(Winelaupo) (inscr. in castle)	Rugo 4, no. 41	VI
(Berardus bp. of Vercelli)	Lanzoni 2: 1041–2	VI/VII
(Raninga) (runes on spear)	Rugo 2, no. 3	VI/VII
(Gaido presbyter, Euda/Geuda presbyter, Grimoaldus presbyter, Guneis presbyter) (catacombs, Rome)	ICUR n.s. 10.26316–20	VI/VII
(Adalbertus presbyter)	Rugo 5, no. 44	?VII
(Vvitu[v]vel. . .) (nr. Vatican)	ILCV 3415a	?
(Sigismundus et Sarra coniunx) (found in Jewish cemetery)	F-S 2F 22	?

None of these names can be dated with any hope of certainty, but are included here for the sake of completeness. Some of these individuals may well have lived under the Ostrogothic regime.

RULERS OF OSTROGOTHIC ITALY, 493–552

★Fl. Theodericus rex	493–526 (king from 470s)
★Athalaricus rex	526–34
★Amalasuintha [regent]	526–34
,, regina	534
★Theodahadus rex	534–6
★Witigis rex	536–40
★Hildebadus rex	540–1
★Erarichus rex	541
★Totila rex	541–52
★Teia rex	552
★Aligernus [never called king]	552–4

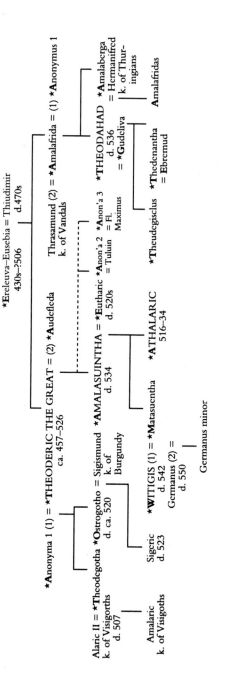

*Boldface with asterisk = see Royal Prosopography
Boldface = see Main Prosopography
CAPITALS = Ostrogothic kings and queens of Italy
*Anon'a = *Anonyma

See *PLRE*2 and *PLRE*3 for information on individuals not included in PA. Dates, included only for guidance, indicate lifespan rather than reigns.

Rulers of Ostrogothic Italy

BIBLIOGRAPHY

NOTES ON CITATION

Works of Ennodius

Cited according to the *Opus* numbers of Vogel, with the Sirmond-Hartel divisions into books in parentheses:
Ennodius, *Op.* 446 (*ep.* 9.23).

Papal letters

For the sake of clarity, cited by JK number and incipit, with edition, number of letter in the edition, and indication of place in *Avellana* or *Arelatensis* if cited according to a different edition:
Hormisdas, JK 819 = *ep.* "Lectis clementiae" (Avellana 168 = Thiel 79, pp. 877–9).

Procopius

Procopius's *Wars* are divided into eight volumes, but are traditionally numbered autonomously within his own sections: *Bellum Persicum* 1–2, *Bellum Vandalicum* 1–2, *Bellum Gothicum* 1–4. For familiarity's sake, I list the section name and its own book number, but include the overall book number in round brackets:
Procopius, BG 2(6).11.3 means *Bellum Gothicum* 2.11.3, *Wars* 6.11.3.

PRIMARY SOURCES

(Note: for inscriptions, papal letters and papyri, see under the respective heading.)

Acta concilii Arausionensis. Ed. Friedrich Maassen. MGM: Concila 1. Concilia aevi Merovingici. Hanover, 1893.
Acta concilii Turonensis a. 567. Ed. C. de Clercq. Concilae Galliae a. 511–a. 695. CCSL 148A. Turnhout, 1963.
Acta synhodorum habitae Romae a. CCCCXCVIIII, DI DII. Ed. Theodor Mommsen. MGH: AA 12: 393–455. Berlin, 1894.
Agathias. *Historiae.* Ed. Rudolf Keydell. Corpus Fontium Historiae Byzantinae, Series Berolinensis 2. Berlin, 1967.
Agnellus of Ravenna (sixth century). *De ratione fidei ad Armenium.* PL 68: 381–6. Paris, 1847.

487

Agnellus of Ravenna (ninth century). *Liber pontificalis Ravennatis.* Ed. O. Holder-Egger. MGH: Scriptores rerum Langobardicarum et Italicarum saec. VI–IX, pp. 275–391. Hanover, 1878.

Ambrose. *De fide ad Gratianum Augustum.* PL 16: 527–698. Paris, 1845.

Anagnosticum regis. Acta synhodi a. DI 5 = *Acta synhodorum habitae Romae*, pp. 425–6.

Anonymus Valesianus pars posterior. Ed. and trans. John C. Rolfe. In Ammianus Marcellinus, *Res Gestae* 3: 531–69. Cambridge, Mass., 1939. [With corrections of J. N. Adams, *The Text and Language of a Vulgar Latin Chronicle*, listed in secondary sources.]

Anthologia Latina 1.1. *Carmina in codicibus scripta: Libri Salmasiani aliorumque carmina.* Ed. D. R. Shackleton Bailey. Stuttgart, 1982.

Arator. *De actibus apostolorum.* Ed. Arthur Patch McKinlay. CSEL 72. Vienna, 1951.

Auctarium Prosperi Havniensis. Ed. Theodor Mommsen. MGH: AA 9. Chronica Minora 1: 304–33. Berlin, 1892.

Auctarii Havniensis Extrema. Ed. Theodor Mommsen. MGH: AA 9. Chronica Minora 1: 339. Berlin, 1892.

Augustine. *De civitate dei.* Ed. Bernard Dombart and Alfonsus Kalb. 1928. 5th edn, Stuttgart, 1981.

   Epistulae. Ed. A. Goldbacher. 5 vols. CSEL 34 [2 parts], 44, 57–8. Prague, Vienna and Leipzig, 1885–1923.

Aurelius Victor. *De Caesaribus.* Ed. Franz Pichlmayr. Leipzig, 1911.

Avitus of Vienne. *Opera.* Ed. Rudolf Peiper. MGH: AA 6.2. Berlin, 1883.

Boethius. *De musica.* Ed. G. Friedlein. Leipzig, 1867.

   De philosophiae consolatione. Ed. and trans. E. K. Rand and H. F. Stewart. 1918. Rev. S. J. Tester. Cambridge, Mass., 1973.

Candidus. *Fragmenta.* Ed. and trans. R. C. Blockley. *The Fragmentary Classicising Historians of the Later Roman Empire* 2: 463–71. ARCA: Classical and Medieval Texts, Papers and Monographs 10. Liverpool, 1983.

Capito. Greek translation of Eutropius, *Breviarium.* Ed. Hans Droysen. MGH: AA 2: 9–182, bottom half of pages. Berlin, 1879.

Cassiodorus. *Chronica.* Ed. Theodor Mommsen. MGH: AA 11. Chronica Minora 2: 120–61. Berlin, 1894.

   Orationes. Ed. Ludwig Traube. MGH: AA 12: 457–84. Berlin, 1894.

   Variae. Ed. Theodor Mommsen. MGH: AA 12. Berlin, 1894.

   De anima. Ed. J.W. Halporn. CCSL 96. Turnhout, 1973.

   Expositio Psalmorum. 2 vols. Ed. M. Adriaen. CCSL 97–8. Turnhout, 1958.

   Institutiones. Ed. R. A. B. Mynors. Oxford, 1937.

   Ordo generis Cassiodororum [= *Anectodon Holderi*]. Ed. Stefan Krautschick. In *Cassiodor und die Politik seiner Zeit*, p. 84. Bonn, 1983.

Codex Iustinianus. Ed. Paul Krueger. Corpus Iuris Civilis 2. 1877. 11th edn, Berlin, 1954.

Codex Theodosianus. Ed. Theodor Mommsen and Paul Krueger. 2 vols. Berlin, 1905.

Collatio beati Augustini cum Pascentio Ariano. PL 33: 1156–62. Paris, 1845.

Collectio Arrianae Veronensis (Verona, Bibl. Capit. MS LI [49]). Ed. Roger Gryson. Scripta arriana latina 1. CCSL 87: 1–145. Turnhout, 1982.

Constitutio Tanta. In *Digesta.* Ed. Theodor Mommsen and Paul Kreuger. Corpus Iuris Civilis 1: 13–22. 1868. 17th edn, Berlin, 1963.

Continuatio Marcellini. Ed. Theodor Mommsen. MGH: AA 11. Chronica Minora 2: 104–8. Berlin, 1894.

Corpus iuris civilis. See *Codex Iustinianus, Digesta, Novellae Iustiniani.*

Cyril of Scythopolis. *Vita Sabae.* Ed. Eduard Schwartz. Texte und Untersuchungen 49.2. Leipzig, 1939. Trans. R. M. Price, with additions from the Georgian and Arabic versions. In *Lives of the Monks of Palestine.* Cistercian Publications 114. Kalamazoo, 1991.

Vita Iohannou Hesychasti. Ed. Eduard Schwartz. Texte und Untersuchungen 49.2. Leipzig, 1939. Trans. R. M. Price, with additions from the Georgian and Arabic versions. In *Lives of the Monks of Palestine.* Cistercian Publications 114. Kalamazoo, 1991.

De viris illustribus urbis Romae. Ed. Franz Pichlmayr. In his edition of Aurelius Victor, pp. 23–74. Leipzig, 1911.

Digesta. Ed. Theodor Mommsen and Paul Krueger. Corpus Iuris Civilis 1. 1868. 17th edn, Berlin, 1963.

Donatio Ansemundi. Ed. Patrick Amory. "The textual transmission of the Donatio Ansemundi." *Francia* 20.1 (1993), 163–83.

Dracontius. *Satisfactio.* Ed. Friedrich Vollmer. MGH: AA 14: 113–41. Berlin, 1905.

Edict of Glycerius to Himelco. Ed. Gustav Haenel. *Corpus legum ab imperatoribus Romanis ante Iustinianum latarum, quae extra constitutionum codices supersunt.* Leipzig, 1857.

Edictum Theoderici regis. Ed. Friedrich Bluhme. MGH Leges in folio 5: 149–70. Hanover, 1875. Reprinted by J. Baviera. Fontes iuris anteiustiniani 2: 683–710. Florence, 1940.

Ennodius. *Opera.* Ed. Friedrich Vogel. MGH: AA 7. Berlin, 1885.

Epistola "Ita se in omnibus gentibus." [= *Epistola legatariis,* or *epistola clericorum Mediolanensium ad legatos Francorum, qui Constantinopolim profiscebantur.*] Ed. Eduard Schwartz. *Vigiliusbriefe* 4. Sitzungsberichte der Bayerischen Akademie der Wissenschaften, philosophisch-historische Abteilung 1940.2. Munich, 1940.

Epistolae Theodericianae Variae. Ed. Theodor Mommsen. MGH: AA 12: 387–92. Berlin, 1894.

Eugippius. *Excerpta ex operibus sancti Augustini.* Ed. P. Knoell. CSEL 9.1. Vienna, 1886.

Vita Sancti Severini. Ed. Rudolf Noll and Emil Vetter. Schriften und Quellen der Alten Welt 11. Berlin, 1963.

Eutropius. *Breviarium ab urbe condita.* Ed. Carlo Santini. Stuttgart, 1979.

Evagrius. *Historia ecclesiastica.* Ed. J. Bidez and L. Parmentier. London, 1898.

Fasti Vindobonenses priores. Ed. Theodor Mommsen. MGH: AA 9. Chronica Minora 1: 274–320. Berlin, 1892.

Fasti Vindobonenses posteriores. Ed. Theodor Mommsen. MGH: AA 9. Chronica Minora 1: 274–334. Berlin, 1892.

Ferrandus Diaconus. *Epistula dogmatica adversus Arrianos aliosque haereticos ad Eugippium.* Ed. Angelo Mai. 1828. Reprinted in PLS 4: 22–35. Paris, 1967.

Vita Fulgentii. PL 65: 118–50. Paris, 1847.

Fragmentum Laurentianum. Ed. Louis Duchesne. In *Liber Pontificalis* 1: 43–6. 1886. 2nd edn, Paris, 1955.

Georgius Cedrenus. *Compendium Historiarum.* Ed. Immanuel Bekker. 2 vols. Corpus Scriptorum Historiae Byzantinae. Bonn, 1838–9.

Gothic Calendar. Ed. and trans. (with facsimile) Peter Heather and John Matthews. In *The Goths in The Fourth Century,* pp. 128–30. Liverpool, 1991.

Gothic glosses on *Collectio Veronensis*. Ed. Roger Gryson. *Le recueil arien de Vérone*. Instrumenta Patristica 13. The Hague, 1982.

"Gothic" [Greek, Catholic] Martyrologies. Ed. H. Delehaye. "Saints de Mésie et de Thrace," *Analecta Bollandiana* 31 (1912), 161–300 at 276, 279. Trans. Peter Heather and John Matthews. In *The Goths in the Fourth Century*, pp. 126–7, 131.

Gregory the Great. *Dialogi*. Ed. Adalbert de Vogüé. 3 vols. Sources chrétiennes 251, 260, 265. Paris, 1978–80.

Gregory of Tours. *Historiae*. Ed. Bruno Krusch and Wilhelm Levison. MGH: SRM 1.1. 2nd edn, Hanover, 1951.

Gloria martyrum 78–9, ed. Bruno Krusch, MGH: SRM 1.2, Hanover, 1885.

Hydatius. *Continuatio Chronicorum Hieronymianorum*. Ed. Theodor Mommsen. MGH: AA 11. Chronica Minora 2: 13–36. Berlin, 1894.

Inscriptions:

Diehl, Ernst. *Inscriptiones Latinae Christianae Veteres*. 3 vols. Berlin, 1925–31.

Fiebiger, Otto. *Inschriftensammlung zur Geschichte der Ostgermanen*, Neue Folge. Denkschriften der Akademie der Wissenschaften in Wien, philosophisch-historische Klasse 70.3. Vienna, 1939.

Inschriftensammlung zur Geschichte der Ostgermanen, Zweite Folge. Denkschriften der Akademie der Wissenschaften in Wien, philosophisch-historische Klasse 72.2. Vienna, 1944.

Fiebiger, Otto and Ludwig Schmidt. *Inschriftensammlung zur Geschichte der Ostgermanen*. Denkschriften der kaiserlichen Akademie der Wissenschaften in Wien, philosophisch-historische Klasse 60.3. Vienna, 1917.

Inscriptiones Italiae. Rome, 1930– .

Le Blant, Edmond. *Inscriptions chrétiennes de la Gaule antérieures au VIIIe siècle*. 2 vols. Paris, 1856–65.

Mommsen, Theodor, et al. *Corpus Inscriptionum Latinarum*. 17 vols. and supplements. Berlin, 1863– .

Mowat, R. "Note sur des bijoux ornés de devises à propos d'une fibule de l'époque ostrogothe." *Mémoires de la Société Nationale des Antiquaires de France* 5th ser. 9 [= 49] (1888), 19–34.

Recueil des inscriptions chrétiennes de la Gaule antérieure à la Renaissance carolingenne. Ed. Henri Irenée Marrou, et al. Paris, 1975–.

Revue des publications épigraphiques, supplement to *Revue archéologique* (1888–1960), now *Année épigraphique* (1961–).

Rossi, Giovanni Battista de. *Inscriptiones Christianae urbis Romae*. 2 vols. Rome, 1857–88.

"Epigrafe d'una illustre donna della regia stirpe degli Amali Ostrogoti." *Bulletino di archeologia cristiana* 5th ser. 4 (1894), 77–82.

Rugo, Pietro. *Le iscrizioni dei secoli VI–VII–VIII esistenti in Italia*. 5 vols. Cittadella, 1974–80.

Silvagni, Angelo et al. *Inscriptiones Christianae urbis Romae, Nova Series*. 10 vols. Vatican City, 1922–.

Iohannes monachus Scytha. *Responsio adversus Hormisdae epistulam*. [Incorrectly attributed to Maxentius abbas.] Ed. Eduard Schwartz. ACO 4.2. Concilium Universale Constantinopolitanum sub Iustiniano habitum 2. Strasbourg, 1914. [See also Maxentius.]

Isidore of Seville. *Etymologiae sive Origines*. Ed. W. M. Lindsay. 2 vols. Oxford, 1911.

Historia Gothorum Wandalorum Sueborum. Ed. Theodor Mommsen. MGH: AA 11. Chronica Minora 2: 267–303. Berlin, 1894.

Jerome. *Epistula ad Ageruchiam = ep.* 123. PL 22: 1046–59. Paris, 1845.

John of Antioch. *Fragmenta.* Ed. Karl Mueller. Fragmenta historicorum Graecorum 4–5. Paris, 1851–1870. [Reattributions to Priscus and Malchus by R. C. Blockley are noted in footnotes.]

John of Biclar. *Chronica.* Ed. Theodor Mommsen. MGH: AA 11. Chronica Minora 2: 211–39. Berlin, 1894.

John the Deacon. *Epistula ad Senarium virum illustrem.* PL 59: 399–408. Paris, 1847.

John Lydus. *De magistratibus.* Ed. and trans. Anastasius C. Bandy. Philadelphia, 1983.

John Malalas. *Chronographia.* Ed. Ludwig Dindorf. Bonn, 1831. Trans. [with new material and improved apparatus] Elizabeth Jeffreys, Michael Jeffreys and Roger Scott. Byzantina Australiensis 4. Melbourne, 1986.

John of Nikiu. *Chronicle.* Trans. R. H. Charles. London, 1916.

Jordanes. *Romana et Getica.* Ed. Theodor Mommsen. MGH: AA 5.1. Berlin, 1882.

Laws of Hammurabi. Ed. and trans. G. R. Driver and John C. Miles. In *The Babylonian Laws.* 2 vols. 1952–5. 2nd edn, Oxford, 1960.

Liber Constitutionum. Ed. Ludwig Rudolf von Salis. MGH: Leges nationum germanicarum 2.1. Hanover, 1892.

Liber Pontificalis. Ed. Louis Duchesne. 1886–1892. 2nd edn, rev. Cyrille Vogel. 3 vols. Paris, 1955–1958. [Contains reconstructed "first edition" of text at 1: 18–108, and surviving "second edition" of text at 1: 117ff.]

Liber de XII gemmis rationalis summi sacerdotis Hebraeorum [of Epiphanius of Constantia (A.D. 315–403)]. Anonymous translation into Latin. Ed. O. Guenther. *Collectio Avellana* 244. CSEL 35, pp. 743–73.

Liberatus. *Breviarium causae Nestorianorum et Eutychianorum.* Ed. Eduard Schwartz. Acta Conciliorum Oecumenicorum 2.5, Concilium Universale Chacedonense 5. Berlin, 1936.

Malchus. *Fragmenta.* Ed. and trans. R. C. Blockley. *The Fragmentary Classicising Historians of the Later Roman Empire* 2: 378–455. ARCA: Classical and Medieval Texts, Papers and Monographs 10. Liverpool, 1983.

Marcellinus comes. *Chronicon.* Ed. Theodor Mommsen. MGH: AA 11. Chronica Minora 2: 60–104. Berlin, 1894.

Marius of Avenches, *Chronicon.* Ed. Theodor Mommsen, MGH: AA 11. Chronica Minora 2: 232–9. Berlin, 1894.

Maxentius. [Incorrectly called Iohannes Maxentius.] *Dialogi contra Nestorianos.* Ed. Eduard Schwartz. ACO 4.2. Concilium Universale Constantinopolitanum sub Iustiniano habitum 2. Strasbourg, 1914.

Maxentius and the Scythian monks. *Maxentii aliorumque Scytharum monachorum necnon Ioannis Tomitanae urbis episcopi Opuscula.* Ed. F. Glorie. Turnhout, 1978. [See also Iohannes monachus Scytha.]

Maximian. *Elegies.* Ed. Emil Baehrens. Poetae latini minores 5: 313–48. Leipzig, 1883. *Poesos Saeculi Sexti Fragmenta Quattuor.* Ed. H. W. Garrod. [Attributed to an anonymous author.] *Classical Quarterly* 4 (1910), 263–6.

Maximinus. See *Scholia Arriana in concilium Aquiliense*, and *Collectio Veronensis.*

Notitia Dignitatum omnium tam civilium quam militarium. Ed. Otto Seeck. Berlin, 1876.

Novellae ad Theodosianum pertinentes. Ed. Paul M. Meyer and Theodor Mommsen. Berlin, 1905.

Novellae Iustiniani. Ed. Rudolf Schoell and Wilhelm Kroll. Corpus Iuris Civilis 3. 1915. 8th edn, Berlin, 1963.

Olympiodorus. *Fragmenta.* Ed. and trans. R. C. Blockley. *The Fragmentary Classicising Historians of the Later Roman Empire* 2: 151–209. ARCA: Classical and Medieval Texts, Papers and Monographs 10. Liverpool, 1983.

Opus imperfectum in Matthaeum. Ed. Bernard de Montfaucon. PG 56: 611–946. Paris, 1862.

Origo gentis Romanae. Ed. Franz Pichlmayr. In his edition of Aurelius Victor, pp. 3–22. Leipzig, 1911.

Orosius. *Historia adversus paganos.* Ed. C. Zangemeister. CSEL 5. Vienna, 1882–9.

Palladius of Ratiara. See *Scholia Arriana in concilium Aquiliense.*

Papal letters:

    Collectio Avellana. Ed. O. Guenther. CSEL 35.1–2. Vienna, 1895–1898.

    Collectio Arelatensis. Ed. Wilhelm Gundlach. MGH: Epistolae 3. Epistolae Merowingici et Karolini aevi 1. Berlin, 1892.

    Ewald, Paul, ed. "Die Papstbriefe der brittischen Sammlung." *Neues Archiv* 5 (1880), 275–414, 503–96.

    Gassò, Pius M. and Columba M. Batlle. *Pelagii I papae epistulae quae supersunt (556–561).* Scripta et documenta 8. Montserrat, 1956.

    Gregory the Great. *Registum epistolarum.* 2 vols. Ed. Paul Ewald and Ludo Moritz Hartmann. MGH: Epistolae 1–2. Gregorii I papae Registrum epistolarum, Libri I–VII, VIII–XIV. Berlin, 1887–99.

    Loewenfeld, Samuel, ed. *Epistulae pontificum Romanorum ineditae.* Leipzig, 1885.

    Praeceptum papae Felicis morientis, Senatusconsultum ann. 530 and *Libellus quem dederunt presbyteri 60.* Ed. Eduard Schwartz. 1914. Reprinted in PLS 3: 1280–2. Paris, 1963.

    Pelagius II. Ed. Ludo Moritz Hartmann. In MGH: Epistolae 2. Gregorii I papae Registrum epistolarum, Libri VIII–XIV. Berlin, 1892–9.

    Schwartz, Eduard. *Vigiliusbriefe.* Sitzungsberichte der Bayerischen Akademie der Wissenschaften, philosophisch-historische Abetilung 1940.2. Munich, 1940.

    Thiel, Andreas. *Epistolae Romanorum pontificum genuinae* 1. [Subsequent volumes never appeared.] Braunsberg, 1868.

    Otherwise unedited letters to and from Felix IV, Boniface II, John II and Vigilius II. PL 62: 91–2; 65: 12–15, 31–4, 40–2; 66: 17–24. Paris, 1847. PL 69: 15–19. Paris, 1848.

Papyri:

    Tjäder, Jan-Olof. *Die nichtliterarischen lateinischen Papyri Italiens aus der Zeit 445–700.* 3 vols. Skrifter Utgivna av Svenska Institutet i Rom [= Acta Instituti Romani Regni Sueciae] series in 4°, 19.1–3. Lund and Stockholm, 1954–82.

Marini, Gaetano. *I papiri diplomatici.* Rome, 1805.

Frösén, Jaakko. In *P. Rainer Cent. Festschrift zum 100-jährigen Bestehen der Papyrus-Sammlung der Österreichischen Nationalbibliothek Papyrus Erzherzog Rainer.* 2 vols., Vienna, 1983, 1: 495–8.

Paschale Campanum. Ed. Theodor Mommsen. MGH: AA 9. Chronica Minora 1: 305–34. Berlin, 1892.

Passio Sancti Sigismundi regis. Ed. Bruno Krusch. MGH: SRM 2: 329–40. Hanover, 1888.

Paul the Deacon. *Historia Romana.* Ed. Hans Droysen. MGH: SRG 49. Berlin, 1879.

    Historia Langobardorum. Ed. Lidia Capo. *Storia dei Longobardi.* Vicenza, 1992.

Pliny the Elder. *Historia Naturalis.* Ed. and trans. H. Rackham, W. H. S. Jones and D. E. Eichholz. 10 vols. Cambridge, Mass., 1938–62.

Pomponius Mela. *De chorographia libri tres.* Ed. K. Frick. Leipzig, 1880.

Praeceptum regis Theoderici. Epistulae Theodericianae Variae 9, p. 392.

Preface to the *Codex Brixianus.* Ed. W. Streitberg. *Die Gotische Bibel,* 2 vols. 1: xlii–xliii. Heidelberg, 1908–10.

Priscian. *De laude Anastasii imperatoris.* Ed. Emil Baehrens. *Poetae latini minores* 5: 264–74. Leipzig, 1883.

Priscus of Panium. *Fragmenta.* Ed. and trans. R. C. Blockley. *The Fragmentary Classicising Historians of the Later Roman Empire* 2: 221–377. ARCA: Classical and Medieval Texts, Papers and Monographs 10. Liverpool, 1983.

Procopius. *Wars.* Ed. J. Haury. Trans. H. B. Dewing. 5 vols. Cambridge, Mass., 1914–28.

The Anecdota or Secret History. Ed. J. Haury. Trans. H. B. Dewing. Cambridge, Mass., 1935.

Buildings. Ed. J. Haury. Trans. H. B. Dewing. Cambridge, Mass., 1940.

Quintilian. *Institutiones Oratoriae.* Ed. Ludwig Radermacher. 2 vols. Leipzig, 1965.

Ravenna Cosmographer. Ed. Joseph Schnetz. *Itineraria Romana* 2. Leipzig, 1940.

Scholia Arriana in concilium Aquiliense in quibus leguntur Maximini episcopi dissertatio et Palladi Ratariensis fragmenta. Ed. Roger Gryson. Scripta arriana latina 1. CCSL 87: 147–96. Turnhout, 1982.

Sidonius Apollinaris. *Carmina et Epistulae.* Ed. and trans. W. B. Anderson and E. H. Warmington. 2 vols. Cambridge, Mass., 1936–65.

Skeireins. Ed. and trans. William Holmes Bennett. *The Gothic Commentary on the Gospel of John: skeireins ai waggeljons thairh iohannen.* Modern Language Association of America Monograph 21. New York, 1960.

Stephanus of Byzantium. *Ethnika.* Ed. August Meineke. 1849. Reprint Graz, 1958.

Suidas. Ed. Ada Adler. 5 vols. Lexicographi Graeci 1. Stuttgart, 1967.

Summa Perusina, adnotationes codicis domni Iustiniani. Ed. Friderico Patetta. *Bulletino dell'Istituto di diritto Romano* 12 (1900).

Tacitus. *De origine et situ Germanorum.* Ed. J. G. C. Anderson. Oxford, 1938.

Themistius. *Orationes* 1. Ed. H. Schenkls. Rev. Glanville Downey and A. F. Norman. Leipzig, 1965.

Theodore Lector. *Epitome historiae ecclesiasticae.* Ed. Guenther Christian Hanson. *Theodoros Anagnostes Kirchengeschichte.* Die griechische christliche Schriftsteller der ersten Jahrhunderte. Berlin, 1971.

Theophanes. *Chronographia.* Ed. Carl de Boor. 2 vols. Leipzig, 1883.

Thesaurus linguae Latinae. Leipzig, 1900–.

Trifolius. *Epistola ad beatum Faustum senatorem contra Ioannem Scytham monachum.* Ed. Eduard Schwartz. In *Publizistische Sammlungen zum Acacianischen Schisma.* Abhandlungen der Bayerischen Akademie der Wissenschaften, philosophisch-historische Abteilung n.s. 10: 115–17. Munich, 1934.

Venantius Fortunatus. *Opera.* Ed. Friedrich Leo. MGH: AA 4. Berlin, 1881–5.

Victor Tonnennensis. *Chronica.* Ed. Theodor Mommsen. MGH: AA 11. Chronica Minora 2: 184–206. Berlin, 1894.

Victor Vitensis. *Historia persecutionis Africanae provinciae sub Geiserico et Hunirico regibus Wandalorum.* Ed. Karl Halm. MGH: AA 3.1. Berlin, 1879.

Vita Caesarii Arelatensis. Ed. Bruno Krusch. MGH: SRM 3. Hanover, 1896.

Vita Hilari Galeatensis. Ed. Daniel Papebroch. Acta Sanctorum, Maii 3: 473–5. Antwerp, 1680.

Zacharias Rhetor. *Historia Ecclesiastica.* Ed. and trans. E. W. Brooks. Corpus scriptorum Christianorum orientalium, 3.5–6. London, 1919–24.

Zosimus. *Historia Nova.* Ed. François Paschoud. 3 vols. Paris, 1971–89.

SECONDARY SOURCES

Adams, J. N. *The Text and Language of a Vulgar Latin Chronicle (Anonymus Valesianus II).* Institute of Classical Studies Bulletin, Supplement 36. London, 1976.

Alföldy, Geza. *Noricum.* Trans. Anthony Birley. London, 1974.

Altaner, Berthold. "Der griechische Theologe Leontius und Leontius der skythische Mönche." 1947. Reprinted in *Kleine patristische Schriften.* Ed. Günter Glockmann. Texte und Untersuchungen 83. Berlin, 1967.

"Zum Schrifttum der 'skythischen' (gotischen) Mönche: Quellenkritische und literarhistorische Untersuchungen." 1947. Reprinted in *Kleine patristische Schriften.* Ed. Günter Glockmann. Texte und Untersuchungen 83. Berlin, 1967.

"Augustinus in der griechischen Kirche bis auf Photius." 1952. Reprinted in *Kleine patristische Schriften.* Ed. Günter Glockmann. Texte und Untersuchungen 83. Berlin, 1967.

Amory, Patrick. "The meaning and purpose of ethnic terminology in the Burgundian laws." *Early Medieval Europe* 2 (1993), 1–28.

"Names, ethnic identity and community in fifth- and sixth-century Burgundy." *Viator* 25 (1994), 1–30.

"Ethnographic rhetoric, aristocratic attitudes and political allegiance in post-Roman Gaul." *Klio* 76 (1994), 438–53.

Anderson, Perry. "Geoffrey de Ste. Croix and the ancient world." 1983. Reprinted in *A Zone of Engagement.* London, 1992.

Arcamone, Maria Giovanna. "I Germani d'Italia: lingue e 'documenti' linguistici." In *Magistra barbaritas: I barbari in Italia.* Ed. Giovanni Pugliese Carratelli. Milan, 1984.

Arnold, C. J. *Roman Britain to Saxon England: An Archaeological Study.* London, 1984.

Bachrach, Bernard S. "Animals and warfare in early medieval Europe." In *L'Uomo di fronte al mondo animale nell'alto medioevo.* 2 vols. Settimane di Studio del Centro Italiano di studi sull'alto medioevo 31. Spoleto, 1985.

Bachrach, Bernard S. Review of *Les Goths* by Michel Kazanski. *Francia* 20.1 (1993), 256.

Bagnall, Roger. *Egypt in Late Antiquity.* Princeton, 1993.

Baldi, Philip. *An Introduction to the Indo-European Languages.* Carbondale, Illinois, 1983.

Balsdon, J. P. V. D. *Romans and Aliens.* London, 1979.

Banniard, Michel. *Viva Voce: Communication écrite et communication orale du IVe au IXe siècle en Occident latin.* Collection des Etudes Augustiniennes, Série Moyen-Age et Temps Modernes 25. Paris, 1992.

Banning, J. van. *Opus imperfectum in Matthaeum: praefatio.* CCSL 87B. Turnhout, 1988.

Barber, Tony. "Young men in no rush to join old battle." *The Independent on Sunday* 76 (7 July 1991), 17.

Barnish, S. J. B. "The *Anonymus Valesianus* II as a source for the last years of Theoderic." *Latomus* 42 (1983), 572–96.

"Taxation, land and barbarian settlement in the Western empire." *Papers of the British School at Rome* 54 (1986), 170–95.

"Pigs, plebeians and *potentes*: Rome's economic hinterland, *c.* 350–600 A.D." *Papers of the British School at Rome* 55 (1987), 157–85.

"Maximian, Cassiodorus, Boethius, Theodahad: literature, philosophy and politics in Ostrogothic Italy." *Nottingham Medieval Studies* 34 (1990), 16–32.

trans. with commentary. *Cassiodorus: Variae.* Liverpool, 1992.

Barnwell, P. S. *Emperors, Prefects and Kings: The Roman West, 395–565.* London, 1992.

Barth, Frederik, ed. *Ethnic Groups and Boundaries: The Social Organization of Cultural Difference.* Boston, 1969.

Barton, Peter F. *Die Frühzeit des Christentums in Österreich und Südostmitteleuropa bis 788.* Studien und Texte zur Kirchengeschichte und Geschichte 1st ser. 1.1. Vienna, 1975.

Battisti, Carlo. "L'elemento gotico nella topomastica e nel lessico italiano." In *I Goti in Occidente: Problemi.* Settimane di studio del Centro Italiano di studi sull'alto medioevo 3. Spoleto, 1956.

Baynes, Norman H. "Justinian and Amalasuntha." 1925. Reprinted in *Byzantine Studies and Other Essays.* London, 1955.

"Eusebius and the Christian Empire." 1933. Reprinted in *Byzantine Studies and Other Essays.* London, 1955.

"The political ideas of St. Augustine's *De Civitate Dei.*" 1936. Reprinted in *Byzantine Studies and Other Essays.* London, 1955.

"The decline of Roman power in Western Europe: some modern explanations." 1943. Reprinted in *Byzantine Studies and Other Essays.* London, 1955.

Becker, Hans-Jürgen. "Edictum Theoderici." In *Handwörterbuch zur deutschen Rechtsgeschichte* 1. Berlin, 1971.

Bennett, William Holmes. ed. and trans. with commentary. *The Gothic Commentary on the Gospel of John: skeireins ai waggeljons thairh iohannen.* Modern Language Association of America Monograph 21. New York, 1960.

Berghe, Pierre L. van den. "Ethnicity and the sociobiology debate." In *Theories of Race and Ethnic Relations.* Ed. John Rex and David Mason. Cambridge, 1986.

Bierbrauer, Volker. *Die Ostgotischen Grab- und Schatzfunde in Italien.* Biblioteca degli studi medievali 7. Spoleto, 1975.

"Aspetti archeologici di Goti, Alamanni e Longobardi," in *Magistra barbaritas: I barbari in Italia.* Ed. Giovanni Pugliese Caratelli. Milan, 1984.

"Archeologia e storia dei Goti dal I al IV secolo." "Archeologia degli Ostrogoti in Italia." Both in *I Goti.* Catalogue of the Exhibition at Milan, Palazzo Reale, 28 January–8 May 1994. Milan, 1994.

"Die Goten vom 1.–7. Jahrhundert n. Chr.: Siedelgebiete und Wanderbewegungen auf Grund archäologischer Quellen." In *Teoderico il Grande e i Goti d'Italia.* Atti del XIII Congresso internazionale di studi sull'alto medioevo. Milan, 2–6 November 1992. Spoleto, 1993.

Bird, H. W., trans. with commentary. *Eutropius: Breviarium.* Liverpool, 1993.

Bishop, M. C. and J. C. N. Coulston. *Roman Military Equipment From The Punic Wars To The Fall of Rome.* London, 1993.

Blockley, R. C., ed. and trans. with commentary. *The Fragmentary Classicising Historians of the Later Roman Empire: Eunapius, Olympiodorus, Priscus and Malchus.* 2 vols.

ARCA: Classical and Medieval Texts, Papers and Monographs 6 and 10. Liverpool, 1981–3.

Blockley, R. C. *East Roman Foreign Policy: Formation and Conduct from Diocletian to Anastasius.* ARCA: Classical and Medieval Texts, Papers and Monographs 30. Leeds, 1992.

Blok, D. P. *Ortsnamen.* Typologie des sources du moyen âge occidental 54. Turnhout, 1988.

Bluhme, Friedrich. Commentary on the *Edictum Theoderici.* In MGH: Leges in folio 5. Hanover, 1889.

Bowman, Alan K. and Greg Woolf. *Literacy and Power in the Ancient World.* Cambridge, 1994.

Brown, Peter. *Augustine of Hippo.* London, 1967.

"Pelagius and his supporters: aims and environment." 1968. Reprinted in *Religion and Society in the Age of Saint Augustine.* London, 1972.

The World of Late Antiquity A.D. *150–750.* London, 1971.

The Cult of the Saints: Its Rise and Function in Latin Christianity. Chicago, 1981.

The Body and Society: Men, Women and Sexual Renunciation in Early Christianity. New York, 1988.

Power and Persuasion in Late Antiquity: Towards a Christian Empire. Madison, 1992.

Brown, T. S. "The church of Ravenna and the imperial administration in the seventh century." *English Historical Review* 94 (1979), 1–28.

Gentlemen and Officers: Imperial Administration and Aristocratic Power in Byzantine Italy, A.D. *554–800.* Rome, 1984.

"Everyday life in Ravenna under Theoderic: an example of his 'tolerance' and 'prosperity?' " In *Teoderico il Grande e i Goti d'Italia.* Atti del XIII Congresso internazionale di studi sull'alto medioevo. Milan, 2–6 November 1992. Spoleto, 1993.

Brunt, P. A. "A Marxist view of Roman history." Review of *The Class Struggle in the Ancient Greek World* by G. E. M. de Ste. Croix. *Journal of Roman Studies* 72 (1982), 158–63.

Buchner, Rudolf. *Die Rechtsquellen.* Supplement to *Deutschlands Geschichtsquellen im Mittelalter: Vorzeit und Karolinger.* Ed. Wilhelm Wattenbach and Wilhelm Levison. Weimar, 1953.

Buchwald, Wolfgang, Armin Hohweg and Otto Prinz. *Dictionnaire des auteurs grecs et latins de l'antiquité et du moyen âge.* 1982. Trans. and rev. Jean Denis Berger and Jacques Billen. Turnhout, 1991.

Buckland, W. W. *A Manual of Roman Private Law.* Cambridge, 1925.

Burgess, M.E. "The resurgence of ethnicity: myth or reality?" *Ethnic and Racial Studies* 1 (1978), 265–85.

Burgess, R. W. Review of *Emperors, Prefects and Kings* by P. S. Barnwell. *Bryn Mawr Classical Review* 4.3 (1993), 1–5.

Burns, Thomas. *A History of the Ostrogoths.* Bloomington, Indiana, 1984.

Barbarians Within The Gates of Rome: A Study of Roman Military Policy and the Barbarians, ca. 375–425 A.D. Bloomington, Indiana, 1994.

Bury, J. B. *History of the Later Roman Empire from the Death of Theodosius I to the Death of Justinian.* 2nd edn, London, 1923.

Cameron, Alan, Jacqueline Long and Lee Sherry. *Barbarians and Politics at the Court of Arcadius.* Berkeley, 1993.

Cameron, Averil. "Agathias on the early Merovingians." *Annali della Scuola Normale di Pisa* 2nd ser. 37 (1968), 95–140.

"Agathias on the Sassanians." *Dumbarton Oaks Papers* 23–4 (1969–70), 1–150.

Agathias. Oxford, 1970.

"Cassiodorus deflated." Review of *Cassiodorus* by James J. O'Donnell. *Journal of Roman Studies* 71 (1981), 183–6.

Procopius and the Sixth Century. Berkeley, 1985.

"History as text: coping with Procopius." In *The Inheritance of Historiography 350–900.* Ed. Christopher Holdsworth and T. P. Wiseman. Exeter Studies in History 12. Exeter, 1986.

"Gelimer's laughter: the case of Byzantine Africa." In *Tradition and Innovation in Late Antiquity.* Ed. Frank M. Clover and R. S. Humphreys. Madison, 1989.

The Mediterranean World in Late Antiquity A.D. 395–600. London, 1993.

Caspar, Erich. *Geschichte des Papsttums von den Anfängen bis zur Höhe der Weltherrschaft* 2. *Das Papsttum unter byzantinischer Herrschaft.* Tübingen, 1933.

Cavanna, Adriano. "Diritto e società nei regno ostrogoto e longobardo." In *Magistra barbaritas: I barbari in Italia.* Ed. Giovanni Pugliese Carratelli. Milan, 1984.

Cecchelli, Carlo. "L'Arianesimo e le chiese ariane d'Italia." In *Le chiese nei regni dell'Europa occidentale e i loro rapporti con Roma sino all'800.* Settimane di Studio del Centro Italiano di studi sull'alto medioevo 7. Spoleto, 1960.

Cesa, Maria. "Etnografia e geografia nella visione storica di Procopius di Cesarea." *Studi classici e orientali* 32 (1982), 189–215.

Chadwick, Henry. *Boethius: The Consolations of Music, Logic, Theology and Philosophy.* Oxford, 1981.

Champion, Timothy. "Theoretical archaeology in Britain." In *Archaeological Theory in Europe: The Last Three Decades.* Ed. Ian Hodder. London, 1991.

Christ, Karl. "Germanendarstellung und Zeitverständnis bei Tacitus." 1965. Reprinted in *Römische Geschichte und Wissenschaftsgeschichte 2. Geschichte und Geschichtsschreibung der römischen Kaiserzeit.* Darmstadt, 1983.

Classen, Peter. *Kaiserreskript und Königsurkunden: Diplomatische Studien zum Problem der Kontinuität zwischen Altertum und Mittelalter.* 1956. Reprint. Thessalonica, 1977.

Claude, Dietrich. "Gentile und territoriale Staatsideen im Westgotenreich." *Frühmittelalterliche Studien* 6 (1972), 1–38.

"Zur Ansiedlung barbarischer Föderaten in der ersten Hälfte des 5. Jahrhunderts." In *Anerkennung und Integration: zu den wirtschaftlichen Grundlagen der Völkerwanderungszeit, 400–600.* Ed. Herwig Wolfram and Andreas Schwarcz. Denkschriften der philosophisch-historischen Klasse 193. Vienna, 1988.

"Zur Begrundung familiärer Beziehungen zwischen dem Kaiser und barbarischen Herrschern." In *Das Reich und die Barbaren.* Ed. Evangelos Chrysos and Andreas Schwarcz. Veröffentlichungen des Insituts für Österreichischen Geschichtsforschung 29. Vienna, 1989.

"Teoderico il Grande nel quadro europeo e mediterraneo: le sue relazioni diplomatiche." In *Teoderico il Grande e i Goti d'Italia.* Atti del XIII Congresso internazionale di studi sull'alto medioevo. Milan, 2–6 November 1992. Spoleto, 1993.

Clifford, James. "Identity in Mashpee." In *The Predicament of Culture: Twentieth Century Ethnography, Literature and Art.* Cambridge, Mass., 1988.

Clover, Frank M. "The pseudo-Boniface and the Historia Augusta." In *Bonner Historia-Augusta Colloquium 1977/1978.* Antiquitas, 4th ser. 14. Bonn, 1980.

"Carthage and the Vandals." In *Excavations at Carthage 1978, Conducted by the University of Michigan 7*. Ed. J.H. Humphrey. Ann Arbor, 1982.

Collins, Roger. *Early Medieval Spain: Unity in Diversity 400–1000*. London, 1983.

Comaroff, John and Jean. *Ethnography and the Historical Imagination*. Boulder, Colorado, 1992.

Connor, Steve. "We know where they're coming from." Review of *The Language of Genes* by Steve Jones. London, 1993.

Conti, Pier Maria. *"Devotio" e "viri devoti" in Italia da Diocleziano ai Carolingi*. Padua, 1971.

Cook, Genevieve Marie, trans. with commentary. *The Life of Saint Epiphanius by Ennodius*. Studies in Medieval and Renaissance Language and Literature 14. Washington, 1942.

Courcelle, Pierre. *Histoire littéraire des grandes invasions germaniques*. 1st ed. Paris, 1948.

"Nouvelles recherches sur le monastère de Cassiodore." 1957. Reprinted in *Opuscula selecta*. Paris, 1984.

"Le tyran et le philosophe d'après la 'Consolation' de Boèce." In *Passaggio dal mondo antico al medio evo da Teodosio a San Gregorio Magno*. Convegno Internazionale dell'Accademia Nazionale dei Lincei, Rome, 25–28 May 1977. Atti dei Convegni Lincei 45. Rome, 1980.

Cramer, Peter. *Baptism and Change in the Early Middle Ages c. 200–c.1150*. Cambridge, 1993.

Croke, Brian. "Mundo the Gepid: from freebooter to Roman general." *Chiron* 12 (1982), 125–35.

"A.D. 476: the manufacture of a turning point." *Chiron* 13 (1983), 81–119.

"Cassiodorus and the *Getica* of Jordanes." *Classical Philology* 82 (1987), 117–34.

"City chronicles of late antiquity." In *Reading the Past in Late Antiquity*. Ed. G. Clarke, et. al. Sydney, 1990.

Cullen, Robert. "Roots." *The New Yorker* (15 April 1991), 55–76.

Cunliffe, Barry. *Greeks, Romans and Barbarians: Spheres of Interaction*. London, 1988.

Dagron, Gilbert. " 'Ceux d'en face': les peuples étrangers dans les traités militaires byzantins." *Travaux et Mémoires* 10 (1987), 207–32.

Dannenbauer, Heinrich. "Die Rechtsstellung der Galloromer im Frankischenreich." In *Grundlagen der mittelalterlichen Welt: Skizzen und Studien*. Zeitschrift "Welt als Geschichte" 194. Stuttgart, 1958.

Dauge, Y.A. *Le barbare: recherches sur la conception romaine de la barbarie et de la civilisation*. Collection Latomus 176. Brussels, 1981.

Deichmann, Friedrich Wilhelm. *Ravenna, Hauptstadt des spätantiken Abendlandes*. 6 vols. Wiesbaden and Stuttgart, 1958–89.

Delbrück, Hans. *History of the Art of War 2. The Barbarian Invasions*. 1921. Trans. Walter J. Renfroe, Jr. Lincoln, Nebraska, 1980.

Delbrueck, Richard. *Die Consulardiptychen und verwandte Denkmäler*. 1 vol. plus plates. Studien zur spätantiken Kunstgeschichte 2. Berlin, 1929.

Demandt, Alexander. "Magister militum." *Real-Encyklopaedie der klassischen Altertumswissenschaft* suppl. 12. Stuttgart, 1970.

"The osmosis of the late Roman and Germanic aristocracies." In *Das Reich und die Barbaren*. Ed. Evangelos Chrysos and Andreas Schwarcz. Veröffentlichungen des Instituts für Österreichischen Geschichtsforschung 29. Vienna, 1989.

Demougeot, Emilienne. *La formation de l'Europe et les invasions barbares de l'avènement de Dioclétien au début du VIe siècle.* 2 vols. Paris, 1979.

"La carrière politique de Boèce." In *Atti del Congresso di Studi Boeziani.* Ed. L. Obertello. Rome, 1981.

"Le partage des provinces de l'Illyricum entre la *pars Occidentis* et la *pars Orientis,* de la tétrarchie au règne de Théodoric." In *La géographie administrative et politique d'Alexandre à Mahomet.* Leiden, 1981.

Detschew, Dimiter. *Die thrakischen Sprachreste.* Österreichische Akademie der Wissenschaften, philosophisch-historische Klasse: Schriften der Balkankommission, Linguistische Abteilung 14. Vienna, 1957.

Drinkwater, John. "The Bacaudae of fifth-century Gaul." In *Fifth-Century Gaul: A Crisis of Identity?* Ed. John Drinkwater and Hugh Elton. Cambridge, 1992.

Dubois, Augustin. *La latinité d'Ennodius.* Paris, 1903.

Duchesne, Louis. "La succession du pape Félix IV." *Mélanges d'archéologie et d'histoire de l'Ecole Française de Rome* 3 (1883), 239–66.

"Vigile et Pélage." *Revue des questions historiques* 36 (1884), 369–440.

L'Eglise au VIe siècle. Paris, 1925.

Dumézil, Georges. *Mitra Varuna: An Essay on Two Indo-European Representations of Sovereignty.* 1948. Trans. Derek Colman. New York, 1988.

Dumville, David. "The West Saxon Genealogical Regnal List and the chronology of early Wessex." *Peritia* 4 (1985), 21–67.

Durliat, Jean. "Le salaire de la paix sociale dans les royaumes barbares (Ve–VIe siècles)." In *Anerkennung und Integration: zu den wirtschaftlichen Grundlagen der Völkerwanderungszeit, 400–600.* Ed. Herwig Wolfram and Andreas Schwarcz. Denkschriften der philosophisch-historischen Klasse 193. Vienna, 1988.

"Qu'est-ce que le Bas-Empire (II)." *Francia* 18.1 (1991), 125–38.

Dütschke, Hans. *Ravennatische Studien: Beiträge zur Geschichte der späten Antike.* Leipzig, 1909.

Dvornik, Francis. *Early Christian and Byzantine Political Philosophy: Origins and Background.* 2 vols. Dumbarton Oaks Studies 9. Washington, 1966.

Dyggve, Ejnar. *History of Salonitan Christianity.* Institutet for Sammenlignende Kulturforskning, ser. A: Forelesninger 21. Oslo, 1951.

Ebling, Horst, Jörg Jarnut and Gerd Kampers. "Nomen et gens: Untersuchungen zu den Führungsschichten des Franken-, Langobarden- und Westgotenreiches im 6. und 7. Jahrhundert." *Francia* 8 (1980), 687–745.

Egger, Rudolf. "Ausgrabungen in Kärnten." *Jahresheft des Österreichischen archäologischen Instituts in Wien* 13 (1910), Beiblatt, 129–75.

Der altchristliche Friedhof Manastirine. Forschungen in Salona 2. Vienna, 1926.

Elton, Hugh. *Warfare in Roman Europe A.D. 350–425.* Oxford, 1996.

Ensslin, Wilhelm. "Der Patricius Praesentalis im Ostgotenreich." *Klio* 29 (1936), 243–9.

Theoderich der Grosse. Munich, 1947.

Des Symmachus Historia Romana als Quelle für Jordanes. Sitzungsberichte der Bayerischen Akademie der Wissenschaften, philosophisch-historische Abteilung 1948.3. Munich, 1948.

Ewald, Paul. "Die Papstbriefe der brittischen Sammlung." *Neues Archiv* 5 (1880), 275–414, 503–96.

Fanning, Steven C. "Lombard Arianism reconsidered." *Speculum* 56 (1981), 241–58.

Fehring, Günter P. *The Archaeology of Medieval Germany: An Introduction.* Trans. Ross Samson. London, 1991.

Finnegan, Ruth. "Oral tradition and historical evidence." *History and Theory* 9 (1970), 195–201.

Förstemann, Ernst. *Altdeutsches Namenbuch.* 3 vols. 2nd. edn, Bonn, 1900.

Foucault, Michel. *The History of Sexuality* 2. *The Use of Pleasure.* 1984. Trans. Robert Hurley. New York, 1985.

Fournier, Paul and Gabriel Le Bras. *Histoire des collections canoniques en Occident depuis les Fausse Décrétales jusqu'au Décret de Gratien.* 2 vols. Paris, 1931–2.

Fraser, P. M. and E. Matthews. *A Lexicon of Greek Personal Names* 1. *The Aegean Islands, Cyprus, Cyrenaica.* Oxford, 1987.

Freeman, E. A. "Race and language." In *Historical Essays* 3. London, 1879.

Frend, W. H. C. "The monophysites and the transition between the ancient world and the Middle Ages." In *Passaggio dal mondo antico al medio evo da Teodosio a San Gregorio Magno.* Convegno Internazionale dell'Accademia Nazionale dei Lincei, Rome, 25–8 May 1977. Atti dei Convegni Lincei 45. Rome, 1980.

Frye, David. "Gundobad, the *Leges Burgundionum,* and the struggle for sovereignty in Burgundy." *Classica et Medievalia* 41 (1990), 199–212.

Fuhrmann, Manfred. "Die Romidee der Spätantike." 1968. Reprinted in *Rom als Idee.* Ed. Bernhard Kytzler. Wege der Forschung 656. Darmstadt, 1993.

Fustel de Coulanges, N. D. "Le colonat romain." In *Recherches sur quelques problèmes d'histoire.* Paris, 1894.

Gamillscheg, Ernst. *Romania Germania: Sprach- und Siedlungsgeschichte der Germanen auf dem Boden des alten Römerreiches* 2. *Die Ostgoten, die Langobarden, die altgermanischen Bestandteile des Ostromanischen, Altgermanisches im Alpenromanischen.* Grundrisse germanischer Philologie 11.2. Berlin, 1935.

Gaudemet, Jean. "A propos du 'droit vulgaire.'" 1963. Reprinted in *Etudes de droit romain* 1. Studi in onore di Biondo Biondi 1. Camerino, 1979.

Geary, Patrick. "Ethnicity as a situational construct in the early Middle Ages." *Mitteilungen der anthropologischen Gesellschaft in Wien* 113 (1983), 15–26.

Gelling, Margaret. "Towards a chronology for English place-names." In *Anglo-Saxon Settlements.* Ed. Della Hooke. Oxford, 1988.

Gensel, P. "Eutropius, Historiker." *RE* 6:1521–7. Stuttgart, 1909.

George, Judith W. *Venantius Fortunatus: A Poet in Merovingian Gaul.* Oxford, 1992.

Giunta, Francesco. "Gli Ostrogoti in Italia." In *Magistra barbaritas: I barbari in Italia.* Ed. Giovanni Pugliese Caratelli. Milan, 1984.

Goebel, Julius. *Felony and Misdemeanour: A Study in the History of Criminal Law.* [Originally published as: *Felony and Misdemeanour: A Study in the History of English Criminal Procedure* 1.] 1937. Reprint. Philadelphia, 1976.

Goffart, Walter. "Zosimus, the first historian of Rome's fall." 1971. Reprinted in *Rome's Fall and After.* London, 1989.

"From Roman taxation to medieval seigneurie: three notes." 1972. Reprinted in *Rome's Fall and After.* London, 1989.

"The date and purpose of Vegetius' *De re militari.*" 1977. Reprinted in *Rome's Fall and After.* London, 1989.

Barbarians and Romans A.D. *418–584: The Techniques of Accommodation.* Princeton, 1980.

"Rome, Constantinople and the barbarians." 1981. Reprinted in *Rome's Fall and After.* London, 1989.

"Old and new in Merovingian taxation." 1982. Reprinted in *Rome's Fall and After*. London, 1989.

"The supposedly 'Frankish' table of nations: an edition and study." 1983. Reprinted in *Rome's Fall and After*. London, 1989.

Review of *Cassiodor* by Stefan Krautschick. *Speculum* 60 (1985), 989–91.

The Narrators of Barbarian History (A.D. 550–800): Jordanes, Gregory of Tours, Bede and Paul the Deacon. Princeton, 1988.

"The theme of '*the* barbarian invasions' in late antique and modern historiography." 1989. Reprinted in *Rome's Fall and After*. London, 1989.

"An empire unmade: Rome, A.D. 300–600." In *Rome's Fall and After*. London, 1989.

Goodman, Martin. "Proselytising in rabbinic Judaism." *Journal of Jewish Studies* 40 (1989), 175–85.

Goody, Jack. "Introduction." In *Literacy in Traditional Societies*. Ed. Jack Goody. Cambridge, 1968.

Gordon, R., Mary Beard et al. "Roman inscriptions 1986–90." *Journal of Roman Studies* 83 (1993), 139–49.

Goubert, Pierre. "Autour du voyage à Byzance du pape S. Jean I." *Orientalia Christiana Periodica* 24 (1958), 339–52.

Graus, František. Review of *Stammesbildung und Verfassung* by Reinhard Wenskus. *Historica* 7 (1963), 185–91.

Gribomont, J. "Jacob of Sarug." In *Encyclopedia of the Early Church*. Ed. Angelo di Berardino. 1982. Trans. Adrian Walford. 2 vols. Cambridge, 1992.

Grierson, Philip and Mark Blackburn. *Medieval European Coinage with a Catalogue of the Coins in the Fitzwilliam Museum, Cambridge* 1. *The Early Middle Ages (5th–10th Centuries)*. Cambridge, 1986.

Gryson, Roger. "Les citations scriptuaires des oeuvres attribuées à l'évêque arien Maximinus." *Revue bénédictine* 88 (1978), 45–80.

Gryson, Roger. *Le recueil arien de Vérone*. Instrumenta Patristica 13. The Hague, 1982.

Haberl, Johann, and Christopher Hawkes. "The last of Roman Noricum: St. Severin on the Danube." In *Greeks, Celts and Romans*. Ed. Christopher and Sonia Hawkes. Archaeology into History Series 1. London, 1973.

Hague, Barry. "Cultures in collision: the barbarization of the western Roman Empire in ideology and reality (c. 370–530 A.D.)." Ph.D. thesis, Cambridge, 1987.

Halsall, Guy. "The origins of the *Reihengräberzivilisation*: forty years on." In *Fifth-Century Gaul: A Crisis of Identity?* Ed. John Drinkwater and Hugh Elton. Cambridge, 1992.

Halsey, A.H. "Ethnicity: a primordial social bond?" *Ethnic and Racial Studies* 1 (1978), 124–8.

Härke, Heinrich. "All quiet on the Western front? Paradigms, methods and approaches in West German archaeology." In *Archaeological Theory in Europe: The Last Three Decades*. Ed. Ian Hodder. London, 1991.

Harnack, Adolf von. "Der erste deutsche Papst (Bonifatius II., 530/32) und die beiden letzten Dekrete des römischen Senats." *Sitzungsberichte der preussischen Akademie der Wissenschaften* (1924), 24–42.

Harries, Jill. "Sidonius Apollinaris, Rome and the barbarians." In *Fifth-Century Gaul: A Crisis of Identity?* Ed. John Drinkwater and Hugh Elton. Cambridge, 1992.

Harrison, Carol. Review of *Baptism and Change in the Early Middle Ages* by Peter Cramer. *Early Medieval Europe* 3 (1994), 78–9.

Hartmann, Ludo Moritz. *Geschichte Italiens im Mittelalter* 1. 2nd edn, Stuttgart, 1923.

Hauck, Karl. "Von einer spätantiken Randkultur zum karolingischen Europa." *Frühmittelalterliche Studien* 1 (1967), 3–93.

"Text und Bild in einer oralen Kultur: Antworten auf die zeugniskritische Frage nach der Erreichbarkeit mündlicher Überlieferung im frühen Mittelalter (Zur Ikonologie der Goldbrakteaten 25)." *Frühmittelalterliche Studien* 17 (1983), 510–99.

Hauptfeld, Georg. "Zur langobardischen Eroberung Italiens: Das Heer und die Bischöfe." *Mitteilungen des Instituts für Österreichische Geschichtsforschung* 91 (1983), 37–94.

Haussig, H.-W. "Anfänge der Themenordnung." In *Finanzgeschichte der Spätantike*. Ed. Ruth Stiehl. Frankfurt, 1957.

Haverfeld, F. "Tacitus during the late Roman period and the Middle Ages." *Journal of Roman Studies* 6 (1916), 196–201.

Heather, Peter. "Cassiodorus and the rise of the Amals: genealogy and the Goths under Hun domination." *Journal of Roman Studies* 79 (1989), 103–28.

Goths and Romans 332–489. Oxford, 1991.

"Literacy and power in the migration period." In *Literacy and Power in the Ancient World*. Ed. Alan K. Bowman and Greg Woolf. Cambridge, 1994.

"Theoderic, king of the Goths." *Early Medieval Europe* 4 (1995), 145–73.

Heather, Peter and John Matthews. *The Goths in the Fourth Century*. Liverpool, 1991.

Hedeager, Lotte. "Kingdoms, ethnicity and material culture: Denmark in a European perspective." In *The Age of Sutton Hoo*. Ed. Martin Carver. Woodbridge, 1992.

Heinzelmann, Martin. *Bischofsherrschaft in Gallien: zur Kontinuität römischer Führungsschichten vom 4. bis 7. Jahrhundert: soziale, prosopographische und bildungsgeschichtliche Aspekte*. Beihefte der Francia 5. Munich, 1976.

"Les changements de la dénomination latine à la fin de l'antiquité." In *Famille et Parenté dans l'Occident médiéval*, Actes du colloque de Paris (6–8 juin 1974). Collection de l'Ecole Française de Rome 30. Rome, 1977.

Heuberger, R. "Das ostgotische Rätien." *Klio* 30 (1937), 77–109.

Hildebrand, Paul. "Die Absetzung des Papstes Silverius (537)." *Historisches Jahrbuch* 42 (1922), 213–49.

Hodder, Ian. *The Spatial Organization of Culture*. London, 1978.

Symbols in Action: Ethnoarchaeological Studies in Material Culture. Cambridge, 1982.

"Archaeological theory in contemporary European societies." In *Archaeological Theory in Europe: The Last Three Decades*. Ed. Ian Hodder. London, 1991.

Hodgkin, Thomas, trans. with commentary. *The Letters of Cassiodorus*. London, 1886.

Italy and Her Invaders. 8 vols. 1880. 2nd edn. Oxford, 1892.

Hoeflich, Michael H. "Gelasius I and Roman law: one further note." *Journal of Theological Studies* n.s. 26 (1975), 114–19.

"The concept of utilitas populi in early ecclesiastical law and government." *Zeitschrift der Savigny-Stiftung für Rechtsgeschichte* 98, Kanonistische Abteilung 67 (1981), 36–74.

Holder, Alfred. *Alt-Celtischer Sprachsatz*. 3 vols. Leipzig, 1896–1907.

Holum, Kenneth G. *Theodosian Empresses: Women and Imperial Dominion in Late Antiquity*. Berkeley, 1982.

Honoré, Tony. *Tribonian*. London, 1978.

Hope, D. M. *The Leonine Sacramentary: A Reassessment of Its Date and Purpose*. Oxford, 1971.

Hunter, M. J. "The Gothic Bible." In *The Cambridge History of the Bible* 2. Ed. G. W. H. Lampe. Cambridge, 1969.

Isaac, Benjamin. "The meaning of the terms *limes* and *limitanei.*" *Journal of Roman Studies* 78 (1988), 125–47.

Jaffé, Phillippe, Samuel Loewenfeld, F. Kaltenbrunner and Paul Ewald. *Regesta Pontificum Romanorum ab condita ecclesia ad annum post Christum natum MCXCVIII.* 2 vols. Leipzig, 1885–8.

Jenkins, Richard. "Social anthropological models of inter-ethnic relations." In *Theories of Race and Ethnic Relations.* Ed. John Rex and David Mason. Cambridge, 1986.

Jones, A. H. M. "The constitutional position of Odoacer and Theoderic." *Journal of Roman Studies* 52 (1962), 126–30.

The Later Roman Empire 284–602: A Social, Economic and Administrative Survey. 1964. 2 vols. Reprint. Oxford, 1973.

Kaegi, Walter Emil, Jr. "Arianism and the Byzantine army in Africa 533–546." *Traditio* 21 (1965), 23–53.

Byzantium and the Decline of Rome. Princeton, 1968.

Kajanto, Iiro. "The problem of names of humility in early Christian epigraphy." *Arctos* 3 (1962), 45–53.

Onomastic Studies in the Early Christian Inscriptions of Rome and Carthage. Acta Instituti Romani Finlandiae 2.1. Helsinki, 1963.

The Latin Cognomina. Societas Scientiarum Fenica: Commentationes Humanarum Litterarum 36.2. Helsinki, 1965.

Supernomina: A Study in Latin Epigraphy. Societas Scientiarum Fenica: Commentationes Humanarum Litterarum 40.2. Helsinki, 1966.

"The emergence of the late single-name system." In *L'onomastique latine.* Colloques internationaux du CNRS 564. Paris, 1977.

Kampers, Gerd. "Anmerkungen zum Lateinisch-gotischen Ravennater Papyrus von 551." *Historisches Jahrbuch* 101 (1981), 141–51.

Kauffmann, Henning. *Ergänzungsband zu Ernst Förstemann, Personennamen.* Hildesheim and Munich, 1968.

Kazanski, Michel. *Les goths (Ier–VIIe siècles après J.-C.).* Paris, 1991.

Klingshirn, William E. *Caesarius of Arles: The Making of a Christian Community in Late Antique Gaul.* Cambridge, 1994.

Koder, Johannes. "Byzanz, die Griechen und die Romaiosyne – eine 'Ethnogenese' der 'Römer'?" In *Typen der Ethnogenese unter besonderer Berücksichtigung der Bayern* 1. Ed. Herwig Wolfram and Walter Pohl. Denkschriften der philosophisch-historischen Klasse 201. Veröffentlichungen des Instituts für Österreichische Geschichtsforschung 12. Vienna, 1990.

Korkkanen, Irma, *The Peoples of Hermanaric: Jordanes, "Getica"* 116. Annales Academiae Scientiarum Fennicae, ser. b, 187. Helsinki, 1975.

Krautschick, Stefan. *Cassiodor und die Politik seiner Zeit.* Habelts Dissertationsdrucke, Reihe Alte Geschichte 17. Bonn, 1983.

"Zwei Aspekte des Jahres 476." *Historia* 35 (1986), 344–71.

Ladner, Gerhart B. *The Idea of Reform, Its Impact on Christian Thought and Action in the Age of the Fathers.* Cambridge, Mass., 1959.

Lanzoni, Francesco. *Le diocesi d'Italia dalle origini al principio del secolo VII (An. 604).* 2 vols. 2nd edn. Studi e Testi 35 bis 1–2. Faenza, 1927.

La Rocca, Cristina. "La politica edilizia di Teoderico." In *Teoderico il Grande e i Goti d'Italia.* Atti del XIII Congresso internazionale di studi sull'alto medioevo. Milan, 2–6 November 1992. Spoleto, 1993.

Lee, A. D. *Information and Frontiers: Roman Foreign Relations in Late Antiquity.* Cambridge, 1993.

Lehmann, Winfred P. *Historical Linguistics.* 3rd edn. London, 1992.

Lemerle, Paul. "Invasions et migrations dans les Balkans depuis la fin de l'époque romaine jusqu'au VIIIe siècle." *Revue Historique* 211 (1954), 265–308.

Levy, Ernst. *West Roman Vulgar Law: The Law of Property.* Philadelphia, 1951.

Liebeschuetz, J. H. W. G. *Barbarians and Bishops: Army, Church and State in the Age of Arcadius and Chrysostom.* Oxford, 1990.

Llewellyn, Peter. *Rome in the Dark Ages.* 1971. Augmented ed. London, 1993.

"The Roman chuch during the Laurentian schism: priests and senators." *Church History* 45 (1976), 417–27.

"The Roman clergy during the Laurentian schism (498–506): a preliminary analysis." *Ancient Society* 8 (1977), 245–75.

Loofs, Friedrich. *Leontius von Byzanz und die gleichnamigen Schriftsteller der griechischen Kirche.* Texte und Untersuchungen 3.1–2. Leipzig, 1887.

Lotter, Friedrich. "Illustrissimus vir Severinus." *Deutsches Archiv* 26 (1970), 200–7.

Severinus von Noricum, Legende und historische Wirklichkeit: Untersuchungen zur Phase des Ubergangs von spätantiken zu mittelalterlichen Denk- und Lebensformen. Monographien zur Geschichte des Mittelalters 12. Stuttgart, 1976.

Lucchesi, Giovanni. "Ellero." In *Bibliotheca Sanctorum* 4. Rome, 1964.

Luiselli, Bruno. "Cassiodoro e la storia dei Goti." In *Passaggio dal mondo antico al medio evo da Teodosio a San Gregorio Magno.* Convegno Internazionale dell'Accademia Nazionale dei Lincei, Rome, 25–8 May 1977. Atti dei Convegni Lincei 45. Rome, 1980.

Storia culturale dei rapporti tra mondo romano e mondo germanico. Biblioteka di Helikon, Rivista di tradizione e cultura classica dell' Universitá di Messina: Nuova Collana di Testi e Studi 1. Rome, 1992.

Maas, Michael. "Roman history and Christian ideology in Justinianic reform legislation." *Dumbarton Oaks Papers* 40 (1986), 17–31.

"Ethnicity, orthodoxy and community in Salvian of Marseilles." In *Fifth-Century Gaul: A Crisis of Identity?* Ed. John Drinkwater and Hugh Elton. Cambridge, 1992.

John Lydus and the Roman Past: Antiquarianism and Politics in the Age of Justinian. London, 1992.

"Terms of inclusion: Christianity and classical ethnography from Justinian to Heraclius." Forthcoming, 1994.

MacCormack, Sabine. "Latin prose panegyrics." In *Silver Latin II.* Ed. T. A. Dorey. London, 1975.

Art and Ceremony in Late Antiquity. Berkeley, 1981.

MacMullen, Ramsay, *Soldier and Civilian in the Later Roman Empire.* Harvard Historical Monographs 52. Cambridge, Mass., 1963.

"The Celtic renaissance." 1965. Reprinted in *Changes in the Roman Empire: Essays in the Ordinary.* Princeton, 1990.

"Provincial languages in the Roman Empire." 1966. Reprinted in *Changes in the Roman Empire: Essays in the Ordinary.* Princeton, 1990.

"Notes on Romanization." 1984. Reprinted in *Changes in the Roman Empire: Essays in the Ordinary.* Princeton, 1990.

Corruption and the Decline of Rome. New Haven, 1988.

"The historical role of the masses in late antiquity." In *Changes in the Roman Empire: Essays in the Ordinary.* Princeton, 1990.

Macpherson, Robin. *Rome in Involution: Cassiodorus' Variae in Their Literary and Historical Setting.* Uniwersytet im. Adama Mickiewicza w Pozananiu, Seria Filologia Kasyczna 14. Poznan, 1989.

Marinetti, Filippo Tomaso. *The Futurist Cookbook.* 1932. Trans. Suzanne Brill. San Francisco, 1989.

Markus, R. A. *Saeculum: History and Society in the Theology of Saint Augustine.* Cambridge, 1970.

"Reflections on religious dissent in North Africa in the Byzantine period." In *Schism, Heresy and Religious Protest.* Ed. Derek Baker. Studies in Church History 9. Cambridge, 1972.

"Carthage – Prima Justiniana – Ravenna: an aspect of Justinian's *Kirchenpolitik.*" *Byzantion* 49 (1979), 277–302.

"Country bishops in Byzantine Africa." In *The Church in Town and Countryside.* Ed. Derek Baker. Studies in Church History 16. Cambridge, 1979.

"Gregory the Great's Europe." *Transactions of the Royal Historical Society,* 5th ser. 31 (1981), 21–36.

"Ravenna and Rome, 554–604." *Byzantion* 51 (1981), 566–78.

"The end of the Roman Empire: a note on Eugippius, *Vita Sancti Severini,* 20." *Nottingham Medieval Studies* 26 (1982), 1–7.

"Chronicle and theology: Prosper of Aquitaine." In *The Inheritance of Historiography 350–900.* Ed. Christopher Holdsworth and T. P. Wiseman. Exeter Studies in History 12. Exeter, 1986.

The End of Ancient Christianity. Cambridge, 1990.

Martindale, J. R. *Prosopography of the Later Roman Empire 2. A.D. 395–527.* Cambridge, 1980.

Prosopography of the Later Roman Empire 3. A.D. 527–641. 2 vols. Cambridge, 1993.

Mastrelli, Carlo Alberto. "I Goti e il gotico." In *I Goti.* Catalogue of the Exhibition at Milan, Palazzo Reale, 28 January–8 May 1994. Milan, 1994.

"Lexical loans and Gothic onomastics: an updating." In *Teoderico il Grande e i Goti d'Italia.* Atti del XIII Congresso internazionale di studi sull'alto medioevo. Milan, 2–6 November 1992. Spoleto, 1993.

Mathisen, Ralph W. "For specialists only: the reception of Augustine and his teachings in fifth-century Gaul." In *Augustine: Presbyter Factus Sum.* Collectanea Augustiniana. Ed. Joseph T. Lienhard, Earl C. Muller and Roland J. Teske New York, 1993.

Matthews, John. "Anicius Manlius Severinus Boethius." In *Boethius: His Life, Thought and Influence.* Ed. Margaret Gibson. Oxford, 1981.

Mayer, Anton. *Die Sprache der alten Illyrier 1. Einleitung, Wörterbuch der illyrischen Sprachreste.* Österreichische Akademie der Wissenschaften, philosophisch-historische Klasse: Schriften der Balkankommission, Linguistische Abteilung 15. Vienna, 1957.

Mazzini, Innocenzo. "*De observantia ciborum:* Un'antica traduzio latina del Περι διαιτεσ pseudoippocratico (1.II) (*editio princeps*)." *Romanobarbarica* 2 (1977), 287–357.

Mazzoleni, Danilo. "Nomi di barbari nelle iscrizioni paleocristiane della Venetia et Histria." *Romanobarbarica* 1 (1976), 159–80.

"Names, personal." In *The Encyclopedia of the Early Church*. Ed. Angelo di Berardino. 1982. Trans. Adrian Walford. 2 vols. Cambridge, 1992.

McCormick, Michael. "Odoacer, the emperor Zeno and the Rugian victory legation." *Byzantion* 47 (1977), 212–22.

Eternal Victory: Triumphal Rulership in Late Antiquity, Byzantium and the Early Medieval West. Cambridge, 1986.

McKitterick, Rosamond. *The Carolingians and the Written Word*. Cambridge, 1988.

(ed.) *The Uses of Literacy in Early Medieval Europe*. Cambridge, 1990.

"The written word and oral communication: Rome's legacy to the Franks." In *Germania Latina*. Ed. R. North and T. Hofstra. Groningen, 1992.

McNally, Robert E. " 'Christus' in the pseudo-Isidorian 'Liber de ortu et obitu patriarchum.' " *Traditio* 21 (1965), 167–83.

Meslin, Michel. *Les Ariens d'Occident, 335–430*. Patristica Sorbonensia 8. Paris, 1967.

Momigliano, Arnaldo. "Cassiodorus and Italian culture of his time." 1955. Reprinted in *Studies in Historiography*. New York, 1966.

"Introduction to a discussion of Georges Dumézil." 1983. Reprinted in *Studies on Modern Scholarship*. Ed. G. W. Bowersock and T. J. Cornell. Berkeley, 1994.

Mommsen, Theodor. "Ostgothische Studien." *Neues Archiv* 14 (1889), 225–49, 453–544. *Neues Archiv* 15 (1890), 181–6.

Moorhead, John. "Boethius and Romans in Ostrogothic service." *Historia* 27 (1978), 604–12.

"The Laurentian schism: East and West in the Roman church." *Church History* 47 (1978), 125–36.

"Italian loyalties during Justinian's Gothic war." *Byzantion* 53 (1983), 575–96.

"The last years of Theoderic." *Historia* 32 (1983): 106–20.

"The Decii under Theoderic." *Historia* 33 (1984), 107–15.

"*Libertas* and *nomen Romanum* in Ostrogothic Italy." *Latomus* 46 (1987), 161–8.

Theoderic in Italy. Oxford, 1993.

Justinian. London, 1994.

Moulton, William G. "Mutual intelligibility among speakers of early Germanic dialects." In *Germania: Comparative Studies in the Old Germanic Languages and Literatures*. Ed. Daniel G. Calder and T. Craig Christie. Woodbridge, Suffolk, 1993, pp. 9–28.

Mowat, R. "Note sur des bijoux ornés de devises à propos d'une fibule de l'époque ostrogothe." *Mémoires de la Société Nationale des Antiquaires de France* 5th ser. 9 [= 49] (1888), 19–34.

Much, Rudolf. "Heruler." In *Reallexikon der germanischen Altertumskunde* 2. Strasbourg, 1913–15.

Muhlberger, Steven. *The Fifth-Century Chroniclers: Prosper, Hydatius, and the Gallic Chronicle of 452*. ARCA: Classical and Medieval Texts, Monographs and Papers 27. Leeds, 1990.

Mühlmann, W. E. "Ethnogonie und Ethnogenese: theoretisch-ethnologische und ideologiekritische Studie." In *Studien zur Ethnogenese*. Abhandlungen der rheinisch-westfälischen Akademie der Wissenschaften 72. Opladen, 1985.

Müller, Klaus Erich. *Geschichte der antiken Ethnographie und ethnologischen Theoriebildung* 2. Wiesbaden, 1983.

Näf, Beat. "Das Zeitbewußtsein des Ennodius und der Untergang Roms." *Historia* 39 (1990), 100–23.

Nehlsen, Hermann. Review of *Edictum Theoderici* by Giulio Vismara. *Zeitschrift der Savigny-Stiftung für Rechtsgeschichte, Germanistische Abteilung* 86 (1969), 246–60.

Sklavenrecht zwischen Antike und Mittelalter: germanisches und römisches Recht in den germanischen Rechtsaufzeichnungen 1. *Ostgoten, Westgoten, Franken, Langobarden.* Göttinger Studien zur Rechtsgeschichte 7. Göttingen, 1972.

Noble, Thomas F. X. "A new look at the *Liber Pontificalis*." *Archivum Historiae Pontificiae* 23 (1985), 347–58.

"Theoderic and the papacy." In *Teoderico il Grande e i Goti d'Italia.* Atti del XIII Congresso internazionale di studi sull'alto medioevo. Milan, 2–6 November 1992. Spoleto, 1993.

Noethlichs, Karl Leo. *Beamtum und Dienstvergehen: Zur Staatsverwaltung in der Spätantike.* Wiesbaden, 1981.

Nonn, Ulrich. "Merowingische Testamente: Studien zum Fortleben einer römischen Urkundenform im Frankreich." *Archiv für Diplomatik* 18 (1972), 1–129.

O'Daly, Gerard. *The Poetry of Boethius.* London, 1991.

O'Donnell, James J. *Cassiodorus.* Berkeley, 1979.

"Liberius the patrician." *Traditio* 37 (1981), 31–72.

"The aims of Jordanes." *Historia* 31 (1982), 223–40.

Page, R. I. *Runes.* London, 1987.

Pagnin, B. "Il codice Giustiniani Recanati in onciale del sesto secolo ed il passo del 'De Trinitate' di S. Agostino in esso contenuto." *Atti e Memorie dell'Accademia Patavina di scienze, lettere ed arti* 90.3 (1977–8), 171–82.

Pape, W. *Wörterbuch der Griechischen Eigennamen.* 3rd edn. Rev. Gustav Eduard Benseler. Handwörterbuch der Griechischen Sprache 3. Braunschweig, 1863.

Paschoud, François. "Le mythe de Rome à la fin de l'empire et dans les royaumes romano-barbares." In *Passaggio dal mondo antico al medio evo da Teodosio a San Gregorio Magno.* Convegno Internazionale dell'Accademia Nazionale dei Lincei, Rome, 25–8 May 1977. Atti dei Convegni Lincei 45. Rome, 1980.

Patlagean, Evelyne. *Pauvreté économique et pauvreté sociale à Byzance, 4e–7e siècles.* Civilisations et Sociétés 48. Paris, 1977.

Pecere, O. "La cultura greco romana in età gota tra adattamento e trasformazione." In *Teoderico il Grande e i Goti d'Italia.* Atti del XIII Congresso internazionale di studi sull'alto medioevo. Milan, 2–6 November 1992. Spoleto, 1993.

Petrucci, Armando. "Aspetti simbolici delle testimonzianze scritte." In *Simboli e simbologia nell'alto medioevo.* Settimane di Studio del Centro Italiano di studi sull'alto medioevo 23. 2 vols. Spoleto, 1976.

Pfeilschrifter, Georg. *Der Ostgotenkönig Theoderich der Grosse und die katholische Kirche.* Kirchengeschichtliche Studien 3. Münster, 1896.

Pietri, Charles. "La géographie de l'Illyricum ecclésiastique et ses relations avec l'Eglise de Rome (Ve–VIe siècles)." In *Villes et peuplement dans l'Illyricum protobyzantin.* Actes du colloque de l'Ecole Française, Rome, 12–14 mai 1982. Collection de l'Ecole Française de Rome 77. Rome, 1984.

"Le sénat, le peuple chrétien et les partis du cirque à Rome sous le pape Symmachus (498–514)." *Mélanges d'archéologie et d'histoire de l'Ecole Française de Rome* 78 (1986), 123–39.

Pohl, Walter. *Die Awaren: Ein Steppenvolk im Mitteleuropa 567–822 n. Chr.* Munich, 1988.

"Conceptions of ethnicity in early medieval studies." *Archaeologia Polona* 29 (1991), 39–49.

"I Goti d'Italia e le tradizioni delle steppe." In *Teoderico il Grande e i Goti d'Italia.* Atti del XIII Congresso internazionale di studi sull'alto medioevo. Milan, 2–6 November 1992. Spoleto, 1993.

"Tradition, Ethnogenese und literarische Gestaltung: eine Zwischenbilanz." In *Ethnogenese und Überlieferung: Angewandte Methoden der Frühmittelalterforschung.* Ed. Karl Brunner and Brigitte Merta. Vienna, 1994.

Prinz, Friedrich. *Frühes Mönchtum im Frankenreich: Kultur und Gesellschaft in Gallien am Beispiel der monastischen Entwicklung (4.–8. Jahrhundert).* 1965. Augmented edn. Munich and Paris, 1988.

Rabinow, "Representations are social facts: modernity and post-modernity in anthropology." In *Writing Culture: The Poetics and Politics of Ethnography.* Ed. James Clifford and George E. Marcus. Berkeley, 1986.

Rasi, Piero. "Sulla paternità del c.d. Edictum Theodorici regis," *Archivio Giuridico* 145 (1953), 105–13.

Reif, Stefan C. "Aspects of mediaeval Jewish literacy." In *The Uses of Literacy in Early Medieval Europe.* Ed. Rosamond McKitterick. Cambridge, 1990.

Rex, John and David Mason, eds. *Theories of Race and Ethnic Relations.* Cambridge, 1986.

Reynolds, L. D., ed. *Texts and Transmission: A Survey of the Latin Classics.* 1983. Corrected reprint. Oxford, 1986.

Richardson, Peter Nichols. *German-Romance Contact: Name-giving in Walser Settlements.* Amsterdamer Publikationen zur Sprache und Literatur 15. Amsterdam, 1974.

Riché, Pierre. *Education and Culture in the Barbarian West from the Sixth to the Eighth Century.* 1962. Trans. John J. Contreni. Columbia SC, 1976.

Rogger, Iginio. "Scavi e ricerche sotto la cattedrale di Trento." *Studi trentini di scienze storiche* 53 (1974), 387–409. *Studi trentini di scienze storiche* 54 (1975), 3–40.

Romm, James S. *The Edges of the Earth In Ancient Thought: Geography, Exploration and Fiction.* Princeton, 1992.

Rossi, Giovanni Battista de. "Epigrafe d'una illustre donna della regia stirpe degli Amali Ostrogoti." *Bulletina di archeologia cristiana* 5th ser. 4 (1894), 77–82.

Ruggieri, Ruggero M. "*Teudisca lingua* e popoli tedeschi, uomini ligi e *barbari leudi* nella prospettiva romano-germanica." *Romanobarbarica* 1 (1976), 243–60.

Rugo, Pietro. *Le iscrizioni dei secoli VI–VII–VIII esistenti in Italia.* 5 vols. Cittadella, 1974–1980.

Rugullis, Sven. *Die Barbaren in den spätrömischen Gesetzen: eine Untersuchung des Terminus "barbarus".* Europäische Hochschulschriften, ser. 3: Geschichte und ihre Hilfswissenschaften 513. Frankfurt, 1992.

Russell, James C. *The Germanization of Early Medieval Christianity: A Sociohistorical Approach to Religious Transformation.* Oxford, 1994.

Ste. Croix, G. E. M. de. *The Class Struggle in the Ancient Greek World from the Archaic Age to the Arab Conquests.* 1981. Corrected impression. London, 1983.

Šašel, Jaroslav. "Antiqui Barbari: Zur Besiedlungsgeschichte Ostnoricums und Pannoniens im fünften und sechsten Jahrhundert nach den Schriftquellen." In *Von der Spätantike zum frühen Mittelalter: Aktuelle Probleme in historischer und archäologischer Sicht.* Ed. Joachim Werner and Eugen Ewig. Vorträge und Forschungen 25. Sigmaringen, 1979.

Scardigli, Piergiuseppe. *Lingua e storia dei Goti.* Manuali di filologia e storia. Florence, 1964.

Die Goten: Sprache und Kultur. 1964. Rev. edn. Munich, 1973.

Schäferdiek, Knut. *Die Kirche in den Reichen der Westgoten und Suewen bis zur Errichtung der westgotischen katholischen Staatskirche.* Arbeiten zur Kirchengeschichte 39. Berlin, 1967.

Schanz, Martin, Carl Hosius and Gustav Krüger. *Geschichte der römischen Litteratur bis zum Gesetzgebungswerk des Kaisers Justinians 4.2. Die römische Litteratur von Constantin bis zum Gesetzgebungswerk Justinians, Die Litteratur des fünften und sechsten Jahrhunderts.* Munich, 1920.

Schmidt, Ludwig. "Die comites Gothorum: ein Kapitel zur ostgotischen Verfassungsgeschichte." *Mitteilungen des Insituts für Österreichische Geschichtsforschung* 40 (1925), 127–34.

"Das germanische Volkstum in den Reichen der Völkerwanderung." *Historische Vierteljahrschrift* 29 (1934), 417–40.

Die Ostgermanen. 2nd ed. Munich, 1941.

Schott, Clausdieter. "Der Stand der Leges-Forschung." *Frühmittelalterliche Studien* 13 (1979), 29–55.

Schönfeld, M. *Wörterbuch der altgermanischen Personen- und Völkernamen.* Germanische Bibliotek 3. Reihe. Heidelberg, 1911.

Schubert, Hans von. *Das älteste germanische Christentum oder der sogenannte "Arianismus" der Germanen.* Tübingen, 1909.

"Arianismus." In *Reallexikon der germanischen Altertumskunde* 1. Ed. Johannes Hoops. 1st edn. Strasbourg, 1911–13.

Schurr, Viktor. *Die Trinitätslehre des Boethius im Lichte der "skythischen Kontroversen".* Forschungen zur christlichen Literatur- und Dogmengeschichte 18.1. Paderborn, 1935.

Schwartz, Eduard. "Capito aus Lykien." *RE* 3: 1527. Stuttgart, 1899.

Publizistische Sammlungen zum Acacianischen Schisma. Abhandlungen der Bayerischen Akademie der Wissenschaften, philosophisch-historische Abteilung, n.s. 10. Munich, 1934.

Vigiliusbriefe. Sitzungsberichte der Bayerischen Akademie der Wissenschaften 1940. Munich, 1940.

Zur Kirchenpolitik Iustinians, Sitzungsberichte der Bayerischen Akademie der Wissenschaften, philosophisch-historische Abeteilung 1940.2. Munich, 1940.

Scott, Roger. "The Byzantine chronicle after Malalas." In *Studies in John Malalas.* Ed. Elizabeth Jeffreys, Brian Croke and Roger Scott. Byzantina australiensia 6. Sydney, 1990.

Seidlmayr, Michael. "Rom und Romgedanke im Mittelalter." 1965. Reprinted in *Rom als Idee.* Ed. Bernhard Kytzler. Wege der Forschung 656. Darmstadt, 1993.

Shanzer, Danuta. "Ennodius, Boethius and the date and interpretation of Maximianus' *Elegia* III." *Rivista di filologia e di istruzione classica* 111 (1983), 183–95.

Simonetti, Manlio. "L'incidenza dell'arianesimo nel rapporto fra romani e barbari." In *Passaggio dal mondo antico al medio evo da Teodosio a San Gregorio Magno.* Convegno Internazionale dell'Accademia Nazionale dei Lincei, Rome, 25–8 May 1977. Atti dei Convegni Lincei 45. Rome, 1980.

Sims-Williams, Patrick. "The settlement of England in Bede and the *Chronicle*." *Anglo-Saxon England* 12 (1983), 1–43.

Sinnigen, William G. "*Barbaricarii, barbari* and the *Notitia dignitatum.*" *Latomus* 22 (1963), 806–15.

"Administrative shifts of competence under Theoderic." *Traditio* 21 (1965), 456–67.

Sivan, H. S. "Sidonius Apollinaris, Theodoric II and Gothic-Roman politics from Avitus to Anthemius." *Hermes* 117 (1989), 85–94.

Smith, Anthony D. "War and ethnicity: the role of warfare in the formation, self-images and cohesion of ethnic communities." *Ethnic and Racial Studies* 4 (1981), 375–97.

The Ethnic Origins of Nations. Oxford, 1986.

"The politics of culture: ethnicity and nationalism." In *Companion Encyclopedia of Anthropology: Humanity, Culture and Social Life.* Ed. Tim Ingold. London, 1994.

Solin, Heikki. *Die griechischen Personennamen in Rom: Ein Namenbuch.* 3 vols. Corpus Inscriptionum Latinarum, Auctarium. Berlin, 1980.

Staab, Franz. "Ostrogothic geographers at the court of Theodoric the Great: a study of some sources of the Anonymous Cosmographer of Ravenna." *Viator* 7 (1976), 27–64.

Stein, Ernst. "Untersuchungen zur spätrömischen Verwaltungsgeschichte." *Rheinische Museum* 74 (1925), 347–94.

"La période byzantine de la papauté." *Catholic Historical Review* 21 (1935), 129–63.

Histoire du Bas-Empire de la disparition de l'Empire d'Occident à la mort de Justinien (476–565). Ed. Jean-Rémy Palanque. 2 vols. Paris, 1949–59.

Sundwall, Johannes. *Abhandlungen zur Geschichte des augehenden Römertums.* Öfersigt af Finska Vetenskaps-Societetens Förhandlingar 60B, 2. Helsinki, 1919.

Supino Martini, Paola. "Le sottoscrizione lucchese." *Bulletino dell'istituto storico italiano* 98 (1992), 87–108.

Sweet, Henry. "Some of the sources of the *Anglo-Saxon Chronicle.*" *Englische Studien* 2 (1879), 310–12.

Teall, John L. "The barbarians in Justinian's armies." *Speculum* 40 (1965), 294–325.

Teillet, Suzanne. *Des Goths à la nation gothique: les origines de l'idée de nation en Occident du Ve au VIIe siècle.* Paris, 1984.

Teoderico il Grande e i Goti d'Italia. Atti del XIII Congresso internazionale di studi sull'alto medioevo. Milan, 2–6 November 1992. Spoleto, 1993.

Thompson, E. A. "Christianity and the northern barbarians." In *The Conflict Between Paganism and Christianity in the Fourth Century.* Ed. Arnaldo Momigliano. Oxford, 1963.

The Visigoths in the Time of Ulfila. Oxford, 1966.

"The Byzantine conquest of Italy: public opinion." In *Romans and Barbarians: The Decline of the Western Empire.* Madison, 1982.

"The end of Noricum." In *Romans and Barbarians: The Decline of the Western Empire.* Madison, 1982.

Tjäder, Jan-Olof. *Die nichtliterarischen lateinischen Papyri Italiens aus der Zeit 445–700.* 3 vols. Skrifter Utgivna av Svenska Institutet i Rom [= Acta Instituti Romani Regni Sueciae], series in 4°, 19.1–3. Lund and Stockholm, 1954–82.

"Il nome dell'antica chiesa Ravennate di S. Michele in Africisco." *Felix Ravenna* 3rd ser. 39 [= 90] (1964), 5–19.

"Der Codex argenteus in Uppsala und der Buchmeister Viliaric in Ravenna." In *Studia Gotica: Die eisenzeitlichen Verbindungen zwischen Schweden und Südosteuropa, Vorträge beim Gotensymposion im Statens Historiska Museum Stockholm 1970.* Kungl. Vitterhets Historie och Antikvitets Akademiens handlingar, Antikvariska serien 25. Stockholm, 1972.

"Note per l'interpretazione del misterioso '*hugsis*' nel Pap. Marini 118 P. Tjäder 8." In *Miscellanea Augusto Campana* 2. Medioevo e umanesimo 45. Padua, 1981.

Todd, Malcolm. *The Northern Barbarians*. London, 1975.

The Early Germans. Oxford, 1992.

Trigger, Bruce G. *A History of Archaeological Thought*. London, 1989.

Trüdinger, K. *Studien zur Geschichte der griechisch-römischen Ethnographie*. Basel, 1918.

Ullmann, Walter. *Gelasius I. (492–496): Das Papsttum an der Wende der Spätantike zum Mittelalter*. Päpste und Papsttum 18. Stuttgart, 1981.

Usener, Hermann. "Das Verhältnis des römischen Senats zur Kirche in der Ostgothenzeit." 1877. Reprinted in *Kleine Schriften* 4. Leipzig, 1913.

van Banning: *see* Banning.

van den Berghe: *see* Berghe.

Van Dam, Raymond. *Leadership and Commmunity in Late Antique Gaul*. Berkeley, 1985.

Vanderspoel, John. Review of *From Empire to Commonwealth: Consequences of Monotheism in Late Antiquity* by Garth Fowden. *Bryn Mawr Classical Review* 5.2 (1994), 13–17.

Vansina, Jan. *Oral Tradition: A Study in Historical Methodology*. 1961. Trans. H. M. Wright. 1965. Reprint. Harmondsworth, 1973.

Vasiliev, A. A. *The Goths in the Crimea*. Medieval Academy of America Publications 29. Cambridge, Mass., 1936.

Velkov, V. "Les campagnes et la population rurale en Thrace au VIe–VIe siècles." *Byzantinobulgarica* 1 (1962), 31–66.

Vellut, Jean-Luc. "Ethnicity and genocide in Rwanda." *Times Literary Supplement* 4763 (15 July 1994), 17.

Veyne, Paul. "Clientèle und corruption au service de l'État: la venalité des offices dans le Bas-Empire romain." *Annales: Economies, Sociétés, Civilisations* 36 (1981), 339–60.

Vidén, G. *The Roman Chancery Tradition: Studies in the Language of the "Codex Theodosianus" and Cassiodorus's "Variae"*. Studia Graeca et Latina Gothoburgensia 46. Göteborg, 1984.

Villes et peuplement dans l'Illyricum protobyzantin. Actes du colloque de l'Ecole Française, Rome, 12–14 mai 1982. Collection de l'Ecole Française de Rome 77. Rome, 1984.

Vismara, Giulio. "Romani e Goti di fronte al diritto nel regno ostrogoto." In *I Goti in Occidente: Problemi*. Settimane di studio del Centro Italiano di studi sull'alto medioevo 3. Spoleto, 1956.

Edictum Theoderici. Ius Romanum Medii Aevi I, 2 b aa α. Milan, 1967.

"Il diritto nel regni dei Goti." In *I Goti*. Catalogue of the Exhibition at Milan, Palazzo Reale, 28 January–8 May 1994. Milan, 1994.

"Il diritto nel regno ostrogoto d'Italia." In *Teoderico il Grande e i Goti d'Italia*. Atti del XIII Congresso internazionale di studi sull'alto medioevo. Milan, 2–6 November 1992. Spoleto, 1993.

Vogel, Cyrille. "Le 'Liber Pontificalis' dans l'édition de Louis Duchesne: état de la question." In *Monseigneur Duchesne et son temps*. Collection de l'Ecole Française de Rome 23. Rome, 1975.

Vogel, Friedrich. "Chronologische Untersuchungen zu Ennodius." *Neues Archiv* 23 (1898), 51–74.

von Harnack: *see* Harnack.

von Schubert: *see* Schubert.

Waal, Alex de. "The genocidal state: Hutu extremism and the origins of the 'final solution' in Rwanda." *Times Literary Supplement* 4761 (1 July 1994), 3–4.
"Ethnicity and genocide in Rwanda." *Times Literary Supplement* 4764 (22 July 1994), 15.
Wagner, Norbert. "Namengebung zur Amalergenealogie." *Beiträge zur Namenforschung* n.s. 14 (1979), 26–43.
"König Theodahad und die amalische Namengebung." *Beiträge zur Namenforschung* n.s. 21 (1986), 433–50.
Wallace-Hadrill, Andrew. "The emperor and his virtues." *Historia* 30 (1981), 298–323.
"*Civilis princeps*: between citizen and king." *Journal of Roman Studies* 72 (1982), 32–48.
Wallace-Hadrill, J. M. *The Barbarian West 400–1000*. 1952. 3rd rev. edn. Oxford, 1967.
Early Germanic Kingship in England and On the Continent. Oxford, 1971.
Ward-Perkins, Bryan. "The towns of northern Italy: rebirth or renewal?" In *The Rebirth of Towns in the West, A.D. 700–1050*. Ed. Richard Hodges and B. Hobley. CBA Research Report 68. Oxford, 1988.
Wattenbach, Wilhelm and Wilhelm Levison. *Deutschlands Geschichtsquellen im Mittelalter: Vorzeit und Karolinger 1. Die Vorzeit von den Anfängen bis zur Herrschaft der Karolinger*. Weimar, 1952.
Weißensteiner, Johann. "Cassiodor/Jordanes als Geschichtsschreiber." In *Historiographie im frühen Mittelalter 1*. Ed. Anton Scharer and Georg Scheibelreiter. Veröffentlichungen des Instituts für Österreichische Geschichtsforschung. Vienna, 1994.
Wenskus, Reinhard. *Stammesbildung und Verfassung: Das Werden der frühmittelalterlichen Gentes*. Cologne, 1961.
Werner, Karl Ferdinand. "Liens de parenté et noms de personne: un problème historique et méthodologique." In *Famille et Parenté dans l'Occident médiéval*, Actes du colloque de Paris (6–8 juin 1974). Collection de l'Ecole Française de Rome 30. Rome, 1977.
Wes, M. A. *Das Ende des Kaisertums im Westen des römischen Reiches*. The Hague, 1967.
Wheeler, Everett L. "Methodological limits and the mirage of Roman strategy." *Journal of Military History* 57 (1993), 7–41, 215–40.
Whitby, Michael. *The Emperor Maurice and His Historian: Theophylact Simocatta on Persian and Balkan Warfare*. Oxford, 1988.
Whitby, Michael and Mary Whitby, trans. with commentary. *Chronicon Paschale, 284–528 A.D.* Liverpool, 1989.
Whittaker, C. R. *Les frontières de l'empire romain*. Trans. Christian Goudineau and Christine Castelnau. Annales Littéraires de l'Université de Besançon 390. Centre de Recherches d'Histoire Ancienne 84. Paris, 1989.
Frontiers of the Roman Empire: A Social and Economic Study. 1989. Rev. edn. Baltimore, 1994.
Wickham, Chris. "The other transition: from the ancient world to feudalism." 1984. Reprinted with revisions in *Land and Power: Studies in Italian and European Social History, 400–1200*. London, 1994.
"Marx, Sherlock Holmes and late Roman commerce." 1988. Reprinted with revisions in *Land and Power: Studies in Italian and European Social History, 400–1200*. London, 1994.
Wieacker, Franz. *Recht und Gesellschaft in der Spätantike*. Stuttgart, 1964.
Wilkes, John. *The Illyrians*. Oxford, 1992.
Winkelmann, Friedhelm. "Die Bewertung der Barbaren in den Werken der oström-

ischen Kirchenhistoriker." In *Das Reich und die Barbaren*. Ed. Evangelos Chrysos and Andreas Schwarcz. Veröffentlichungen des Insituts für Österreichischen Geschichtsforschung 29. Vienna, 1989.

Winter, E. K. *Studien zum Severinsproblem*. Klosterneuberg, 1959.

Wirszubski, Chaim. *Libertas as a Political Idea at Rome*. 1950. Reprint. Cambridge, 1960.

Wolfram, Herwig. *Intitulatio* 1. *Lateinische Königs- und Fürstentitel bis zum Ende des 8. Jahrhunderts*. Mitteilungen des Instituts für Österreichische Geschichtsforschung, Ergänzungsband 21. Graz, 1967.

"The shaping of the early medieval kingdom." *Viator* 1 (1970), 1–20.

"Gotische Studien I: Das Richtertum Athanarichs." *Mitteilungen des Instituts für Österreichische Geschichtsforschung* 83 (1975), 1–32.

"Gotische Studien II: Die terwingische Stammesverfassung und das Bibelgotisch (1)." *Mitteilungen des Instituts für Österreichische Geschichtsforschung* 83 (1975), 289–324.

"Gotische Studien III: Die terwingische Stammesverfassung und das Bibelgotisch (2)." *Mitteilungen des Instituts für Österreichische Geschichtsforschung* 84 (1976), 239–61.

"Gotisches Königtum und römisches Kaisertum von Theodosius dem Großen bis Justinian I." *Frühmittelalterliche Studien* 13 (1979), 1–28.

"Gothic history and historical ethnography." *Journal of Medieval History* 7 (1981), 309–19.

"Zur Ansiedlung reichsangehöriger Föderaten." *Mitteilungen des Instituts für Österreichische Geschichtsforschung* 91 (1983), 5–35.

"Ethnogenese im Donau- und Ostalpenraum (6.–10. Jahrhundert." In *Frühmittelalterliche Ethnogenese im Alpenraum*. Ed. Helmut Beumann and W. Schröder. Nationes: historische und philologische Untersuchungen zur Entstehung der europäischen Nationen im Mittelalter 5. Sigmaringen, 1985.

Review of *Des Goths à la nation gothique* by Suzanne Teillet. *Francia* 13 (1985), 724–6.

History of the Goths. 1979. 2nd rev. edn. Trans. Thomas J. Dunlap. Berkeley, 1988.

"Einleitung oder Überlegungen zur Origo Gentis." In *Typen der Ethnogenese unter besonderer Berücksichtigung der Bayern* 1. Ed. Herwig Wolfram and Walter Pohl. Denkschriften der philosophisch-historischen Klasse 201. Veröffentlichungen des Instituts für Österreichische Geschichtsforschung 12. Vienna, 1990.

Review of *Goths and Romans* by Peter Heather. *Francia* 20.1 (1993), 257–8.

"Il regno di Teoderico in Italia e nelle area adiacenti." In *Teoderico il Grande e i Goti d'Italia*. Atti del XIII Congresso internazionale di studi sull'alto medioevo. Milan, 2–6 November 1992. Spoleto, 1993.

"*Origo et religio*: ethnic traditions and literature in early medieval texts." *Early Medieval Europe* 3 (1994), 19–38.

Wood, Ian. "Avitus of Vienne: religion and culture in the Auvergne and the Rhône valley, 470–550." Diss., Oxford, 1980.

"The end of Roman Britain: continental evidence and parallels." In *Gildas: New Approaches*. Ed. Michael Lapidge and David N. Dumville. Woodbridge, Suffolk, 1984.

"Disputes in late fifth- and sixth-century Gaul: some problems." In *The Settlement of Disputes in Early Medieval Europe*. Cambridge, 1986.

"Ethnicity and ethnogenesis of the Burgundians." In *Typen der Ethnogenese unter besonderer Berücksichtigung der Bayern* 1. Ed. Herwig Wolfram and Walter Pohl. Denkschriften der philosophisch-historischen Klasse 201. Veröffentlichungen des Instituts für Österreichische Geschichtsforschung 12. Vienna, 1990.

The Merovingian Kingdoms 470–751. London, 1994.

Woolf, H. B. *The Old Germanic Principles of Name-Giving*. Baltimore, 1939.

Wrede, Ferdinand. *Über die Sprache der Ostgoten in Italien*. Quellen und Forschungen zur Sprach- und Culturgeschichte der germanischen Völker 68. Strasbourg, 1891.

Yinger, J. Milton. "Intersecting strands in the theorisation of race and ethnic relations." In *Theories of Race and Ethnic Relations*. Ed. John Rex and David Mason. Cambridge, 1986.

Zecchini, Giuseppe. "I 'gesta de Xysti purgatione' e le fazioni aristocratiche a Roma alla met à del V secolo." *Rivista di storia della Chiesa in Italia* 34 (1980), 60–74.

"Il 476 nella storiografia tardoantica." *Aevum* 59 (1985), 3–23.

Zeiller, Jacques. "Les églises ariennes de Rome à l'époque de la domination gothique." *Mélanges d'archéologie et d'histoire de l'Ecole Française de Rome* 24 (1904), 17–33.

"Etude sur l'arianisme en Italie à l'époque ostrogothique et à l'époque lombarde." *Mélanges d'archéologie et d'histoire de l'École Française de Rome* 25 (1905), 127–46.

Les origines chrétiennes dans le province romaine de Dalmatie. Bibliothèque de l'Ecole des Hautes Etudes: Sciences historiques et philologiques 155. Paris, 1906.

Les origines chrétiennes dans les provinces danubiennes de l'empire romain. Bibliothèque des Ecoles Françaises d'Athènes et de Rome 112. Paris, 1918.

Zimmermann, Odo John. *The Latin Vocabulary of Cassiodorus*. 1944. Reprint. Hildesheim, 1967.

Zöllner, Erich. "Zusammenfassung: Noricum und Raetia I." In *Von der Spätantike zum frühen Mittelalter: Aktuelle Probleme in historischer und archäologischer Sicht*. Ed. Joachim Werner and Eugen Ewig. Vorträge und Forschungen 25. Sigmaringen, 1979.

INDEX

Boldface initials indicate individuals included in the Prosopographical Appendix. Not every individual in the Prosopographical Appendix mentioned in the text is indexed here. See under the individual's name in the Appendix for further cross-references. Modern spellings of names are given in square brackets when they differ from the spelling of the entry in the Prosopographical Appendix.

Cambridge Studies in Medieval Life and Thought
Fourth Series

Titles in series

*Also published as a paperback